To Touch the Text

To Touch the Text

Biblical and Related Studies
in Honor of
Joseph A. Fitzmyer, S.J.

Edited by
Maurya P. Horgan
and
Paul J. Kobelski

Crossroad • New York

1989

The Crossroad Publishing Company
370 Lexington Avenue, New York, NY 10017

Printed in the United States of America

Library of Congress Cataloging-in-Publication Data

To touch the text.

    Includes bibliographical references.
    1. Bible—Criticism, interpretation, etc.
2. Fitzmyer, Joseph A. I. Fitzmyer, Joseph A.
II. Horgan, Maurya P., 1947-   . III. Kobelski,
Paul J., 1946-   .
BS540.T58 1989   220.6   89-25127
ISBN 0-8245-0897-1

Contents

v

Part II: Hebrew Bible

Part III: Dead Sea Scrolls

Part IV: New Testament

Preface

In evangelicis sermonibus semper litterae iunctus est spiritus; et quidquid primo frigere videtur apectu, si tegigeris, calet.

In the words of the Gospels the Spirit has been joined to the letter; and whatever at first sight seems to be cold, if you touch it, grows hot.

   Jerome, *In Matth.* 2.14.14; see Fitzmyer, *Luke*, 2. xi.

THIS COLLECTION OF STUDIES is offered with esteem and gratitude to Professor Joseph A. Fitzmyer, S.J. The title of the volume, *To Touch the Text,* is a phrase from Father Fitzmyer's conclusion of the preface to the second volume of his commentary on the Gospel of Luke (*The Gospel According to Luke* [Anchor Bible 28, 28A; Garden City, NY: Doubleday, 1981, 1985] 2. xi): "May hearts of readers still be set on fire by reading about the risen Christ in the Gospel of Luke who begs them to touch the text of his words." It is fitting that this book bear a title in the honoree's own words; it conveys the heart of his endeavor in the spheres of scholarly research, teaching, and the life of the church.

This is the second volume in recent years that has been published to honor Professor Joseph A. Fitzmyer, S.J. The first was a special issue of the *Catholic Biblical Quarterly* entitled *A Wise and Discerning Heart: Studies Presented to Joseph A. Fitzmyer, S.J. In Celebration of His Sixty-Fifth Birthday* (ed. Raymond E. Brown, S.S., and Alexander A. Di Lella, O.F.M.; *CBQ* 48/3 [July 1986]). Readers are referred to the *CBQ* volume for a biographical sketch of Father Fitzmyer by Myles M. Bourke, which offers a testimony to Fitzmyer's influence on biblical studies within the Roman Catholic tradition (pp. 375–78). Although the present volume was begun independently about the same time as the special issue of *CBQ,* it was not propelled with the efficiency of that journal issue; it comes to light at long last now on the eve of Father Fitzymer's seventieth birthday. The intervening years have served only to enhance the renown of this distinguished scholar and to increase the fervor with which the tribute is offered.

In the summer of 1985 we invited colleagues and former students of Father Fitzmyer to contribute to this volume articles that treated the topic of how ancient extrabiblical writings illuminate the biblical text. We thought this an appropriate theme because of Father Fitzmyer's own pioneering work in Aramaic studies and the Qumran literature, especially as these areas relate to the background of the New Testament. The studies in this collection are grouped into four parts: Language, Hebrew Bible, Dead Sea Scrolls, and New Testament. An emphasis on mastering the languages of the ancient world as the basis for biblical interpretation characterizes Father Fitzmyer's work in such major studies as *The Genesis Apocryphon of Qumran Cave I* (##137 and 218 in the bibliography), *The Aramaic Inscriptions of Sefire* (#160), and *A Manual of Palestinian Aramaic Texts* (coauthored with Daniel J. Harrington, S.J.; #341), and in his presidential addresses to the Catholic Biblical Association in 1970, "The Languages of Palestine in the First Century A.D." (#212), and to the Society of Biblical Literature in 1979, "The Aramaic Language and the Study of the New Testament" (#368). Knowledge of the Hebrew Bible and the history of its interpretation within Jewish and Christian traditions is integrated into Professor Fitzmyer's study of the Dead Sea Scrolls and the New Testament (e.g., ##53, 143, 145, 344, 397). Father Fitzmyer's many studies of the Qumran literature as evidence of the Palestinian background of the New Testament writings are well known, and his comprehensive works on Luke and Paul command the attention and study of all New Testament scholars. Professor Fitzmyer's championing of historical criticism as a method of studying and interpreting the Bible is evident throughout his writings on the New Testament. In a recent article he pointed out the ecumenical significance of the use of this method by Roman Catholic scholars: "[It] had much to do with the preparation of the Church for the developments at the Second Vatican Council. On the heels of the Council emerged ecumenical dialogue with many Christian ecclesial communities. No little reason for that emergence of dialogue was precisely the fact that Catholic interpreters of the Bible were pursuing the same kind of interpretation of the Bible that was in current use among many non-Catholic interpreters" ("Historical Criticism: Its Role in Biblical Interpretation and Church Life" [#480]). The truth of this assessment is borne out by the international and inter-confessional acclaim accorded Father Fitzmyer's work and by the backgrounds of the contributors to this volume.

There is another important area that this volume seeks to acknowledge. Father Fitzmyer serves the academic world tirelessly in the professional societies and in their publication projects. He initiates his students not only into careful research directed toward scholarly publishing but also into the practical life of the professional by encouraging students to join the societies and sponsoring them for membership. He instructs students how to prepare and submit articles for publication in scholarly journals and how to see works properly through the publication process. The editors of this volume have benefited greatly from this practical instruction over the years. When Father Fitzmyer was editor of *JBL* and *CBQ*, we worked with him as proofreaders and began to learn copyediting skills and the stages of journal and book publishing. These seeds grew to fruition in our partnership, The Scriptorium, which specializes in copyediting, typesetting, and proofreading in the area of biblical studies. We have a special debt of gratitude to Father Fitzmyer for this.

To the distinguished contributors we offer our gratitude for their fine studies and for their patience with the editors. Manuscripts for most of the articles were submitted in 1986 and 1987, and consequently the authors were unable to take full advantage of publications of the last two to three years, though during the proofreading stage some additions were made to update the research. We make here one final apology to the contributors for the delays.

To Frank Oveis of Crossroad, who is himself a former student of Father Fitzmyer, we offer our thanks for supporting the project and for awaiting its completion.

We give special thanks to Father Fitzmyer for supplying his complete bibliography for publication in this volume.

On behalf of the contributors we are pleased to set this volume awing, to present this gift, so that it may be a record of our high regard for Professor Joseph A. Fitzmyer, S.J.

MAURYA P. HORGAN
PAUL J. KOBELSKI

Abbreviations

AcOr	*Acta Orientalia*	BGBE	Beiträge zur Geschichte der
AER	*American Ecclesiastical Review*		biblischen Exegese
AfO	*Archiv für Orientforschung*	BH	Biblical Hebrew
AHw	W. von Soden, *Akkadisches Handwörterbuch*	BHT	Beiträge zur historischen Theologie
ALGHJ	Arbeiten zur Literatur und Geschichte des hellenistischen Judentums	*Bib*	*Biblica*
		BibOr	Biblica et orientalia
		BJRL	*Bulletin of the John Rylands Library*
AnBib	Analecta Biblica		
ANEP	*Ancient Near East in Pictures,* ed. J. B. Pritchard (Princeton: Princeton University Press, 1954)	BK	*Bibel und Kirche*
		BN	*Biblische Notizen*
		BR	*Biblical Research*
		BSac	*Bibliotheca Sacra*
ANET	*Ancient Near Eastern Texts,* ed. J. B. Pritchard (Princeton: Princeton University Press, 1950)	BT	*The Bible Translator*
		BTB	*Biblical Theology Bulletin*
		BZ	*Biblische Zeitschrift*
		BZAW	Beihefte zur *ZAW*
AnGreg	Analecta gregoriana	BZNW	Beihefte zur *ZNW*
AOAT	Alter Orient und Altes Testament	CAD	*The Assyrian Dictionary of the Oriental Institute of the University of Chicago*
AOS	American Oriental Series		
ASOR	American Schools of Oriental Research	CBQ	*Catholic Biblical Quarterly*
		CBQMS	Catholic Biblical Quarterly Monograph Series
ATANT	Abhandlungen zur Theologie des Alten und Neuen Testaments	CIL	*Corpus inscriptionum latinarum*
		ConNT	*Coniectanea neotestamentica*
ATR	*Anglican Theological Review*	CSEL	Corpus scriptorum ecclesiasticorum latinorum
AusBR	*Australian Biblical Review*		
BA	Biblical Aramaic	CTA	A. Herdner, *Corpus des tablettes en cunéiformes alphabétiques*
BA	*Biblical Archaeologist*		
BARev	*Biblical Archaeology Review*		
BASOR	*Bulletin of the American Schools of Oriental Research*	EBib	Etudes bibliques
		EKK	Evangelisch-katholischer Kommentar
BDB	F. Brown, S. R. Driver, and C. A. Briggs, *Hebrew and English Lexicon of the Old Testament* (Oxford: Oxford University Press, 1952)	EstBíb	*Estudios bíblicos*
		ETL	*Ephemerides theologicae lovanienses*
		ExpTim	*Expository Times*
BDF	F. Blass, A. Debrunner, and R. W. Funk, *A Greek Grammar of the New Testament and Other Early Christian Literature* (Chicago: University of Chicago Press, 1961)	FRLANT	Forschungen zur Religion und Literatur des Alten und Neuen Testaments
		GRBS	*Greek, Roman, and Byzantine Studies*
		GTA	Göttinger theologische Arbeiten
BETL	Bibliotheca ephemeridum theologicarum lovaniensium	HAR	*Hebrew Annual Review*

HNT	Handbuch zum Neuen Testament	*LTK*	*Lexikon für Theologie und Kirche*
HNTC	Harper's New Testament Commentaries	*MUSJ*	*Mélanges de l'Université Saint-Joseph* (Beirut)
HSM	Harvard Semitic Monographs	NCB	New Century Bible
		NCE	*New Catholic Encyclopedia*
HSS	Harvard Semitic Studies	*NJBC*	*The New Jerome Biblical Commentary*, ed. R. E. Brown, J. A. Fitzmyer, and R. E. Murphy (Englewood Cliffs, NJ: Prentice Hall, 1990)
HTKNT	Herders theologischer Kommentar zum Neuen Testament		
HTR	*Harvard Theological Review*		
HTS	Harvard Theological Studies	*NovT*	*Novum Testamentum*
HUCA	*Hebrew Union College Annual*	*NRT*	*La nouvelle revue théologique*
HUCAMS	*Hebrew Union College Annual* Monograph Series	NTA	New Testament Abstracts
		NTAbh	Neutestamentliche Abhandlungen
ICC	International Critical Commentary	NTD	Das Neue Testament Deutsch
IDB	*The Interpreter's Dictionary of the Bible*, ed. G. A. Buttrick (Nashville: Abingdon, 1962)	NTM	New Testament Message
		NTS	*New Testament Studies*
		NTTS	New Testament Tools and Studies
IEJ	*Israel Exploration Journal*	OBO	Orbis biblicus et orientalis
JAAR	*Journal of the American Academy of Religion*	*OCD*	*Oxford Classical Dictionary*
		OLP	*Orientalia lovaniensia periodica*
JAOS	*Journal of the American Oriental Society*	*OrAnt*	*Oriens antiquus*
JARCE	*Journal of the Research Center in Egypt*	OTA	*Old Testament Abstracts*
		PRU	*Le Palais royal d'Ugarit*
JBC	*The Jerome Biblical Commentary*, ed. R. E. Brown, J. A. Fitzmyer, and R. E. Murphy (Englewood Cliffs, NJ: Prentice Hall, 1968)	PSTJ	Perkins School of Theology Journal
		PW	Pauly-Wissowa, *Real-Encyclopädie der classischen Altertumswissenschaft*
JBL	*Journal of Biblical Literature*		
JJS	*Journal of Jewish Studies*	*Qad*	*Qadmoniot*
JNES	*Journal of Near Eastern Studies*	*RB*	*Revue biblique*
JNSL	*Journal of Northwest Semitic Languages*	RechBib	Recherches bibliques
		RevQ	*Revue de Qumran*
JQR	*Jewish Quarterly Review*	*RevScRel*	*Revue des sciences religieuses*
JR	*Journal of Religion*		
JSNT	*Journal for the Study of the New Testament*	RNT	Regensburger Neues Testament
JSOT	*Journal for the Study of the Old Testament*	*RSR*	*Recherches de science religieuse*
JSS	*Journal of Semitic Studies*	SANT	Studien zum Alten und Neuen Testament
JTC	*Journal for Theology and the Church*	SBLDS	Society of Biblical Literature Dissertation Series
JTS	*Journal of Theological Studies*		
KAI	H. Donner and W. Röllig, *Kanaanäische und aramäische Inschriften* (Wiesbaden, 1962–64)	SBLMS	Society of Biblical Literature Monograph Series
		SBLSBS	Society of Biblical Literature Sources for Biblical Study
KAT	Kommentar zum Alten Testament	SBT	Studies in Biblical Theology
		SC	Sources chrétiennes
KlT	Kleine Texte	SD	Studies and Documents
LCL	Loeb Classical Library	*SEÅ*	*Svensk exegetisk årsbok*

SJLA	Studies in Judaism in Late Antiquity	*TWAT*	*Theologisches Wörterbuch zum Alten Testament*, ed. G. J. Botterweck and H. Ringgren (Stuttgart: Kohlhammer, 1970-)
SNTS	Studiorum Novi Testamenti Societas		
SNTSMS	Studiorum Novi Testamenti Societas Monograph Series	*TWNT*	*Theologisches Wörterbuch zum Neuen Testament*, ed. G. Kittel and G. Friedrich (Stuttgart: Kohlhammer, 1933-)
SP	Samaria Papyrus		
STDJ	Studies on the Texts of the Desert of Judah		
SUNT	Studien zur Umwelt des Neuen Testament	*TynBul*	*Tyndale Bulletin*
SVTP	Studia in Veteris Testamenti pseudepigrapha	*UF*	*Ugarit-Forschungen*
		UT	C. H. Gordon, *Ugaritic Textbook*
TDNT	*Theological Dictionary of the New Testament*, ed. G. Kittel and G. Friedrich (Grand Rapids, MI: Eerdmans, 1964-76)	*VT*	*Vetus Testamentum*
		VTSup	Supplements to *VT*
		WMANT	Wissenschaftliche Monographien zum Alten und Neuen Testament
TDOT	*Theological Dictionary of the Old Testament*, ed. G. J. Botterweck and H. Ringgren (Grand Rapids: Eerdmans, 1977-)	*ZAW*	*Zeitschrift für die alttestamentliche Wissenschaft*
		ZDPV	*Zeitschrift des deutschen Palästina Vereins*
TLZ	*Theologische Literaturzeitung*	*ZNW*	*Zeitschrift für die neutestamentliche Wissenschaft*
TRU	*Testi Rituali di Ugarit*		
TRu	*Theologische Rundschau*	*ZTK*	*Zeitschrift für Theologie und Kirche*
TS	*Theological Studies*		
TU	Texte und Untersuchungen		

Part I

Language

Chapter 1   Aleph as a Vowel Letter in Old Aramaic

Francis I. Andersen
University of Queensland

David Noel Freedman
The University of Michigan
University of California, San Diego

There is no convincing evidence that *aleph* was used regularly, systematically, and deliberately as a vowel letter, an assertion that can be made and sustained for the three genuine vowel letters: *he, waw,* and *yod.*

IN 1952 F. M. CROSS AND D. N. FREEDMAN concluded that "there is no evidence for the use of aleph as a *mater lectionis*" in any of the Old Aramaic inscriptions which they studied.[1] In 1956 G. Garbini reported a somewhat diffuse use (*uso piuttosto diffuso*) of all four *matres lectionis* in the Zkr Inscription, citing אשא (I:11) as evidence for *aleph* as *mater lectionis* in word-final position.[2] In 1962 J. J. Koopmans claimed that Cross and Freedman's statement cannot be correct (*kann das doch nicht richtig sein*).[3] His reason: It has not been proved that the definite article was pronounced -*a*'. In 1975 S. Segert similarly asserted that *aleph* was a *mater lectionis* in the Sefire inscriptions.[4] In 1967 J. A. Fitzmyer studied the use of *aleph* in the Sefire inscriptions and concluded: "We find no reason to regard *aleph* in this stele as anything but consonantal, and consequently the emphatic ending as -*a*'."[5] Note the word "consequently."

---

[1] F. M. Cross and D. N. Freedman, *Early Hebrew Orthography: A Study of the Epigraphic Evidence* (AOS 36; New Haven: American Oriental Society, 1952) 28.

[2] G. Garbini, *L'aramaico antico* (Memorie Accad. Naz. dei Lincei, Classe di scienze morali, stori e filologi VIII, Vol. VII, 5; 1956) 252.

[3] J. J. Koopmans, *Aramäische Chrestomathie, Ausgewählte Texte (Inschriften, Ostraka, Papyri)* (Leiden: Nederlands Instituut voor het Nabije Oosten, 1962) 7.

[4] S. Segert, *Altaramäische Grammatik* (Leipzig: Verlag Enzyklopädie, 1975).

[5] J. A. Fitzmyer, *The Aramaic Inscriptions of Sefire* (BibOr 19; Rome: Pontifical Biblical Institute, 1967) 147.

R. Degen recognized only *he, waw,* and *yod* as *matres lectionis* in Old Aramaic inscriptions, stating categorically: "' ist im Aa. noch keine *mater lectionis* für - ā."[6]

In view of this ongoing debate and discussion of the possible use of *aleph* as a vowel letter in early Aramaic inscriptions, it seemed advisable to consider and evaluate the available evidence and the arguments on both sides of the debate. Our conclusions will not differ appreciably from those previously arrived at, but this discussion may clarify the issues by examining the underlying presuppositions, weighing the methods used, and testing the results.

To begin with, there is the question of definition. What is a vowel letter? And how is it to be distinguished from consonantal letters? Our frame of reference is the so-called Phoenician alphabet and the Northwest Semitic inscriptions of the Iron Age, including the proto-Canaanite inscriptions of the twelfth-eleventh centuries and the major corpus of substantial inscriptions in Phoenician and related dialects of the tenth century and following, as well as the group of Aramaic inscriptions of the same general period. Originally the alphabet was entirely consonantal: every letter had a consonantal value and words were spelled in accordance with their consonantal values. Naturally the words included vowels, but these were not indicated in the orthography. It was, therefore, a form of shorthand or a conventional means for indicating certain sounds (the consonants) while leaving the recognition or reproduction of the vowel sounds to the knowledge, skill, or ingenuity of the reader or speaker. All of the earliest inscriptions (twelfth, eleventh centuries) from Canaan reflect this pattern, and the Phoenician inscriptions for the major part of their history and certainly covering the period of our interest preserve the pattern of purely consonantal spelling. There are no vowel letters in Phoenician inscriptions.

In the related language groups for which the Phoenician alphabet was adopted and adapted, we cannot be sure whether there was an initial period of pure consonantism—and for the purposes of this paper it is not a matter of significance. All of the inscriptions in Old Aramaic (as well as inscriptions in Canaanite dialects such as Moabite and Hebrew) exhibit the use of vowel letters. What this means is that certain letters, originally and regularly representing consonantal sounds, were also used to represent certain vowels, perhaps with corresponding or compatible values. It is universally agreed that three of these letters were so used: *he, waw,* and *yod. Waw* and *yod* were used in both final and medial positions to represent the vowels *û* and *î* respectively, whereas *he* was used only in the final position. Its primary and perhaps chief function was to represent the vowel -*â*, but it also reflects other vowel

---

[6] R. Degen, *Altaramäische Grammatik der Inschriften des 10.-8. Jh. v. Chr.* (Wiesbaden: Komissionsverlag Steiner, 1969) 25.

sounds: $\bar{e}$ and $\bar{o}$. Unlike the case of $\hat{u}$ and $\hat{\imath}$, medial -$\bar{a}$- was not represented in the orthography.

It is immediately clear that the system was neither complete nor flawless, since it handled only certain vowels and used letters that already functioned and would continue to function as consonants. An ambiguity arises, since the same letter cannot be both a consonant letter and a vowel letter in the same occurrence, but it is not always clear which it is in any given instance. In theory at least the three letters listed above can be either consonants or vowel letters wherever they appear, but in most cases the choice can be made without great difficulty or much contention.

In this analysis a question might be raised about diphthongs, e.g., *ay* and *aw*. In principle and in practice these are represented by their consonantal elements, *yod* and *waw* respectively, and therefore diphthongs are treated as consonants. In the case of contracted diphthongs, *ay>ê, aw>ô*, the result is a vowel, either *ê* or *ô*, and if the *yod* or *waw* is retained in the spelling, then that sign, which remains the same, has nevertheless changed from representing a consonant (the consonantal element in the diphthong) to a vowel letter. Although this apparent sleight of hand actually takes place and can be documented, it nevertheless poses serious problems for scholars. On the basis of orthography alone, it is impossible to tell whether the letter is a consonant or a vowel letter: we need to know whether the contraction of the diphthong has actually taken place.

If the diphthong has been contracted, then we might expect the letter (*yod* or *waw*) reflecting the diphthong to be dropped. Thus, in languages where the contraction has occurred the word for "house," originally *bayt,* is spelled *bt* (for *bêt*), whereas in those in which it is not contracted the word is spelled *byt* (for *bayt*). In cases where the phonetic shift has occurred after the spelling *byt* has been fixed, this *yod* might be retained in the spelling, producing the equation *byt = bêt,* a hybrid form.

This effect or outcome is called "historical spelling," and it results in a new phonemic value for the letter used. Thus *waw* can represent *ô* and *yod* can represent *ê* as well as their previously established consonantal (*y* and *w*) and vowel (*î* and *û*) indications. Without external evidence (from inscriptions in a writing system using vowels, or a vocalization system such as the Masoretic Text) it is difficult to evaluate historical spelling. In order to establish the new values for a vowel letter derived or developed in this manner, we normally require substantial evidence that the same equivalence or equation occurs apart from historical spelling. In other words, if we are going to maintain that *waw = ô* (along with *û* or *aw*) and *yod = ê* (along with *î* and *ay*), then we must be able to demonstrate the utilization of these values in the spelling of words in which the *waw* or *yod* is not part of the root form and does not have a continuous history of use, first for the primal consonant and now for the resultant vowel. In short, the argument from historical spelling is often tainted by these ambiguities and continuities, and so without external supporting data we cannot accept any such cases of historical spelling by themselves as decisive or persuasive.

In the case of *aleph* practically all of the instances for which it is claimed that *aleph* is a vowel letter are cases of historical spelling in which it is claimed that *aleph* has lost its consonantal force and has become a vowel letter representing this or that vowel. What is needed is evidence that *aleph* has been introduced into a word where it had no previous consonantal function and serves purely as a vowel marker. Thus, words derived from the root *rʾš*, "head," generally continue to be written with the etymological *aleph*, even after the consonant sound has ceased to be pronounced (is "quiescent") in such words. The practical outcome of such a change in pronunciation without a corresponding change in spelling is that *aleph* comes to function virtually as a vowel letter in words like *rō(ʾ)š* or *rē(ʾ)š* or *rī(ʾ)š*, *rā(ʾ)šîm*, etc. But this is only evidence that in later texts the *aleph* is preserved by historical spelling; that is, such an *aleph* has a merely passive association with various vowels because it has lost its consonantal force. To qualify as a vowel letter in the strict sense, however, *aleph* must be used for these or other vowels in words in which it never had consonantal force or an etymological base; e.g., *qāʾm* (Hos 10:14). Since the root is *q(w)m*, the *aleph* in such a spelling is a genuine vowel letter, but this is a very rare and late phenomenon in Biblical Hebrew. F. I. Andersen and A. D. Forbes report only sixteen specimens.[7] It is even rarer and quite anomalous in the Old Aramaic inscriptions.

When it comes to the possible use of *aleph* as a vowel letter in early Aramaic inscriptions, we must evaluate the following data, and follow these procedures:

(1) Exclude from consideration all instances in which *aleph* is a root or stem consonant or in which it serves as a prefix in verbal and nominal forms. In this category we must likewise include all cases of possible historical spelling, since the most that can be said for such instances is that the *aleph* has quiesced and has been preserved as a passive marker of the accompanying vowel. This at once cancels Garbini's use of אשא in Zkr I:11 as evidence of *aleph* as *mater lectionis* in word-final position.[8] It is only when such a practice is regularized and extended to cases in which there is no etymological *aleph* in the word and the same vowel or vowels are indicated by *aleph* that we can speak of *aleph* as a vowel letter in the sense that has been demonstrated for *he*, *waw*, and *yod*.

[7] F. I. Andersen and A. D. Forbes, *Spelling in the Hebrew Bible* (BibOr 41; Rome: Biblical Institute Press, 1985) 83–84.

[8] Garbini, *L'aramaico antico*, 252.

(2) Evaluate the remaining cases in which *aleph* appears as a vowel marker (opposed to vowel bearer, which signifies that it must be a consonant). The issue then is whether the form in question involves *aleph* as a consonant or as a vowel letter. We can divide this group into two parts: (a) the appearance of the *aleph* at the end of nouns (substantives and adjectives) in the emphatic state. Since this is the most frequent and regular usage of *aleph* in a syllable- or word-terminal position and is the form about which much of the dispute has turned, it deserves to be looked at carefully. The suffix -*ā'* as an indicator of definiteness, while semantically equivalent to the definite article in Hebrew and other Canaanite dialects (*ha-* prefixed to nouns), seems to be unique to Aramaic. Its derivation is unknown. But to say that because the etymology is not known the terminal *aleph* must be only or actually a vowel letter is a *non-sequitur*. The natural presumption is that it is a consonant, since all letters are potentially consonantal and it is reasonable to begin at that point with *aleph* as with all other letters. What needs to be shown is that it *is* a vowel letter, and such a conclusion cannot be drawn from the evidence of the inscriptions.

In the first place, there is a perfectly good letter (*he*) available to represent final *â*, and it is used regularly for all words ending in -*â* in Aramaic inscriptions, while in those inscriptions in which the noun in the emphatic state occurs, the distinction in spelling is maintained systematically. The final *aleph* is used always in the case of the emphatic state, while *he* is used in all cases in which the word ends in the vowel -*â*. The inference is almost inescapable that the *aleph* is not a vowel letter but a consonant, while *he* is used as a vowel letter. At most we might say that the *aleph* has quiesced and thus serves as a passive vowel marker (regardless of the actual vowel). What still needs to be shown is that *aleph* is used where we would expect *he* to be used, and vice versa. That would show that they were interchangeable vowel letters and that the *aleph* had quiesced. But this phenomenon (use of either *he* or *aleph* to spell the same vowel) is not attested in the early inscriptions at all, and even as late as the most recent of the Samaria Papyri (335 B.C.E.) the complementary distribution between the emphatic ending (-*ā'*) and words ending in -*â* (just the vowel) is rigorously maintained. That means that in all likelihood the *aleph* was still pronounced as a consonant and the distinction was both phonemic and orthographic. The use of *aleph* with the emphatic state of the noun throughout the whole period of extant inscriptions in turn argues strongly for its being an original and essential part of this enclitic and not simply the result of an arbitrary choice of *aleph* as a vowel letter (instead of *he*) to represent final -*â*. Alternatively the *aleph* may have been appended to the definite article for reasons unknown to us. There is no basis for doubt that it was pronounced as a consonant, at least in the entire period under consideration, and possibly even beyond it.

(b) What remains for investigation are a handful of anomalous and idiosyncratic cases which may or may not be instances of *aleph* as a vowel letter, but which in any case only serve to demonstrate that *aleph* was in an entirely different category from the three standard vowel letters, *he, waw,* and *yod,* which are used extensively throughout the whole inscriptional corpus.

One theoretical possibility may be considered before turning to the actual examples. The vowel-letter system is slightly skewed by the fact that *waw* and *yod* are used both at the ends of words and also medially, while *he* appears only in the terminal position. That leaves a gap in the system, i.e., there is no representation of medial -*ā*-, and theoretically at least this gap could have been filled by *aleph.* This in fact is what eventually did happen, as we have already pointed out in the discussion above. But indubitable specimens of this usage turn up only toward the very end of the period under study, and then only sporadically. The earliest certain attestation of the use of *aleph* as a vowel letter for medial -*ā*- (not in historical spelling, which we have excluded as not germane) is in the Dead Sea Scrolls. There is no unambiguous evidence for such usage in the early inscriptions, and hence we can infer that there was no apparent reason to use *aleph* at all as a vowel letter.

We now turn to the examples in the early inscriptions of *aleph* alleged to be a vowel letter. First, we dispose of two cases that are equivocal either from the point of view of decipherment or in terms of morphological interpretation. Garbini adduced *mlkh,* "the king" (which he read in *KAI* 203), as evidence that the emphatic suffix could be spelled with *he* and therefore was pronounced -*â,* even when it was spelled with *aleph,* as it was routinely. But the letter is not clear. Koopmans reads *mlk',* which is what we would expect. Second, the noun "night" occurs in Hebrew as *lyl* and *lylh.* Both *lyl'* and *lylh* are found in Old Aramaic. One cannot simply declare that these are the same and that therefore *he* and *aleph* can be used interchangeably for the spelling of -*â.* The consistent and contrasting use of *he* and *aleph* everywhere else, as well as the distinctive morphology of this word, points to *lylh* as adverbial ("by night") while *lyl'* is determined ("the night").

The other cases of the use of *aleph* in Old Aramaic inscriptions allegedly to represent *ā* are restricted to particles. This is a most interesting fact, and it raises a number of important methodological considerations. Particles are notoriously difficult to track etymologically or to analyze into ancestral parts. They are also characteristically unruly when it comes to obeying the laws of regular sound changes which are discovered by research in historical-comparative grammar. Regular sound changes, such as the quiescence of *aleph* in certain positions in the syllabic structure of words, take place systematically in words that belong to classes of large membership, notably nouns and verbs. Such changes are fostered and also regulated by paradigmatic analogies. It is otherwise with words that belong to classes of small membership and do not group into paradigms, notably particles. Some of these—for example, the negative *lā'*—are the only members of their class. Their evolution is less constrained by analogy; their phonetic development is often erratic. In Northwest Semitic there are several such particles which have only one root consonant—*l, w, z, š, p*—and they are more labile than words with stable roots; they are susceptible to the production of alloforms which use *aleph*, either before or after the primal consonant, so as to yield a closed syllable.

Among these particles the most conspicuous is the negative *lā'*. Whatever the historical status of an alternative form spelled simply with *l* and presumably pronounced *lā*, the form spelled with *aleph* is standard and widespread and stable over the entire period in which we are interested. A typical comment is that of Z. Zevit. He cites *l'*, "not," as evidence that *aleph* was used as a vowel letter in preexilic Hebrew, "since the *'alep* in this word is not etymological."[9] Presumably the same argument would apply to Aramaic, but this begs the whole question and it does not address the real problem. If *aleph* in *l'*, "not," is just another way of writing *-â*, why is the negative particle never spelled *lh*?

The consistent spelling of both the emphatic suffix and the negative particle points to the existence in Old Aramaic of a word-terminal *aleph* actually pronounced as a consonant. The fact that these particular *alephs* cannot be traced to primal origins does not mean that they could never have emerged in the language; and the fact that in due time they would become quiescent does not mean that they never were pronounced. We conclude that there were four distinct paths along which phonetic and/or orthographic *aleph* developed in Aramaic (see Table 1). Some primal *alephs* continue to be pronounced throughout the entire history of the language, and these are written as consonantal *aleph* (column 1). Some *alephs* originally pronounced eventually become quiescent, and when *aleph* is still written at that point, the spelling is historical in the strict sense (column 2). When *aleph* is eventually used to write a vowel in a word that never had a consonantal *aleph* at that point, the *aleph* is a vowel letter (column 4). Column 3 presents an intermediate category; although not demonstrably etymological, it emerged as a real consonant at a certain stage of the language and was written by means of *aleph*, the consonant letter. When such an *aleph* eventually quiesced but was still shown in the spelling, the result was a vowel marker similar in function to the historical spellings in column 2, but differing from them in ancient historical origins. We need the development shown in column 3 to explain the history of the spelling of the suffix of the emphatic state and of the

[9] Z. Zevit, *Matres Lectionis in Ancient Hebrew Epigraphs* (ASOR Monograph Series 2; Cambridge, MA: ASOR, 1980) 22.

Table 1
***Aleph* in Aramaic**

	Etymological		Non-etymological	
	1 Stable	2 Quiescing	3 Emerging	4 Never Pronounced
Primal Stage	An original root consonant or stem preformative, pronounced as a consonant.		Not shown to be present in the early language.	No *aleph* was ever pronounced at this point in the word.
Middle Stage Old Aramaic	Still pronounced; the written *aleph* is a consonant letter.		A phonetic innovation to close certain syllables at word end or at morpheme juncture; *aleph* represents a consonant.	No certain attestation of the use of *aleph* as a vowel letter.
Late Stage	Consonant is still pronounced and written *aleph*.	*Aleph* quiesces, written as historical spelling; passive vowel marker.		*Aleph* used to write a vowel as such.

negative particle. They are not the only cases, although they are the most abundant.

Other examples are *w'*, alternative spelling of *wa-*, "and"; *p'*, alternative spelling of *pa-*, "and"; *z'*, alternative spelling of *z-*, demonstrative/relative. These have been adduced as evidence of the use of *aleph* as a vowel letter in Old Aramaic. These *aleph*s are evidently not etymological. But we contend once more that this does not necessarily prove that they were never pronounced as a consonant. We consider it significant that these *aleph*s turn up in the writing of particles. It should also be emphasized that their occurrence is sporadic and very limited.

The spelling of "and" as *w'* occurs apparently twice in Panamuwa II (*KAI* 215). Line 5 has *w'gm* (compare with *wgm* in line 16). To read this as *wāgam* is only one possibility; and this would still require an explanation of the lengthening of the vowel in this proclitic position. Giving first preference to reading the *aleph* as a consonant, we have either *wa'-gam* (the glottal stop is articulated and marks juncture between the two conjunctions), or *wa-'agam* (*'gm* being an allomorph of *gm* with prosthetic *aleph*). KAI 215:9 has *w'z*, which does not have to be read as *wā-z(i)*, since it could be *wa'-z(i)* or *wa-'az*.

The word *p'* occurs three times. The simple *p-* occurs ten times in Old

Aramaic. (For the purposes of this paper, the exact dialectal affiliation of the texts is irrelevant. The conjunction is found in other Semitic languages, notably Arabic.) The three occurrences of *p'* are *p' γ'mr* (*KAI* 214:17); *p' yšrh* (*KAI* 214:33); *p' hdd* (*KAI* 215:22). By assuming that this is no more than an alternative spelling of simple *p-*, it is argued that in these three instances the *aleph* has been added as a vowel letter and that the word should be transcribed as *pā-* instead of *pa'*. But the question arises again: Why didn't they use *he*? Even if the words are originally of common derivation, the *aleph*, developed secondarily, could still be consonantal, written because it was pronounced. As with the analogous *w'-*, the secondary form with *aleph* was in free fluctuation with the prime form, and seems to have had a transitory existence in a regional dialect. If it had taken over, or even survived as an alloform, and then the *aleph* quiesced but was still written, it would be no more than another example of historical spelling and would not qualify as a vowel letter in the strict sense.

The demonstrative/relative is variously *z, zy, z'*. A reading *zh* has been claimed in line 19 of the Asshur ostracon (*KAI* 233), but this is uncertain, and *wg . . .* is preferred.

There is, then, some variety in the spelling of these particles in Old Aramaic. We wish to be careful not to overstate our argument, but we think it is more likely that this reflects an accurate spelling of a real fluidity in the pronunciation of these words rather than an inconsistency in the spelling system. And even if these *aleph*s were used as vowel letters rather than the well-established *he,* the practice was restricted to a few special particles and very circumscribed in both space and time; that is, it cannot possibly be recognized as a central and lasting contribution to Aramaic spelling. On the contrary, by taking these *aleph*s at their face value and interpreting them as we do all other *aleph*s of the period, namely, as consonant letters, we recover some interesting data about the phonological and morphological developments of these particles in Old Aramaic.

Table 2
Secondary *aleph* in Northwest Semitic

'l	l	l'
'p	p	p'
'z	z	z'
'w	w	w'
'gm	gm	
'š (Phoen.)	š	

This interpretation receives further support when we add other evidence from Northwest Semitic to the picture. Some of these particles, and other similar particles, are attested with prosthetic as well as following *aleph*. See

Table 2. The development of energic *nun* in Canaanite is not understood well enough to connect it with the insistent Hebrew particle *nā'*, not to mention the exclamation *'ānnā'*.

Conclusions

For Old Aramaic the orthographic (vowel-letter) system can be explained or described in essentially simple terms: *he, waw, yod* for final long vowels, and *waw, yod* for internal long vowels, in particular *û* and *î* respectively. There was no natural or ordinary place for a fourth vowel letter in this system, and it is clear that neither *aleph* nor any other letter had such a function.

Practically every occurrence of *aleph* in the inscriptions is to be explained on the basis of its natural consonantal value. All cases in which *aleph* is initial in a syllable are to be explained in that fashion, and the same should be maintained for most, if not all occurrences in which it closes a syllable or word. In these cases *aleph* is either part of the root system or it serves as an indicator of some particle, such as the ending of the emphatic state. The most that can be said of such examples is that the *aleph* may have quiesced and hence, not being pronounced, serves as a vowel marker. Since, however, it can be and is associated with a wide range of vowels, its real value is zero, and hence it does not function in the way that a true vowel letter does. (If any given vowel letter is not dedicated to the representation of one kind of vowel, but can indiscriminately represent any kind of vowel, it does not tell the reader anything. In the classical system *yod* represents front vowels, *waw* represents back vowels, *he* represents central vowels. In complete contrast to this workable system, *aleph* in historical spellings is found associated with any and every kind of vowel.)

There remains a small and anomalous residue of instances of *aleph* which do not yield easily to analysis or interpretation. With respect to the negative particle, it seems easier and more reasonable to recognize in *lā'* a vocable separate from the preserved negative *l*, just as the particle *'al* is recognizably different. Ultimately they may have derived from the same root form = *l*, which is expanded by a prefixed *aleph* (*'al*), or by one that is affixed at the end (*lā'*). If the *aleph* in the latter case were no more than a vowel letter, then it is not clear why *aleph* was used for this purpose rather than the standard and normative *he*. The case here cannot be proved beyond doubt, but the assumption or assertion that *aleph* is only a vowel letter here is questionable at best.

Out of all the examples of *aleph* in the Old Aramaic inscriptions there remains only the barest handful that still challenge the hypothesis presented here and remain doubtful. These examples are the words *wā'* and *p'*, which are presumably and apparently equivalent to *w-* and *p-*, well-known particles serving as conjunctions in the Old Aramaic inscriptions. Since the conjunctions are attached directly to the following word, the insertion of the *aleph* makes it appear like an internal *mater lectionis*, not a terminal one. Nevertheless it comes at a juncture point and may have been used to distinguish between or separate the two components of the word or phrase, in pronunciation as well as writing—in pronunciation first, and then, therefore, in writing. It should also be reiterated that the phenomenon is quite rare, *w'* and *p'* occurring only in the Panamuwa inscriptions and not used anywhere else in this limited corpus. We would argue that the usage here is like that of *lā'*, the negative particle, in relation to *l-*, and that *w'* and *p'* are by-forms of *w-* and *p-*, and that the differences are phonetic and phonemic and not merely orthographic. Admittedly it is a difficult case, but even if it were agreed that the *aleph* in these circumstances is a vowel letter rather than a consonant, then it should also be noted that this usage of *aleph* was experimental, sporadic, and evanescent, since it was not carried forward in the standard spelling procedures of later Aramaic inscriptions. All that would be left in future centuries would be the fossilized form *lā'*, where *aleph* might once have been a vowel letter. But even so, all these cases can be explained as autonomous by-forms or secondary developments resulting from the addition of a genuine consonantal (i.e., glottal stop) *aleph*, either before the root consonant (i.e., *'al, 'aw, 'ap*) or after it (*la', wa', pa'*).

There is no convincing evidence that *aleph* was used regularly, systematically, and deliberately as a vowel letter, an assertion that can be made and sustained for the three genuine vowel letters, *he, waw,* and *yod*.

The attested uses of *aleph* as a vowel letter in any of the Northwest Semitic languages came much later. Thus, *aleph* is used as a medial vowel letter in the *Genesis Apocryphon* (Freedman and Ritterspach 1967) to represent the vowel *a*, but only after *waw* and *yod*, and then to indicate that the preceding letter is a consonant and not itself a vowel letter.[10] Similar usage may be inferred in forms such as *ky'* (= *kiya'*) in the Dead Sea Scrolls for Masoretic *ky* (= *kî*). Contrariwise, the *aleph* in the words *hw'h* (Dead Sea Scrolls) and *hw'* (Masoretic Text) is not a vowel letter at all, but a consonant in both instances: it is clearly meant to be pronounced in the longer form (*hû'â*), although it probably had quiesced in the familiar shorter form (*hû'*).

---

[10] D. N. Freedman and A. Ritterspach, "The Use of Aleph as a Vowel Letter in the Genesis Apocryphon," *RevQ* 22 (1967) 293–300.

Bibliography

Andersen, F. I., and A. D. Forbes, *Spelling in the Hebrew Bible.* BibOr 41. Rome: Biblical Institute Press, 1985.

Cross, F. M., and D. N. Freedman, *Early Hebrew Orthography: A Study of the Epigraphic Evidence.* AOS 36. New Haven: American Oriental Society, 1952.

Degen, R., *Altaramäische Grammatik der Inschriften des 10.-8. Jh. v. Chr.* Wiesbaden: Komissionsverlag Steiner, 1969.

Fitzmyer, J. A., *The Aramaic Inscriptions of Sefire.* BibOr 19. Rome: Pontifical Biblical Institute, 1967.

Freedman, D. N., and A. Ritterspach, "The Use of *Aleph* as a Vowel Letter in the Genesis Apocryphon." *RevQ* 22 (1967) 293–300.

Garbini, G., *L'aramaico antico.* Memorie Accad. Naz. dei Lincei, Classe di scienze morali, stori e filologi VIII, Vol VII, 5; 1956.

Koopmans, J. J., *Aramäische Chrestomathie, Ausgewählte Texte (Inschriften, Ostraka, Papyri).* Leiden: Nederlands Instituut voor het Nabije Oosten, 1962.

Segert, S., *Altaramäische Grammatik.* Leipzig: Verlag Enzyklopädie, 1975.

Zevit, Z., *Matres Lectionis in Ancient Hebrew Epigraphs.* ASOR Monograph Series 2. Cambridge, MA: American Schools of Oriental Research, 1980.

The Spelling of Samaria Papyrus 1

David Noel Freedman
The University of Michigan
University of California, San Diego

Francis I. Andersen
University of Queensland

Two key factors make the papyri especially important: they are official documents and they are dated precisely.

THE RECENT PUBLICATION of the Samaria Papyri is to be welcomed for many reasons. These documents will shed new light on legal customs and practices in that region during the last decades of Persian rule, as well as many related historical, social, and economic matters. The papyri will also provide much useful information about the Aramaic language of this period, its vocabulary, grammar, and syntax. They will also have significant value for the disciplines of epigraphy and orthography. Two key factors make the papyri especially important: they are official documents and they are dated precisely. For epigraphic research, they provide a fixed point (or points) in the evolutionary charts and thus will be of enormous value in dating the many other written documents from this and adjoining periods. In like fashion, they will enable us to fix the orthographic patterns for official Aramaic documents and establish the prevailing practices for the middle decades of the fourth century B.C.E. Thus, we are in a position to place these documents in the long evolutionary sequence of alphabetic orthography among the Northwest Semitic dialects,

We wish to thank Dr. William H. Propp for substantial criticism and assistance with this paper.

especially Aramaic, and at the same time measure and evaluate comparable documents that for the most part lack dates and may not have had official status.

Our purpose in the present study is to examine the orthography of the first Samaria Papyrus (SP 1), summarize the findings, and present a sketch of spelling practice and principle in the third quarter of the fourth century B.C.E. According to the editor of the document, its date can be fixed precisely to 19 March 335 B.C.E., and that is the point from which we will begin.[1] In what follows, we will list each readable word of the inscription, transcribe it with appropriate vocalization according to the best information and opinion that we have, and provide an attested or presumed vocalization in Biblical Aramaic. On occasion, we have cited a Hebrew form if an Aramaic parallel is lacking. Since our objective is to determine actual orthographic practice, we restrict ourselves to certain or highly probable readings, although there is no doubt that Frank Cross's reconstruction of the document is correct in all major respects.

1. (1:1) *b 20.*
2. (1:2) *l'dr*—*la'adar* (BA *la'ădār*), "of Adar."
3. (1:3) *šnt 2*—*šanat* (BA *šĕnat*), "in the second year."
4. (1:4) *r'š*—*ri'š* (BA *rē'š*), "the first" = "accession year." The vocalization in Biblical Aramaic indicates that the *aleph* has quiesced and the vowel therefore changed and lengthened from -*i* to *ē*. There is no clear evidence that the change had already occurred by this time, but even if the *aleph* had quiesced it would have been preserved by historical spelling, as is the case in Biblical Aramaic. Only if there were instances in which the word were spelled without *aleph* could we be certain that the *aleph* was no longer pronounced. Even then, the *aleph* should not be regarded as a vowel letter but only as a passive vowel marker (i.e., the result of historical spelling).
5. (1:5) *mlkwt*—*malkût* (BA *malkût*), "of the reign." The *waw* serves as a vowel letter representing -*û*.
6. (1:6) *(d)ryhws*—*darayahaweš* or *darayahûš* (BA *dārĕyāweš*). The name appears as *darayava'ush* in Old Persian; it is transcribed in Elephantine Aramaic as *drywhwš*, which can be vocalized as *darayawahûš*. As can be seen, there are different ways in which to represent this non–Semitic name, and therefore we cannot be certain as to the precise value accorded the letters, which may be either consonants or vowels. The *he* is certainly to be regarded as a consonant (representing the ' of Old Persian), while the *waw* may be either a consonant (as clearly in BA) or a vowel letter for -*û*, reflecting the vocalization of the final syllable of the name in Old Persian.

[1] F. M. Cross, "Samaria Papyrus 1: An Aramaic Slave Conveyance of 335 B.C.E. Found in the Wadi Ed-Daliyeh," in *Nahman Avigad Volume* (ed. B. Mazar and Y. Yadin; Eretz-Israel 18; Jerusalem: Israel Exploration Society, 1985) 10*.

7. (1:7) *mlk'* — *malka'* (BA *malka'*), "the king." In Biblical Aramaic, the final *aleph* has quiesced, and the preceding vowel lengthened. Just when this change took place, and whether it had occurred by the time of our document cannot be determined. In any case, we are dealing with an originally consonantal *aleph*, which ultimately quiesces and then serves as a passive vowel marker. So it does not qualify as a true vowel letter. If the *aleph* had quiesced and thus had become a vowel letter for final -*ā*, then we might have expected both confusion and contamination with the letter *he*, which is regularly used for that purpose. It so happens that in all clear cases, *he* is a vowel letter for final -*â*, while *aleph* is used only where it had originally consonantal status. The implication is that the distinction between the two letters was still being observed in these papyri.

8. (1:8) *bšmry(n)* — *bišamaray(n)* (BA *bĕšāmĕrāyin*), "in Samaria." In Biblical Aramaic, the diphthong -*ay* has been resolved into the bisyllabic -*ayi-*. That may be the case with the reading in the papyrus, but since the development in question is specific to Biblical Hebrew and Aramaic, it is more likely that the diphthong has simply been preserved in SP 1 (-*ayn*). It is even less likely that the diphthong has been contracted, -*ay* > *ê;* in that case, the preservation of the *yod* would be an instance of historical spelling.

9. (2:1) *lyhwhnn* — *liyahawahanan* (BH *yĕhôhānān*), "Jehohanan." The analysis and interpretation of this familiar biblical Yahwistic name are difficult. In view of its universal and persistent occurrence, we are convinced that the *waw* in the sequence *yhw* was originally consonantal, and therefore we question the traditional explanation of the preformative *yĕhô*- as a back-formation from an original *yahu* > *yaw* > *yô* and then with the restoration of the original *he*, *yĕhô-*. We must start further back in the series with the full name *yahweh* and postulate a combining form such as **yahwi-* and then **yahw-*. From this basic element, there could be a natural development to *yahaw-*, from which the two biblical forms can easily be derived: *yahaw-* > *yĕhô* (for the older form of the name) and *yahaw* > *yaw* > *yô*. In defense of this approach, it should be noted that in all early texts *yĕhô*-names are always spelled *yhw-*, never *yh-* (without orthographic indication of the *ō*). The preservation of the *waw* in all surviving forms of the name, biblical and otherwise, strengthens the case for its original consonantal character, whether as a root consonant of the divine element, or as a diphthong in the development of the form. There is no evidence, therefore, that the diphthong had contracted by the time of this papyrus, or that *he* of the preformative had been lost and was reintroduced at or before this time. We therefore favor the pronunciation *yahaw-hanan* in this period as being in harmony with the consistent spelling of the name. The shorter form of the name would have been *yawhanan*. Whenever the diphthong was contracted, the spelling of either form would have remained the same.

10. (2:2) *šmh—šumih* (BA *šĕmēh*), "his name." The *he*, representing the 3rd masc. sg. suffix, is consonantal, as confirmed by the spelling in Biblical Aramaic.

11. (2:3) *br—bar* or *bir* (BA *bar*), "the son of."

12. (2:4) *š'lh—ša'ilâ* (cf. BH *šĕ'ēlâ* and BA *šĕ'ēlĕtā'*, which is derived from the same basic form), "Shaila." The root is found in other names such as the familiar *šā'ûl* (Saul). Closer to the time of the papyrus, the name *šĕ'āl* occurs in Ezra 10:29 (K). In addition the masculine name *š'yl'* occurs in Palmyrene. The spelling with medial *yod* for -*î* may imply that the name in the papyrus is written defectively, but we cannot be sure that the name is precisely the same in both cases. We have assumed that the form of the name in the papyrus is *qatil,* or basically the same as in the biblical common noun, rather than *qatîl* as in the Palmyrene name. The final *aleph* in the Palmyrene name shows that the name belongs to a large class of apparently hypocoristic names ending in *aleph*. There can be little doubt that the *aleph* in all of these cases was originally consonantal (as shown by the occurrence of the same type of name with the same spelling in Phoenician, which has no vowel letters) although in the course of time the *aleph* may have quiesced. After the *aleph* quiesced, it served as a passive vowel marker for the final vowel, presumably -*ā*. Once that shift had taken place (from a' to *ā*), then it would be possible to substitute the normal vowel letter for final -*ā*, namely, *he*. It is conceivable, then, that the name *š'lh* in the papyrus is equivalent to the name *š'(y)l'* attested in Palmyrene, and that the original *aleph* has quiesced and been replaced by a pure vowel letter, *he,* but it does not seem likely. Throughout this text, *aleph* is used as consonant, or at most is preserved as historical spelling where it was once a consonant, while *he* is used as a vowel letter when that is appropriate. It seems better to regard the name here as different in form from the one in Palmyrene ending in *aleph*. It may be that the name here is not that of the father, but that of the mother, and the final syllable reflects the feminine ending -*â*.

13. (2:5) *dnh—dinâ* (BA *dĕnâ*), "this one." The final *he* is a vowel letter for -*â*.

14. (2:6) *'bd—'abad* (BA **'ăbad* or *'ābēd*), "a slave."

15. (2:7) *zylh—zîlih* (BA *dî - lēh*), "of his" (lit., "who belongs to him"). Although the letters are written together to form a single unit we actually have a compound of two terms, so the medial *yod* could be regarded as originally a terminal vowel letter. At this period, the letter *yod* is used both in the final and the medial positions for the vowel -*î*. The *he* retains its consonantal force here, as attested in Biblical Aramaic.

16. (2:8) *tmym—tamîm* (BH *tāmîm*), "whole, sound, unblemished." The medial *yod* is a vowel letter for -*î*. The word does not occur in extant Biblical Aramaic, but is well attested in other Aramaic dialects.

In interpreting line 2 of the text, we take the demonstrative *dnh* as modifying the personal name *yhwḥnn* and render the passage as follows: "This Jehohanan, whose (sur)name is bar-Shaila, a slave who belongs to him (i.e., Hananyah), unblemished . . ."; cf. the phrase *lyhwḥnn zk* in line 10.

17. (3:1) *šḥrṣ—šiḥariṣ,* "the exact price."[2] The editor's analysis of the word combination is undoubtedly correct, but his proposal concerning the vocalization of the resultant form in Aramaic may be questioned. If the development actually was *šim > šiw > šû-,* then, since there is a consonantal *waw* in the word at a certain point in the sequence, we would expect it to be preserved in the spelling from that time on, even when it had become the vowel *-û*. Since this vowel is represented elsewhere in the orthography—and always when it is derived from consonantal *waw* (by way of a diphthong)—the word should then have been spelled **šwḥrṣ*. A defective spelling is always possible, especially with an unusual expression (e.g., we might have expected a *yod* to represent the second vowel of *ḥārîṣ*). At the same time, there are other possibilities, and these should be explored. Perhaps the *m/w* at the end of the first syllable was assimilated to the following *ḥ*.

18. (3:2) *dmyn—damîn* or perhaps more likely *damiyîn.* In Talmudic Aramaic, the word is plural and is written *dāmîn,* with the meaning "payment," "equivalent," "price." It seems clear, therefore, that we have a masc. pl. ending in *-în,* and ordinarily we would regard the *yod* as a vowel letter for the final vowel *-î*. Curiously, however, in this document, and presumably in the other Samaria Papyri, the masc. pl. ending (*-în*) is not indicated by a vowel letter. In all the other occurrences in SP 1, the expected *yod* does not appear, so it may be questioned whether the *yod* here is a simple vowel letter for *-î*. In view of the fact that the root of this word is *dmy* (i.e., III-*yod*), it seems more likely that the *yod* here represents the original consonant of the root. Thus, the word would have been written *dmyn* as we have it; then there should have been a time when it was written with two *yods: dmyyn,* but with the loss of the consonantal *yod* the spelling would have reverted to *dmyn.* The omission of the vowel letter *yod* to represent the masculine plural in *-în* is unusual and apparently reflects archaic usage, frozen into official documents of this sort. The spelling of this form with the vowel letter (*yod*) is attested as early as the Aramaic inscription from Tell Fekheryeh, but it remains sporadic throughout most of Aramaic inscriptional history, being sparse in the Elephantine papyri and other documents of the Persian period.[3] By contrast, the use of *yod* as a vowel letter in masc. pl. forms in the Hebrew Bible

---

[2] Ibid., 11*.

[3] We have a detailed study of the orthography of the Tell Fekheryeh Aramaic inscription in the *Text and Context: Old Testament and Semitic Studies for F. C. Fensham* (ed. W. Claassen; JSOTSup 48; Sheffield: JSOT Press, 1988) 9–49.

is practically universal and must have been adopted as a general practice quite early in the postexilic period.

19. (3:3) *gmyrn—gamîrîn* (BA *gĕmîr*, peal pass. ptc.). In view of the discussion above concerning *dmyn*, there can be little doubt that the form of this adjective is also masc. pl. and should be read with the standard *-în* ending. It will be noted that the word contains a vowel letter, *yod*, representing *-i* in the second syllable, which shows that this long vowel was regularly represented in the spelling. Its omission before *n* at the end of the word is surprising, but we have pointed out that the omission is regular and consistent in this document, and therefore the reading and the vocalization can be sustained: *damiyîn gamîrîn*.

20. (3:4) *ksp'—kaspa'* (BA *kaspā'*), "the silver." Cf. no. 7.

21. (3:5) *(zn)h—zinâ* (BA *dĕnâ*), "this." The *he* is used here as a vowel letter for final *-â*, in contrast to the preceding word, where *aleph* is used to indicate a consonantal sound at the end of the noun in the emphatic state. Cf. no. 13.

22. (3:6) *š* 35—"35 shekels."

23. (3:7) *ḥnnyh—ḥananyâ* (BA & BH *ḥănanyâ*), "Hananiah." Note that the *yod* is consonantal, while the *he* is a vowel letter for *-â* at the end of the word.

24. (4:1) *lh—lih* (BA *lēh*), "for him." The *he*, representing the 3rd masc. sg. suffix, was originally consonantal and has retained its consonantal force according to the Masoretic tradition.

25. (4:2) *wlbnwhy—walibanawhî* (BA *ûbĕnôhî*), "and for his sons." In Biblical Aramaic the medial *waw* serves as a vowel letter for *-ô*, but it is likely that this is historical spelling for an original consonant or diphthong, as reflected in Syriac. The traditional explanation is that the *-ô* vowel connecting the plural noun with the suffix (*hî*) is the vestigial remainder of a 3rd masc. sg. suffix: *-ahu > -aw > -ô*, to which then another 3rd masc. sg. suffix was added (*hî* presumably from *hû* through dissimilation). While such an explanation is barely possible, it does not seem likely, and it would be advantageous to seek a more plausible and less complicated solution. What we propose, based on a suggestion made by Frank Cross—who should be given credit if the idea proves sound, but not held responsible if the idea does not work—is that the plural form *bnw* is an alternate to the normal form represented by *bny* (reflecting the basic difference between the nominative and oblique cases of the primitive Semitic noun). According to this analogy the common form *banay* would become *bĕnê* in Masoretic vocalization, whereas the unusual form *banaw* would become *bĕnô*. The 3rd masc. sg. suffix would normally be *-hû*, but as a result of dissimilation an earlier *banawhû* ends up as *bĕnôhî*. It may be that the presence of *waw* and *yod* in plural forms originally derives from III-weak roots with these as third stem consonants, but the usage spread to other nouns, so that either *waw* or *yod* turns up in plural forms of nouns generally. We can point to the attested phenomenon of plural nouns with

waw in the Tell Fekheryeh inscription and elsewhere, as well as the frequent occurrence of *-wāt* in feminine plural forms as evidence for the presence of a plural using *waw* along with the common *yod*. In this document, therefore, we would read the plural form of this noun with the suffix as *banawhî*, which can be compared and contrasted with the form used with a different suffix: *baynayhōn* (BA *bênêhôn*).

26. (4:3) *mn—min* (BA *min*), "from." The preposition is idiomatic in this context and combines with *'hry* to produce the following pattern:

bnwhy mn 'hrwhy	"his sons (from) after him"
bnyk mn 'hryk	"your sons (from) after you"
bny mn 'hry	"my sons (from) after me"

27. (4:4) *'hrwhy—'aharawhî* (BA, if the form occurred, would presumably have *'ahărôhî*), "after him." We interpret the form here on the analogy of *bnwhy*, discussed under no. 25. Instead of the normal ending of the preposition in *-ay > ê*, we have an ending in *waw*, which on the analogy of the regular form would have been *-aw > ô*. The usage seems to be restricted to forms with the 3rd masc. sg. suffix, which itself is modified from a presumably original *-hû* to *-hî*. The *yod* at the end of the word is the standard vowel letter for *-î* (cf. no. 25).

28. (4:5) *l'lm'—li'ālama'* (BA *lĕ'ālĕmā'*), "in perpetuity." The *aleph* at the end of the word represents the emphatic state of the noun and was originally consonantal. Cf. no. 20.

29. (4:6) *šlyt—šallît* (BA *šallît*), "having mastery, exercising authority." The *yod* is an internal vowel letter for *-î*.

30. (4:7) *yhwnwr—yahawnûr* (the biblical form of the name would be *yĕhônûr*, if it occurred), "Yehonur: Yahweh is (my) lamp." For the initial component, *yhw*, we prefer the vocalization *yahaw*, recognizing the originally consonantal force of the *waw* (see the discussion under no. 9). For the last syllable of the word, *nwr*, the *waw* is clearly a vowel letter for *-û*.

31. (4:8) *lyh(whnn)—liyahawhanan* (BH *yĕhôhānān*), "Jehohanan." See the discussion of this name under no. 9.

32. (5:1) *hqymw—haqîmû* (BA *hăqêm* and *wahăqîm*), "they established." The *yod* surely represents the characteristic *-î* of the H-stem in Aramaic as well as other Northwest Semitic languages. The vacillation in the MT between *-î* and *-ê* seems to be a secondary internal development, and does not reflect a by-form **haqaymû > haqêmû* along with *haqîmû*. The *waw* is a vowel letter for final *-û*.

33. (5:2) *bynyhm—baynayhum* (BA *bênêhôn*), "between them." In both cases, the *yod* represents an original diphthong *-ay*, which in Biblical Aramaic has been contracted to *-ê*, cf. Dan 7:8 *bynyhwn* (*kĕtîb;* the *qĕrē'* is *bênêhen*, presumably reflecting a different orthography without the *waw* in the last syllable). According to F. Rosenthal the suffixes in Biblical Aramaic are: *hm* or *hwn* (3rd

masc. pl.), *km* or *kwn* (2nd masc. pl.).[4] The spelling in SP 1 coincides with the first form of Biblical Aramaic in this instance, and could reflect the older pronunciation -*hum,* before the tone-lengthening to -*hōm* had occurred.

34. (5:3) *zy—zî* (BA *dî*), "that, to wit." The *yod* represents final -*î*.

35. (5:4) *hn—hin* or *hēn* (BA *hēn*), "if, whether." The vowel, originally short, may have been lengthened under the tone, but is not represented in the orthography.

36. (5:5) *'nh—'anâ* (BA *'ănâ*), "I." The *he* represents final -*â*.

37. (5:6) *ḥnnyh—ḥananyâ* (BH and BA *ḥănanyâ*), "Hananiah." Once again, the *he* represents final -*â*. Cf. no. 23.

38. (5:7) *br—bir* or *bar* (BA *bar*), "son of." In any case, the vowel is short and not represented in the orthography.

39. (5:8) *b[y]d'l—biyad'ēl,* "Biyad'el." None of the vowels is indicated in the orthography. The first two remain short, while the third, originally -*i,* may have been lengthened to -*ē* under the tone.

40. (6:1) *yhwnwr—yahawnûr* (or later *yĕhônûr*), "Yehonur." In our view the first *waw* represents the diphthong -*aw*, while the second is a vowel letter for -*û*. Cf. no. 30.

41. (6:2) *w'm—wa'im* (BH *wĕ'im*), "and with." Neither vowel is indicated in the orthography.

42. (6:3) *bnyk—banayk* (BA would probably have been *bĕnayik* or *bĕnêk* if the word occurred; i.e., the diphthong might well have been contracted or resolved into two syllables, but in either case the *yod* would have been preserved as a consonantal element or by historical spelling), "your sons."[5] Here the *yod* represents the original diphthong of the construct plural ending, which was later contracted in BH and BA. In our opinion, there is no possibility that the form spelled with final -*k* could have been pronounced -*kā*. If it were, it would be the only instance in this text of a word-terminal -*ā* spelled defectively.

43. (6:4) *mn—min* (BA *min*), "from." Cf. no. 26.

44. (6:5) *'ḥryk—'aḥarayk* (BA *'aḥărê* and *'aḥărêhôn*), "after you." The *yod* represents the original diphthong, which was probably preserved in SP 1. In Biblical Aramaic, the related forms (given above) reflect contraction of the diphthong, but preservation of the *yod* through historical spelling. For the same ending, cf. no. 42, and for a different form of the preposition, cf. no. 27.

---

[4] F. Rosenthal, *A Grammar of Biblical Aramaic* (Wiesbaden: Harrassowitz, 1974) 20.

[5] In Biblical Aramaic the *kĕtîb* is written -*yk* while the *qĕrē'* is vocalized -*āk*. It is not clear just how the *kĕtîb* would have been pronounced, but the original form was doubtless a diphthong, pronounced -*ayk*. The original diphthong would have been represented in the orthography by *yod,* and even if or when the diphthong was contracted, the *yod* would have remained in place through historical spelling.

45. (6:6) *'nh* — *'anâ* (BA *'ănâ*), "I." Cf. no. 36.
46. (6:7) *hnnyh* — *hănanyâ* (BA and BH *hănanyâ*), "Hananiah." Cf. nos. 23 and 37.
47. (6:8) *wbny* — *wabanay* (BA *ûběnay*), "and my sons."
48. (6:9) *mn* — *min* (BA *min*), "from." Cf. nos. 26, 43.
49. (6:10) *'hry* — *'aharay* (BA *'ahăray*), "after me." Cf. nos. 27, 44.
50. (7:1) *'mk* — *'immak* (BA *'immāk*), "with you." Neither of the vowels is represented in the orthography. In Biblical Aramaic tone-lengthening of the second vowel (-ā) has taken place, and this change may also have taken place in SP 1, although we cannot be sure. The orthography is not affected.
51. (7:2) *'nt* — *'ant* (BA *'ant* as the *qěrē'* consistently, but the anomalous *'nth*, presumably for *'antâ* in the *kětîb*), "you." The spelling of SP 1 supports that of the *qěrē'* in Biblical Aramaic. The *kětîb* of BA reflects a longer form, comparable to Biblical Hebrew *'attâ*.
52. (7:3) *yhwnwr* — *yahawnûr*, "Yehonur." Cf. nos. 30, 40.
53. (7:4) *bmly'* — *bamillayya'* (BA *millayyā'*), "by, with, or in these words." There are no vowel letters in this word. The final *aleph* was originally consonantal and may have retained that force in SP 1, although it has quiesced in Biblical Aramaic (with attendant lengthening of the preceding vowel -ā). For further discussion of the *aleph* representing the emphatic state in nouns, see nos. 7, 20, and 28.
54. (7:5) *'lh* — *'ille(h)* (BA *'ělleh*), "these." The final *he* is a vowel letter for -e.
55. (7:6) *['nt]n* — *['inti]n* (BA *'entēn*), "I shall give." There are no vowel letters in this word. Whether the second vowel has been lengthened under the tone, as in Biblical Aramaic, is uncertain.
56. (7:7) *lk* — *lak* (BA *lāk*), "to you." Tone-lengthening has occurred in Biblical Aramaic, and is possible in SP 1. Since medial -a (whether long or short) is not represented in the orthography of this document, the spelling is not affected.
57. (7:8) *'nt* — *'ant* (BA *qěrē'* *'ant*), "you." Cf. no. 51.
58. (7:9) *yhwnwr* — *yahawnûr*, "Yehonur." Cf. nos. 30, 40, 52.
59. (8:1) *l'* — *la'* (BA *lā'*), "not." It is our position that the *aleph* in this word (as in other particles) was originally consonantal and later quiesced as in Biblical Aramaic (and also Biblical Hebrew, with a different vocalization). It is difficult to determine whether the *aleph* was still pronounced at the time of SP 1, but the fact that in the manuscript *aleph* is used exclusively in such particles and the emphatic state of nouns indicates that it was pronounced; otherwise, it might easily have been interchanged with the normal vowel letter for final -ā, namely, *he*. An example of such an interchange (*lh* for the negative particle *l'*) occurs in Dan 4:32, showing that the *aleph* had quiesced. The consistency and accuracy of the spelling in SP 1 argue against the quiescence of *aleph* in this document.

60. (8:2) *mqbl—muqabbil* (BA **mĕqabbēl*), "accept." There are no vowel letters in this word.

61. (8:3) *'nh—'anâ* (BA *'ănâ*), "I." The *he* represents final *-â.* Cf. nos. 36, 45.

62. (8:4) *mnk—minnak* (BA *minnāk*), "from you." There are no vowel letters in this word. The second vowel has been lengthened under the tone in BA, but whether this change has taken place in SP 1 is not certain. The orthography is not affected. For the same suffix with other prepositions, see nos. 50, 56.

63. (8:5) *'w—'aw* (BH *'ô*), "or." While the original diphthong in this word has been contracted in Biblical Hebrew (which retains the *waw* of the diphthong as historical spelling), there is no reason to suppose that the contraction has occurred in SP 1. In either case, the *waw* represents the original consonant.

64. (8:6) *ksp'—kaspa'* (BA *kaspā'*), "the silver." Cf. nos. 7, 20.

65. (8:7) *š 35*—"35 shekels."

66. (8:8) *zy—zî* (BA *dî*), "which." Cf. no. 34.

67. (8:9) *yhb[t]—yahabt* (BA *yĕhabt*), "you gave." There are no vowel letters in this word.

68. (9:1) *w'ḥr—wa'aḥar* (BH *wĕ'aḥar*), "and afterwards." There are no vowel letters in this word.

69. (9:2) *ḥyb—ḥayyāb* (Talmudic *ḥayyāb*), "one who is liable, debtor." A predicate noun is desiderated in combination with the pronoun *'nh* ("I"). The *yod* is clearly consonantal and therefore there are no vowel letters present.

70. (9:3) *'nh—'anâ* (BA *'ănâ*), "I." Cf. nos. 36, 45, 61.

71. (9:4) *ḥnnyh—ḥananyâ* (Biblical *ḥănanyâ*), "Hananiah." Cf. nos. 23, 37, 46.

72. (9:5) *'šlm—'ašallim* (BA has examples of this verb, but not in the Pael form; in BH the form would be: *'ăšallēm*), "I will repay." Tone lengthening occurs in the biblical verbs, and is possible in SP 1.

73. (9:6) *'ntn—'intin* (BA **'entēn*), "I will give." Cf. no. 55, which is the same word, reconstructed on the basis of its appearance here.

74. (9:7) *lk—lak* (BA *lāk*), "to you." Cf. no. 56.

75. (9:8) *'nt—'ant* (BA *qĕrē' 'ant*), "you." Cf. nos. 51, 57.

76. (9:9) *yhwnwr—yahawnûr*, "Yehonur." Cf. nos. 30, 40, 52, 58.

77. (10:1) *zy—zî* (BA *dî*), "which, that." Cf. nos. 34, 66.

78. (10:2) *l'—la'* (BA *lā'*), "not." Cf. no. 59.

79. (10:3) *dynn—dînîn* (BA sg. *dîn*), "judgments, lawsuits." The Targum confirms that the vocalization should be *dînîn* (masc. pl. of *dîn*). The spelling is unusual; we would expect a second *yod* (*dynyn*), since the second vowel is primitive and "pure-long." We have already observed, however, that in the masc. pl. form of nouns the expected vowel letter (which occurs as early as

the Tell Fekheryeh inscription of the tenth or ninth century) *yod* does not appear (cf. nos. 18, 19). This idiosyncrasy may reflect archaic usage and highly traditional and conventional language, handed down in its original form for centuries. It is also possible that the scribe wished to avoid the use of two *yods* in the same short word (cf. *dmyn* in line 3, no. 18, and *gmyrn* in line 3, no. 19). The reasoning would not apply to the word *ḥwbn*, where the *waw* is presumably not a vowel letter; and note the repeated spelling of *yhwnwr*, with *waw* written twice.

80. (10:4) *wl'*—*wala'* (BA *lā'*), "and not." Cf. nos. 59, 78.

81. (10:5) *ḥwbn*—*ḥawbīn*, "obligations, debts." The word occurs in both a feminine (*ḥôbâ*) and a masculine (*ḥôb*) form with generally similar meanings. Here the plural form could be either *ḥôbīn* (masc.) or *ḥôbān* (fem.); in the context, however, and in association with the preceding *dīnīn* it is more likely to be *ḥôbīn*. As we have seen, the spelling in this inscription does not offer help in resolving the issue, since the plural in *-īn* is not indicated by the expected *yod*. The *waw* reflects the original diphthong *-aw* in this word, although it has contracted in Biblical Aramaic.

82. (10:6) *ksp*—*kasap* (BA *kĕsap*), "silver." There are no vowel letters in this word.

83. (10:7) *mnn 7*—*manīn* (BH *mānīm*), "seven minas." Once again we seem to have a masculine plural form of the noun (in *-īn*) without the expected orthographic indication (*yod* as a vowel letter for *-î*).

84. (10:8) *lyhwḥnn*—*liyahawḥanan* (BH *yĕhôḥānān*), "Jehohanan." Cf. nos. 9, 31.

85. (10:9) *zk*—*zēk* (BA *dēk*), "that (one)." There are no vowel letters in this word. The word always follows the noun it modifies, in this case the personal name "Jehohanan."

86. (10:10) *l'*—*la'* (BA *lā'*), "not." Cf. nos. 59, 78.

87. (11:1) *mn*—*min* (BA *min*), "from." Cf. nos. 26, 43, 48.

88. (11:2) *'ḥryk*—*'aḥarayk*, "after you." Cf. no. 44.

89. (11:3) *lqbl*—*laqubil* (BA *loqŏbēl*), "by reason of, on account of." There are no vowel letters in this word.

90. (11:4) *znh*—*zinâ* (BA *dĕnâ*), "this." Cf. no. 21, and also 13.

91. (11:5) *'sr'*—*'isara'* (BA *'ĕsārā'*), "covenant, binding agreement." The *aleph* at the end of the word is the sign of the emphatic state and was originally consonantal. It has quiesced in Biblical Aramaic, but there is no clear evidence that it had quiesced at the time of SP 1. Cf. nos. 7, 20, 28, 53, 64.

92. (11:6) *hqymw*—*haqîmû* (BA **hăqîmû*), "they established." Cf. no. 32.

93. (11:7) *bynyhm*—*baynayhum* or possibly *baynayhōm* (BA *bênêhôn*), "between them." Cf. no. 33.

94. (12:1) *yḥtmwn*—*yaḥtumûn* (BA **yaḥtĕmûn*), "they seal, affix seals." The

form seems to be the peal imperf. 3rd masc. pl. The *waw* is a vowel letter for medial *-û.*

95. (12:2) *hmw* — *himmô* (BA *himmô*), "they." This word is the independent pronoun, 3rd masc. pl. Biblical Aramaic also has a by-form *himmôn.* This is the only example of *waw* as a vowel letter for *-ô* in the inscription, unless we suppose that the diphthong *-aw* has been contracted in the numerous cases in which it occurs. In those cases, however, we can explain the presence of the *waw* as an instance of historical spelling and not as a true vowel letter. If the final *-ô* in this word is explained as deriving from an original *-u,* which seems most likely, then it would be the only example of the use of *waw* as a true vowel letter for final *-ô < u.* There is no evidence to support an original reading of *himmaw* for this pronoun. This usage may imply that the contraction has already taken place in the diphthong and that we are witnessing the initial stage of the extension of the result of historical spelling to situations in which the *waw* was not originally present in the word. At the same time, we can assert that this practice has not been extended to the interior of words in which an *-ō* vowel derived from *-u* has developed (e.g., *bynyhm* for *bênêhōm*).

96. (12:3) *mhymnn* — *muhaymanīn* (BA *měhêmān*), "trustworthy." The form is a haphel pass. ptc. masc. pl. We note that the *yod* represents the original diphthong in this form of the verb, *-ay,* which has been contracted in Biblical Aramaic. We also note that the expected *yod* in the masc. pl. form of the ptc. does not appear. Apparently the *aleph* in the verbal root (*'mn*) has been lost; this is also true of the surviving forms in Biblical Aramaic.

Conclusions

Samaria Papyrus 1 contains 96 usable words, which we number serially for ease of reference. Of these, 21 have minimal interest for orthographic studies, since they end in a consonant and contain only short vowels originally (in some cases these are reduced to *shewa* in Biblical Aramaic, and hence it may not be clear just what the original vowel was). These are the following: no. 2, *l'dr;* no. 3, *šnt;* nos. 11, 38, *br;* no. 14, *'bd;* nos. 26, 43, 48, 87, *mn;* no. 41, *w'm;* no. 50, *'mk;* nos. 51, 57, 75, *'nt;* nos. 56, 74, *lk;* no. 62, *mnk;* no. 67, *yhbt;* no. 68, *w'ḥr;* no. 69, *ḥyb;* no. 82, *ksp.* There are three numerical expressions that are not relevant to our interest: nos. 1, 22, 65.

1. Before proceeding to a consideration of the three genuine vowel letters in the classical Aramaic spelling system (*he, waw,* and *yod*), we can make an observation about the use and distribution of word-terminal *aleph:* in six cases in the inscription, *aleph* serves as the determiner, marking the emphatic state of the noun. The examples are as follows: no. 7, *mlk';* nos. 20, 64, *ksp';*

no. 28, *l'lm'*; no. 53, *bmly'*; no. 86, *'sr'*. The remaining four instances involve the negative particle *l'*, nos. 59, 78, 80, 91.

2. In twelve cases, word-terminal *he* is the vowel letter for *-â*.

Pronouns: no. 13, *dnh*; nos. 21, 90, *znh*; nos. 36, 45, 61, 70, *'nh*.

Names: no. 12, *š'lh*; nos. 23, 37, 46, 71, *ḥnnyh*. In one instance word-terminal *he* represents the vowel *e:* no. 54, *'lh*.

There are three other words with final *he:* in each of these cases the *he* represents the pronoun suffix, 3rd masc. sg., and is consonantal.

In all cases in which a word ends in *-â*, the vowel letter representing that sound is *he*. As we have pointed out, the case with terminal *aleph* is different, since it is used only for the emphatic state and the negative particle, and we believe that it has retained its original consonantal function in both of these sets. Had *aleph* quiesced and been in use as a vowel letter, we would have expected *he* and *aleph* to have been used indiscriminately or interchangeably for the same vowel. That is not the case.

3. Word-terminal *yod* represents *-î* (no. 25, *wlbnwhy*; no. 27, *'ḥrwhy*; nos. 34, 66, 77, *zy*) or *-ay* (no. 49, *'ḥry*).

4a. Within a word, *yod* may be consonantal (no. 69, *ḥyb*) but is otherwise a vowel letter for *-î:* no. 15, *zylh*; no. 16, *tmym*; no. 19, *gmyrn*; no. 29, *šlyṭ*; nos. 32, 92, *hqymw*; no. 79, *dynn*. The *yod* in no. 84 was originally consonantal and therefore cannot be counted as a vowel letter: *wyhwḥnn*, which in Masoretic vocalization might come out *wîḥôḥānān*. The *yod* in no. 18 is probably conso-nantal: *damiyîn* rather than *dāmîn* as in later Aramaic (in this inscription that word would probably have been spelled without *yod* at all: *dmn*).

4b. In contrast to this consistent usage of *yod* as a medial vowel letter, we apparently have six masculine plural nouns in all of which the final long vowel (*-î*) is not represented in the orthography: no. 18, *dmyn* (?); no. 19, *gmyrn*; no. 79, *dynn*; no. 81, *ḥwbn*; no. 83, *mnn*; no. 96, *mhymnn*.

5a. In the medial position *yod* represents the original diphthong *-ay*, which in Biblical Aramaic regularly is contracted to *-ê*. We cannot tell whether this development has taken place in the Aramaic of the papyri, since there is no difference in the spelling. Alongside the consistent use of *yod* in all cases where there was an original diphthong, which may have been contracted, there is equally consistent omission or non-use of *yod* in cases in which in Biblical Aramaic the original vowel *-i* has been changed and lengthened to *-ē* (see 5b). We cannot tell whether this tone-lengthening and qualifying process has taken place in the Aramaic of SP. The point, however, is that this constant complementary distribution corresponds to the derivation of the two vowel sounds and shows either that the phonetic changes described above: *-ay>-ê* and *-i>-ē* have not yet taken place, or, if they have, then historical spelling has been strictly preserved. Here are the examples: no. 8, *bšmry[n]*; nos. 33, 93, *bynyhm*; no. 42, *bnyk*; nos. 44, 88, *'ḥrk*; no. 96, *mhymnn*.

5b. Where Masoretic vocalization indicates the vowel -*ē* from -*i*, the spelling in the document is always defective: no. 4, *rē'š;* no. 35, *hēn;* no. 85, *zēk;* no. 39, *bĕyad'ēl;* nos. 55, 73, *'intēn;* no. 60, *mĕqabbēl;* no. 72, *'ašallēm;* no. 89, *loqōbēl.* This consistent usage indicates that no. 12 is to be pronounced *šĕ'ēlâ* or even *ša'ilâ.*

6. Word-terminal *waw* represents -*û* (nos. 32, 92, *hqymw*), or -*aw* (-*ô*) (no. 63, *'w*), or -*ô* presumably from -*u* (no. 95, *hmw*).

7a. Within a word, *waw* represents -*û:* no. 5, *mlkwt;* nos. 30, 40, 52, 58, 76, *yhwnwr* (*yahawnûr*); no. 94, *yḥtmwn.* It is also possible that *waw* in no. 6 represents -*û;* the uncertainty arises from the variety of possible spellings of the Persian king's name.

7b. This usage makes it unlikely that the first vowel of no. 17 is -*û.*

8a. Otherwise *waw* within a word is used for the original diphthong -*aw.* We prefer to vocalize with the older form (the diphthong), although it is possible that the diphthong has contracted as in Biblical Aramaic. It is the same situation as described for the diphthong -*ay* > -*ê* in paragraph 5a. These are the instances: nos. 9, 31, 84, *yahawḥanan* or *yĕhôḥānān;* nos. 30, 40, 52, 58, 76, *yahawnur* or *yĕhônûr;* no. 81, *ḥawbīn* or *ḥôbīn;* no. 25, *walibnawhî* or *wĕlibnôhî;* no. 27, *'aḥarawhî* or *'aḥărôhî.*

8b. In two cases of a form in which Masoretic pronunciation and comparative grammar point to -*ō* from -*u*, the spelling is defective: nos. 33, 93, *bênêhōm.* But compare no. 95, where in the final position *waw* seems to represent -*ô* from -*u*.

The spelling of SP 1 is generally consistent and regular, with only one notable exception. In the final position, *he, waw,* and *yod* are used to represent *â, û,* and *î* respectively. It is to be noted that in single instances, *he* represents final -*ē* and *waw* apparently represents final -*ô* as well. *Waw* is used to represent -*û* in medial positions as well as the diphthong -*aw,* whether or not the latter has been contracted. And in the medial position, *waw* is not used for -*ō. Yod* is used for the diphthong -*ay,* whether or not it has been contracted, and it is never used for -*ē* derived from -*i.* It is also used to represent -*î* internally, but there is a major exception to this practice: while all the cases are not equally decisive, it appears that in the case of all six instances of the masculine plural noun (in -*īn*), the *yod* representing the final long vowel does not appear.

Summary of the Orthographic Analysis of SP 1

The occurrences and functions of *aleph, he, waw,* and *yod*

1. *Aleph*

    A. In the final position (after -*a*): nos. 7, 20, 28, 53, 59, 64, 78, 80, 86, 91.

    B. In the medial position: nos. 2, 4, 12, 39, 68.

Aleph was originally a consonant and is still treated as one in all positions: initial, medial, and final. Although it may have quiesced in certain words, it functions only as a passive vowel marker, not as an active vowel letter.

2. *He*
   A. In the final position:
      i. For -*â*: nos. 12, 13, 21, 23, 36, 37, 45, 46, 61, 70, 71, 90.
      ii. For -*e*: no. 54.
      iii. As a consonantal suffix: nos. 10, 15, 24.
   B. In the medial position:
      i. As a consonant: nos. 6, 9, 25, 27, 30, 31, 33, 40, 52, 58, 67, 76, 84, 93, 96.

He is used as a vowel letter in the final position only; it represents -*â* predominantly, but may also represent other vowels, such as -*ē* from -*i*. In any other position, initial or medial, it is a consonant.

3. *Waw*
   A. In the final position:
      i. For -*û*: nos. 32, 92.
      ii. For -*ô* (from -*u*): no. 95.
      iii. As the consonantal element in the diphthong -*aw* (which may have been contracted to -*ô*): no. 63.
   B. In the medial position:
      i. For -*û*: nos. 5, 6(?), 30, 40, 52, 58, 76, 94.
      ii. For the diphthong -*aw*- (which may have been contracted to -*ô*-): nos. 9, 25, 27, 30, 31, 40, 52, 58, 76, 81, 84.
      iii. As a consonant: no. 6(?).
      iv. Apparently the vowel -*û*- from -*u*- is not represented in the orthography: nos. 33, 93.

Waw occurs as a vowel letter in both the final and medial positions. It represents the vowel -*û*- in both positions, and the vowel -*ô* in the final position only, if that is the correct interpretation of no. 95. It also represents the consonantal element in the diphthong -*aw*- in both positions. Whether the diphthong was preserved or contracted at the time of the Samaria Papyri, the spelling (with *waw*) was not affected.

4. *Yod*
   A. In the final position:
      i. For -*î*: nos. 25, 27, 34, 66, 77.
      ii. For -*ay* (possibly contracted to -*ê*): nos. 47, 49.
   B. In the medial position
      i. For -*î*-: nos. 15, 16, 18(?), 19, 29, 32, 79, 84(?), 92. In a number of instances, the same vowel is not represented in the orthography: nos. 18(?), 19, 79, 81, 83, 96. These are all cases involving the masculine plural -*în*.[6]

[6] It is possible that no. 17, *šḥrṣ*, belongs on this list. If the expression is derived from Neo-Babylonian *šīm harīṭ*, as proposed by the editor, then the final vowel would be -*ı*. We might well have expected the long vowel in that position to be represented by *yod* as in a number of instances in the inscription. However, its omission can be justified on the basis of the regular

    ii. For -*ay*- (possibly contracted to -*ê*-): nos. 8, 33(bis), 42, 44, 88, 93(bis), 96.

    iii. As a consonant: nos. 6, 9, 18(?), 23, 31, 37, 46, 53, 69, 71, 84.

    iv. Apparently the vowel -*ē*- from -*i*- is not represented in the orthography: nos. 12, 17(?), 24, 35, 39, 55, 60, 72, 73, 85, 89.

Yod occurs as a vowel letter in both the final and medial positions. It represents the vowel -*î*- in both positions. It also represents the consonantal element in the diphthong -*ay*- or *ay*>*ê* in both positions. One important anomaly is to be reported. Contrary to the regular practice of representing -*ī*- in the medial position by *yod*, probably all six instances of the masculine plural form of nouns omit the expected *yod*. The exact reason or explanation for this unusual circumstance remains to be determined.

The Spelling of SP 1

List of Words in SP 1

1. (1:1) *b 20*
2. (1:2) *l'dr* (*la'adar* > *la'ădār*): 1.B
3. (1:3) *šnt 2* (*šanat* > *šēnat*)
4. (1:4) *r'š* (*ri'š* > *rē'š*): 1.B
5. (1:5) *mlkwt* (*malkût*): 3.B.i
6. (1:6) *(d)ryhwš* (*darayahaweš* or *darayahûš*): 2.B.i, 3.B.i or 3.B.iii, 4.B.iii
7. (1:7) *mlk'* (*malka'* > *malkā'*): 1.A
8. (1:8) *bšmry(n)* (*bišamarayn* > *bĕšāmĕrāyin*): 4.B.ii
9. (2:1) *lyhwḥnn* (*liyahawḥanan* > *lîhôḥānān*): 2.B.i, 3.B.ii, 4.B.iii
10. (2:2) *šmh* (*šumih* > *šĕmēh*): 2.A.iii
11. (2:3) *br* (*bir* or *bar*)
12. (2:4) *š'lh* (*ša'ilâ* > *šĕ'ēlâ*): 1.B, 2.A.i
13. (2:5) *dnh* (*dinâ* > *dĕnâ*): 2.A.i
14. (2:6) *'bd* (*'abad* > *'ăbad*)
15. (2:7) *zylh* (*zîlih* > *zîlēh*): 2.A.iii, 4.B.i
16. (2:8) *tmym* (*tamîm* > *tāmîm*): 4.B.i
17. (3:1) *šḥrṣ* (*šim ḥariṣ* > *siḥarīṣ* > *šēḥārīṣ*): 4.B.i, 4.B.iv
18. (3:2) *dmyn* (*damiyīn* > *dāmīn*): 4.B.i, 4.B.iii
19. (3:3) *gmyrn* (*gamîrīn* > *gĕmîrîn*): 4.B.i
20. (3:4) *ksp'* (*kaspa'* > *kaspā'*): 1.A
21. (3:5) *(zn)h* (*zinâ* > *zĕnâ*): 2.A.i
22. (3:6) *š 35*

---

practice in the same inscription of omitting the *yod* in the final syllable where we undoubtedly have a long vowel: -*ī* in the masculine plural form of nouns. Given the uncertainty of the vocalization of a loanword, we hesitate to pursue this point or to classify the form.

23. (3:7) *ḥnnyh* (*ḥananyâ* > *ḥānanyâ*): 2.A.i, 4.B.iii
24. (4:1) *lh* (*lih* > *lēh*): 2.A.iii, 4.B.iv
25. (4:2) *wlbnwhy* (*walibanawhî* > *wĕlibĕnôhî*): 2.B.i, 3.B.ii, 4.A.i
26. (4:3) *mn* (*min*)
27. (4:4) *ʾḥrwhy* (*ʾaḥarawhî* > *ʾaḥărôhî*): 2.B.i, 3.B.ii, 4.A.i
28. (4:5) *lʿlm* (*liʿālama* > *lĕʿālĕmāʾ*): 1.A
29. (4:6) *šlyṭ* (*šallîṭ*): 4.B.i
30. (4:7) *yhwnwr* (*yahawnûr* > *yĕhônûr*): 2.B.i, 3.B.i, 3.B.ii
31. (4:8) *lyh[wḥnn]* (*liyahawḥānān* > *lîhôḥānān*): 2.B.i, 3.B.ii, 4.B.iii
32. (5:1) *hqymw* (*haqîmû* > *hăqîmû* or *hăqêmû*): 3.A.i, 4.B.i
33. (5:2) *bynyhm* (*baynayhum* > *bênêhōm*): 2.B.i, 3.B.iv, 4.B.ii
34. (5:3) *zy* (*zî*): 4.A.i
35. (5:4) *hn* (*hin* > *hēn*): 4.B.iv
36. (5:5) *ʾnh* (*ʾanâ* > *ʾănâ*): 2.A.i
37. (5:6) *ḥnnyh* (*ḥananyâ* > *ḥānanyâ*): 2.A.i, 4.B.iii
38. (5:7) *br* (*bir* or *bar*)
39. (5:8) *bydʾl* (*biyadʾil* > *bĕyadʾēl*): 1.B, 4.B.iii, 4.B.iv
40. (6:1) *yhwnwr* (*yahawnûr* > *yĕhônûr*): 2.B.i, 3.B.i, 3.B.ii
41. (6:2) *wʿm* (*waʿim* > *wĕʿim*)
42. (6:3) *bnyk* (*banayk* > *bĕnêk*): 4.B.ii
43. (6:4) *mn* (*min*)
44. (6:5) *ʾḥryk* (*ʾaḥarayk* > *ʾaḥărêk*): 4.B.ii
45. (6:6) *ʾnh* (*ʾanâ* > *ʾănâ*): 2.A.i
46. (6:7) *ḥnnyh* (*ḥananyâ* > *ḥānanyâ*): 2.A.i, 4.B.iii
47. (6:8) *wbny* (*wabanay* > *ûbĕnay*): 4.A.ii
48. (6:9) *mn* (*min*)
49. (6:10) *ʾḥry* (*ʾaḥaray* > *ʾaḥăray*): 4.A.ii
50. (7:1) *ʿmk* (*ʿimmak* > *ʿimmāk*)
51. (7:2) *ʾnt* (*ʾant*)
52. (7:3) *yhwnwr* (*yahawnûr* > *yĕhônûr*): 2.B.i, 3.B.i, 3.B.ii
53. (7:4) *bmlyʾ* (*bamillayyaʾ* > *bĕmillayyāʾ*): 1.A
54. (7:5) *ʾlh* (*ʾille[h]* > *ʾēlleh*): 2.A.ii
55. (7:6) [*ʾnt*]*n* (*ʾintin* > *ʾentēn*): 4.B.iv
56. (7:7) *lk* (*lak* > *lāk*)
57. (7:8) *ʾnt* (*ʾant*)
58. (7:9) *yhwnwr* (*yahawnûr* > *yêhônûr*): 2.B.i, 3.B.i, 3.B.ii
59. (8:1) *lʾ* (*laʾ* > *lāʾ*): 1.A
60. (8:2) *mqbl* (*muqabbil* > *mĕqabbēl*): 4.B.iv
61. (8:3) *ʾnh* (*ʾanâ* > *ʾănâ*): 2.A.i
62. (8:4) *mnk* (*minnak* > *minnāk*)
63. (8:5) *ʾw* (*ʾaw* > *ʾô*): 3.A.iii
64. (8:6) *kspʾ* (*kaspaʾ* > *kaspāʾ*): 1.A
65. (8:7) *š 35*
66. (8:8) *zy* (*zî*): 4.A.i

67. (8:9) *yhb*[*t*] (*yahabt* > *yĕhabt*)
68. (9:1) *w'ḥr* (*wa'aḥar* > *wĕ'aḥar*)
69. (9:2) *ḥyb* (*ḥayyāb*): 4.B.iii
70. (9:3) *'nh* (*'anâ* > *'ănâ*): 2.A.i
71. (9:4) *ḥnnyh* (*ḥananyâ* > *ḥănanyâ*): 2.A.i, 4.B.iii
72. (9:5) *'šlm* (*'ašallim* > *'ăšallēm*): 4.B.iv
73. (9:6) *'ntn* (*'intin* > *'entēn*): 4.B.iv
74. (9:7) *lk* (*lak* > *lāk*)
75. (9:8) *'nt* (*'ant*)
76. (9:9) *yhwnwr* (*yahawnûr* > *yĕhônûr*): 2.B.i, 3.B.i, 3.B.ii
77. (10:1) *zy* (*zî*): 4.A.i
78. (10:2) *l'* (*la'* > *lā'*): 1.A
79. (10:3) *dynn* (*dînīn*): 4.B.i (bis)
80. (10:4) *wl'* (*wala'* > *wĕlā'*): 1.A
81. (10:5) *ḥwbn* (*ḥawbīn* > *ḥôbîn*): 3.B.ii, 4.B.i
82. (10:6) *ksp* (*kasap* > *kĕsap*)
83. (10:7) *mnn* (*manīn* > *mĕnîn*): 4.B.i
84. (10:8) *lyhwḥnn* (*liyahawḥanan* > *lîhôḥānān*): 2.B.i, 3.B.ii, 4.B.iii
85. (10:9) *zk* (*zik* > *zēk*): 4.B.iv
86. (10:10) *l'* (*la'* > *lā'*): 1.A
87. (11:1) *mn* (*min*)
88. (11:2) *'ḥryk* (*'aḥarayk* > *'aḥărêk*): 4.B.ii
89. (11:3) *lqbl* (*laqubil* > *loqŏbēl*): 4.B.iv
90. (11:4) *znh* (*zinâ* > *zĕnâ*): 2.A.i
91. (11:5) *'sr'* (*'isara'* > *'ĕsārā'*): 1.A
92. (11:6) *hqymw* (*haqîmû* > *hăqîmû*): 3.A.i, 4.B.i
93. (11:7) *bynyhm* (*baynayhum* > *bênêhôm*): 2.B.i, 3.B.iv, 4.B.ii
94. (12:1) *yḥtmwn* (*yaḥtumûn* > *yaḥtĕmûn*): 3.B.i
95. (12:2) *hmw* (*himmu* > *himmô*): 3.A.ii
96. (12:3) *mhymnn* (*muhaymanīn* > *mĕhaymĕnîn*): 2.B.i, 4.B.i

Bibliography

Abou-Assaf, A., P. Bordreuil, and A. R. Millard, *La Statue de Tell Fekheryeh*. Etudes Assyriologiques 7. Paris: Recherche sur les civilisations, 1982.

Cross, F. M., "Samaria Papyrus 1: An Aramaic Slave Conveyance of 335 B.C.E. Found in the Wadi Ed-Daliyeh." In *Nahman Avigad Volume*, 7*–17*. Ed. B. Mazar and Y. Yadin. Eretz-Israel 18. Jerusalem: Israel Exploration Society, 1985.

Rosenthal, F., *A Grammar of Biblical Aramaic*. Wiesbaden: Otto Harrassowitz, 1974.

Phonological Phenomena in the Greek Papyri Significant for the Text and Language of the New Testament

Francis T. Gignac, S.J.
The Catholic University of America

THIS IS A COMPANION PIECE to my contribution to *A Wise and Discerning Heart;*[1] one article does not suffice to show the great esteem I have for my confrere, colleague, and friend Joseph A. Fitzmyer, S.J.

As I did there for morphology, I shall here select from my grammar of the papyri[2] some interesting phonological phenomena that shed light on the text and language of the New Testament. Before presenting individual examples, however, it might be helpful to show how we establish the phonology of ancient languages and how Greek was actually pronounced in the Greco-Roman world, including Palestine, in the first century A.D.

In most ancient languages—and Greek is an outstanding example—the significant sounds or phonemes can be reconstructed for early stages by means of comparative studies of cognate sounds in related languages. These sounds cannot be assigned precise phonetic values, but phonemic oppositions can be established. A given sound can be distin-

Τῷ τιμιωτάτῳ μου ἀδελφῷ πλεῖστα χαίρειν. πρὸ μὲν πάντων εὔχομαί σε ὑγιαίνειν καὶ ὁλοκληρεῖν διὰ παντὸς παρὰ τῷ κυρίῳ θεῷ.

Common greeting in a papyrus letter

---

[1] "Morphological Phenomena in the Greek Papyri Significant for the Text and Language of the New Testament," in *A Wise and Discerning Heart: Studies Presented to Joseph A. Fitzmyer, S.J. in Celebration of His Sixty-fifth Birthday* (ed. Raymond E. Brown, S.S., and Alexander A. Di Lella, O.F.M. = *CBQ* 48/3 [July, 1986]) 499–511.

[2] F. T. Gignac, *A Grammar of the Greek Papyri of the Roman and Byzantine Periods.* Vol. 1, *Phonology* (Testi e Documenti per lo Studio dell' Antichità 55; Milan: Cisalpino—La Goliardica, 1976).

guished from other sounds that are significant in the language at a particular place and time, and relative phonetic values for these sounds can be drawn up to within certain definite articulatory positions. With the current state of development of the sound system easily ascertainable from the modern spoken form of the language, the general framework of the sounds of that language over the transitional periods as a whole is clear.

The pronunciation of a dead language at a particular time and place is determined primarily by an analysis of spelling variations. This method is based on the observation that letters are not generally confused in writing unless the sounds they represent are identified in speech. A sporadic interchange of letters may not be phonologically significant; but if certain letters or groups of letters interchange frequently in all types of documents, this points to a corresponding reality in the speech of the writers concerned. Indiscriminate confusion of symbols indicates an identity of the sounds they represent.

This observation can be confirmed by an analysis of spelling mistakes today. Over the years I have maintained lists of misspellings by students ranging from third-form boys at an English Jesuit Grammar School (a collection I made for purposes of comparison when writing my dissertation), to adults from educationally deprived backgrounds in the United States, to supposedly highly literate college students in Chicago, New York, and Washington. Nearly 95 percent of these mistakes are phonetic, involving the substitution of a letter or group of letters with precisely the same sound as the correct spelling, e.g., *annoint* (*nn* and *n* both = /n/), *recieve* (*ie* and *ei* both = /i/), *reverance* (*a* and *e* here both = / ə /), *shure* (*sh* and *s* here both = / ʃ /), *reunight* (*-ight* and *-ite* both = /ait/). Very few mistakes fail to reflect the actual pronunciation, and these can generally be explained on orthographic grounds as visual spelling analogies (*hugh* for *huge*), inversions (*signle* for *single*), haplographies (*repetion* for *repetition*), or dittographies (*accepteted*).

With allowances made for less literate societies with less exposure to writing and less adherence to a fixed standard of orthography, spelling variations in ancient documents are similarly instructive for the pronunciation of a language, especially one like Koine Greek, in which there was a disparity between spelling and pronunciation analogous to that of present-day English.

When we find both short and long ι confused with ει in thousands of different words in all types of documents from all areas of the Hellenistic world from the third century B.C. on,[3] we are forced to the conclusion that

---

[3] E.g., πόλι (for πόλει) PHib. 110 V.82 (ca. 255 B.C.); εἵνα (for ἵνα) PCairZen. 243.7 (252 B.C.). See further E. Schwyzer, *Griechische Grammatik* (Handbuch der Altertumswissenschaft; Munich: Beck, 1953) 1. 184, 191–94, 196; M. Lejeune, *Phonétique historique du mycénien et du grec ancien*

the different sounds once represented by these symbols[4] had coincided in a single phoneme /i/.

Similarly, there is an interchange of the diphthong αι with the simple vowel ε from the second century B.C. on,[5] and this confusion of symbols becomes nearly as frequent as that of ει and ι by the first century A.D., indicating the identification of the sounds they represented in one phoneme /ε/, as in Modern Greek today. The diphthong οι interchanges sporadically with υ in the papyri of Ptolemaic Egypt;[6] the convergence of the sounds once represented by these symbols, probably in the sound /y/ inherited by the Koine from Attic,[7] seems complete by the first century A.D., when a widespread confusion of οι and υ is found in papyri from Egypt.[8]

The pronunciation of the other vowels and diphthongs in the Greek of the first century A.D. as indicated by orthographic variations in papyri, ostraca, and inscriptions from Egypt and elsewhere in the Mediterranean world is as follows. The classical Greek diphthongs were uniformly reduced to simple vowels. The long diphthongs ᾱι, ηι, and ωι show evidence of having been reduced to their corresponding simple vowels by the end of the second century B.C.[9] By the first century A.D., these diphthongs are more often than

---

(Tradition de l'Humanisme 9; Paris: Klincksieck, 1972) §§240, 246–57; K. Meisterhans–E. Schwyzer, *Grammatik der attischen Inschriften* (3d ed.; Berlin: Weidmann, 1900) 48–49; E. Schweizer, *Grammatik der pergamenischen Inschriften* (Berlin: Weidmann, 1898) 52–53, 72–74; E. Nachmanson, *Laute und Formen der magnetischen Inschriften* (Uppsala: Almqvist & Wiksells, 1904) 34–36; E. Rüsch, *Grammatik der delphischen Inschriften*, 1. *Lautlehre* (Berlin: Weidmann, 1914) 65–75, 80–100; E. Mayser, *Grammatik der griechischen Papyri aus der Ptolemäerzeit, 1.² 1, Einleitung und Lautlehre*, bearb. von H. Schmoll (Berlin: de Gruyter, 1970) 60–70; G. Crönert, *Memoria Graeca Herculanensis* (Leipzig: Teubner, 1903) 26–34; BDF §23.

[4] ι represented Indo-European /i/; ει originally represented the inherited short diphthong /ei/. This latter merged with the long closed /e/ arising from contraction and compensatory lengthening that it came to represent (the so-called spurious diphthong) by the seventh century B.C. in Corinthian and by the fifth century B.C. in Attic-Ionic. See Schwyzer, *Griechische Grammatik*, 1. 191–94, 346–48; Lejeune, *Phonétique* §§240, 246–47; C. D. Buck, *The Greek Dialects* (Chicago: University of Chicago Press, 1955) §28.

[5] E.g., παλεοῦ (for παλαιοῦ) UPZ 94.8 (159 B.C.); βαίνεται (for βαίνετε impt.) PWeil VI b.8 (before 160 B.C.). See further Schwyzer, *Griechische Grammatik* 1. 194–96; Lejeune, *Phonétique* §242; Meisterhans-Schwyzer, *Grammatik*, 34; Rüsch, *Grammatik*, 76–80; Schweizer, *Grammatik*, 77–78; Nachmanson, *Laute*, 37; Crönert, *Memoria*, 24; Mayser, *Grammatik*, 1.² 1, 85–86; Gignac, *Grammar*, 1. 191–93.

[6] E.g., ἠνυγμένων (for ἠνοιγμένων) PFrankf. 3.19 (ca. 213 B.C.); λοιμαινομένων (for λυμαινομένων) PHamb. 92.3 (181–145 B.C.). See further Mayser, *Grammatik*, 1.² 1, 89–90.

[7] Schwyzer, *Griechische Grammatik*, 1. 181–84; Lejeune, *Phonétique* §252.

[8] E.g., λυπόν (for λοιπόν) POxy. 1480.13 (A.D. 32); χοιρίου (for κυρίου) PMich. 351.34 (A.D. 44). See further Gignac, *Grammar*, 1. 197–99, 201.

[9] Meisterhans-Schwyzer, *Grammatik*, 67–68; Mayser, *Grammatik*, 1.² 1, 95–117; Schweizer,

not written without the -ι, and conversely an -ι is often added erroneously to a simple α, η, or ω in words in which it was not etymologically present.[10] The diphthong υι, identified with υ already in Attic inscriptions of the fifth and especially the fourth centuries B.C.,[11] shows little evidence of confusion with the simple vowel in the Koine before the Roman period.[12] But from the first century A.D. on, this identification is attested directly by the omission of the -ι[13] and indirectly by the expansion of the second element to -ει, which served graphically to represent the vowel glide that occurs before another vowel.[14] There is sporadic evidence already in the Ptolemaic papyri for the reduction of the second element of the diphthongs αυ and ευ to a consonantal sound.[15] A more exact chronology of this phonetic shift can be deduced from the papyri of the Roman and Byzantine periods, throughout which the second element continues to be omitted.[16] The closure of the second element to a /w/ sound is indicated by the occasional expansion of αυ and ευ to αου and εου, sometimes even to αυου and ευου,[17] while the later occasional interchange of the second element with β (pronounced at that time like the Spanish bilabial voiced fricative) points to its further closure to /β/, a sound midway between the original [u] and the Modern Greek [v] or [f].[18] The diphthong

---

Grammatik, 59–66, 89–91; Nachmanson, *Laute,* 49–59. See further Schwyzer, *Griechische Grammatik,* 1. 201; Lejeune, *Phonétique* §§235–36; Buck, *Greek Dialects* §38.

[10] E.g., τῇ ἐνεστώσῃ ἡμέρα (for τῆι ἐνεστώσηι ἡμέραι) *PSI* 203.3 (A.D. 87); ἔχωι (for ἔχω) *PMich.* 523.9 (A.D. 66). See further Gignac, *Grammar,* 1. 183–86.

[11] Meisterhans-Schwyzer, *Grammatik,* 59–60.

[12] Cf. Rüsch, *Grammatik,* 114–17; Schweizer, *Grammatik,* 85–86; Nachmanson, *Laute,* 46–48; Mayser, *Grammatik,* 1.² 1, 91–92.

[13] E.g., ὑός (for υἱός) *SB* 7031 = *PMich.* 186.36 (A.D. 72); ἐδύης (for εἰδυίης) *PLond.* 289 (2. 184–85).37 (A.D. 91). See further Gignac, *Grammar,* 1. 202.

[14] E.g., υειός (for υἱός) *PCornell* 22.7, etc. (early 1st cent.); εἰδυεῖαι (for εἰδυῖα) *PMich.* 346a.10 (A.D. 13). See further Gignac, *Grammar,* 1. 203, 207.

[15] E.g., ῥάυδους (for ῥάβδους) *UPZ* 12.32; 13.25 (158 B.C.); ἀτῶν (for αὐτῶν) *PTebt.* 812.9 (192 B.C.?); βασιλέοντος (for βασιλεύοντος) *PEleph.* 5.15 (284 B.C.). See further Mayser, *Grammatik,* 1.² 1, 92–95; Meisterhans-Schwyzer, *Grammatik,* 62; Schweizer, *Grammatik,* 82–84; Nachmanson, *Laute,* 59–61; Rüsch, *Grammatik,* 136–41; Schwyzer, *Griechische Grammatik,* 1. 197.

[16] E.g., ἀτοῦ (for αὐτοῦ) *SB* 7032 = *PMich.* 187.38 (A.D. 75); ἀλῆς (for αὐλῆς) *CPR* 198.17 (A.D. 139); σκέων (for σκεύων) *PPrinc.* 163.8 (2d cent.); δετέρου (for δευτέρου) *SB* 9427.5 (A.D. 162). See further Gignac, *Grammar,* 1. 226–29.

[17] E.g., αουτοῦ (for αὐτοῦ) *PMich.* 259.14,15 (A.D. 33); θησαουρῷ (for θησαυρῷ) *BGU* 2026.6 (2d cent.); ὑπογραφεούς (for ὑπογραφεύς) *PMich.* 311.24–25 (A.D. 34); σκεουει (for σκεύη) *PMich.* 343.5 (A.D. 54/55); ταυοῦτα (for ταῦτα) *BGU* 615.7 (2d cent.); αυουτά, αυουτῇ, αυουτῶν *PRein.* 118.8,11,14–15 (late 3d cent.); δευουδέρου (for δευτέρου) *CPR* 198.5 (A.D. 139); δουλευούετε (for δουλεύετε) *SB* 6263.20 (Rom.). See further Gignac, *Grammar,* 1. 230–31.

[18] E.g., προσαγορέβσε (for προσαγορεῦσαι) *PJand.* 101.9 (5th/6th cent.); οἰχουσκεβῆ (for οἰχοσκευῆς) *PLond.* 1610.57 (A.D. 705–9); ἐνδόμη (for ἐβδόμη) *PLond.* 1914.47 (A.D. 335?); ναύιαν, ναύια (for ναύβιον, ναύβια) *PMich.* 596.5,17 (A.D. 328/43). See further Gignac, *Grammar,* 1. 69–70, 231–33.

ου had been identified by the beginning of the Koine with the sound /u/ represented by υ in all dialects except Attic-Ionic,[19] the sound it has preserved to the present day.

The simple vowels for the most part preserved their classical pronunciation, except for the loss of quantitative distinction at least by the end of the second century B.C., when long vowels and diphthongs interchange frequently with short vowels. The diphthong ει interchanges with an etymologically short ι as well as with a long ι; αι interchanges with ε, οι with υ, and, most frequently, ω interchanges with ο in all kinds of words and in all phonetic conditions. This loss of quantitative distinction reflects in turn a change in the nature of the Greek accent from pitch to stress. Classical Greek had a pitch accent,[20] and meter was determined by quantity. With the change from pitch to stress, the word accent becomes dominant and forms the metrical ictus, with quantity transferred and subordinated to the accent.[21] A strong stress accent is reflected in writing by a very frequent interchange of vowels in unaccented syllables.[22] The change in the nature of the Greek accent came about in the Koine primarily through the transfer by non-native Greek speakers of their own accentual patterns to their Greek.

The determination of the sounds represented by the letter η presents a special problem. Its sound or sounds would be expected to be somewhere intermediate between its classical [æ] sound and its Modern Greek identification with the /i/ vowels. There is on the one hand considerable evidence in all types of documents from the first century A.D. on of a confusion of η with ι and ει,[23] suggesting that η may already have been pronounced [i]. On

---

[19] The inherited diphthong /ou/ had been reduced to a long /o/ by the seventh century B.C. in Corinthian and by the fifth century B.C. in Attic-Ionic, when the spurious diphthong ου was adopted to represent the long closed /o/ arising from contraction and compensative lengthening. It had shifted to /u/ by fourth-century B.C. Boeotian. See Schwyzer, *Griechische Grammatik*, 1. 191–94; Lejeune, *Phonétique* §241; Buck, *Greek Dialects* §§24–25.

[20] Each syllable had a rising intonation, with the main word accent rising to about a musical fifth above the ordinary level of the other syllables. See Schwyzer, *Griechische Grammatik*, 1. 180, Zusatz; 371–76, 391–95; Lejeune, *Phonétique* §§191, 322, 336–50, 383.

[21] Neglect of vowel quantity in poetry is attested in Roman times in Attic inscriptions (Meisterhans-Schwyzer, *Grammatik*, 68) and a stress accent is indicated elsewhere in later Greek inscriptions (Schweizer, *Grammatik*, 129–30). The earliest signs of accentual versification are found in Antipator of Sidon (150–120 B.C.), Philip of Thessalonica (ca. 50 B.C.), and especially Babrius (2d cent. A.D.). See Schwyzer, *Griechische Grammatik*, 1. 394; P. Maas, *Greek Metre* (Oxford: Clarendon, 1946) §§19–25; A. Dihle, "Die Anfänge der griechischen akzentuierenden Verskunst," *Hermes* 82 (1954) 182–99.

[22] E.g., τεσσεράκοντα (for τεσσαράκοντα) *BGU* 68.16 (A.D. 113/14); τέσσαρος (for τέσσαρας) *PPrinc.* 142.6 (ca. A.D. 23); σύνθασις (for σύνθεσις) *POxy.* 2407.22 (late 3d cent.); ἀνόματα (for ὀνόματα) *PCairIsidor.* 29.3 (1st half 4th cent.); τρίτεν (for τρίτον) *SB* 7031 = *PMich.* 186.34 (A.D. 72); ἔγραφος (for ἔγραφες) *PFay.* 117.22 (A.D. 108). See further Gignac, *Grammar*, 1. 278–92, 306–10.

[23] E.g., μέρι (for μέρη) and μί (for μή) *SB* 5109 = *PRyl.* 160d, i.2,7 (A.D. 42); πᾶσι βεβαιώσῃ (for

the other hand, η interchanges frequently with ε[24] and also with υ,[25] not only in the first century but virtually throughout Roman and Byzantine times. These data indicate that η was at least bivalent; this came about in Egypt through bilingual interference.[26]

The pronunciation of the consonants in Greek of the first century is as follows. The classical voiced stops /b g d/ represented by β, γ, δ were probably voiced fricatives /β γ-j ð/ throughout the Koine except in Egypt. The labial stop represented by β had begun to shift to a fricative dialectically already in the fifth century B.C.,[27] and by the early Roman period it serves to transliterate the Latin ν[28] and eventually interchanges in Greek words with -υ in the αυ/ευ diphthongs.[29] The original velar stop represented by γ shows a fricative pronunciation from the fourth century B.C. on,[30] probably [ɣ] (like

---

πάσῃ βεβαιώσει) PMich. 280.6 (1st cent.); εἰμῖν (for ἡμῖν) PSI 917.4 (1st cent.); εἴμισυ (for ἥμισυ) PMich. 563.27–28 (A.D. 128/29); ἡδίου (for ἰδίου) BGU 830.6 (1st cent.); ἤσασει (for ἴσασι) BGU 597.5 (A.D. 75); ἡμί (for εἰμί) POxy. 1481.3 (early 2d cent.); σπονδήου (for σπονδείου) SB 5252.20 (A.D. 65). See further Gignac, Grammar, 1. 235–42.

[24] E.g., μέ (for μή) PIFAO ii, 28.6 (1st cent.); ταύτες (for ταύτης) PLond. 333 = MChr. 176.7 (A.D. 166); ἔμισους (for ἥμισυ) BGU 765.6 (A.D. 166?); σπουδές (for σπουδῆς) POxy. 1837.10 (early 6th cent.); ἠάν (for ἐάν) POxy. 1480.13,24 (A.D. 32); ἠνιαυτόν (for ἐνιαυτόν) SB 9636.4, sim. 13 (A.D. 136); ἐννῆα (for ἐννέα) WO 46.7 (A.D. 97); εὐεργήτου (for εὐεργέτου) SB 4669.3 (A.D. 614). See further Gignac, Grammar, 1. 242–49.

[25] E.g., ὑμῖν (for ἡμῖν) PMich. 293.2 (A.D. 14–37); μό (for μή) BGU 153.38 (A.D. 152); ἡπέρ (for ὑπέρ) POxy. 1145.3 (1st cent.); νῆν (for νῦν) PSI 66.18 (5th cent.?); cf. also ὀγδοοίκοντα (for ὀγδοήκοντα) SB 10724.13–14 (3d cent.); ἐτήμασον (for ἑτοίμασον) OMeyer 65.6 (3d cent.). See further Gignac, Grammar, 1. 262–67.

[26] In Coptic, H was bivalent. In all dialects it represented an allophone of / i/ before or after sonants as well as the phoneme /ε/ (long or short). In Bohairic, it also represented an allophone of /æ/. See J. Vergote, Grammaire copte, 1a. Introduction, phonétique et phonologie, morphologie synthématique: Partie synchronique (Louvain: Peeters, 1973) §§42–44. See also T. O. Lambdin, "The Bivalence of Coptic Eta and Related Problems in the Vocalization of Egyptian," Journal of Near Eastern Studies 17 (1958) 177–93.

[27] Evidence is found in fifth-century B.C. inscriptions from Laconia and the Argolid and fourth-century inscriptions from Crete (Schwyzer, Griechische Grammatik, 1. 207–8; Lejeune, Phonétique §44). A fricative pronunciation is first reflected in Attic and Asia Minor inscriptions ca. the beginning of the first century A.D. (Meisterhans-Schwyzer, Grammatik, 77; Schweizer, Grammatik, 105). In the Ptolemaic papyri, the spellings in n. 15 above point to a fricative pronunciation; see further Mayser, Grammatik, 1.& 1, 151.

[28] E.g., βιάτικον viaticum BGU 423 = WChr. 480.9 (2d cent.); πρεβέτοις privatus BGU 781 vi.7 (1st cent.); Φλαβία Flavia BGU 1893.404 (A.D. 149). See further Gignac, Grammar, 1. 68–69.

[29] See above, n. 18.

[30] E.g., Pamphilian μηειάλαν = μεγάλην (Schwyzer, Griechische Grammatik, 1. 209; Lejeune, Phonétique §44), and ὀλίος (for ὀλίγος) frequent in Attic inscriptions from 300 B.C. on (Meisterhans-Schwyzer, Grammatik, 75). Cf. from papyri of the Roman period ὑιῆ and ὑγῆ (for ὑγιῆ), e.g., POxy. 729.23 (A.D. 137); PMich. 312.32 (A.D. 34); μναγεῖα (for μναεῖα) SB 7816 = PSI 1263.20 (A.D. 166/67); Τραγιανοῦ Trajanus PBrem. 69.12 (A.D. 98); ἔραφεν (for ἔγραφεν) PMich.

the *g* in Spanish *luego*) before back or rounded vowels and [j] (as in English *yes*) before front vowels. Evidence for the fricative pronunciation of the dental stop is found considerably later, beginning in the first century A.D.[31] In Semitic-speaking areas, these fricative sounds would have corresponded to the fricative pronunciation of the *begadkepat* letters; in Egypt, the fricative pronunciation was found only in certain phonetic conditions, because the voiced velar and dental stops were widely identified with their corresponding voiceless stops /k t/ through bilingual interference (Coptic has only the voiceless order).[32] The classical aspirates /k^h t^h p^h/ represented by χ, θ, φ were probably still pronounced as voiceless aspirated stops. Evidence for the fricative pronunciation of these aspirates begins to appear in the first century A.D. but it is infrequent and ambiguous;[33] in Egypt, this shift was hindered by the identification of these aspirates with their corresponding voiceless stops (only in the Bohairic dialect were aspirated stops distinct phonemes).[34]

The liquids, represented by λ and ρ, remained phonemically distinct except in Egypt, where there was widespread confusion of λ and ρ at all times, not only in documents from the Fayum (in the Fayumic dialect of Coptic, λ generally stands for ρ of other dialects[35]) but also in those from other areas of Egypt.[36] Elsewhere in the Koine, however, there is evidence of the shift of preconsonantal λ to ρ,[37] as generally in Modern Greek.

304.10 (A.D. 42?); θυάτηρ (for θυγάτηρ) *PTebt*. 397.29 (A.D. 198). See further Gignac, *Grammar*, 1. 71–75.

[31] Early evidence for a dental fricative in the classical dialects is inconclusive (Schwyzer, *Griechische Grammatik*, 1. 208–9; Lejeune, *Phonétique* §44), and there are no indications of it in the Attic or Asia Minor inscriptions or in the Ptolemaic papyri. Cf. from papyri of the Roman period δά (for διά) *PRyl*. 160c, ii.41 (A.D. 32); δώρυγος (for διώρυγος) *SB* 9480 (1) = *PMilVogl*. 167.11 (A.D. 110); ζώρυγα (for διώρυγα) *PMeyer* 20.18 (1st half 3d cent.); ζαχοσίας (for διαχοσίας) *POxy*. 1646.31 (A.D. 268/69); ζιά (for διά) *PLond*. 413 = *PAbinn*. 6.22 (ca. A.D. 346); etc. See further Gignac, *Grammar*, 1. 75–76.

[32] See Gignac, *Grammar*, 1. 76–86.

[33] E.g., transcriptions of Latin *f*: φίσκου *fiscus SB* 8444.21 (A.D. 98–138); φούνδαν *funda PHamb*. 10.33–34,38–39 (2d cent.). See further Gignac, *Grammar*, 1. 88–101; Schwyzer, *Griechische Grammatik*, 1. 204–7.

[34] See Gignac, *Grammar*, 1. 86–98.

[35] W. H. Worrell, *Coptic Sounds* (Ann Arbor: University of Michigan, 1934) 68, 84; J. Vergote, *Phonétique historique de l'égyptien*. 1, *Les consonnes* (Bibliothèque du Muséon 19; Louvain, 1945) 109–10; *Grammaire*, 1a. §30.

[36] E.g., χαθαλά (for χαθαρά) *PRyl*. 166.22 (A.D. 26); θέρης (for θέλης) *POxy*. 1291.9 (A.D. 30); ὑπέλ (for ὑπέρ) *SB* 5110 = *PRyl*. 160d ii.34 (A.D. 42); ἐξερθῖν (for ἐξελθεῖν) *PMich*. 204.5–6 (A.D. 127). See further Gignac, *Grammar*, 1. 102–7.

[37] This shift is found especially before labials already in second-century A.D. Delphian Δερφοί (Rüsch, *Grammatik*, 201), Lydian Εὐέρπιστος (K. Hauser, *Grammatik der griechischen Inschriften Lykiens* [Basel: E. Birkhäuser, 1916] 60 n. 2), and third-century A.D. Attic ἐρπίς, ἀδερφοί (Schwyzer, *Griechische Grammatik*, 1. 213). Cf. Modern Greek ἀδερφός, ἦρθα, ἐρπίδα (A. Thumb,

The nasals were somewhat unstable in the Koine. Final -ν was frequently omitted regardless of the nature of the following sound (movable -ν was used irregularly),[38] and, at least in Egypt, medial nasals were also frequently dropped or assimilated to a following stop.[39] In Modern Greek, final nasal is usually pronounced only in words like the definite article that are closely connected syntactically with the following word when this begins with a stop consonant or a vowel.[40]

The inherited voiceless sibilant /s/, represented by σ, retained its pronunciation, though becoming [z] before a voiced consonant,[41] as already earlier in dialectal inscriptions.[42] The interchange of σ and ζ in other phonetic conditions is virtually limited to Egypt, where it parallels the lack of distinction between voiced and voiceless stops.[43]

Aspiration at the beginning of a word was lost in the course of the Koine.[44] Evidence for its loss in individual words and the false aspiration of others, perhaps through analogy, is widespread even by the first century A.D.[45]

There is considerable fluctuation in the use of the spellings -ρσ-/-ρρ- and -σσ-/-ττ-, reflecting the diverse dialectal heritage of the Koine.[46] The inherited

---

A Handbook of the Modern Greek Language [trans. from the 2d German ed. by S. Angus; Chicago: Argonaut, 1964] §31).

38 E.g., τὴ τιμήν *OFay.* 7.2 (A.D. 4); ἐ μηνεί (for ἐν μηνί) *BGU* 910 ii.39–40 (A.D. 71); καθ' ἑκάστη (for ἑκάστην) ἡμέραν *POxy.* 1769.4–5 (3d cent.). See further Gignac, *Grammar*, 1. 111–16.

39 E.g., ἀπενέχαι (for ἀπενέγχαι) *POxy.* 119.8 (2d/3d cent.); ἀνήνεχχεν (for ἀνήνεγχεν) *SB* 9190.16 (A.D. 131); πάτων (for πάντων) *PPrinc.* 73.3 (3d cent.); πέπτῳ (for πέμπτῳ) *BGU* 2066.6 (A.D. 73/74); μεταλαββάνων (for μεταλαμβάνων) *POslo* 153.10 (early 2d cent.). See further Gignac, *Grammar*, 1. 116–19, 165–72.

40 Thumb, *Handbook* §34; A. Mirambel, *Grammaire du grec moderne* (Paris: Klincksieck, 1949) 21, 29.

41 This is indicated by such spellings as νομίζματος (for νομίσματος) *OStrassb.* 776.7 (early Rom.); ἀμφιζβητήσεως (for ἀμφισ-) *PMilVogl.* 129.2–3 (A.D. 135); ζμύρνης (for σμύρνης) *PRossGeorg.* v 52.4 (2d cent.). See further Gignac, *Grammar*, 1. 120–22.

42 Cf. Attic ἀναβαζμούς 329 B.C. (Meisterhans-Schwyzer, *Grammatik,* 92), Delphian πρεζβυτάς, etc. (Rüsch, *Grammatik,* 206), and Ζμύρνα, etc. passim (Schwyzer, *Griechische Grammatik,* 1. 217).

43 E.g., ἄζημος (for ἄσημος) *BGU* 854.10 (A.D. 44/45); ἴζου (for ἴσου) *StudPal.* iii 384.3 (5th/6th cent.); μίσονος (for μείζονος) *PAmh.* 130.16 (A.D. 70); σῷα (for ζῷα) *PAmh.* 150.21 (A.D. 592). See further Gignac, *Grammar*, 1. 123–24.

44 Lejeune, *Phonétique* §321. It has not survived into Modern Greek.

45 E.g., μετ' ὅρχου *PMich.* 123 V, IV.13–14,21 (A.D. 45–47); ἐπ' ὑποθήχῃ *PFlor.* 81.6 (A.D. 103); χατίστημι *POxy.* 2474.20–21 (3D CENT.); καθ' ἔτος *BGU* 197.13, etc. (A.D. 17); ἐφ' ἐνιαυτόν *PMich.* 585.29 (A.D. 87); ἐφ' ἐλπίδων *PMich.* 466.30 (A.D. 107). See further Gignac, *Grammar*, 1. 133–38.

46 Assimilation to /-rr-/ was regular in Attic, West Ionic, and Northwest Greek except where the influence of analogy was strong, but in other dialects the /-rs-/ cluster was generally preserved (Schwyzer, *Griechische Grammatik,* 1. 284–85). Attic, along with Boeotian, Cretan, and Euboean (partially), shows the /-tt-/ cluster and initial /t-/, except in loanwords, while Ionic and the other dialects show /-ss-/ and /s-/ (Schwyzer, *Griechische Grammatik,* 1. 317–22).

/-rs-/ cluster occurs in relatively few words, in which both spellings are found;[47] -σσ- tends to predominate in all words except those that are specifically Attic.[48] The later prevalence of -ρρ- and -ττ- spellings reflects the influence of Atticism in the Roman and Byzantine periods.

Single and double consonants were no longer distinguished in speech (just as in English, where *embarrass* is often misspelled with only one *r*, whereas in Spanish there is a phonemic distinction between single and double *r*, e.g., *pero* "but"; *perro* "dog"). This is reflected in writing by the frequent simplification or converse gemination of consonants[49] and corresponds to the loss of quantitative distinction in vowels that occurred under the influence of the stress accent.

Throughout the Koine there is considerable irregularity in the orthographic practice of representing the assimilation of a nasal to a following consonant. In general, unassimilated spellings always predominate in word junction but are relatively rare within a simple word.[50] In word composition, however, the practice varies greatly, as unassimilated spellings gradually give way over time to assimilated spellings. In the first century A.D., unassimilated spellings still predominate over assimilated spellings in word composition at a ratio of ten to one.[51] This reflects an orthographic tendency to isolate individual word elements and represents the conflict between phonetic and historical spelling observed elsewhere in Greek from archaic to Koine.[52] Actual assimilation in speech is indicated by evidence for the complete assimilation in writing of a nasal, sometimes even in composition, to the following consonant.[53] Similarly, the preposition ἐx is frequently written ἐγ

---

[47] E.g., θαρρῶ *PSI* 717.7 (2d cent.); θαρσῶν *BGU* 1080 = *WChr.* 478.14 (3d cent.); ἄρρενα *PSI* 38.6 (A.D. 101); ἄρσενα *POslo* 160.6 (2d half 3d cent.). See further Gignac, *Grammar*, 1. 142–45.

[48] Thus almost always τέσσαρες, etc., but ἐλαττόω; most words fluctuate, e.g., ἧσσον *PMich.* 262.31 (A.D. 35/36) and ἧττον *PLond.* 853a = *PSarap.* 98.4 (early 2d cent.); θαλάσσης *POxy.* 1067.29 (3d cent.) and θαλάττης *POslo* 126.4 (A.D. 161 or later); φυλάσσειν *PMich.* 123 R II.17 (A.D. 45–47) and φυλάττειν *PLond.* 1178 = *WChr.* 156.35 (A.D. 194). See further Gignac, *Grammar*, 1. 145–54.

[49] E.g., ἄλα (for ἄλλα) *PMich.* 312.21 (A.D. 34); γράματα (for γράμματα) *POxy.* 728.34 (A.D. 142); ἐνέα (for ἐννέα) *PMich.* 322a.26 (A.D. 46); ἵπον (for ἵππον) *PSI* 39.5 (A.D. 148); θέλλεις (for θέλεις) *POslo* 53.12 (2d cent.); ἄρρον (for ἄρον) *POxy.* 119.10 (2d/3d cent.); ἔσσχον (for ἔσχον) *PRossGeorg.* v, 19.2 (A.D. 236); ἔχχτης (for ἔχτης) *BGU* 1049.26 (A.D. 342). See further Gignac, *Grammar*, 1. 154–65.

[50] E.g., ἐὰν μή passim but ἄμ μή *POxy.* 119.8,14 (2d/3d cent.); ἔπεμψα passim but ἔπενψα *POxy.* 1155.12 (A.D. 104). See further Gignac, *Grammar*, 1. 165–72.

[51] E.g., συνχωρῶ *POxy.* 104.10 (A.D. 96); ἔνπροσθεν *PMich.* 345.16 (A.D. 7); συνλαβεῖν *PMich.* 421.22 (A.D. 41–54); ἐνμεῖναι *POxy.* 38 = *MChr.* 58.16 (A.D. 49–50); συνσταθμίαν *PMerton* 12.17 A.D. 58).

[52] Cf. Schwyzer, *Griechische Grammatik*, 1. 213–14; Lejeune, *Phonétique* §143.

[53] E.g., συππεφωνημένης (for συμπεφωνημένης) *CPR* 220.5 (1st cent.); πασσόφωι (for πανσόφωι)

before a voiced consonant.[54] This indicates that the final sound was voiced [g] at least at the time of adoption of this orthography.[55] Whether the actual voicing of this stop still took place during the Roman period is not clear. It may have been only a relic of an older orthographic practice.

Perhaps a table summarizing the pronunciation of Greek in the first century might be useful. I shall here indicate the phonetic value(s) of each letter of the Greek alphabet. I do this in preference to presenting the phonemic structure of the language according to the points of articulation of the various vowels and consonants, not to resuscitate the *Buchstabenlehre* of prescientific grammars but to provide a handy reference to scholars more accustomed to the traditional orthography. I give the equivalents in symbols of the International Phonetic Alphabet, with examples from modern languages.

α	[a]	= the *a* in *father*
β	[β]	= the *b* in Spanish *Habana*
	[j]	= the *y* in *yes*
γ {	[ɣ]	= the *g* in Spanish *luego*
	[ŋ]	= the *ng* in *sing*
δ	[ð]	= the *th* in *this*
ε	[ɛ]	= the *e* in *get*
ζ	[z]	= the *z* in *zoo*
	[i]	= the *i* in French *si*
η {	[e]	= the *e* in French *thé*
	[ɛ]	= the *e* in *get*
θ	[tʰ]	= the *t* in *tin* (aspirated)
ι	[i]	= the *i* in French *si*
κ	[k]	= the *k* in *skin* (unaspirated)
λ	[l]	= the *l* in *light*
μ	[m]	= the *m* in *might*
ν	[n]	= the *n* in *night*
ξ	[ks]	= the *x* in *ax*
ο	[o]	= the *o* in French *mot*
π	[p]	= the *p* in *spin* (unaspirated)
ρ	[r]	= the *r* in Spanish *pero*

PHermRees 3.1,V (4th cent.). See n. 39 above for analogous examples of complete assimilation of nasals in simple words.

[54] E.g., ἐγ δίκης *PMich.* 340.63 (A.D. 45/46); ἐγ βορρᾶ *POxy.* 2240.50 (A.D. 211); ἐγ γειτόνων *POxy.* 1675.9 (3d cent.); see further Gignac, *Grammar*, 1. 172–76.

[55] In the Ptolemaic papyri, ἐκ is regularly assimilated to ἐγ before voiced consonants in both word junction and composition (Mayser, *Grammatik*, 1.² 1, 199–202).

σ/ς	[s]	= the *s* in *sing*
τ	[t]	= the *t* in *still* (unaspirated)
υ	[y]	= the *u* in French *lune*
φ	[pʰ]	= the *p* in *pin* (aspirated)
χ	[kʰ]	= the *k* in *kin* (aspirated)
ψ	[ps]	= the *ps* in *apse*
ω	[o]	= the *o* in French *mot*
αι	[ε]	= the *e* in *get*
ει	[i]	= the *i* in French *si*
οι	[y]	= the *u* in French *lune*
υι	[y]	= the *u* in French *lune*
αυ	[aw]	= the *ow* in *now*
ευ	[εw]	= similar to above with *e* as in *get*
ηυ	[ew]	= similar to above with *e* as in French *thé*
ου	[u]	= the *ou* in French *tout*

Some practical applications of the phonology of the Koine to the text and language of the New Testament may now be made.

Awareness of the elimination of the classical Greek diphthongs serves to confirm the reading in Phlm 12 adopted by UBSGNT³ and Nestle-Aland²⁶, ὃν ἀνέπεμψά σοι, αὐτόν, τοῦτ' ἔστιν τὰ ἐμὰ σπλάγχνα, attested in ℵ* A 33. By the first century A.D., the classical short diphthong /oi/ represented in writing by οι had become a monophthong and coincided in pronunciation with the simple vowel υ in the phoneme /y/. The third word, σοι, was pronounced /sy/, exactly the same as σύ, the nominative singular. What may have happened in the transmission of this text was that a scribe (whether reading aloud or from dictation) heard /sy/ and understood it as nominative σύ, which he wrote with a connective δέ; this is the reading of Ggr: ὃν ἀνέπεμψα, σὺ δὲ αὐτόν, τοῦτ' ἔστιν τὰ ἐμὰ σπλάγχνα. The syntax of this was elliptical; a verb was needed, and προσλαβοῦ was introduced from v 17: ὃν ἀνέπεμψα, σὺ δὲ αὐτόν, τοῦτ' ἔστιν τὰ ἐμὰ σπλάγχνα προσλαβοῦ: this is the reading of ℵc (Dc 104) K P 81 326 330* 436 614 630 1241 1739 1881 1984 1985 2495 *Byz Lect*m itdiv,f, z* vgww syrh goth John-Damascus. The other variants are conflations of these three readings: ὃν ἀνέπεμψά σοι, τοῦτ' ἔστιν τὰ σπλάγχα τὰ ἐμὰ προσλαβοῦ 629; ὃν ἀνέπεμψά σοι αὐτόν, τοῦτ' ἔστιν τὰ ἐμὰ σπλάγχνα προσλαβοῦ C*; ὃν ἀνέπεμψά σοι, σὺ δὲ αὐτόν, τοῦτ' ἔστιν τὰ ἐμὰ σπλάγχνα προσλαβοῦ C² (D* 88) itar, c,x,zc vgcl (syrp Chrysostom Jerome etc.); ὃν ἀνέπεμψα· σὺ δὲ αὐτὸν προσλαβοῦ, τοῦτ' ἔστιν τὰ ἐμὰ σπλάγχνα 330mg 451 2492 (69 431 462 προσλαβοῦ αὐτόν) syrpal Theodoret; ὃν ἀνέπεμψά σοι, σὺ δὲ αὐτὸν προσλαβοῦ, τοῦτ' ἔστιν τὰ ἐμὰ σπλάγχνα (048) itg (copsa,bo προσλαβοῦ αὐτόν) (arm eth). Thus the variants may all be derived from the reading established in our critical editions in light of the evidence of the pronunciation of σοι as /sy/.

The widespread identification of simple vowels led to manifold textual variants in the manuscript tradition. One notorious example is the reading κάμιλον, "ship's hawser," "cable," for κάμηλον, "camel," at Mark 10:25 (13 28 pc) // Luke 18:25 (S ƒ¹³ 1010 1424 al) // Matt 19:24 (no v.l.). The word κάμιλος is not attested in Greek until late (scholiast on Aristophanes' Frogs and Suidas), but it does correspond to the Arabic jummal, "ship's cable." Despite later rabbinical parallels (Str-B 1. 828) about an elephant going through the eye of a needle and gratuitous assumptions of the existence of a city gate in Jerusalem or elsewhere called the Needle's Eye, through which camels had to kneel to pass, κάμιλον remains an intriguing possibility here that is phonologically acceptable. Both κάμιλον and κάμηλον would have been pronounced the same in first-century Palestine. Reading κάμιλον does not reduce the hyperbole of the saying of Jesus; it just makes it less illogical and grotesque.

The bivalence of η and the pronunciation of υ as a rounded front vowel /y/ foreign to many speakers, especially in a bilingual situation, led to a widespread confusion of η and υ. This is reflected in the manuscript tradition especially in the confusion of forms of the first and second personal pronouns in the plural. Thus, ἡμεῖς fluctuates with ὑμεῖς at Gal 4:28; ἡμῶν fluctuates with ὑμῶν at John 8:54; Acts 3:22, 25; 7:39; 19:37; 28:25; Rom 14:16; 1 Cor 15:14; 2 Cor 1:11; 3:2; 8:7; Gal 4:6; Col 1:7; 3:4; Heb 9:14; 1 Pet 2:21; 1 John 1:4; 2 John 12; Jude 3; etc.; ἡμῖν fluctuates with ὑμῖν at Acts 7:38; 13:26; 16:17; Heb 13:21; 1 Pet 2:21; 1 John 2:25; ἡμᾶς fluctuates with ὑμᾶς at Rom 13:11; 15:7; 1 Cor 7:5; Eph 5:2; Col 1:12; 2:13; 1 Pet 3:18. Similarly, ἡμέτερον fluctuates with ὑμέτερον at Luke 16:12; sim. Acts 27:34; 1 Cor 15:31. While a possible confusion of person is undoubtedly a factor in many of these passages, the disproportionate frequency of variant readings involving forms of these pronouns indicates a basis in phonology. Evidence from the papyri corroborates the widespread confusion of η and υ throughout the Roman and Byzantine periods.

In consonants, some forms of οὐδείς and μηδείς are spelled in the NT with θ in place of δ, with or without variants. Thus, οὐθενός occurs at Luke 22:35; 2 Cor 11:9; οὐθέν is found at Luke 23:14; Acts 15:9; 19:27; 26:26; 1 Cor 13:2; μηθέν is read at Acts 27:33. Similarly, the verb is always ἐξουθενέω (Luke 18:9, etc.). The spellings with θ preserve an orthography prevalent in Attic and other dialects from 378 B.C. on,[56] where the θ arose to represent the assimilation of /d/ before a rough breathing (the feminine is always οὐδεμία, etc.).

---

[56] Meisterhans-Schwyzer, Grammatik, 104–5; Schweizer, Grammatik, 112–14; cf. Schwyzer, Griechische Grammatik, 1. 408.

These spellings with θ are quite common in the Ptolemaic papyri[57] but are found only occasionally in the Roman period, rarely after the second century.[58]

In our critical editions of the NT, ἐλπίς is printed with initial aspiration in ἐφ' ἐλπίδι at Rom 8:20 with P⁴⁶ ℵ B* D* F G Ψ (*v.l.* ἐπ' ἐλπίδι P²⁷ A B² C D² *pm*). Elsewhere the critical editions print the unaspirated spelling ἐπ' ἐλπίδι at Acts 26:6, Rom 5:2, and 1 Cor 9:10 (twice: both LXX) without variants and at Titus 1:2 with the variant ἐν ἐλπίδι F G H 365 *pc* and κατ' ἐλπίδα at Titus 3:7. This is one of the words that occurs frequently with false (new) aspiration in the Koine, indicated in writing by the change of a preceding π, κ, τ to φ, χ, θ in word junction or composition. This aspirated spelling is found only once in the nonliterary papyri (ἐφ' ἐλπίδων *PMich.* 466.30 [A.D. 107]), but it is attested in the Herculaneum papyri and in codices of Josephus, Hippolytus, Ptolemaeus, etc.[59] It also appears as a loanword in Coptic in the aspirated spelling ⲞⳈⲈⲗⲡⲓⲥ in both the Sahidic and Bohairic dialects.[60] Perhaps the aspirated spelling should be uniform in the NT.

Many other examples involving vowels and consonants could be adduced to illustrate the value of a study of the phonology of the papyri. Nearly all of the linguistic phenomena singled out above have implications for the text and language of the NT. Thus, the process of elimination of the diphthongs is reflected in such manuscript spellings as υει for υι in ἐληλυθεῖαν at Mark 9:1 W and εου for ευ in χαλκεούς at 2 Tim 4:14 D.[61] The loss of quantitative distinction and the consequent identification of ο and ω is reflected in the frequent confusion of indicative and subjunctive forms, often with considerable exegetical significance, e.g., at Rom 5:1 ἔχομεν ℵ¹ B² F G P Ψ 0220vid 6 88 104 365 1506 1739 1881 2464 *pm*, with ἔχωμεν ℵ* A B* C D K L 33 81 1175 *pm*, and at 1 Cor 15:49 φορέσομεν B I 6 88 630 945*v.l.* 1881 *al Lect*, etc., with φορέσωμεν P⁴⁶ ℵ A C D F G K P Ψ 075 0243 33 81 *pm*, etc. The interchange of λ and ρ is reflected in the variant μέλους D* Ψ t vg syʰ for μέρους at 1 Cor 12:27. The voicing of σ before a following voiced consonant is reflected in such manuscript spellings as ζβέννυτε at 1 Thess 5:19 B* D* F G, ἄζβεστον at Mark 9:43 N, and Ζμύρναν, Ζμύρνη at Rev 1:11, 2:8, and even σζμύρνης at John 19:39 in the Codex Sinaiticus.[62] The NT manuscripts

⁵⁷ Mayser, *Grammatik*, 1.² 1, 149.
⁵⁸ Gignac, *Grammar*, 1. 97.
⁵⁹ Crönert, *Memoria*, 150[-1] and n. 5; Mayser, *Grammatik*, 1.² 1, 176.
⁶⁰ A. Böhlig, *Die griechischen Lehnwörter im sahidischen und bohairischen Neuen Testament* (Studien zur Erforschung des christlichen Ägyptens, Heft 2; Munich, 1954) 112; W. E. Crum, *A Coptic Dictionary* (Oxford: Clarendon, 1939) s.v. 632.
⁶¹ BDF §§8, 9.
⁶² BDF §10.

likewise reflect the contemporaneous practices of the papyri in the use of movable -ν and movable -ς, in the simplification and gemination of consonants, and in the indication of assimilation, especially in composition. But these examples may serve to illustrate the importance of a good knowledge of the pronunciation of Greek during the early Christian centuries for the practice of NT textual criticism. The ample evidence from some 50,000 nonliterary papyri, ostraca, and inscriptions from this period is now available to students of the Greek Bible. The data gleaned from them should constitute an external control in dealing with the vagaries of the manuscript tradition.

Chapter 4   Idiomatic Ancient Aramaic

Jonas C. Greenfield
The Hebrew University of Jerusalem

She [wisdom] is also precious to the gods; her kingdom is forever; she is set in the heavens, for the lord of the holy ones has taken her.

Aḥiqar l. 95

THE STUDENT OF ARAMAIC has at the present time various dictionaries, word lists, and glossaries to turn to when looking for the meaning of a word or phrase, or when examining the spread of a verbal root or nominal form in the various Aramaic dialects. These dictionaries vary greatly in completeness, and for the earlier periods they are out of date. Even the best of these, however, usually list the individual vocables and rarely give them together with other elements with which they are associated—such as the combination of verb with a particular particle, or of verb and noun—that so often constitute an idiomatic expression. The basic meaning of a vocable, noun or verb, is modified by its companion; the ensuing idiomatic expression often, but not always, has a parallel in cognate languages. This article will attempt to gather together those known to us from Early and Ancient Aramaic. I use these designations for this collection with a degree of hesitancy and have included both the framework story and the proverbs of Aḥiqar, and also Biblical Aramaic, but for various reasons have not included the legal documents from Elephantine, the epistolary material of the Persian period from Egypt, and other texts in Official Aramaic.[1]

[1] For the stages of Aramaic, see the important essay by J. A. Fitzmyer, "The Phases of the Aramaic Language," reprinted in *A Wandering Aramean* (SBLMS 25: Missoula, MT: Scholars Press, 1979) 57–84. My own designations diverge slightly, introducing various distinctions. The lack of references to the Tell Fekherye inscription is due to the lack of Aramaic idioms in it.

1. *'bd šm: l'bdt 'šmhm* (Sfire II B 7), lit., "to destroy the name," i.e., "to anni-
hilate." In Aramaic the verb is in pael, but Biblical Hebrew knows both
piel (*wĕ'ibbadtā 'et šĕmām* [Deut 12:3]) and hiphil (*wĕha'abadtā 'et šĕmām*
[Deut 7:24]), both indicating total destruction.[2]

2. *'ḥz ḥṭr* (Hadad lines 15, 20, 25), lit., "to hold the scepter," i.e., "to rule."
The Biblical Hebrew phrase is *tōmēk šebeṭ*, used in Amos 1 of the ruler of
Bit Adini (v. 5) and of Ashkelon (v. 8). The Akkadian equivalent is *tāmiḥ
ḥaṭṭi*, known first from the times of Aššur-rēš-iši (1133–1116), although
the scepter as a symbol of royalty is known from much earlier times.[3] The
phrase *tamiḥ ḥaṭṭi* may very well be a calque on the Aramaic.

3. *'ḥz bknp* (Panamuwa line 11), lit., "to seize the corner of the garment," i.e.,
"to acknowledge the sovereignty of. . . ." Taking hold of the corner of the
garment of a ruler was, especially in the Mari texts where it is phrased
as *sissiktam* or *qannam ṣabātum,* an acknowledgment of his overlordship.
It is interesting to find this expression in an inscription of the Assyrian
period since in Assyrian texts the orientation of the phrase has shifted to
the sphere of religion, where it was a form of submission to a particular
god. The phrase *'ḥz bknp lbš* occurs in Aḥiqar 171, but is to be taken
literally there.[4]

4. *'ḥz pm* (Nerab 2 line 4), found in the passive: *pmy l't'ḥz mn mln,* "my
mouth was not closed from words," i.e., "I was not silent."

5. *'kl qrṣyn* (Dan 3:8; 6:25), lit., "to eat the pieces," i.e., "to slander"; a calque
on Akkadian *karṣa akālu.*[5]

6. *'mr qrṣyn* (Carpentras line 2), lit., "to say the pieces of," the full quotation
being *qrṣy 'yš l' 'mrt,* "she spoke no slander of any one." This is undoubtedly a development of the previous phrase. It is not an innovation
in Aramaic since the phrase *qābi karṣiya,* "my calumniator," is known from
an Amarna text (252 line 14).[6]

7. *'mr bnbšh* (Sfire II B 5), lit., "says to himself," i.e., "thinks." In Biblical
Hebrew the idiom is *'amār bĕlibbô* (Ps 41:1). In Sfire it is found together
with *'št,* "to think."

8. *b'š 'l* (Dan 6:15), "to feel bad about," "grieve." The expression is found also
in the *Genesis Apocryphon* (1QapGen 21:7): *wb'š 'ly dy prš Lwṭ br 'ḥy mn
lw'ty,* "and I was grieved that Lot my nephew had parted from me."

---

[2] I have dealt with this and other idiomatic expressions in the Sfire inscriptions in "Stylistic
Aspects of the Sefire Treaty Inscriptions," *AcOr* (1965) 1–18.

[3] See M.-J. Seux, *Epithètes royales akkadiennes et sumériennes* (Paris: Cerf, 1967) 337.

[4] I shall deal with the proverb in lines 171–72 in a forthcoming article to appear in the William
Moran Festschrift.

[5] See *CAD* "K", pp. 222–23, s.v. *karṣu.*

[6] Ibid., sections (b) and (c), from which it is clear that a secondary development of *karṣu* as
"calumny," "slander," was known already in the Old Babylonian period.

The Biblical Hebrew equivalent *r* ‘ ‘ *’l* in *wayyera*‘ *’el Yonā* (Jonah 1:4) seems to be a calque on Aramaic.

9. *bl,* "mind"

   (a) *’th ‘l bl* (Ahiqar 97), "to come to mind," for which Biblical Hebrew has *bā’ ‘al lēb* (2 Chr 7:11).

   (b) *śm bl ‘l* (Dan 6:15), "to attend to," "pay attention to." Compare the Biblical Hebrew *śwm lb / lbb* and *šyt lb.*

   (c) *yhb bl.* This idiom, known from the three Palestinian dialects — Jewish, Samaritan, and Christian — and also Syriac, may stand behind the enigmatic *bl’ hbh l . .* in *Pap. Padua* II line 3. It means "pay attention to," "beware of" and usually as "beware" is governed by *min.* There are grammatical problems, to be sure, but this may simply mean "pay attention to X."[7]

10. *br btn* (Ahiqar 139), "child," "progeny"; cf. Biblical Hebrew *bn btn* (Isa 49:15), *bēnê bitnî* (Job 19:17), and the Aramaicizing *br btn* (Prov 31:2).

11. *bny rb‘* (Nerab 2 line 5), "fourth generation," used as an expression for longevity; cf. *ribbē‘îm* and *’arbā‘ā dōrōt* (Job 42:16), so too in Nabonidus's mother's tomb inscription (*ANET*[3], p. 561b).[8]

12. *yd,* "hand"

    (a) *mḥ’ byd* (Dan 4:32), lit., "smite the hand," i.e., "to prevent." Found in the Mishna *Baba Batra* 2:3 and elsewhere.

    (b) *mṭ’ yd* (Hermopolis 4.3; 6.6), lit., "the hand reaches," i.e., "is able"; cf. Biblical Hebrew *māṣ’ā yādô* (Lev 12:8; 25:28).

    (c) *nś’ yd ’l* (Zakkur A 11), lit., "to lift one's hand," i.e., "to pray"; cf. Biblical Hebrew *bēnāś’î yādî.*

    (d) *hskr byd* (Sfire III lines 2–3), "hand over"; cf. Biblical Hebrew *siggēr bēyād* (1 Sam 24:19; 26:8), *hisgîr bēyād* (1 Sam 17:46; Ps 31:9).

    (e) *šlḥ yd b* (Sfire I B 25), lit., "set one's hand against," i.e., "to kill"; cf. Biblical Hebrew Gen 37:22; 1 Sam 23:7.

    (f) idem (Sfire I B 34), "to take"; cf. Exod 22:7.

    (g) *šlḥ yd l* (Ezra 6:12), "set one's hand to," i.e., "to undertake" (with negative intent); cf. Biblical Hebrew 2 Sam 1:14.

    (h) *šlḥ byd* (Hermopolis 3.6), "to send by means of"; cf. Biblical Hebrew 2 Sam 10:2.

13. *ywm,* "day"

    (a) *ywm bywm* (Ezra 6:9), "daily"; so too in Biblical Hebrew and Syriac.

---

[7] The material in the Aramaic dialects was clarified by S. Lieberman, *Greek in Jewish Palestine* (New York: Jewish Theological Seminary, 1942) 135–37. For the Padua Papyri, see J. A. Fitzmyer, "Phases of the Aramaic Language," 219–30, especially 227–28. The troublesome *hbh* may be the imper. masc. sg. as in Biblical Hebrew *hbh* (*hābâ*); cf. too CAP 42 line 6.

[8] As noted by B. Landsberger many years ago.

(b) *bl' bywm* (Aḥiqar 102): [b]l' bywmyk, "before your time," "prematurely"; cf. Biblical Hebrew Job 15:32 (bēlō' yōmô).

14. *lbb*, "heart"

    (a) *ḥdh lbb b* (Aḥiqar 106), "to rejoice in," "be happy about"; cf. Biblical Hebrew *śāmaḥ libbô b* (Ps 33:21).

    (b) *yhb lbb l* (Aḥiqar 169), "to pay attention to"; cf. Biblical Hebrew *nātan lēb l* (Prov 23:26).

    (c) *hwqr lbb* (Aḥiqar 98), lit., "make the heart heavy/precious," i.e., "to be discreet about."[9]

    (d) *slq 'l lbb* (Sfire III lines 14, 15), lit., "to ascend the heart," i.e., "to think"; cf. Biblical Hebrew *'ālâ 'al lēb* (2 Kgs 12:5; Jer 3:16).

    (e) *'st blbb* (Sfire II B 5), lit., "to think in the heart," i.e., "to plot"; cf. Biblical Hebrew *ḥsb blb* (Zech 7:10; 8:17).

15. *mḥ' 'l . . . . mṣr* (Zakkur I 15), "to set siege to." Biblical Hebrew has a similar expression, *nātan 'al . . . māṣōr* (Ezek 4:2) but no true cognate.

16. *ml' lbh* (Ashur Ostracon, line 19; Hermopolis 1.6; *Pap. Padua* I r.3), "to be angry," a calque on Akkadian. It has long since been seen as standing behind *mâ 'amullâ libbātēk* in Ezek 16:30.[10]

17. *nṭl 'yn 'l* (Aḥiqar 169), lit., "to lift one's eye on," i.e., "to pay attention to." It is different from Biblical Hebrew *nāsā' 'ayin 'el*, which means "to look at."

18. *nsk lḥm* (Sfire I B 38; III 5), lit., "to pour out food," i.e., "to provide food." Biblical Hebrew uses *yṣq* in a similar manner; cf. 2 Sam 13:9; 2 Kgs 4:40–41.

19. *nqm dm mn yd* (Sfire III 12, "avenge the blood"; cf. Biblical Hebrew *nāqam dām miyyad* (Deut 32:43; 2 Kgs 9:7).

20. *ns' 'l śptym* (Sfire III 16), lit., "lift up, bear on lips," i.e., "to mention," "say." The same idiom is found in Biblical Hebrew (Ps 16:4).

21. *pny b'śr* (Sfire III 7), lit., "to turn in the place/back," i.e., "to turn toward." There is a similar rection of *btr* rather than the expected *'al* or *l* in the Targum of Lev 19:4.

22. *pqḥ 'yn* (Sfire I A 13), "to open the eyes"; cf. Biblical Hebrew 2 Kgs 19:16.

23. *qwm 'm* (Zakkur I 3), "to stand by." The usual Biblical Hebrew idiom is *qwm l*, but Samaritan Aramaic and Jewish Palestinian Aramaic both have *qwm 'm* with this meaning.[11]

---

[9] See James M. Lindenberger, *The Aramaic Proverbs of Ahiqar* (Baltimore: Johns Hopkins University Press, 1983) 75 with reference to J. N. Epstein, *ZAW* 32 (1912) 134.

[10] See J. A. Fitzmyer, "A Note on Ez 16:30," *CBQ* 23 (1961) 460–62.

[11] Cf. Lieberman, *Greek in Jewish Palestine*, 64–66, and this writer in *Bib* 50 (1969) 100 and in "The Zakir Inscription and the Danklied" in *Proceedings of the Fifth World Congress of Jewish Studies* I (Jerusalem: World Congress of Jewish Studies, 1972) 176–77 and n. 12.

24. *qwm qdm* (Aḥiqar 107), lit., "to stand before," i.e., "to withstand"; cf. Biblical Hebrew *qûm lipnê* (Num 16:2); *ʿāmad lipnê* (Nah 1:6; Ps 76:6).[12]

25. *šqr l* and *šqr b* both are found in the Sfire inscriptions, and there is a meaningful distinction between the two. Thus, *šqr b* (Sfire I B 38) is used when lack of faithfulness to the treaty or covenant is intended; and *šqr l* (Sfire III 14, 23) when unfaithfulness to the gods witnessing the treaty is meant. This distinction is kept in Biblical Hebrew. Thus, *šqr bibrīt* (Ps 44:18; cf. too 89:34), while *šqr l* is used for unfaithfulness with a party to the covenant, as in Gen 21:23.

There can be no doubt that a study of the material not covered in this article, and of later material too, would add to our knowledge of idiomatic Aramaic.[13]

---

[12] See Lindenberger, *Aramaic Proverbs,* 93.

[13] In a forthcoming article I deal with some idioms and other lexical matters in the Aramaic texts from Qumrān.

Chapter 5

Of Beginnings, Ends, and Computers in Targumic Studies

Stephen A. Kaufman
Hebrew Union College

טוב אחרית דבר מראשיתו
The end of something is better
than its beginning.
Qoheleth 7:8

PROF. J. A. FITZMYER IS A SCHOLAR who has always insisted upon the application of philological rigour to the study of Palestinian Jewish Aramaic texts and of their relationship to Christian Scriptures.[1] In particular, he has been in the forefront of those who have cautioned against careless assumptions about the relationship between the Aramaic of the Palestinian targums and the Aramaic dialects of Judea in the first century C.E. At the outset of our work together on the new, computerized Comprehensive Aramaic Lexicon (CAL) project, I am pleased to be able to offer in his honor this small contribution to targumic studies in which I hope to describe a typical way in which computer based methods of textual analysis can help to strengthen the foundations of the philological approach.

The purpose of this study is to illustrate the validity of an intuitively obvious but heretofore largely ignored tripartite principle: (1) The more often a text has been copied, the greater the degree of both scribal corruption and, especially in the case of Jewish texts, scribal modification to which the text has been exposed. (2) The earlier portions of a heavily tradited text have, in general, been copied more often than have later portions of the

[1] This study was written while the author was a fellow of the Institute for Advanced Studies of the Hebrew University of Jerusalem.

same text. Therefore, (3) the later portions of such a text should preserve a better textual tradition. Once demonstrated, the principle can serve as an analytical tool contributing to our understanding of the scribal history of targumic and other texts.

My interest in this subject was aroused by the publication of David M. Golomb's monograph on the grammar of *Targum Neofiti*. The monograph is based on a dissertation devoted to the grammar not of the manuscript as a whole, but just of the book of Genesis.[2] If one is to study just a sample of a large work, does it not make better sense, I thought, to begin at its end rather than at its beginning, especially in the case of medieval Jewish texts?

Students of rabbinic texts, like students of Bible versions, are agonizingly well aware of the sometimes seemingly insoluble problems of manuscript variation. In the case of relatively poorly known Hebrew and Western Jewish Aramaic texts in particular, it has long been recognized that the late MSS and all printed editions are heavily contaminated because of the scribes' familiarity with the classic Jewish texts—the Bible and the Babylonian Talmud.[3] In the case of targumic texts, *Targum Onqelos* (and *Jonathan* to the Prophets) also played a similar classic role. The orthography, grammar, and even lexicon of such texts are regularly altered in accommodation to the better-known traditions. Naturally, the more frequent the copying of a given text, the more frequent the opportunity for scribal error, but also more frequent the opportunities for intentional scribal modification. Morevover, since many scribes were careful and tried to avoid common scribal errors—but few hesitated to "improve" their text as they copied it—such scribal "improvements" were liable to multiply much more readily than did scribal errors. Since scribes, like readers, usually begin at the beginning but do not always reach the end, we must expect to find greater evidence of scribal tampering at the beginning of a lengthy text than at its end. Moreover, there is a tendency for scribes to "correct" a form the first few times it is encountered; after several such encounters, however, they may realize that the form is actually correct and stop modifying it.[4] Eventually, after many generations of such activity, these corrections will have made their way well into the text. Thus, in general, the later you are in a MS, the more reliable the text you should expect to find.

In a previous study on the Targumim to the Decalogue, I was able to demonstrate that the text of the Decalogue in chap. 5 of Deuteronomy in MS

---

[2] D. M. Golomb, *A Grammar of Targum Neofiti* (HSM 34; Chico: Scholars Press, 1985).

[3] This was perhaps best demonstrated by the late E. Y. Kutscher in his *Studies in Galilean Aramaic* (from *Tarbiz* 21–23 [1950–52] in Hebrew; English edition translated and annotated by Michael Sokoloff; Ramat-Gan: Bar-Ilan, 1976) see particularly pp. 1–4.

[4] I learned this principle from the late E. Y. Kutscher, though I cannot recall ever having seen it demonstrated in print.

Neofiti I is far superior to that preserved in chap. 20 of Exodus in the same MS.[5] In terms of scribal error, the Deuteronomy text is preferable to that of Exodus in a ratio of about 3 to 2. In terms of intentional scribal modification, however, the ratio jumps to over 6 to 1 in favor of Deuteronomy![6] The aligned text of the two chapters illustrating the differences is repeated here as Table 1. The most straightforward explanation for these differences is that the text underlying the version in Deuteronomy 5 has undergone fewer generations of scribal transmission.

Here I wish to present additional, graphic evidence supporting the general thesis, demonstrating as well that this tendency is neither confined to the Decalogue nor due to the fact that in MS *Neofiti I* Exodus 20 and Deuteronomy 5 were copied by different scribes. Such statistical analyses can easily be replicated by anyone with access to a personal computer and machine-readable text files of the Targumim. For the latter, I was able to make use of preliminary versions of text files supplied to the data base of the CAL by Profs. M. Sokoloff (in the case of all the Palestinian Pentateuchal Targumim) and, for *Pseudo-Jonathan,* by Prof. E. G. Clarke.[7]

The main text of MS *Neofiti I* has been divided into 42 sections of approximately equal size (ca. 15,000 characters), taking into account previously known, demonstrable scribal differences. Thus, sectors 1 (Gen 1:1–3:4) and 42 (Deut 29:17–34:12) constitute the portions of the MS that have been copied from a source that elsewhere served rather as a source for some of the marginalia.[8] Of the three main hands, sections 1–4 and 21–24 are of the First, 5–20 the Second, and 25–42 the Third.[9]

---

[5] S. A. Kaufman and Y. Maori, "The Targumim to Exodus 20: Reconstructing the Palestinian Targum" (to be published in the proceedings of the Seminar on Targumic and Cognate Studies at the Institute for Advanced Studies of the Hebrew University, Jerusalem, 1986).

[6] For the justification for the decision as to the superiority of one text over the other in the individual cases the reader is referred to the previously cited article.

[7] When these files have been fully incorporated into the CAL data base, they, like all our texts, will be made available to qualified scholars. For information, contact the Comprehensive Aramaic Lexicon, Department of Near Eastern Studies, The Johns Hopkins University, Baltimore, MD, 21218.

The analysis and charting of data were done using a few simple Turbo Pascal programs. For copies, contact the author c/o the CAL.

[8] See S. Lund and J. Foster, *Variant Versions of Targumic Traditions within Codex Neofiti I* (SBL Aramaic Studies 2; Missoula, MT: Scholars Press, 1977).

[9] The first verses of each of the sections are: (1) Gen 1:1; (2) Gen 3:5; (3) Gen 7:1; (4) Gen 13:1; (5) Gen 18:19; (6) Gen 23:1; (7) Gen 28:1; (8) Gen 32:1; (9) Gen 36:1; (10) Gen 41:1; (11) Gen 44:1; (12) Gen 48:1; (13) Exod 1:1; (14) Exod 7:1; (15) Exod 13:1; (16) Exod 16:1; (17) Exod 20:1; (18) Exod 26:1; (19) Exod 30:1; (20) Exod 35:1; (21) Lev 1:1; (22) Lev 6:1; (23) Lev 11:1; (24) Lev 15:1; (25) Lev 22:3; (26) Lev 25:1; (27) Num 1:1; (28) Num 5:1; (29) Num 8:1; (30) Num 12:1; (31) Num 16:1; (32) Num 21:1; (33) Num 24:1; (34) Num 29:1;

In each chart the location of the asterisk indicates the occurrences of the first form as a percentage of the total occurrences of both forms. Thus, sections wherein the asterisk is further to the right have a greater percentage of the first feature, while an asterisk on the left indicates a greater percentage of the second feature. If no examples of the given feature are attested in that section, its line is blank.

One of the better-known distinctions between Eastern and Western Aramaic texts is orthographic: Final long *a*, be it the emphatic ending or the marker of the feminine absolute, is spelled with *aleph* in all Eastern orthographic traditions, whereas in the Western texts and inscriptions *heh* is used. The best Genizah MSS of the Palestinian Targum, like the best texts of the Palestinian Talmud and Midrashim, regularly have final *heh* here. Thus, Chart A depicts the distribution of final *aleph* vs. final *heh* in MS *Neofiti*.[10] Chart B, more limited in scope and hence, perhaps, more graphic in its results, depicts the relationship between the plural emphatic nominal ending spelled איי and the more Western spelling with ייה. Chart C compares the spellings final אי- and יי-, indicating three different morphemes: 1st com. sg. suffix on pl. nouns, gentilic masc. sg. absolute noun, and gentilic pl. determined noun. In each chart, then, an asterisk to the right indicates generally Eastern orthography; on the left—Western orthography.

Though the distribution of each feature is quite different, they all reflect a basic pattern equally demonstrable with many other such features: a relatively high proportion of "Eastern" or "Literary" forms at the beginning, diminishing somewhat though the last part of Exodus. At Exodus 35 (beginning of *Wayaqhel*) there is a relatively sharp decrease, and through Numbers 7 (end of *Naso*) there is a fairly constant "Western" orthography wherein the distribution of the features generally corresponds to that in the best Genizah MSS of the Palestinian Targum, as illustrated in Charts D and E.[11] Thereafter

---

(35) Num 33:1; (36) Deut 1:1; (37) Deut 5:1; (38) Deut 9:1; (39) Deut 13:1; (40) Deut 19:1; (41) Deut 25:1; (42) Deut 29:17.

[10] My intention has been to demonstrate "quick and dirty" computerized approaches to otherwise tedious tasks; therefore, I have made no effort to count only those final *heh*s that are the emphatic ending, which, at this point, would have meant going through the machine-readable text word by word. (When the texts have been completely analyzed for the CAL, we shall obviously be able to perform more sophisticated analyses with greater ease.) In this case, the absence of morphological screening should not affect the general validity of our data. But care is required! Were one to wish to study the relationship of the orthographic alternation יה- vs. ה- for the 3d masc. sg. pronominal suffix, for example, the progressive relative increase in the number of final *heh*s in general on the emphatic forms would significantly skew the distribution under investigation.

[11] The Y axis numbers here correspond to the 38 different MSS recognized by Michael Klein in his forthcoming edition of the Genizah texts, where 1 through 6 correspond to Kahle's A

the percentage of Easternism remains low, but does evidence a gradual increase as one moves toward the end of Deuteronomy.

As we should expect, this internal, orthographic division of the MS into three quite different sections does not correspond to the division of the MS into its main hands. It reflects, rather, an earlier stage of scribal activity. (On the other hand, sections 1 and 42, copied from a different source, do stand out a bit from their immediate neighbors.) What the divisions do reflect, however, is how frequently the various pericopes of the Palestinian Targum were copied over time. The central section, with few unique, Palestinian expansions, was copied only infrequently. Indeed, although it constitutes about 24 percent of the entire Palestinian Targum (as it is preserved in Neofiti), only about 6 percent of all of the Palestinian Targum corpus from the Genizah comes from this portion of the Pentateuch. Another 6 percent of the Genizah texts corresponds to our sections 29-40. Only at Deuteronomy 26 do the examples begin to increase, although they remain far less numerous that the number of MSS available for most of Genesis and Exodus. Since, as we have seen, the orthographic practice of Neofiti reflects these frequencies, it seems quite clear that at some stage in the history of its transmission the connected main text preserved in Neofiti was put together from other, fragmentary MSS.[12]

Our principle, once demonstrated, can provide important new evidence towa.d the solution of rather knotty problems. Herewith an example:

The Targum to Qoheleth, like the Hagiographic Targumim in general, is widely known only from printed editions and late MSS whose grammar and orthography have been accommodated to Onqelos-type Aramaic. Yet certain lexical features (like an occasional ארום instead of ארי) seem to suggest a similarity to the Palestinian Pentateuchal Targum. There exists, however, one known MS of Targum Qoheleth that generally has certain Palestinian-like features throughout—Paris 110.[13] For example, Paris 110 usually employs the verb חמי for "to see," whereas all the other witnesses almost always have forms of חזי. Does this mean that Paris 110 is a very good MS that has often, in contrast to other MSS, preserved the original form of this literary work, or

---

through F. Excluded from consideration are the so-called "tosephta" targums, i.e., those written in Onqelos-like orthography and language.

[12] Had it always been copied as a complete MS, it should evidence much greater uniformity. The scribal practice of correcting only the first few encountered forms (see above) could not be totally responsible for the patterns demonstrated here.

[13] My thanks to Prof. E. G. Clarke and the Institute for Advanced Studies for making a machine-readable version of this and other Qoheleth MSS available to me. Paris 110, of course, also contains other Hagiographic Targums and, in a different script, the important Fragment Targum P to the Torah. Also significant as a sign of the antiquity of its tradition is the fact that Paris 110 is the only major MS of the Hagiographic Targumim without vocalization.

has an *Onqelos*-like targum been "Westernized" just in this single MS? (That is, has original חזי been changed to חמי?) And if Paris 110 is a good witness to the original text, was that original text an early Palestinian Targum, or was it written in a much later period in what I have elsewhere termed Late Jewish Literary Aramaic?[14]

Charts F and G graphically demonstrate the application of our principle to this problem.[15] As we move through this MS the instances of חזי dramatically decrease. This suggests, if it does not prove, that the original text of the targum had חמי, which was replaced near the beginning of the text by חזי.[16] In the case of final *a,* however, if anything there is a tendency to increased use of *aleph* as we progress through the MS! Certainly Paris 110 offers us no evidence that Targum Qoheleth ever existed in a purely Western orthography, something that may be viewed as demonstrated as regards the Palestinian Targum to the Pentateuch.[17] All of this, of course, is consistent with an origin in the Late Jewish Literary Aramaic milieu that spawned Targum *Pseudo-Jonathan* and the other Hagiographic Targumim.[18]

Here I have tried to demonstrate just one small way in which the computers in our offices can contribute far beyond mere word processing to our philological endeavors. Moreover, unlike the implications of some recent work in Biblical Studies, one need not be a trained mathematician in order to discover important patterns in one's data or to assess the general validity of those patterns. The limits are only those of our imaginations.

---

[14] "התרגום המיוחס ליונתן והארמית היהודית הספרותית המאוחרת," M. Goshen-Gottstein Festschrift (Ramat-Gan: Bar-Ilan, in press).

[15] Numbers on the Y axis refer to chapters.

[16] In fact, of the 12 instances of חזי (vs. 48 of חמי), 5 are in the distinctive use of the passive חזי ל- meaning "proper to" (including the maverick example in chap. 11). Only once does חמי ל- occur in that meaning. This is a biblicism (Dan 3:19) that should probably be treated as a special case. Eliminating it would make the evidence of distribution emphatically clear.

[17] I use the term *the* Palestinian Targum intentionally. See Kaufman and Maori, "Targumim to Exodus 20."

[18] Cf. Kaufman, "התרגום"; and Edward Morgan Cook, "Rewriting the Bible: The Text and Language of the Pseudo-Jonathan Targum" (Ph.D. diss., UCLA, 1986) 266–80.

A. FINAL א as percent of final א and final ה in Neofiti

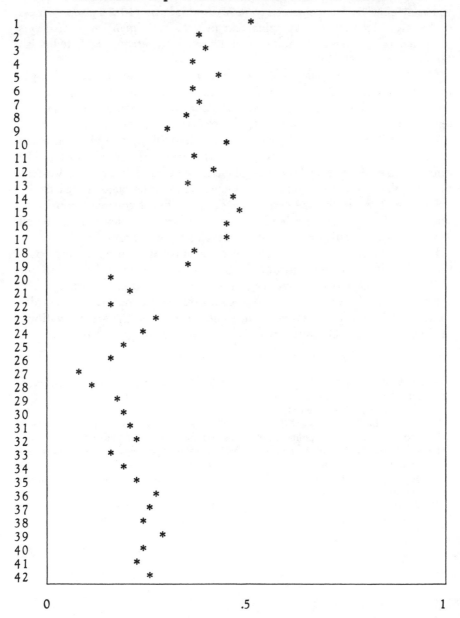

B. FINAL ייא as percent of final ייא and final ייה in Neofiti

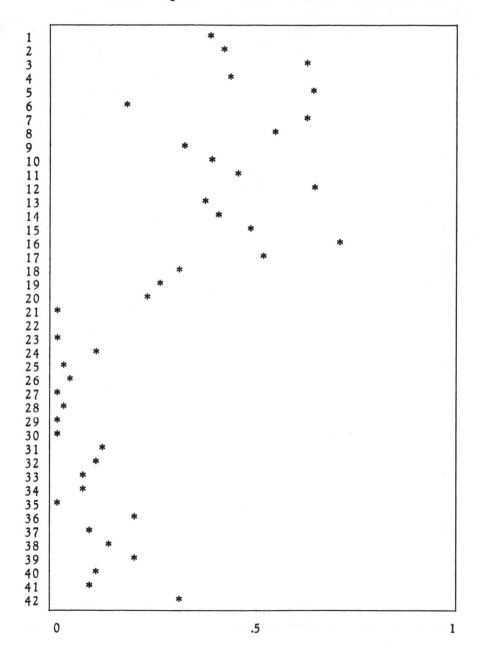

C. FINAL אי as percent of final אי and final יי in Neofiti

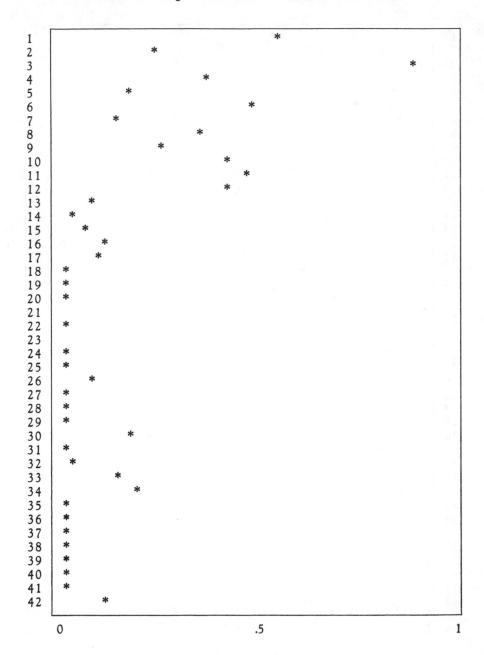

D. FINAL א as percent of final א and final ה in Genizah Targum MSS

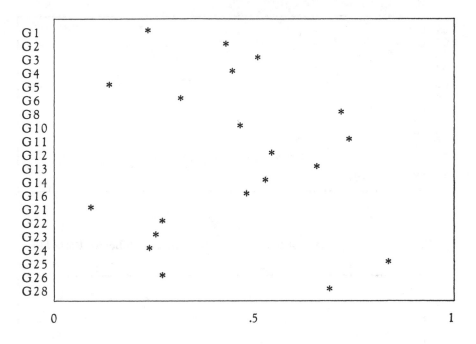

E. FINAL ייא as percent of final ייא and final ייה in Genizah Targum MSS

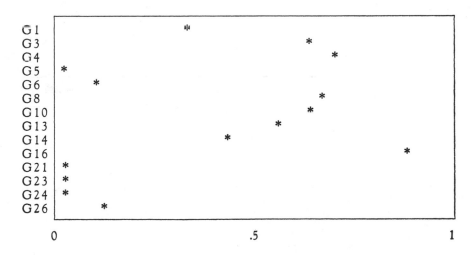

F. Root חזי as percent of חזי and חמי in Tg. Qoheleth Paris 110

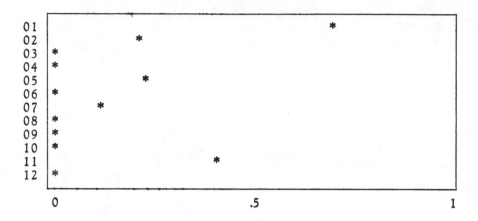

G. FINAL א as percent of final א and final ה in Tg. Qoheleth Paris 110

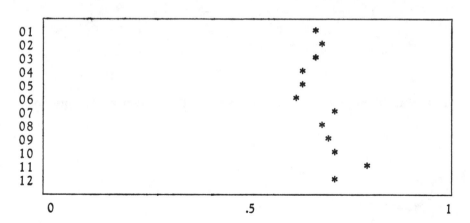

TABLE I

The Decalogue according to Targum *Neofiti,* Exodus and Deuteronomy

Orthographically and grammatically "unimproved" forms are in double-underlined type.
Single underlining indicates a preferable text tradition.

20:02

NeoEx דבורייא קדמיא   דהוה נפיק מן פום קודשא יהא   שמה מבורך היך זיקין והיך ברקין והיך למפדין

NeoDt דב י רה קדמיה כד הוה נפק מן פם קודשא יהא שמיה מברך היך זיקין והיך ברקין והיך למפדין

NeoEx דנוזר למפד דנור מן ימיניה ולמפד דאשא מן שמאליה פרח וטייס באויר שמייא

דנור מן ימיניה ולמפד דאשה מן שמאליה פרח וטייס באויר שמיא

NeoEx וחזר וכל ישראל חמיין יתיה ודחלין וחזר והוה חזר ומתחקק על תרין לוחי קיימא ואמר עמא בני [ ]

NeoEx וחזר ומקף על משרייותיהון דישראל וחזר ומתחקק   על לוחי קיימא

NeoDt וחזר ומקף על משרייתהון דישראל וחזר ומ(הה)נתחן]קק על לוחי קיימה

NeoEx וכל ישראל חזיין יתיה בכן הוה צווח ואמר עמי בני ישראל

NeoDt _____ וכן הוה צוה ואמר עמי בני ישראל

NeoEx אנה הוא יי אלהכון די פרקת ואפקת יתכון פריקין מן ארעא דמצרים מן בית   עבדי:

NeoDt אנה הוא יי אלהכון די פרקית ואפקית יתכון פריקין מן ארעה דמצרים מן בית שעבוד עבדיה:

20:03

NeoEx דבירא תנינא כד הוה נפק מן פום קודשא יהא   שמה מברך היך זקין והיך ברקין והיך למפדין דנור

NeoDt דבירה תנינה כד הוא נפק מן פם קדשה יהי(ה) שמיה מברך היך זיקין והיך ברקין והיך למפדין דנור

NeoEx למפד דנורא מן ימינה ולמפד דאשא מן שמאלה פרח וטייס באויר שמיא

NeoDt   מן ימינה ולמפד דאשה מן שמאליה פרח וטייס באויר שמייא

NeoEx וחזר וכל ישראל חמיין יתיה ודחלין והוה חזר ומתחקק על תרין לוחי קיימא ואמר עמי בני [ ]

NeoEx וחזר ומקף על משרייותיהון   דישראל וחזר ומתחקק על לוחי קיימא וכל ישראל חזיין יתיה וכן הון[ה]
צווח ואמר

NeoDt וחזר ומקף על משרייתהון דבני ישראל וחזר ומתחקק על לווחי קיימה _____ וכן הוה
צווח ואמר

NeoEx עמי בני ישראל לא יהווי לך אלה אחרא בר מני:

NeoDt עמי בני ישראל לא יהווי לבון אלה אחרן בר מני:

20:04

NeoEx לא תעבדון לבון [צלם וצורה] וכל דמות די בשמייא מלעיל ודי בארעא מן לרע ודי במיא מן תחות לארעא
מן תחות:

NeoDt לא תעבדון לבון [צלם וצורה] וכל דמו די בשמייא מן לעיל ודי בארעא מן לרע   לארעא:

1. Erased in both texts. Note how the hand of the censor does not fail to reach all the way to Deuteronomy.

20:05

NeoEx יי אלההכן אלה קניי וכורען דמתפרע בקנא   לא תסגדון להון ולא תפלחון קדמיהון ארום אנה
NeoDt יי אלההכן אלה קניי _ופורען מתפרע בקנאה   לא תסגדון להון ולא תפלחון קדמיהון ארום אנה הוא

NeoEx מן   רשיעיא על בנין מרדין על דר תליתיא ועל דר רביעיא לשנאי
NeoDt מדכר חובי אבהן רשיעין   על בנין מרדין על דר תליתי ועל דר רביעי

NeoEx כד יהוון במייא משלמין בחטאה   בתר אבהתהון להון אנה קרא שנאיי:
NeoDt כד   משלמין בחטא קדמיי   לשנאיי:

Exod 20:06

NeoEx ברם נטר חסד אנה חסד וטיבו לאלפין דרין לרחמוי צדיקיא ולנטורי פיקודיא:
NeoDt ונטר   חסד וטבו לאלפין דרין לרחמיי צדיקיה ולנטרי   מצוותה דאורייתי:

Exod 20:07

NeoEx עמי בני ישראל לא יסב נבר מנכון ית שמה דייי אלהיה על מגן ארום לא מזכי ייי ביום דינא רבא
NeoDt עמי בני ישראל לא יסב אנש מנכן   שמה דייי אלהכן על מגן ארום לא יזכי ייי ביום דינה רבה

NeoEx ית מן די יסב   שמה דייי   אלהיה על מגן:
NeoDt ית מן די יסב ית שמה דייי קדישה   על מגן:

Exod 20:08

NeoEx עמי בני ישראל הוון דכירין   ית יומא דשבתא למקדןשׁא יתיה:
NeoDt עמי בני ישראל   טורו ית יומא דשבתה למקדשה יתיה (היך מה די פקד יתכן ייי אלהכן:)

Exod 20:09

NeoEx שיתא יומין תפלחון ןתעבדון כל עבדתכן:
NeoDt שיתה יומין תפלחון ותעבדון כל עבידתכן:

Exod 20:10

NeoEx ויומא שביעיא שבא וניח קדם ייי אלהכן לא תעבדון כל עובדה
NeoDt וביומא שביעיה שבה וניח קדם ייי אלהכן לא תעבדון על עבידה

NeoEx אתון ובניכון ובנתכון ועבדכון אמהתיכן   ובעירכם וגיוריכן די בקריויכן
NeoDt אתון ובניכון ובנתכון ועבדיכן ואמהתכן תוריכון וחמריכון וכל בעיריכן וגיורכן די בקרויכן

(differing texts omitted for end of Sabbath commandment)

Exod 20:12

NeoEx עמי בני ישראל הוון זהירין   נבר   ביקרריה דאבוי ובאיקרה דאימיה
NeoDt עמי בני ישראל   יוקר   כל אנש מנכן   ית אבוי   וית אמיה היך מה דפקד
ייי אלההכן

NeoEx מן בגלל דיסנן יומיכון   על ארעא דייי אלהכן יהב לכן:
NeoDt מן בגלל דיסנן יומיכון (ומן בגלל דייטיב לכן) על ארעא דייי אלהכן יהב לכן:

Exod 20:13

NeoEx עמי בני ישראל לא תהוון קטולין לא חברין ולא שותפין עם קטוליא ולֹא יתחמי בכנישתיהון דישראל עם
קטולין

NeoDt עמי בני ישראל לא תהוון קטולין ולא חברין ולא שותפין עם קטולין ולא יתחמי בכנישתהון דישראל עם
קטולין

NeoEx דלא יקומון בניכון מן בתריכון וילפון לחוד אינון למהוי   עם קטולין ארום בחובי קטוליא חרבא נפיק
על עלמא:

NeoDt דלא יקומון בניכון מן בתריכון וילפון לחוד אינון למיהוי עם קטולין ארום בחובי קטוליֵה חרבה נפק
על עלמא:

Exod 20:14

NeoEx עמי בני ישראל לא תהוון ניוורין לא חברין ולא שותפין עם ניוורין ולא יתחמי בכנישתהון דישראל
עם ניוורין

NeoDt   (omit by haplog.)   עמי בני ישראל לא תהוון ניוורין ולא חברין ולא שותפין עם ניוורין

NeoEx דלא יקומון בניכון מן בתריכון וילפון לחוד אינון למהוי   עם ניוורין ארום בחובי ניוורא מותנא אתא
על עלמא:

NeoDt דלא יקומון בניכון מן בתריכון וילפון לחוד אינון למיהוֵי עם נֵיווריֵן ארום בחובי נֵייוריֵיה מותנה מותנה   נפק
[על] עלמא:

Exod 20:15

NeoEx עמי בני ישראל לא תהוון גנבין   לא חברין ולא שותפין עם גנבין ולא יתחמי בכנישתהון דישראל עם גנבין
דלא יקומון

NeoDt עמי בני ישראל לא תהוון גנבין ולא חברין ולא שותפין עם גנבין ולא יתחמי בכנישתהון דישראל עם גנבין
דלא יקומון

NeoEx בניכון מן בתריכון וילפון לחוד אינון למהוי עם גנבין ארום בחובי גנביא כפנא אתי   לעלמא:
NeoDt בניכון מן בתריכון וילפון לחוד אינון למהוי עם גנבין ארום בחובי גנבייֵה כפנה אתי על   עלמא:

Exod 20:16

NeoEx עמי בני ישראל לא תהוון   סהדי שקר לא חברין ולא שותפין עַם סהדי שקרא
NeoDt עמי בני ישראל לא תהוון מַשהדֵין סהדי דֵשקר לא חברין ולא שותפין   לֵשהדי שקרא

NeoEx ולא יתחמי בכנישתהון דישראל עם סהדי שיקרא דלא יקומון בניכון מן בתריכון וילפון לחוד אִינֵן
NeoDt ולא יתחבר   עם מַשהדי שַקר דלא יקומון בניכון מן בתריכון

NeoEx למיהוי עַם   סהדי שקרא ארום בחובי סהדי שקרא חיות ברא מתכלה בבני אינשא:
NeoDt לַמהוי מַסהדֵין מַ[ס]הדי דֵשקר   ארום בחובי סהדי שקרא חיות ברא מיתנֵריֵה בבני אֵנשא:

Exod 20:17

NeoEx עמי בני ישראל לא תהוון חמודין לא חברין ולא שותפין עם חמודין ולא יתחמי בכנישתהון דישראל עם חמודין

NeoDt עמי בני ישראל לא תהוון חמודין לא חברין ולא שותפין   לחמודיה

NeoEx דלא יקומון בניכון מן בתריכון וילפון לחוד אינון למהוי עם חמודין לא יתחמד גבר מנכון

NeoDt דלא יקומון בניכון מן בתריכון וילפון לחוד אנון למהוי עם חמודין ולא יתחמד אנש מנכון

NeoEx ביתא דחבריה ולא אתתיה דחבריה   ולא עבדיה ולא אמהתי ולא תוריי ולא חמריה

NeoDt   ית אתתה דחבריה ולא יתחמד בייתיה דחבריה לא חקלה ולא עבדה ולא אמהתיה ולא תוריה ולא חמריה

NeoEx ולא כל מה די לחברך ארום בחובי חמודייה

NeoDt ולא כל מה די לחברך ארום בחובי חמודיה עננין סלקין ומטר לא נחת ובצורתה אתייה על עלמא

NeoEx מלכותא   מתגריין בבני אנשא:

NeoDt ומלכוותה מתגריין בבני אנשא וחמדין נכסיהון וג(ס)(ס)כנבין יתהון:

The Historical Present in the Gospel of Mark

Elliott C. Maloney
St. Vincent Archabbey

Scriptura non potest intellegi
theologice, nisi antea intellecta
sit grammatice.
Ascribed to Melanchthon

IT IS WELL KNOWN THAT the historical present tense appears with great frequency in the Gospel of Mark. This study will examine the nature of this usage and point out its significance for the ongoing redaction and source criticism of the Gospel. The first question we must ask is whether the historical present is the result of Semitic interference (Semitism) of some kind, especially in the case of the verb "to say," because the Gospel of Mark uses the historical present λέγει/λέγουσιν a total of seventy-two times.

Whether or not it is a Semitism, the historical present is clearly a peculiarity of the Gospel of Mark. In part II of the paper we shall examine its use to see if we can make some observations about the manner in which it is used and whether or not it is part of the evangelist's own style.

Part I. The Historical Present: A Semitism?

The Historical Present in Hellenistic Greek

The historical present (hereafter h.p.) refers to the use of the present indicative form of the verb to introduce an action in past time. It replaces the usual aorist tense in order to vivify the action and bears a punctilinear *Aktionsart* (no nuance of continuing or repetitive action) otherwise not characteristic of the present tense.[1]

[1]We are not convinced by Stephen M. Reynolds's presentation of the present tense in Hellenistic Greek as a "zero tense," the complete semantic equivalent of the aorist (*Westminster*

There is a great variety of opinion regarding the normalcy of the h.p. in postclassical, Hellenistic Greek. S. Thompson holds that the h.p. "was never used on a large scale" in the Koine.[2] J. H. Moulton maintained the exact opposite view: "It is by no means true that it was 'by no means common in Hellenistic Greek.' "[3] There is a considerable list of scholars who hold that the frequent use of the h.p. in the Gospels of Matthew, Mark, John, and the book of Revelation is the result of at least indirect influence from Aramaic and/or Hebrew.[4] The majority, however, hold that the phenomenon is perfectly at home, if a bit on the vulgar side, in Hellenistic Greek.

The h.p. was quite usual in classical Greek narrative, especially among the historians. It vivified a special moment in the narrative, the circumstantial and secondary actions of the tale being expressed in the aorist (or the imperfect where an iterative effect was sought), e.g., οἱ δὲ Ἐπιδάμνιοι οὐδὲν αὐτῶν ὑπήκουσαν, ἀλλὰ στρατεύουσιν ἐπ' αὐτοὺς οἱ Κερκυραῖοι, "The Epidamnians paid [aorist] no heed to them, but the Corcyraeans attacked [h.p.] against them" (Thucydides 1.26.4). Often a string of vivid actions is narrated with the h.p., e.g., ἀκούσας δὲ τούτων ὁ Θῶνις πέμπει . . . ἀντιπέμπει . . . συλλαμβάνει . . . καὶ κατίσχει . . . τοῦτον ἀνήγαγε, "having heard this Thonis sent [h.p.] . . . [Proteus] sent back [h.p.] . . . [Thonis] seized [h.p.] . . . and held [h.p.] . . . but brought [aorist] him" (Herodotus 2.114–15). Note the punctilinear *Aktionsart* in each case.

In the postclassical writers of the Hellenistic Age of Greek (ca. 300 B.C.E. to 300 C.E.), the use and frequency of the h.p. vary greatly, from its complete lack of use in Diodorus Siculus to nearly one h.p. for every page of text in Dionysius Halicarnassus, both of whom wrote in the first century B.C.E.[5]

Theological Journal 32 [1969–70] 68–69). Reynolds says that in narrative the present tense alternates with the aorist merely to avoid monotonous style, and not for a heightened vividness in the story. His conclusion, however, is accepted by J. M. Voelz, "The Language of the New Testament," in *Aufstieg und Niedergang der römischen Welt*, 2.25.2. *Prinzipat* (ed. W. Haase; Berlin & New York: de Gruyter, 1984) 947.

[2] S. Thompson, *The Apocalypse and Semitic Syntax* (SNTSMS 52; Cambridge: University Press, 1985) 36–37.

[3] J. H. Moulton, *A Grammar of NT Greek. Vol. I, Prolegomena* (3d ed.; Edinburgh: T. & T. Clark, 1908) 121, somewhat unfairly quoting J. C. Hawkins, who had said: "The employment of the historic present had been up to this time by no means common *with the writers of sacred story* in the *Koinē* or Hellenistic Greek" ([italics added] *Horae Synopticae* [2d ed.; Oxford: Clarendon, 1909] 143).

[4] In recent scholarship, the following maintain Semitic interference in the frequency with which the historical present appears in the NT: M. Black, *An Aramaic Approach to the Gospels and Acts* (3d ed.; Oxford: Clarendon, 1967) 130; F. Blass and A. Debrunner, *A Greek Grammar of the NT and Other Early Christian Literature* (ed. and trans. R. W. Funk; Chicago: University of Chicago Press, 1961) §321; V. Taylor, *The Gospel According to St. Mark* (2d ed.; London: Macmillan, 1966) 46; Thompson, *Apocalypse*, 35–36; N. Turner, *A Grammar of NT Greek. Vol. III, Syntax* (Edinburgh: T. & T. Clark, 1963) 5; *Vol. IV, Style* (Edinburgh: T. & T. Clark, 1976) 20; M. Zerwick, *Untersuchungen zum Markus-Stil* (Rome: Biblical Institute, 1937) 73.

[5] On Diodorus Siculus, see G. D. Kilpatrick, review of L. Rydbeck, *Fachprosa, vermeintliche*

Although the content and style of many of the papyri do not give much opportunity for use of the h.p., E. Mayser points out that it occurs quite often as a "dramatische Form" with a preceding or following aorist in vivid narrative.[6] This occurs especially in chancery style reports of criminal behavior, e.g., κατέλυσα ἐν τῶι ᾿Ανουβιείωι . . . καί . . . τις σπασάμενος λέπει με τῆι μαχαίραι εἰς τὸ σκέλος, "I lodged [aor.] in the Anubeum . . . and someone, having drawn (a sword), struck [h.p.] me with the sword in the leg" (*P.Par.* 12.8–16).

The h.p. is common in the nonliterary papyri as well, especially in vivid reports of dreams and religious experiences,[7] e.g., ἀνύγω [= ἀνοίγω] . . . ὁρῶ . . . κλαίγω . . . ἐπορευόμην . . . καὶ ἔρχομαι . . . ἔλεγον, "I opened [h.p.] . . . I saw [h.p.] . . . I wept [h.p.] . . . I was going [imperfect] . . . and I came [h.p.] . . . I was saying [imperfect]" (*P.Par.* 51.7–17; see also 23.9ff.; 50.3ff.).

Verbs of saying, especially λέγει/λέγουσιν and φησίν/φασίν, when used to introduce direct discourse, appear in the h.p. frequently in Hellenistic writers, e.g., Dionysius Halicarnassus (λέγει, *Ant.* 1.73.4; 81.4; 86.4; φησίν, 1.82.6; ἀποκρίνεται, 1.83.1; but ἔφη, 1.82.1); Arrian's *Discourses of Epictetus* (throughout; see especially 1.1.20, 30; 1.19.26–27; 1.26.12); occasionally in Plutarch (e.g., *Vit. Alex.* 28.1).

G. D. Kilpatrick has maintained, along with others, that the h.p. was viewed as a vulgarism among literary Hellenistic authors. Its reintroduction in later Hellenistic writers like Arrian (second century C.E.) and Achilles Tatius (fourth century C.E.), he claims, is the result of Atticism, the classicist revival of the Attic style among writers from the second century on.[8] In response, one must point out the numerous examples of the h.p. in the chancery language of official papyri throughout the Hellenistic period,[9] not to mention its use by literary writers like Dionysius Halicarnassus and Polybius in the second and first centuries B.C.E.

Volkssprache und NT, JBL 88 (1969) 355; for Dionysius Halicarnassus, see K. Eriksson, "Das Praesens Historicum in der nachklassischen griechischen Historiographie" (Diss., Lund, 1943) 39, cited in Turner, *Syntax,* 61. Other statistics are Polybius (from 1 h.p. per 6 pages of text to 1 per 23 pages) in J. A. de Foucault, *Recherches sur le langue et style de Polybe* (Paris: Belles Lettres, 1972) 127; Arrian's *Anabasis* (1 h.p. per 0.6 pages) and Josephus (*Antiquities* book 5 [1 h.p. per .28 pages] and *Jewish Wars* bk. 1 [1 h.p. per .37 pages] in Eriksson, cited by Turner, *Syntax,* 61.

[6] E. Mayser, *Grammatik der griechischen Papyri aus der Ptolemäerzeit* (Berlin and Leipzig: W. de Gruyter, 1926–38) 2.1.131; Mayser gives several examples on pp. 131–32. B. G. Mandilaras points out that the h.p. is found "as a rule" in petitions to high officials to present a vivid effect (*The Verb in the Greek Non-Literary Papyri* [Athens: Hellenistic Ministry of Culture and Science, 1973] 109).

[7] Mayser, *Grammatik,* 2.1.131.

[8] G. D. Kilpatrick, "The Historic Present in the Gospels and Acts," *ZNW* 68 (1977) 258.

[9] This chancery language belongs to the technical Greek style (*Fachprosa*) which L. Rydbeck calls a middle layer (*Zwischenschicht*) between the more literary language of the rhetoricians and historians and the common prose of the popular papyri (*Fachprosa, vermeintliche Volkssprache und NT* [Acta Universitatis Upsaliensis: Studia Graeca 5; Uppsala: University of Uppsala, 1967] 57; see also 13–16.

Conclusion

The use of the historical present to enliven a narrative was common in Hellenistic Greek in its literary, technical, and more popular styles, but varied widely according to the personal choice of an author.

The Semitic Evidence

Hebrew and Its Greek Translators

In Hebrew a participle can act as the predicate in an independent noun clause "to represent *past* actions or states,"[10] usually describing an action or state circumstantial to the main action, e.g.,

לא ידעו כי מיהוה היא כי תאנה הוא מבקש מפלשתים,

"(They) did not know that it was from the Lord, for he *was seeking* an occasion against the Philistines" (Judg 14:4; other examples: ישב, Gen 19:1; האמר, Gen 32:10; ראים, Exod 20:18). However, the Hebrew participle is normally not used to introduce a past action with the punctilinear *Aktionsart* characteristic of the Greek h.p. The neo-classical and Proto-Mishnaic Hebrew texts of the Dead Sea Scrolls generally use participles in the same way as Biblical Hebrew.[11]

In a few cases the Old Greek (LXX) may translate such a participle with the present tense, e.g., ὅτι ἐκδίκησιν αὐτὸς ζητεῖ (B)/ἐκζητεῖ (A) ἐκ τῶν ἀλλοφύλων, "because he sought [h.p.] an occasion against the foreigners" (Judg 14:4). We do not, however, concur with Thompson, who adduces this single example of an h.p. translating a Hebrew participle and concludes that "the Hebrew participle with a past durative sense is obviously responsible" for the translation with the h.p. (ἐκ)ζητεῖ.[12] It is much more likely that the translators used (ἐκ)ζητεῖ here as a punctilinear and vivifying h.p. because of their own stylistic preference and interpretation of the text. In his well-known study, J. C. Hawkins pointed out that the use of the h.p. by the translators of the Old Greek varied tremendously from book to book. He

---

[10] E. Kautzsch, *Gesenius' Hebrew Grammar* (rev. A. E. Cowley; Oxford: Clarendon, 1910) §116(m) and (o).

[11] Cf. S. J. De Vries, "The Syntax of Tenses and Interpretation in the Hodayoth," *RevQ* 19 (1965) 412.

[12] Thompson, *Apocalypse*, 36. We find no evidence whatsoever that "doubtless the frequence of the picturesque participle in Heb. narrative, which tended to be translated by the present indic., contributed to its popularity in Biblical Greek" (Turner, *Syntax*, 61) or that since the h.p. turns up over 330 times in the LXX, "thus Hebrew influence is very apparent" (Turner, *Style*, 20).

found that of the 337 instances of the h.p. in the entire Old Greek Bible, 232 occur in 1–4 Kingdoms, and that fully 151 of these appear in 1 Kingdoms.[13] When one inspects the Greek text of 1 Kingdoms, chaps. 3–4, 8–9, 12–13 (chosen at random), one turns up 17 instances of the h.p. as the main verb in narrative. All of these translate Hebrew preterites (imperfects with *waw* conversive or perfects), except at 1 Sam 13:5 (without *Vorlage* in the Hebrew text).

With regard to the verb "to say," we should point out here that when it is used as the main verb in these chapters of 1 Samuel, it is always the preterite indicative in Hebrew. In the entire Old Greek book of 1 Kingdoms it occurs 53 times; in 51 cases it is the aorist εἶπεν/αν/ον, and twice the h.p. λέγουσιν (9:11 and 12, translating the Hebrew imperfect with *waw* conversive).

Conclusion

The usage of the h.p. in Greek translations from Hebrew does not depend on the form of the Hebrew verb. The frequency of the h.p. we have studied in the Old Greek version depends, as we have shown, on the stylistic preference of the particular translator and not on the presence of the Hebrew participle.

Middle Aramaic and Its Greek Translators

In Biblical Aramaic, and *only* in the book of Daniel, there is a special use of the participle as a kind of independent tense to introduce onetime events,[14] e.g.,

,בֵּאדַיִן נָפְקִין שַׁדְרַךְ . . . מִן גּוֹא נוּרָא

"then Shadrach, (Meshach and Abed-nego) came forth from the midst of the fire" (Dan 3:26). There is no durative or circumstantial quality here, but an important moment of the story is emphasized.[15]

With regard to other Middle Aramaic texts,[16] in a few cases the participle

---

[13] Hawkins, *Horae Synopticae*, 143.

[14] H. Bauer and P. Leander, *Grammatik des Biblisch-Aramäischen* (Tübingen: Niemeyer, 1927) 129(r).

[15] Ibid., 294(s). F. Rosenthal explains that the use of the participle to indicate the immediate present "led to the widespread use of the participle to indicate an action that is simultaneous with the main action. This led further to the free use of the participle as a narrative tense" (*A Grammar of Biblical Aramaic* [Porta Linguarum Orientalium 5; Wiesbaden: Harrassowitz, 1968] 55).

[16] Only contemporaneous Aramaic literature should be used to determine the grammar of the first century. Here we follow J. A. Fitzmyer's division of the Aramaic language: Old Aramaic (925–700 B.C.E.), Official (Imperial) Aramaic (700–200 B.C.E.), Middle Aramaic (200 B.C.E.–200 C.E.), Late Aramaic (200–700 C.E. [or later]), Modern Aramaic (today); see J. A. Fitzmyer, *The*

may be used in this way, e.g.,

והא מרובין שבעה שפכין [. . .] והא הדרין פתיחו

"and, behold, seven sluices poured out [participle] ... and, behold, the chambers were opened [perf.]" (4QEnᵉ 4 i 16–17);

ותוריא שקעין וטבעין [. . .] וערבה פרחה עלא מן מיא
וכל תוריא [. . .] ופיליא ירו מי[ן]

"and the oxen sank [part.] and drowned [part.] ... and the ship floated [part.] above the waters and all the oxen [and wild asses and camels] and elephants sank [perf.] in the waters" (4QEnᵉ 4 i 19–21; also possibly וֹנֹחֹתין in 4QEnᵉ 4 ii 3 — not clearly read). However, when one inspects two rather lengthy texts, the *Genesis Apocryphon* and the Aramaic fragments of the books of *Enoch* collected by J. T. Milik, one finds that, apart from the two texts just cited, participles denoting past time in nominal clauses are iterative, circumstantial, and subordinate to the main action of the text.[17]

With regard to the verb "to say" (אמר), in Middle Aramaic narrative this verb usually occurs in the perfect, with exception in the book of Daniel of the phrase ענה ואמר (if the Masoretic pointing as two participles is correct — two perfects would look the same in an unpointed text — 23 times) and its plural ענו ואמרין (with ענו as a finite verb in Dan 2:7, 10; 3:9, 16; 6:14) or ענין ואמרין (two participles, only in Dan 3:24). The perfect of אמר is used 17 times in Daniel, and exclusively to express past action in the *Genesis Apocryphon* (20 times) and in the Aramaic fragments of *Enoch* (8 times).[18]

Genesis Apocryphon of Qumran Cave I (2d rev. ed.; BibOr 18a; Rome: Biblical Institute, 1971) 22 n. 60.

[17] See in the *Genesis Apocryphon* משתני (2:2), ממללין (20:8), נחתן (20:12). שביק and קטיל in 19:16 and 22:3 are probably not participles but perfect passives. The participles in 22:4 and 8 are verbal adjectives, not the predicates of nominal clauses. In the fragments of the books of *Enoch* published by J. T. Milik (*The Books of Enoch* [Oxford: Clarendon, 1976]), the narrating verb is generally in the perfect while the periphrastic (the verb "to be" with a participle) occurs in 4QEnᵃ 1 iii 16, 17, 19; 4QEnᵇ 1 ii 22 (corrected), 25; 4QEnᶜ 1 vi 20; 4QEnᶜ 4.1, 6; 4QEnᵈ 2 ii 30; 4QEnᵉ 4 i 18, 19. Participles occur as the predicate in a nominal clause in 4QEnᵃ 1 iv 5 (in a subordinate clause); 4QEnᶜ 1 vi 6 (*bis*), 22; 4QEnᶜ 4 i 16, 19 (*bis*); 4QEnᵉ 4 ii 3 (not clearly read).

[18] In the *Genesis Apocryphon* the participle of אמר occurs three times: once in a nominal clause in present time: וכען לכא אנה אמר, "and now I say to you" (5:9) and once in the periphrastic construction: דלמא תהוה אמר, "lest you say" (22:22). The usage in 2:25 is not clear because of the fragmentary nature of the text. In the Enochic material the participle of אמר occurs once as the predicate of a nominal clause: וכען לכן אנה אמר, "and now I say to you" (4QEnᵍ 1 v 24 — again as a "present tense") and once as a verbal adjective: נסב חֲנוך מתלה אמר, "Enoch [took up] his discourse saying ..." (4QEnᵍ 1 iii 19). It is unlikely that here we have the perfect form of אמר in asyndeton because that is not a feature found elsewhere in this material.

Greek translation of the Aramaic participle expressing past action shows little correlation with the use of the h.p. by a translator. Of the roughly 100 participles in Daniel which C. F. Burney showed as describing a past action,[19] Theodotion has translated with a Greek h.p. only six times (λέγει in 2:27; λέγουσιν in 2:10; 6:12, 14, 16; συνάγονται in 3:27), and the translator of OG Daniel never uses the h.p.! The Greek translation of the book of *Enoch* does not use the h.p. either.

Conclusion

The use of the Aramaic participle as a kind of punctilinear past tense was a matter of personal style of an author, just as the h.p. was in Greek. Even in the book of Daniel, and even in the case of the verb "to say," and even in Theodotion, who uses λέγει/λέγουσιν five times (as noted above), it is not the Aramaic participle itself that seems to have caused the translator to use the h.p.[20]

TABLE

P = historical present; a = aorist
P̱ = h.p. of λέγειν; i = imperfect

1 Prologue—John the Baptist (1:1–8) aiiia	7 The Leper (1:40–45) PaP̱aaaP̱aii
2 Baptism and Temptation (1:9–13) aaaaaP̱iii	8 The Paralytic (2:1–12) aaiP̱aP̱P̱iP̱P̱aa
3 Summary (1:14–15) a	9 Call of Levi (2:13–17) aiiaP̱aP̱iiiiP̱
4 Call of Disciples (1:16–20) aiaaaaa	10 Question of Fasting (2:18–22) iP̱P̱a
5 Capernaum Synagogue (1:21–28) P̱iiiiaaaaa	11 Plucking Grain (2:23–28) aaaP̱i
6 Simon's House (1:29–39) aiP̱aaiiiaaiaaiaaP̱P̱a	12 The Withered Hand (3:1–6) aiiP̱P̱iP̱aai

[19] C. F. Burney, *The Aramaic Origin of the Fourth Gospel* (Oxford: Clarendon, 1922) 88–89.

[20] Black has claimed that the h.p. λέγει/λέγουσιν, when used asyndetically in the Gospels, is the result of Aramaic interference (*Aramaic Approach*, 57). In Mark the usage occurs once: πόσους κοφίνους . . . ἤρατε; λέγουσιν αὐτῷ· Δώδεκα. " 'How many baskets . . . did you take up?' They said to him: 'Twelve' " (8:19). We have elsewhere pointed out that asyndeton is a frequent feature of many classical and Hellenistic Greek writers, especially with verbs of saying which introduce direct discourse (*Semitic Interference in Marcan Syntax* [SBLDS 51; Missoula, MT: Scholars Press, 1981] 77). As a matter of fact, we have shown that asyndeton is not a common feature of Middle Aramaic (*Semitic Interference*, 79). M.-J. Lagrange's five examples of asyndetic אמר in the Elephantine papyri do not prove the contrary since they belong to the Official Aramaic phase of the language (*Évangile selon Saint Matthieu* [Paris: Gabalda, 1927] xcii).

13 Summary (3:7–12)
aa[a]aaiii

14 Choosing the Twelve (3:13–19)
PPaa[a]aa

15 Jesus' Relatives (3:20–21)
PPai

16 Jesus and Beelzabul (3:22–30)
ii

17 Arrival of Relatives (3:31–35)
PaiPPP

18 Parable Discourse (4:1–34)
aPiiiiiiPiiiiiii

19 Storm at Sea (4:35–41)
PPiPiiPPaaaaaai

20 Gerasene Demoniac (5:1–20)
aaiiiaaPiiPiiaaaaiaaaPPaaaiaPaaai

21 Request of Jairus (5:21–24)
aiPPPaii

22 Woman with Hemorrhage (5:25–34)
aiaaiiiaaaa

23 Jairus' Daughter (5:35–43)
PPaPPPiPPPaiiaaa

24 In Nazareth (6:1–6)
aPPaiiiiii

25 Sending of Apostles (6:7–13)
Paiaiaiii

26 Herod and John (6:14–29)
aaiiiiaaiiiiiiiiiiaaaaaaaaaaaaaaaa

27 Return of Apostles (6:30–33)
PaPiiaaaaa

28 Multiplication of Loaves (6:34–44)
aaaiaPPPaaaaiaaaai

29 Walking on Water (6:45–52)
aaiPiaaaaaPaaiai

30 Summary (6:53–56)
aaaaiii

31 Ritual Purity (7:1–23)
PPaiiiiPi

32 Syrophoenician Woman (7:24–30)
aiaaiiiaPaa

33 Deaf and Dumb Man (7:31–37)
aPPaaaPaaiaii

34 Multiplication of Loaves (8:1–10)
PaiaPaiaiaaaia

35 Demand for a Sign (8:11–13)
aaPa

36 Leaven of Pharisees (8:14–21)
aiiiPPPi

37 Blind Man (8:22–26)
PPPaiiaaaia

38 Recognition of Messiah (8:27–30)
aiaiPa

39 Jesus Foretells Death (8:31–9:1)
aiaaPai

40 Transfiguration (9:2–8)
PPaaaiPiaaaa

41 Question about Elijah (9:9–13)
aaii

42 Boy with Dumb Spirit (9:14–29)
aaiaaaPaaiaaaiaaaaia

43 Second Passion Prediction (9:30–32)
iiiiii

44 In Capernaum (9:33–37)
aiiaaPaa

45 Discourse (9:38–50)
ia

46 Teaching about Divorce (10:1–12)
PPiiaaaiP

47 Blessing Children (10:13–16)
iaaai

48 Rich Young Man (10:17–22)
iaaaai

49 Wealth and Poverty (10:23–31)
PiPiPai

50 Third Passion Prediction (10:32–34)
iiiia

51 Sons of Zebedee (10:35–45)
PaaaaaaP

52 Blind Man (10:45–52)
PiaiiaPaaaaai

53 Entrance into Jerusalem (11:1–11)
PPaaPiaaPPaaiaa

54 Cursing the Fig Tree (11:12–14)
aaaiai

55 Cleansing the Temple (11:15–19)
Paaiiiaiiii

56 Withered Fig Tree (11:20–25)
aPP

57 Question of Jesus' Authority
(11:27–33)
PPiaiiiPP

58 Parable of Vineyard (12:1–12)
aiaaa

59 Taxes to Caesar (12:13–17)
PPaaPaai

60 Question about Resurrection
(12:18–27)
Pii

61 Great Commandment (12:28–34)
aaaaai

62 Question about David's Son
(12:35–40)
iii

63 Widow's Mite (12:41–44)
iiaa

64 Eschatological Discourse (13:1–37)
Paia

65 Anointing in Bethany (14:1–11)
iiiaiiaaaai

66 Preparation for Passover (14:12–16)
PPPaaaa

67 Last Supper (14:17–25)
Paaaaaaaa

68 Peter's Denial Foretold (14:26–31)
aPiPii

69 Gethsemane (14:32–42)
PPPaPiiiPPPaaiiPP

70 Betrayal and Arrest (14:43–52)
PPaaaaaaiPa

71 Trial before Sanhedrin (14:53–65)
aPaiiiiiiaiaiPaPaaa

72 Peter's Denial (14:66–72)
PPaa[a]aiiaaai

73 Trial before Pilate (15:1–15)
aaaPiiaiiaaiaiaiaaa

74 Crowning of Thorns (15:16–20a)
aPPPaiiiaa

75 Way of the Cross (15:20b–27)
PPPiPPiaiP

76 Jesus on the Cross (15:29–41)
iiiaaiiaaai

77 Burial of Jesus (15:42–47)
aaaaaaaai

78 At the Tomb (16:1–8)
aPiPiaaPaiai

II. Use of the Historical Present in the Gospel of Mark

In the Gospel of Mark the historical present occurs 149 or 150 times in independent clauses,[21] and only once in a subordinate clause.[22] It does not

---

[21] This depends on whether κατευλογει (10:16) is the present tense κατευλογεῖ or the imperfect κατευλόγει (as marked in the UBS text). The root verb εὐλογέω is attested in the imperfect both as εὐλόγουν and ηὐλόγουν, but the compound form κατευλογέω occurs only very rarely in the pertinent literature. In addition to the present participle in Plutarch (Mor. 66A, 1069C) and the aorist (κατευλόγησεν) in Tobit 11:17, only the same ambiguous form κατευλογει turns up in Hellenistic Greek, in Tob 10:14, as far as we can tell. Now since the book of Tobit has forms of the h.p. (only) in 3:17 (ἐπιβάλλει) and in 10:6 and 9 (λέγει), the form κατευλογει in 11:17 could be either the (historical) present or the imperfect. As we shall see below (n. 25), κατευλογει (Mark 10:16) is probably the imperfect form if the verb is used consistently with the rest of the Gospel.

[22] Mark 11:1, ὅτε ἐγγίζουσιν, in a pericope full of instances of the h.p. Present tense forms in indirect discourse may not be considered examples of the h.p., of course, since in this construction in Greek the tense of the original (direct) discourse is used. Two other present-tense verbs occur in subordinate clauses, but they are not *historical* presents: ἕως ἀπολύει (6:45) is probably a proleptic present (= present for future; see A. T. Robertson, *A Grammar of the Greek NT in the*

turn up in direct discourse or in the evangelist's parenthetical remarks. In order to make some observations on this usage we found it helpful to update and correct M. Zerwick's table of main verb tenses in Mark's narrative material.[23]

Zerwick claims that almost all the pericopes in Mark (as enumerated in the table) fall into six categories: (1) with no instances of the h.p., (2) with only λέγειν as h.p., (3) with only ἔρχεσθαι as h.p., (4) with only λέγειν and ἔρχεσθαι as h.p.'s, (5) pericopes containing h.p.'s following and influenced by the h.p. of ἔρχεσθαι, (6) pericopes with h.p.'s following and influenced by an h.p. (other than ἔρχεσθαι and λέγειν) which introduce a new turn in the story. Zerwick admits that these categories do not give sufficient consideration to the text of Mark as a whole, but he states that they do show a wide-reaching uniformity in Marcan usage.[24] We must point out that many of the pericopes contain combinations of Zerwick's categories—a fact that he does not point out. However, his overall conclusion on the use of the h.p. has much to commend it. He holds that often in a Gospel story, although introductory activities are narrated in preterite tenses of the verb, the real and important beginning of a story is told in the h.p., while the conclusion occurs in the preterite once again.[25]

With a fresh look at the evidence, we may now make the following observations:

1. The h.p. is used in the Gospel to vivify past events in the telling of a story, a practice common among various literary, technical, and nonliterary first-century writers of Greek. As in those authors, it has a punctilinear *Aktionsart*.

2. A pattern does emerge in the use of the h.p., much as explained by Zerwick: the important action of a pericope often begins with a h.p. or a string of h.p.'s, with λέγει/λέγουσιν (occurs 72 times in Mark), ἔρχεται/ἔρχονται (occurs 23 times in Mark), or some other verb of coming or going, bringing,

---

Light of Historical Research [3d ed.; New York: Hodder & Stoughton, 1919] 975–76 and Blass-Debrunner-Funk §383.1). In Mark 12:41, πῶς ὁ ὄχλος βάλλει, we are dealing with an indirect question (see Robertson, *Grammar*, 1032).

[23] Zerwick, *Untersuchungen*, 49–57. Zerwick uses the Westcott-Hort Greek text and bases his pericope divisions on the paragraphs and subparagraphs of that edition of the Gospel (pp. 49–50). Zerwick's table is full of typographical errors. We have corrected these and preferred the UBS text of Mark, but have retained Zerwick's enumeration of the pericopes as a working model in full realization of its limitations and sometime arbitrariness.

[24] *Untersuchungen*, 54.

[25] Thus, on the premise that the usage would be consistent throughout the Gospel, we uphold the common opinion that κατευλογει in 10:16 is the imperfect tense, since it clearly belongs to the conclusion of the pericope. In a similar vein, we uphold the Westcott-Hort division, followed by Zerwick, of pericopes #74 and #75 (see chart) between 15:20a and 15:20b because of the h.p. ἐξάγουσιν in 15:20b.

leading, or gathering. The story almost always continues or concludes in the past tense (there are no pericopes with all h.p.'s.).[26] A new turn in the story may be signaled by a second (or third) instance or series of h.p.'s, always to be concluded in the past tense—with one exception:

3. While λέγει/λέγουσιν is used normally as an h.p.,[27] and often introduces the main action or a new and important turn in the story which will be concluded in the past tense (see table), in pericopes ##9, 17(*bis*), 46, 51, 56, 57, and 69, the h.p. λέγει introduces the main action or a new turn in the story which is concluded by a saying of Jesus (and not by a verb in a past tense). The words καὶ λέγει αὐτοῖς appear in each of these cases (αὐτοῖς is lacking in 3:34 but occurs in 3:33).

4. In twenty-two of the pericopes (##1, 3, 4, 13, 16, 22, 26, 30, 41, 43, 45, 47, 48, 50, 54, 58, 61, 62, 63, 65, 76, 77) there are no h.p.'s. Of these we point out that #1 is the Marcan introduction; ##3, 13, and 30 are Marcan summaries; ##43 and 50 are the second and third passion predictions redacted by the evangelist; ##16, 22, 26, 54, 58, and possibly 41 and 77 are examples of Marcan intercalation (stories "sandwiched" into the middle of another story). It is tempting to draw some conclusions about the possible redactional nature of ##4, 45, 47, 48, 61, 62, 63, 65 (#76 may be the conclusion of #75; see n. 24), but we are well aware of the amount of other evidence to be examined before such conclusions should be attempted.[28] We are not, however, willing to go as far as Zerwick when he maintains that the choice between the h.p. λέγει/λέγουσιν and the aorist εἶπεν/αν/ον depends more on the content of the saying it introduces and its psychological impact than on its origin as source or redaction.[29]

---

[26] The only exception to this general rule for the use of the h.p. (apart from λέγει; see below) would be #75 in our table, since we have dropped 15:[28] from the text of Mark (with the UBS text) as an intrusion of Luke 22:37. As Zerwick pointed out, it may be better to take #75 (The Way of the Cross, 15:20b–27) together with the next section #76 (Jesus on the Cross, 15:29–41), the two forming a single pericope beginning the action with h.p.'s and concluding it (at the death of Jesus) with aorists and an imperfect (*Untersuchungen*, 55). D. Senior also treats the combined sections as one pericope (*The Passion of Jesus in the Gospel of Mark* [Wilmington: Glazier, 1984] 114).

[27] Zerwick (*Untersuchungen*, 55) and Turner (*Style*, 20) overdistinguish when they claim that in Mark the form λέγει/λέγουσιν is not fully an h.p. Λέγει/λέγουσιν clearly indicates the main action or a new turn in the story, and it has the requisite punctilinear *Aktionsart*, even when it is the last verb in a narrative (see below).

[28] J. J. O'Rourke has already warned that in itself the use or nonuse of the h.p. cannot prove authorship or literary unity in conclusive fashion ("The Historical Present in the Gospel of John," *JBL* 93 [1974] 588).

[29] Zerwick makes a very credible observation that the imperfect καὶ ἔλεγεν in 2:27; 3:23; 4:2, 9, 11, 21, 24, 26, 30; 6:4, 10; 7:9, 14, 20; 9:1 is redactional, since there it (and never λέγει or εἶπεν) adds a new and independent teaching, always of Jesus. He points out that in 9:31; 11:17; 12:35, 38, καὶ . . . ἔλεγεν is juxtaposed with the Marcan favorite διδάσκω/διδαχή, and is probably

Conclusions

1. The use of the historical present in the Gospel of Mark is *not* the result of Semitic interference. As in other Hellenistic documents, the phenomenon in the Gospel is the result of the stylistic preference of the evangelist, a redactor, or the (Greek) sources of the Gospel.

2. When the historical present is used in the Gospel, it signals in vivid fashion the main action of a story or a new turn of events in a story already begun with an h.p.

3. Since the use of the historical present is so widespread and so uniform in the Gospel, it is unlikely that the phenomenon is the chance result of the oral traditions that gave rise to a written Gospel.

4. However, since the historical present is conspicuously absent from 22 (or 21) out of 78 (or 77) pericopes of the Gospel, the phenomenon proves to be a very important stylistic feature in determining the redactional activity and the variety of sources of the Gospel writer(s).

5. Examination of the use of the historical present, however, cannot by itself determine source or redaction, but must be used in conjunction with a complete discussion of the style of each Marcan pericope for such a determination.

---

also redactional. For the remaining texts in the Gospel which have ἔλεγεν (5:8, 30; 7:27; 8:21) Zerwick is not convincing (*Untersuchungen*, 60–61).

Chapter
7

(Rather Dim but Nevertheless Appreciable) Light from (a Very Obscure) Ugaritic (Text) on (the) Hebrew (Bible)

Dennis Pardee
The University of Chicago

אשרי אדם מצא חכמה
ואדם יפיק תבונה
Proverbs 3:13

A RECENT REEDITION of the Ugaritic text that deals with abnormal births of sheep and goats[1] relied extensively on the Akkadian versions of these texts, as was to be expected because this is a standard Mesopotamian *genre*[2] while the Ugaritic version almost certainly represents an importation in the West. But being a version written in Ugaritic, still a relatively poorly attested western Semitic language, its elucidation also had to rely to some extent on Biblical Hebrew lexical and syntactic parallels. The elucidation has not been one-sided, however, and it is the purpose of this contribution in honor of Prof. Fitzmyer to present for biblical scholars the principal features of the Ugaritic text that

---

[1] D. Pardee, "The Ugaritic *šumma izbu* Text," *AfO* 33 (1986) 117–47. See this article for discussion of the many textual difficulties (my text differs markedly from the previous editions cited below in this note) and for parallels with the Akkadian *šumma izbu* texts. The Ugaritic text was originally edited by A. Herdner, "Nouveaux textes alphabétiques de Ras Shamra—XXIVᵉ campagne, 1961," *Ugaritica* VII (Mission de Ras Shamra 18; Paris: Geuthner, 1978) 1–74, esp. 44–60. See also the independent edition of this text by M. Dietrich, O. Loretz, and J. Sanmartín, "Der keilalphabetische *šumma izbu*-Text RS 24.247 + 265 + 268 + 328," *UF* 7 (1975) 133–40, and the inclusion of this text in the same authors' collection of the Ugaritic texts: *KTU* 1.103 and 1.145. The edition by Dietrich, Loretz, and Sanmartín was followed closely by P. Xella and A. M. G. Capomacchia, "Tre testi ugaritici relativi a presagi di nascite," *OrAnt* 18 (1979) 41–58; see also Xella's reedition with some changes in *I testi rituali di Ugarit. I, Testi* (Studi Semitici 54; Rome: Consiglio Nazionale delle Ricerche, 1981) 191–206.

[2] E. Leichty, *The Omen Series Šumma Izbu* (Locust Valley, NY: Augustin, 1970).

elucidate, corroborate, or are simply parallel to Hebrew words and texts. The notes below are arranged in order of the occurrence of the Ugaritic word(s) in the omen text.

The Double Feminine Morpheme
on Feminine Plural Nouns

The Ugaritic text begins *ṯ'att ṣ'in [kt]ldn! 'abn m'adtn tqln b ḥwt*, "As for the ewes of the flock, (if) [they give bi]rth to a stone, many[3] will fall in the land." *ṯ'att* is either a mistake for *ṯ'at*, "ewe," or a plural.[4] If the latter analysis is correct, we have an example in Ugaritic of a feminine plural morpheme added to a singular stem which already included the feminine morpheme. This phenomenon has been noted and many examples have been gathered for Biblical Hebrew[5] but it has not yet appeared in Ugaritic.[6]

The Postposition of the Hypothetical Particle
in Leviticus 13

In the first line of the Ugaritic text quoted in the previous section the hypothetical particle *k* is reconstructed as appearing after the subject. The reconstruction itself is very likely, for the Ugaritic text dealing with omens based on abnormal human births[7] begins (and the phrase is repeated before each section) *k tld 'a[tt]*, "If a woman gives birth to . . ." (with the hypothetical particle in first position). T. Seidl has recently explained the postposing of the hypothetical particle in Lev 13:2 (*'ādām kî yihyeh . . .*) as follows: "Die Voranstellung von *'adam* im Rahmen einer C[onstructio] P[endens] geschieht mehr aus inhaltlichen und kompositionellen Gründen, um die Aussagen über den 'Aussatz' am Menschen von den späteren Einheiten des 'Kleider'- und

---

[3] For the usage of -*n* on the first word of the apodosis (if singular absolute) in this text, see J. Hoftijzer, "Quodlibet Ugariticum," *Zikir šumim. Assyriological Studies Presented to F. R. Kraus on the Occasion of his Seventieth Birthday* (ed. G. van Driel et al.; Leiden: Brill, 1982) 121–27, esp. 121–23.

[4] The verb form *tldn!* does not help to decide the matter because it is actually written *[t]ld'at* (that is, the third wedge of {*n*} was written separately from the first two resulting in what appears to be {'*a*} + {*t*}) and the -*n* could, in any case, be "energic" -*n* on a singular verb). The plural of *ṯ'at* is not attested in Ugaritic, but the plural of the corresponding word in Old Aramaic is attested as both ṣ'*n* (Sefire) and *s'wn* (Fakhariya); see D. Pardee and R. D. Biggs, *JNES* 43 (1984) 256; and J. A. Fitzmyer, *JBL* 103 (1984) 266.

[5] E. J. Wiesenberg, "Rabbinic Hebrew as Aid in the Study of Biblical Hebrew Illustrated in the Exposition of the Rare Words רחת and מורה," *HUCA* 47 (1976) 143–80, esp. 171–78. Cf. also *mś'tt* in Punic, the plural of *mś't*, "gift, offering" (*KAI* 69, 74 *passim*).

[6] I know of no other example and S. Segert mentions none in his recent *A Basic Grammar of the Ugaritic Language* (Berkeley: University of California Press, 1984) 50.

[7] Herdner, *Ugaritica* VII (1978) 60–62 = *KTU* 1.140 (also reedited in my article cited in n. 1).

'Häuseraussatzes' abzuheben und zu kennzeichnen."[8] Because the Ugaritic tablet deals with only animal births, Seidl's explanation of the word order in Leviticus 13 is certainly not applicable here. Nor, on the basis of present data, can one say that this tablet formed a series with other types of omens and that the series would have had the structure of Leviticus 13, for in the only other Ugaritic omen text (just cited) the subject is not fronted. The Ugaritic word order cannot be accounted for by its probable Akkadian original, for the Akkadian texts begin either BE U₈ . . . Ù . TU, "If a ewe gives birth . . . ," or BE (DIŠ in Old Babylonian) *iz-bu*, "If the anomaly . . . ," that is, with the hypothetical particle in first postition in both formulas.[9] I do not have an explanation for the fronting of the subject in the Ugaritic and Hebrew texts cited, but the lack of both contextual and comparative motivations for the Ugaritic example leads me to believe that the reasons for the Hebrew example may be more complex than the one that Seidl has proposed.

Ugaritic *ql* ~ Hebrew *npl*, "to Fall"

The similarity in usage of Hebrew *npl*, Akkadian *maqātu*, and Ugaritic *ql* in epistolary formulae was pointed out long ago by S. E. Loewenstamm.[10] The first line of the Ugaritic *šumma izbu* text (cited above) provides a parallel for another usage of Hebrew *npl*, that of falling in battle. BDB state that there are about 96 usages of *npl* to denote violent death. The closest parallel to the Ugaritic text that I have found is 2 Sam 1:4 *wĕgam-harbēh nāpal min-hā'ām wayyāmūtû*, "Many have fallen from the people and they have died." Here as in the Ugaritic text there is a word denoting "many"; the syntax is, however, different (*harbēh* = adverb; *m'adtn* = subject), and the Hebrew text adds the specification that the fallen ones have died. Akkadian *maqātu*, not surprisingly, is again used in similar ways.[11]

b'r, "to Destroy"

In an excellent study of Hebrew *b'r*, "faire disparaître," P.-E. Dion has cited the relevant passages from the Ugaritic *šumma izbu* text[12] and has

---

[8] *Tora für den 'Aussatz'-Fall. Literarische Schichten und syntaktische Strukturen in Levitikus 13 und 14* (Arbeiten zu Text und Sprache im Alten Testament 18; St. Ottilien: EOS Verlag, 1982) 78.

[9] See Leichty, *Šumma Izbu*, 73, 84, and 201, for examples (Tablet V has the first formula; Tablets VI ff. and the Old Babylonian version, the second).

[10] S. E. Loewenstamm, "Prostration from Afar in Ugaritic, Accadian and Hebrew," *BASOR* 188 (1967) 41–43.

[11] See *CAD* M₁, p. 243, for similar usages in omens.

[12] P.-E. Dion, "Tu feras disparaître le mal du milieu de toi," *RB* 87 (1980) 321–49, esp. 332, 341–42.

correctly given to the verb *b'r* the meaning "destroy" in all three previously known occurrences in this text (lines 41', 56', 58').[13] As a quite hypothetical but not implausible restoration in line 2, I have suggested the reading *t'tbr*, to be parsed as a D_t form of the root, with passive meaning. The first part of the line is badly damaged but the entire line seems to say that if the anomaly consists of a piece of wood (*'s*, cf. *'abn*, "stone," in line 1) the cattle will be destroyed (*bhmth*[14] *t'tbr*).

ḫr, "Pierce" ≠ *ḥr*, "Be Hot"

The meaning "hole" for *ḫr*, already cited by Gordon[15] on the basis of a personal communication from C. Virolleaud, is corroborated by the complete editions of the text. The word occurs in the phrase *ḫr 'apm*, "holes of the nostrils," in lines 6 and 30. An anatomical part *ḫr* occurs in this same text (lines 54', 58') but in broken contexts, and its meaning is uncertain. I have tentatively suggested the meaning "vulva," for which the only parallel that I am aware of is Arabic *ḥirrun* (√*ḥrr*, "be hot"). Whatever the meaning of the latter word may be, BDB's etymology for Hebrew *ḥōr*, "hole," as derived from a proto-Hebrew root *ḫrr* is validated by the Ugaritic word *ḫr*.

dll Denoting Physical Prostration

BDB list five examples, three in the qal (Pss 79:8; 116:6; 142:7), two in the niphal (Isa 17:4; Judg 6:6 — both forms could be "quasi-Aramaic" qal imperfects), of *dll* with the meaning "be low," "be brought low," "be laid low." This root occurs twice in the Ugaritic anomaly text; unfortunately both occurrences are defective, one because of context, the other apparently because of scribal error. The first is in line 7: *[w]'in [   ]mlkn y'iḫd ḥw[t 'ibh w']mrḥy mlk tdlln*, "[And] (if) there is no [   ] the king shall seize the lan[d of his enemy

---

[13] As opposed to Dietrich, Loretz, and Sanmartín (*UF* 7 [1975] 135) and Xella (*OrAnt* 18 [1979] 52; *TRU* I [1981] 195–96, 206) who translate "destroy" ("wird . . . ausrotten"/"sterminerà") in line 58' but "abandon" in lines 41' and 56' ("werden . . . verlassen"/"abbandoneranno"). In a separate article on the root *b'r* ("Die keilalphabetischen Belege für *B'R* I und *B'R* II," *UF* 7 [1975] 554–56), Dietrich, Loretz, and Sanmartín, though classifying all occurrences in the Ugaritic anomaly text under one main heading, divide them into the subheadings "abandon" (G-stem ?) and "force to abandon" (D-stem: "wird . . . zum Aufgeben zwingen"), with the latter corresponding to their translation "ausrotten" in their study of the anomaly text. Dion's arguments that *b'r* is in the same semantic field as *ḫlq*, "perish," "destroy" are more convincing.

[14] Because of the damaged state of the line, the referent of the pronominal suffix on *bhmt* is uncertain.

[15] *UT* §19.998. This is probably a different root from the one behind *ḫr* in the Ugaritic hippiatric texts, cited also in §19.998 by Gordon. See D. Pardee, *Les textes hippiatriques* (Ras-Shamra-Ougarit 2; Paris: Editions Recherche sur les Civilisations, 1985) 51–52.

and ?] the weapon[16] of the king shall lay it low." Here the problem is linking the part of the line that precedes the lacuna with the part that follows the lacuna, for the latter segment is written on the edge of the tablet and almost on the vertical axis of the tablet, making the assignment of these and other ends of lines difficult. The other occurrence is in line 46': [   ] *mlkn yd ḫrdh yddll*, "[And (if) . . . ,] the king will lay low the power of his *ḫurādu*-troops." Here the problem is with the form, for unless *yddll* is a very anomalous passive form, it must be emended to *ydll*.[17] Other scribal errors appear in this text; that factor and the similarity of the signs {*d*} and {*l*} make the emendation likely. These usages corroborate BDB's analysis of the forms cited above, for the context of the Ugaritic references (note especially the subject *mrḥy* in the first example) indicate that the notion is one of physical prostration rather than of economic poverty.

šq, "Thigh"

On the basis of a personal communication from Virolleaud, Gordon was able to include the entry *šq*, "thigh" or "leg," in *UT* (§19.2393a). The occurrences are in lines 9 and 26' of the anomaly text, almost certainly with reference to the left and right thighs, respectively, and almost certainly with respect to the upper portion of the leg, the "haunch/loin/thigh" (~Akkadian *pēmu*). This Ugaritic usage corresponds to biblical Hebrew *šôq* as a sacrificial term.

qṣrt as an Anatomical Term

Though not of immediate interest for Biblical Hebrew, the appearance of Ugaritic *qṣrt* (line 10: *ẇ 'in qṣr[t šm]'al*, "And (if) it has no lower left leg . . .") as the almost certain correspondent to *qṣrt* in the Marseilles Tariff[18] is of interest for West Semitic sacrificial terminology. The word probably refers to the portion of the animal leg between the foot and the "ankle," corresponding to the flat of the human foot. The Akkadian functional equivalent, if not the etymological one, is *kursinnu*.

ṭḥl, "Spleen"

Though again not of immediate interest to Biblical Hebrew, the occurrence of *ṭḥl*, "spleen," in the Ugaritic anomaly text (line 12: *ṭḥl 'in bh*, "(If) it

---

[16] *mrḥy* is almost certainly another form of the Ugaritic word *mrḥ* "spear," "lance," as is established by *šumma izbu* parallels.

[17] The form may be passive even if emended to *ydll*. The meaning would be "the king will be laid low by (that is, with respect to) the power of his *ḫurādu*-troops."

[18] So identified by Xella, *OrAnt* 18 (1979) 51; *TRU* I (1981) 202–3.

has no spleen . . .") is worth noting here, for only Herdner of the authors cited above in n. 1 read and identified the word correctly. Corresponding forms occur in postbiblical Hebrew (*těḥôl*) and Aramaic (*ṭaḥălâ/ṭěḥôlâ*) as well as in Akkadian (*ṭulīmu*) and in Arabic (*ṭiḥâlun*).

pq "to Obtain"

Because the meaning of *pq* in its best-known occurrence in Ugaritic (*CTA* 14:12 *'aṯt ṣdqh l ypq*) has been in dispute, the less ambiguous cases in the omen text may be cited:

13) *mlkn . l ypq* ⌜ š ⌝ *[p]ḥ* "The (= our) king will not obtain offspring."
29') *l ypq špḥ* "[. . .] will not obtain offspring."

This usage of *pq* provides a general parallel to Hebrew *hēpîq*,[19] "to obtain" (e.g., Prov 3:13 *'ašrê 'ādām māṣā' ḥokmâ wě'ādām yāpîq těbûnâ*, "Happy the man who finds wisdom, the man who obtains understanding").

'uškm, "Testicles"

Because there was only one previous occurrence of *'ušk*, "testicle," in Ugaritic (in a context that was not overly encouraging for that interpretation[20]) to provide a parallel to Hebrew *'āšek* (pausal) in Lev 21:20, the unequivocal appearance of the dual form *'uškm* in line 14 of the Ugaritic anomaly text (*[w] 'in 'uškm bḥ̊*, "[And] (if) it has no testicles . . .") may be cited.

yd, "Foreleg"

The word *yd* occurs twice in the Ugaritic omen text, probably with the meaning "foreleg": *ẘ'in kr' yd̊h š[m'al]* and *w 'in kr' ydh [ymn]*, "And (if) the middle portion of the left/right leg is missing . . ." (lines 15, 28'). Because *p'n(t)* is apparently used for the hindlegs and/or for all four legs (lines 39', 52'), it is contextually likely that *yd* in lines 15 and 28' refers to the forelegs. Such a usage occurs in Biblical Hebrew, but only in passages where *yd* also has the metaphorical notion of "grasp," "power" (1 Sam 17:37, of a lion and a bear; Ps 22:21, of a dog; cf. also Gen 9:5, where the reference is to responsibility for shed blood placed on an animal).

Ugaritic *ḫrsp* ~ Hebrew *ḥarṣubbôt?*

Herdner already toyed with the explanation of the phrase *w 'in ḫrsp bk[. . .]*,

---

[19] Already cited by Gordon, *UT* §19.2030, on the basis of oral information from Virolleaud.
[20] See *UT* §19.397; the text is *UT* 132: 2 = *CTA* 11: 2 = *KTU* 1.11:2.

"And (if) it has no *ḫrṣp* . . ." (line 27'), on the basis of Hebrew *ḥarṣubbôt* (Isa 58:6) but abandoned it.[21] Xella made the same suggestion independently and retained it in his translation ("articolazioni/giunture").[22] A. Caquot, probably on the basis of Herdner's study, also made the connection between the Hebrew and Ugaritic words and gave for the Ugaritic term the plausible interpretation "tendon."[23] If the correspondence is valid, it is for the moment a purely etymological one, for Hebrew *ḥarṣubbôt* clearly refers to "bonds" with no immediate reference to an older (?) meaning "tendon." Moreover, the meaning "tendon" lacks parallels in the Akkadian *šumma izbu* texts. Though not impossible, therefore, both the meaning of Ugaritic *ḫrṣp* and a possible connection with Hebrew *ḥarṣubbôt* must for the moment remain in doubt.

qṣr + ym for Shortening of Days

Though the Ugaritic text is again lacunary and uncertain, it is plausible that *pnh pn 'irn 'u[. . .]tqṣrn ymy b'l* (lines 33'-34') is to be translated "(If) it has the face of a *'irn*, [. . .] will shorten the days of the lord (of the homeland). . . ." The subject of *tqṣrn* is probably contained in the lacuna before that word, for the apodosis in the extant portions of this text always begins with the subject; it is perhaps "the power of the enemy" or the like. Transitive expressions of shortening the days containing the verb *qṣr* are attested in Ps 102:24 (the only occurrence of the piel in Hebrew; the Ugaritic form is probably also D-stem) and Ps 89:46 (hiphil).

šdd, "Devastate"

UT contains no entry *šdd*. A verbal form based on that root is attested twice in the Ugaritic anomaly text, in mirror-image omens:

35') *w 'in 'udn ymn b[h 'ibn y]šdd ḥwt*
36')   *[[24] w y]ḥslnn*
37') *w 'in 'udn šm'al b[h]mlkn [y]šdd ḥwt 'ib[h]*
38') *w yḥslnn*

35') "And (if) it has no right ear, [the enemy will] devastate the land
36')   [. . . and will] consume[25] it.

---

[21] Herdner, *Ugaritica* VII (1978) 51.

[22] *OrAnt* 18 (1979) 45, 51; cf. *TRU* I (1981) 194, 204 ("tendini").

[23] *SDB* 9 (1979) 1412.

[24] There is room in the lacuna to restore *mlk*, "king," if a precise mirror-image to the following omen is desired.

[25] See below on Deut 28:38 for this verb.

37′) And (if) [it] has no left ear, the king [will] devastate the land of [his] enemy

38′) and will consume it."

šdd is, of course, frequent in Biblical Hebrew for devastating political entities, e.g., Jer 51:55 *kî šōdēd YHWH 'et-bābel,* "Yahweh is destroying Babylon."

God Burning or Destroying

The gods are twice said to *b ʿr* a land in this text: *ẇ 'apḣ k 'ap 'ṣr 'ilm tb ʿr̈n ḥwt [. . .],* "And (if) its nose is like the 'nose' of a bird, the gods will destroy the land . . ." (line 41′); *w ʿ[. . .] 'ilm tb ʿrn ḥwt hyt,* "And (if) [it has (but) one?] e[ye,?] the gods will destroy that land." For the meaning of *b ʿr* and the many parallels in Biblical Hebrew, see note above to *t ʿtbr̈* (line 2) and Dion's article cited there (note 12).

rps, "to Tread Under"

The Ugaritic passage is again damaged, but the root letters *rps* are entirely preserved in line 50′: *[. . .] l̈'aṭrt ʿnh w ʿnh b lṣbh ['ibn y]rps ḥwt,* "[And (if) its ears? are] in place of its eyes and its eyes are in its forehead, [the enemy will] tread the land under." The Hebrew attestations of the corresponding root are relatively rare and the forms are spelled with both *šin* and *samech.* The Ugaritic form with {s} provides an additional argument for *samech* as the original third root letter and the etymological connection with Arabic *rfs,* "to kick," is established.[26] Semantically, the Ugaritic usage is closer to Akkadian "schlagen," "(ver)dreschen"[27] than to Biblical Hebrew usage, where the clearest references are to befouling water (with the feet).

prš, "Be Scattered" in Ezek 17:21

Because of the structure of the Ugaritic anomaly text in comparison with the Akkadian versions, Herdner was almost certainly correct in translating *ḥwtn tprš* (line 53′) negatively ("sera écrasé").[28] The phrase *wĕhanniš'ārîm lĕkol-rûaḥ yippārēšû* in Ezek 17:21 and the frequency of the notion of scattering in the Akkadian omen series[29] make the notion of "scattering" likely for the Ugaritic text as well.

[26] See J. Blau, *On Pseudo-Corrections in Some Semitic Languages* (Jerusalem: Israel Academy of Sciences and Humanities, 1970) 122; idem, " 'Weak' Phonetic Change and the Hebrew *šin,*" *HAR* 1 (1977) 67–119, esp. 94.

[27] *AHw,* 954–55.

[28] Herdner, *Ugaritica* VII (1978) 50, 57.

[29] The notion even occurs in an omen which may have the same protasis as the Ugaritic one. The Ugaritic protasis is *w[—]lšnh,* which is perhaps to be restored *w[tt] lšnh* "And (if) its tongue(s) is/are two," closely parallel to Akkadian [BE ÁB Ù].TU-*ma* 2 EME MEŠ-*šú* GIŠ . . GU

hšlym (')l in Josh 11:19 and Job 5:23

The apodosis in line 54′ reads *mlkn yšlm l 'ibh*, "The king (of the homeland) will make peace with his enemy." Josh 11:19 states that *lō' hāyĕtâ 'îr 'ăšer hišlîmâ 'el-bĕnê yiśrā'ēl*, "Not one city sued for peace with Israel . . . ," and Job 5:23 that *ḥayyat haśśādeh hošlĕmâ-lāk*, "The beasts of the field have been put at peace with you." The Ugaritic form is probably G-stem, like Akkadian *salāmu*.

zr' + ḥsl in Deut 28:38

One of the curses in Deuteronomy 28 is expressed *zera' rab tôṣî' haśśādeh ûmĕ'aṭ te'ĕsōp kî yaḥsĕlennû hā'arbeh*, "You will take much seed-grain out to (your) fields but will only gather (= harvest) a small amount, for the locust(s) will consume it." Though common in the Aramaic dialects with various nuances of ending, the verb *yaḥsĕlennû* is a *hapax legomenon* in Deut 28:38, and the root is otherwise known in Biblical Hebrew only from the noun *ḥāsîl*, a kind of locust. M. Held presented very clearly the case for the equivalence of Hebrew *ḥsl* and the word *ḥa-zi-lu*, attested once as a so-called Canaanite gloss in an Amarna text (EA 263:13).[30] Herdner correctly interpreted *ḥsl* in the Ugaritic text and compared Deut 28:38.[31] The close parallel between the verb and the entity destroyed, *dr'/zr'*, in both texts has not been pointed out, however.

The relevant line in the Ugaritic text reads as follows: *w 'i[n -]k̂bm bh ḏr' ḥwt hyt yḥsl*, "And (if) it has no -KB (literally, "and there are no -KB in it"), the seed(-grain) of that land will be consumed" (line 55′). The phrase "that land" refers to the preceding omen, just discussed (*mlkn yšlm l'ibh*). The missing body part was expressed by the partially destroyed word which comes after the negative particle. It was in all probability a dual or plural form (-M) and consisted of three consonants of which the second and third were -K- and -B-, though it is not certain that a letter is missing and another possible reading of the {k̂} is {r̂}. Thus, the word may have been -KBM, KBM, -RBM,

---

. ZAN I Š-*ni* É. GAL NUN BIR [. . .] "If a cow gives birth and (the calf) has two tongues—the throne will change; the palace of the prince will be scattered" (Leichty, *Šumma Izbu*, 178, Tablet XIX 12′).

[30] M. Held, "Studies in Comparative Semitic Lexicography," in *Studies in Honor of Benno Landsberger* . . . (Assyriological Studies 16; Chicago: University of Chicago Press, 1965) 395–406, esp. 398–401. The word is preceded by the *Glossenkeil* but the sign only indicates a local word here, for it is not glossing an Akkadian word present in the text.

[31] Herdner, *Ugaritica* VII (1978) 50, 58. Line 30 in Herdner's edition, line 55 in *KTU*.

or RBM, with preference for the first form. I have been unable to find a reconstruction that fits the traces and the context. It could have been any organ or limb, internal or external.

Regarding the word $\underline{d}r^c$, there is general agreement that it is cognate to Hebrew *zera*[c], "seed," not to Hebrew *zĕrōa*[c], "arm,"[32] but all of the authors cited above, apparently including Herdner,[33] give to $\underline{d}r^c$ the nuance of "offspring" in this line and in its two previous occurrences in this text (both in lines even more broken than this one[34]). But the very close parallel with the Deuteronomy passage has led me to believe that the reference in the Ugaritic text may well be to "seed-grain" or simply to "grain" in all three occurrences, with the strongest case to be made for line 55′.[35] Unfortunately, the modality of destruction is not stated as explicitly in the Ugaritic passage as in Deuteronomy 28. We know from such texts as *PRU* V 59 that $\underline{d}r^c$ was shipped by sea and was thus liable to destruction by water.[36] Was *ḥsl* so general that such forms of destruction would have been understood as subsumed under a statement like $\underline{d}r^c$ *ḥwt hyt yḥsl* or does the development of a word for locust in Hebrew based on that root imply a nuance of destruction by devouring? The Amarna text refers to general destruction (cities are destroyed) as do the other two uses of the verb in the Ugaritic text under discussion[37] and data are at present insufficient, therefore, for a definite answer to that question. In my translation of the Ugaritic omen text, I have

---

[32] In addition to the authors cited in n. 1, see P. Bordreuil, A. Caquot, "Les Textes en cunéiformes alphabétiques découverts en 1978 à Ibn Hani," *Syria* 57 (1980) 343–73, esp. 357, dealing with the occurrence of $\underline{d}r^c$ in a letter in the Ugaritic language from Ras Ibn Hani.

[33] I say "apparently" because she uses only the word "seed" (*semence*) in her translation and commentary, but cites two texts in support of that sense, in one of which "seed" has the nuance of "offspring" (the Merneptah stele; see, for example, *ANET*[2,3], p. 378, n. 18) in the other that of "(seed-)grain" (part of this text is cited here below in n. 36).

[34] 14) *[w] 'in 'uškm bḥ* $\underline{d}\dot{r}[^c$------]̣

"[And] (if) it has no testicles, the see[d(-grain?) . . .]"

. . .

43′) *[*   *] lr'iš̌h* $\underline{d}r^c$*mlk hwt*
44′) *[*   *]ḥ̣*

43′) "[. . .]on its head, the seed(-grain)? of that king (44′) [. . .]."

[35] The case of line 43′ is less clear, for the verb is missing; it is not at all impossible that the nuance there is "progeny." The reference could, however, be to plantings in the king's fields or, if $\underline{d}r^c$ had taken on the nuance of a commodity, the $\underline{d}r^c$ of the king could refer to a commercial undertaking (cf. next note).

[36] C. Virolleaud, *Le Palais Royal d'Ugarit* (Mission de Ras Shamra 11; Paris: Klincksieck, 1965) text 59 = *KTU* 2.38. Lines 10–18 READ (MY COLLATION): 10) *'anykn dt* (11) *l'ikt mṣrm* (12) *hndt b ṣr* (13) *mtt by* (14) *gṡm 'adr* (15) *nškḥ* (16) *rb tmtt* (17) *lqḥ kl* $\underline{d}r^c$ (18) *bdnḥm*, "The ship which you sent to Egypt was disabled off Tyre. They were caught in a bad storm. The salvage-master has removed all of the (seed-?)grain in their containers."

[37] The other two occurrences are in lines 35–38, cited above, note to *šdd* (line 35′).

preferred the translation "consume" because of the Deuteronomy passage and in order to provide lexical relief in a text characterized by verbs of destruction.[38]

Whether or not the verb *ḥsl* has the specific meaning "to consume," the association of *ḥsl* and of *ḏr'/zr'* in the Ugaritic and Hebrew texts is mutually illuminating because of the common features of the two contexts. Though the omen *genre* certainly is not identical to the curse *genre* in Deuteronomy 28, they share a common "if . . . then" perspective.[39] Moreover, the prognosis in both *genres* may be either positive or negative; the deciding factor is legal/cultic/ethical in Deuteronomy, quasi-magical in the omen literature. In the two texts being compared and contrasted here, *ḥsl* applied to *ḏr'/zr'* constitutes a negative prognosis. This shared perspective on cause and effect and the shared negativity of the prognosis in both cases are sufficient to provide quite a specific background to the Deuteronomy passage: at Ugarit, if a lamb or a kid was born without any -KB, the seed, the grain, or the seed-grain would be consumed/destroyed; in Israel, if YHWH's statutes were not observed, the seed-grain would be consumed by locusts.

'zz 'l in Judg 3:10

Again on the basis of a personal communication from Virolleaud, Gordon[40] was able to cite the phrase *mlkn y'zz 'l ḥpṯ* (line 57′), "The king (of the homeland) will prevail over his *ḥupṯu*-troops," and he cited as a parallel Judg 3:10 *wattā'oz yādô 'al kûšan riš'ātayim*, "His power prevailed over Kushan Rishatayim."

Some of these comparisons were original with me; most were not. I sincerely hope that this accumulation of parallels from an obscure Ugaritic text for several words and passages in Biblical Hebrew and in other dialects will have been relatively complete and that the collection of minor lights will constitute a light bright enough to irradiate with philological pleasure a few moments of Prof. Fitzmyer's life.

---

[38] *ql*, "to fall"; *b'r* ,"to burn/destroy"; *ḥlq*, "to perish/destroy"; *dll*, "to languish/lay low"; *šdd*, "to devastate"; *špl*, "to be/lay low"; *rps*, "to tread under"; *prš*, "to scatter," are all attested in this relatively brief and badly damaged text.

[39] Deut 28:1, *wĕhāyâ 'im-šāmôa' tišma';* v. 15, *wĕhāyâ 'im-lō' tišma'*. The hypothetical particle is not extant in the present state of the main Ugaritic omen text cited here but is almost certainly to be restored in line 1 (see remarks here above).

[40] *UT* §19.1835.

Part II

Hebrew Bible

Narrative and Lament in Isaiah 63:7-64:11

Richard J. Clifford, S.J.
Weston School of Theology

Then Moses his servant
remembered the days of old.
Isaiah 63:11

IN A COLLECTION OF PROPHETIC SPEECHES in which the boundaries of virtually every one are contested, the scholarly consensus that 63:7–64:11 forms a single composition is remarkable. Consensus is possible, one suspects, because the passage contains all the conventions of a communal lament, satisfying scholars who prefer form criticism for analyzing Third Isaiah, and also artistically develops a single theme, satisfying scholars whose method is stylistic and rhetorical analysis.[1] This essay affirms the case for unity by pointing out several features of the genre and of the rhetoric that have gone unnoticed or been given a different interpretation. Our discussion will suggest that at least some of the supposed glosses and additions are in fact part of the original composition.

It is a pleasure to explore an OT theme in honoring Father Joseph A. Fitzmyer, S.J., whose scholarly interests and competence range far beyond his well-known specialties of New Testament and Aramaic language and literature.

---

[1] Many form critics, to be sure, see the composition as the final stage of several redactions. K. Pauritsch has a good review of the literature (*Die neue Gemeinde: Gott sammelt Ausgestossene und Arme (Jesaia 56–66)* [AnBib 47; Rome: Pontifical Biblical Institute, 1971] 144–71). Claus Westermann suspects that 63:11 began the psalm, in its older form (*Isaiah 40–66* [Philadelphia: Westminster, 1969] 386). R. Kuntzman believes that vv 8–10 were written later than vv 11–14 ("Une relecture de 'salut' en Is. 63,7–14," *RevScRel* 51 [1977] 22–39).

We restrict our detailed observations to the two sections of the composition that are most controverted, the historical recital of 63:7–14 and the prayer for the heavens to open in 63:19c–64:4b (Eng. 64:1–5b).

63:7–14 is a historical recital, a regular feature of communal laments (Pss 44:2–9; 74:12–17; 77:12–21; 80:9–12; 83:10–13; 89:2–38). To put into their proper context the several text-critical and interpretive problems of the Isaian text, we first examine the function of historical recitals in communal laments. The presence of such recitals in communal laments has long been noted; they are generally interpreted as highlighting the tragedy of the present by con- trasting it with the glorious past.[2] Such an explanation, however, does not go far enough. It explains neither the length of the historical recitals in relation to the whole lament nor their enormous variety of detail. The historical part of Psalm 77, for example, vv 12–21 (counting the invocation), is fully one half the psalm; it describes the cosmic battle, passage through the Sea, and appointment of Moses and Aaron as leaders. Ps 89:2–38 describes Yahweh's victory over Sea and ordering of the universe climaxing in the installation of the king; it is two-thirds of the lament.[3] Psalm 74 devotes six of its twenty- three verses (vv 12–17) to Yahweh's slaying of Leviathan and arrangement of the world. Ps 80:9–12, the transplanting of the vine in Canaan, is a fifth of that psalm. The history recital in Isa 63:7–64:11 is close to 40 percent of the lament. Surely if the psalmists intended simple contrast of past glory and present misery, they could have done so directly and economically by an allu- sion to the glorious events of the past. As an explanation for the elaborate and diverse histories, contrast alone is insufficient.

The answer to the question why the psalmists put such emphasis and artistry into the historical recital can only be that they carefully tailored the historical recital to fit the aim of the lament. Selection of details of the "days of old"–the exodus-conquest (or the cosmogonic victory) that founds Israel – differs in each lament according to what is being lamented. Psalm 89, lamenting the defeat of the Davidic king by his enemies, "remembers" Yahweh's sharing the fruits of his cosmogonic victory with David, making him 'elyôn among the kings of the earth[4] by an unconditional oath; the history

---

[2] H. Gunkel, *Einleitung in den Psalmen* (3d ed.; Göttingen: Vandenhoeck & Ruprecht, 1977) 129–30; S. Mowinckel, *The Psalms* (New York: Abingdon, 1967) 1. 196–97, 205; C. Westermann, *The Praise of God in the Psalms* (Richmond: Knox, 1965) 55–57. The authors see the psalms' mention of the old saving events as motives to persuade God to act now in like manner. None explores in detail how the history is related to the prayer.

[3] For discussion and recent bibliography, see my "Psalm 89: A Lament over the Davidic Ruler's Continued Failure," *HTR* 73 (1980) 35–47.

[4] J.-B. Dumortier demonstrated the point-by-point sharing of the cosmogonic victory with David ("Un rituel d'intronisation: Le Ps LXXXIX:2–38," *VT* 11 (1962) 187).

raises in acute form the problem of royal defeats. Psalm 74 retells the divine ordering of the paired elements of the universe that is now threatened by the destruction of one of its basic elements, the Temple. Psalm 77, sung by an individual for the community doubting the ancient promises to the people, recites the story of Yahweh's visible superiority over all gods and nations by his bringing the people through the hostile waters to their land and appointing their leaders. It poses the question: Why is the founding event without effect now? Psalm 44 tells of Yahweh's conquest of the land as it asks why Israel's enemies move at will through Canaan.

The freedom in selecting details is all the more remarkable since it is essentially the same event that is recalled in all the psalms: the creation of Israel as Yahweh's people, shown to be Yahweh's by their living in his land (or around his shrine) according to his law and under his leaders.[5] That creative act can be depicted in a variety of ways, e.g., the transplanting of his vine from Egypt to Canaan (Psalm 80), the defeat of chaotic Waters and the installation of the king (Psalm 89), but most frequently as the exodus-conquest, depicted either from a "suprahistoric" perspective of the defeat of Sea (which bars the people from their land), or from a "historic" perspective of predominantly human actors, Moses, Aaron, the people, Pharaoh, the Egyptians.

Isaiah 63:7-14

Isa 63:8-14, like the psalmic laments, narrates its own version of the founding events: the divine choosing and guidance from Egypt by Yahweh's presence (*pānāyw*). It differs from most laments, however, by including among the founding events the people's apostasy, Moses' intercession, and the return of the presence (in the form of Yahweh's holy spirit and glorious arm). In this it resembles Psalm 106, a communal lament, which also records the people's sin and Moses' (and Aaron's) successful intercession.[6] As in other historical recitals in laments the selection of details—Yahweh's gracious presence, his withdrawal because of sin, and his return (*tērēd*, "[the spirit] descended," in 63:14b; see the translation below) after Moses' intercession—

---

[5] "What is 're-presented' are not isolated incidents in history but rather something that had happened which was on-going and all-inclusive, viz., the deliverance at the beginning, as for example in the Credo of Deut. 26 where it is told as a unified story. It is a history which takes place between God and the people. It is to this on-going event that the 're-presentation' of historical events in the Psalms refers, even if only a single event is named" (Claus Westermann, "The 'Re-presentation' of History in the Psalms," in *Praise and Lament in the Psalms* [trans. K. R. Crim and R. N. Soulen; Atlanta: Knox, 1981] 246).

[6] There are several features common to the two laments: rebellion, *mārâ* (Ps 106:7; Isa 63:10); Yahweh acting for the sake of his name (Ps 106:8; Isa 63:12, 14); the privileges of Moses (Ps 106:16-18; Isa 63:11-12); and his intercession (Ps 106:23; Isa 63:11-12).

is tailored to the aim of the lament. The prayer following the recital, 63:15–64:11, asks that Yahweh in heaven come down (*yāradtā*, 63:19) to the people from his holy and glorious dwelling (63:15), precisely the adjectives describing the divine presence in vv 10–12. The prayer repeats other elements of the recital: the question "where?," *'ayyēh*, the divine epithet *gō'ēl*, "redeemer"; it also alludes to *bānîm*, "children," of v. 8. 63:17–64:11 complains that the people's meeting place with Yahweh, the Temple, is in ruins (63:18; 64:9, 10), dramatizing God's absence. The ancient story of Moses' success in persuading Yahweh to come down among the people is exactly appropriate to the prayer of a people experiencing God's absence.

The brief review of the function of historical recitals in communal laments has been necessary to establish a context for examining the details of 63:7–14. Verse 7 is the speaker's invocation and vv. 8–14 are what the speaker "remembers" (*'azkîr*); the meaning of the term is the same as in Ps 77:12–13, in which the speaker remembers vv. 14–21. Verses 8–14 are given unity and shape by artistic repetition, shown below by the transliterated Hebrew: repetition of key words (*hēmmâ, yĕmê 'ôlām*) and of similar sounding phrases (*lāhem lĕmôšîa'* and *lāhem lĕ'ôyēb, hû' gĕ'ālām* and *hû' nilham bām*); note also the shift from *pānāyw* to *rûah qodšô* and *zĕrôa' tipartô*).

> ⁷The loving deeds of Yahweh I will remember,
>   the praiseworthy acts of Yahweh —
> For all that Yahweh did for us,
>   the great goodness to the house of Israel —
> Which he did in accord with his mercy,
>   in accord with his great love.
> ⁸He said, "Surely my people are they (*hēmmâ*),
>   children who will not deal falsely."
> He became their Savior (*lāhem lĕmôšîa'*)
>   ⁹in all their adversities.
> No envoy, no messenger,
>   but his presence (*pānāyw*) saved them.⁷
> In his love and his pity,
>   he redeemed them (*hû' gĕ'ālām*).
> He picked them up and carried them,
>   all the days of old (*yĕmê 'ôlām*).
> ¹⁰But they (*hēmmâ*) rebelled and grieved
>   his holy spirit (*rûah qodšô*).
> He turned to become their enemy (*lāhem lĕ'ôyēb*).
> He made war against them (*hû' nilham bām*).

---

⁷ The OG *ou presbys oude angelos all'autos kyrios esōsen autous* correctly interprets Hebrew *ṣr* as defectively written *ṣîr*. So most commentators.

[11]Then remembered the days of old (*yĕmê 'ôlām*)
Moses his servant.[8]
"Where is the one who brought up[9] from the Waters
the shepherd[10] of his people?
Where is the one who placed in his midst[11]
his holy spirit (*rûaḥ qodšô*)?
[12]The one who caused to walk at the right hand of Moses
his glorious arm (*zĕrôa' tipartô*)?
(Where is) the one who split the Waters before them,
to make for himself an eternal name,
[13]the one who caused them to walk through the deeps
like a horse in the steppe?
They did not stumble,
[14]like a beast in the plain."[12]

---

[8] The MT is senseless with "Moses his people (*mōšeh 'ammô*)." The OG omits *mōšeh 'ammô* '*ayyēh*, "Moses his people where," either from haplography of *mēm*, or, more probably, to avoid a senseless reading. At any rate, it smooths out the sense in *kai emnēsthē hēmerōn aiōniōn ho anabibasis ek tēs gēs*. The best solution is to assume that the original *bêt* and *dālet* of '*abdô* were read as *mēm*, which could easily have happened in the "archaic proto-Jewish" hand of the mid-third century B.C., in which the *bêt* resembles the right stroke of the *mēm*, and the slant of the *dālet* and its open top resemble the left downward stroke of the *mēm*. For the illustration of the script, see. F. M. Cross, "The Development of the Jewish Scripts," in *The Bible and the Ancient Near East: Essays in Honor of William Foxwell Albright* (ed. G. E. Wright; Garden City, NY: Doubleday, 1961) 175, fig. 1, line 3. Presumably the confusion arose before the Greek translation, since the Greek presupposes confusion here.

The resulting word order, "remembered the days of old Moses his servant," is exceptional: verb-object-subject. It serves to emphasize *yĕmê 'ôlām* as the frame of v. 10.

The crucial question is: Who is the subject of *yizkōr*—Moses, the people, or Yahweh? The people cannot be the subject syntactically since they are referred to in the plural in the immediately preceding verse and in v. 12. It cannot be Yahweh since the complaints of vv. 11c–14a would be left hanging without a speaker. Moses is the obvious subject. He intercedes as he does in the Pentateuchal laments. *Yizkōr* is used precisely as in Ps 77:12—to recall the founding events of the past.

[9] The final *mēm* of *hamma'ālēm* could be dittography or a final *mî* particle. The reference may be to the pulling of Moses out of the water in Exodus 2; more probably, it is a conventional expression for rescuing from straits, as in Pss 18:17; 40:3; 30:4; 71:20; Jonah 2:7.

[10] We read *rō'eh* for MT *rō'ê*, according to sense.

[11] Hebrew *bĕqirbô* seems to refer to Moses, deferentially referring to himself in the third person; the people elsewhere are referred to in the plural. In Ps 51:12, *wĕrûaḥ nākôn haddēš bĕqirbî*, the psalmist refers to himself as *bĕqirbî*. The OG, with *en autois*, "among them," fails to understand the sequence—Moses, then the people—of the complaint.

[12] We depart from the MT order and the order of most modern translations and follow the OG *katebē pneuma para kyrios*. The corrected division yields an AB/AB pattern for vv. 13–14a. "They did not stumble" parallels "causes to walk." "Not to stumble" parallels verbs of motion in Isa 5:26–27; 40:30–31; Prov 4:12. Jer 31:9 is the best parallel: *'ôlîkēm 'el naḥălê mayim // bĕderek yāšār lō' yikkāšēlû bāh*, "I will cause them to walk by brooks of water, // in a straight path they

> Yahweh's spirit came down,[13]
> and gave him rest.[14]
> Thus did you lead your people,
> to make for yourself a glorious name.

Verses 8-9 describe a specific act: the divine declaration that makes the people Yahweh's, like the divine declarations in Exod 3:7-8; 19:5-6; 20:2-3; Yahweh will be their saving God, *wayĕhî lāhem lĕmôšîa*.[15] Divine choice means God's very self, *pānāyw*, will guide them, which, as vv. 11-12 show, is mediated through the person of Moses. That presence is expressed in the following verses as "his holy spirit" (vv. 10, 11) and "his glorious arm" (v. 12). The lifting and carrying of the people in v. 9 draw on ancient traditions like Exod 19:4 and Deut 32:11; Second Isaiah exploits the image in 40:11 and especially in chap. 46. Verse 10 collapses into a single act the rebellions that are recorded separately in Exodus 32-34, Numbers, and Deuteronomy 1-2.[16] (Verses 11-14 similarly condense the punishments and Mosaic

---

shall not stumble." *'Ôlîkēm*, therefore, is "to cause to walk *freely*." There is an equal syllable count in the redivision: 8:5//5:8.

[13] Verse 14b-d is the response to Moses' complaint of vv. 11-14a: the presence comes down as spirit. *Yārad*, "come down," admittedly is not used elsewhere in the OT to describe the descent of the spirit of God, but in Exod 33:9 the pillar of cloud "comes down" upon the Tent whenever Moses enters it, and in Num 11:25 Yahweh "comes down" and takes some of the spirit from Moses to share with the seventy elders. One must assume the *wāw* conversive before *tērēd* has dropped out, perhaps through haplography of the last part of the preceding *hē* or the first part of the succeeding *tāw*, possibilities in the third-century script mentioned in n. 8.

[14] The MT *tĕnîhennû* ("gave him rest") makes acceptable sense. Like the speech of Yahweh to Moses in Num 33:14, "My presence will go and give you rest," Moses receives the assurance of the divine presence for the whole people. For the verb with suffix, see Prov 25:17. In our understanding, the spirit rests on Moses as representative of the people. The Greek *ōdēgēsen autous*, "it led them," and the Syriac and targum seem to have read *tanḥēm*, "it led them."

[15] Some scholars separate vv. 8-10 from vv. 11-14 on the grounds that it is a general history of the chosen people ending in division from God and that vv. 11-14 are a specific historical retrospect, depicting particulars of the ancient days, e.g, Paul Volz, *Jesaia II* (KAT 9/2; Leipzig: School, 1932) 267. Volz also corrects *yizkōr* to *'azkîr*, to make it a reprise of v. 7a. P. D. Hanson follows Volz's emendation (*The Dawn of Apocalyptic* [Philadelphia: Fortress, 1975] 81, 84). R. Kuntzman does not emend but considers vv. 8-10 a later meditation based on vv. 11-14 ("Une relecture," 28). Such a disjunction fails to recognize the specificity of v. 8; the divine declaration is not a summary but an act, like the declarations in Exodus 19 and Deuteronomy 32.

[16] Several scholars understand the rebellion in v. 10 to be general, "referring in general terms to Israel's whole history of rebellion and its culmination in the disasters of the Assyrian and Babylonian conquests which are seen as due to Yahweh's deliberate instigation" (R. N. Whybray, *Isaiah 40-66* [NCB; Grand Rapids: Eerdmans, 1981] 258). So also Paul D. Hanson, *The Dawn of Apocalyptic*, 89; and P.-E. Bonnard, *Le Second Isaie* (EBib; Paris: Gabalda, 1972) 450. Bernhard Duhm refers the rebellion primarily to the Mosaic age, but includes in it the rebellions of the tribal and monarchic periods (*Das Buch Jesaja* [5th ed.; Göttingen: Vandenhoeck &

intercessions). Verse 10 is central in vv.7–14 not only by its position (eight bicola precede and eight follow it) but also by its careful reprise of vv. 8–9 (shown in the transliterations above) and by its shifting the traditional *pānāyw* of v. 9 to *rûaḥ qodšô* of vv. 10–11. It is framed by *yĕmê 'ôlām* of vv. 9 and 11.[17]

The complaint of Moses in vv. 11–14a is remarkable in that in vv. 11c–12b he appeals first to his own privilege as servant,[18] and only then in vv. 12c–14a speaks directly of the salvation of the people that involves the public honor of Yahweh (*šēm 'ôlām* in v. 12d and *šēm tiparet* in v. 14d). The same distinction between Moses' appeal to his own relationship to God and his appeal to God's honor for the sake of the people is found also in Moses' intercessions in Exodus.

> On the next day Moses said to the people, "You have committed a great sin. Yet now I will go up to Yahweh; perhaps I can atone for your sin." And Moses went back to Yahweh and said, "Alas, this people has committed a great sin by making for themselves gods of gold. And now, please forgive their sin. If not, blot me out, I pray, from the book you have written." And Yahweh said to Moses, "Only the one who has sinned against me will I erase from my book. Go now and lead the people where I have told you. See, my angel will go before you." (Exod 32:30–34)

> And now, if perhaps I have found favor in your eyes, show me please your way, that I may know you and find favor in your eyes. Realize too that this nation is your people. And he said, "I (*pānay*) will go with you and I will give you (sg.) rest." And he said to him, "If you yourself (*pāneykā*) do not go, do not bring us up from here. How shall it be known that I have found favor in your eyes, I and your people. . . ." (Exod 33:13–16)

> And he said, "If I have found favor in your eyes, O Lord, may the Lord go in our midst. Yes, they are a stiff-necked people. Pardon our iniquities and sins and take us as your own." (Exod 34:9).

In the Exodus passages, Moses reminds God of his commitment to his servant. How can God call him, equip him for leading the people, and then

---

Ruprecht, 1968] 467). In our view, since Moses is the intercessor in vv. 11–14, the rebellion must have occurred during his ministry. The text does not say which rebellion is meant among the many of the Pentateuch. Deut 1:26–2:16 interprets the refusal to enter the land (Numbers 13–14) as a rebellion punished by Yahweh's fighting against them as their enemy; it might have served as the model for v. 10.

[17] As is shown by the transliterations in the translation, v. 10 sums up what has gone before. *hēmmâ* picks up *hēmmâ* of v. 8a; *rûaḥ qodšô* picks up *pānāyw* of v. 9 and points forward to *rûaḥ qodšô* of v. 11f. and to *zĕrôa 'tipartô* of v. 12b; *wayyēhāpēk lāhem lĕ'ôyēb* reverses *wayĕhî lāhem lĕmôšîa'* of v. 8c; *hû' nilḥam bām* echoes *hû' gĕ'ālām* of v. 9e.

[18] The servant's reference to himself in the third person is well attested, e.g., 1 Sam 26:19–20 and 2 Sam 7:18–29. Samuel even refers to himself by name in his speech in 1 Sam 12:11.

allow him to fail in his task?[19] Speaking in the third person appropriate to a servant speaking to his lord, he complains of the absence now of the one who drew him up from danger to be the shepherd of his people (v. 11cd), the one who made him the mediator of his holy spirit (v. 11ef), the one who accompanied him with his glorious arm (v. 12ab). Only then does he speak of the divine deeds on behalf of the people, the splitting of the sea and the guidance in the wilderness (vv. 12c–14a), which were performed to glorify his name (*šēm 'ôlām*), precisely the distinction of the Pentateuchal sources cited above.

The lament of the people under Moses has a happy result (v. 14b): a fresh descent of the spirit to guide the people. The giving of the spirit brings about renewed guidance in v. 14 and, by implication, safe arrival and settlement in the land where Yahweh dwells. Later in the lament, in 64:9–10, the people will complain that the shrine is in ruins, with the implied question: Will you let the sacred precincts to which you led your people remain in ruins?

The history, therefore, has been designed with an eye to the aim of the entire lament. The presence (*pānāyw*), which in the course of the recital becomes the spirit and the arm of Yahweh, is as central in the recital as it will be in the prayer that follows in 63:15–64:11. It is to descend among the beleaguered people and guide them along the right path.

Isaiah 63:19c–64:4b

We now turn to one section of the prayer to see how the historical recital has influenced it. The prayer continues the strategy of the recital. The coming down of the spirit that leads Israel home in 63:14 prepares for the prayer of 63:15–19b to "God above." The prayer emphasizes that God is in the heavens like another exilic prayer, 1 Kgs 8:46–51. The address to God as Father in 63:16 is one of the few addresses to Yahweh under that title in the OT. As the reprise of the term in 64:7 shows, father means creator, the one who brought forth the "children" of 63:8. God has brought the people into being by his declaration that they are his children.[20] The prayer asks: Will you, the creator, remain distant from your creation?

The prayer section also speaks several times of Yahweh's hostility to the people (63:17–19; 64:4cd, 6cd, 8, 11), a reference back to Yahweh's fighting against them in the history (63:10): "He turned to become their enemy. He

---

[19] Moses' prominence may have a Deutero-Isaian meaning. It is generally recognized that the Deutero-Isaian servant has Mosaic traits; in 49:1–12, for example, the servant is called to lead a new exodus–conquest. For further reflections on the role of Moses from the perspective of the party strife in the period, see Hanson, *Dawn of Apocalyptic*, 94–98.

[20] The OT avoids the term "father" probably because it has the sense of divine begetting that it has when used of El and Asherah in the Ugaritic texts. El is called there "the father of gods and humans."

made war against them." The prayer declares the people to be in the same situation of enmity to God that the ancestors were in before their lament was answered.

63:19c-64:4b impressively prays for the spirit to descend (*yāradtā*) as in days of old; "that you would come down" echoes *tērēd* in 63:14.

> 63:19Oh that you would split the heavens and come down,
>   that before you the mountains would quake—
> 64:1As fire enkindles brushwood,
>   causing water to boil21 —
> To make known your name to your enemies,
>   that the nations might tremble before you.
> 2As you do wonders we do not expect,22
>   —you came down, before you mountains quaked—
> 3what was never heard of,
>   nor perceived by the ear,
> what no eye had seen, O God, except yours,
>   who act for those who wait for you.
> 4Oh23 that you would encounter24 those who rejoice in doing good
>   who remember your ways.25

The psalmist hopes that the community lament will be answered by a theophany as in days of old—the return of the presence of Yahweh in the

---

21 The verse seems corrupt. The picture may resemble Ps 18:13 and Ps 83:15.

22 The verse seems to rework Isaiah 48.

> 6I declare new things at the present time,
>   well-guarded secrets you do not know.
> 7Now they are created, not in the time of old,
>   before today, you have not heard them,
>   so you could say, "I already knew it."
> 8You have not heard, you have not known,
>   your ears were not opened hitherto.

The hoped-for descent of God from the heavens is an instance of the Deutero-Isaian "new things," utterly new, not predicted. The lament prays for full realization of the Deutero-Isaian promises.

23 Reading *lû'*, omitted by haplography, with several commentators.

24 The verse is controverted. Some take *pāga'tā* in a hostile sense—that is, God is so much an enemy as to attack even those who do good—and join the verse to the following complaint in vv. 5c-7 (*NJV*). "To meet," like other Hebrew verbs of solemn encounter (e.g., *qaddēm*), can be used in a hostile or friendly sense; here it probably means "encounter (favorably) in a shrine," as in Gen 28:32. The shrine is the normal place of solemn divine–human encounter. It thus concludes the prayer for Yahweh's coming.

25 With the OG *kai tōn hodōn mnēsthēsontai*, "and remember your ways." The verse could be an allusion Moses' remembering in 63:11; God will descend on those who remember his deeds, or ways, of old.

midst of the people, a presence that will make possible divine–human encounter.

The lament, like other exilic and postexilic prayers, imagines apostasy and forgiveness to be part of the formative ancient days. It presents the pattern of gracious divine deed, popular apostasy, Mosaic intercession and return of the spirit, to the contemporary community as a sign of hope and a model of prayer. The lamenter, who may even see himself playing the role of the Deutero-Isaian Moses-like servant, asks that the spirit come down on the people today as it came upon the people of old.

Chapter 9 Eighth-Century Prophets and Apodictic Law

Joseph Jensen, O.S.B.
The Catholic University of America

Hear the word of the Lord,
Princes of Sodom!
Listen to the instruction of
our God, people of Gomorrah!

. . . .

Cease doing evil;
learn to do good.
Make justice your aim:
Redress the wronged.
Hear the orphan's plea,
defend the widow.

Isaiah 1:10, 16–17

NOT TOO MANY YEARS AGO it seemed that Israel's legal tradition was the only one taken into account in assessing OT ethical teaching, often to the neglect of the prophets and the wisdom tradition.[1] One author went so far as to say that "everything the prophets have to say on social responsibility seems to presuppose the tradition of the law" and went on to conclude that "this makes it possible to discuss the subject of social responsibility in the OT without looking into the prophets."[2] One of the criticisms of the OT section of the CTSA report on human sexuality[3] was that it dealt too exclusively with legislation, to the neglect of the wisdom and prophetic traditions.[4] Some authors not only attempt to trace prophetic exhortations to Israel's legislation, but even specifically to apodictic law.

---

[1] The "not too many years ago" qualification would not even apply in some cases; the fairly recent work of W. C. Kaiser, whose title, *Toward Old Testament Ethics* (Grand Rapids: Zondervan, 1983), suggests covering the whole OT field, has four chapters on the principal law codes but no explicit treatment of the prophets or wisdom.

[2] H. Eberhard von Waldow, "Social Responsibility and Social Structure in Early Israel," *CBQ* 32 (1970) 182. In spite of this rather incautious statement, there is much that is excellent in the article, and the author does, in fact, deal with the prophets (pp. 203–4), though even here the reference is to "the will of God, which was known by the legal tradition" and to the legal tradition being "the basis for the doom" which the prophets announce.

[3] A. Kosnik et al., *Human Sexuality* (New York: Paulist, 1977).

[4] J. Jensen, O.S.B., and Carroll Stuhlmueller, C.P., "The Relevance of the Old Testament," in *Dimensions of Human Sexuality: A Critical Response* (New York: Doubleday, 1979) 5–7.

Thesis of Bach, Bergren, and Others

R. V. Bergren,[5] for example, taking his starting point from a work of R. Bach, who held that accusations of Amos based on law were based solely on *apodictic* law,[6] asks whether the same is true of prophetic accusation in general, and comes to the conclusion that where law is the basis of a prophetic accusation, such accusation is grounded solely in apodictic law.[7] Bach had contented himself with investigating specific examples in Amos and concluding that parallels were found only in apodictic law, never in casuistic law;[8] he concluded that in Amos's day these two streams were still separate and that Amos's use of apodictic law shows his preaching to have been closely connected with the covenant.[9] Bergren's approach goes far beyond this. He accepts Mendenhall's distinction between "policy" and "technique" with reference to law (pp. 32–34) and, using Mendenhall terminology, asserts that the prophetic judgment speech presupposes a situation where legal sanctions and legal techniques have failed, a situation in which an offense has been committed that the deity will punish because the community failed to use the means available for protecting itself (p. 41). The framework that validates the laws is the Sinai tradition of covenant between Israel and Yahweh (p. 44). Elsewhere he asserts that "the law was part of the covenant between Yahweh and Israel" (pp. 91, 101, 125). Details of his argumentation relate to (1) use of

---

[5] Bergren, *The Prophets and the Law* (HUCAMS 4; Cincinnati and New York: Hebrew Union College-Jewish Institute of Religion, 1974).

[6] Bach, "Gottesrecht und weltliches Recht in der Verkündigung des Propheten Amos," *Festschrift für Günther Dehn* (ed. W. Schneemelcher; Neukirchen: Verlag der Buchhandlung des Erziehungsvereins Neukirchen Kreis Moers, 1957) 23–34.

[7] Bergren, *The Prophets,* 76. Bergren goes so far as to assert that Jer 34:13–20 is the only possible instance of prophetic judgment based on casuistic law (cf. Exod 21:2–6 and Deut 15:12–18), but then he concludes that that is not the case, that the violation of the covenant is the sufficient explanation here (ibid.).

[8] Bach, "Gottesrecht," 33–34. It can be pointed out that the sort of accusations Amos makes are most often in more general terms (mistreatment of the poor, etc.), the kind of thing we find in apodictic law, rather than the specific kind of cases casuistic law treats of. Moreover, Bach never asks if parallels exist outside the legal tradition, e.g., in wisdom. He does see an allusion to casuistic law in Amos 3:12 (cf. Exod 22:12), but not as a basis for accusation.

[9] It is difficult to conceive how Bach dates the Covenant Code, which incorporates both apodictic and casuistic law and is usually dated to the period of the Tribal League. The attempt of A. Phillips ("Prophecy and Law," in *Israel's Prophetic Tradition: Essays in Honor of Peter R. Ackroyd* [ed. R. Coggins, A. Phillips, and M. Knibb; Cambridge: Cambridge University Press, 1982] 233—already asserted in *Ancient Israel's Criminal Law* [New York: Schocken, 1970] 159–61) to see the Covenant Code as "a handbook of justice for the new Davidic state" runs counter to most scholarly opinion and rests largely on the assumption that similarity of content identifies the source—the kind of assumption that is being questioned in the present article. See below pp. 105, 114, and esp. n. 45.

the term *peša'*, which he claims "is a treaty expression which signifies a treaty has been violated" (p. 117); (2) use of the verb *yd'*, which also "has a treaty background" (p. 118); (3) treaty curse parallels in announcements of disaster (p. 95); and (4) examples of the covenant lawsuit in the prophets (pp. 126–27). Antecedent to and concomitant with these arguments, he also gives examples of prophetic parallels to specific apodictic laws.

One methodological objection can be raised at the outset. These authors seldom ask about the dating of the collections of laws they cite, much less about individual laws; yet before parallels with specific laws can be claimed, there should be adequate reason for holding that that law was in force at the time in question. Place should also be a consideration to be taken in conjunction with time. The Covenant Code, for example, is usually conceded to be early, from the time of the Tribal League;[10] however, it seems to have been largely a northern code, and the extent to which it was in effect in Judah is a matter of doubt. The promulgation of the Deuteronomic Code was in Judah in the late seventh century; some of its provisions are undoubtedly older, but it cannot be assumed that they all are. So also many provisions of the Holiness Code were no doubt earlier than the sixth-century date assigned to its final crystallization, but it is a matter of determining which ones. The point being made here is that it is not legitimate to assume that any time a prophet condemns behavior forbidden in an apodictic (or any other kind of) law, he is basing his condemnation on that law. As H. McKeating points out, it is normal for the same offense to be discouraged by whole batteries of sanctions, operating in a variety of social spheres, and that lawmakers, prophets, and wisdom writers may all appeal to different sets of sanctions.[11]

This brings us to a further methodological consideration. A prophet's condemnation of a crime cannot be related to an apodictic (or other) law because they both relate to the same crime, but only if (and even then, not necessarily) there is close similarity in terminology. For example, Bergren cites four law texts, Exod 22:20–21; 23:9; Lev 19:13; and Deut 24:14 as the Pentateuchal legislation for three Isaiah texts concerning oppression of the poor, Isa 1:17; 3:15; and 10:1. In fact, the only terminology the Isaiah passages have in common with the four law texts are the words for "widow" and "orphan" in Exod 22:21 and Isa 1:17 and *'ānî* in Deut 24:14 (sg.) and Isa 3:15 (pl.). If one extends his last Isaiah text a verse to 10:1–2, another reference to "widow," "orphan," and *'ānî* (all pl.) can be added. There is no coincidence

---

[10] This does not prevent von Waldow from seeing a number of Priestly reinterpretations added, which he relates to a later period ("Social Responsibility," 197–203).

[11] McKeating, "Sanctions against Adultery in Ancient Israelite Society, with Some Reflections on Methodology in the Study of Old Testament Ethics," *JSOT* 11 (1979) 57–72.

of verbs from any of the legal texts to any of the Isaiah texts. This is meager grounds for claiming apodictic law as the grounds for Isaiah's accusations!

Bergren is no better off in arguing for a covenant connection because of the use of *pešaʿ*. He asserts that *pešaʿ* indicates an action which violates a treaty relationship and that in the prophets the content of *pešaʿ* is often apodictic law.[12] It is true that *pešaʿ* sometimes occurs in a context in which the crime involved would amount to infringement of covenant, but this is far from providing a basis for asserting that its use necessarily points to a covenant violation. In fact, it is used in countless instances where there is no reason to suspect covenant influence.[13] Basically *pešaʿ* is a very general term for a wicked act, as the words with which it is used in parallel[14] indicate, which in some cases (probably a minority of cases) designates a transgression against the covenant. Bergren pays special attention to use of *pešaʿ* in Amos 2:6-8. He numbers five "rebellions" and parallels them with apodictic laws (pp. 100-110) but gives scant attention to the fact that not only *pešaʿ* but even the same formula is used for indictments of pagan nations around Israel (1:3-2:3), stating that he does not wish to engage in a discussion of the relationship of Yahweh to other nations in Amos (pp. 107-8 n. 2).

But to sustain his argument Bergren would have to show that covenant breaking is involved in each instance of *pešaʿ*, though in fact that cannot be done. Any attempt to justify *pšʿ* as treaty terminology by appealing to any actual or supposed relationship between Israel and the nation involved is self-defeating: the *pšʿ* is not against Israel but against Yahweh, and the nations are not Yahweh's covenant partners. As H. W. Wolff, commenting on Amos 1-2, says, the crimes are not presented as violations of Israelite political interests; the oracular framework shows clearly that it is Yahweh's will which has been violated,[15] and even specifically points out that "oracles of accusation never quote words of Yahweh which derive from the ancient divine law or from covenant proclamation" (p. 102). Specifically discussing the *pšʿ* root, he notes that it is rare and unusual in the Pentateuch and that its relative frequency in Amos is matched by its frequency in Proverbs; his conclusions are that Amos's use of the term reflects oral clan tradition, that the translation "crime" (not "rebellion") seems appropriate, and that it regularly involves "infractions of property and person rights, deeds which deliberately violate

---

[12] Bergren, *The Prophets*, 106. Bergren bases himself, in part, at least, on D. R. Hillers, *Covenant: The History of a Biblical Idea* (Baltimore: Johns Hopkins, 1969); and M. Fishbane, "The Treaty Background of Amos 1:11 and Related Matters," *JBL* 89 (1970) 313-18.

[13] Gen 31:36; 50:17; 1 Sam 24:12; 25:28; Job 14:17; 35:6; Ps 32:1, 5; 36:2; 51:3, 5; etc.

[14] With *ḥaṭṭāʾt* (Gen 31:36; Ps 51:5), *rāʿâ* (1 Sam 24:12), *šeqer* (Isa 57:4), *ḥaṭṭāʾt*, *ʿawôn* (51:3-4), *ʿawôn* (Job 14:17), *mādôn* (Prov 10:12; 29:22).

[15] Wolff, *Amos and Joel* (Hermeneia; Philadelphia: Fortress, 1977) 146.

communal standards" (pp. 152–53).[16] Although the major attention on this point has been given to Bergren, he is only one among many to have argued along these lines, as the works he cites indicate.[17]

Bergren is on somewhat better ground in arguing from the use of *yāda'*, for serious studies have related it to treaty usage,[18] where it may mean (1) to recognize the legitimacy of a suzerain or vassal and (2) to recognize treaty stipulations as binding. However, we are again dealing with an extremely common OT term (close to 800 times in the qal alone) which is used in a wide variety of contexts, and its force in any particular case can be determined only from the particular context. No one would assert that in Gen 4:1, when the man "knows" his wife and she conceives, he is acknowledging her as either vassal or suzerain. One cannot assert treaty connection on the basis of the occurrence of the term alone, but only on the basis of some other argument from the context. Thus, to argue from the use of *yāda'* in Amos 3:2 to covenant connection could be valid, but it may also simply refer to the bestowal of Yahweh's favor.[19]

---

[16] It is to be noted that "communal standards" are expressed in many ways other than legal formulations. Much of Israel's ethic was earlier than any legal formulation and was sometimes expressed in terminology that said "such a thing is not done in Israel" or that it is *nĕbālâ* in Israel (Gen 34:7; 2 Sam 13:12; Deut 22:21). See J. Jensen, "Does *porneia* Mean Fornication?" *NovT* 20 (1978) 161–84. The article of G. M. Tucker, "The Law in the Eighth Century Prophets," in *Canon, Theology, and Old Testament Interpretation,* ed. G. M. Tucker, D. L. Petersen, and R. R. Wilson (Philadelphia: Fortress, 1988) 201–16, which appeared while the present article was awaiting publication, aims "to draw a profile of the law . . . which these prophets knew and used" (p. 203), and in the main his conclusions are prudently restrained (p. 213); further, I would agree that "already in the eighth century B.C. there was a considerable body of legal, moral, and religious tradition that the prophets considered valid" (ibid.). Too frequently, however, it seems to me, he too easily identifies the source of the prophets' strictures with specific laws from specific collections, even while resorting in the same context to much vaguer expressions such as "expectations" or "binding expectations" (pp. 203, 204, 211, 214), "traditions concerning land ownership" or "ancient tradition of . . . land tenure" (pp. 205, 206). Not everything that the prophets considered binding on their hearers needs to be classified as law.

[17] See also, among others, F. H. Seilhamer ("The Role of Covenant in the Mission and Message of Amos," in *A Light Unto My Path: Old Testament Studies in Honor of Jacob M. Myers* [ed. H. N. Bream et al.; Philadelphia: Temple, 1974] 435–51), who argues along much the same lines, though often with less critical sense than Bergren. He holds, e.g., that the use of *tôrâ* indicates covenant context; in this regard he cites Amos 2:4, a text all critics hold to be a later addition. See the response of E. W. Davies (*Prophecy and Ethics: Isaiah and the Ethical Tradition of Israel* [JSOTSup 16; Sheffield: JSOT Press, 1981] 42–61) to similar allegations with reference to Isa 1:2–3 and the further literature he cites.

[18] H. B. Huffmon, "The Treaty Background of Hebrew *Yāda'*," *BASOR* 181 (Feb. 1966) 31–37; H. B. Huffmon and S. B. Parker, "A Further Note on the Treaty Background of Hebrew *Yāda'*," *BASOR* 184 (Dec. 1966) 36–38.

[19] See Wolff, *Amos,* 76–77. If Bergren were correct on *yāda'* and *peša'*, we should by all means expect Yahweh in this text to speak of punishing Israel for *pĕšā'îm,* whereas in fact the term is *'āwōnôt.*

Influence of Mendenhall

Much of the argumentation of those who have been discussed rests on parallels, or supposed parallels, from extrabiblical literature. In all this the influence of the work of G. E. Mendenhall, mainly in a single article,[20] but taken up by D. R. Hillers and others, has been immense. As is well known, Mendenhall argued that Israel's Sinai covenant, even as embodied in the Decalogue formulation of Exodus 20, revealed the influence of the Hittite suzerainty treaty formulation, after which it was patterned. Since, he argued, this treaty formulation was not in use after the fall of the Hittite Empire around 1200 B.C., its presence in the Sinai covenant account demonstrated the antiquity and Mosaic origins of that covenant formulation. This is of particular interest to the present study because the "stipulations," one of the characteristic parts of the Hittite suzerainty treaty, the part in which the obligations of the vassal under the treaty were set forth, were sometimes in apodictic form; this is the grammatical form in which the commandments of the Decalogue and many of Israel's other laws are cast.[21] Mendenhall could thus assert that it was through the treaty pattern that the apodictic form came to be used for Israel's legal formulations. Other vistas opened up from the treaty form. D. R. Hillers, in particular, has attempted to show that the curses connected with treaty violation are reflected in prophetic oracles of doom.[22] Hillers begins almost at the very outset to speak of the influence of Mendenhall in this matter (pp. 1–2); he states that his own study was suggested by Mendenhall's work but adds that it is not dependent on the correctness of Mendenhall's views (p. 3). Others have gone on to suggest that the prophets adapt legal terminology connected with the treaties in what has come to be called the "covenant lawsuit" or the rîb-pattern. H. B. Huffmon

[20] Mendenhall, "Covenant Forms in Israelite Tradition," BA 17 (1954) 50–76; this work has been reprinted more than once and perhaps now is most readily accessible in Biblical Archaeologist Reader 3 (ed. E. F. Campbell and D. N. Freedman; Garden City, NY: Doubleday, 1970) 25–33. See also his "Covenant," IDB 1. 714–23. K. Baltzer (Das Bundesformular [WMANT 4; Neukirchen: Neukirchener Verlag, 1960]) reached similar conclusions and is often cited along with Mendenhall.

[21] The term "apodictic" was applied by A. Alt ("The Origins of Israelite Law," in Essays on Old Testament History and Religion [Oxford: Blackwell, 1966] 79–132) to diverse forms that really need to be differentiated, as pointed out by E. Gerstenberger (Wesen und Herkunft des "apodiktischen Rechts" [Neukirchen-Vluyn: Neukirchener Verlag, 1965] 22–76); with specific reference to the apodictic form in the treaty tradition, see D. J. McCarthy, Treaty and Covenant: A Study in Form in the Ancient Oriental Documents and in the Old Testament (2d ed.; AnBib 21a; Rome: Biblical Institute Press, 1978) 60–61.

[22] Hillers, Treaty-Curses and the Old Testament Prophets (BibOr 16; Rome: Pontifical Biblical Institute, 1964).

was the first to suggest this,[23] and his debt to Mendenhall is explicitly acknowledged more than once. He is closely followed by J. Harvey,[24] who builds upon his work and also makes reference to Mendenhall. Harvey even seems to use the pattern to argue for a Mosaic date for the Song of Moses in Deuteronomy 32. His argument supposes that the covenant that goes back to Moses was patterned on the treaty formula.[25] Some authors are sufficiently convinced of the existence of this form that they use it to solve thorny questions of literary composition.[26]

Response of McCarthy and Others

If the starting point for this whole development was analysis of nonbiblical treaties by Mendenhall and Baltzer, a very substantial reaction against it can be traced to the analysis of the same sort of documents by D. J. McCarthy. J. A. Fitzmyer had already stressed the importance of the dating of the treaty form for Mendenhall's thesis: "It is crucial to Mendenhall's thesis that the Old Testament covenant forms are related to the Hittite style of the suzerainty treaty. For him this is an indication of the date of the tradition and the legal pattern which are being used—they must have been introduced into the history of Israel at an early date."[27] But McCarthy's careful analysis has shown that the treaty form, far from having been restricted to the period of the Hittite Empire that ended in the thirteenth century, is found well into the first millennium. He finds that in the late treaties the characteristic features of the Hittite treaties, the stipulations, the invocation of the gods, the curses, always appear.[28] Even (and in certain respects, most importantly) the history is found in the later texts: "Our few and broken texts from Assyria are enough after all to show that an historical citation could form part of an Assyrian treaty. While they are common in the Hittite treaties, such citations

---

[23] Huffmon, "The Covenant Lawsuit in the Prophets," *JBL* 78 (1959) 285–95.

[24] Harvey, "Le 'Rib-Pattern,' requisitoire prophétique sur la rupture de l'alliance," *Bib* 43 (1962) 172–96.

[25] Having asserted that the *rîb* of chap. 32 is the reverse side of a diptych of which the covenant is the obverse, he says that the mediator, especially in his final words, had to foresee the possible rupture of the covenant and so add the *rîb* referred to in 31:19, 21; but if one of the tablets of a diptych, the covenant, dates back to Moses, the corresponding *rîb* should also (pp. 184–85).

[26] For example, both J. J. M. Roberts ("Form, Syntax, and Redaction in Isaiah 1:2–20," *Princeton Seminary Bulletin* 3 [1982] 293–306) and J. T. Willis ("The First Pericope in the Book of Isaiah," *VT* 34 [1984] 63–77) argue for the unity of Isa 1:2–20 from the formal elements which are supposed to be found in the covenant lawsuit.

[27] Fitzmyer, *The Aramaic Inscriptions of Sefîre* (BibOr 19; Rome: Pontifical Biblical Institute, 1967) 122–23.

[28] McCarthy, *Treaty and Covenant*, 120.

were not peculiar to them" (p. 120). Analysis, he says, does not bear out the claim "that the Assyrian and other treaties of the first millennium B.C. are entirely different in structure from the Hittite form in the second millennium" (p. 122).

Thus, even if one accepts that the Sinai covenant is expressed in terms of the treaty form, the argument for a Mosaic date falls to the ground. McCarthy rightly holds that the Exodus account of the Sinai covenant does not display the treaty form, whether one thinks in terms of the Decalogue alone or the broader context. It has been argued that "who brought you out of the land of Egypt, that place of slavery" (Exod 20:2b) is secondary in its present context; however, even if it is original, "it is not necessarily an historical prologue in the strict sense as found in the Hittite treaty. There we have as a rule an extended recounting of the past to motivate obedience to the stipulations which follow" (p. 251). Nor does the Decalogue have one of the indispensable elements, the curses and blessings. Even if one looks to the broader context, the treaty form does not emerge. At the end of the Covenant Code there are promises concerning Yahweh's conduct of Israel into the Promised Land (Exod 23:20–33), but nothing that resembles the blessings and curses of the treaties; in any case it is universally conceded that the Covenant Code did not originally stand in its present place in the Sinai narrative.

Thus, stricter methodology and literary criticism leave very little of the treaty form at Sinai. This is not to say that there was no Mosaic covenant, but it was a different concept than that which would emerge from one patterned on the treaty form. McCarthy sees the emphasis at Sinai placed on the terror-inspiring theophany as motive for the covenant and Israel's obedience to its stipulations.[29] It is clear that at a later stage Israel came to present the covenant in terms of the treaty form, but this emerges only with the advent of the Ur-Deuteronomium (Deuteronomy 5–28).[30]

This conclusion carries an important methodological consequence for those authors who cite Jeremiah as though his preaching reveals witness to ancient apodictic law and reflects a treaty form of the Sinai covenant. Since Jeremiah is contemporary with the promulgation of Deuteronomy under Josiah and since it is widely conceded that the book bearing his name reveals the heavy imprint of the deuteronomic school,[31] the covenant and law

---

[29] McCarthy's detailed treatment is found in chap. 12, "Sinai" (pp. 243–76), but see also pp. 277–79 and *passim;* my brief relation of it necessarily truncates and oversimplifies.

[30] See especially McCarthy's chap. 9, "Deuteronomy: The Central Discourse" (pp. 157–87) and also pp. 290–93 under "Conclusions."

[31] As set forth, e.g., by E. W. Nicholson, *Preaching to the Exiles: A Study in the Prose Tradition in the Book of Jeremiah* (Oxford: Blackwell, 1970).

concepts found there may be reflecting only what has come to the fore with Deuteronomy.[32]

McCarthy and others have had their impact, and it is not surprising to see scholars modifying their positions accordingly. R. E. Clements, for example, having discussed, among other matters, Mendenhall's hypothesis concerning covenant and treaty form, comes to the conclusion that "for a clear under-standing of what such covenant traditions may have meant to the prophets we must adhere to those passages where explicit reference is made to such covenant traditions," and he adds, "in this regard I should now wish to modify the tendency in my earlier study, *Prophecy and Covenant,* to bring together a considerable variety of Israel's religious traditions into a relatively uniform covenant theology."[33] In the same context he treats as unproved the assertions about prophetic threats and treaty curses,[34] covenant lawsuit,[35] and "love" and "know" as OT terminology derived from the treaty tradition.[36]

Substantial modification can be seen also through the four editions of B. W. Anderson's widely used text, *Understanding the Old Testament.*[37] In all four editions Anderson says that new light has been thrown upon the rela-tionship between covenant and law by the study of the Hittite treaties of the late second millennium. In the first edition (1957) he alludes to three elements

---

[32] Thus, Bergren's methodology is open to objection in that he lumps together the four prophets that he is particularly concerned with (Amos, Micah, Isaiah, and Jeremiah), without ever asking whether Jeremiah really fits all that well with the other three. The methodologically questionable procedure of lumping together laws from all of the codes without raising questions of date has already been referred to. For examples of both, see Bergren's chart, *The Prophets,* 182–83.

[33] Clements, *Prophecy and Tradition* (Atlanta: John Knox, 1975) 8–23; the quoted material is found on pp. 22 and 23.

[34] He sees the similarities that may exist as explicable "simply on the recognition that descrip-tions of evil and misfortune were bound to show a considerable degree of similarity because all peoples were subject to essentially similar threats to life and security. There is nothing of a specifically covenantal, or treaty, character about this" (*Prophecy,* 19).

[35] The material simply represents the application of vocabulary and imagery drawn from the processes of law to this particular situation, without the necessity of introducing the form and contents of the treaty curses (*Prophecy,* 19–20), citing the arguments given by E. von Waldow in *Der traditionsgeschichtliche Hintergrund der prophetischen Gerichtsreden* (BZAW 85; Berlin: A. Töpelmann, 1963). See also the more recent study of M. de Roche, "Yahweh's *rîb* Against Israel: A Reassessment of the So-Called 'Prophetic Lawsuit' in the Preexilic Prophets," *JBL* 102 (1983) 563–74, with the conclusion, "for this reason the terms 'prophetic lawsuit' and 'covenant lawsuit' should be abandoned" (p. 574).

[36] "We simply do not need to turn to such treaties to explain these basic religious concepts, which are intelligible enough in the context of Israel's own religious history and life" (Clements, *Prophecy,* 20–21).

[37] Englewood Cliffs, NJ: Prentice-Hall.

of the treaties and comments, "this political form was appropriated for the expression of Israel's covenant faith" and speaks of the Decalogue being "prefaced with a brief historical prologue" (pp. 56–57). The second edition (1966) mentions McCarthy's *Treaty and Covenant* in a footnote, though otherwise the treatment seems unchanged. The third and fourth editions (1975 and 1986) list the usual six characteristic parts of the Hittite suzerainty treaty and comment that the correlation with the Mosaic covenant is so striking that "many scholars" (3rd edition; 4th edition: "some scholars") have concluded that it must have provided the model for the Israel–Yahweh relationship. But he refers to elements missing in the Sinai account and then goes on to say that this political analogy would not have been particularly meaningful to wanderers in the wilderness and that it is likely that it had its greatest influence later on, after the settlement, and now cites McCarthy's *Old Testament Covenant*. Thus McCarthy's study, and works of others, have had their impact, though not all have embraced their implications.[38]

Other Approaches to Apodictic Law

Other lines of development which have undermined Mendenhall's position are those developed by E. Gerstenberger and W. Richter, whose differing approaches converge to somewhat similar conclusions. One of the aspects of Mendenhall's position that had appealed to many was its explanation of how apodictic law, virtually unknown in other ancient Near Eastern law codes, had entered Israelite legislation, but these authors present a more convincing alternative. Gerstenberger, referring to what McCarthy had established in the 1963 edition of his book, argued that the treaty stipulations were essentially links between the compact and the curse which sanctioned them and that the OT apodictic commandments do not show any trace of being covenant stipulations in that sense, and he explicitly rejected Mendenhall's position. Treaty stipulations are all ordered to the end for which the treaty is made; they redound to the advantage of the sovereign, arrange to make peace and combat common enemies. Of the OT prohibitives, Gerstenberger sees only those against "other gods," images, and cursing, and the law of the altar as possibly being rooted in a covenant ceremony. He argues that

---

[38] Bergren is remarkably ambivalent and inconsistent in his response to McCarthy and Gerstenberger. On pp. 37–40 he calls McCarthy's criticism of Mendenhall "cogent" and seems to accept it without reservation, but on p. 92, he lumps together what Mendenhall says of Sinai and what McCarthy says of Deuteronomy 5–28 and then declares that all this establishes "an awareness of the treaty form in the biblical material." His overall approach ignores the implications of what he had earlier embraced. He is soon back to speaking of the "covenant conceived of as a treaty between God and Israel" (p. 148), and this is his background in assessing the use of *peša'* and *yāda'* and in validating the concept of the "lawsuit of God" (pp. 106–50) and treaty-curse parallels (pp. 95–106).

most of the others suppose a seminomadic or small-town society. The original speaker in such cases was not Yahweh nor the priest nor the prophet but the father, the tribal head, the wise man, and, secondarily, the court official. He sees them rooted in clan ethic (*Sippenethos*), with the Semitic clan as the place of origin. They were, therefore, the authoritative orders of the clan or family head; but they take their worth not so much from the power of the clan chieftain but rather from the sanctified rule-of-life (*Lebensordnung*) that they represent. He appeals to the example of the Rechabites (Jer 35:6–7), where it is a question of a command given by the clan father, and the form is *lō'* + imperfect (5 times). He looks at the wisdom literature and notes the similarities to be found and concludes that negative wisdom admonitions (*Warn- und Mahnworte*) and the legal prohibitives had the same origin, from which they developed independently, namely, the *Lebensordnung* of the clan. This *Gattung*, once released from its natural origin, was taken into a new context and developed further; this explains the distinction between the two branches of the negative prescription. When such formulations were taken into law, and especially when put into the (literary) context of the Sinai covenant, the speaker is now understood to be Yahweh.[39]

Richter's approach is somewhat different, but there is a good deal of congruence in his conclusions. While the prohibitive (*lō'* + imperfect) is found mainly in law and the vetitive ('*al* + jussive) is found mainly in wisdom, the two forms are closely related, both in terms of content and in having motivations attached to them, and he concludes that there is a connection between the two forms in that they have a common *Sitz im Leben* in the wisdom school of the upper middle class (and the content therefore represents *Gruppenethos*).[40] There is congruence between the two positions in that after Israel's settlement in their land, and especially after the establishment of the monarchy, the task of training the youth of the upper-class families would have migrated from the clan-family structure to the school and to other mechanisms and structures of the wisdom circles.

A Sounder Approach

Given the impact of studies such as those of McCarthy, Gerstenberger, and Richter, there is now little basis for speaking of the eighth-century prophets thinking of the covenant in terms of treaty form or Israel's apodictic formulations being necessarily connected with it. R. Sonsino remarks (following G. Fohrer) that the order "do this" and "do not do that" is very

---

[39] This brief summary draws on both "Covenant and Commandment," *JBL* 84 (1965) 38–51, and *Wesen und Herkunft* (see above, n. 21).

[40] Richter, *Recht und Ethos: Versuch einer Ortung des weisheitlichen Mahnspruches* (SANT 15; Munich: Kösel, 1966).

common and is found almost everywhere; he points out that there are examples of the second-person apodictic in a variety of extrabiblical texts: in Syrian treaty stipulations as well as Hittite, in wisdom instructions, in disciplinary warnings, in royal instructions, in sepulchral inscriptions, etc.[41] He emphasizes that whereas in extrabiblical texts examples of the form are found scattered among other modes of expression, in biblical legislation it usually appears as part of a series, and he finds the closest parallel to this in wisdom literature, both biblical and extrabiblical, giving examples from Egyptian, Akkadian, and Sumerian (p. 38).

It is necessary here to develop further a methodological point raised earlier, namely, the inadequacy of claiming that a prophet's condemnation of a crime rests on apodictic law simply because both relate to the same crime. The prophets condemn Israel's crimes in an astonishing variety of formulations, including woe oracles, rhetorical questions, indicative statements, etc. Sometimes the prophet speaks in the imperative to tell Israel what it should do and has not been doing (e.g., "cease doing evil; learn to do good. Make justice your aim: redress the wronged . . ." [Isa 1:17]). But seldom or never does such imperative address resemble the apodictic commands of the legal tradition in terms of form and terminology (aside from common terms such as "widow," "orphan," "justice," and terms for specific crimes such as murder and adultery), so that the similarity is simply in terms of content. This is not to say that the eighth-century prophets were not familiar with the Sinai covenant concept or with Israel's legal tradition. Hosea refers to covenant twice (Hos 6:7 and 8:1), and it seems likely that his marriage analogy rests upon it. Amos, who exercised his prophetic ministry only a little earlier, also in the north, would also have been familiar with it, and from him we have the reference to "garments taken in pledge" (Amos 2:8), a probable allusion to Exod 22:25–26 in the Covenant Code. Isaiah probably would not have been ignorant of such things, though he speaks mainly from traditions at home in Jerusalem and we find in him no reference to Moses, Sinai, or covenant. It is not clear what legal tradition might have been in force in Judah at this time. Deuteronomy had not yet been promulgated and the Covenant Code seems to have been largely a northern collection (see above). For this reason it seems unwise to see as based on law, whether apodictic or not, prophetic accusations which happen to deal with the same material. The content of the ethical teachings of the prophets could have been drawn from a number of areas and undoubtedly were.

One area that deserves to receive much attention is the wisdom tradition. Whereas there used to be much said about the self-serving nature of wisdom

---

[41] Sonsino, *Motive Clauses in Hebrew Law: Biblical Forms and Near Eastern Parallels* (SBLDS 45; Chico, CA: Scholars, 1980) 37–38.

instruction, now more is said about the lofty ideals that are inculcated, especially those that relate to what we would call social justice. The older materials found in the book of Proverbs give us an idea of the sort of thing contained in the curriculum that the young nobles were educated in. Moreover, if it is recognized that those who underwent this sort of instruction were primarily those destined to become officials of the court, we can see that those ideals were not for the private practice of virtue; rather they were for the guidance of those who would be responsible for the administration of justice. The appeal in these instructions is not to law but to what is right and fitting and, sometimes, what is pleasing to God. In the cases in which law and wisdom touch on the same areas—and they are many—it is unwise to say that the prophet is appealing to law; more likely he is reminding the leaders of the manner of administering justice that had been inculcated during their schooling.[42] Law was of little use if those who administered it were corrupt or even used their position to enact statutes that served their own selfish purposes (Isa 10:1–2).

Thus, when the prophets condemn unjust weights and measures (Amos 8:5; Mic 6:10–11), rather than looking to Lev 19:35–36 and Deut 25:13–15, as Bergren does, we ought perhaps to think of Prov 16:11 and 20:10. In Proverbs we have strictures in very religious terms against condemning the just ("he who condones the wicked, he who condemns the just, are both an abomination to the Lord" [17:15]), oppressing the poor ("he who oppresses the poor insults his Maker" [14:31]), false witnessing (21:28), etc. The wisdom tradition is all the more relevant in that here we find warnings concerning the evil effects of unbridled drinking, including its adverse impact on just judgment (Prov 20:1; 23:20–21, 29–35; 31:4–5), as we do in the prophets (Isa 5:11–12, 22–23; 28:1, 7–8; Amos 6:6), and the uselessness of unworthy sacrifice (Prov 15:8; 21:27), as we do in the prophets (Isa 1:11–17; Amos 5:21–24), though neither of these concerns is reflected in the

---

[42] See especially Isa 1:17, 23; Amos 5:12; Mic 3:1, 9. For Isaiah the remedy for Jerusalem's harlotry was the restoration of the judges and counselors to their earlier, uncorrupted condition (1:26). On the existence of such schooling, see, among others, J. P. J. Olivier, "Schools and Wisdom Literature," *JNSL* 4 (1975) 49–60. J. L. Crenshaw, reviewing the evidence for the existence of schools in Israel during the period of the monarchy and avowedly taking a "minimalist perspective," opts for the bulk of education being carried out in the family home, but concedes that it would be unwise to insist that all occurred there and that "for a chosen few, special scribal training may have been provided in Hezekiah's court" ("Education in Ancient Israel," *JBL* 104 [1985] 601–15). However, Crenshaw makes no mention of the emphasis given to items in the wisdom tradition that seem to be directed specifically to those responsible for the administration of justice. See, more recently, J. D. Pleins ("Poverty in the Social World of the Wise," *JSOT* 37 [1987] 61–78), who argues that wisdom thought (as found in Proverbs) is grounded in the educational background of the urban elite and makes a difference in their vocabulary for poverty from that of the prophets.

law codes. There is, in fact, so much similarity to the wisdom tradition in the things denounced by prophets in their woe oracles that this has been used as an argument for a wisdom origin for the "woe" form.[43]

Extrabiblical texts in the Egyptian "instruction" form are particularly instructive on this point for a number of reasons. For one, they are characterized by the second-person address with frequent use of the imperative, and no one (to my knowledge) has attempted to relate them to the treaty form. Second, since no law codes have been found in Egypt, these texts can hardly be claimed to derive from a legal tradition (as it has sometimes been claimed of the exhortations in Israel's wisdom tradition[44]). Third, the manner in which these "instructions" present themselves shows clearly that they are intended to give guidance to those who administer justice for the state. Fourth, the basis on which they rest seems to be simply that which is "meet and just" and that which is pleasing to God, especially where it is a case of concern for the widow, the poor, and other *personae miserables*,[45] truth in giving witness, honest scales, etc., even to the point of judgment on the acceptability of sacrifice.[46] The "Tale of the Eloquent Peasant" gives an interesting, if largely fictional, account of how such ideals might be applied in a concrete case, specifically when an official uses naked power to abuse the rights and confiscate the property of a simple peasant. Some of those hearing the case were inclined to side with their crony, but the higher authority saw

[43] By Gerstenberger, W. J. Whedbee, and others, though this is a position I reject; see the discussion in J. Jensen, *The Use of tôrâ by Isaiah: His Debate with the Wisdom Tradition* (CBQMS 3; Washington DC: Catholic Biblical Association, 1973) 101–2.

[44] See, e.g., A. Robert, "Les attaches littéraires bibliques de Prov. I-IX," *RB* 43 (1934) 42–68, 172–204, 378–84; 44 (1935) 344–65, 502–25.

[45] It is this concern for the widow, poor, etc. in the settled Egyptian culture which renders very doubtful von Waldow's argument that Israel's concern for the *personae miserables must* go back to its nomadic days, *before* its settlement in the land ("Social Responsibility," 86–87). The same is to be said of the argument of A. Phillips ("Prophecy and Law," 223) that the humanitarian provisions in the Covenant Code "reflect the break-up of a clan-dominated society. . . ."

[46] To cite just some of the commonest examples (page numbers are from *ANET*): in "The Instruction of the Vizier Ptah-hotep": commendation of justice and warning of punishment for its transgression (p. 412), the attention to be paid to petitioners, against being greedy for or covetous of someone else's property (p. 413), against being miserly with wealth (p. 414); in "The Instruction for King Meri-ka-re": against covetousness, oppressing the widow, supplanting anyone from inherited property, impairing officials in their work, punishing wrongfully (p. 415), uprightness better than sacrifice (p. 417); King Amen-em-het claims that he gave to the destitute and brought up the orphan (p. 418); in "The Instruction of Amen-em-opet" (which, even though it may date later than the eighth century, reveals the ideals of the tradition): against encroaching on the land of others, particularly the widow (p. 422), being greedy for the property of a poor man, falsifying weights and measures (p. 423), perversion of justice in the lawcourt, accepting bribes, oppressing the disabled, and commending compassion toward the widow (p. 424).

to it that justice was done.[47] No doubt it did not always happen so in Egypt any more than it always did in Israel. But the procedure would not have been all that different in Israel, and the role of the prophet would not have been so much to speak from Israel's tradition of apodictic law as to urge that oppressive rulers rule the way it was universally known they should rule.

In the eighth century this universal conviction would have been rooted in various traditions; these certainly included both the legal tradition and the wisdom tradition. Those matters relating to ideals of "social justice" would have had a complex history. It may very well be the case that the origins lie in a clan ethic that found its way both into apodictic law and the wisdom tradition by different routes, maintaining identity of content and similarity of expression, but by the eighth century the traditions of Israel's wisdom circles would have received ample cross-fertilization from Egypt,[48] especially, and also from Mesopotamia.

Israel's convictions concerning social justice were not unique in the ancient Near East, if one looks to the wisdom traditions of neighboring cultures. B. Gemser points out that in some ancient cultures proverbs can have the force of legal maxims.[49] Israel, too, may have operated more in terms of general and ethical norms than in terms of collected laws. But such norms would not have remained simply those of the ancient world, for they had been given a place within the context of the national religion of Yahwism. What was unique was Israel's apprehension of Yahweh's character, especially as revealed by the prophets. It was not sufficient to hold up justice and compassion for the poor as an ideal; the prophets present Yahweh as a God who zealously enforces these things, at least in the sense that the responsible human agents can expect to be punished as severely for neglecting them as for idolatry or any other crime, even to the extent of the total destruction of the nation.

---

[47] *ANET,* 407–10.

[48] See, most recently, N. Shupak, "Egyptian Terms and Features in Biblical Wisdom," *Tarbiz* 54 (1984/85) 475–83 (in Hebrew; English summary in *OTA* 9 [1986] #693).

[49] Gemser, "The Importance of the Motive Clause in Old Testament Law," in *Congress Volume: Copenhagen, 1953* (VTSup 1; Leiden: Brill, 1953) 64–65.

Yahweh's Asherah

Robert North, S.J.
Pontifical Biblical Institute

And mooned Ashtaroth,
Heav'ns Queen and Mother
  both,
Now sits not girt with Tapers'
  holy shrine.
      Milton, *Christ's Nativity*

1. To HONOR THE EPIGRAPHIC ACHIEVEMENTS of Father Fitzmyer, we were invited to contribute something on inscriptions in biblical research. Certainly the most sensational recent OT development has been the discovery in at least three places of inscriptions speaking apparently of "Yahweh's Asherah."

It has been debated first whether that is really the reading at all; and we may modestly claim to present here the first legible 'Ajrud facsimile with letter-decipherment comparable to the several which have appeared for Qôm.

Second, Hebrew *'ašera,* though undoubtedly prominent in and outside the Bible as the name of a goddess, has also some chance of being a common noun meaning either "representation" or "holy place/worshiper." In relation to that possibility there is a third debate, as to whether Hebrew usage permits the use of a possessive with a personal name. Finally, the experts have well aired the question of just what place "Yahweh's Asherah" would occupy in the biblical background, whether as female paredra of the El whose place had been taken over by Yahweh, or at any rate as a breakthrough in the hitherto monolithically patriarchal character of Hebrew religion.

What has *not* been seriously asked in the already extensive literature is whether the inscriptions are truly "cultic," or what constitutes a "cultus." The term would seem to imply some sort of regulated practice, not just *any* kind of use of the name of a divinity, as

118

for instance in cursing. Admittedly even in blasphemous or contemptuous uses we have clues as to what the normative practice was; and in any case the expressions of "popular religiosity" often stray very far from theological and priestly preferences. Nevertheless, the degree to which the expressions are properly cultic would seem to enter into any conclusions about the "place of the feminine within Israel's object of worship."

2. The 'Ajrud Pithos and Its Context

2.1 Usually taken as outset, because likeliest though not chronologically first, are the lines scribbled on a jar found in 1976 by Z. Meshel at Kuntillet Ajrud, located about forty miles south of Kadesh-barnea at survey-grid points 093.957. The importance of the site was due to its situation at the crossing-point of three desert tracks, one of which is the Darb el-Ghazzeh.[1]

The site was known to the Palestine Exploration Fund surveyors as Contillet Koreiyah, in an article which does not mention the name 'Ajrud, but does note that several large ancient pithoi (not said to be decorated) were then still in use to hold water for the dwellers nearby.[2] Meshel notes without reference that Edward Palmer visited the site in 1869 and identified it as a stop called Gypsaria on the road from Gaza to Eilat. *Kuntilla* is said to mean "an isolated hill," not verifiable in Belot or Lane or Wehr dictionary; its *k* seems to be clearly *kaf*, though Koreiyah's is *qof*; see below on Qôm. *'Ajrud* is said to mean "wells."[3] Meshel emphasizes that the name is an apt one, because there are several in the neighborhood. We will follow him in giving the name of the site sometimes simply as 'Ajrud.

2.2 Already in 1967 Meshel visited here and recognized surface-sherds dating the ruin to the later Iron Age; then in 1975–76 in excavating for Tel Aviv University he discovered the inscribed pithos-fragments and the building in which they stood. His *BARev* article gives an admirably clear description of the whole small excavated area on the flat top of a mound; our Fig. 1 gives his plan, oriented to correspond to his excellent color-photo from

---

[1] Ze'ev Meshel, "The Israelite Religious Centre of Kuntillet 'Ajrud," *Bulletin of the Anglo-Israel Archaeological Society* 2 (1983–3) 52(–55); with Carol Meyers, "The Name of God in the Wilderness of Zin," *BA* 39 (1976) 6–10.

[2] Neither *kuntilla* nor *'ajrûd* seems to be in the *Survey of Western Palestine* volume *English and Arabic Name Lists* by Edward H. Palmer (London, 1881); but in the volume *Special Papers*, by Palmer and others (also 1881) p. 15 treats "Contellet Garaiyeh." (*Qurayya* means "small building.")

[3] *'Ajar* means "be thick"; *'ajara*, "protuberance." *'Ajrad* means "denude," "strip naked"; there is also a verb *jarad*, "be naked"; as noun, "field without vegetation"; also *jârûd*, "evil (man or year)." No *'ajrûd* plural or other form is indicated.

There is a root *qunna*(t), "mound," and another, *qinnît*, "(water-) skin, container," also *kanît*, "solid," as qualifier of a water-container; nothing else approaching *kuntillet*.

the air.[4] In the foreground (below, east) are scarcely recognizable ruins of what was presumably another building carried away by erosion. The west building is a large rectangle of 75 x 45 ft. (23 x 13 m.) with walls surviving to a height of 5 ft.

There was nothing of interest in the large central room; the southeast and northeast corners (left and right respectively) contained ovens at three successive occupation-stages. West of these corners were long narrow rooms for storage of food. The square constructions at the far west corners were towers. Their walls were of rough unhewn limestone interspersed by binder-courses of tamarisk, which the excavator rather remotely compares to the "cedar-beams between (every three) courses of hewn stones" in 1 Kgs 2:12.

The entrance to the building, at the east, was once decorated with linear and floral frescoes and was protected by a sort of half porch at its north and east. Immediately inside and on both sides of the entrance, separating it from the large main room, was a long room containing a white-plastered bench along the whole wall adjacent to the entrance on either side. Meshel's plan shows more convincingly than his photo that the west wall of the bench-room is also the east wall of the large main room. The north and south of the bench-room gave access to small corner rooms. Meshel characterized the whole building or site as an "Israelite religious center," but this seems to *depend upon,* rather than to help determine, the interpretation of the drawings and inscriptions on the fragments found in the bench-room and the small corner-rooms near it.

"The most dramatic discoveries were on two pithoi [each a meter high and weighing some 30 pounds or 13 kg.] which were restored from sherds found in the bench-room. Both pithoi were densely covered with drawings as well as inscriptions . . . frequently overlapped. Most were executed in red ink."[5] Neutron analysis later showed that the pottery was not locally made, but came from the coast, or from Judah or even North-Israel.[6]

On a large pithos, then, showing also drawings other than on our Fig. 2, was the inscription which we there give on a larger scale, but in roughly the position in which it was found.

---

[4] Z. Meshel, "Did Yahweh Have a Consort? The New Religious Inscriptions from the Sinai," *BARev* 5,2 (1979) 24–35.

[5] Ibid., 30. There is no page-numbering or documentation in his *Kuntillet 'Ajrud, a Religious Centre from the Time of the Judaean Monarchy on the Border of Sinai* (Israel Museum Catalog 175; Jerusalem, 1978); briefer statements in *IEJ* 27 (1977) 52–53; *RB* 84 (1977) 270–73; *Qad* 9 (1976) 119–24; *Expedition* 20,4 (1978) 50–54; *MDB* 10 (1979) 32–36.

The mention by Diethelm Conrad in E. Würthwein Festschrift, *Textgemäss* (Göttingen, 1979) 32, is too brief to be of use.

[6] Jan Gunneweg, Isadore Pearlman, Ze'ev Meshel, "The Origin of the Pottery of Kuntillet Ajrud," *IEJ* 35 (1985) 270–83.

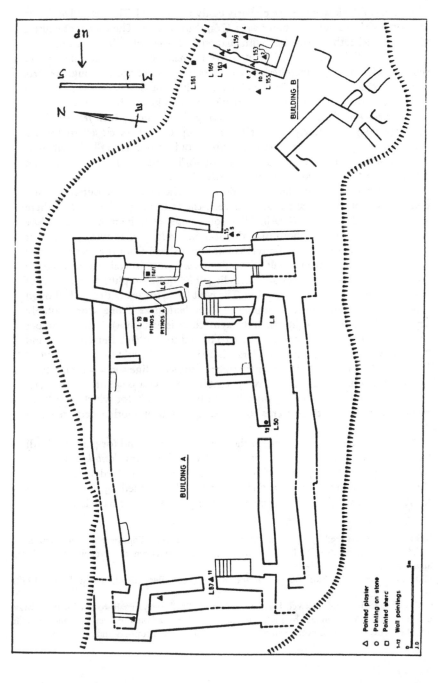

Fig. 1. Kuntillet ʿAjrud, Z. Meshel plan, from (P. Beck) *Tel Aviv Journal* 9 (1982) 5. Reprinted by permission of Professor Z. Meshel and *Tel Aviv Journal*.

> '*mr.*' ...*h.k.* '*mr.lyhl...wlyw*'*šh.w*
> [*brkt.*'*tkm* not in drawing] *lyhwh.šmrn.wl*'*šrth*

The letters of the lower line can be fairly easily recognized. The *yod* and *he* forms are notably similar to each other as at Qôm but smaller. The *waw* looks like a Greek ghimel rather than staff with diagonal cross-stroke. In the right-hand open space of the helmet can be perceived a *resh;* the *mem* preceding it and separating it from *šin* is uncontested; a *nûn* is scarcely perceptible, though experts debate whether *šmrn* is for *šōmᵉrēnû* "our guardian" or *Šōmrōn* 'of Samaria'.[7] In the space to the lower left of the helmet's upper spike can be seen *lamed,* then less clearly *aleph,* then *šin* somewhat covering the left horn, then *resh* (without open triangle), *tau* clearly, and *he* (its two top cross-bars closed to form a triangle). This final -*h*, if a pronoun-suffix, would more naturally be taken as feminine -*âh* 'her(s)', but could also be -*ôh* (for -ô) 'his (Ašeraᵗ'); however it could also be for a feminine absolute ending, Aširtâh.

The upper line is more difficult to decipher. The *mem* at the outset is just a comma, without its usual zigzag. Between the following *resh* and *aleph* there seems to be a dot or outset-slash. What follows seems to be more clearly *above* the helmet-peak on the photo than the drawing indicates; anyway just at that place (about 1 cm before and after) is missing a sherd from the reconstructed pithos, along with the upper half of some otherwise unmistakable letters. To the left of the helmet-peak can be seen the alleged *he* (quite simplified) and a sort of comma not noted in the transcription. The next word begins with a *kaph,* though reduced in size and low in alignment. Then '*mrlyhl* as if one word notably separated from *wlyw*'*šhw* (in which the ayin-circle is just a dot). From the upper line thus we get only "Say to . . . say to Yhl and to Yw'*šh*". Between this and "for Yahweh of Samaria and his Ašera" there is said to be *brkt* '*tkm* "I bless you" [with ? (I.PN)]; in the photo rather far right of the *lower* line and at a higher level is another break in the pithos leaving visible the lowest edge of some letters. There is also supposed to be a *further* line with only *h.* . . .'*t*, for which *hšlm* '*t* has been proposed.[8] But there seems to be also question of another occurrence of Ašera.

At any rate there is elsewhere on the pithos a clear second (or perhaps third) "and for his Ašera" in the inscription '*mryw* '*mrl.*'*dny h...brktk.lyhwh.* .. *wl*'*šrth.ybrk.wysmrk wyhy* '*m.*'*dnw* (the '*dny* seems to be 'my lord' or 'sir' rather than Adonai, and the "from Yahweh" is separated by something from "and for his Ašera").[9] The "Yo'aš(h)" of the main inscription seems to have been at least

---

[7] "Protector" is favored by Volkmar Fritz, "Kadesch Barnea—Topographie und Siedlungsgeschichte im Bereich der Quellen von Kadesch und Kultstätten des Negeb während der Königszeit," *BN* 9 (1979) (45–)50.

[8] Debra A. Chase, "A Note on an Inscription from Kuntillet 'Ajrūd," *BASOR* 246 (1982) 63–67.

[9] Meshel renders ("Did Yahweh Have a Consort?" 32) "Amaryau said to my lord: . . . May you be blessed by Yahweh and by his Asherah. Yahweh bless you and keep you and be with you." The form "I bless you in the name of . . ." as found in the prophets and especially Balaam

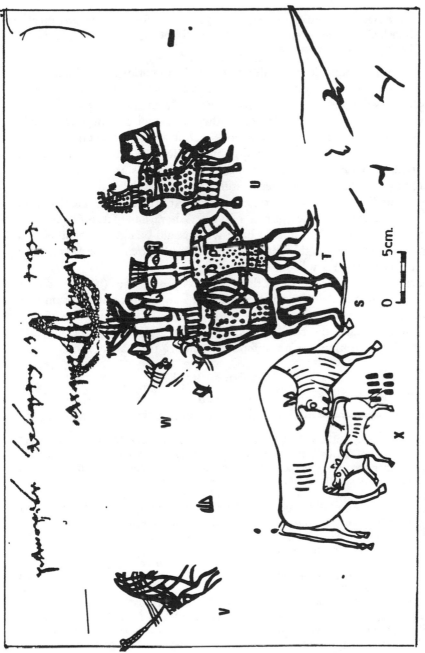

Fig. 2. 'Ajrud Pithos I, from P. Beck, *Tel Aviv Journal* 9 (1982) 9, with inscription added, enlarged from (M. Gilula) *Shnaton la-Miqra'* 3 (1978–79) 137. Reprinted by permission of Professor Z. Meshel and *Tel Aviv Journal*.

originally a factor in the dating; the epigraphic dating before 800 now proposed by Meshel, Cross, and Naveh is not so very different from Lemaire's *after* 800 (to 725, as the Samaria ostraca).[10]

2.3 It seems reasonable to inquire whether the intention of the inscription is related to that of the drawing, like the caption of an illustration (even though it was put there later, or even earlier).[11] The image on the right is that of a woman playing the lyre: "the find that could not be," in journalese — meaning not the scandalous Yahweh-consort but simply the fact that musical instruments are relatively unattested in archaeology.[12] (The lyre is attested as an attribute of Qudšu, equivalent of the Phoenician Astarte/Aṭṭira.) On the left are two standing figures; their features have been claimed to be bovine, to represent Qudšu as Hathor, or more likely (both) Bes, a male divinity. Gilula holds that the middle figure is a dwarf, Ashera, and that its phallus was added later.[13] In fact both figures have what could be either a phallus or a tail. King seems to imply that the (larger) standing figure may be a lion, since Ashera was called "Lady Lion."[14]

Maier's judicious treatment of these various possibilities (below) and his resolute conclusion that they have nothing to do with the inscription lose considerable force from the fact that among his illustrations is none of this, which would allow the reader to judge of his arguments. Undoubtedly though, the inscription was not intended as an original part of the drawing.

3. The Qôm Epitaph

3.1 The Khirbat al-Qôm inscription had in fact been found earlier, by W. G. Dever at a tomb in 1967, but was published without combining the

Num 22–24 is treated by Alessandro Catastini, "Le iscrizioni di Kuntillet 'Ajrud e il profetismo," *AION* 42 (1982) 127–34. The pithos with the *'dnw* inscription contains also four abecdaries, with *pe* preceding *'ayin*, as at Izbet Sarta: A. Demsky, M. Kochavi, "An Alphabet from the Days of the Judges," *BARev* 4,5 (1979) 23.

[10] André Lemaire (see n. 18 below), "Date et origine des inscriptions paléo-hébraïques et phéniciennes de Kuntillet 'Ajrud," *Studi Epigrafici e Linguistici* 1 (1984) 134; 131–143; his further (earlier) claim that we have a scribal school at Kuntillet 'Ajrud (*Les écoles et la formation de la Bible dans l'ancien Israël* [OBO 39; Fribourg/Göttingen, 1981] 30) was queried by E. Puech at the 1984 Jerusalem Congress: *Biblical Archaeology Today* (Jerusalem, 1985) 363.

[11] Amply illustrated study by Pirhiya Beck, "The Drawings from Horvat Teiman (Kuntillet 'Ajrûd)," *Tel Aviv (Univ.) Journal* 9 (1982) 3–86. Our Fig. 2 (without its inscription) is taken from p. 9; our Fig. 1 (Meshel's plan) from p. 5.

[12] Bathja Bayer, "The Finds that Could Not Be," *BARev* 8,1 (1982) 20–33.

[13] Mordechai Gilula, "Lyhwh šmrn wl'šrth," *Shnaton la-Miqra'* 3 (1978–79) 129–37; Eng. xv–xvi, "To Yahweh Shomron and his Asherah." Less firmly the figure to the left of central Asherah is said to be of Yahweh himself. From the drawing of p. 137, many times enlarged, is the inscription of our Fig. 2.

[14] Philip J. King, "The Contribution of Archaeology to Biblical Studies," *CBQ* 45 (1983) 13; now Ruth Hestrin, "A note on the 'lion bowls' and the Asherah," *IsrMusJ* 7 (1988) 115–18.

letters which were later taken to form "his Asherah."[15] The site is located nine miles west of Hebron, at grid-points 1465.1045; it is quite often spelled *Kom*, even by the experts.[16] Dever dated also this inscription to the eighth century and published it as follows:

> *l'ryhw.hqšb.ktbh*
> *brk.'ryhw.lyhwh*
> *wm'rk.yd.l'šr.thwš. 'lh.*
> *l'nyh.*

"For Uriahu: pay attention to [*qšb*, presuming the *beth* a mistake for *resh*] his inscription; and cursed be the hand 'of whoever defaces it'[17] [*l'šr th(wš*) being the letters later taken by others as 'for Aširtâh' or 'for his *ašerâ*']; for Oniyahu." The inscription is on a sherd, and beneath it is the drawing of a hand (Fig. 4), which Dever's early publication did not show, nor apparently put into any relation with the *yd* of his decipherment.

3.2 A thorough study by Lemaire makes the rather extreme supposition that the scribe should have written *l'šrth* at the beginning of its line, but erroneously put it after the first letters, which he reads as *wmṣryh;* he also finds trace of a further *l'šrth* after *l'nyh:* "Blessed be Uriahu by Yahweh and [by his Asherah] he has saved him from his enemies; by Oniahu and his Asherah." He explains the bracketed (misplaced) word to mean that popular religion did indeed reckon with a blessing "by Yahweh and his Asherah," but *ašerâ* is left equally capable of meaning a *maṣṣebâ* (post, representation), possibly of Yahweh himself.[18] Jaroš, along with his own drawing of the inscription and a helpful table of the letters, retains the essential of Lemaire's decipherment without its massive emendation, "from his enemies (Yahweh) by his *ašerâ* has saved him."[19]

---

[15] William G. Dever, "Iron Age Epigraphic Material from the Area of Khirbet el-Kom," *HUCA* 40–41 (1969–70) 158; 139–204.

[16] It is hard to imagine experts mistaking Arabic *kaf* for *qof; kaf* is pronounced like our *k* by city-dwellers, but by villagers or bedouin like our *ch* (*č*). *Qof* is pronounced like our hard *g* by bedouin, and not at all (or by a barely perceptible throat-movement) by city-dwellers. The root *qôm* as in Hebrew means "rise"; but in Arabic it seems never applied to "rising ground"; rather "a group of people" or "a stop on the route." *Kôm* means "mound," and is often found as a toponym-prefix like *tell* or *khirba*.

[17] Giovanni Garbini, "Su un' iscrizione ebraica da Khirbet el-Kom," *AION* 38 (1978) 191–93, proposes that *'šrt* as a fem. participle with *yad* means "bless" but euphemistically for curse, thus synonymous with *m'rr*.

[18] André Lemaire, "Les inscriptions de Khirbet el-Qôm et l'Ashérah de Yhwh," *RB* 84 (1977) 595–608.

[19] J. Jaroš, "Zur Inschrift Nr 3 von Hirbet el-Qôm," *BN* 19 (1982) 36; 30–41; 39, table of the letters; see the similar table(s) of J. Brian Peckham, *The Development of the Late Phoenician Scripts* (Harvard Semitic Series, 20; 1968) 104. Our Fig. 3 gives our stylized form of only the letters occurring at 'Ajrûd and Qôm, with our transcription for them.

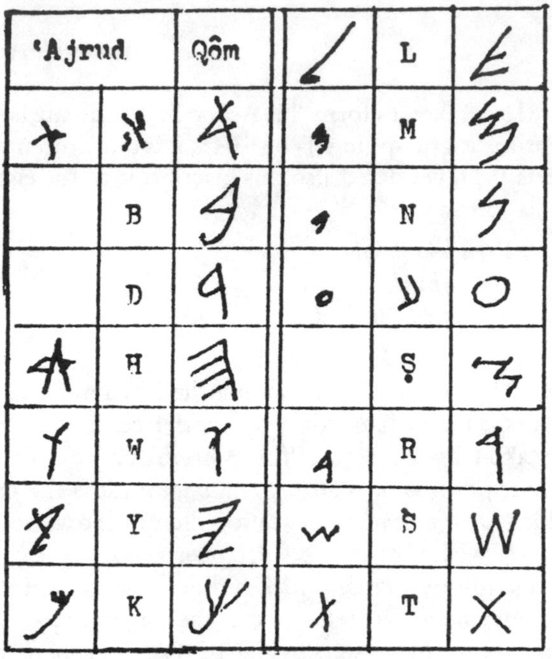

'Ajrud		Qôm			L	
					M	
	B				N	
	D				Ṣ	
	H					
	W				R	
	Y				Š	
	K				T	

Fig. 3. 'Ajrud/Qôm letters

Fig. 4. Qôm tomb sherd inscription from S. Mittmann, *ZDPV* 97 (1981) 140. Reprinted by permission of Prof. S. Mittmann and the publisher, Otto Harrassowitz Verlag.

3.3 Mittmann with admirable care and objectivity (except perhaps in choosing a title which begs the question) transcribes thus:

> 'ryhw.h[d]šr.ktbh.
> brk.'ryhw.lyhwh
> wmmṣr.ydh.l'l.šrth.hwš'.lh

"Uriah the singer wrote this: blessed is Uriahu by Yahweh, and from distress he praises the *El* of his cultus who saves him," omitting from consideration the final line about Oniahu.[20]

Mittmann admits that in the first line between *he* and *šin* there is undoubtedly a *daleth,* prolonged by the diagonal scratch through all three lines; he claims the *daleth* is canceled by the writer himself with the two vertical lines which we see on the drawing. Thus he avoids the *aleph* of Lemaire's *ha'ašer* "the wealthy," unsuitable to a tomb-inscription, an incitement to tomb-robbers. The third line begins with *waw,* then *mem* twice, intentionally (not by correction as Lemaire held). Ashera disappears because a second *lamed* is clearly recognizable on our drawing (taken from Mittmann); the "hand" becomes just part of *yōdēh* "praising."[21] The *šrth* which is left is "(his) Dienst," which we have rendered "cultus," *šrt,* "service," a common liturgical term. (One might have thought that a derivation from *šîr* might have been at least considered here, in relation to *šr* of the first line.)

3.4 One must conclude regretting that Mittmann does not give sufficient attention to the fact that whatever slight possibility there may be of finding *l'šrth* in the Qôm inscription is greatly enhanced by its similarity to 'Ajrud. This is safeguarded by Zevit, in his entirely different approach. He regards the goddess name as Ašeratâ, three times, equivalent to the attested Aširta: "I blessed Uriahu to Yahweh; and from his enemies, O Ašerata, save him .. by Abiyahu [for Oniyahu] and to Ašerata .. Ašerata."[22] A similar rendition had been independently proposed by Angerstorfer: Aširta is to be taken as a feminine noun without suffix, as Abdi-Aširta in the Amarna letter to Byblos.[23] This solution must not be omitted from our consideration, though it will doubtless recommend itself chiefly to those who antecedently find "Yahweh's Asherah" repugnant; and will be rejected by those who find it titillating.

[20] Siegfried Mittmann, "Die Grabinschrift des Sängers Uriahu," *ZDPV* 97 (1981) 139–52; our Fig. 4 is from his p. 140.

[21] S. Schroer ("Zur Deutung der Hand unter der Grabinschrift von Chirbet el Qom," *UF* 15 [1983] 191–99) holds that the hand is not as specifically "Israelite" as is claimed by Mittmann in the large portion of his article devoted to this question. Lemaire in *BARev* 11,2 (1985) 78 (cf. n. 55 below) comments on V. Parnass's proposal to relate the inscription to the hand.

[22] Ziony Zevit, "The Khirbet el-Qôm Inscription Mentioning a Goddess," *BASOR* 255 (1984) 43; 39–47; now Judith M. Hadley, "The Khirbet el-Qôm inscription," and M. O'Connor, "The poetic inscription from Khirbet el-Qôm," *VT* 37 (1987) 50–62; 224–30.

[23] Andreas Angerstorfer, "Ašerah als 'consort of Jahwe' oder Aširtah?" *BN* 17 (1982) 7–16.

4. Yahweh of Teman and His Asherah

4.1 A third inscription, or group of inscriptions, mentions "Yahweh of Teman and his Asherah," which thus far is documented chiefly or only by this fleeting declaration attributed by Weinfeld to Meshel: " 'Several times' [two? or more?] among 'the' inscriptions [which ones? presumably those of Meshel's Sinai survey] is found *yhwh tmn w'šrth*, important because of Hab 3,3 [Yahweh comes from Teman]."[24]

Such inscriptions, if they really exist, are indeed important, in part as justifying the rendition "Yahweh of Samaria" for 'Ajrud. This is the point chiefly focused by Emerton's erudite study, incidentally calling in question the common understanding of *yhwh ṣĕbā'ôt* (see below).

Even more important perhaps is the fact that such Teman mentions would go far to establish a genuine "parallel" between the undoubted mention of "Yahweh and his Asherah" at 'Ajrud and its very dubious mention in a quite differently situated inscription at Qôm.

5. Asherah as Name of a Divinity

5.1 Asherah, occurring forty times in the Bible, or an equivalent, is so often attested as the name of a goddess that it seems perfectly objective and fair to agree that the burden of proof must be on those who claim that in the apparently (though varyingly) cultic context of 'Ajrud and Qôm it has one of the more "dilutedly cultic" senses which we will examine below. We are fortunate in possessing a very recent Harvard doctoral dissertation, surveying all that is known about the goddess Asherah from outside the Bible, including the 'Ajrud and Qôm references. It is chiefly concerned, however, with the validity of literary data from Philo Byblius and Lucian, and with the equating of goddess-Asherah with Ugaritic Athirat and/or with (fertility-figurine) Qudšu, Ba'alat Gebal, Tanit, and Derketo.[25]

5.2 *The Phoenician History* was written probably around A.D. 100 by Philo of Byblos.[26] Chiefly the first book, a theogony, is preserved in Eusebius's

---

[24] M. Weinfeld (in Hebrew) additions to the inscriptions of 'Ajrud, *Shnaton la-Miqra'* 4 (1980) (280–)284; 5–6 (1982) 237–39. Meshel now renders [even the 'Ajrûd inscription?!] "Amaryahu [*one* only] said to his lord, 'May you be blessed by Yahweh of Teiman and his Asherah'": *IOSOT Jerusalem meeting summaries 1986*, p. 92; and see now his "The Israelite Religious Centre of Kuntillet Ajrûd, Sinai" in *Archaeology and Fertility Cult in the Ancient Mediterranean* (ed. A. Bonanno; Malta conference Sept. 1985; Amsterdam: Gräner, 1986) 237–39.

[25] Walter A. Maier, "The Study of 'Ašerah: The Extrabiblical Evidence," Harvard dissertation 1984 (Ann Arbor service copy) 73. Previously the chief treatment of Asherah was by William L. Reed, *The Asherah in the Old Testament* (Fort Worth, 1949); see nn. 33 and 49 below.

[26] Harold W. Attridge, Robert A. Oden, *Philo of Byblos, the Phoenician History* (CBQMS 9; Washington: CBA, 1981). The article of *Der kleine Pauly* (Stuttgart, 1967), by Hans Gärtner, must be sought under "Herennios Philon," 2. 1059–60.

Preparation for the Gospel. Philo's account purports to be largely a translation from Trojan-War era Sanchuniathon, who by Porphyry is also dated near to the Trojan War; but the gods are humanized in a "euhemerist" way more characteristic of Philo's contemporaries.[27] In *Praep. Ev.* 1.10–24, Astarte is like Rhea and Dione daughter of Ouranos; she is espoused by Kronos after he foils their plot to kill him. Kronos then has seven daughters by Astarte, and two sons; he had also seven sons by Rhea and two daughters by Dione. Maier limits his interest in this passage to proving that an originally single divinity, Ašera = Elat, is divided into two, Rhea = Ašera and Dione = Elat = Baaltis/Baalat. Astarte is thus tacitly left separate from the similar-sounding Ašera, who "does not play a greater role than Astarte." Farther on in *Praep. Ev.* (33–35) Kronos divinizes one of his sons by Rhea named Muth; and there is a parenthetical note that Ouranos "invented *baitylia* by contriving vivified stones."[28] Though this event is not put in any special relation to Astarte (or noticed at all by Maier), there is reason for maintaining that baitylion (or "bethel"!) became a variant for the *maṣṣēba* or cultic stela, which is one of the possible meanings of *ašera*.

5.3 *The Syrian Goddess,* though written in an Ionic dialect perhaps mocking Herodotus, remains attributed to Lucian of Samosata despite recent impugning.[29] The essay concerns the cult of the goddess Hera or Juno at Hierapolis.[30] Names in the context are equivalents of Semitic mythic figures (Kombabos is the Ḫumbaba of Gilgameš); the bearded Apollo is held to be El, and Zeus as Syrian Hera's consort is equated with Ba'al Hadad. Syrian Hera herself is shown from *other* sources to be Atargatis; either this entire name or only Atar- is 'Ateret/Astarte; -gatis may represent either an ending -'t, or an Anatolian Attis or (as most now hold with Albright) 'Anat.[31] Maier

---

[27] "Neither fully ancient nor fully recent" concludes James Barr, "Philo of Byblos and his 'Phoenician History,'" *BJRL* 57 (1974) 21; 17–63. On Sanchuniaton: Lynn R. Clapham, "Sanchuniaton: The First Two Cycles," Harvard dissertation, 1969; Otto Eissfeldt, "Phönikische und griechische Kosmogonie," *Kleine Schriften* 3 (1966) 501–12; Carl Clemen, "Die phönikische Religion nach Philo von Byblos," *Mitteilungen der Vorderasiatisch-Aegyptischen Gesellschaft* 42/3 (1939) 1–16.

[28] Jean-Marie Durand, "Le culte des bétyles en Syrie," *Miscellanea Babylonica* (Festschrift Maurice Birot; ed. Durand; Paris: Recherche sur les Civilisations, 1985) 79–84; W. Fauth, "Baitylia," *Der kleine Pauly* (Stuttgart, 1964) 1. 806–8; M.-J. Lagrange, "Pierres sacrées, dites bétyles," *RB* 10 (1901) 223–32; 231, "derivation from Bethel highly unlikely."

[29] R. A. Oden, *The Syrian Goddess: Studies in Lucian's De Syria Dea* (Harvard Semitic Monographs, 15; Missoula, MT: Scholars Press, 1977).

[30] Equated with Mabbug = Membij: D. G. Hogarth, "Hierapolis Syriae," *Annual of the British School at Athens* 14 (1907–8) 183.

[31] William F. Albright, "The Evolution of the West-Semitic Divinity 'An– 'Anat– 'Attā," *AJSL* 41 (1925) 73–101; further pp. 283–85; and 43 (1927) 233–36.

concludes agreeing with Oden that Atargatis is a conflation of the three major Canaanite goddesses: 'Aštart, 'Anat, and 'Ašerah.[32]

5.4 Further light on the Ašera/Astarte thus known from Lucian and Philo Byblius is found by Maier in a wide range of Ugaritic texts, often reinterpreted with the aid of his mentor Frank Cross. His chief conclusion is that the qdš of CTA 14,14,197 is an epithet of Atirat. This conclusion then dominates the epigraphic material which he examines, and in which qdš (as in four Egyptian portrayals) is identified with the nude-goddess figurines found "in almost every excavated site in Palestine."[33] She is further equated by Maier with Egyptian Hathor. This Ašera-qdš is then more deviously related to Tannit and Ba'alat-Gebal, "the Lady of Byblos," thus also Derketo.

5.5 Not prominent in Maier is the title "Lady Lion," which we noticed above for Ašera (why not Lioness? otherwise rather "Lion-Lady"). Lion-Lady is noted by Oden, and by Cross as an equivalent of 'Anat(?-Ašera).[34] Maier's pages vii and 203 mention, apparently as equated with Ašera, the Hittite El-Kunirša. This Elkunirša in an earlier dissertation unmentioned in Maier's bibliography was as at Ugarit "El's consort not yet in a perfectly marital relationship."[35] Influences which we would expect from the Egyptian pantheon are not forthcoming.[36]

Both Lipiński and Lemaire casually use the title Atirat ("Ašera under Canaanite influence replacing Atirat") in a way which would seem to support this reading instead of "her/his Ašera" at 'Ajrud. At Sidon, Ašera began to be more important than Astarte, though not *clearly* identified with Élat as

[32] R. Patai, "The Goddess Asherah," *JNES* 24 (1965) 37–52; on p. 38 it is noted that the Bible gives us the names of the three, assuming that 'Anat is "the Queen of Heaven," Jer 7:18.

[33] James B. Pritchard, *Palestine Figurines in Relation to certain Goddesses Known through Literature* (AOS 24; New Haven, 1943); examples in his *ANEP*, fig. 467, 469. Urs Winter, *Frau und Göttin: exegetische und ikonographische Studien zum weiblichen Gottesbild im Alten Israel und in dessen Umwelt* (OBO 53; Fribourg/Göttingen, 1983) 110, on qudšu-type nude female figurines; on p. 490, after treating the question "Did Yahweh have a paredra?" concludes "never a partner of Yahweh; at most an assistant (subordinate *Hilfsgrösse*)."

[34] Frank M. Cross, Jr., "The Origin and Early Evolution of the Alphabet," *ErIsr* 8 (1967) 13*; "The name 'servant of the Lion-lady' (i.e., 'Anat) is well-known from a list of names of an archers' guild of the period"; in "The Evolution of the Proto-Canaanite Alphabet," *BASOR* 134 (1954) 20 n. 17, he identifies Asherah with Élat.

[35] Tadanori Yamashita, "The Goddess Asherah," Yale dissertation, 1964; summary in *Studia Biblica et Theologica* 11 (1981) 229s. John Day's "Asherah in the Hebrew Bible and Northwest Semitic Literature" (prize essay of the 1984 Doubleday competition in honor of Mitchell Dahood [*BARev* 11,2 (1985) 73]; *JBL* 105 [1986] 385–408) shows extrabiblical usages both for goddess and for cult-object.

[36] Maier's appendix C follows up his brief earlier mentions of Hathor; see now Michel Gitton, *Les divines éspouses de la 18e dynastie* (Paris: Centre de Recherche d'Histoire Ancienne. 1984); H.-P. Müller, "Aštoret," *TWAT* 6. 453–63.

consort of Ešmun.[37] The resounding title of another recent research conveys information mostly from Lagrange.[38]

6. Ašerâ as a Common Noun

6.1 Here too another study is very serviceable, that of Emerton. He claims at the outset that the primary and immediate importance of the 'Ajrud-related inscriptions is as our very earliest example of *yhwh* written (not as in the Meša-stone) by an "Israelite."[39] He then emphasizes that *yhwh šmrn,* especially if confirmed by *yhwh tmn,* sheds new light on a very old problem of Biblical Hebrew. *Yahweh ṣĕbā'ôt* has been explained as an ellipsis or a kind of apposition for *Yahweh 'ĕlohê ṣĕbā'ôt,* since in Biblical Hebrew a proper name cannot stand in the construct state, despite some evidence from *place*-names or extrabiblical Semitic.[40] Ultimately, however, Emerton does not exclude ellipsis of *'elohê* after *yahweh:* indeed holds the possibility rather heightened by the new find.

6.2 A more urgent issue is whether Ašera as a personal name can have a grammatical possessor, or must be taken as a common noun if the final *-h* is regarded as "his" (likelier than "hers"). The Aširtâ alternative (*-h* being ending of a feminine noun in the absolute state) does not seem to have been noticed by Emerton. In any case, *ašerâ* as a common noun is frequent in the Bible for "a *maṣṣēbâ*-type sacred post or tree-trunk," in some cases as symbol of the goddess Ašerah (often with crudely-carved breasts); in other cases not (or even with masculine-phallic character).[41] There is grammatically no difficulty in the rendering "for Yahweh and for his cult-symbol," whether the symbol represented Yahweh himself, or one of the Elim demoted to "his footstool," or something more specifically feminine with which he is put in relation.

An interesting reversal of the development from goddess into post was offered recently by Dohmen, who claims that the Hebrew word *semel,* normally taken to mean "statue," conveys instead a "Geleit- Funktion," either a "worshiper," or a "consort, paredra" (*Begleiterin,* e.g., 2 Chr 33:7, 15).[42]

[37] John W. Betlyon, "The cult of 'Ašerah/'Élat et Sidon," *JNES* 44 (1985) 53–56.

[38] Pierre Lévêque, "Astarté s'embarque pour Cythère" [in 12th century becomes Aphrodite], *Hommages à Lucien Lerat,* ed. Hélène Walter (Annales Litt. Besançon 294, Hist.anc. 55; Paris: Les Belles Lettres, 1984) 451–60; M.-J. Lagrange, *Études sur les religions sémitiques* (Paris, 1903) 378; 351–93, "Les mythes phéniciens" (Philo, Sanchuniathon).

[39] J. A. Emerton, "New Light on Israelite Religion: The Implications of the Inscriptions from Kuntillet 'Ajrûd," *ZAW* 94 (1982) 1–20.

[40] G. R. Driver, "Reflections on Recent Articles," *JBL* 73 (1954) 125–36.

[41] J. R. Engle, "Pillar Figurines of Iron Age Israel and Ashérah-Ashérim," dissertation, 1979; p. 82 on Qôm; R. North, "Malsteine," *LTK* (Freiburg: Herder, 1961) 6. 1335–36.

[42] C. Dohmen, "Heisst *semel* 'Bild, Statue'?" *ZAW* 96 (1984) 263–66.

Though this insight seems at first to support "Yahweh's consort," it would also prove that the same word may be used for both a person and a cult-object. "His *ašera*" is thus taken by Lemaire as "a sacred tree or grove, but on the way to being personified."[43]

6.3 The Mishnah seems to regard the despised Ašera as a *live* tree.[44] An *evergreen* tree was specified by Wellhausen in his interpretation of Hos 14:9 (below). The sense of "grove," *temenos,* for ašera, as an extension of "tree (-stump)" seems suggested by the dictionary for 2 Chr 19:3; 33:2; Isa 27:9 and a dozen other texts. But these are mostly negative, praise of a ruler who did not make, or who uprooted, "asherahs" (often *ašerîm* rather than *ašerôt;* Exod 34:13 = Deut 7:5, "you shall break their *maṣṣebôt* and uproot their *ašerîm*").

A further extension from "grove" to "*any* (cultic) enclosure" is favored by Lipiński. He alleges Judg 6:25, but the next verse certainly fits "(dead) wood post" better; no more cogent is Deut 16:21. His other evidences taken from the Bible are reinterpreted in the light of Akkadian cognates which designate "shrines, chapels, sanctuaries." He also adduces Phoenician examples. Ultimately he seems to hold with Albright that the root sense is just "place," not specially "holy" nor connected with "wood."[45]

7. Specific Exegetical Applications

7.1 Before drawing conclusions as to the likeliest interpretation and biblical relevance of "Yahweh's Asherah," we may briefly call attention to the specific texts to which the new finds have been applied. As noted above (and shown on Fig. 2) the two figures with tail or phallus have to the left of them two much more evident bovines. These are claimed to be the "oppressor cows of Bashan in Samaria" (Amos 4:1) against which are the standing figures of Yahweh and Asherah.[46] No one seems to have suggested a connection with Yahweh represented under the form of a bull even in the Jerusalem Temple or the "golden calf" of Exod 32:4; 1 Kgs 12:28 according to insights of Albright widely though not universally accepted.[47] In Hos 8:5 "the calf

[43] A. Lemaire, "Who or What was Yahweh's Asherah?" *BARev* 10,6 (1984) 51. See now David N. Freedman, "Yahweh of Samaria and his Asherah," *BA* 50 (1987) 241–48.

[44] Mishna *Orla* 1,7,8; ʿ*AbodZar* 3,7,9; *Sukka* 3,1–3.

[45] E. Lipiński, "The Goddess Atirat in Ancient Arabia, in Babylon, and in Ugarit," *OLP* 3 (1972) 101–19.

[46] Paul F. Jacobs, " 'Cows of Bashan'—A Note on the Interpretation of Amos 4:1," *JBL* 104 (1985) 109–10.

[47] Moses Aberbach and Leivy Smolar, "Aaron, Jeroboam, and the Golden Calves," *JBL* 86 (1967) 129–40; Samuel E. Loewenstamm, "The Making and Destruction of the Golden Calf," *Bib* 48 (1967); W. F. Albright, *From the Stone Age to Christianity*[2] (Garden City, NY: Doubleday, 1957) 299; R. North, "Jeroboam's Tragic Social-Justice Epic," *Homenaje a Juan Prado* (Madrid,

of Samaria," as symbol of its opposition to Judah's Yahweh, is spurned and broken.

7.2 The possible association of Yahweh and Asherah with Samaria at 'Ajrud has been further taken as an exemplification of the fact that prophets opposed associating Yahweh not only with Asherah but also with *cities*.[48] This insight could be of value in tracing below the transit from a stage in which the El of Abraham or Bethel was put in vague parallel with the El of other cities.

7.3 We may also advert to Hos 14:8 (Hebr 9), "O Ephraim, what are idols to me any more? *'ănî 'anîtî wa-ăšûrennû* (RSV, "it is I who answer and look after you"; *JerB*[2], "when I hear him and watch over him"); I am like an evergreen fir." For the Hebrew terms above, Wellhausen had proposed "I am his 'Anah and his Asherah."[49] This bold conjecture anticipates some of the issues here discussed in relation to "a consort of Yahweh." We admit also the relevance further noted to Hos 4:12, blaming the people which consults its wood: "this could refer to the *ašerâ*" frequently in parallel with *maṣṣebâ*.[50]

8. Religionsgeschichtlich Evaluation

8.1 The glittering headlines "Did Yahweh have a consort?" and "Asherah, consort of Yahweh?" involve really two separate questions. One is whether in some circles of Canaan/Israel Yahweh was thought to have a *paredra* or mate, not necessarily divine, as was the case of the numerous matings of Zeus and other Greek divinities with attractive humans. A quite different question, and even more ominous, is whether Asherah was considered to share in the *divinity* of Yahweh, to be (equally, or at least somehow) divine. Prior to this double problem we must resolve the question of whether the new graffiti are really "cultic" at all.

8.2 Naveh begins with the correct observation that graffiti in modern times are quite different from those known in antiquity.[51] Most of the personal (as distinct from political) graffiti of which we have actual experience are either scurrilous (scatological) or amorous. Perhaps the Pompei

---

1975) 191–214; disputed in the dissertation of my student T. Brzegowy, *Les prophètes contre le sanctuaire royal de Bethel* (Rome: Gregorian University, 1975); Manfred Weippert, "Gott und Stier," *ZDPV* 77 (1961) 93–117.

[48] Knud Jeppesen, "Micah V 13 in the Light of a Recent Archaeological Discovery," *VT* 34 (1984) 462–66.

[49] Wellhausen, *Skizzen und Vorarbeiten* (&1983) 5,131; Moshe Weinfeld, "Kuntillet 'Ajrud Inscriptions and their Significance," *Studi Epigrafici e Linguistici* 1 (1984) 122; 121–130.

[50] J. C. de Moor, "*Ashērāh*," *TDOT* 1. (438–)444. K. A. D. Smelid, *Behouden Schrift; historische documenten uit het Oude Israel* (Baarn: Ten Have, 1984) 151 compares Num 6:24 for the blessing formula; see also n. 9 above.

[51] Joseph Naveh, "Graffiti and Dedications," *BASOR* 235 (1979) 27–30.

inscriptions already fit into these categoreis. From our background we are led to question whether the 'Ajrud-Qôm inscriptions really belong to cultus at all, or just use the divine name in blasphemous or simply vehement expression of strong emotion, like "god-damned."

It must be admitted, however, that a large proportion of the graffiti known from antiquity, even the "John loves Mary" type, are really cultic: "John" being the name of the scribbler, and "Mary" the name of a divinity as object of unmistakable respect and veneration, as in the Sinaitic inscriptions. Unless ancient examples are forthcoming, we must consider it unlikely that the 'Ajrud-Qôm uses of the divine name were intended to be just blasphemous or vulgar, as if "his Asherah" were in derisive contempt of Yahweh's alleged purity and spirituality.

Even if not profane, the graffiti could be the expression of unorthodox "popular religiosity" or ill-informed syncretism. Even a sincere worshiper of the graffito-writing type may have had only vague ideas of the religion(s) which surrounded him, but wanted to be on the good side of whatever higher powers there might be. His combining of two incompatible divinities could therefore have been the kind of ignorant syncretism which does not point to any real existing "cultus" at all. After reflecting on this possibility, we are forced to conclude that although this might be true of any of the new-found inscriptions taken singly, they nevertheless *can* fall into a pattern too distinct to be dismissed as random, even apart from the Teman evidence which we are not yet in a position to judge.

8.3 As for Yahweh's consort, what is really at stake here is how fully the biblical era theologians' equating of Yahweh with El/Elohim had been worked out and penetrated into the popular consciousness. We needed no new inscriptions to be aware that within our Bible are plainly preserved indications that "Yahweh is greater than all the Elohim" (Exod 14:11).

The Bible in some passages clearly states that there are other "gods" (*elim*) besides Yahweh: *elim* whose existence and divinity is neither affirmed nor denied. But it is rather firmly stated that Yahweh is "greater than those other gods."[52] "Give glory to Yahweh, you *elim*" (Ps 29:1). "Every nation will walk in the name of its El, and we will walk in the name of Yahweh our Elohim forever" (Micah 4:5).

Taking similar expressions along with what is said about God making the Elim his footstool or his messenger, there has long been a widespread conviction that the tribes later known as Israel had recognized as their supreme divinity an *El* ("of the patriarchs"; "of the covenant," Judg 9:46; "of Bethel," Gen 35:7; "Shaddai," Exod 6:2) but were not exactly clear whether or to what

---

[52] On the ultimate orthodoxy of these formulations see F. X. Kortleitner, *De Hebraeorum ante exsilium Babylonium* (Innsbruck, 1910) and a number of his similar booklets.

extent their El was identical with the El worshiped by rival tribes.[53] It is only gradually made clearer within the Bible that any being called El other than Yahweh had been demoted to serve as his footstool; only later that such an El had no reality whatsoever. But even if we find in our Bible the unequivocal statement "Yahweh alone is El," we must recognize this as the culmination of a development of many things which were earlier believed about "the El of our fathers."

If, ultimately, Yahweh is El, then to some extent the question of whether Yahweh had a paredra in early Hebrew belief becomes a question of whether El had a paredra. Actually we do not have within the Bible indication of any paredra even for those *Elim* to which not all reality is denied.[54] But we possess Ugaritic and Phoenician indications that 'Anat or another female divinity was closely associated with El or Baal. Lemaire perhaps puts the case too strongly, "If Yahweh replaced El, it would seem logical to suppose that Ašera [under Canaanite influence replacing Athirat] functioned as the consort or wife of Yahweh"; he adds that Judg 3:7 and 1 Kgs 18:19 "fit" this view.[55] Rather than "logically suppose" that Asherah in fact functioned as Yahweh's consort, we should say with Albright that there was a stage, reflected in our Bible, during which even sincere worshipers of Yahweh as "the supreme El" were not exactly sure as to the status of the closest associates of "any other El."

8.4 Proceeding to the question of whether Asherah was worshiped as a *divinity* within Israel (quite apart from whether she was *also* considered "Yahweh's consort"), we find that this is what Dever really focused in the article that had "consort" in its title:

> The "silence" regarding Asherah as the consort of Yahweh, successor to Canaanite El, may now be understood as the result of the near-total suppression of the cult by 8th-6th century reformers. As a result, references to "Asherah," while not actually expunged from the consonantal text of the MT, were misunderstood by later editors or re-interpreted to suggest merely the shadowy

---

[53] Albright, *FSAC* (n. 47 above) 248, 271. The problem is somewhat differently posed by José Alonso Díaz, "Los 'dos Yahves' incompatibles o dos antropologías bíblicas contropuestas," in N. Fernández Marcos, ed., *Simposio bíblico español,* Salamanca 1982 (Madrid: Univ. Complutense, 1984) 371–91; Eng. 392: the "Yahweh of the prophets" is so different from the "Yahweh of the cult" because a "baalization of Yahwism" took place at Israel's entry into Canaan; further O. Loretz, *Psalm 29, Kanaanäische El- und Baaltraditionen in jüdischer Sicht* (Altenberge, 1984); O. Keel, ed., *Monotheismus im Alten Israel und seiner Umwelt* (Biblische Beiträge 14; Fribourg: Swiss KBW, 1980) 168–71; George E. Mendenhall, "The Worship of Baal and Asherah: a study in the social bonding functions of religious systems" *Biblical and Related Studies* (Festschrift for S. Iwry; ed. A. Kort, S. Morschauser; Winona Lake, IN: Eisenbrauns, 1985) 147–58.

[54] J. Chopineau, "Être libéré des dieux," *Foi et Vie* 82,2 (1983) 83–96, includes Asherah among those associates of Baal from which Israel had to be liberated.

[55] A. Lemaire, "Who or What was Yahweh's Asherah?" *BARev* 10,6 (1984) 46 (42–47.50–51).

image of the goddess . . . "innocent deception" . . . Nearly all later commentators, Jewish and Christian, have interpreted the [forty] texts in a "minimalist" fashion.[56]

The question of whether the Bible conveys information about a female being who was supposed to be God(dess) has next been subtly metamorphosed into the currently popular question of whether feminine traits also must be recognized in Israel's true and only God. Raurell seems clearly to regard the ʿAjrud-Qôm data as relevant to this problem, though he concludes only that Yahweh was never genealogically integrated into the pantheon of ʿAjrud or Qôm, and notes with Cohen that "the two figurines" at ʿAjrud are bisexual.[57] There are more than two, in fact (assuming that his "figurines" are painted representations rather than, as normally, statuettes), but two have a protuberance which could be either phallus or tail (but hardly both; in any case possibly added later).

More nuanced is the position taken by E. Jacob in "feminine traits in the portrayal of the God of Israel." He construes "*his* ašera" to be necessarily a common noun, but not consort; apparently rather "a feminine divinity; a goddess," because Athart and ʿAnat are goddess-names within the Bible as well as at Ugarit.[58] But he introduces a different factor. The Bible does indeed undeniably stress the role of God as spouse. The feminine partner is rather Israel, and this does not point to any feminine trait within God. But Jacob finds it important that Israel itself is shown as taking over the role once held by a goddess. He judiciously concludes, "to speak of God as 'father in heaven and mother on earth' would be harmful; but the Father should be invoked in relation to Eve as mother of all the living."

---

[56] William G. Dever, "Asherah, Consort of Yahweh? New Evidence from Kuntillet ʿAjrud," *BASOR* 255 (1984) 31; 21–37; further, "Recent Archaeological Confirmation of the Cult of Asherah in Ancient Israel," *Hebrew Studies* 23 (Madison, 1982) 37–43. Mark S. Smith ("God Male and Female in the OT; Yahweh and his 'Asherah,'" *Theological Studies* 48 [1987] 333–40 on p. 334s) does not distinguish paredra as divine or beloved human. See now Ruth Hestrin, "The Lachish Ewer and the ʾAsherah," *IEJ* 37 (1987) 212–23; Jeffrey H. Tigay, *You Shall Have No Other Gods: Israelite Religion in the Light of Hebrew Inscriptions* (HSS 31; Atlanta: Scholars Press, 1987); K. M. Alomia, *Lesser Gods of the Ancient Near East and Some Comparisons with Heavenly Beings of the OT* (Andrews dissertation, Berrien Springs, MI, 1987).

[57] Frederic Raurell, "Il mito della maschilità di Dio come problema ermeneutico," *Laurentianum* 25 (1984) 26; 3–77.

[58] E. Jacob, "Traits féminins dans la figure du Dieu d'Israël," *Mélanges bibliques et orientaux en l'honneur de M. Mathias Delcor* (AOAT 217; Kevelaer/Neukirchen, 1985) 227; 221–30; citing Kurt Lüthi, *Gottes neue Eva. Wandlungen des Weiblichen* (Stuttgart: Kreuz, 1978). [On p. 237–53 of the Delcor volume, Bernhard Lang, "No sex in heaven; the logic of procreation, death, and eternal life in the Judaeo-Christian tradition," is not about God but about the survivor.]

Other inquiries into "the feminine dimension of the divine" have perhaps wisely emphasized tender providence or wisdom[59] — instead of the 'Ajrud-Qôm type portrayals, which ultimately focus rather the question of feminine sex-object of a thoroughly masculine God.

8.5 What has just been said above about either consort or goddess is applicable chiefly if we regard "his Asherah" as a personal name. Even if we take Ašîrtah as an *absolute* goddess-name (not "his/Yahweh's"), its pairing with Yahweh remains challenging. The challenge might seem to vanish if we find it plausible to take the common noun ašera as merely temenos or shrine. But if—and this is what all in all we consider likeliest—*ašera* is a common noun meaning like *maṣṣebâ* a cult-post, then it does trail along with it enough relation to its origins to make the question of atavistic goddess or consort not altogether irrelevant.

An ordinary worshiper, not uncouth or crassly ignorant, but just average theologically unsophisticated, might well have been impelled, upon sighting an obelisk-like cult-stela or tree trunk, to formulate a pious invocation "for Yahweh (of Samaria) and his symbol." He may even have known that it was frowned upon to admit any kind of symbol to represent Yahweh, precisely because such symbols trailed polytheistic or feminine associations. But he may well have felt the need to show respect for what in some quarters was taken as a "representation" of God. It required no new inscriptions to assure us that such practices were fairly common among the worshipers for whom our Bible was written.

[59] Christa Mulack, *Die Weiblichkeit Gottes: Matriarchale Voraussetzungen des Gottesbildes* (Berlin: Kreuz, 1983); J. C. Engelsman, *The Feminine Dimension of the Divine* (Philadelphia: Westminster, 1979).

Part III

Dead Sea Scrolls

Matt 18:15-17 in Relation to Three Texts from Qumran Literature (CD 9:2-8, 16-22; 1QS 5:25-6:1)

Timothy R. Carmody
Spring Hill College

He shall instruct the Many in the works of God and shall teach them his wonderful, mighty deeds.

Damascus Document 13:7-8

IT IS COMMON FOR COMMENTATORS on Matt 18:15–17 to draw a parallel between that text and texts from Qumran literature (1QS 5:24–6:1; CD 9:2–8; CD 9:16–22).[1] Some just mention the parallel.[2] Others see one or the other point of similarity and interest.[3] Some would see an almost exact parallel,[4] and others have even suggested direct influence or even dependence.[5] Yet with all the references to the parallels from QL, very little careful comparison between the texts has been done. It is the purpose of this paper to go a small

[1] It is assumed that Qumran literature (QL) was written by the Essenes. Based on the fragments found at Qumran, we are also assuming that the *Damascus Document* from the Cairo Geniza belongs to QL.

[2] P. Gaechter, *Das Matthäus Evangelium* (Innsbruck: Tyrolia-Verlag, 1963) 599–600; L. Mowry, *The Dead Sea Scrolls and the Early Church* (Chicago: University of Chicago Press, 1962) 33; G. Strecker, *Der Weg der Gerechtigkeit* (3d ed.; FRLANT 82; Göttingen: Vandenhoeck & Ruprecht, 1971) 223 n. 5.

[3] D. Catchpole, "Reproof and Reconciliation in the Q Community: A Study of the Tradition-history of Mt 18,15–17.21–22/Lk 17,3–4," *Studien zum Neuen Testament und Seiner Umwelt* 8 (1983) 83–84; J. Gnilka, "Die Kirche des Matthäus und die Gemeinde von Qumran," *BZ* nf 7 (1963) 55–56.

[4] J. Daniélou, *The Dead Sea Scrolls and Primitive Christianity* (Baltimore: Helicon, 1958) 40; W. Pesch, *Matthäus der Seelsorger* (SBS 2; Stuttgart: Katholisches Bibelwerk, 1966) 39–40; L. Schiffman, "The Qumran Law of Testimony," *RevQ* 8 (1972–75) 611–12.

[5] W. D. Davies, *The Setting of the Sermon on the Mount* (Cambridge: University Press, 1964) 221–23; J. Schmitt, "Contribution à l'étude de la discipline pénitentielle dans l'église primitive à la lumière des textes de Qumran," *Les manuscrits de la mer Morte: Colloque de Strasbourg 25–27 Mai 1955* (Bibliothèque des Centres d'Études supérieures spécialisés; Paris: Presses universitaires de France, 1957) 99.

distance in making that comparison. By presenting a brief study of the three Essene texts and then showing the striking similarities and equally striking differences of Matt 18:15–17 to these texts, we hope to show that Matthew had the Essene legal code in mind when he wrote 18:15–17 as a rebuttal to their view of law.

Three Texts from Qumran Literature

Both passages from CD (9:2–8, 16–22) are from the section called the "Former Ordinances."[6] According to J. Murphy-O'Connor this section of CD consists of the ordinances written by the Essene community living in the Diaspora, perhaps Babylonia, prior to 165 B.C. and prior to the Essenes' ever coming to Kirbet Qumran.[7]

This section of CD gives a picture of a community internally well defined and hierarchically ordered. Every camp had an overseer, usually a priest, whose job included instructing the community (13:7–10), examining and admitting new members (13:11–13), and recording the offenses of members of the community (9:17–22). Besides the overseer, there were ten judges in each community (10:4–5), who were responsible for legal judgments (9:9–10). They heard witnesses and may have pronounced the death penalty (9:23–10:1).

At this stage the eschatological view of the community was not highly developed. There was an expectation of the coming of the Messiah of Aaron and Israel (12:23–13:1; 14:19), who was to perform some sort of judgment (14:2, 19). Yet the community does not seem at all preoccupied with the future judgment and carries out present judgment in the community based on its interpretation of the law and not on any eschatological motivation.

The law was the overwhelming preoccupation of this community. They viewed themselves as having received special knowledge to interpret the law correctly and fully (15:5–15; 16:1–9). The first half of the "Former Ordinances" deals with explicating vague or anomalous points of the law.

The first passage with which we are concerned is CD 9:2–8:[8]

(2) And concerning what is said, "you shall not take revenge and you shall not bear a grudge against the sons of your people," every man from among those who have entered the (3) Covenant who brings a case against his fellow and has not reproved him before witnesses (4) or brings the accusation in the heat of

---

[6] J. Murphy-O'Connor, "La genèse littéraire de la *Règle de la Communauté*," *RB* 76 (1969) 531; "The Essenes in Palestine," *BA* 40 (1977) 121; see also, "A Literary Analysis of Damascus Document VI, 2–VIII, 3," *RB* 78 (1971) 216–17.

[7] Murphy-O'Connor, "Essenes in Palestine," 121.

[8] Unless otherwise noted, the translation of passages from QL follows the text as reconstructed and pointed by E. Lohse (*Die Texte aus Qumran* [Munich: Kösel, 1971]).

anger or recounts it to his elders so that he (the offender) is despised, he (the accuser) is one who takes revenge and bears a grudge. (5) Is it not written that only "he (God) takes revenge on his foes and bears a grudge against his enemies." (6) And if he keeps silent to him from one day to the next and in the heat of his anger speaks against him in a capital matter, (7) he has witnessed against himself because he did not uphold the commandment of God that says, "you shall certainly (8) reprove your neighbor, and you shall not bear sin because of him."

The passage is an attempt to explicate the precise meaning of Lev 19:17–18, parts of which are quoted at the beginning and the end of the passage. The community was concerned with following the law of Moses fully and asked what it meant to take revenge or bear a grudge and when a man must reprove his fellow. The three examples of taking revenge given in lines 3 and 4 (one of which has to do with reproof) are all related to the process of bringing an accusation before a court, and reproving one's fellow is again linked to the judicial process in lines 6–8. Lev 19:15, which prohibits rendering dishonest judgments, may have provided the clue to the community for interpreting the reproof in 19:17–18 as applying to the judicial process.

Although this passage is not directly concerned with the judicial process, it does give a good deal of information about it. The passage indicates that before a case could be brought to court the accuser must reprove the offender before witnesses. Lev 19:17 mentions the reproof of one's fellow as a means that might be required in order to avoid bearing a grudge, but it does not state that reproving is the *necessary* means to that end. The Essenes made the reproof in Lev 19:17 a necessary part of their legal system.[9]

They have also added the requirement that the reproof be before witnesses. Although no number of witnesses is mentioned, this requirement is probably based on the requirement of two or three witnesses for a legal case (Deut 19:15).[10] Thus the passage links together Lev 19:17 and Deut 19:15.

This passage is concerned with showing when an accuser acts improperly and bears a grudge. It describes what was required by law to bring a case to court properly. There is no indication here that the reproof was meant to bring the offender to repentance, only that it was to keep the accuser from acting out of revenge.

Line 4 discusses the case where the accuser "recounts it to his elders." Since the context deals with the legal process, this too probably refers to part of that process. The first two examples of bearing a grudge speak of what is necessary before bringing a case (*yābî' . . . dābār; wehēbî'ô*) to court. Since this

---

[9] L. Schiffman says that the Essenes were unique in developing reproof as a forensic procedure (*Sectarian Law in the Dead Sea Scrolls: Courts, Testimony and the Penal Code* [Brown Judaic Studies 33; Chico, CA: Scholars Press, 1983] 96).

[10] Catchpole, "Reproof," 80; Davies, *Setting*, 223; Schiffman, *Sectarian Law*, 96.

third example is not cited as a precondition to bringing the case, it probably refers to that stage of the process when the case is already in court and the accuser is giving testimony against the accused in such a way as to make the judges (elders) despise the accused.[11]

Thus there were at least two steps in the legal process. (1) The accuser was required to reprove the offender before witnesses. (2) The case was brought to court where it was heard by the elders/judges. It is possible that there was also another step involving reproof alone at the beginning of the process. Line 6 says that a person has not fulfilled the commandment to reprove his neighbor if he keeps silent from one day to the next. The person's keeping silent clearly refers to his not reproving the offender as required, since this section concludes by quoting Lev 19:17 about reproving.[12] It is possible to argue that the reproof that was to take place on the same day is not the same as the reproof before witnesses, but a complete study of this possibility will have to wait until all three texts have been presented.

The second important passage from the "Former Ordinances" is CD 9:16–22:

> (16b) For every matter in which a man is unfaithful (17) to the Law and his neighbor, being alone, sees him, if it is a capital offense, he (the neighbor) must report it (18) to the overseer, with the offender present as a reproof. The overseer will write it down in his own hand until he (the offender) should do it (19) again before another one who in turn reports it to the overseer. If the offender is caught again before (20) one, his judgment is complete. And if they are two and they are witnessing to (21) one matter,[13] the man shall be separated from the purification, only if they are trustworthy (22) and report it to the overseer on the same day that they see the man.

This passage is clearly meant to give an interpretation of Deut 17:6 and 19:15, even though neither text is cited. Deut 19:15 requires that two or three witnesses are necessary to convict an offender of a crime, while Deut 17:6 says that two or three witnesses are required for putting a person to death.

---

[11] Schiffman says that the elders constitute a court (*Sectarian Law*, 94).

[12] A. Dupont-Sommer assumes that keeping silent means not rebuking (*The Essene Writings from Qumran* [Cleveland: World, 1961] 149).

[13] The text reads 'ḥr, but with Lohse (*Texte*, 84) we read 'ḥd. Yet the emendation makes little difference for this discussion. The arguments concerning lines 20b–22a and whether they deal with two witnesses to the very same offense, two occurrences of the same offense, or two different offenses, are not our concern here. For those arguments see B. Jackson, "Damascus Document IX, 16–23 and Parallels," *RevQ* 9 (1977–78) 445–46; J. Neusner, " 'By the Testimony of Two Witnesses' in the Damascus Document IX, 17–22 and in Pharisaic-Rabbinic Law," *RevQ* 8 (1972–75) 199–201; C. Milikowsky, "Law at Qumran: A Critical Reaction to Lawrence H. Schiffman, *Sectarian Law in the Dead Sea Scrolls: Courts, Testimony and the Penal Code*," *RevQ* 12 (1985–86) 243–44.

The Essenes concluded that three witnesses were necessary to convict of a capital offense (9:16–20), while only two were necessary in matters of property (9:22–23).[14] However, the most important and unique aspect of CD 9:16–22 is that it allows for the combination of witnesses from separate offenses.[15]

Even though this passage does not set out to describe the community's legal procedure but only to discuss the possibilities for fulfilling one of its requirements (two or three witnesses), it does provide a glimpse of that legal procedure, since line 20 speaks of his judgment (*mišpāṭô*) being complete (*šālēm*).

Reproving is again considered a necessary part of the legal process. Although this passage is based on Deut 19:15 and is concerned with witnesses, it contains a reference to reproving from Lev 19:17, just as CD 9:2–3, based on Lev 19:17, was concerned with reproving and contained an allusion to the witnesses of Deut 19:15. The similarity found in the linking of reproving and witnesses is not negated by the fact that the witnesses (*'ēdîm*) in CD 9:3 are to the reproof and in 9:16b–20a they are to the offense.[16] In fact it is this difference in the roles of the witnesses in the two passages that draws attention to the linking of Lev 19:17 and Deut 19:15 in both.

It is possible that 9:16–22 also contains a parallel to the reproof before witnesses. In 9:16–22 the reproof apparently does not take place before the reporting of the crime to the overseer but concurrent with it. C. Milikowsky maintains that this contradicts the procedure described in 9:2–8, which calls for the reproving to take place before taking the case to court.[17] However, the reporting of the offense to the overseer is not to be compared to bringing the case to court, since CD 10:1 indicates that the judges, and not the overseer, passed the death sentence. When the overseer had obtained the written testimony of three witnesses to separate occurrences of the same offense, then the case could be taken to court and tried before the judges. In this analysis, the reproving before the overseer would take the place of reproof before witnesses,[18] and the judicial process would be the same in 9:2–8 and 9:16–20: The accuser must reprove the offender before witnesses (or the overseer), and

---

[14] Jackson, "Damascus Document IX, 16–23," 446; Milikowsky, "Law at Qumran," 243; Schiffman, "Qumran Law," 607.

[15] Jackson, "Damascus Document IX, 16–23," 445; Neusner, "Testimony," 201–2; Schiffman, "Qumran Law," 610.

[16] The noun *'ēd* is not used in lines 16b–22 but does occur in line 23 referring to the witnesses of an offense.

[17] Milikowsky, "Law at Qumran," 244.

[18] Schiffman (*Sectarian Law,* 98) has suggested that there are witnesses present with the overseer when the offense is reported.

only then may he bring the case to trial before the judges (elders). There are again two steps in the legal process that are described.

As in CD 9:2–8, this passage gives no indication that the reproof is meant to bring the offender to repentance but only that it is a necessary part of the judicial process. It also highlights the community's preoccupation with the law. The offense that is being discussed is a capital offense (*děbar māwet*), but it is first described generally as "a matter in which a man is unfaithful to the law" (*dābār 'ăšer yim'al 'îš battôrâ*). The community was not only concerned that the offense was unfaithfulness to the law; they were also concerned that the legal proceedings be completely faithful to the law. They made explicit what was vague and joined together different prescriptions in the law in order to make sure that the law was meticulously followed.[19]

The third passage that is relevant to Matt 18:15–17 is 1QS 5:25–6:1. This passage is from a section of the *Rule of the Community* that J. Pouilly assigns to Stage IV.[20] Following J. Murphy-O'Connor, Pouilly maintains that Stage IV was written by the Essenes who were living at Qumran during the latter part of archaeological period 1b.[21] The period is marked by new construction and an increase in population that is dated to the first quarter of the first century B.C.[22] Pouilly maintains that the literature of this stage offers no new disciplinary code.[23] Rather it is concerned with members of the community who are not fervent in their adherence to the existing codes. Laxity and apostasy are the major concerns, and they have reached crisis proportions.[24]

The text of 1QS 5:25–6:1 reads as follows:

[19] B. Levin has suggested that the combination of witnesses as an interpretation of Deut 19:15 is derived by analogy from Exod 21:29, which requires the death penalty for the owner of an ox who gores someone to death, if that ox has previously gored someone and the owner, though warned, fails to confine the ox properly ("Damascus Document IX, 17–22: A New Translation and Comments," *RevQ* 8 [1972–75] 196). Y. Yadin talks about the same tendencies in 11QTemple to combine laws that seem to refer to the same matter, to explicate vague laws in light of other laws, and to get rid of inconsistencies (*The Temple Scroll* [3 vols.; Jerusalem: Israel Exploration Society, the Institute of Archaeology of the Hebrew University of Jerusalem and the Shrine of the Book, 1983] 1. 73–81).

[20] Pouilly, *La règle de la communauté de Qumran: Son évolution littéraire* (Cahiers de la Revue biblique 17; Paris: Gabalda, 1976) 82–83.

[21] Pouilly, *Règle*, 65–66; Murphy-O'Connor, "Genèse," 548–49. These periods have been assigned and dated by R. de Vaux (*Archaeology and the Dead Sea Scrolls* [London: Oxford University Press, 1973] 3–24).

[22] R. de Vaux, *Archaeology*, 19; J. Murphy-O'Connor, "The Essenes and Their History," *RB* 81 (1974) 239.

[23] Pouilly, "L'évolution de la législation pénale dans la communauté de Qumran," *RB* 82 (1975) 550.

[24] Pouilly, "Evolution," 550–51; Murphy-O'Connor, "Essenes and Their History," 242; "Essenes in Palestine," 124.

(25) A man shall not speak to his fellow in anger or in murmurings (26) or obstinately or in jealousy or in a spirit of evil, and he shall not hate him in the perversity of his heart for he shall reprove him on the same day and he shall not (6:1) bear guilt because of him. A man shall also not bring a case against his fellow before the Many who has not reproved him before witnesses.

This passage contains many of the same elements as CD 9:2–8; in fact, 6:1 follows CD 9:3 almost verbatim, but its context is quite different.[25] The context in 1QS deals with the order or rank of members according to their intelligence and works (5:23). Each year a special session of the community is to examine the works of each member and to promote some in rank because of the perfection of their conduct and demote others because of their faults (5:24). It is in the context of this demotion in rank based on faults that the necessity of reproof is mentioned. Each member of the community is "to reprove his fellow in truth and humility and loving charity" (5:24–25). The concern here is not with the law of Moses but with the internal workings of the community. The reproof's being made in loving charity also shows a concern for the offender that is not found in the previous two passages. (Perhaps the reproof is now being used as a means of encouraging those who are lacking in fervor.) Following this passage are other prescriptions for the proper ordering of the community at work and at meals (6:1–8).

Even though 6:1 does refer to bringing a case before the Many, the context would suggest that it is not so much a trial for an infringement of the Mosaic law as it is part of the yearly reckoning of faults against the ordinances of the sect.[26] However, the legal formula of CD 9:2–8, which requires reproof before witnesses prior to bringing a case to court, is intact and gives the passage a legalistic overtone.

As in the previous two texts, there are at least two steps in the procedure: (a) reproof before witnesses and (b) bringing the case before the Many (6:1).[27] However, 5:26 speaks of reproving in loving charity and with the goal of not bearing guilt. Is this the same reproof as the one mentioned in 6:1, which takes place before witnesses prior to the case's being brought before the Many?

In order to resolve the question of how many reproofs there are, all three of the texts need to be considered. Both CD 9:2–8 and 1QS 5:25–6:1 speak of the reproof on the same day and the reproof before witnesses separately.

---

[25] 1QS 6:1 is considered secondary to CD 9:2–8 based on the dating of the two texts by Pouilly.

[26] Schiffman suggests that both CD 9:2–3 and 1QS 6:1 refer to offenses against sectarian organizational rules ("Qumran Law," 612).

[27] Schiffman sees the same legal procedure in CD 9:2–8 and 1QS 5:25–6:1 (*Sectarian Law*, 94).

In CD 9:3 reproving before witnesses is part of the interpretation of Lev 19:18, which forbids taking revenge. Also reproving before witnesses is a necessary step in bringing a case to court. In CD 9:6 reproving on the same day is part of the interpretation of Lev 19:17, which requires a reproof so that a person does not bear a sin.

In 1QS 5:25–6:1 the order in which the reproofs are mentioned is switched, but the motive for each reproof stays the same. 1QS 5:26 requires that the reproof be made on the same day, and this is followed by a modified quotation of Lev 19:17 (the author has changed *ḥṭ'* to *'wn*). The motive of this reproof is not to bear guilt. 1QS 6:1 required that a reproof be made before witnesses. Although there is no reference to Lev 19:18 as there is in CD 9:2–3, the reproof before witnesses is again the necessary step in bringing the case to court.

In another text, CD 7:2–3,[28] the reproof on the same day is mentioned without any reference to a reproof before witnesses. In that case there is an allusion to Lev 19:18 about not bearing a grudge: CD 7:2, *wĕlō' linṭôr;* Lev 19:18, *wĕlō' tiṭṭōr 'et-bĕnê 'ammekā*. Even though the allusion is to 19:18 (in CD 9:2, Lev 19:18 is associated with reproof before witnesses, which has the motive of making the case legal), the motive for the reproof on the same day is that the accuser not bear a grudge, which would involve sin.

These facts point to the conclusion that there are two different reproofs, one on the same day, which presumably involves only the offender and the accuser, and another before witnesses.[29]

However, CD 9:16–22 is not easily reconciled with this interpretation. CD 9:17–18 requires that the accuser report the offense to the overseer in the presence of the offender as a reproof. We have concluded that this reproof before the overseer takes the place of the reproof before witnesses. However, 9:22 indicates that the reporting of the offense to the overseer (and therefore also the reproof before the overseer) is to take place on the same day as the offense. This text would indicate that the reproof on the same day and the reproof before witnesses are not two separate things. Based on CD 9:16–22

---

[28] This text belongs to what Murphy-O'Connor calls the Memorandum, written just prior to 152 B.C. when the Essenes had returned to Palestine but before their move to Qumran. Its purpose was to remind the community of its ordinances and ideals (see "Literary Analysis," 216–20).

[29] It is a common opinion that there are three steps (two reproofs and bringing the case to trial) in the Essene legal procedure: W. H. Brownlee, *The Dead Sea Manual of Discipline* (BASOR Supp. Studies 10–12; New Haven, CT: American Schools of Oriental Research, 1951) 23 n. 3; Daniélou, *Dead Sea Scrolls*, 40; Davies, *Setting*, 223; Catchpole, "Reproof," 83; D. Hill, *The Gospel of Matthew* (NCB; London: Oliphants, 1972) 275; E. Schweizer, *The Good News according to Matthew* (Atlanta: John Knox, 1975) 370.

it is very likely that there is only one reproof, and it is to be made on the same day as the offense and before witnesses.[30]

However, the two texts which are more explicitly concerned with the reproof (CD 9:2-8; 1QS 5:25-6:1) reveal that there is a separate motive and OT text behind each of the two requirements for the reproof. Behind the requirement that the reproof be made on the same day is the motive that the accuser not bear sin. Behind the requirement that the reproof be made before witnesses is the motive of ensuring that the case be properly brought to court. Because there are two distinct requirements for the reproof, linked to two distinct motives, it is legitimate to speak of *two* reproofs. Even though they may refer to the very same event, there is the reproof that is made the very same day and keeps the accuser from bearing sin, and there is the reproof that is made before witnesses that is necessary in order to bring a case to court.

There are several observations to be made from the study of the Essene texts.

(1) The "Former Ordinances" show a consistent linking of Lev 19:17 and Deut 19:15 in such a way that reproving is always part of the judicial process and linked to witnesses.

(2) The use of the term "witnesses" in the judicial process is not exactly defined. It can refer to witnesses to the offense or witnesses to the reproof.

(3) In all three Essene texts "reproving" is a necessary step in bringing a case to court (the assembly). In that sense it is a judicial term.[31]

(4) There is a definite change in 1QS 5:25-6:1 from the two texts in CD. 1QS 5:25-6:1 has made the reproof part of the process of community ranking, and this has resulted in the reproof being more concerned with the offender and the "trial" more concerned with community ordinances than with Mosaic law.

(5) The evidence from 1QS shows that even though the community has changed and the nature of legal trials is different, the judicial process has remained intact in the community.

(6) Even though it is tenuous to hold that these texts describe a clear three-step legal procedure, involving reproof alone, reproof before witnesses, and bringing the case to court, the evidence is quite clear that there are two

---

[30] Schiffman, *Sectarian Law*, 98.

[31] H. van Vliet, *No Single Testimony* (Utrecht: Kemink & Zoon, 1958) 58. Schiffman is correct to say that it is a forensic procedure that must be executed in accord with specific legal norms, but that it probably does not mean "prove." (*Sectarian Law*, 95). S. Schechter (*Documents of Jewish Sectaries* [reprinted with a prolegomenon by J. A. Fitzmyer; New York: Ktav, 1970] 78, 79) and P. Wernberg-Møller (*The Manual of Discipline* [STDJ 1; Leiden: Brill, 1957] 101) incorrectly translate the root *ykh* as "prove."

distinct requirements for the reproof (on the same day, before witnesses) coupled with two distinct motives (not to bear sin, to bring the case to court). For this reason it is fair to say that there are, in a sense, two reproofs even though they may involve the same action.

Matthew 18:15-17

If your brother ever sins, go and reprove him, you and him alone. If he listens to you, you have gained your brother. If he does not listen, take along with you one or two others, so that "on the words of two or three witnesses every matter may be confirmed." But if he ignores you, speak to the church. If he ignores the church, let him be to you as a Gentile and a toll collector.

There are many significant parallels between Matt 18:15-17 and the three texts from QL.

(1) Both Matthew and the Essene texts are dealing with the offense of a member. CD 9:16 begins with the case of a man who is unfaithful to the law (yim'al 'îš battôrâ), and Matthew begins with the case of a brother who sins (hamartēsē ho adelphos sou).[32]

(2) Both CD 9:17 and Matt 18:15 treat a situation where the offender and his fellow member are alone.

(3) Matt 18:15-17 involves a three-step process similar to the one in CD 9:2-8 and 1QS 5:25-6:1 that involves reproof alone, reproof before witnesses, and bringing the case to the full assembly or its judging body.

(4) Both Matthew and the Essene texts are concerned with reproof. In fact, 1QS 6:1 and CD 9:2-3 are concerned with reproof before witnesses as is Matt 18:15-17. In this all three differ from any passage of the OT. In the first part of this paper it was noted that the Essene texts consistently combine Lev 19:17 and Deut 19:15. That same combination of reproving and (two or three) witnesses is found in Matthew.

(5) All of the texts involve a final step of taking the matter to the full assembly or its judging body. In 1 QS 6:1 as the final step the case is taken to the Many, in CD 9:4 it is taken before the elders, and in CD 9:20 when the case is complete it is most likely taken before the judges (see 9:10; 10:1, 4-10). In Matthew the last step is to tell the church (ekklēsia).[33]

---

[32] *Eis se,* which if it is part of the text makes the sin a personal offense, is probably not original but a later addition harmonizing the text with v. 21 and Luke 17:4. It is omitted by MSS ℵ B f¹ copsa,bo. For a summary of the argument, see W. G. Thompson, *Matthew's Advice to a Divided Community: Mt. 17,22-18,35* (AnBib 44; Rome: Biblical Institute, 1970) 176 n. 1.

[33] J. Gnilka maintains that the texts from QL and Matt 18:18 all explicitly describe or imply the role of a single person to whom is delegated full authority and responsibility in judging ("Kirche," 56). This is certainly not the case in Matt 18:17, 1QS 6:1, or CD 9:4. Even in CD 9:16-20, the role of the overseer is defined only as inscribing the names of offenders and

(6) There is some kind of judgment implied or stated in all of the texts. CD 9:16–22 is concerned with the death penalty and separation from purification; CD 9:7 only with the death penalty. The "judgment" in 1QS 5:25–6:1 is probably a demotion within the ranks of the community. Matthew 18:17 calls for the offender to be "as a Gentile and a toll collector."

It is, however, at these very points of similarity that the author of Matthew 18:15–17 makes what appear to be deliberate changes from the Essene penal code or at least constructs his text in such a way as to highlight his contrasting point of view.

(1) The contrast between "sin" and "unfaithfulness to the law" may not appear great on the surface, but two important differences stand out. (a) Sin in Matthew is almost always linked to forgiveness. Except for 26:45, sinners (*hamartōloi*) are those to whom Jesus addresses his message of forgiveness (9:10, 11, 13; 11:19), and sin (*hamartia*) is what Jesus forgives (1:21; 9:2, 5, 6; 12:31; 26:28). Of the two times besides this passage that Matthew uses the verb *hamartanō*, one is clearly concerned with forgiving (18:20). There is little doubt, considering the context of this passage and Matthew's perspective on sin, that forgiveness and repentance are the foremost concerns in this passage as well. In contrast, unfaithfulness in CD 9:16–22 is a matter of breaking the law and is dealt with by giving the punishment prescribed by the law itself. Even in 1QS 5:25–6:1 and CD 9:2–8, where there are no descriptions of the offenses, the contexts show that the focus of both passages is entirely on the exact fulfillment of the law (1QS 5:21–22; CD 9:7).[34] (b) Matthew consistently shows Jesus as the one who surpasses the law. As will be seen later in the paper, Matthew is showing that something greater than the law is involved for the Christian community that is dealing with a person who sins.

(2) In CD 9:17 a member of the community is alone (*wĕhû' 'eḥād*) when he observes the transgression of another. As pointed out earlier, this text is concerned with showing how the law in Deut 19:15, requiring three witnesses to an offense, can be applied to a situation where there is only one witness. The answer of the Essene community involves the combination of witnesses: three separate offenses with only one witness apiece add up to an offense with three witnesses.

Matt 18:15 is not concerned at all with how many persons witness the offense. Nowhere does the Matthean text say that the person to whom the text is directed is the only one to witness the offense. In fact, the text never

---

witnessing the reproof. Based on CD 9:10 and 10:1 it is likely that the judges, and not the overseer, were responsible for judging.

[34] See I. Robinson, "A Note on Damascus Document IX, 7," *RevQ* 9 (1977–78) 238–39.

even states that he has actually witnessed the offense; it only says, "If your brother sins . . ." Matthew is clearly not concerned with witnesses to the offense. However, Matt 18:15 does state that the person should be alone with the offender (*sou kai autou monou*) when he reproves him. Commentators quite rightly note that the first reproof is made alone so that the offender is not embarrassed and is therefore more likely to be open to the reproof.[35] In Matthew, "being alone" is the result of a concern for the offender and his repentance. In CD 9:17 "being alone" is the cause of a concern for obtaining a legal conviction. In QL it is part of the problem, in Matthew part of the solution.

(3) Even if the reproof made on the same day as the offense is separate from the reproof made before witnesses and there are, therefore, three steps in the Essene procedure similar to the three steps in Matthew, the three steps play very different roles in the two communities. In 1QS 5:25–6:1 and CD 9:2–8 the first reproof is always associated with keeping the accuser from hating the offender. The reproof is a way of rescuing the accuser from sin (*ht'*) or guilt (*'wn*). In Matthew the first reproof is not at all concerned with the accuser. It is an attempt to rescue the offender from his sin and gain him as a brother.[36] Anger and hatred on the part of the one who reproves are not even mentioned. In Matt 18:21–35 the attitude and response of the one offended are discussed. In that case no reproof is mentioned, only forgiveness.

For the second reproof, CD 9:3 and 1QS 6:1 require a man to reprove an offender before witnesses before he can bring a case against the man. In CD 9:16–20 the reproof takes place at the same time that the formal complaint is made to the overseer and the offender's name is inscribed. These reproofs in QL are with the express purpose of bringing the case to court legally. The witnesses can testify that the reproof was legally fulfilled.[37] In Matthew the first reproof, the reproof alone, is with the express purpose of gaining the brother if he listens (*ean sou akousē ekerdēsas ton adelphon sou*). The second reproof is before witnesses and takes place if the offender does not listen (*ean de mē akousē*). A third reproof is initiated if the offender again fails to listen (*ean de parakousē autōn*). The clear implication is that all three reproofs have the same purpose: to gain a brother by getting him to listen to the reproof and admit his sin.

Thus, in Matthew the reproof alone and the reproof before witnesses have exactly the same purpose, while in QL the reproof alone and the reproof

---

[35] F. V. Filson, *A Commentary on the Gospel according to St. Matthew* (HNTC; New York: Harper & Row, 1960) 201; W. Trilling, *Hausordnung Gottes* (Düsseldorf: Patmos, 1960) 44.

[36] Davies, *Setting*, 223.

[37] Schiffman, *Sectarian Law*, 94–95.

before witnesses have quite different purposes. In QL the reproof alone is intended to keep the accuser from bearing sin (as the law dictates), and the reproof before witnesses fulfills the requirement of reproving before a case is filed. In QL both reproofs are derived from different interpretations of Lev 19:17–18. The first reproof follows Lev 19:17 closely and is concerned about the possible sin of the accuser. The second reproof interprets Lev 19:17–18 in terms of Lev 19:15 and sees the reproof as necessary for acting honestly in rendering judgment. Keeping the law exactly is the motive for the reproofs in the Essene texts. Gaining a brother (even with attempts that surpass the demands of the law) is the motive for the reproofs in Matthew.[38]

(4) Matt 18:16b quotes Deut 19:15, which says that every matter must stand on two or three witnesses. Verse 16a, however, requires that the person take along one or two. Some commentators see a discrepancy between the numbers in v. 16a and the quotation from Deut 19:15.[39] For this reason they consider v. 16b to be added later, perhaps by Matthew, to an original exhortation involving three levels of fraternal correction. According to these commentators, Matthew has added the quotation in order to make the exhortation into a three-step disciplinary code, similar to the Essene code, with the one or two others as the witnesses of the second step. Yet if the action in Matthew is parallel to the legal action described in the texts from QL, the number of witnesses before whom the reproof is made would only be one or two and not two or three as Deut 19:15 requires. In order to get two or three, the person who first reproves must be included. But this raises several questions. (a) If the first person is to be considered as a witness, then how does Matthew conceive of the legal process requiring three witnesses when one is the accuser? (b) If the first person is to be included as a legal witness, why does Matthew continue the process and describe a third reproof? (c) Yet if Matthew sees the three reproofs as the full number that makes the judgment complete, why would he place the quotation after the one or two others when there is not a legal judgment made at that point?

B. Jackson has offered an intriguing interpretation of 2 Cor 13:1 that perhaps can lead to a solution to these questions.[40] In 2 Cor 13:1 Paul says, "This is the third time I shall be coming to you. 'On the words of two or three witnesses every matter will be confirmed.' " Some commentators maintain that Paul is referring to his third visit as the third time that he will have

---

[38] For these reasons it seems that the contention of W. Trilling (*Das Wahre Israel* [SANT 10; Munich: Kösel, 1964] 114) that *elenchein* in Matt 18:15 has a strong disciplinary and juridical character is not correct. Matthew has deliberately changed the nuance of this word.

[39] Catchpole, "Reproof," 80–81; Gaechter, *Matthäus,* 599; Strecker, *Weg,* 223.

[40] Jackson, "*Testes Singulares* in Early Jewish Law and the New Testament," in *Essays in Jewish and Comparative Legal History* (SJLA 10; Leiden: Brill, 1975) 193–201.

accused members of the community of sinning (see 12:20–21). Paul's third accusation on the planned third visit will, by the combination of witnesses similar to CD 9:16–20, make the legal number of three witnesses necessary for a conviction and judgment.[41] Jackson, however, maintains that the witnesses to which Paul is referring are not witnesses to an offense, whose testimony will lead to a conviction, but witnesses to a theological fact leading (hopefully) to belief or acceptance of a truth.[42]

In v. 3 Paul says, "You are after all looking for a proof of the Christ who speaks in me." It is Jackson's contention that the three witnesses that Paul speaks of are his three visits, during the first two of which he has reprimanded the sinners and during the third of which he will not spare them (13:2). These visits witness not to the sin of the offenders but to Paul's claim that he is an apostle and that Christ speaks in him.[43] Paul quotes Deut 19:15 to show that even though the Corinthians do not accept his claim to be an apostle just based on one or two visits in which he spoke with Christ's authority, they must surely accept it based on three visits. These three visits constitute the three witnesses that Deuteronomy says confirm a matter.

The case is similar in Matthew. The first reproof is made alone in the hopes that the offender, with the least amount of embarrassment, will admit his sin and be gained as a brother. If, however, on the word of only one he refuses to admit that he has sinned, then the first reprover is to take along one or two others. Together they comprise two or three, and on their word the matter should be considered proved to the offender. Not "proved" so that he will be convicted but "proved" so that he will listen. According to this interpretation, v. 16b would have been an original part of the text. The text could be considered a deliberate attempt, using Deut 19:15, to contrast the role of reproof in Matthew's community with its role in the Essene community.

Matthew uses the quotation as an important ingredient in the concentrated effort to win the offender back. Many have argued that the one or two witnesses are meant to give support to the reproof of the first person, to convince the offender of his sin, and thus to gain him as a brother; but they do not give Matthew enough credit for his use of the quotation of Deut 19:15.[44] Matthew uses the one or two others not just to support the reproof

---

[41] C. K. Barrett, *A Commentary on the Second Epistle to the Corinthians* (HNTC; New York: Harper & Row, 1973) 333; V. P. Furnish, *II Corinthians* (AB 32a; Garden City, NY: Doubleday, 1984) 575; van Vliet, *Testimony,* 96 n. 8.

[42] Jackson, "*Testes Singulares,*" 196.

[43] Ibid., 195–96; R. H. Strachan, *The Second Epistle of Paul to the Corinthians* (MNTC; New York: Harper, 1935) 38.

[44] G. Barth, "Auseinandersetzungen um die Kirchenzucht im Umkreis des Matthäusevangeliums," *ZNW* 69 (1978) 172–73; Gnilka, "Kirche," 54; R. H. Gundry, *Matthew, A Commentary on His Literary and Theological Art* (Grand Rapids: Eerdmans, 1982) 368; V. Pfitzner, "Purified

of the first but to add up to two or three witnesses in order actually to *prove* the point to the offender. Matthew uses this legal language not because he is thinking of this as a legal proceeding[45] or because he expects these witnesses to testify in the trial before the church[46] but to show that the *legal number of witnesses* is used to convince the offender and not to convict him. Matthew's use of the quotation from Deut 19:15 at this point in the passage, instead of making the three-step process more legal, makes it less legal.

The combination of witnesses in Matthew is used to prove the offender's fault to him. This is very different from CD 9:16–20 in which the witnesses combine to prove the offender's fault to the court. It is also different from CD 9:2–8 and 1QS 5:25–6:1 in which the witnesses are to be present at the reproof. In these Essene texts the witnesses are not described as having any function on behalf of the offender; the function of the witnesses is to allow for the case to be legally brought to court. The real difference in the texts is that the witnesses prove the offense to the *offender* in Matthew and to the *court of the community* in QL.

It must also be noted that even when the person has had his offense "legally" proved to him (on the word of two or three witnesses), Matthew calls for making a third and even greater effort to convince him of his fault and gain him back. The passage is rebelling against the legal thinking reflected in the codes from QL. The Essene attempt to be completely legal in convicting an offender is replaced in Matthew by the attempt to surpass the legal and be completely thorough in trying to bring the offender back.

(5) Even though we are dealing with different stages of the Essene community with significantly different structures (in the "Former Ordinances" there are the twelve judges and in Stage IV of 1QS there is the Many), all the Essene texts agree that after an offender is reproved before witnesses the case can be brought before the assembly of judges or the Many, where a judgment will be made. In QL, in the matter of an offender, the assembly gathers to try the case and pass judgment. In Matthew even after the failure of the two or three witnesses to prove the point, the community makes *another* attempt at reproving the offender in order to win him back. Instead of gathering to pass judgment, the assembly of Christians gathers to make an attempt to gain a brother.

Community—Purified Sinner: Expulsion from the Community according to Matthew 18:15–18 and 1 Corinthians 5:1–5," *AusBR* 30 (1982) 40; Thompson, *Advice*, 183.

[45] Against G. Strecker (*Weg*, 223) and P. Gaechter (*Matthäus*, 599), who maintain that Matthew's addition of Deut 19:15 to the original text is to make the original brotherly reproof into a legal procedure. See also Pesch, *Matthäus*, 39–40.

[46] Against J. P. Meier, *Matthew* (NTM; Wilmington, DE: Glazier, 1980) 205.

When commentators are comparing the three-step process in Matthew and QL, they fail to emphasize this point: in Matthew the third step is not a judgment but another reproof. This seems to be a deliberate reaction to the careful legalism of the Essenes. When the legal number of witnesses is present and the case is brought to the assembly, the expected action would be judgment, but Matthew deliberately flouts that expectation and calls for another reproof with the purpose of getting the offender to listen. Matthew means the action of the church to be contrasted with the action of the Many or the judges, just as he means the action of the witnesses who are trying to gain a brother to be contrasted with the action of the witnesses who are part of a legal process.

(6) In QL there is a strict legal code set down; and when a person violates the law and is convicted before the Many or the judges, he automatically receives the punishment set down in the law (1QS 6:24).[47] The judges or the Many convict the offender and give the sentence prescribed by the law.

In Matt 18:17 we have a very different case. The matter has been brought before the church so that they can make one final attempt at convincing the offender of his sin. Then the text says, "Let him be to you as a Gentile and a toll collector." A detailed study of this verse is impossible at this point, but in relation to the texts from QL that we have studied there are several points about this verse that should be noted. (a) Between the reproof of the church and the "sentence" there is a lack of any statement that the church is to try the case, make a judgment, or give a sentence. Matthew's text says that the church is to make a third attempt at a reproof and then the person is a Gentile or a toll collector to them. This is not a legal judgment and sentence comparable to that in the texts from QL. (b) Instead of describing an action on the part of the community, Matthew uses the third person singular imperative. Instead of the church *doing* anything, the offender *is* something.

What is the offender? He is a Gentile and a toll collector. Does this mean that he is excluded from the community? It certainly means that he is no longer a member by his own choice,[48] but there is another, more important implication. As pointed out, in the Essene texts the offender who broke the law is judged as one who is under the law and punished accordingly. In Matthew's community, instead of a law by which a member is judged, they have a community in which a member participates or not. Matthew is saying that when a person refuses to listen to the church, the church, unlike the

---

[47] Following 6:24 is a list of offenses and their punishments. This is also a great deal of the content of CD 9–16, the "Former Ordinances." In the "Former Ordinances" the punishments follow the OT law very closely and include the death penalty. In 1QS 6 the offenses and punishments have mostly to do with the internal rules of the community.

[48] Pfitzner, "Purified Community," 39.

Essenes, does not punish that person under the rules of the community or the law but merely considers that person outside of the community and the law. Many have noted that the very negative connotation given here to Gentiles and toll collectors does not fit with some of the other sayings of Matthew, but it appears that Matthew has used this group deliberately, not just because they are excluded from Judaism but because they are not under the law. They do not fulfill it, and in the present they are not judged by it.

Matt 10:14-15 confirms this analysis. That passage is also concerned with the case of one (a household or a town) who does not listen (*mēde akousē*). The advice that Jesus gives his disciples is to shake the dust of that town from their feet and go on. In other words they are merely to consider it the same as pagan territory or a Samaritan town, which they have already been told not to enter (10:5). They are sent out "after the lost sheep of the house of Israel" (10:6). These verses are part of Matthew's redaction of the Marcan text, and 10:6 calls to mind the parable in 18:10-14 about the shepherd seeking after the lost sheep. Matthew also drops the statement found in Mark and Luke that the disciples are to shake the dust from their feet "in witness against them" (*eis martyrion autois*). Matthew may have deleted this because he intended a close connection between this passage and chap. 18 and did not want the witnesses in chap. 18 to be construed as witnesses *against* someone, leading to judgment. Matthew also makes an interesting addition at 10:15. He speaks of the punishment of the town on judgment day. In a similar fashion in chap. 18 he relates the "judgment" that the offender is like a Gentile and a toll collector to the final judgment (18:18).

Matthew perceives the process of reproving a brother as being the same as missionary work—it is a seeking after the lost sheep. If the missionary work inside the community fails, it is the same as a town or household that refuses to listen to the good news—the offender is considered as one outside. When judgment day comes, all those who have rejected Christ, a would-be Christian who refuses to repent or a town or household of Israel that refuses to listen, will be liable to punishment. Matthew makes a point of the community refusing to pass sentence because the only sentence that can be passed is the final judgment.[49] The community, however, can decide that every attempt at seeking out the lost has been made and can leave the person, household, or town as lost to be judged and punished by Christ on the last day.[50]

[49] G. Forkman (*The Limits of the Religious Community* [ConBNT 5; Lund: Gleerup, 1972] 131) and Strecker (*Weg*, 225-26) stress that the decision of the church in no way usurps the final judgment, and F. W. Beare (*The Gospel according to Matthew* [San Francisco: Harper & Row, 1981] 380) notes that it is only at the final judgment that the church's decision is confirmed.

[50] Perhaps the explanation for the singular (*sou*) in v. 17 is that Matthew does not want this passage to be construed as a legal judgment by the church but an action on the part of the offender that leaves each Christian with no further responsibility to him.

There are several points that can be made by way of conclusion. (a) The commentators who cite the Essene text as parallels to Matt 18:15–17 are certainly correct. In fact, there are many more parallels between the two groups of texts than are usually mentioned. (b) There is no evidence that this involves direct dependence, and yet the author of Matt 18:15–17 seems to be familiar with at least the content of that aspect of the Essene penal code dealing with the discipline of an offending member. (c) It is at the very points where the texts are parallel that Matthew seems to have made a deliberate attempt to alter some aspect of the code in order to create an entirely different attitude toward internal discipline. (d) Matt 18:15–17 is an original unity, and the quotation of Deut 19:15 in v. 16b is not a later addition. We cannot be certain that Matthew is the author of this passage, but from its connections to other parts of the Gospel that are Matthean redaction, this is likely. (e) The passage is a unified attempt to show that the Christian response to an offending member relies on the law (Lev 19:17 and Deut 19:15) just as the Essene penal code does, yet the Christian interpretation of these texts has to do with trying every means to win the brother back. The reproof, the two or three witnesses, the witness being alone, the assembly of the community, and the concluding "judgment" all have a very different purpose in Matthew. The follower of Jesus fulfills the law by a missionary attitude that seeks out the lost sheep and forgives, and not by a casuistic definition of the demands of the law. (f) In its concern for charity toward the offender, 1QS 5:25–6:1 is closer to Matt 18:15–17 than the other two texts are, and yet it is still much closer to the other Essene texts than to Matthew. It is still concerned with law (even though it may be the ordinances of the community). The reproofs are still for the benefit of the accuser and for the legal process, and there is still a judgment made by the community based on its laws. (g) It seems that part of the difference between Matthew's attitude toward an offending member and the Essene's may be due to the difference in their eschatologies. In QL, whether the end-time is considered as still future or is present, the final judgment is clear to the Essenes, who have been given the full and correct interpretation of the law. As adherents of the law, they are, and will always be, exempt from final judgment. In Matthew, the final judgment is still in the future. It belongs to Jesus Christ; and although the criteria for it are clear, it is impossible to predict the verdict of any case. Forgiveness and repentance, not judgment, belong to the present time. When forgiveness and repentance are refused, then the one who refuses is left to face the final judgment alone.

The Origin of the Qumran Community: A Review of the Evidence

John J. Collins
University of Notre Dame

ויקם להם מורה צדק
להדריכם בדרך לבו
Damascus Document 1:11

AFTER FOUR DECADES OF STUDY, the origin of the Qumran community is still the subject of widely diverse hypotheses.[1] The reason is, of course, that the evidence of the scrolls is very elliptic on this subject. The imminent publication of 4QMMT, the supposed letter of the Teacher of Righteousness to the Wicked Priest, may cast some new light on the issue.[2] For the present, however, it is worthwhile to review the available evidence and try to clarify how far the main current hypotheses can claim a textual basis. I will focus on three issues: (1) the causes of dissension between the Dead Sea sect and the rest of Judaism; (2) the time at which the sect emerged as a distinct organization; and (3) the opposition to the Teacher associated with the Man of Lies.

1. The Causes of Dissension

The *Damascus Document* addresses the issues which distinguished the sect from the rest of Israel in three passages. In CD 3:12 we are

---

[1] For a sampling of recent proposals see B. Z. Wacholder, *The Dawn of Qumran* (Cincinnati: Hebrew Union College, 1983); P. R. Davies, *The Damascus Covenant* (Sheffield: JSOT, 1983); R. Eisenman, *Maccabees, Zadokites, Christians and Qumran* (Leiden: Brill, 1983); B. E. Thiering, *Redating the Teacher of Righteousness* (Sydney: Glenburn, 1979). N. Golb ("Who Hid the Dead Sea Scrolls?" *BA* [June, 1985] 68–82) denies that Qumran was an Essene settlement but fails to account for the community described in 1QS or Pliny's reference to an Essene settlement between Jericho and Ain Gedi (*Nat. Hist.* 5.15).

[2] E. Qimron and J. Strugnell, "An Unpublished Halakhic Letter from Qumran," in *Biblical Archeology To-Day: Proceedings of the International Congress on Biblical Archeology* (Jerusalem: Israel Exploration Society, 1985) 400–407.

told that "with those who held fast to the commandments of God, those who were left over of them, God established his covenant with Israel forever, to reveal to them the hidden things (nistārôt) in which all Israel strayed: he manifested to them his holy sabbaths, his glorious feasts, the testimonies of his righteousness and the ways of his truth and the desires of his will which man must do and by which he must live." In this passage the "covenant with Israel" is restricted to a remnant and requires a new revelation.[3] The content of that revelation is primarily the cultic calendar. Presumably the "desires of his will" include other matters besides, but the only matters mentioned specifically are the observance of sabbaths and feasts.

The issues between the sect and the rest of Israel are elaborated in the discussion of the "three nets of Belial" in CD 4:15–5:12. These are fornication, riches, and profanation of the Temple. The author admits that other people see these practices as "three kinds of righteousness." They are seen as sinful only in light of the distinctive halakhah of the sect. The fornication in question consists of taking two wives in their lifetime (either polygamy or divorce). In support of the halakhah, Gen 1:27 and Deut 17:17 are cited. Neither passage carried this implication in its biblical context, but a similar prohibition is found in the Temple Scroll, in the "law of the king."[4] Profanation of the temple is said to result from failure to observe purity laws—lying with a woman during her period, and marrying nieces. Here again CD extends the evident range of the biblical text (Lev 18:13), again in accordance with the Temple Scroll (66:16–17).

This passage does not clarify the second net of Belial, "wealth," but it adds a further grievance against the enemies of the sect. They say the ordinances of the covenant are not sure. Rejection of the sectarian claim of revelation is construed as blasphemy.

The third passage in CD which discusses the points of dissension between the sect and the rest of Judaism is in CD 6:11–7:6. Those who enter the covenant are forbidden to enter the Temple to light its altar in vain. While this need not imply a total boycott of the Temple, it surely involves a refusal to participate in the official Temple cult.[5] Instead, they should "act according to the exact interpretation of the Law during the age of wickedness." This involves "separation from the sons of the pit" and avoidance of "the unclean

---

[3] L. H. Schiffman (The Halakha at Qumran [Leiden: Brill, 1975] 22–32) argues that the nistar is the sectarian interpretation of the Torah, through divinely inspired exegesis.

[4] 11QT 57:17–18. Wacholder (The Dawn of Qumran, 119–24) argues that the "three nets of Belial" are derived from the Temple Scroll, which he regards as the Torah of Qumran. His case is strongest on the marriage laws.

[5] See the discussion of this passage by Davies, The Damascus Covenant, 134–40; J. Murphy-O'Connor, "The Damascus Document Revisited," RB 92 (1985) 234–38.

riches of wickedness acquired by vow or anathema or from the temple treasure." This comment clarifies the second net of Belial in the earlier passage. The enemies of the sect are implicitly accused of robbing the poor of the people by exploitation of Temple offerings.[6] Those who enter the covenant are further enjoined to observe the difference between sacred and profane and keep the sabbath and festivals "according to the findings of the members of the new covenant in the land of Damascus."

This third passage in CD, then, recapitulates the points of dissent as envisaged by the document. These are the cultic calendar and Temple cult, certain purity laws and wealth that is considered unclean.

According to the preliminary report, a more direct and elaborate account of the issues separating the sect from the rest of Judaism is found in 4QMMT, which is characterized by the editors as "a polemic-halakhic letter," which was "probably written immediately after the separation of the sect."[7] The original document must be pieced together from the surviving fragments, but it apparently contained (1) an opening formula, (2) a calendar, (3) a list of distinctive Qumran *halakhot,* and (4) an epilogue discussing the reasons for the sect's withdrawal. The prominence of the calendar is an obvious point of resemblance to CD. The specific *halakhot* described by Strugnell and Qimron do not correspond to those in CD but they share common concerns with ritual purity and marital status. Some topics are also concerned with tithes offered to the priests, an issue which may be related to the "unclean riches of wickedness" denounced in CD.

Calendrical considerations are also prominent in 1QS. There we are told that those who enter the covenant must live "in accordance with all that has been revealed concerning their appointed times" (1:8), and are forbidden to "depart from any command of God concerning their times; they shall be neither early nor late for any of their appointed times (1:14–15). Elsewhere in 1QS we are told that the Council of the Community "shall be an agreeable offering, atoning for the land and determining the judgment of wickedness" (8:10, compare 5:6) and we might infer from this that the community did not rely on the official Temple cult. 1QS 8 goes on to say that none of the things hidden from Israel but discovered by the interpreter of the law should be concealed from those who have been confirmed for two years in the community. In 1QS, as in CD 3, the sectarian understanding of the covenant involves the new revelation of matters hidden from the rest of Israel.

Thus far, the primary issue between the sect and the rest of Israel would seem to be the cultic calendar, although other matters of ritual purity also

---

[6] Compare 1QpHab 12:6 where the Wicked Priest is said to have stolen the wealth of the poor ones.

[7] Qimron and Strugnell, "An Unpublished Halakhic Letter," 401.

impinge on the status of the Temple and its cult. It is worth noting, however, what issues are *not* mentioned in these documents. The most widely held explanation of the separation of the sect from the rest of Judaism is that it was triggered by the usurpation of the high priesthood by the Maccabees. This explanation is held not only by the classic consensus of Cross, Vermes, Milik, and others,[8] but also by scholars like Murphy-O'Connor, who hold that the sect had an earlier origin but that a quarrel over the high priesthood precipitated the move to Qumran.[9] The right of succession to the high priesthood is an issue of primary importance for those scholars who hold that the Teacher of Righteousness was the high priest in Jerusalem and was ousted by Jonathan Maccabee. It is with some surprise, then, that we note that neither CD nor 1QS suggests that the legitimacy of the high priest was an issue. Neither does it appear to be an issue in 4QMMT according to the published report, although that letter is apparently addressed to a leader of Israel.

There is, however, another source of information about the origin of the Qumran community—the *pesharim*. These compositions are usually dated somewhat later than 1QS and CD—about the middle of the first century B.C.E. This dating rests in part on the palaeography of the documents, of which only single exemplars have been found (i.e., there are no multiple copies of any *pesher*) and in part on the historical allusions in 4QpNahum, which transparently refer to Alexander Jannaeus (103–76 B.C.E.) and events in the first half of the first century (compare also the *pesher* on Hosea). We cannot assume, however, that all the *pesharim* were composed at the same time or that the extant documents are autographs.[10] The *pesher* on Habakkuk could, in principle, be older than that on Nahum. Even if it is not, its evidence should not be slighted, since it may preserve old traditions of the community.

The passages that concern us in the *pesharim* are those related to the Teacher of Righteousness and the Wicked Priest. Like most scholars, I hold that the Wicked Priest should be identified as Jonathan Maccabee. The clearest allusions are those to the death of the Wicked Priest in 4QpPs^a 4:8–10 and 1QpHab 9:8–12, which say that God gave him into the hands of his enemies (1QpHab), who are specified in 4QPs^a as "the ruthless ones of the Gentiles." Most scholars agree that this can only refer to the death of Jonathan at the

---

[8] F. M. Cross, *The Ancient Library of Qumran* (Garden City, NY: Doubleday, 1961) 109–60; G. Vermes, *The Dead Sea Scrolls: Qumran in Perspective* (Philadelphia: Fortress, 1981) 151; J. T. Milik, *Ten Years of Discovery in the Wilderness of Judaea* (London: SCM, 1959) 80–83; H. Stegemann, *Die Entstehung der Qumrangemeinde* (Bonn: published privately, 1971) 204–26.

[9] J. Murphy-O'Connor, "The Essenes and their History," *RB* 81 (1974) 229–30.

[10] See M. P. Horgan, *Pesharim: Qumran Interpretations of Biblical Books* (Washington: CBA, 1979) 3–4.

hand of Trypho (1 Macc 12:39–53; 13:23).[11] It must be said, however, that other allusions do not seem especially apt for Jonathan, and the passage which says that he "walked in the ways of drunkenness" (1QpHab 11:13–14) is more easily applied to either Simon[12] or Alexander Jannaeus.[13] It is certainly possible that the title is applied to more than one individual. The attempt of van der Woude to assign each reference in the Habakkuk commentary to a different individual is unconvincing,[14] but the possibility that more than one high priest is involved cannot be dismissed. The fact that the reference is to high priests is assured by the wordplay *rš'* (Wicked)/*r'š* (Head).

Two passages in the *pesharim* bear directly on the causes of the rift between the Teacher and his followers and the high priesthood. The first is in 1QpHab 8:9–13, where Hab 2:5–6 is interpreted with reference to the Wicked Priest, "who was called by the true name at the beginning of his course, but when he ruled in Israel, he became arrogant, abandoned God, and betrayed the statutes for the sake of wealth. He stole and amassed the wealth of the men of violence who had rebelled against God and he took the wealth of peoples to add to himself guilty sin. And the abominable ways he pursued with every sort of unclean impurity."[15] The interpretation of this passage has been much debated. To be "called by the name of truth" has been taken to mean either that his name had honorable associations (e.g., for Jonathan, the son of Saul; for Simon, Simon the Just)[16] or that he was a legitimate priest,[17] or simply that he had a good reputation.[18] The phrase translated "at the beginning of his course" (*bětěhillat 'mdw*) is often rendered "when he first arose."[19] Milik

---

[11] E.G., G. VERMES, *The Dead Sea Scrolls*, 151; A. S. van der Woude, "Wicked Priest or Wicked Priests? Reflections on the Identification of the Wicked Priest in the Habakkuk Commentary," *JJS* 33 (1982) 356.

[12] So Cross, *The Ancient Library*, 152. Cross's identification of the Wicked Priest as Simon rests largely on a passage in the Testimonia, which refers not to the Wicked Priest but to "a cursed man, one of Belial."

[13] Van der Woude, "Wicked Priest or Wicked Priests?" 358; W. H. Brownlee, "The Wicked Priest, the Man of Lies, and the Righteous Teacher," *JQR* 73 (1982) 5. According to Josephus, Alexander Jannaeus became ill from overdrinking at the end of his life (*Ant.* 13.15.5 [398]).

[14] Some of the allusions provide no basis for a specific identification. The proposal that the first wicked priest was Judas Maccabee is very dubious since it relies on a confused passage in Josephus which says that Judas was high priest after Alcimus (Ant 12.11.2 [434]). Brownlee, "The Wicked Priest," also favors multiple "Wicked Priests."

[15] Trans. Horgan, *Pesharim*, 17.

[16] Cross, *The Ancient Library*, 142.

[17] Horgan, *Pesharim*, 41.

[18] G. Jeremias, *Der Lehrer der Gerechtigkeit* (Göttingen: Vandenhoeck & Ruprecht, 1963) 36–40; G. W. E. Nickelsburg, "Simon—A Priest with a Reputation for Faithfulness," *BASOR* 223 (1976) 67–68.

[19] See G. Vermes, *The Dead Sea Scrolls in English* (Harmondsworth: Penguin, 1968) 240.

contends that "'*amad* is a general term which refers to the performance of any office, political, religious or eschatological."[20] We must note, however, that it is often used for priestly service, and, since the antecedent here is "priest," the reference is most naturally to the priestly office.[21] The verb *māšal* is rightly taken to indicate civil authority but not kingship, and therefore to be appropriate for the early Hasmoneans.[22] Many scholars have argued that the passage refers to the two stages of Jonathan's rise to power: he became "ruler and leader" after the death of Judas (1 Macc 9:30) but was appointed high priest by the Syrian king Alexander Balas in 152 B.C.E. (1 Macc 10:20). This assumption of the high priesthood is the reason most widely posited for the rift between the Qumran sect and the Jerusalem priesthood. Hans Burgmann finds an allusion to the usurpation of the priesthood in the text of Habakkuk cited here, "woe to him who multiplies what is not his own," but the *pesher* conspicuously fails to make this association.[23] Instead "what is not his own" is interpreted as "the wealth of the men of violence" and "the wealth of the peoples." Stegemann claims that *hakkōhēn hārāšā'* must be translated "the illegitimate priest" and that priestly illegitimacy can only result from cultic abuses or from the wrong ancestry.[24] He finds the cultic charges against the Wicked Priest too general and concludes that his ancestry must have been the issue, although he admits that this is never stated in the scrolls.[25] The assertion that "wicked" here means "illegitimate" is not necessarily compelling, however—there are no parallels to establish the usage. Moreover, both Stegemann and Burgmann, and indeed most scholars who have addressed this question, base their argument on deductive rather than inductive reasoning: they assume that the usurpation of the high priesthood *must* have been the reason why Jonathan was designated "Wicked Priest." However plausible this deduction may seem, we must recognize that it is never supported by the explicit statements of the texts, although 1QpHab 8:9–13 provided a golden opportunity for making the charge.[26] Moreover, this passage in the *pesher* can plausibly be construed to exclude this reason for the rift. We have noted already that '*md* is often used for specifically priestly service. If it carries this connotation here, the wicked priest enjoyed a good reputation at the beginning of his service as *high priest*. This is not conceivable if he was thought

[20] Milik, *Ten Years*, 65.

[21] Horgan, *Pesharim*, 41. Compare the use of *ma'amad* for priestly service, 1QM 2:3, Mishnah *Ta'anit* 4:2, Y. Yadin, *The Scroll of the War of the Sons of Light Against the Sons of Darkness* (Oxford: Oxford University Press, 1962) 202–7.

[22] Milik, *Ten Years*, 65–66.

[23] H. Burgmann, *Zwei lösbare Qumranprobleme* (Frankfurt: Lang, 1986) 75.

[24] Stegemann, *Die Entstehung*, 110–11.

[25] Ibid., 111. Compare Milik, *Ten Years*, 83.

[26] Brownlee, "The Wicked Priest," 17.

to be illegitimate because of descent or, parenthetically, if he had ousted the Teacher of Righteousness from the office. In any case, the charges against him here concern usurpation of wealth and cultic impurity. The accusation of ill-gotten wealth is also made against "the last priests of Jerusalem" in 1QpHab 9:4, while the Wicked Priest is said to defile God's sanctuary in 12:9. We have seen that these offenses also figured prominently in CD.

The second crucial passage is found in 1QpHab 11:4–8. There we are told that the Wicked Priest pursued the Teacher to his place of exile and attempted to disrupt his celebration of the Day of Atonement. This passage conveys two important pieces of information. First, the Teacher was observing a different cultic calendar than the high priest (who otherwise would have been officiating in Jerusalem). In view of the prominence of the calendar as an issue in CD, this is not surprising. In view of this fact, however, it is surely unlikely that the Teacher had recently been officiating as high priest in the Jerusalem Temple. There is no evidence that Jonathan, or any of the Has-moneans, introduced a new calendar, and the Teacher can scarcely have switched calendars when he went to Qumran. The second piece of informa-tion in 1QpHab 11 is that the high priest took the initiative in attempting to suppress the sect. This is confirmed by other passages. 1QpHab 9:9 speaks of the wrong done to the Teacher and his followers. 1QpHab 12:6 says that the Wicked Priest plotted to destroy completely the poor ones, and 12:10 adds that he stole their wealth. A fragmentary passage in 4QpPs^a 4:8–10 has been reconstructed to say that the Wicked Priest tried to kill the Teacher. A much-quoted passage from a supposed Teacher-hymn in the *Hodayot* says that the author was driven out "like a bird from his nest" (1QH 4:8–9). We should not then suppose that the secession of the Teacher and his followers was a unilateral decision. At least some of the initiative lay with the "wicked" high priest.

Once further piece of evidence from the *pesharim* has potential significance for the feud between the Teacher and the Wicked Priest. Both the Teacher of Righteousness (in 1QpHab 2:8; 4QpPs^a 2:19; 3:15) and the Wicked Priest (in 1QpHab 8:16; 9:16; 11:12) are referred to as "the priest." Hartmut Stegemann has insisted that this title is a technical term and that it proves that both of these figures were high priests.[27] The argument has recently been formulated succinctly by Murphy-O'Connor: "The available evidence reveals that *hakohen* is always used in a 'titular' or 'non-titular' sense. In the latter the meaning is 'the aforementioned priest.' However, in the Scrolls the sense is always 'titular' and elsewhere this absolute usage always designated

---

[27] Stegemann, *Die Enstehung,* 102 nn. 328 and 329. He further claims that the title cannot be used merely for a claim to high priesthood but only for one who actually held the office.

the High Priest. . . ."[28] Hence the conclusion that the Teacher must have been an otherwise unknown high priest who officiated in the Jerusalem Temple during the so-called Intersacerdotium[29] and was displaced by the "Illegitimate Priest," Jonathan.

The bold assertions of Stegemann and Murphy-O'Connor are not sustained by the evidence, even as that evidence is presented by Stegemann.[30] Many instances of the titular usage refer to the priest of a specific shrine in the preexilic period, but this fact does not invalidate Stegemann's claim for the postexilic usage. He acknowledges a problem in the case of Ezekiel, who is identified as "the priest" in Ezek 1:3. He claims, however, that "the priest" is used absolutely to refer to "the Aaronid High Priest" in the following cases: Ezra (Ezra 7:11; 10:10, 16; Neh 8:2, 9; 12:26), Meremoth (Ezra 8:33), Eliashib (Neh 13:4), Shelemaiah (Neh 13:13), and Simon (Sir 50:1). Only two of these five priests (Eliashib and Simon) are generally recognized to have been high priests. It has indeed been suggested that Ezra came to Jerusalem as high priest,[31] but this suggestion lacks direct evidence and is open to the objection that Ezra is not listed in the line of high priests in Nehemiah 12.[32] Moreover, on his arrival in Jerusalem he is said to have delivered gold, silver, and vessels to Meremoth son of Uriah, the priest (Ezra 8:33). It is difficult to see how "the priest" can designate "high priest" simultaneously in the case of both Ezra and Meremoth. The argument that the absolute titular use of "the priest" must designate high priest is unfounded. There is no basis, then, for a sharp distinction between the usage in the *pesharim* and such usage as we find in CD 14:7 which refers to "the priest who is appointed at the head of the many." All we can infer is that the Teacher was regarded as the priest par excellence by his own followers. The expression "the priest" obviously could mean the high priest, and probably does so in the case of the "Wicked Priest," but it is not in itself evidence that the Teacher of Righteousness ever functioned as high priest in Jerusalem. Since the scrolls never assert either

---

[28] Murphy-O'Connor, "The Damascus Document Revisited," *RB* 92 (1985) 239.

[29] Josephus, *Ant.* 20.10.4 [357] says the office was vacant for seven years (between Alcimus and Jonathan). Elsewhere he says that Judas Maccabee had functioned as high priest and that the interval was only four years.

[30] Stegemann, *Die Entstehung,* A 79–82 n. 328.

[31] K. Koch, "Ezra and the Origins of Judaism," *JSS* 19 (1974) 190–93.

[32] H. G. M. Williamson, *Ezra, Nehemiah* (Word Bible Commentary 16; Waco: Word, 1985) 91. Williamson judges Koch's suggestion "most improbable." Similarly D. J. Clines (*Ezra, Nehemiah, Esther* [The New Century Bible Commentary; Grand Rapids: Eerdmans, 1984] 99) asserts that Ezra "was not high priest, but simply a member of the high-priestly family." For a reconstruction of the High-Priestly lineage in the Persian period, see F. M. Cross, "A Reconstruction of the Judean Restoration," *JBL* 94 (1975) 17. The list does not include Ezra, Meremoth, or Shelemaiah.

that he had so functioned or that his opponent had usurped the high priest-hood, and in view of the calendrical difference between the Essenes and the Jerusalem Temple, the theory that the Teacher was a displaced high priest must be judged highly improbable.[33]

The primary reason why scholars have thought that the usurpation of the high priesthood was a factor in the secession of the Qumran sect is that it seems (to modern scholars) to be the development in the early Hasmonean period which was most likely to cause such a split. Our examination of the evidence, however, fails to confirm this hypothesis. The theory is not thereby rendered impossible, but we must ask whether it is necessary. The scrolls provide adequate reasons for the rejection of the Jerusalem cult: the difference in calendar, halakhic matters concerning purity and marriage, and the ill-gotten wealth of the ruling priests. The break may have been precipi-tated by the Teacher's criticism of the high priest or by the attempt on the part of the authorities to suppress the variant calendar. It may be that the Teacher and his followers had been able to observe their own cultic calendar during the Intersacerdotium,[34] but that when Jonathan became high priest he insisted on uniformity. This suggestion too is hypothetical, but it requires us to make fewer assumptions beyond the actual evidence than does the customary view about a dispute over the priesthood.

2. The Time of the Emergence of the Sect

Even if the secession of the Qumran community was not a reaction to the usurpation of the high priesthood, the origin of the settlement by the Dead Sea is dated to the early Hasmonean period on archaeological grounds. Moreover, if the original Wicked Priest was Jonathan Maccabee, the activity of the Teacher of Righteousness must be dated to his time. The main debate has been whether the Essenes had already been in existence as an organized group before this time and for how long. As usual, the lack of consensus reflects the paucity of the evidence.

To begin with, there is some ambiguity as to what is meant by the emer-gence of the sect. It is important to distinguish between the traditions of a group, however distinctive, and a sectarian form of organization. Despite the claim in CD 3 that the distinctive requirements of the "new covenant" were revealed, most scholars have assumed that they were derived from older

---

[33] See also H. Burgmann, "Das umstrittene intersacerdotium in Jerusalem 159–152 v. Chr.," *JSJ* 11 (1980) 135–76.

[34] This does not require that the Teacher or another Essene leader was *de facto* high priest. At most the Teacher would have functioned as high priest for his own group, but we do not know whether in fact they performed ceremonies which required a high priest (e.g., on the Day of Atonement).

traditions. It is certainly true that the 364-day calendar is found in documents which were not demonstrably composed by Essenes (the Astronomical Book of *Enoch* and *Jubilees*). This was presumably a tradition shared with other Jewish groups and one which was quite probably older than any organization of Essenes. The books of *Enoch* reflect a tradition which goes back at least to the middle of the third century, but provides no evidence as to how the tradents were organized. The Enoch tradition is part of the religious legacy inherited by the Qumran community, but it is not itself evidence for pre-Qumran Essenes since it lacks the distinctive organization of the sect.[35] Similarly, arguments that some Essene traditions (interest in divination and astrology, Iranian themes) can be traced to a Babylonian setting cannot be taken as evidence that the organization of the Essene sect should be localized there.[36]

The *Damascus Document* describes the emergence of the sect in three places. Column 1 is the only passage which gives indications of dates. As the text now stands we are told that God "visited" the remnant of Israel "in the age of wrath, three hundred and ninety years after he had given them into the hand of Nebuchadnezzar" and caused "a root of cultivation" to spring from Israel and Aaron.[37] Yet we are told that these were like blind men for twenty years until the coming of the Teacher of Righteousness. In this passage, then, there is a clear distinction between two stages in the emergence of the community, although they are not far apart.

The emergence of the "root of cultivation" here has often been correlated with other groups of the postexilic period, who are mentioned in apocalyptic literature, most notably "the chosen righteous from the eternal plant of righteousness" in the Apocalypse of Weeks (*1 Enoch* 93:10). The other passages in CD, however, suggest a more distin : form of organization than can be inferred from the apocalypses. In CD 3:13 we read that God established his covenant with Israel by revealing the hidden things. Yet the recipients of this revelation were still defiling themselves until God pardoned them and built them a sure house. Finally in CD 6 we are told that God remembered the covenant of the forefathers and raised from Aaron men of understanding and from Israel men of wisdom. In this case there is no reference to a further period of error, but a figure called the Searcher of the Law is said to set up ordinances for the whole period of wickedness.[38] This figure is

---

[35] See further J. J. Collins, *The Apocalyptic Imagination* (New York: Crossroad, 1984) 56–63.

[36] J. Murphy-O'Connor, "The Essenes and Their History," *RB* 81 (1974) 222–26; "The Damascus Document Revisited," *RB* 92 (1985) 228–29. It is not apparent to me that any of the points listed requires a Babylonian setting.

[37] This is the standard interpretation of the passage, exemplified in the translation of Vermes.

[38] The Searcher of the Law is identified as the "staff" of Num 21:18 (*měḥoqeq*) while the statutes are *měḥoqěqot*.

usually identified as the Teacher of Righteousness.[39] The passage goes on to speak of a covenant which involved a rejection of the Temple cult.

The passages in cols. 3 and 6 do not distinguish as clearly as does col. 1 between two stages: the initial formation of the group and the advent of the Teacher. Col. 3 is most easily understood to say that the initial stage involved a covenant, while a second involved the "sure house." In col. 6 the elect from Aaron and Israel must be correlated with the first stage in col. 1. The covenantal agreement not to use the Temple "in vain" is mentioned after the "Searcher of the Law" and could be one of his ordinances, but the passage sees no discontinuity between this figure and the initial men of Aaron and Israel. It seems likely, then, though not certain, that the formation of the "new covenant" which was the hallmark of the Qumran sect preceded the advent of the Teacher by a short period (the 20 years of col. 1), although he may have finalized the ordinances and completed the separation from the rest of Judaism.[40]

As we have noted, the only explicit indications of date in CD are the figures "390 years" and "20 years" in col. 1. These figures are controversial for two reasons. On the one hand, they disrupt the rhythmical balance of the parallel lines and are quite probably glosses. On the other hand, the precise meaning of the passage is open to question. To say that the numbers are added as glosses, however, does not give us license to disregard them. They are evidently ancient glosses and reflect the sect's own calculation of its origin.[41] The interpretation of the passage presents the more serious problem. The figure 390 is derived from Ezek 4:5, where it refers to the punishment of the house of Israel.[42] This is a schematic figure, however, and cannot

---

[39] Davies (*The Damascus Covenant,* 123–25) identifies him with an earlier leader, before the rise of the "Teacher of Righteousness" but this is to multiply figures without cause. See my discussion in *The Apocalyptic Imagination,* 125–26.

[40] In 1QS 8 the motifs of "planting" and "Aaron and Israel," which are used of the first stage in CD 1 and the "house" (stage 2 in CD 3) are all used with reference to the group which "prepares in the desert the way of the Lord" (possibly the pioneering settlers at Qumran). The fusion of terminology here again suggests that the emergence of the sect was remembered as a continuous process.

[41] It has been suggested that if we add the 390 years and 20 years of blindness, allow the biblical figure of 40 years for the career of the Teacher, and add the 40 years from his death to the destruction of his enemies (CD 20:15), we arrive at 490 years, the 70 weeks of years of Daniel 9 (F. F. Bruce, "The Book of Daniel and the Qumran Community," *Neotestamentica et Semitica* [ed. E. E. Ellis and M. Wilcox; Edinburgh: Clark, 1969] 232; G. Vermes, *The Dead Sea Scrolls,* 147–48). If this suggestion is correct, it would point to a date for the end of the age a century after the first emergence of the sect. The chronological data in CD would then presumably have been inserted within that century and before the *pesher* on Habakkuk, which discusses the delay of the end, was composed.

[42] Vermes (*The Dead Sea Scrolls,* 158) says that we may "safely discard" this derivation since

be taken as chronologically exact, as we can see by comparison with Daniel 9, where the period from the destruction of the Temple to the Maccabean era is calculated as 490 years.[43] At most we can assume that such figures as 390 years and 490 years could only be plausible several hundred years after the exile and so point to a date in the Hellenistic era.

Moreover, there are problems with the standard translation of CD 1. The verb *paqad*, "visit," which is usually taken in a benign sense here, is used elsewhere in CD in the sense of "punish."[44] The expression *ltytw 'wtm* is usually translated here as "after he had given them," which is an unusual construal of the preposition.[45] The Hebrew could be construed differently, by taking the 390 years as equivalent to "the epoch of wrath" and *ltytw 'wtm* as indicating the manner of punishment (to give them, or by giving them, into the hand of Nebuchadnezzar). On this interpretation the 390 years do not necessarily indicate the time of the emergence of the sect, but only identify the "age of wrath" with the period prophesied by Ezekiel.

Even if we disallow any chronological value to the 390 years, however, CD 1 contains valuable information in the statement that those in the elect group were like blind men for twenty years, presumably a round figure for half a generation. This blindness is relieved by the advent of the Teacher of Righteousness.[46] If the Teacher was a contemporary of Jonathan Maccabee, as most scholars infer from the *pesharim*, then the "plant root" can scarcely be dated earlier than 172 B.C.E. While this information is neither as clear nor as exact as we would wish, it does reflect the community's own recollection of its history. To overrule this evidence, we would need to find passages in the scrolls which *require* (and not merely *permit*) a different calculation.

Jerome Murphy-O'Connor and Philip Davies claim to find such evidence in CD. Their reconstruction of Essene origins is "based on the conviction that CD unambiguously pointed to the Exile in Babylon as the time and place of the origin of the Essene movement."[47] This conviction has been subjected to a thorough and careful critique by Michael Knibb,[48] and there is no need to

---

the document shows no interest in the fate of northern Israel. This is to lose sight of the symbolic understanding of scripture in the scrolls, where the original reference is often disregarded.

[43] Vermes (*The Dead Sea Scrolls,* 158–59) gives several illustrations of the unreliability of the chronology of ancient Jewish writers.

[44] CD 5:15; 7:9; 8:2, 3.

[45] See Davies, *The Damascus Covenant,* 65.

[46] Ibid., 175, 200. Davies regards the reference to the Teacher in 1:11 as secondary, but he is led to this conclusion by his reconstruction of the history of the sect and of CD, not by any textual evidence.

[47] Murphy-O'Connor, "The Damascus Document Revisited," 226.

[48] M. Knibb, "Exile in the Damascus Document," *JSOT* 25 (1983) 99–117.

repeat all the arguments here. I will focus only on what seems to me to be the central issue, especially since Murphy-O'Connor has attempted a rebuttal of Knibb on this point.[49]

The central issue is the interpretation of the three passages in CD 1, 3, and 6 which recount the emergence of the sect. In cols. 3 and 6 the rise of the new group follows directly on a reference to the exile. This would also be true in col. 1 if the chronological data were excised. Knibb explains the abrupt transition by reference to "the same theological pattern that we find in other literature of the period, namely that which sees the condition of exile as lasting beyond the return at the end of the sixth century and being brought to an end only in the events of a much later period."[50] This pattern is exemplified in Daniel 9 and *1 Enoch* 93. Murphy-O'Connor counters that this pattern is not found in any of the source documents of CD (from which he excludes col. 1). In the apocalypses the exile is followed by a period of lawlessness, which comes to an end in the writer's generation, when, in *1 Enoch* 93, a new group emerges. In CD, there is no interval of lawlessness.[51]

Murphy-O'Connor has correctly perceived that the understanding of history in CD is different from that of the apocalypses. In the apocalypses, the rise of a movement heralds the end of an era. CD emphasizes that Belial is let loose upon Israel during the time of the existence of the sect. The different emphasis here may well derive from the dualistic world view which is expounded in 1QS and only hinted at in CD.[52] It does not follow, however, that the sect must have arisen during the exile or at the start of the postexilic period. CD 5:17–21 moves directly from "ancient times" when Moses and Aaron arose to "the epoch of the desolation of the land."[53] We do not infer that the author placed the desolation in the premonarchic period. Knibb's argument does not require complete correspondence between the theological patterns of CD and the apocalypses. The significant parallel is that the condition of exile persists beyond the sixth century.[54] Therefore, a

---

[49] "The Damascus Document Revisited," 227–28. Murphy-O'Connor makes a major concession to his critics when he accepts the translation "converts of Israel" (rather than returnees) for *šby yiśrā'ēl* (ibid., 233), although he makes an exception for CD 19:33–34.

[50] Knibb, "Exile in the Damascus Document," 110.

[51] "The Damascus Document Revisited," 227.

[52] On the dualism of CD see my essay "Was the Dead Sea Sect an Apocalyptic Movement?" in *Qumran Studies in Memory of Yigael Yadin* (forthcoming).

[53] The authenticity of the reference to Moses and Aaron here has been questioned by J. Murphy-O'Connor ("An Essene Missionary Document? CD II, 14–VI, 1," *RB* 77 [1970] 224) but is accepted by Davies (*The Damascus Covenant*, 121). In either case the extant text shows that contiguous references do not necessarily imply immediate historical continuity.

[54] The closest parallel to CD is neither *1 Enoch* 93 nor Daniel but *Jub.* 1:13–15, which says that when God scatters Israel they will forget the laws, and specifically the calendar (compare CD 3:13–15).

passage like CD 3, which mentions no intervening events between the exile and the rise of the sect, does not necessarily date the latter event to the sixth century.[55] The evidence of CD (apart from col. 1) is compatible with an exilic date but does not require it. It cannot then overrule the explicit evidence of col. 1 for a later date.

I conclude then that the two stages of the emergence of the sect, the "plant root" and the advent of the Teacher, must be dated in close proximity to each other, most probably in the second century. Nothing requires an earlier date for an organized community or for a "new covenant," although various traditions of the sect can undoubtedly be traced to a much earlier time.

3. The Man of the Lie

A third area of dispute in the area of Qumran origins concerns the figure of the "Man of the Lie," also known as the Scoffer and the Spouter of Lies.[56] Some scholars still assume that this figure is identical with the Wicked Priest, but G. Jeremias and H. Stegemann have made a strong case for his separate identity.[57] Whereas the Wicked Priest is said to "rule in Israel" (1QpHab 8:9–10), the Liar is the leader of a group which rejected the authority of the Teacher. Both are enemies of the Teacher, but only the Wicked Priest is accused of defiling the sanctuary (1QpHab 12:8–9). The feud with the Man of the Lie concerns the true teaching:[58] he is said to have led Israel astray and caused them not to listen to the Teacher (CD 1:15; 4QpPs37 1:25).

Various hypotheses have been advanced about the identity of this figure and his relation to the Teacher. Hans Burgmann identifies him with Simon Maccabee, brother of the Wicked Priest Jonathan, and credits him with founding the Pharisaic sect.[59] For Stegemann, he was a Hasidic leader who refused to accept the authority of the Teacher and led a break-away group

---

[55] Davies (*The Damascus Covenant*, 202) grants that an "exilic origin" does not necessarily imply a sixth century B.C.E. date, but then it is difficult to see what is the chronological value of an exilic origin.

[56] This figure appears in CD 1:14; 8:13; 19:26; 20:15 (compare also CD 4:19 which refers to "Precept," a "spouter"). 1QpHab 2:1f.; 5:9–12; 10:1–13; 4QPss[a] 1:26; 4:14. The text of 1QpMic 10:2 has been reconstructed to yield another reference, but this suggestion should be rejected (Horgan, *Pesharim*, 60).

[57] G. Jeremias, *Der Lehrer der Gerechtigkeit* (SUNT 2; Göttingen: Vandenhoeck & Ruprecht, 1963) 79–126; H. Stegemann, *Die Entstehung*, 41–53. Stegemann corrects some of Jeremias's arguments but confirms his main thesis.

[58] The designation "Man of the Lie" may have overtones of Persian dualism. In Yasna 30 the evil spirit is "he who was of the Lie," and his followers are "the followers of the Lie" (See P. J. Kobelski, *Melchizedek and Melchireša'* [CBQMS 10; Washington: CBA, 1981] 89).

[59] H. Burgmann, *Zwei lösbare Qumranprobleme*, 13–256.

which became the Pharisees.[60] Murphy-O'Connor, in contrast, sees the "Man of the Lie" as the leader of "non-Qumran Essenism" which refused to follow the Teacher to the desert,[61] and has even suggested that he be identified with Judah the Essene.[62]

Recent discussion of the "Man of the Lie" has been heavily influenced by the work of Jeremias and Stegemann. Jeremias argued that the Man of the Lie and the Teacher were originally members of the same community.[63] Stegemann modified this argument and argued that the Man of the Lie was originally leader of his own community and that the Teacher may originally have belonged to it.[64] Both scholars relied primarily on 1QpHab 5:8–12, where Habakkuk 1:13b is interpreted as follows: "The interpretation of it concerns the House of Absalom and their partisans, who were silent at the rebuke of the Teacher of Righteousness and did not support him against the Man of the Lie — who rejected the Law in the midst of all their council." There are three notorious problems in this passage: the identity of the House of Absalom, the antecedent of "their council" and the question whether the Teacher was administering or suffering the rebuke.

Stegemann is surely right that the "House of Absalom" is, syntactically, the most natural antecedent of "their council."[65] He proceeds to argue that the silence of the "House of Absalom" was understood to indicate support for the Man of the Lie and must therefore have been his community. This argument is not persuasive. The *pesher* reflects disappointment that the House of Absalom failed to help the Teacher, and help could scarcely have been expected from the community of the Man of the Lie. Moreover, if the House of Absalom had actually taken the side of the Man of the Lie, it would surely have been accused of something more than silence. The simplest interpretation of the passage is that the "house of Absalom" was, and remained, neutral ground. Its identity remains uncertain, but it is noteworthy that 1 Maccabees identifies two supporters of Jonathan Maccabee as "sons of Absalom."[66] It is

[60] Stegemann, *Die Entstehung*, 227–28. The statement of Murphy-O'Connor that Stegemann regards the "Man of the Lie" as "a leader in the Essene movement" is not quite accurate, since Stegemann, quite correctly, refrains from using the name Essene at this stage of the development of the sect (J. Murphy-O'Connor, "The Judean Desert," in *Early Judaism and its Modern Interpreters* [ed. R. A. Kraft and G. W. E. Nickelsburg; Atlanta: Scholars Press, 1986] 141).

[61] J. Murphy-O'Connor, "The Essenes and their History," *RB* 81 (1974) 235.

[62] J. Murphy-O'Connor, "Judah the Essene and the Teacher of Righteousness," *RevQ* 10 (1981) 579–86.

[63] Jeremias, *Der Lehrer*, 86–87.

[64] Stegemann, *Die Entstehung*, 48–52.

[65] Stegemann (*Die Entstehung*, 49) against Jeremias (*Der Lehrer*, 86), who takes it as the congregation of the Teacher and the Man of the Lie.

[66] 1 Macc 11:70; 13:11; D. N. Freedman, "The 'House of Absalom' in the Habakkuk Scroll," *BASOR* 114 (1949) 11–12.

possible that the "house of Absalom," was the actual name of a clan and that the symbolic associations of the name were fortuitous.

The reference to "the rebuke of the Teacher of Righteousness" is ambiguous. Jeremias correctly established that the word in question (*twkḥt*) means rebuke, as in 1QS 6:1; CD 7:2; 9:2-8,[67] not physical punishment as in Burgmann's theory.[68] He proceeds to argue from 1QS 9:16-18 that such remonstrance would only have taken place between two members of the same community.[69] This point is not well founded: it is not apparent that the directive of 1QS 9 was already in force when this encounter took place. We have a possible clue as to the nature of the rebuke in 1QpHab 5:11-12. We are told that the Man of the Lie rejected the Torah in the midst of the assembly. If the Teacher was rebuking the Man of the Lie, the rebuke was probably in accordance with this Torah. We may compare 4QpPs[a] 4:8-9, which says that "the Wicked Priest sought to murder the Teacher . . . and the law which he sent to him." From this it would seem that the Teacher made an attempt to win over his enemies by presenting them with a Torah (perhaps analogous to 4QMMT, the so-called "Letter of the Teacher of Righteousness to the Wicked Priest"). The effort was evidently unsuccessful, and the experience of rejection may have led him to formulate the rule of 1QS 9:16-18. On the other hand, if the Man of the Lie was administering the rebuke, this would presumably be related to his rejection of the law and of the divine authority of the Teacher. The use of *twkḥt* in 1QpHab 5:4 would seem to favor an active rather than a passive use and so that the Teacher was the one administering the rebuke.

Other evidence strengthens the impression that the feud was not an inner sectarian one. In CD 1:14 the man of mockery is said to spout waters of falsehood "*to Israel*" and lead them astray. He did not merely resist the claims of the Teacher but actively preached a different message. His audience was not just a congregation or community, but Israel. In CD 4:19-20 the "builders of the wall" who have followed the spouter are said to be trapped in two of the nets of Belial, in which he traps Israel. The disagreement then is not only over the authority of the Teacher but involves some of the halakhic issues which separated the sect from the rest of Israel. It is probable that those whom the Man of the Lie "led astray" included some who had hitherto been followers of the Teacher. CD 20:14-15 speaks of "the men of war who turned back with the Man of the Lie."[70] The same column says that

---

[67] Note also the use of the term in 1QpHab 5:4 where *twkḥt* convicts the wicked ones of the people.

[68] *Zwei lösbare Qumranprobleme*, 84.

[69] Jeremias, *Der Lehrer*, 85-86.

[70] The designation "men of war" is derived from Deut 2:14.

those who rejected the "new covenant in the land of Damascus" would receive the same judgment as their companions who turned back with the men of scoffing. These traitors to the new covenant should not, however, be simply identified with the followers of the Scoffer. Indeed 1QpHab 2:1–10 distinguishes three groups of traitors: the "traitors together with the Man of the Lie" (2:1–2) who did not accept the words of the Teacher; the traitors to the new covenant, who were unfaithful to it; and the traitors at the end of days.[71] Here again there seems to be a distinction between those who followed the Man of the Lie instead of the Teacher and those who were members of the new covenant.[72]

The *pesharim* emphasize the success of the Man of the Lie.[73] He led many astray (4QpPs[a] 1:26; 1QpHab 10:9) and built a city of vanity and established a congregation with deceit (1QpHab 10:10).[74] From this it would seem that he was credited with building up a movement, not merely retaining the loyalty of an old movement against the challenge of the Teacher, and not merely with causing a split within a sect. Murphy-O'Connor's view that the Man of the Lie and his followers represent "non-Qumran Essenism"[75] is implausible on several counts. To begin with, we have found no evidence that the Liar was ever an "Essene." Further, there is no evidence that the "Qumran Essenes" were ever at variance with other settlements of the sect.[76] Finally, there is evidence that the reverse was true. The *Damascus Document*, which clearly comes from a community loyal to the Teacher, legislates for "those who live in camps following the order of the land" (7:6–9),[77] and

---

[71] For discussion of this passage see Jeremias, *Der Lehrer*, 79–82. He concludes that there were three distinct groups, but not necessarily at three distinct times.

[72] CD 1:17 says the Scoffer caused "the curses of his covenant" to cling to those he led astray. This is usually understood as God's covenant. If it were the Scoffer's covenant it would indicate that he had a distinct covenant which was "his."

[73] Stegemann, *Die Entstehung*, 44–45.

[74] This passage might be thought to lend support to Burgmann's identification of the Liar with Simon (*Zwei lösbare Qumranprobleme*, 175–83). Cross described Simon as "the builder par excellence" (*The Ancient Library of Qumran*, 150; see 1 Macc 13:10, 33, 52; 14:33, 37) and identified him with the cursed "man who rebuilds this city" in the Testimonia. Jeremias, however, has pointed out that in 1QpHab the reference to building a city is derived from the biblical text. The *pesher* reinterprets it as building a congregation. The passage does not necessarily have the same reference as the one in the Testimonia.

[75] "The Essenes and their History," 235.

[76] See further my comments in "Was the Dead Sea Sect an Apocalyptic Community?" Philo and Josephus speak of one sect with many settlements. They do not, of course, mention Qumran. Qumran is identified as an Essene community primarily because of Pliny's reference to an Essene sect by the Dead Sea (*Nat. Hist.* 5.15) and the correspondences between the *Community Rule* and the account in Josephus.

[77] This passage is sometimes regarded as redactional, but Davies (*The Damascus Covenant*, 142) makes a case for its authenticity. Rules for the "camps" also appear in CD 12–14.

therefore provides for "non-Qumran Essenes" within the Teacher's movement. The view of Vermes, that 1QS and CD reflect the different branches of the Essenes reported by Josephus and that these were complementary and not schismatic, remains the most probable theory.[78]

Stegemann's thesis that the followers of the Man of the Lie became the Pharisees[79] has some evidence to support it. This evidence consists of the use of stereotypical designations such as "seekers after smooth things" and "Ephraim." In the *pesher* on Nahum the "Seekers after smooth things" appear as opponents of the "Lion of Wrath" who hanged men alive. They are also said to have advised "Demetrius, king of Greece" to enter Jerusalem. The Lion is clearly identifiable as Alexander Jannaeus, and in this context the "seekers" are clearly the Pharisees.[80] Ephraim is identified as "the seekers after smooth things at the end of days" and the *pesher* also refers to "those who lead Ephraim astray" and "lead many astray." Stegemann points out that "leading astray" (*ht'h*) is a motif associated with the Man of the Lie.[81] Also in CD 1, the followers of the Spouter are said to have sought smooth things. The question is whether stereotypical language necessarily has the same referent in different contexts or may have been applied at various times to different opponents of the sect.[82]

The only passage which may contain information about the halakhic views of the Man of the Lie is found in CD 4:19–5:12. There we are told that the followers of "Precept," a spouter, are caught in two of the three nets of Belial. These are fornication by marrying "two women in their lifetime" and profanation of the Temple by breach of purity and marriage laws. The purity laws in question (sleeping with a menstruating woman) are too general to be helpful.[83] It is interesting, however, that Louis Ginzberg regarded the marriage laws in this passage as a clear exception to what he perceived as the Pharisaic character of the book.[84] He argued that, despite thousands of differences between rabbis on other matters, "there is not a single case of incestuous marriage on which they are not unanimous." Hence the halakha of the sect would indeed be in conflict with the rabbis on this matter. Against

---

[78] Vermes, *The Dead Sea Scrolls*, 105–9.

[79] Stegemann, *Die Entstehung*, 250.

[80] See E. Schürer, *The History of the Jewish People in the Age of Jesus Christ* (rev. and ed. G. Vermes and F. Millar; Edinburgh: Clark, 1973) 1. 219–28.

[81] Stegemann, *Die Enstehung*, 69–72.

[82] See the objections of Murphy-O'Connor, "The Essenes and their History," 240–41.

[83] *M. Niddah* 1: 1–7 shows that the definition of menstrual impurity was subject to various interpretations.

[84] L. Ginzberg, *An Unknown Jewish Sect* (New York: Jewish Theological Seminary, 1970) 127–30.

this line of argument, we cannot assume that the views of the earliest Pharisees are accurately reflected in the Mishnah and Talmud, and so the halakhic issues in CD cannot confirm the proposed identification of the followers of the Man of the Lie as Pharisees. That identification does, however, remain possible, even if it cannot be proved conclusively.

The Evidence of the Teacher Hymns

Thus far we have made little reference to a body of material which many scholars regard as the work of the Teacher of Righteousness himself—the so-called Teacher Hymns.[85] While the ascription of these hymns is necessarily hypothetical, it is plausible.[86] The presumed author claims to be a mediator of revelation in a way that is only attested in the case of the Teacher (1QpHab 7:4). Unfortunately, these hymns contain very little biographical information. The most informative passage is found in 1QH 4:5–5:4.[87]

Perhaps the most noteworthy claim advanced in this hymn is that "teachers of lies" have banished the author from his land "like a bird from its nest" (1QH 4:8–9). While the hymn does not focus on the individual "Man of the Lie," he is surely included among these teachers, who are also described as "lying prophets" and "seers of falsehood." The charges against these people are very similar to what we found in the *Damascus Document*. They have schemed "to exchange the Law engraved on my heart by Thee for the smooth things (which they speak) to Thy people." Their errors concern "feast days" (compare CD 3:14–15), their teachings are described as "snares" (*mĕṣudot*) and "designs of Belial" (1QH 4:12–13; compare the three *mĕṣudot* of Belial in CD 4:15), and they say of the vision of knowledge "it is not sure" (1QH 4:18; compare CD 5:12). Their offense includes rejection of the Teacher, but is not only a question of authority. We read in another hymn that the Teacher encountered rebellion within his own community (1QH 5:23–25), and that some who were bound by his testimony were deceived (6:19). While the "lying prophets" may have made inroads among the Teacher's followers, however, there is no indication that the dispute was primarily an inner-sectarian one. The reasons why the Teacher was driven out were apparently the halakhic ones which are said to have caused the separation of the sect in CD and 4QMMT.

---

[85] Jeremias, *Der Lehrer*, 168–267. H. W. Kuhn (*Enderwartung and gegenwartiges Heil* [SUNT 4; Göttingen: Vandenhoeck & Ruprecht, 1966] 23) lists the most widely accepted Teacher Hymns: 2:1–19; 4:5–29; 5:5–19; 5:20–6:36; 7:6–25; 8:4–40. Jeremias also includes 2:31–39; 3:1–18 and extends two other hymns: 4:5–5:4 and 5:20–7:5.

[86] Jeremias (*Der Lehrer*, 172–73) contrasts the terminology of the Teacher Hymns with that of the rest of the *Hodayot*.

[87] Jeremias, *Der Lehrer*, 211.

It is noteworthy that neither 1QH nor CD makes reference to the Wicked Priest, who figures so prominently in the *pesharim*. This fact is anomalous for the widely held views that a dispute over the priesthood caused the emergence of the community, or that the Teacher was a displaced high priest when he encountered the Man of the Lie. One possible explanation for the absence of the Wicked Priest in these documents is that the feud with the "teachers of lies" came first and that the Teacher's community had already crystallized as a separate entity before its feud with the high priest.[88]

Conclusion

Our review of the evidence for the origin of the Qumran community has led us to question several widely held hypotheses. The claim that the sect originated in the Babylonian Exile contradicts the most explicit evidence of the *Damascus Document*, without adequate warrant. The view that the withdrawal of the sect was caused by a dispute over the high priestly succession lacks textual evidence to support it. The thesis that the Teacher of Righteousness functioned as high priest during the Intersacerdotium is not only unsupported, but implausible. There is no evidence that the "Man of the Lie" was an Essene leader.

The identity of both the Teacher and the "Man of the Lie" remains enigmatic and will probably continue to remain so, unless new evidence is found. We know that both were prophetic figures in the mid-second century B.C.E. They were largely concerned with halakhic matters, although this should certainly not be taken to exclude a concern for metaphysical beliefs or for eschatology.[89] Attempts to identify either one with figures otherwise known have hitherto been unsuccessful.[90] Given the sketchiness of our knowledge of ancient Judaism, this is hardly surprising. While the results of our review have been negative, they may perhaps clear the way for a more realistic appraisal of our limited knowledge on this fascinating topic.

[88] According to the preliminary report the epilogue to 4QMMT states "we have separated ourselves from the majority of the people . . . from intermingling in these matters and from participating with them in these [matters]" (Qimron and Strugnell, "An Unpublished Halakhic Letter from Qumran," 402).

[89] See further my article "Was the Dead Sea Sect an Apocalyptic Community?"

[90] The attempt of J. Carmignac to identify the Teacher with Judah the Essene ("Qui etait le Docteur de Justice?" *RQ* 10 [1980] 235–46) has been refuted at length by Burgmann (*Zwei lösbare Qumranprobleme*, 231–56) and Murphy-O'Connor ("Judah the Essene and the Teacher of Righteousness," *RQ* 10 [1981] 579–86).

The Hodayot (1QH)
and New Testament Poetry

Maurya P. Horgan
The Scriptorium

Paul J. Kobelski
The Scriptorium

ברוך אתה אדוני
Blessed are you, my Lord!
1QH 10:13

εὐλογητὸς κύριος ὁ θεός
Blessed be the Lord God!
Luke 1:68

IN 1957, TEN YEARS AFTER the initial discovery of the Qumran scrolls, Charles Kraft noted briefly in an early study of the Qumran hymns that the sectarian psalms may be "important for an understanding of what New Testament writers regarded as poetry."[1] At about the same time, in the first edition of *The Ancient Library of Qumran,* Frank Cross stated: "Analysis of the literary types, the prosody, and the language and theological motifs of these documents will greatly expand our knowledge of the development of late Old Testament psalmody on the one hand, and will illuminate on the other hand difficult problems in the study of the literary types and prosodic canons of the New Testament psalms (especially in the prologue of Luke) and poetry." In a footnote Cross charged: "The failure of New Testament scholars to recognize this development has hindered advances in the analysis of poetic materials embedded in the New Testament, notably in the Gospels."[2] The suggestion that the poetic material from the Dead Sea Scrolls may form a bridge between the poetry of the Hebrew Bible and poetic passages in the New Testament is the starting point for this article,

[1] C. F. Kraft, "Poetic Structure in the Qumran Thanksgiving Psalms," *BR* 2 (1957) 16.
[2] F. M. Cross, *The Ancient Library of Qumran and Modern Biblical Studies* (Garden City, NY: Doubleday, 1958) 166 and n. 8.

which offers a preliminary description of some of the literary features of this poetic bridge.

Prophecy and Poetry

The larger contexts of this limited treatment are poetic language in general and Hebrew poetry in particular. James Kugel gives a concise definition of poetry: "evocative compositions that communicate more by connotation than denotation."[3] In every age one can point to works that exhibit this special use of language. The ancient poetry of the Hebrews, like the poetic oracles of other ancient religions, was the language the people used to verbalize their understanding of divine communications and to respond in liturgy and ritual.[4] Poetry was, for them, the vehicle of revelation. David Noel Freedman, in his presidential address to the Society of Biblical Literature in 1976, traced the thread of poetic communication through the ancient Yahwistic poets to the prophets, who, he said, "were the inheritors of the great poetic tradition of Israel's adventure in faith and maintained, enhanced, renewed, and recreated it."[5] He pointed out that the authors of the old poems were identified as prophets. For example, Exod 15:20 calls Miriam a prophet; Judg 4:4 calls Deborah a prophet; and David is named as the composer of a number of poems, and is called a prophet in Acts 2:30. Conversely, according to Freedman, there are hints that the prophets composed poems: Samuel in 1 Sam 15:23; Nathan in 2 Sam 12:1-4; Micaiah in 1 Kgs 22:17; and Elisha in 1 Kgs 13:27.[6] There is, then, some special identification between prophecy and poetry as vehicles of revelation.

When classical prophecy declined, a new type of poetic prophecy grew up in the form of apocalyptic.[7] This is not the place to recount the debate about the origins of apocalyptic or its relation to prophecy and wisdom, about which much has been written in recent years. It is here assumed that it is on this continuum—ancient poetry, prophecy, apocalyptic—that the poetry of the Dead Sea Scrolls stands, especially the *Thanksgiving Hymns* or *Hodayot,* the document identified as 1QH. These hymns are sometimes attributed to the

[3] Kugel, "poetry," in *Harper's Bible Dictionary* (ed. P. J. Achtemeier; San Francisco: Harper & Row, 1985) 804.

[4] David Noel Freedman, "Pottery, Poetry, and Prophecy: An Essay on Biblical Poetry," *JBL* 96 (1977) 15, 20.

[5] Ibid., 21.

[6] Ibid.

[7] Ibid., 23–26; see also Paul D. Hanson, *The Dawn of Apocalyptic: The Historical and Sociological Roots of Jewish Apocalyptic Eschatology* (rev. ed.; Philadelphia: Fortress, 1979) 8–31; John J. Collins, "Old Testament Apocalypticism and Eschatology," in *The New Jerome Biblical Commentary* (ed. R. E. Brown, J. A. Fitzmyer, and R. E. Murphy; Englewood Cliffs, NJ: Prentice Hall, 1990; off the press in August 1989) 298–304.

Teacher of Righteousness (or Righteous Teacher), the founder of—or surely an important figure in—the Dead Sea community.[8] Though not called a prophet, the Teacher was described as an inspired interpreter, one "to whom God made known all the mysteries of the words of his servants the prophets" (1QpHab 7:2). The community believed that the Teacher possessed prophetic powers in the sense that he could discern the divine power and plan and its working in human history—past, present, and future.

In the same prophetic and apocalyptic line, some of the NT writings point to a new prophetic age being realized in eschatological fulfillment. Though largely a collection of prose works, the New Testament is interspersed with poetic compositions of various types. Hymns are found scattered throughout the letters and epistles; the book of Revelation is filled with poems of various lengths; and in the Gospel of Luke the pronouncements of angels and inspired persons are in the form of poetry. Thus, as Freedman proposed, the community's perception of revelation stretched from the ancient poets and prophets, through the apocalyptic visionaries and the inspired interpreters of the Dead Sea Scrolls, to the prophetic and poetic sayings of Jesus in the New Testament and the poems and hymns of the early Christian community.

Hebrew and Greek

Against this background, we are able to describe several strands of the poetic and prophetic thread by examining briefly the *Thanksgiving Hymns* or *Hodayot* of the Dead Sea Scrolls and two NT hymns, the Magnificat (Luke 1:47–55) and the Benedictus (Luke 1:68–79). The literary features treated here are themes, structure, use of biblical language, parallelism, and grammatical phenomena.

The question arises immediately: How can the poetic material of the New Testament, which is in Greek, be compared with the poetry of the Dead Sea Scrolls, which is in Hebrew? From the NT material that might be described as poetic, we have chosen the Magnificat of Mary and the Benedictus of Zechariah, because they have generally been understood as Jewish, or Jewish-Christian, compositions, and it is therefore assumed that they have the same general cultural heritage as the hymns from Qumran.[9] In fact, some

---

[8] On this figure, see, e.g., J. Carmignac, *Christ and the Teacher of Righteousness* (Baltimore: Helicon, 1962); G. Jeremias, *Der Lehrer der Gerechtigkeit* (SUNT 2; Göttingen: Vandenhoeck & Ruprecht, 1963); J. Murphy-O'Connor, "The Judean Desert," in *Early Judaism and Its Modern Interpreters* (ed. R. A. Kraft and G. W. E. Nickelsburg; The Bible and Its Modern Interpreters 2; Atlanta: Scholars Press, 1986) 140–41; H. Stegemann, *Die Entstehung der Qumrangemeinde* (Bonn: privately published, 1971); and see the article by John J. Collins in this volume, "The Origin of the Qumran Community: A Review of the Evidence," 159–78, esp. 177–78.

[9] R. E. Brown, *The Birth of the Messiah: A Commentary on the Infancy Narratives in Matthew and*

have argued on the basis of their unmistakable tone and flavor that the two Lucan poems were translated into Greek from a Semitic—Aramaic or, more likely, Hebrew—original.[10] This is not impossible, but some of the poetic devices used by the author suggest that these hymns were original Greek compositions. Martin Dibelius showed, in his treatment of the Epistle of James, that Christian writings from the latter part of the first century, although heavily influenced by traditional Jewish attitudes about the piety of the "poor ones," were composed in Greek.[11] Moreover, studies of bilingual interference in the Greek of the eastern Mediterranean world in the Roman and Byzantine periods have shown that interference phenomena affected all areas of the language. The effects of bilingualism on the NT writings, just as on Egyptian papyri, were not limited to the linguistic patterns of those who actually were bilingual. Interference phenomena so filtered through the language of the area that they influenced even the non-bilingual speakers and writers.[12] Furthermore, the infancy narrative of Luke's Gospel is testimony to the possibility of a Greek writing being composed with Semitic syntactical and lexical interference because of the author's dependence on the Greek Old Testament. Consequently, the probability that the Magnificat and the Benedictus were originally Greek compositions does not preclude a comparison of them with Hebrew poetic compositions. We are inquiring whether there are any specific features of thought and language shared by the two bodies of poetic material that could be described as a poetic bridge, and whether there are definable ways in which the poetic material of the New Testament shares in the legacy of the poetic, prophetic, and apocalyptic movements that produced the lyrical compositions of the Hebrew Bible and the Dead Sea Scrolls.

Biblical Hebrew Poetry

The backdrop against which the poetic traditions of the Qumran community and early Christianity play out their roles, putting into words their respective community's responses to history, is the poetry of the Hebrew Bible. Including as much as one-third of the Hebrew Bible, Hebrew poetic literature is a vast maze, and every avenue seems to end in a virtually insoluble problem. But though significant areas of difficulty persist—especially

---

Luke (Garden City, NY: Doubleday, 1977) 349–50; J. A. Fitzmyer, *The Gospel According to Luke I–IX* (AB 28; Garden City, NY: Doubleday, 1981) 359–62.

[10]See, e.g., the discussion in D. R. Jones, "The Background and Character of the Lukan Psalms," *JTS* 19 (1968) 19–50.

[11]Martin Dibelius, *James* (Hermeneia; Philadelphia: Fortress, 1976) 39–45.

[12]F. T. Gignac, *A Grammar of the Greek Papyri of the Roman and Byzantine Periods.* Vol. 1, *Phonology* (Testi e Documenti per lo Studio dell'Antichità 55; Milan: Cisalpino–La Goliardica, 1976) 47.

concerning textual problems of the Hebrew poems, the lack of consensus about the nature of the rhythms of the poetic compositions, and disagreement over the extent to which and the ways in which the Ugaritic poetic materials may illuminate biblical poems—progress has been made in describing the poetic features and themes of the Hebrew lyrical material; and it is this area that is important for the comparisons offered here.[13] The poetic characteristic about which most scholars agree, though there are different descriptions of the phenomenon, is the use of what has usually been termed "parallelism" in Hebrew poetry. The description of this feature of biblical Hebrew poetry is usually traced to Bishop Robert Lowth in the mid-eighteenth century. Studies during the ensuing century refined—or over-refined—the concept of parallelism to the point that it did not serve well as a description of a fundamental feature of biblical Hebrew poetry. The literary phenomenon that is usually intended by the term "parallelism" is a sentence of two or more parts (or a series of short sentences[14]) in which the second or later part(s) in some way echo, expand, strengthen, or complete the first. Kugel uses the terms "seconding" and "extending," rather than parallelism, to describe this feature of Hebrew poetry, and A. Fitzgerald calls it "balance."[15] This parallelism or seconding or balance is a prominent feature also of the Qumran poetry.

The question of the meter or rhythm of biblical Hebrew poetry is a matter of much debate, but a glance at the Qumran material shows that the rhythm of the Qumran poems is quite different from that of the biblical material. The issue of rhythm need not be addressed here, since the comparisons offered concentrate on other poetic features and literary devices.

---

[13]Recent studies of biblical Hebrew poetry include Aloysius Fitzgerald, "Hebrew Poetry," in *The New Jerome Biblical Commentary,* 201–8; R. Alter, *The Art of Biblical Poetry* (New York: Basic Books, 1985); A. Berlin, *The Dynamics of Biblical Parallelism* (Bloomington: Indiana University Press, 1985); David Noel Freedman, *Pottery, Poetry and Prophecy: Studies in Early Hebrew Poetry* (Winona Lake, IN: Eisenbrauns, 1980); James L. Kugel, *The Idea of Biblical Poetry* (New Haven: Yale University Press, 1981); idem, "poetry," in *Harper's Bible Dictionary* (ed. P. J. Achtemeier; San Francisco: Harper & Row, 1985) 804–6; M. P. O'Connor, *Hebrew Verse Structures* (Winona Lake, IN: Eisenbrauns, 1980); Erhard S. Gerstenberger, "The Lyrical Literature," in *The Hebrew Bible and Its Modern Interpreters* (ed. D. A. Knight and G. M. Tucker; The Bible and Its Modern Interpreters 1; Chico, CA: Scholars Press, 1985) 409–44; James H. Charlesworth, "Jewish Hymns, Odes, and Prayers (ca. 167 B.C.E.–135 C.E.)," in *Early Judaism and Its Modern Interpreters,* 411–36; *Directions in Biblical Hebrew Poetry* (ed. Elaine R. Follis; JSOTSup 40; Sheffield: JSOT Press, 1987).

[14] A. Fitzgerald states that the basic building blocks of Hebrew verse are short sentences ("Hebrew Poetry," 202). As will be seen below, this does not describe the Qumran poems, which are made up of longer lines.

[15] Kugel, "poetry," 805; Fitzgerald, "Hebrew Poetry," 204–5; see also D. J. A. Clines, "The Parallelism of Greater Precision: Notes from Isaiah 40 for a Theory of Hebrew Poetry," in *Directions in Biblical Hebrew Poetry,* 77–100.

Poetry of the Qumran Literature

Turning to the poetry of the Qumran community, we are faced first with the task of identifying the poetic material from among the documents of the Dead Sea discoveries. The scrolls contain many copies of biblical poetic material, and there are sectarian poems as well; but none of these works is divided into poetic lines that would distinguish it from prose. In modern-language versions of the sectarian documents, translators have divided some of the material into poetic lines. For example, Geza Vermes translates in poetic lines cols. 10 and 11 of the *Community Rule* or *Manual of Discipline* (1QS), cols. 10, 12, 13, and 19 of the *War Scroll* (1QM), the so-called *Angelic Liturgy* (4QŠirŠabb), 4QLament over Jerusalem (4Q179), and 4Q184 and 4Q185, which he describes as wisdom poems.[16] André Dupont-Sommer went even further, dividing into poetic lines most of the *Manual of Discipline,* the *Damascus Document,* and the *War Scroll.* He comments in his introduction to the *Manual of Discipline:* "The verse form is intended to emphasize, whenever it is sufficiently recognizable, the characteristics of this style with its long sententious and oratorical periods, and also the parallelism of the poetic sections."[17] Thus, there is much material that could be examined for the purpose of analyzing the poetic features used in this literature, but the clearest examples must be the sectarian poems called the *Thanksgiving Hymns* or *Hodayot.* The sections of this document are recognized by virtually all commentators as poems or psalms or hymns.

The scroll known as 1QH preserves parts of eighteen columns and some sixty fragments.[18] The script of the scroll is dated from the mid-first century B.C., that is, about the same time as the *War Scroll* (1QM) and the *pesher* on Habakkuk (1QpHab), to the mid-first century A.D.[19] The date of the

---

[16] G. Vermes, *The Dead Sea Scrolls in English* (3d ed.; Sheffield: JSOT Press, 1987).

[17] A. Dupont-Sommer, *The Essene Writings from Qumran* (trans. G. Vermes; Gloucester, MA: Peter Smith, 1973) 72.

[18] The *editio princeps* of this document is E. L. Sukenik, *The Dead Sea Scrolls of the Hebrew University* (Jerusalem: Hebrew University and Magnes Press, 1955) pls. 35–58; for the Hebrew transcription with Masoretic pointing (and German translation), see E. Lohse, *Die Texte aus Qumran* (Munich: Kösel, 1971) 109–75; see also George S. Glanzman, "The Sectarian Psalms from the Dead Sea," *TS* 13 (1952) 487–524; S. Holm-Nielsen, *Hodayot: Psalms from Qumran* (Acta Theologica Danica 2; Aarhus: Universitetsforlaget, 1960); D. Dombkowski Hopkins, "The Qumran Community and 1Q Hodayot: A Reassessment," *RevQ* 10 (1981) 323–64; B. Pedrotti Kittel, *The Hymns of Qumran* (SBLDS 50; Chico, CA: Scholars Press, 1981); M. Mansoor, *The Thanksgiving Hymns: Translated and Annotated with an Introduction* (STDJ 3; Grand Rapids: Eerdmans, 1961); Y. Thorion, "Der Vergleich in 1Q Hodayot," *RevQ* 11 (1983) 193–217.

[19]See the introductions and commentaries; see also A. A. Birnbaum, "How Old Are the Cave Manuscripts? A Paleographical Discussion," *VT* 1 (1951) 91–109; F. M. Cross, "The Development of the Jewish Scripts," in *The Bible and the Ancient Near East: Essays in Honor of William Foxwell Albright* (ed. G. E. Wright; Garden City, NY: Doubleday, 1961) 133–202.

composition of the hymns is not known, but some of the hymns are believed to have been composed by the Teacher of Righteousness. The question of the date of the composition of the hymns is thus tied to the problem of the identity of the Teacher and the uncertainty about the early history of the Qumran sect. These questions, however, need not be discussed here. The scroll contains portions of some twenty-five psalms or poems that are individual prayers of praise, thanksgiving, and lament.

The Hodayot and the Lucan Hymns

Themes

The prominent themes of the hymns are traditional biblical ideas, as well as some sectarian beliefs that appear also in the other Qumran writings. Some of the same themes occur in the Magnificat and the Benedictus:

1. *Praise of God and thanksgiving.* Like the poems of the canonical Psalter that were categorized by H. Gunkel as psalms of individual thanksgiving, the *Hodayot* begin with formulas of praise or blessing, followed by the reason for the praise.

1QH 3:19–20:

אודכה אדוני כי פדיתה נפשי משחת
ומשאול אבדון העליתני לרום עולם

I thank you, my Lord, for you have redeemed my life from the Pit,
and from Sheol Abaddon you have brought me up to everlasting height.

With this can be compared the opening lines of the Benedictus:

Luke 1:68–69:
Εὐλογητὸς χύριος ὁ θεὸς τοῦ Ἰσραήλ,
ὅτι ἐπεσχέψατο χαὶ ἐποίησεν λύτρωσιν τῷ λαῷ αὐτοῦ
χαὶ ἤγειρεν χέρας σωτηρίας ἡμῖν
ἐν οἴχῳ Δαυὶδ παιδὸς αὐτοῦ

Blessed be the Lord God of Israel,
for he has visited and redeemed his people,
and has raised up a horn of salvation for us
in the house of his servant David.

2. *Knowledge*—in two senses. First, the omniscience of God:

1QH 1:7–8:
ובטרם בראתם ידעתה כול מעשיהם לעולמי
. . . ולא יודע בלוא רצונכה

Before you created them, you knew all their deeds forever,
. . . and nothing is known without your will.

Second, God's gift of knowledge to chosen interpreters:

1QH 2:13:

ותשימני נס לבחירי צדק
ומליץ דעת ברזי פלא

You have set me up as a banner for the righteous elect,
and a knowledgeable interpreter of wonderful mysteries.

Compare Luke 1:76–77:

Καὶ σὺ δέ, παιδίον, προφήτης ὑψίστου κληθήσῃ,
προπορεύσῃ γὰρ ἐνώπιον κυρίου ἑτοιμάσαι ὁδοὺς αὐτοῦ,
τοῦ δοῦναι γνῶσιν σωτηρίας τῷ λαῷ αὐτοῦ
ἐν ἀφέσει ἁμαρτιῶν αὐτῶν

And you, child, will be called the prophet of the Most High;
for you will go before the Lord to prepare his ways,
to give knowledge of salvation to his people
in the forgiveness of their sins.

   3. *The lowliness and sinfulness of the human creature in contrast to the might and glory of God.* This theme occurs throughout the Qumran poems:

1QH 1:21–23:

ואני יצר החמר ומגבל המים
סוד הערוה ומקור הנדה
כור העוון ומבנה החטאה
רוח התועה ונעוה בלא בינה
. . .

And I, a shape of clay, kneaded in water,
a ground of shame and a source of pollution,
a melting-pot of wickedness and an edifice of sin,
a straying and perverted spirit of no understanding
. . .

Or again, 1QH 11:3–4:

אודכה אלי כי הפלתה עם עפר
וביצר חמר הגברתה

I thank you, my God, for you have done wonders with dust,
and in a creature of clay you have manifested strength.

Compare Luke 1:48:

ὅτι ἐπέβλεψεν ἐπὶ τὴν ταπείνωσιν τῆς δούλης αὐτοῦ.

For he has regarded the low estate of his handmaiden.

Or Luke 1:52:

καθεῖλεν δυνάστας ἀπὸ θρόνων
καὶ ὕψωσεν ταπεινούς

He has put down the mighty from their thrones
and exalted those of low degree.

4. *Salvation.* For example, 1QH 2:32:

פדיתה נפש אביון

You have redeemed the soul of the poor one.

1QH 5:6:

ותעזור משחת חיי

You have saved my life from the Pit.

1QH 7:22:

ותרם קרני על כול מנאצי

You have lifted my horn above those who insult me.

Compare Luke 1:47:

καὶ ἠγαλλίασεν τὸ πνεῦμά μου
ἐπὶ τῷ θεῷ τῷ σωτῆρί μου

My spirit rejoices in God my Savior.

Luke 1:68–69:

ὅτι ἐπεσκέψατο καὶ ἐποίησεν λύτρωσιν τῷ λαῷ αὐτοῦ,
καὶ ἤγειρεν κέρας σωτηρίας ἡμῖν
ἐν οἴκῳ Δαυὶδ παιδὸς αὐτοῦ

He has visited and redeemed his people
and has raised up a horn of salvation
in the house of his servant David.

The similarities of the themes point to a common cultural, theological, and literary heritage.

Structure

When we compare the structure of the poetry of the *Hodayot* with the two New Testament hymns, we find some similarities. The structure of the Qumran psalms is often determined by changes in content rather than by meter or clear poetic lines. Of the poems whose limits are certain, the length varies from nine lines to more than twenty. The poems begin with a formula—either אודכה אדוני ("I thank you, my Lord") or ברוך אתה אדוני ("Blessed are you, my Lord"). Compare Luke 1:68: Εὐλογητὸς κύριος ὁ θεὸς τοῦ Ἰσραήλ ("Blessed be the Lord God of Israel").

Within the Qumran poems independent subject pronouns (which are sometimes preceded by extra spaces in the scroll) mark the most obvious divisions of the poem. For example, in the poem that is partially preserved in col. 1 of the *Hodayot,* after a long section praising God, the poet begins a personal section with the signal ואני, "and I" (1:21), and the poem returns to the second person, addressing God with אתה, "you" (1:27). In Luke 1:76 a similar structure is used. The poem changes from the beginning prayer, which describes God's saving acts in the third person, to the second person with καὶ σύ, but here the address is to the child John.

Other words that mark new sections within a poem are the interrogatives מה ("What?") and מי ("Who?"), the conjunctions כי ("because") and לכן ("therefore"), and the particle הנה (traditionally translated "behold," but perhaps better "now"). The conjunction כי appears frequently after an opening formula to introduce the reason for praise and thanksgiving. For example, 1QH 3:19: "I thank you, O Lord, for (כי) you have redeemed my soul from the Pit." Compare Luke 1:47–48: "My soul magnifies the Lord . . . , for (ὅτι) he has regarded the low estate of his handmaiden." Or Luke 1:68: "Blessed be the Lord God of Israel, for (ὅτι) he has visited and redeemed his people." The use of the particle הנה to mark divisions in the Qumran hymns can be compared with Luke 1:48: "For behold (ἰδοὺ γάρ), henceforth all generations will call me blessed." Within the units marked off by these signal words, poetic images are often constructed by the use of parallel infinitives, which will be treated below under grammatical features.

Use of Biblical Language

Like the *Hodayot,* the Magnificat and Benedictus are composed almost entirely of biblical expressions and phrases, though there are few phrases in the Lucan hymns that could be called OT quotations. Most of the biblical reminiscences consist of only a few words that exactly parallel the Septuagint (LXX) passages that have proposed as models for the poems.[20]

Magnificat: 1:46 Μεγαλύνει ἡ ψυχή μου τὸν κύριον,
              1:47 καὶ ἠγαλλίασεν τὸ πνεῦμά μου ἐπὶ τῷ θεῷ τῷ σωτῆρί μου,

Ps 34:9 (LXX)   ἡ δὲ ψυχή μου ἀγαλλιάσεται ἐπὶ τῷ κυρίῳ,
                  τερφθήσεται ἐπὶ τῷ σωτηρίῳ αὐτοῦ

ἡ ψυχή μου, the subject of μεγαλύνει in Luke, is identical to the subject of ἀγαλλιάσεται in Ps 34:9; however, the verb that follows ἡ ψυχή μου in Ps 34:9 is not the same verb that is used in Luke 1:46. Rather, it is the verb ἀγαλλιάω that occurs in 1:47. Note also ἐπὶ τῷ κυριῷ and σωτηρίῳ in Psalm 34 and ἐπὶ τῷ θεῷ and τῷ σωτῆρι in Luke. A number of other OT passages such as 1 Sam 2:1–2; Hab 3:18; and Ps 94:1 have been proposed as possible sources of the biblical allusions in Luke 1:46–47. An examination of the tables of parallels in the older commentary of Creed or in Brown's more recent study of these hymns in *The Birth of the Messiah* provides ample evidence of the richness of the NT poet's use of biblical language and the ability to evoke so many past meanings that are now brought to bear in a new context.[21]

The biblical language used by the NT poet also uses traditional words in ways that expand the significance of the terms. For example, the use of ταπείνωσις, "lowliness" or "low estate" in 1:48 calls to mind the use of ταπείνωσις in the Greek Old Testament to describe the infertility of Hannah, Sarah, and Leah. Although this is not the reason for Mary's "lowliness" in Luke, the use of ταπείνωσις to described Mary's status as the Lord's handmaiden (δούλη) situates her among those women in Israel's past whom God favored with sons—in spite of human impossibility.

Similarly, the vocabulary of the *Hodayot* and of the Qumran literature in general uses numerous biblical words and phrases in ways that have expanded their significance. To cite only one example: בליעל in the Hebrew Bible has traditionally been rendered "a worthless or base person," or "wickedness, destruction." The word assumes a rather important additional meaning in the *Hodayot* and throughout the Qumran writings when it becomes the name of the leader of the forces of evil.

Two final examples will illustrate the free, though unmistakable, use of biblical phrases and expressions in the Lucan hymns and in the *Hodayot:*

Luke 1:51   Ἐποίησεν κράτος ἐν βραχίονι αὐτοῦ,
              διεσκόρπισεν ὑπερηφάνους διανοίᾳ καρδίας αὐτῶν.
Ps 88:11   σὺ ἐταπείνωσας ὡς τραυματίαν ὑπερήφανον
(LXX)   καὶ ἐν τῷ βραχίονι τῆς δυνάμεώς σου διεσκόρπισας τοὺς
              ἐχθρούς σου.

---

[20] S. Holm-Nielsen, *Hodayot: Psalms from Qumran*, 301, esp. n. 1.
[21] J. M. Creed, *The Gospel according to St. Luke: The Greek Text, with Introduction, Notes, and Indices* (London: Macmillan, 1930) 303–4; Brown, *The Birth of the Messiah*, 358–60, 386–89.

Luke 1:51b combines the verb διασκορπίζω (in the third person) from Ps 88:11b (where it occurs in the second person) with the complement ὑπερή-φανος (now in the plural) from Ps 88:11a. Other words from this psalm have echoes in the Magnificat: ἐταπείνωσας, δυνάμεώς. Moreover, in close proximity to this psalm verse in Ps 88:9 we read: δυνατὸς εἶ, κύριε. Luke 1:49 refers to God as ὁ δυνατός.

A similar use of biblical language occurs throughout the *Hodayot*. For example, 1QH 1:7–13 contains many reminiscences of Jeremiah 10:12–16 but is not an exact quotation of Jeremiah. The interplay of the biblical words and images in this passage can be illustrated by looking at one verse, Jer 10:12, and the echoes in 1QH:

Jer 10:12		1QH	
עֹשֵׂה אֶרֶץ בְּכֹחוֹ	1:13	אתה בראתה ארץ בכוחכה	
מֵכִין תֵּבֵל בְּחָכְמָתוֹ	1:7	ובחכמתכ[ה] ה[	עולם]
וּבִתְבוּנָתוֹ נָטָה שָׁמָיִם	1:9–10	ואתה נטיתה שמים לכבודכה	

Jer 10:12	1QH
It is he who made the earth by his power	1:13 You created the earth by your strength
who established the world by his wisdom	1:7 By your wisdom [ ] forever
and by his understanding stretched out the heavens.	1:9–10 You spread out the heavens for your glory.

Almost every line from the Magnificat and the Benedictus—1:76–78 of the Benedictus being the only exceptions—contains phrases that are used elsewhere in the Greek OT, and in the majority of these lines it could be argued that two or three Greek OT passages have equal claim to being the model for the NT poet. This use of traditional language in new contexts is not a sign of a lack of originality, but it is testimony to the art of the poet who can take language already laden with meaning for people familiar with the heritage of the Greek OT and use it to describe a new situation.[22]

Parallelism or Balance

In the Lucan hymns there are some very carefully constructed examples of parallelism in consecutive clauses that themselves form a chiasm:

1:52 καθεῖλεν δυνάστας ἀπὸ θρόνων
      καὶ ὕψωσεν ταπεινούς,
1:53 πεινῶντας ἐνέπλησεν ἀγαθῶν
      καὶ πλουτοῦντας ἐξαπέστειλεν κενούς.

---

[22] Pace Creed, *The Gospel according to Luke*, 306–7.

He has put down mighty rulers from their thrones
and he has exalted the lowly.
The hungry he has filled with good things,
and the rich he has sent away empty.

Each verse shows a contrast in the two parts of the sentence, and the whole of vv. 52 and 53 also forms a larger chiastic parallel in thought (mighty, lowly, hungry, rich) and in structure (in v. 52 the verbs καθεῖλεν and ὕψωσεν are in the first position in each line followed immediately by the verb complements δυνάστας and ταπεινούς; in v. 53 the verb complement is in the first position followed immediately by the verb in the second position in each line (πεινῶντας ἐνέπλησεν, πλουτοῦντας ἐξαπέστειλεν). Moreover, rhyme (θρόνων, ἀγαθῶν/ταπεινούς, κενούς) and assonance and alliteration (ταπεινούς, the last word of v. 52, πεινῶντας, the first word of v. 53) tie the whole together.

There are examples also in the Lucan hymns of the generally looser balance that is found in the *Hodayot;* this differs from the clean and concise expressions of the canonical Psalter:

1:68   ὅτι ἐπεσκέψατο καὶ ἐποίησεν λύτρωσιν τῷ λαῷ αὐτοῦ,
1:69   καὶ ἤγειρεν κέρας σωτηρίας ἡμῖν
        ἐν οἴκῳ Δαυὶδ παιδὸς αὐτοῦ

1QH 3:32

ויבקעו לאבדון נחלי בליעל
ויהמו מחשבי תהום בהמון גורשי רפש

and the torrents of Belial will burst into Abaddon
and the schemers of the pit will roar, in turmoil the stirrers of the slime

As in the example above from the Benedictus, the parallel lines in the *Hodayot* are frequently of unequal length:

1QH 3:19–20:

כי פדיתה נפשי משחת
ומשאול אבדון העליתני לרום עולם

For you redeemed my life from the Pit
and from Sheol Abbadon you have brought me up to everlasting height.

In Luke 1:68–69, the two finite verbs in the aorist in the first line show alliteration and assonance (ἐπεσκέψατο and ἐποίησεν with the augmented *epsilon*s followed by the labial *pi* and then, after other vowels, *sigma*s). This may also account for the choice of ποιέω as the verb, which has as its complement λύτρωσιν, a combination that is not found in the Greek Old Testament.

In 1:69, the often-noted unusual combination of ἐγείρω and κέρας may be similarly explained. In both words the initial consonant is a velar that is followed by a liquid. In Egyptian papyri, the *gamma* and *kappa* are often confused because of the similarity of their pronunciation during this period.[23]

In the same way, 1QH 3:32 shows repetition of the same sounds, *b, h, m, š,* and *ō* in several words.

Some Grammatical Features

Among the similarities between the *Hodayot* and NT poetry is the extensive use of nonverbal sentences and of infinitive clauses in the poetic lines. For example:

Luke 1:49b–50:
καὶ ἅγιον τὸ ὄνομα αὐτοῦ.
καὶ τὸ ἔλεος αὐτοῦ εἰς γενεὰς καὶ γενεὰς
τοῖς φοβουμένοις αὐτόν.

Examples are frequent in other NT poetic passages: Luke 2:14–15: Δόξα ἐν ὑψίστοις θεῷ, καὶ ἐπὶ γῆς εἰρήνη ἐν ἀνθρώποις εὐδοκίας. Other examples occur regularly in the book of Revelation (e.g., 15:3; 19:1). The frequency of the nonverbal sentence in NT poetry is not, however, significantly greater than in the canonical Psalms.

One of the most striking differences between the *Hodayot* and the canonical Psalter is the use of infinitive clauses or phrases one after the other (e.g., 1QH 7:26–33, which contains four infinitives; 3:19–36, which contains eight).

1QH 3:21–23:

ורוח נעוה טהרתה מפשע רב
להתיצב במעמד עם צבא קדושים
ולבוא בין . .] עם עדת בני שמים
ותפל לאיש גורל עולם עם רוחות דעת
להלל שמכה ביחד [. . .]
ולספר נפלאותיכה לנגד כול מעשיכה

For a perverted spirit you purified from much sin
to stand in attendance with the host of the holy ones
and to enter into [the community] with the council of the sons of heaven,
and you allotted to each an eternal lot with the spirits of knowledge
to praise your name in the community [. . .]
and to recount your wonders along with all your works

---

[23] Gignac, *A Grammar of the Greek Papyri*, vol. 1, *Phonology*, 76–80.

In other places in the *Hodayot* the frequent use of infinitives creates syntactical problems that make translation difficult. This is also the case in the Benedictus (1:69–75), which contains only one finite verb, two subordinate clauses, and four epexegetical or purpose infinitives:

1:72:	ποιῆσαι ἔλεος
	μνησθῆναι διαθήκης
1:73–74:	τοῦ δοῦναι ἡμῖν . . . ῥυσθέντας
	λατρεύειν αὐτῷ.

At the end of the Benedictus (1:76–79) the construction is similar: two finite verbs in 1:76 (κληθήσῃ and προπορεύσῃ) are followed by infinitive clauses:

1:76	ἑτοιμάσαι ὁδοὺς αὐτοῦ
1:77	τοῦ δοῦναι γνῶσιν σωτηρίας
1:79	ἐπιφᾶναι τοῖς ἐν σκότει
1:79	τοῦ κατευθῦναι τοὺς πόδας

The Magnificat and the Benedictus were most likely earlier compositions that the author of the Gospel of Luke inserted into the infancy narrative.[24] Many would argue that Luke interpolated several lines into these hymns to bring them more into line with the themes of the narrative and with the Gospel as a whole. The verses most frequently discussed as Lucan inserts are 1:48 of the Magnificat, 1:70 and 1:76–77 of the Benedictus. If these are in fact Lucan inserts, they are testimony to the author's familiarity with characteristics of poetic composition during this period. Note in particular the use of ὅτι and ἰδού in Luke 1:48 and of καὶ σύ in 1:76 to introduce a new division in the poem.

From this brief examination of a small portion of the poetic material from Qumran and from the New Testament, we conclude that there are detailed ways—structure, language, and use of biblical materials—in which the Qumran material can be said to form a poetic bridge. Further delineation of the poetic bridge might come from studying, for example, the *Psalms of Solomon*, the *Odes of Solomon*, the poems in the book of Revelation, and other poetic materials of the Qumran literature.

---

[24] Fitzmyer, *The Gospel according to Luke I–IX*, 309.

The New Covenant in the Letters of Paul and the Essene Documents

Jerome Murphy-O'Connor, O.P.
Ecole Biblique de Jérusalem

God has qualified us to be ministers, not of a new covenant of the letter, but of a new covenant of the spirit.

2 Cor 3:6

ONE OF THE FEW MATERIAL CONTACTS between the Pauline letters and the Essene documents found at Qumran is the mention of a new covenant. In the epistles it appears only in the Corinthian correspondence (1 Cor 11:25; 2 Cor 3:6), while at Qumran, if we except a plausible reconstruction of 1QpHab 2:3, it is used only in the *Damascus Document* (6:19; 8:21 = 19:33; 20:12). Even in the palmy days of pan-Qumranism, when it was common to see Essene influence throughout the NT, no one suggested that Paul had borrowed the new covenant concept from the Essenes. It was clear that Christianity had adequate grounds for an independent exploitation of Jer 31:31–33. S. E. Johnson, however, hypothesized that in 2 Cor 3:6 Paul might be reacting against the Essene concept of the new covenant.[1] W. D. Davies was rightly skeptical of this view,[2] but his reaction betrays his conviction that the new covenant was an important category in Paul's theology.[3] In this he is but a faithful representative of the current consensus. While few would accord the new covenant theme the centrality in Pauline

---

[1] Johnson, "Paul and the Manual of Discipline," *HTR* 48 (1955) 159.

[2] Davies, "Paul and the Dead Sea Scrolls: Flesh and Spirit," in his *Christian Origins and Judaism* (London: Longman, Darton, & Todd, 1962) 175.

[3] See his *Paul and Rabbinic Judaism: Some Rabbinic Elements in Pauline Theology* (London: SPCK, 2d ed., 1955/1962) 224–26, 259–60.

thought that W. C. van Unnik[4] and T. J. Deidun[5] claim for it, the majority of scholars would agree with V. P. Furnish that "the concept of a 'new covenant' is fully at home in Paul's thought."[6]

The purpose of this note is to suggest that this consensus is not as well-founded as the number of adherents would make it appear. I shall argue that the concept of a new covenant was fundamentally alien to Paul's theology, and that his use of it was a grudging concession to external pressure. His reason for finding the concept unpalatable is illustrated by the attitude of the Essenes to their new covenant.

Ministers of a New Covenant

The one passage in which Paul himself employs the concept is *hikanōsen hēmas diakonous kainēs diathēkēs ou grammatos alla pneumatos*, "(God) qualified us to be ministers of a new covenant not of (the) letter but of (the) spirit" (2 Cor 3:6). Most commentators treat this verse as if Paul's concern was to distinguish between a "covenant of the letter" and a "covenant of the spirit." The controlling factor in such an assessment is manifestly the following section, though few are explicit as C. J. A. Hickling, who baldly asserts that "vv. 7–19 form an extended, and itself rapidly burgeoning, exegesis of the phrase *diakonous kainēs diathēkēs*."[7]

Were such the case, however, one would have expected Paul to use *kainē diathēkē* at least once in 2 Cor 3:7–18, especially since he does employ *palaia diathēkē*, "the old covenant" (v. 14), yet it never appears. His repeated use of *diakonia* (four times in 3:7–9) rather betrays a deliberate intention to avoid *diathēkē*, and this conclusion is confirmed by Bultmann's acute observation apropos of 3:7, "Dabei ist der Ausdruck insofern inkorrekt, als natürlich nicht die *diakonia*, sondern die *diathēkē entetypōmenē lithois*."[8] A "ministry" cannot be "engraved in stone." Paul could have spoken of "a covenant of death engraved in letters on stone," and the logic of the *qal wahomer* argument would have obliged him to contrast it with "a covenant of the spirit" (3:8). Given the current understanding of 3:6, this should have been perfectly acceptable to

[4] Van Unnik, "La conception paulinienne de la nouvelle alliance," in *Littérature et théologie pauliniennes* (RechBib 5; Bruges: Desclée, 1960) 109–26.

[5] Deidun, *New Covenant Morality in Paul* (AnBib 89; Rome: Pontifical Biblical Institute, 1981).

[6] Furnish, *II Corinthians* (AB; Garden City, NY: Doubleday, 1984) 198–99. See also D. E. H. Whiteley, *The Theology of St. Paul* (Oxford: Blackwell, 1964) 75–77.

[7] Hickling, "The Sequence of Thought in II Corinthians, Chapter Three," *NTS* 21 (1974–75) 384. See also C. K. Barrett, *A Commentary on the Second Epistle to the Corinthians* (HNTC; New York: Harper, 1973) 113; R. Bultmann, *Der zweite Brief an die Korinther* (MeyerK; Göttingen: Vandenhoeck and Ruprecht, 1976) 82; Furnish, *II Corinthians*, 225.

[8] Bultmann, *Der zweite Brief an die Korinther*, 83.

Paul. In fact, however, it was not. Paul deliberately switched from "covenant" to "ministry," and this alone justifies taking a new look at 2 Cor 3:6.

Grammatically, *ou grammatos alla pneumatos*, "not of the letter but of the spirit," qualifies *kainē diathēkē*, "new covenant," and not, as the current consensus assumes, *diathēkē* alone. Windisch's[9] stress on this obvious point is echoed by Furnish, who nonetheless continues, "the Spirit is identified with a new covenant, and what is *written* (the letter) is identified with the old covenant."[10] The logic of such exegesis is, to put it mildly, disconcerting. What Paul in fact does is make a distinction between *two types of new covenant*, one which he sees as characterized by "letter" and the other by "spirit." Given what is said about the new covenant in the OT, the need for such a distinction is not at all evident; the originality of the new covenant is precisely that it is spiritual. The need for the distinction, therefore, must have been forced upon Paul by something in the situation at Corinth, and we catch a hint of what he had in mind if we paraphrase 3:6 thus, "we are not letter-ministers but spirit-ministers of the new covenant."[11]

There were some at Corinth who were using the new covenant in a sense that Paul could not accept. In consequence, he called them "letter-ministers." These were certainly Christians; otherwise they would not have invoked the new covenant theme. They were also intruders, for they had come to Corinth with letters of recommendation (2 Cor 3:1). More importantly, they were Judaizers. This is clear, not only from the use of *gramma*, "letter," in 3:7, but also from the unexpected appearance of *en plaxin lithinais*, "on tablets of stone," in 3:3. Having written *engegrammenē ou melani alla pneumati theou zōntos*, "inscribed not with ink but by the Spirit of the living God," it would have been natural for Paul to continue *ouk en membranais all'en kardiais sarkinais*, "not on parchments but on hearts of flesh" in order to round off the contrast between two types of letters of recommendation, one a written document and the other a community (3:1–2). Attempts to explain this shift by a complicated interplay of OT texts[12] are unconvincing because they ignore the polemic/apologetic character of 2:17–3:6. Justice is done to this aspect only by J.-F. Collange's suggestion that it was prompted by something in the situation at Corinth. The connotation of "on tablets of stone" (3:3) and

---

[9] Windisch, *Der zweite Korintherbrief* (MeyerK; Göttingen: Vandenhoeck & Ruprecht, 1924) 110.

[10] Furnish, *II Corinthians*, 199. See also H.-J. Klauck, *2. Korintherbrief* (Neue Echter Bibel 8; Würzburg: Echter, 1986) 37.

[11] This suggestion is based on A. Plummer, *A Critical and Exegetical Commentary on the Second Epistle of Paul to the Corinthians* (ICC; Edinburgh: Clark, 1915) 88.

[12] So, for example, M. Rissi, *Studien zum zweiten Korintherbrief: Der alte Bund—Der Prediger—Der Tod* (ATANT 56; Zurich: Zwingli, 1969) 22 n. 32; E. Richard, "Polemics, Old Testament, and Theology: A Study of II Cor., iii, 1–iv, 6," *RB* 88 (1981) 344–49.

of "engraved in letters on stone" (3:7) is unambiguous. The intruders were appealing to the law, and so must be identified as members of a Christian law-observant mission.[13]

It is obvious why such Judaizers would have used the new covenant theme. It furnished them with a perfect argument for maintaining the validity of the law, while at the same time acknowledging the inauguration of the eschaton in Christ. Jeremiah had written, "This is the covenant which I will make with the house of Israel after those days, says the Lord: I will put *my law* within them, and I will write it upon their hearts, and I will be their God, and they shall be my people" (31:33). The point is that the internalization of the law will ensure perfect obedience. The eschaton will differ from the present in that the people will be holy in fact, and not merely in theory.[14] While sensitive to the force of this position, Paul could not accept the practical conclusions that the Judaizers drew, as A. Jaubert acutely observed, "Il n'est pas impossible que, dans la *IIe aux Corinthiens,* Paul réagisse consciemment contre la conception d'une 'nouvelle alliance' qui demeurcrait fidèle à la Loi, d'une 'nouvelle alliance' qui resterait celle de la lettre."[15]

Paul, however, was not in a position to reject the concept of a new covenant outright. Not only was it rooted in a tradition that he believed to be sacred, but it was also part of the eucharistic liturgy that he had introduced into Corinth. The Words of Institution that he had handed on to them contained the phrase, "This cup is the new covenant in my blood" (1 Cor 11:25). It is far from improbable that the Judaizers made capital of this point, because H. Schürmann has argued with some plausibility that the Pauline and Lucan version of the word over the cup is more primitive than that of Mark and Matthew.[16] Such being the case, the only avenue open to Paul was to make a distinction between an authentic and an inauthentic vision of the new covenant, a distinction that would permit him to move the discussion with the

[13] Collange, *Enigmes de la deuxième épître de Paul aux Corinthiens: Etude exégétique de 2 Cor. 2:14–7:4* (SNTSMS 18; Cambridge: University Press, 1972) 55. This is not the place to go into an extended discussion of the complex question of Paul's opponents in 2 Corinthians, of which an excellent summary is given in Furnish, *II Corinthians,* 48–54. In my view the intruders were Judaizers of Palestinian origin, who at Corinth assumed certain Hellenistic traits in order to win the support of disaffected elements within the Corinthian community. See my study "*Pneumatikoi* and Judaizers in 2 Cor 2:14–4:6," *AusBR* 24 (1986) 42–58.

[14] The prevalence of this theme in Judaism is well documented in I. de la Potterie—S. Lyonnet, *La vie selon l'Esprit condition du chrétien* (US 55; Paris: Cerf, 1965) 199–204.

[15] Jaubert, *La notion d'alliance dans le Judaïsme aux abords de l'ère chrétienne* (Patristica Sorbonensia 6; Paris: Seuil, 1963) 447. R. P. Martin has perceptively noted that "it does seem clear that he [Paul] has to overcome some misunderstanding of what the '*new*' covenant entailed, specifically, that it was not a sign of renovated Judaism but of a new chapter in God's dealing with humankind" (*2 Corinthians* [Word Biblical Commentary 40; Waco, TX: Word Books, 1986] 54).

[16] Schürmann, *Der Einsetzungsbericht, Lk 22,19–20. II. Teil. Eine quellenkritischen Untersuchung des lukanischen Abendmahlberichtes, Lk 22,7–38* (NTAbh 20/4; Münster: Aschendorf, 1955) 104.

Judaizers to a level more favorable to himself. This he does with the lapidary formula "the letter kills but the Spirit gives life" (3:6). It is this phrase *alone* that serves as the basis for the development in 3:7–18.

The Essene New Covenant

The only formal, certain references to a new covenant in the Essene documents so far published appear in the *Damascus Document*. Even though they differ in their delineation of the sources, all scholars who have worked seriously on CD recognize that it is a compilation and not a homogeneous literary production.[17] According to my analysis, the allusion to a new covenant in CD 6:19 belongs to an Essene document that antedates the Qumran settlement,[18] whereas the other references (CD 8:21 = 19:33; 20:12) occur in a text composed at Qumran.[19]

This dating of the documents has been confirmed by P. R. Davies's recent study of CD.[20] Davies, however, argues that the qualification of the covenant made in the land of Damascus as "new" derives from the Qumran branch of the Essenes, and that it was added after the split in the Essene movement in order to justify the claim of the Qumranites to be the heirs of the original inspiration.[21] His sole argument is the formulation of CD 20:11–12, "they rejected the covenant and the bond which they affirmed in the land of Damascus, that is, the new covenant." The final phrase certainly looks like a gloss, but no such uncertainty attaches to the use of the adjective "new" in CD 6:19 or 8:21 = 19:33. If a glossator had inserted "new" so neatly in these latter texts, one would have expected him to treat 20:12 in the same way. The gloss, therefore, should be explained either as the correction of a scribe who had accidentally omitted the adjective, or as a later effort to bring 20:12 into line with the other two texts that associate "new covenant" with the "land of Damascus." The new covenant formula, in consequence, belongs to the prehistory of the Qumran community, and in my view is associated with the origins of the Essene movement in Babylon during, or shortly after, the exile.[22] Its importance in the ideology of the sect is underlined by the fact that it remained in use for almost 600 years.

[17] For a survey see my article "The Judean Desert," in *Early Judaism and Its Modern Interpreters* (The Bible and Its Modern Interpreters 2; ed. R. A. Kraft and G. W. E. Nickelsburg; Atlanta: Scholars Press, 1986) 132–34.

[18] Murphy-O'Connor, "A Literary Analysis of *Damascus Document* vi, 2–viii, 3," *RB* 78 (1971) 210–32.

[19] Murphy-O'Connor, "A Literary Analysis of *Damascus Document* xix, 33–xx, 34," *RB* 79 (1972) 544–64.

[20] Davies, *The Damascus Covenant: An Interpretation of the "Damascus Document"* (JSOTSup 25; Sheffield: JSOT Press, 1983), which I have reviewed in *RB* 92 (1985) 274–77.

[21] Davies, *Damascus Covenant,* 130, 176–77.

[22] Murphy-O'Connor, "The *Damascus Document* Revisited," *RB* 92 (1985) 224–30.

The oldest reference to the new covenant (CD 6:19) occurs in a document that is essentially a list of precepts (CD 6:11–7:4) followed by a hortatory epilogue (CD 7:4–8:3). The way in which a number of the precepts are formulated indicates that their function was to serve as reminders of points in a more detailed body of legal material, namely, the laws contained in CD 9–16. Thus, for example, the admonition "Keep the sabbath day according to its exact rules" (CD 6:18) is meaningless without the precise legislation of CD 10:14–11:18.[23] This legislation mentions two other covenants, the "covenant of Abraham" (CD 12:11) and the "covenant which Moses concluded with Israel" (CD 15:8–9). The relationship between these two covenants need not detain us here; it has been discussed thoroughly by R. F. Collins.[24] What is important is the relationship between the Mosaic covenant and the new covenant.

The context of the allusion to the Mosaic covenant furnishes a partial answer:

> Likewise is the ruling during the whole epoch of wickedness with regard to everyone who turns from his corrupt way. On the day that he speaks to the overseer of the Many, they shall muster him with the oath of the covenant which Moses concluded with Israel, namely, the covenant to return to the Law of Moses with all his heart and all his soul. (CD 15:6–10)

It is evidently a question of the reception of a new member into the Essene community, an interpretation that is confirmed by the retention of the central element in the reception ceremony at Qumran:

> When they join the community, let whoever comes to the council of the community enter into the covenant of God in the presence of all the volunteers, and let him undertake by oath of obligation to be converted to the Law of Moses according to all of his commands, with all his heart and all his soul. (1QS 5:7–9)

To enter the new covenant is to commit oneself totally to the law of Moses (cf. CD 16:1–2).

However, if the legislation in CD 9–16, corresponding to the list of precepts in CD 6:11–7:4, is compared with the Holiness Code (Leviticus 17–26) on which it is based, it becomes clear that the Essene interpretation of the law contained additional specifications that made it much more rigorous. It is generally, and rightly, recognized that these are "the hidden things in which all Israel had strayed," and which were revealed to the remnant that received the new covenant (CD 3:13–14). In addition to perfect obedience,

---

[23] For details, see the article cited in n. 18, pp. 212–17.

[24] Collins, "The Berith-Notion of the Cairo Damascus Document and its Comparison with the New Testament," *ETL* 39 (1963) 555–94, esp. 556–65.

therefore, the new covenant involved "the exact interpretation of the Law" (CD 6:14; cf. 4:8). In essence the new covenant was but a renewal of the Mosaic covenant revitalized by the exploitation of its virtualities (cf. CD 5:8–11).

The intimate connection of the Essene new covenant with the law is confirmed by the other references in a later stratum of CD:

> All who entered the new covenant in the land of Damascus and who returned, and who acted treacherously and departed from the well of living water, shall not be reckoned in the council of the people and shall not be written in their records from the time the Teacher is gathered in until the arrival of the Messiah from Aaron and from Israel. (CD 19:33–35)

> They shall receive the same judgment as their companions who turned back with the men of scoffing, for they spoke heresy against the ordinances of righteousness and rejected the covenant and bond which they affirmed in the land of Damascus, that is, the new covenant. (CD 20:11–12)

In the first text those who have acted treacherously with respect to the new covenant are those who have turned away from "the well of living water," which is a symbol for the law, as CD 6:4 formally states (cf. CD 3:16–17). Equally, in the second text, "the ordinances of righteousness" define the content of the law. It goes without saying that in both cases it is a question of the law as understood by the Essenes.

The new covenant in CD is not thought of as the fulfillment of the prophecy of Jer 31:31,[25] and it is doubtful that it had any eschatological connotation in pre-Qumran usage. The period in which the new covenant is operative is defined as "the time of wickedness" (CD 6:14). By their obedience the members of the new covenant belong to "the sure house" (CD 3:19), and so are protected both from the errors of their ancestors (CD 2:17–3:12) and from the current "snares of Belial" (CD 4:12–19). They are in God's favor and can anticipate the future with confidence, but salvation is not guaranteed, as the appeal for continuing fidelity demonstrates (CD 7:4–8:3). There is no hint that the future has broken into the present in the form of a realized eschatology.[26]

The situation in the Qumran period is somewhat different, at least at the beginning. I have been persuaded by P. R. Davies's analysis of CD 6:2–11[27] that the high priest, who led some of the Essenes to exile at Qumran,

---

[25] R. F. Collins, "The Berith-Notion," 571–75.

[26] See J. Carmignac, E. Cothenet, H. Lignée, *Les textes de Qumran traduits et annotés* (Paris: Letouzey et Ané, 1963) 2. 144. P. R. Davies thinks that the eschatology of CD contains "an element of anticipation and of realization" ("Eschatology at Qumran," *JBL* 104 [1985] 52), but I cannot find this in the text.

[27] Davies, *Damascus Covenant,* 123–24.

appropriated the eschatological title of "Teacher of Righteousness" (CD 6:11) because of his conviction that the end was imminent.[28] His followers, who must have shared his belief that the fulfillment of Isa 40:3 was at hand (cf. 1QS 8:13–14), would have seen the new covenant as the last stage before the end, and would have given it a heightened eschatological coloration.

There is also another significant difference. Each time the new covenant is mentioned in the Qumran stratum of CD (19:33; 20:12), it appears in close association with the Teacher of Righteousness (cf. also 1QpHab 2:3), and this suggests that the content was not precisely the same as for those Essenes who did not follow the Teacher. To the "former ordinances" that constituted the pre-Qumran new covenant the Teacher of Righteousness had added the "latter ordinances" that were binding on the Qumran branch of the Essenes,[29] and thus became an integral part of their new covenant (cf. CD 20:8–9, 28–33; 1QpHab 2:2).

Among the Essenes, therefore, the new covenant evolved, not only in content but also in its eschatological connotation. Nonetheless, obedience to its precepts remained a constant. Only those who submitted themselves to "the ordinances of the covenant" (CD 20:29) belonged to the new covenant.

This insistence on the quality of the human response should not cause us to lose sight of the fact that it is preceded by a divine invitation. It is clear from CD 3:13–17 that the new covenant was not simply a matter of Jews binding themselves anew to the observance of the Mosaic covenant. The initiative lay with God, who "established his covenant with Israel forever, revealing to them the hidden things in which all Israel had strayed. . . . He opened to them and they dug a well of copious waters." Similarly, "God remembered the covenant of the fathers and he raised from Aaron men of understanding and from Israel men of wisdom, and he let them hear (his voice) and they dug the well" (CD 6:2–3). The secret knowledge, which made the exact interpretation of the law possible, was given through divine revelation accorded to those chosen by God. For the Essenes, therefore, the demand for total obedience is set within the framework of gratuitous election, a theme that receives much greater emphasis in 1QH than in CD, because of the difference in literary form.[30]

Paul and the New Covenant

If Paul accepted the overarching concept of divine election (Rom 8:28–30), it seems unreasonable, given his Jewish background, to suggest that he

---

[28] Murphy-O'Connor, "The Damascus Document Revisited," 239–45.

[29] See the article cited in n. 19, pp. 547–48.

[30] E. P. Sanders, Paul and Palestinian Judaism: A Comparison of Patterns of Religion (Philadelphia: Fortress, 1977) 292.

would have repudiated the concept of a new covenant. Yet this is what is indicated by 2 Cor 3:6–18. The explanation, I believe, lies in the only way that election and covenant commandments can be reconciled. The best statement of the relationship between the two at Qumran is that of E. P. Sanders:

> The emphases on God's choice *and* on human commitment ("volunteering") *both* reflect the *crucial significance of election and membership in the covenant for salvation.* Once in the covenant, members took upon themselves to *obey its regulations.* . . . *Obedience to the commandments* was not thought of as earning salvation, which came rather by God's grace, but was nevertheless required as a *condition of remaining in the covenant;* and not obeying the commandments would damn. Although all humans are sinful and are seen as such in comparison with God, the explicit *sinfulness* which would either keep one out of the community or remove one from it was conceived as *transgression of commandments.*[31]

The complexity of this formulation, which is necessary if the gratuity of the divine initiative is to be respected, highlights the problem. It is impossible for the average person to live on the intellectual tightrope of such a subtle distinction. The human mind instinctively and inevitably simplifies. If disobedience to the covenant commandments caused damnation, then it was simpler to consider that obedience to such precepts caused salvation, rather than to think that it maintained one in a situation in which gratuitous grace was available. Thus, while lip service was paid to the fundamental concept of election, in practice all attention was concentrated on observance of the commandments. To stress covenant, which necessarily involves law,[32] leads inevitably to legalism. A religion of grace that expresses itself in covenant form quickly becomes a religion of works, certainly in the popular mind if not in the dissertations of theologians. This tendency is graphically illustrated by the quick development of casuistry at Qumran.[33]

The Essenes, of course, were not unique in this regard; the phenomenon is evident in every religion that places a significant emphasis on law. As a Pharisee (Phil 3:5–6), Paul would have experienced covenantal nomism, not only in its theoretical articulation, but also in its practical consequences. The tension between the two is highlighted by his divergent attitudes toward the law. On the one hand, it is "holy and just and good" (Rom 7:12), while on the other hand, it is "the law of sin and death" (Rom 8:2). The apparent contradiction is resolved by Bultmann's neat distinction, "Paul does not criticize the law from the standpoint of its *content,* but with respect to its

---

[31] Sanders, *Paul and Palestinian Judaism,* 320.

[32] See W. Eichrodt, "Covenant and Law: Thoughts on Recent Discussion," *Int* 20 (1966) 302–21.

[33] See my "La genèse littéraire de la Règle de la Communauté," *RB* 76 (1969) 528–49, and J. Pouilly, "L'évolution de la législation pénale dans la communauté de Qumran," *RB* 82 (1975) 522–51.

significance for man."[34] Paul's experience had persuaded him that if commandments were given any role in a religious community they tended to push
God's gracious choice and mercy to the unconsidered periphery of human
life (cf. Rom 7:10).

It is against this background that Paul's grudging acceptance of the new
covenant theme becomes intelligible. It is not something that he would have
introduced on his own initiative, because it would have given the law a
foothold in his community and he had reason to fear that it would eventually
displace from its central position the saving grace of God in Christ.[35]

Paradoxically, confirmation for this view is provided by the one section
in the Pauline letters, which at first sight might seem to constitute a decisive
objection, namely, Paul's positive attitude toward covenant in Galatians 3–4.
Here it is even clearer than in 2 Corinthians that Paul is reacting against
Judaizers, who justified their law-observant mission to the pagan world by
appealing to the promise that in Abraham all the nations would be blessed
(Gen 12:3 = Gal 3:8).[36] It was they who introduced the idea of covenant, and
once again Paul could not simply reject it out of hand. Even though the
expression of his response is much more complex than the distinction of
2 Cor 3:6, its basic thrust can be summed up very simply: he divorces law
from covenant.

First, he associates covenant with freedom. Christians are the children of
the Jerusalem above (Gal 4:26), which is identified with Sara, and thus belong
to the covenant of the free woman (Gal 4:31); this is the antithesis of the
covenant of the slave woman associated with Mount Sinai (immediately
evocative of the law) and the present Jerusalem (Gal 4:22–25). This covenant
of freedom is the covenant of Abraham (Gal 3:17) which, Paul insists, is
essentially promise (Gal 3:16–18, 21; 4:28). An intention to transform the
idea of covenant is manifest.

Second, in order to break the association in the popular mind of covenant
and law, Paul insists that the two are not indissolubly linked. The law was
not part of God's original plan, because it first appeared only 430 years after
the covenant/promise (Gal 3:17). Moreover, the law was not ordained by
God but by angels (Gal 3:19), and so it cannot modify in any way the
covenant/testament drawn up by God.[37] Finally, the law does not enjoy the
permanency of the covenant/promise, because it was given for only a limited

---

[34] Bultmann, "Paulus," *RGG²*, 4.1036.
[35] See C. K. Barrett, *Freedom and Obligation: A Study of the Epistle to the Galatians* (London: SPCK, 1985) 44, 49.
[36] See in particular J. Louis Martyn, "A Law-observant Mission to Gentiles: The Background of Galatians," *Michigan Quarterly Review* 22 (1983) 221–36.
[37] See Barrett, *Freedom and Obligation*, 27.

time (3:19); its role ceased once the promise had been fulfilled in Christ (Gal 3:14).

Paul, therefore, was prepared to accept the idea of covenant, and *a fortiori* that of new covenant, provided that it was completely divorced from law. In this he broke with a millennial tradition that his opponents were striving to maintain, and whose weight he feared. He could live with a new covenant that was entirely of the spirit and in no way marked by the letter of the law (2 Cor 3:6), but it was not a category that he adopted with enthusiasm, and he certainly did not give it a key role in his theology.

Part IV

New Testament

Chapter 15 Newborn Babes and Living Stones: Literal and Figurative in 1 Peter

Paul J. Achtemeier
Union Theological Seminary, Richmond

The question of when the author of 1 Peter uses figurative language and when not is aided by a clear understanding of the controlling metaphor and the underlying thematic structure of the letter.

NEGLECT OF THE STUDY OF 1 PETER, to which attention was called some years ago,[1] appears to have been overcome, at least to some extent, in the time since that observation was made. A sure sign that interest has increased lies in the fact that some former convictions about the letter have been called severely into question, and new forms of consensus have begun to crystallize. Yet there are basic areas of scholarly disagreement that remain. A number of them center on the one hand around lack of clarity about the underlying structure of the letter and thus about its theme, and on the other hand around a basic misunderstanding of the letter's controlling metaphor and hence of the extent of its figurative language. Indeed, much recent debate has centered around the extent to which the reader is allowed, or compelled, to take certain concepts as literal descriptions of the original readers' situation or as metaphorical descriptions of the situation of Christians in the first century.

Part of the solution to this problem lies in a careful consideration of sources lying outside the perimeters of the letter, or even of the NT itself. It is therefore a most appropriate

---

[1] John H. Elliott, "The Rehabilitation of an Exegetical Step-Child: 1 Peter in Recent Research," *JBL* 95 (1976) 243–54; republished in *Perspectives on First Peter* (ed. C. H. Talbert; NAPBR Special Studies Series 9; Macon, GA: Mercer University Press, 1986) 3–16. Prof. Fitzmyer's own work in 1 Peter ("The First Epistle of Peter" in *The Jerome Biblical Commentary* [Englewood Cliffs, NJ: Prentice-Hall, 1968] 2. 362–68), which preceded Elliott's article by some years, shows that for him at least it had not in fact become an "exegetical step-child."

207

topic to address in a volume honoring your own contributions to NT studies, particularly those contributions which have been made out of your vast knowledge of the extrabiblical Aramaic materials. For one who has, in addition to profiting from your erudition, enjoyed your friendship over the past decades, it is at once a privilege and a pleasure to share in this volume honoring your contributions to biblical studies.

Problems in Interpreting 1 Peter

Areas of Emerging Consensus

Some four or five decades ago, there was a general consensus among critical scholars that 1 Peter had as its core a baptismal homily or liturgy preserved in some form or another which had been adapted, because of the pressure of persecutions instigated by the Roman government, into a general letter of encouragement to besieged Christians in Asia Minor who were suffering as a result of this imperial action. Research in the intervening time has called severely into question each of the elements of that consensus.

There is, first, the notion that the bulk of 1 Peter consists of some sort of primitive baptismal homily or liturgy. This view, based on what were taken to be allusions to baptism within the letter,[2] had become all but axiomatic.[3] Further reflection, however, has convinced a number of scholars that the evidence on which this consensus rested will not bear its weight. There is the fact that "baptism" is mentioned but once in the letter,[4] and the added fact that such other references as there are show no greater attention to baptism, perhaps even less, than other NT letters which are clearly not baptismal homilies.[5] The notion that 1 Peter is based on a primitive baptismal homily,

---

[2] In addition to the one reference to baptism in 1 Pet 3:21, references to new birth (e.g., 1:3, 23; 2:2) and to the new situation of Christians (e.g., 1:14, 18, 22; 4:3, 4) were taken to point to this conclusion. F. L. Cross (*1 Peter, a Paschal Liturgy* [London: A. R. Mowbray, 1954], taking clues from 2:3 and from the many references to the suffering of Christ, concluded that the setting was a paschal baptismal liturgy. A convenient summary of Cross's argument may be found in David Hill, "On Suffering and Baptism in 1 Peter," *NovT* 18 (1976) 181–89, esp. 182.

[3] For example, Herbert McCabe, "What is the Church?—VIII," *Life of the Spirit* 18 (1963) 162–74, esp. 163; R. P. A. Vanhoye, "L'Epître (1P 2, 1–10): La maison spirituelle," *Assembleés du Seigneur* 43 (1964) 16–29, esp. 16; Francis Wright Beare, *The First Epistle of Peter* (Oxford: Basil Blackwell, 1947) 6; Edward Gordon Selwyn, *The First Epistle of St. Peter* (London: Macmillan, 1955²) 19. For a good summary of this view and the scholars who espoused it, see John H. Elliott, *The Elect and the Holy* (Leiden: Brill, 1966) 12–13 n. 3; see also W. C. van Unnik, "Christianity according to 1 Peter," *ExpTim* 68 (1956–57) 79–83, esp. 79; F. W. Danker, "1 Peter 1:24–2:17—A Consolatory Pericope," *ZAW* 58 (1967) 93–102, esp. 94 n. 6.

[4] See, for example, the discussion in David Hill, "On Suffering and Baptism," 186.

[5] See Hill, "On Suffering," 181; he notes further that "the meaning of baptism is never far away from the surface when Christians are being exhorted to maintain the integrity of their

or the liturgy that accompanied that act, has therefore become unconvincing to more recent students of that letter.[6]

Implied in the theory of an adapted baptismal homily as the core of 1 Peter was the notion that the letter represented a composite literary entity. The benediction in 4:11, along with what seemed to be a new tack in 4:12, namely, that the readers were presently undergoing persecution (cf. 3:14, where the optative mood seemed to imply that persecution was only a possibility) led many to find there a literary seam. If one posited 1:1–2 as an epistolary addition, one found the basis of the homily to consist roughly in 1:3–4:11, with 1:1–2 and 4:12–5:14 added to adapt the homily to the situation of the readers of 1 Peter. The fact that no further references to baptism were found after 4:11 seemed further confirmation.[7]

Once again, however, further reflection has brought scholars to see 1 Peter more as a unified composition than as an epistolary adaptation of earlier baptismal material. The break between the material preceding 4:11 and following 4:12 is not so clear when one takes into account the discussion of common themes in both parts.[8] The supposed contrast between the possibility (3:14, 17) and the reality (4:12) of suffering is also shown to be exaggerated when one considers the references to suffering, and to the conflict

---

commitment to Christ's way" (185), as they are in this letter. See also Danker, ("1 Peter 1:24–2:17," 101), who lists Rom 6:1–4; Gal 3:27; Eph 4:24; Col 2:12. One may add Heb 6:1–8.

[6] The fact that "the baptismal homily theory has not proved convincing" (J. Francis, " 'Like New-born Babes'—The Image of the Child in 1 Peter 2:2–3," *Studia Biblica* 3 [1978] 111–17, esp. 111) which surfaced as early as the early 1950s (e.g., Eduard Lohse, "Parenesis and Kerygma in 1 Peter," trans. J. Steely; chap. 3, *Perspectives on First Peter* [ed. C. H. Talbert; NAPBR Special Studies Series 9; Macon, GA: Mercer University Press, 1986] 48), has since emerged as something of a new consensus; e.g., Leonhard Goppelt, *Der erste Petrusbrief* (KEK; Göttingen: Vandenhoeck & Ruprecht, 1978) 40; Norbert Brox, *Der erste Petrusbrief* (EKK vol. 21; Cologne: Benziger, 1979) 24; David W. Kendall, "The Literary and Theological Function of 1 Peter 1:3–12," *Perspectives on First Peter* (ed. C. H. Talbert; NAPBR Special Studies Series 9; Macon, GA: Mercer University Press, 1986) 118. Those who accept 1 Peter as a unified composition also tend to deny the baptismal homily theory.

[7] A good summary of this position can be found in F. W. Beare, *The First Epistle*, 6–8; cf. also E. G. Selwyn, *The First Epistle*, 17–23.

[8] Earl Richard ("The Functional Christology of First Peter," *Perspectives on First Peter*, [ed. C. H. Talbert; NAPBR Special Studies Series 9; Macon, GA: Mercer University Press, 1986]) finds the break after 4:11 to be no greater than that after 2:11 and hence an insufficient basis on which to posit literary disunity for 1 Peter. In another vein, L. Goppelt (*Der erste Petrusbrief*, 41, 43) argues for a unified letter on the basis of similar themes and an identical presumed situation. A similar argument, with additional evidence, is proposed by F. W. Danker ("1 Peter 1:24–2:17," esp. 100–101 n. 38), who also cites the "tightly-structured arguments" as further evidence of its unity (101). W. C. van Unnik argues for the unity between 1:1–2 and the body of the letter ("The Redemption in 1 Peter I 18–19 and the Problem of the First Epistle of Peter," *Sparsa Collecta* [Supplements to the New Testament XXX, part 2; 1980] 3–82) and on that basis endorses the idea of 1 Peter as a literary unity (62–63).

between Christians and non-Christians which eventuates in suffering, references which occur throughout the letter.[9] Nor must the optative bear only the meaning of potentiality often attributed to it by proponents of a composite 1 Peter.[10] It appears therefore that a further consensus is taking shape around the notion that 1 Peter as we have it is a unitary composition, probably intended as a circular letter for readers in Asia Minor.[11]

The notion, third, that the Christians in Asia Minor to whom 1 Peter is addressed were suffering as a result of official persecution by the Romans has also fallen by the wayside. Instead of attempting to decide whether 1 Peter reflects the persecutions carried out against Christians under Nero, Domitian, or Trajan,[12] persecutions which were neither empire-wide nor the reflection of some official policy applicable in all cases, scholars have now come to the conclusion that the suffering these readers underwent was the result of sporadic, rather than regular, persecutions.[13] Further, it is now

[9] D. W. Kendall ("The Literary and Theological Function," 115 n. 24) finds references to such suffering-producing conflict in 1:6–7; 2:4–8, 12, 18–20; 3:1–2, 9, 14, 15, 17; 4:1–2, 12–19; 5:8–9, 10. W. C. van Unnik ("Christianity according to 1 Peter," *ExpTim* 68 [1956–57] 79–83, esp. 80) finds no difference in the way suffering is considered in 1:1–4:11 from the way it is discussed in 4:12–5:14; see also L. Goppelt, *Der erste Petrusbrief,* 41–42.

[10] F. W. Danker ("1 Peter 1:24–2:17," 100 n. 38) argues that the optative in 3:14 points not to what may be possible but to what is desirable, namely, to suffer for righteousness' sake. Earl Richard ("The Functional Christology," 125) argues the optative in 3:14 may be due to "the writer's delicate, indirect approach to the reality of suffering." E. Lohse ("Parenesis and Kerygma," 50–51 n. 68) points out that whatever the optative may mean in regard to suffering in 3:14 and 17, suffering was described earlier (but in the same supposed original portion of the letter!) as a reality (1:6), thus obviating the notion that suffering is presumed a reality only after 4:12.

[11] L. Goppelt (*Der erste Petrusbrief,* 44–45) argues that 1 Peter was intended as a *Rundbrief,* such as is found in 2 Macc 1:1–9; 1:10–2:18; Jer 29:4–23; *syrBar* 78:1–86:2. On this point see also N. Brox, *Der erste Petrusbrief,* 22.

[12] Thus, Beare (*The First Epistle of Peter,* 15) could argue that 1 Peter must be dated under the reign of Trajan, when that emperor supported the official persecution of Christians instigated by Pliny in the years 110–111. Trajan was simply continuing official policy, however, since "we may suppose that the action of Nero had made the profession of Christianity illegal throughout the Empire." For the whole discussion of the date in relation to persecutions, see 10–16.

[13] So N. Brox (*Der erste Petrusbrief,* 27), who terms the notion of an empire-wide persecution "phantastisch"; N. Lewis amd M. Reinhold (eds., *Roman Civilization: Sourcebook II: The Empire* [New York: Harper & Row, 1966] 596) note that the first systematic persecution of Christians in the Roman Empire did not occur until the time of the Emperor Decius in A.D. 249–51; E. A. Judge (*The Social Pattern of Christian Groups in the First Century* [London: Tyndale, 1960] 48; see also 71) speaks of "popular alarmism drag(ging) halting public authorities into a series of haphazard actions against Christians"; see also E. Richard ("The Functional Christology," 126); John H. Elliott, "1 Peter, its Situation and Strategy: A Discussion with David Balch," *Perspectives on First Peter* (ed. C. H. Talbert; NAPBR Special Studies Series 9; Macon, GA: Mercer University Press, 1986) 62; W. C. van Unnik, "Christianity according to I Peter," 80; van Unnik also suggests ("The Redemption in 1 Peter," 3–82, esp. 78) that the persecution was carried on not by Romans but by "the Synagogue."

widely held that such persecutions occurred not as the result of official policy although, as the Pliny-Trajan correspondence shows, government officials could become involved, but rather as a result of the pressure of localities who saw in the Christians a nonconformist group who threatened the stability of the normal way of life.[14] It was therefore as nonconformists who threatened the religious, and hence the sociopolitical, status quo[15] that Christians suffered, not as enemies of the state who sought to practice an "illegal religion."[16]

One can therefore speak of a new emerging consensus, quite different from that of some decades ago, a consensus that would now agree that 1 Peter represents a literary unity with no particular relationship to an earlier baptismal liturgy or homily, and that it was designed to encourage Christians in Asia Minor to maintain their faith during a period of social hostility and religious antagonism toward them as people who by their acts threatened the stability of the communities in which they lived.

Areas of Continuing Debate

That is not to say, however, that there is general agreement on all the problems related to 1 Peter. A number of significant disagreements remain within the scholarly community in regard to this letter. No discussion of problems in 1 Peter, for example, can avoid mention of the complex of ideas found in 3:18–22, with its accompanying problems. There is the problem posed by the contrasting formal parallelism of v. 18c (*sarki, pneumati*), which apparently does not submit to a comparable contrasting parallelism of meaning. There is the problem of the prototypical relationship between Noah's rescue through water by means of the ark and the Christian's rescue by means of water through baptism (v. 21). There is the problem of the identity of the "spirits in prison"; the problem of the possible source(s) and/or underlying references to well-known, or even lesser-known, traditions for the entire

[14] So D. Hill, "On Suffering," 182; Charles H. Talbert, "Once Again: The Plan of 1 Peter," *Perspectives on First Peter* (ed. C. H. Talbert; NAPBR Special Studies Series 9; Macon, GA: Mercer University Press, 1986) 145; E. Richard, "The Functional Christology," 127; Everett Falconer Harrison, "Exegetical Studies in 1 Peter," *BSac* 97 (1940) 200–9, esp. 204; W. C. van Unnik, "Christianity according to 1 Peter," 80; N. Brox, *Der erste Petrusbrief,* 29; E. G. Selwyn, *The First Epistle,* 55.

[15] Modern Western readers need constantly to keep in mind that in the Roman Empire of the first and second centuries of our era, religion and politics were simply not separable entities for the average person, and both were intimately related to the social fabric of the community. Hence, to be a religious nonconformist is at the same time to attack the political stability of the community.

[16] There continues to be much confusion about "legal religion(s)" in the Roman Empire; suffice it to say that normal practice was to allow an indigenous people to practice their religion in peace so long as it was not perceived as a threat to Roman hegemony over the area.

complex, as well as for such individual verses as 20 or 22. The literature on these problems is vast and not without ingenious solutions, but there is nothing even approaching a consensus on the problems in this passage.[17]

A related problem which continues to be discussed is the extent to which the author of 1 Peter is dependent on traditions which had already been formulated, whether in written or oral form. Contrary to earlier conclusions that the author of 1 Peter knew and used the letters in the Pauline corpus,[18] scholars now are more inclined to attribute similarities between them not to any dependence of 1 Peter on Paul[19] but rather to their common dependence on the OT and/or early Christian tradition.[20] The extent to which the author of 1 Peter drew directly on the OT[21] or was influenced by such other traditions as those of Qumran[22] continues to be debated, however, as does the

[17] The most thorough treatments of this passage are those of Bo Reicke, *The Disobedient Spirits and Christian Baptism* (Copenhagen: Ejnar Munksgaar, 1946) and William Joseph Dalton, *Christ's Proclamation to the Spirits* (AnBib 23; Rome: Pontifical Biblical Institute, 1965). A glance at the more recent commentaries such as those of N. Brox (163–82, esp. the excursus on the "Nachgeschichte" of 3:19–20, 182–89) or L. Goppelt (239–64, esp. the excursus on its "religionsgeschichtlichen Zusammenhang," 250–54) on this passage will provide a notion of more recent work and give further bibliography.

[18] So, e.g., F. W. Beare (*The First Epistle*, 25), who found "clear dependence upon the Epistles of St. Paul" from an author "steeped in the Pauline letters" who wrote numerous verses that "are a kind of mosaic of Pauline words and forms of expression."

[19] For representative arguments against such a dependence, see E. Lohse, "Parenesis and Kerygma"; Klyne R. Snodgrass, "I Peter II. 1–10: Its Formation and Literary Affinities," *NTS* 24 (1977) 97–106; John H. Elliott, "The Rehabilitation," 7–8; H. G. Meecham, "A Note on 1 Peter ii. 12," *ExpTim* 75 (1953–54) 93; C. N. Hillyer, " 'Rock-Stone' Imagery in I Peter," *TynBul* 22 (1971) 58–81.

[20] This is a very common conclusion; see as examples E. Lohse, "Parenesis and Kerygma"; John H. Elliott, "The Rehabilitation," 8–9, who gives a brief survey of this position; H. G. Meecham, "A Note on 1 Peter ii. 12"; Wolfgang Nauck, "Probleme des frühchristlichen Amtsverständnisses," *ZNW* 48 (1957) 200–220; Gerhard Delling, "Der Bezug der christlichen Existenz auf das Heilshandeln Gottes nach dem ersten Petrusbrief," *Neues Testament und christliche Existenz* (ed. H. D. Betz, L. Schottroff; Tübingen: Mohr-Siebeck, 1973) 95–113; Horst Goldstein, *Paulinische Gemeinde im Ersten Petrusbrief* (Stuttgarter Bibelstudien 80; Stuttgart: KBW, 1975).

[21] Those who argue for direct dependence on OT materials refer most frequently to the image of "rock" found in Isa 8:14; 28:16 or Ps 118:22; e.g., K. Snodgrass, "I Peter II.1–10"; C. N. Hillyer, " 'Rock-Stone' Imagery"; an exception to this is Thomas D. Lea ("How Peter Learned the Old Testament," *Southwestern Journal of Theology* 22 [1980] 96–102), who argues that the apostle Peter, the author, got the image directly from Jesus himself. For others who argue for Petrine dependence directly on the OT, see F. W. Danker ("1 Peter 1:24–2:17," esp. 101), who argues against a collection of "testimonia" in favor of direct dependence on the OT; Ernest Best, "I Peter II 4–10—A Reconsideration," *NovT* 11 (1969) 280–93; Gerhard Delling, "Der Bezug der christlichen Existenz."

[22] L. Goppelt (*Der erste Petrusbrief*) finds pervasive influence from Qumran in the first half of 1 Peter. E. Best ("I Peter II 4–10") and E. Lohse ("Parenesis and Kerygma") also find Qumranian influence, while K. R. Snodgrass ("I Peter II.1–10"), on the basis of careful comparison, denies it; for further bibliographical material, see Snodgrass, 101–2.

identification of specific phrases or verses in 1 Peter as coming from early hymnic or confessional traditions of whatever source.[23]

Other currently debated traditional-theological issues around which no real consensus has formed concern the extent to which the idea of Christ's descent into hell is to be found in 1 Peter 3:18–22,[24] or whether the idea of the "priesthood of all believers," as a basis from which can be derived a special ministry of some representatives of the whole community, can legitimately be grounded in 1 Pet 2:1–10.[25] Finally, there are the problems with which this essay is concerned, namely, that of the controlling metaphor with its concomitant problem of identifying where figurative use of language is intended, and the problem of the underlying structure of the letter. It is to those last two problems we must now turn our attention.

Date of 1 Peter

Although the question of the date of 1 Peter is not of central concern to this essay, we do need to review the arguments mounted by W. C. van Unnik in favor of a date within the historical Peter's lifetime.[26] His argument is important not so much for the date he proposes as for the evidence he uncovers along the way concerning the OT background of 1 Pet 1:18–19.[27]

Van Unnik sets out to determine the correct understanding of the idea of redemption by Christ's blood which is found in 1 Pet 1:18–19. After reviewing the explanations given by a number of scholars, van Unnik notes six unresolved difficulties: (1) *lytroō* is normally translated "ransom" in v. 18 because of the presence of *argyrion* and *chrysion,* even though "ransom" is

---

[23] Still the most careful study is that of Rudolf Bultmann, "Bekenntnis- und Liedfragmente im ersten Petrusbrief," *ConNT* 11 (1947) 1–14. For a more recent such analysis, see Earl Richard, "The Functional Christology," esp. 128–29. For further bibliographical information, see his note 22, page 128.

[24] See especially W. J. Dalton, *Christ's Proclamation to the Spirits,* and N. Brox, *Der erste Petrusbrief,* "Exkurs: Zur nachgeschichte von 1 Petr 3,19f/4,6 (Der 'Höllenabstieg' Christi)," 182–89.

[25] The strongest argument against it is J. H. Elliott's *The Elect and the Holy;* for similar arguments, see F. W. Danker, "1 Peter 1:24–2:17," 97 n. 19; E. Best ("I Peter II 4–10"), in an article generally critical of Elliott's book, finds defensible the argument for individual minister/priests, but only as people who exercise priestly functions as members of a group each of whom exercises the same function (287). A similar tack is taken by John S. Marshall, " 'A Spiritual House and Holy Priesthood' (I Peter ii. 5)," *ATR* 28 (1946) 227–28; R. P. A. Vanhoye, "L'Epitre (1P 2, 1–10); La maison spirituelle"; A Feuillet, "Les 'sacrifices spirituels' du sacerdoce royal des baptises (1P 2, 5)," *NRT* 94 (1974) 704–28.

[26] Van Unnik, "The Redemption in 1 Peter I 18–19 and the Problem of the First Epistle of Peter."

[27] There will be no attempt to reproduce the argument in detail; only the broad outlines need to be recited in any case in order to determine what is important for the argument of this article.

never used with regard to a sacrifice (v. 19), and the verb can also mean "deliver"; (2) *phthartois* is translated as "perishable things," even though in its five other occurrences in the NT it means "corruptible," and even though its antithesis in v. 19 (contrary to every other occurrence in the NT, including 1 Pet 1:23) is not *aphthartō* but rather *timiō*; (3) the explanation of *anastrophē*, a neutral word meaning "way of life," is interpreted in terms of enslavement under the power of sin, even though the notion of "slave to sin," so familiar from Paul, does not appear in 1 Peter; (4) there is confusion about exactly what *amnos* means and to what it refers; (5) there is confusion about the apposition Christ-lamb which involves a simile that interrupts a genitive link (*aimati hōs amnou . . . christou*), a confusion indicated by the automatic addition of "the" to "blood" despite the absence in the Greek of the definite article; and (6) there is lack of clarity about the contextual link with v. 17, indicated by the participial construction of v. 18. Of these, the notion that *lytroō* must mean "ransom" lies at the root of these difficulties.

Van Unnik begins his solution by defining two contrasting kinds of *anastrophē*: a futile one (*anastrophē mataia* [v. 18]) which characterized the readers' former lives as pagans, and a Christian one (*anastrophē en phobō* [v. 17]) which must characterize their present lives. When and by what means did this conversion from one form of life to another take place? Clearly the answer has to do with the statement in v. 19, where, however, van Unnik insists that given the present form of the phrase, Christ is to be understood as an explanation of the lamb, not vice versa. Noting that the words *aspilos* and *amomos* do not occur in Greek sacrificial terminology, but that *amomos* does occur in the LXX, van Unnik locates the background of this verse in OT cultic terminology, specifically Lev 22:17–25. Here van Unnik finds a key point: in Lev 22:25 LXX *phtharta* is used[28] as a synonym for *momos*, both of which in this context can only mean "blemished" or "that which is corrupt." This in turn provides the key to 1 Pet 1:18: it is to be interpreted in a cultic sacrificial sense, and it provides the clue to the meaning of *phthartois* in the same verse: it means not perishable or even corruptible things, but rather things unacceptable (to God) in cultic context.

The next question van Unnik asks is: where do we find sacrifice mentioned in connection with a conversion from one way of life to another? The answer: in the conversion from paganism to Judaism, accompanied by the proselyte's sacrifice as one of the three elements (baptism, circumcision, and sacrifice) essential to every conversion of that kind.

That leaves one unresolved problem: the meaning of *timios* in v. 19. Why is the blood of the proselyte's sacrifice precious? The answer: it is precious

---

[28] Rahlfs prefers *phtharmata* in LXX Lev 22:25b to the *phtharta* (Alexandrinus, corrected reading in Vaticanus) that van Unnik reproduces (37), but the meaning is the same in either case.

because it can save one from Gehenna (here is becomes clear as well that *lytroō* can mean both "deliver" and "ransom").

Such an interpretation of 1:18–19, based on OT cultic terminology, also solves the problem of the *hos* of v. 19; the one who has converted to Christianity has been delivered not by means of something unacceptable — gold or silver — but with the precious blood "like that of an unblemished (and thus acceptable) lamb" in the proselyte conversion, except that in the present Christian context, that sacrificed lamb is Christ.[29]

From all of this, van Unnik concludes that since the metaphor contained in these verses would have made sense only during a period when such proselyte offering was still taking place, something that ended after A.D. 70, the letter must have been written before that cessation.[30] While this conclusion cannot stand — applying its logic would necessitate the conclusion that the Gospel of Matthew was written prior to A.D. 70 since Matt 5:23–25 also presume the practice of the sacrificial cultus[31] — his study has the value of pointing us to the OT as a significant background against which to understand the metaphorical language of 1:18–19,[32] even though the letter was admittedly written to pagans. The value of the OT background for understanding metaphorical language in 1 Peter will become increasingly apparent as our argument proceeds.

Social Situation of 1 Peter

Another area of current debate which has importance for the question of the controlling metaphor and the use of figurative language in 1 Peter concerns the social situation of the intended readers of this letter. While it is admittedly difficult to determine specific details of the social situation of Christian readers of 1 Peter who lived in Asia Minor in the first century of our era, that situation surely had important bearing on how they understood the language of this letter, and hence on what functioned for them as figurative language and controlling metaphor. Therefore even a general grasp of that social situation will be of help in this matter.

---

[29] Van Unnik has a long section on "Further Traces of Proselytism in I Peter" (53–68; he finds 15 such traces), but it does not materially affect his argument, and hence no account of it will be included.

[30] Even if proselyte sacrifice were being practiced, how can we assume that *pagans* in *Asia Minor* would necessarily know about it from sources other than Christian tradition?

[31] The solution to 1:18–19 is the same as for Matt 5:23–25: a later document can easily contain traditions which did originate in an earlier time. It is not 1 Peter, but the tradition alluded to in 1:18–19, which is to be dated prior to A.D. 70.

[32] Other scholars have pointed to the OT background of 1:17–18, e.g., G. Delling ("Christliche Existenz," 100) suggests Lev 17:11; Earl Richard ("The Functional Christology," 134) suggests Isaiah 52, but none with the amount of evidence or careful argumentation of van Unnik.

The two scholars who have done the most work in this aspect of research on 1 Peter are John H. Elliott and David L. Balch, and a review of their work will prove helpful.

Elliott's argument can be seen more readily in his work on the sociological exegesis of 1 Peter.[33] He comes to the conclusion that the difficulties reflected in 1 Peter are the result of social conflicts which pitted the readers as rural dwellers against the city culture of Asia Minor, pitted the poor community against the rich society, eventuated in social separation rather than accommodation and conformity, set the house of God against the forces of evil, and set the proletarian against the bourgeoisie.[34] Thus the *Sitz im Leben* of 1 Peter is the "situation of acute homelessness and the feeling of not belonging."[35] The letter seeks to combat the deleterious effects both of the conflicts outlined above and of the resulting social alienation of the Christian community by encouraging its members to remain faithful members of the household of God. Elliott thus affirms that the controlling metaphor (although he does not use that term) is "household or family of God"; it is the *oikos* terminology of the letter which "*coordinates* the traditional metaphors" employed in 1 Peter.[36]

There is nore than metaphorical language involved here, however. Elliott makes explicit the fact that he holds the term *paroikos,* which he suggests be translated as "resident aliens,"[37] to be a description of the social status of the readers prior to their conversion to the Christian faith,[38] as well as a description of their standing in society as members of that community of faith. The point against which Elliott is primarily concerned to argue here is the notion that Christians in 1 Peter are "exiles" from their true home in heaven,[39] a view

---

[33] *A Home for the Homeless* (Philadelphia: Fortress, 1981). I do not propose to repeat my evaluation of the argument as a whole; cf. my review in *JBL* 103 (1984) 130–33. See also his "1 Peter, its Situation and Strategy"; for his sociological models, see *Home,* 96 n. 57; "1 Peter," 69 n. 10.

[34] I have drawn this summary of the social conflicts Elliott discusses in *A Home* from David L. Balch, "Hellenization/Acculturation in 1 Peter," *Perspectives on First Peter* (ed. C. H. Talbert; NAPBR Special Studies Series 9; Macon, GA: Mercer University Press, 1986) 83; he documents the discussion of each of the conflicts in his notes to that page. Elliott later argued that all of these are subordinate to the fundamental contrast "between the Christian community and the external non-Christian society" ("1 Peter," 64).

[35] "Rehabilitation," 15.

[36] *Home,* 228, emphasis his; see also "I Peter," 77, where Elliott emphasizes the "familial terminology and metaphors," and "The Rehabilitation," 15, where he had earlier affirmed that "in Christ the homeless ones are members of the *oikos tou theou.*"

[37] *Home,* 47; he suggests *paroikia* be translated "alien residence" or "residence as aliens."

[38] See *Home,* 42–43, 47.

[39] For an expression of this widely held view, see E. F. Harrison, "Exegetical Studies," 206–7; Paul E. Deterding, "Exodus Motifs in First Peter," *Concordia Journal* 7 (1981) 58–65, esp 63; van Unnik, "Christianity," 82. This view is not universally held, however; see Christian Wolff, "Christ und Welt im 1. Petrusbrief," *TLZ* 100 (1975) 334–42, esp. 337.

which in his estimate would eliminate any sociological implications for the status of the readers and hence for the message of 1 Peter.[40]

In the course of his linguistic study, which includes a good deal of research on the words related to the *paroik-* stem, Elliott makes no attempt to evaluate the fact that the word *paroikia* does not appear in Hellenistic Greek literature except in Jewish or Christian writers.[41] Again, Elliott is silent on the significance of fact that in the verse where *paroikous* is used, it is combined with a second word, *parepidēmous* (2:11).[42] Not only is this latter word rare in nonbiblical Greek, but it represents with *paroikos* a combination that occurs in Greek literture for the first time in the Septuagint (Gen 23:4; Ps 38:12 [39:13]), and thereafter only in literature influenced by the biblical usage (Philo, Clement of Alexandria, and the Cappadocian theologians Gregory of Nazianzus and Basil).[43] The author of 1 Peter therefore reproduced a phrase which came from the OT and was otherwise unknown in secular Greek, a fact which would render that phrase rather inappropriate to describe political status in the Hellenistic world.

The phrase would, however, be particularly appropriate if the author of 1 Peter wanted to compare the current status of the Christian community as people of God with the fate of that other people of God, namely, Israel. That of course is precisely what he has done in 2:9–10. To continue that metaphor in 2:11 would then seem most natural.[44] That in turn would point not to the

---

[40] *Home,* 42; reinforced in private conversation with Elliott. I share his evaluation of this mistaken notion.

[41] *Home,* 43. The word occurs in authors writing during the period including the first century B.C. to the second century A.D. only in Clement of Alexandria (*Paedagogus* 3.12.85; *Stromata* 4.26.166), Clement of Rome (*2 Cor.* 5:1), Irenaeus (*Adv. Haer.* 5.3.15, 19), Origen (*Com. Ev. Joan.* 6.41.211, 213; 10.12.63; *Philocalia* 13.2; *Frag. in ev. Matt.* 16.14; *Ep. ad Greg. Thaum.* 2; *Frag. ex com. in ep. i ad Cor.* 89; *Frag. ex com. in ep. ad Eph.* 31; *Frag. in Ps.* 118.54), Theophilus of Antioch (*Ad Autolycum* 3.28) and Philo (*De Conf. Ling.* 80). It also appears some 20 times in the LXX, and one other time in the NT (Acts 13:17). This information is based on the literature encompassed in the Thesaurus Linguae Graecae Pilot CDRom disc (hereafter "TLG disc").

[42] *Home,* 30.

[43] Philo uses the phrase as a quotation from Genesis 23 (*De Confusione* 79; he employs the combination a second time in *De Conf.* 76, but not as a phrase); Clement used it twice in the *Stromata,* once as a quotation from Gen. (4.26.165.2), once as a quotation from 1 Peter (3.11.75.1); Gregory quoted it from LXX Ps 38:13 (*Funebris oratio* 49.3) as did Basil (*Homiliae super Psalmos* 29.252). This information is again based on the TLG disc. Van Unnik also noted the appearance of this phrase in the Septuagint ("The Redemption," 72), as did M.-A. Chevallier, "Condition et Vocation des Chretiens en Diaspora: Remarques Exegetiques sur la 1ʳᵉ Epitre de Pierre," *RevScRel* 48 (1974) 387–400, esp. 394, but did not draw the same conclusions from it that I shall. See also P. E. Deterding, "Exodus Motifs," 61.

[44] One should similarly understand the reason for the combination of *parepidēmois* with *diasporas* at the very beginning of the letter, surely an appropriate place to begin to use one's controlling metaphor.

contrast *oikos-paroikos* as the controlling metaphor, but rather to a different metaphor, one that embraced within itself both *oikos* and *paroikos,* namely, the metaphor of the Christians as the new chosen people of God. We will need to return to this topic.

The second scholar whose work is important for this discussion is David Balch, who looks at 1 Peter from the perspective of social adaptation and acculturation.[45] Balch examines the household code in 1 Pet 2:13–3:7 and concludes that, despite the evident desire of the author of 1 Peter for peaceful households, the "*experience* was of *divided* households, unjust masters, and many pagan husbands."[46] This meant tension between Christian communities and Hellenistic society, a trait of every NT letter in which a household code is included.[47]

Such tension was the result of the different kind of behavior exhibited by Christians, particularly those in socially subordinate roles (wives, slaves), who did not as a matter of course worship the gods of the Roman household. That opened Christians up to the kind of slanderous objections directed by Hellenistic society against any belief that altered what the Greco-Roman culture took to be the natural roles in the family (subordination of wives to husbands, slaves to masters, children to parents).[48]

It was the effort to counteract that kind of accusation, Balch argues, that accounts for the plea in 1 Peter to its readers that they be prepared to offer an apologetic for Christian behavior to any who would listen (3:15).[49] The point of the combination of apology and household code was to assure non-Christians that the beliefs of the Christian community did not in fact threaten the traditional roles within the household of those who constituted it.[50]

If that apologetic intention were true, and Balch does not doubt that it was, then that means that a significant change in the nature of the Christian faith has occurred. Acculturation of Christianity to the extent Balch finds in 1 Peter can only mean that "Petrine Christianity accepted hellenistic social values in tension with important values in Jewish tradition (in the Torah)

---

[45] See *Let Wives be Submissive: The Domestic Code in 1 Peter* (SBLMS 26; Chico, CA: Scholars Press, 1981) and his article "Hellenization/Acculturation in 1 Peter."

[46] "Hellenization/Acculturation," 99; author's italics. See also 95.

[47] Ibid., 99.

[48] *Let Wives,* 118; see also "Hellenization/Acculturation," 81–82.

[49] *Let Wives,* 118–19. It is a repeated assertion of Balch's argument that 3:15 be construed with the household code as the reason for its inclusion; see "Appendix I. The Structure of 1 Peter," 123–31. E. A. Judge (*The Social Pattern,* 73) holds a similar view on the need of early Christians for social apology.

[50] In this they shared the defense of Jews and devotees of Isis who suffered similar accusations; "Hellenization/Acculturation," 82, 90, 93.

and even in tension with the early Jesus movement."[51]

Balch finds further confirmation for his thesis that 1 Peter represents a decisive attempt to acculturate Christianity to Greco-Roman family values in the source for the kind of household codes of which portions are reproduced in 1 Pet 2:13–3:7. That source is to be found in Hellenistic, indeed in classical Greek, culture in the writings of Aristotle; such codes were then used and developed by political philosophers and ethicists and so spread through the entire Hellenistic world.[52] Such codes, with the emphasis on subordination of certain groups of people, were appropriated by the Romans as an ideological defense of their imperialistic policies and as a means of maintaining order in their rapidly expanding empire.[53] For that reason, inclusion of such a code in 1 Peter would strike a particularly empathetic note among the Romans and would echo sentiments familiar and accepted by the Hellenistic world in general. It would prove Christians could be faithful Christians without failing to be good citizens of Hellenistic society and the Roman Empire.

To be sure, the household code in 1 Peter is not a pure representation of the *genre*. Significant portions are absent—parent–child relationships, for example[54]—and the motivation has been altered: it is now not good citizenship or the natural order, but the example of the subordination/suffering of Christ to which appeal is made for the desirable behavior. Balch observes that "the final and characteristic basis for the ethical exhortations is Christological,"[55] a point which, as we will see, if taken seriously would point in another direction in interpreting the household codes of 1 Peter.

There are several considerations, some indicated by Balch himself, which call his conclusions into question. Perhaps foremost is the fact that if one gains any impression from the whole of 1 Peter, it would have to be that the farthest thing from the author's mind is accommodation to Hellenistic culture; 4:1–4 ought to make that clear enough. Indeed, it is not the danger of avoiding acculturation, but the temptation to lapse into acculturation that seems uppermost in our author's mind. The contrast between "formerly" and "now," which recurs repeatedly throughout the letter, with the implication of lesser value of "formerly," combined with the equally clear indications that such "former" conduct was precisely the sort of thing advocated by Greco-

---

[51] Ibid., 81; see also 97. Balch feels that those changes were so basic that they "raise questions about the continuity and identity in early Christianity" (81).

[52] See his arguments in *Let Wives,* chap. II, "Plato, Middle Platonists, and Stobaeus," 23–31, and chap. III, "Aristotle, the Peripatetics, and Three Dependent Writers," 33–49.

[53] "Hellenization/Acculturation," 81–82.

[54] Such a relationship is included in Eph 6:1–4 and Col 3:20–21, showing that it could also be included in a Christian household code.

[55] "Hellenization/Acculturation," 100.

Roman culture (esp. 4:3–4), present a telling argument against Balch's interpretation.[56]

Again, the fact that Christians approved as good values which were also generally so regarded in the contemporary culture is hardly evidence of acculturation, or the desire for it. There would be no reason for early Christians not to expect to find what was good operating in Hellenistic culture, along with what was base. They knew God had created the world (e.g., Acts 17:24; Rom 1:20) and had not left himself without witnesses in it (e.g., Acts 14:17; cf. Rom 1:19–20); Paul had been quite sure that even without divine revelation, people were capable of doing what was good (Rom 2:14–15); and tradition remembered Jesus making the same point (cf. Luke 11:13). It would thus be quite natural for Christians to welcome and receive any evidences of good conduct on the part of non-Christians and do what they could to encourage it in them.[57] Such acceptance and encouragement would not mean necessary accommodation to all secular values, or even to those values that would promise surcease of persecution, as 1 Peter shows.

Indeed, the purpose for which elements of household codes were cited in 1 Peter seems to be not so much for the purpose of cultural accommodation as for the purpose of providing exemplary modes of conduct for all Christians. The clue is the exhortation with which the code begins (2:13): it is subordination, an act which is quite in accordance with God's will (2:15, 16, 19, 20; 3:4, 17). The fact that the suffering Christ is cited as the primary example of such subordination points in the same direction. Further evidence is provided by the groups of people singled out for extended address; they are: everyone who lives in that culture (2:13–17), slaves (2:18–25), and wives (3:1–7).[58] In each instance, the group chosen provides an example of those at the mercy of others, who can inflict punishment on them, arbitrarily if they so desire. Thus those who did not belong to the ruling class were strictly subordinate; their "only duty . . . was loyalty to their betters."[59] Slaves were regarded as property, with no rights as individuals;[60] wives were to be ruled over by their husbands, and their duty and virtue lay in obedience to such rule.

---

[56] So also Elliott, "1 Peter," 72–73. Elliott appropriately warns that "keeping open the channels of communication between believers and nonbelievers ought not to be confused with an advocacy of social assimilation" (72).

[57] Balch himself is aware of this ("Hellenization/Acculturation," 86, 87); see also C. H. Talbert, "Once Again," 146, 148; J. H. Elliott, "1 Peter," 73.

[58] Husbands are also addressed (3:8), but only very briefly. The fact that they are mentioned in relation to wives, but masters are not mentioned with slaves, or rulers with ruled is an important point; see below.

[59] E. A. Judge, The Social Pattern, 73.

[60] See Balch, Let Wives, passim. For examples of unjust suffering of slaves, see Tacitus Annales 12.32; Petronius Satyricon 57; Seneca "On Mercy" 1.18.1; 26.1; Epistle 47.11.

The very choice of such groups of people therefore seems dictated by the author's desire to show all Christians their proper conduct toward God, and hence toward those who in their own culture had the power to persecute them. Following Christ's example (2:21; 3:17; 4:1, 12, 15), they were to suffer rather than strike back.

There is additional evidence that points away from the notion that the household codes are employed in 1 Peter to foster cultural accommodation. There is the question of the source of the code here used. Both the form, and the groups of people included, are rather unlike ordinary codes. Slaves, for example, are simply not addressed in such household codes from the Greco-Roman world.[61] Again, unlike even the codes in Ephesians and Colossians, slaves are addressed with no reference to masters. Ordinary people are addressed, but no advice is given to the rulers, encouraging them to be just and equitable. Again, the normal pair of parents/children is omitted, contrary to the normal codes, even those in Ephesians and Colossians.

Again, there is the substance of the "commands." The source of the material addressed to the wives is anything but Hellenistic. Not only is the example of correct conduct (3:5–6) drawn from the OT (Gen 18:12), but the language of the preceding admonitions (3:1–4) reflects far more closely the language of Isa 3:18 than anything in Hellenistic sources.[62] The fact that the material addressed to slaves (2:22–25) reflects the language of Isa 53:5–12 makes the likelihood of that same book being the source for the wives all the more probable.

There is, finally, the matter of those groups not mentioned in the adaptation of the household code in 1 Peter. We have already noted the absence of the customary groups of parents and children. We have also noted the absence of any words addressed to the master of slaves, all the more striking because some words are addressed to husbands, if only in passing. How are we to account for this?

Surely, given the pressure in Hellenistic culture to keep slaves subordinate and "in their place," one would expect some advice to Christian masters to keep their slaves sufficiently disciplined, lest impudent or too-familiar slaves give the Christian faith a bad name. Absence of advice to slave owners would be especially surprising if, as Balch thinks, Christians like the author of 1 Peter themselves owned slaves.[63]

---

[61] See James W. Thompson, " 'Be Submissive to your Masters': A Study of I Peter 2:18–25," *Restoration Quarterly* 9 (1966) 66–78, esp. 70.

[62] The combination of *emplok-*, *imat-*, and *kosm-* occurs only in Isa 3:18; 1 Pet 3:2, and Clement of Alexandria *Paedagogus* 3.11.66, information again gleaned from the literature encompassed in the TLG disc.

[63] "Hellenization/Acculturation," 95. The evidence that allows Balch to conclude that "the educated author of this letter *certainly* owned slaves" (italics mine) is unavailable to me.

Yet again, the need to keep orderly subordination within the family and the household is not the point of advice to the husbands. They are not counseled to keep the wives subordinate, something accommodation to Hellenistic culture would dictate. Rather, the advice to the husbands is the opposite; they are advised *not* to exercise their cultural right of power over their wives. In short, there is little in the admonitions contained in 1 Peter 2–3 to certain classes of people within the Christian communities which would lead one to conclude the author intended to accommodate the Christian conduct to Hellenistic culture as represented in secular household codes.

Once again, however, we have been pointed to the OT as a source from which the author of 1 Peter drew, in this case Isaiah. If Balch does not suggest a controlling metaphor for understanding the other figurative language in 1 Peter, he has called attention to materal which, contrary to his assumptions, nevertheless seems to be used in a metaphorical way for all Christians, and its content has again pointed us to the OT. We must now turn to the task of identifying the controlling metaphor of 1 Peter which will allow us to understand the remaining figurative language in 1 Peter and do justice to the hints we have received concerning the source in the OT of language as well as images used in this letter.

Figurative Language in 1 Peter

One of the more difficult problems with 1 Peter, as the work of J. H. Elliott has shown, is how to determine when the author is using figurative language, and when he wants to be taken literally. Even the most cursory reading of 1 Peter will make evident the author's abundant use of metaphor and simile.[64] In some instance, the content of the phrase makes clear that the language must be figurative, as when the readers are addressed as "newborn babes" (2:2) or as "living stones" (2:5). In other cases, the terminology makes it equally clear that we are to take the language literally, as when the readers are addressed as "Christians" (4:16) or some of them as "fellow elders" (5:1). How are we to determine which is which?

Content is an obvious indicator. Those phrases that speak of people as "stones" is one example. In this instance the author is employing imagery already abundantly used in the OT,[65] a source already indicated in the

---

[64] So L. Radermacher, "Der erste Petrusbrief und Silvanus; mit einem Nachwort in eigener Sache," *ZNW* 25 (1926) 287–99, esp. 289. For a discussion of the letter's style, see H. G. Meecham, "The First Epistle of St. Peter," *ExpTim* 48 (1936–37) 22–24; for a discussion of figurative language used to describe the church, see Kenneth O. Gangel, "Pictures of the Church in I Peter," *Grace Journal* 10 (1969) 29–35.

[65] For a discussion of this imagery in the OT and in 1 Peter, see C. N. Hillyer, " 'Rock-Stone' Imagery," *passim*. Association of this imagery with the messiah is indicated in Justin Martyr *Dialogue with Trypho* chap. 36.

discussion of Elliott and Balch. Another example is the cluster of references which address the readers as newborn infants. In this case, there are two other indications of figurative use: the adjective *logikos* which has as one of its meanings "metaphorical" and which may be used in that sense in 2:2,[66] and the pun on *chrēstos/christos* in 2:3. These nourishment images may also have an OT substratum, in this instance the Exodus.[67] A third example is references that are historically impossible; the sprinkling of the readers with Christ's blood (1:2) is such a reference. This language is itself a figure for the crucifixion and the benefits derived from it. Again, the background of that figure of "sprinkling with blood" is drawn from the OT, in this case Exodus 24.[68] The figure of "house" or "temple" applied to people is yet another instance; here there is doubled figurative language, since even the word "house" is qualified by the adjective "spiritual" (2:5). Once more, the background is from the OT, as the further reference to "(spiritual) sacrifices" makes evident.[69] Other references which most commentators find to be figurative, given the meaning of the word or phrase, are Babylon as the point of origin of the letter (5:13), the reference to Mark as "my son" (5:13), and diaspora (1:1).[70]

Does the author give us any other, more general clues about when we are to take the figure literally, and when we are not? The use of the particle *hōs,* used 23 times in 1 Peter, is clearly one clue; most of the obviously figurative expressions are introduced by it (e.g., 1:14, 19, its addition in 1:24; 2:2, 4, 24; 5:11). It is not an infallible clue, however, since many words meant to be taken literally are also introduced by it (e.g., 2:13–14; 3:5; 4:16). Another

---

[66] J. H. Moulton and G. Milligan ("Lexical Notes from the Papyri: XVI," *The Expositor* 7th Series, 7 [1909] 559–68, esp. 560) specifically find this use in 1 Pet 2:2. See also J. Francis, " 'Like Newborn Babes,' " *passim;* Eugene A. LaVerdiere, "A Grammatical Ambiguity in 1 Pet 1:23," *CBQ* 36 (1974) 89–94.

[67] F. W. Danker ("1 Peter 1:24–2:17," 95) cites Exod 1:7, where "Israel grew up."

[68] Cf. Daniel C. Arichae, Jr., "God or Christ? A Study of Implicit Information," *BT* 28 (1977) 412–18, esp. 12–13.

[69] R. P. A. Vanhoye, "L'Epitre (1P 2, 1–10); La maison spirituelle," 21. C. N. Hillyer (" 'Rock-Stone' Imagery") calls attention to the metaphorical use of building in the OT (74) and of "spiritual" sacrifices at Qumran (75).

[70] Even here, there have been those who understand these as literal. That Babylon meant the city on the Euphrates, see Henry Alford, *The Greek Testament,* rev. E. G. Harrison (IV vol.; Chicago: Moody Press, 1958) IV.128–31; that the Mark mentioned in 5:13 was actually Peter's physical child, see R. S. T. Haselhurst, " 'Mark, My Son,' " *Theology* 13 (1926) 34–36; that "diaspora" meant the letter was sent to Jewish Christians who lived outside Palestine, see Robert Leighton, *A Practical Commentary upon the First Epistle General of St. Peter* (2 vols.; London: Religious Tract Society, n.d. (Leighton lived in the 17th century —ed.]) 1.20–21. I owe this reference to Robert W. Thurston, "Interpreting First Peter," *Journal of the Evangelical Theological Society* 17 (1974) 171–82, esp. 174; Thurston argues the diaspora refers to Christians who fled from Rome to Asia Minor during Nero's persecution.

suggestion consists in the observation that, when the word or phrase is one which could be taken literally but is meant by the author to be taken figuratively, it is accompanied by one or more adjectives, or by a qualifying phrase, designed to make clear the author's intention and to indicate how the figure is to be taken.[71] This is helpful, but one cannot rule out the possibility that some terms without such qualifying words or phrases may be meant figuratively (e.g., 2:11), simply because they belong to a larger metaphor being employed by the author.

Identifying that larger metaphor would be most helpful of all. Knowledge of that basic metaphor would aid us in determining on a case-by-case basis whether a given term is to be understood literally or figuratively, where content or use does not solve that problem. There have been attempts to locate that controlling metaphor—the notion that baptism, for example, provided the clue to the language, including the metaphors, of this letter,[72] or the *oikos-paroikos* contrast,[73] or the Exodus and the terminology associated with it in the OT,[74] or the notion of "people of God" as found in 2:9–10[75]—but no attempt, to my knowledge, has been made either to isolate it specifically as controlling metaphor, or to apply it to our problem of interpreting when and how the author of 1 Peter uses figurative language. It is to a sketch of that procedure that we must now turn.

The thesis, which we will consider in more detail in what follows, is this: The controlling metaphor to be found in this letter is the *Christian community as the new people of God constituted by the Christ who suffered (and rose)*. From the first half of this metaphor flows the language reminiscent of Israel as God's chosen people set apart from himself, not only the language of 2:4–10 but also the language reflecting separation from other peoples and their customs: exiles, aliens, Gentiles. From the second half of the metaphor flows the language that describes Christians as finding a pattern for their behavior in the suffering Christ, including the descriptions of Christians in terms of powerless social classes that also exist in circumstances of suffering in 2:13–3:6.

---

[71] E. Best, "I Peter II 4–10," 292–93; he cites a number of examples.

[72] See note 2 above.

[73] J. H. Elliott, *A Home;* see the discussion above.

[74] P. E. Deterding, "Exodus Motifs," makes a case, albeit at times somewhat tenuous and farfetched, for that event as the basic underlying metaphor for 1 Peter, although again he does not use that term.

[75] E. Best ("I Peter II 4–10," 276–78) argues for its importance; M.-A. Chevallier ("Condition et Vocation," 390) argues that no NT author speaks so penetratingly of Christians as the people of God, and notes that this latter term is applied "globally" by the author to issues concerning Gentile believers, but restricts himself to a consideration of the initial verses of chap. 2; cf. also E. Richard ("The Functional Christology," 123) on this matter.

A *New* People

The theme of newness appears at the very outset of the letter, when in v. 3 it is announced that God has caused the Christians to be "born anew," followed by a description of the new inheritance into which such newly born people have come (1:3b–4). This new birth, accomplished by their accepting the word of God when the gospel was preached to them (1:23), must be understood in terms of the activity of Israel as God's people, since that activity already pointed forward to this new people (1:10–12). For that reason, they are called upon to fulfill the task given to Israel when it was called: "You shall be holy, for I am holy" (1:16).[76]

In that way, the newness is made thematic for all that follows. It is in this category of newness that that language belongs which had led earlier commentators to find baptism to be the controlling metaphor. It is not, however, baptism which underlies this discussion, but the newness of God's new people, who individually begin their careers as members of this people by baptism. The reference to infants (2:2) again does not belong to a baptismal homily or liturgy, but to the basic emphasis of God's *new* people, as new in this new people of God as are infants in the human race. That is also why baptism is mentioned only once and then as an illustration of salvation rather than rebirth (3:21); the point of the discussion in 1 Peter is newness, illustrated by metaphors of new birth and infant status, not by baptism, illustrated by allusions more or less appropriate to it. That is also why the metaphor of Christians as newborn babes (2:2) is followed immediately by metaphors of Christians as chosen people (2:4–10). The ruling metaphor is God's new people, not baptism, and hence newness is meant to comment on that rather than on the ritual of baptism.

The emphasis on newness of the existence of the individual member of the Christian community as new chosen people may also be reflected in the language reminiscent of the rituals connected with admitting proselytes into Israel and their legal status upon admission. Perhaps most important in this context is the fact that, in Judaism, the proselyte was legally equivalent to a

---

[76] Unlike Paul, 1 Peter does not seem to envision Christians as being incorporated into Israel, or its "calledness," as it were. Rather, for 1 Peter, the Christian community has supplanted Israel as chosen people. Whereas Paul makes it clear in Romans 9–11 that Israelites, if at present only in limited numbers, are included in that chosen people, and indeed that anyone belonging to that people is grafted into the "root" (Rom 11:17–18) which is Israel's irrevocable call (11:28b–29), the author of 1 Peter does not speak in those terms. For whatever reason, there is no discussion of the future fate of Israel, whether that future means inclusion in the new people of God (cf. Rom 11:26) or not. Nor is there any mention of Christians by ethnic origin, i.e., Jewish or gentile. 1 Peter assumes a homogeneity in his readers which, as we shall see, probably means they are all of gentile origin.

newborn child.[77] That fact may indicate that the status of the proselyte as a new member of the people of God functioned as a metaphor for the status of the new member of the Christian community. W. C. van Unnik has called attention to a number of other allusions to proselyte status as well, allusions which include specific language[78] as well as broader concepts.[79]

Whether or not the metaphor of the proselyte operates in the language of 1 Peter, there can be no question that the metaphor of the newborn child strongly emphasizes the newness of God's new people, in which all members are newly born.

A New *People of God*

If newness is characteristic of the Christian community, so is the fact that they are the people of God. In fact, it is the people of God that lie at the heart of the controlling metaphor of this epistle. That becomes most evident in the collection of terms in 2:9 which in the OT (Isa 43:20–21; Exod 19:6 or 23:22) were applied to Israel as God's chosen people. The same is true of the quotation from Hos 2:25 (see also Hos 1:6, 9; 2:3) in 2:10 which is used to describe the coming into being of the new people of God.[80] The way for those verses was in turn prepared by the discussion beginning in 1 Pet 2:4 (see the repetition of phrases there and in v. 10) and then continued in vv. 5–8.[81]

Allusions to this controlling metaphor of people of God are not limited to this important passage, however. In addition to such terms as "flock" (5:3; cf. 2:25: this is again language used of Israel in the OT) or "household of God" (4:17), there is the quotation of God's statement to Israel as his people: "You shall be holy, for I am holy." This phrase, as important as any contained in 2:4–10, occurs repeatedly in Leviticus (LXX 11:44, 45; 19:2; 20:7, 26) as the description of that characteristic of Israel that sets them apart from all other nations, and hence makes of them the chosen people (see esp. Lev

---

[77] See Karl Georg Kuhn, "*prosēlytos*," *TWNT* 6 (1959) 727–45, esp. 739. His discussion of the concept in the NT does not include any reference to 1 Peter, however.

[78] *prosagō* in 3:18 ("Christianity according to I Peter," 81); see "The Redemption in I Peter," 55–56, where he cites Josephus, *BJ* VII 45; *proserxomai* in 2:3 ("Redemption," 54, 56).

[79] In addition to 1:18–19, van Unnik ("Redemption," 68) finds "fifteen points at which we find traces reminiscent of proselytism," although he admits the cumulative effect is needed to be persuasive (*idem*). For his discussion of the material, including detailed consideration of Philo's material in particular, *De Specialibus Legibus* I 51–53, see 55–68.

[80] The same quotation is used the same way in Rom 9:25; it seems to have belonged to common Christian tradition. 1 Peter's dependence on Romans seems unlikely in light of the explicit inclusion of Jews in the new people in Romans (cf. 9:24).

[81] Elliott found the controlling metaphor (*oikos/paroikos*) in this passage, specifically from the reference to *oikos* in 2:5. *oikos* is surely important in 1 Peter, but a part of the larger metaphor of chosen people.

20:26, where this is made doubly explicit by the use of *aphorisas* as well as *agioi*). This statement not only grounds the ethical admonitions contained in 1 Peter, but also accounts for the priestly and sacrificial terminology in 2:5: only the special people can offer sacrifices acceptable to God. In terms of the controlling metaphor, those sacrifices now become spiritual sacrifices, the new sacrifice offered by the new people.

Terminology in 1 Peter other than that specifically related to Israel as people of God also points to the importance for our author of the Christian community as the new people of God. One of those terms is the word "gentile," used by the author of 1 Peter to designate those "outside" the Christian community. This use of the word is strange, since there is little question in the mind of most recent commentators that the readers to whom the letter is addressed are themselves neither Jews nor Christians of Jewish heritage; they themselves surely belong among the "gentiles."[82] Why would the author warn *gentiles* to avoid "*gentile behavior*" (2:12; 4:3; cf. 1:18)?[83] The answer is best given in terms of the controlling metaphor of the letter, namely, the people of God. The author has so immersed himself in this metaphor and thinks of the Christian community so totally in terms of Israel as chosen people that "outsiders" present themselves to him conceptually in terms of those who were outsiders for that chosen people, namely, the "gentiles."

The same logic was operating, I would urge, in the case of the opening of the letter, when the readers are addressed as members of the "diaspora." Again, the controlling metaphor has caused the author of the letter to understand his Christian readers in terms of Israel, and their status as strangers in their surrounding culture (1:1 *parepidēmois*—"displaced persons") presents itself to him as an analogy to those members of the chosen people who also

---

[82] This is conceded even by van Unnik ("The Redemption," 32) who argues for a pre-70 date for the letter; he finds 1:14 and 4:3 decisive on this score. For a review of the opinion of some who suggested Jewish Christian readers, see 71. Daniel J. Harrington ("The Church as a Minority Group," *God's People in Christ* [Philadelphia: Fortress, 1980] 81–94, esp. 83) finds 2:10 and the reference to "once you were no people" to be evidence for the conclusion that "Gentiles constituted a large part, if not practically the whole" of the original readership of the letter; see also Victor Paul Furnish, "Elect Sojourners in Christ: An Approach to the Theology of I Peter," *PSTJ* 28 (1975) 1–11, esp. 3.

[83] The rare adjective *patroparadotos* is not used either by Philo or Josephus; it is used by Christian authors (Clement of Alexandria *Paedagogus* 3.12.85; Origen *Commentarium in evangelium Matthaei* 16.8, both quoting 1 Pet 1:18; its use in Origen's *Fragmenta in Psalmos 1–150* 29.10, may also be drawn from the language of that verse; Theophilus of Antioch *Ad Autolycum* 2.34), as well as by secular writers (Diodorus Siculus *Bibliotheca historica* 4.8 ["ancestral piety"]; 15.74 and 17.2 ["ancestral way of thinking"]; 17.4 ["ancestral hegemony"]; Dionysius of Halicarnassus *Antiquitates Romanae* 5.48 ["ancestral status"]). Its use therefore tends to confirm that the readers are gentile rather than Jewish; the word to describe their former behavior is one drawn from outside the Jewish tradition.

lived as strangers within a surrounding culture, namely, members of the historic Diaspora.[84] This also explains the reference to "Babylon" at the close of the letter. The author shares with his readers the status of stranger in the surrounding culture, and the analogy again of the Jewish diaspora presents itself to his mind, this time in terms of the nation in which deported Jews were forced to dwell. References to the historic fate of Israel when it became dwellers in a foreign culture, the situation in which our author sees his readers, thus form an *inclusio* for the whole letter (*diasporas*, 1:1; *Babylōni*, 5:13), reinforcing the idea that "chosen people" forms the controlling metaphor for our author's understanding of the reality of the Christian community.

It is now possible to evaluate properly the significance of the phrase "exiles and aliens" (*paroikous kai parepidēmous*) which occurs in 2:11. This phrase as noted above[85] occurs, apart from in our letter, only in those writers influenced either by Genesis 23 or Psalm 38. In those passages, the phrase describes the progenitor of the chosen people, Abraham, as stranger in the very land God had promised to him (Gen 23:4), or the Psalmist (David, according to the superscription) who likewise was not at home in the place where he found himself (Ps 39:12; LXX 38:13). It seems evident, therefore, that this phrase is drawn not from the political arena of the Greco-Roman world to describe the political status of the readers both before and after their conversion, as Elliott had argued,[86] but rather is again chosen under the influence of the controlling metaphor, the chosen people, and applied to the Christians.[87]

A New People of God Constituted by the Christ Who Suffered (and Rose)

The third important element included by the author of 1 Peter in his

---

[84] M.-A. Chevallier ("Condition et Vocation," 398) argues that the author understands the Christian diaspora to be a prolongation of the Jewish diaspora, but for Christians it is presented not "comme une contingente et deplorable condition, mais comme une necessair et lumineuse vocation."

[85] See note 42.

[86] See note 38; *paroikos* would not have been a particularly appropriate word to describe people estranged from their surrounding culture, since there is good evidence that the word described a class of people whose status was recognized by the state, and whose names were contained in an official register; see Hans Schaefer, "Paroikoi," in Pauly-Wissowa, *Realencyclopädie der classischen Altertumswissenschaft* 36th halbband XVIII,4 cols. 1695–1707, esp. cols. 1698–99. Elliott cites this article, but does not interpret this information as I have.

[87] C. H. Talbert ("Once Again," 144), for example, agrees that the phrase is figurative language; M.-A. Chevallier ("Condition et Vocation," 394) affirms that according to our author the phrase is true of *all* Christians (emphasis his); D. J. Harrington ("The Church," 81) affirms that the phrase shows the author "drew upon imagery expressing ancient Israel's sense of peoplehood" to express the Christians' "own consciousness as a community."

understanding of the Christian community as an analogy to Israel as chosen people is the role played in constituting that new community by the Christ who suffered for sin. The author of course knew that Christ also rose from the dead, and it is in fact an important point for him (cf. 1:3), but the suffering of Christ plays a more developed role in the argument of the letter.

At key points in the letter, the author cites Christ who suffered as the example for those who follow him (2:21; 4:1; cf. 2:23; 4:13); because he suffered through no fault or failing of his own, so must the Christian be ready for that eventuality (2:19, 20a; cf. 4:19). Indeed, Christians must be prepared to suffer precisely because they do what is right (3:14; 3:17), again as was the case with Christ (3:18). Such suffering is therefore to be understood as part of the vocation of the Christian; it was predicted long before it occurred (1:11) and is now required of all Christians (5:9; cf. 5:10, perhaps also 5:1). To suffer for wrongdoing on the other hand falls outside the purview of Christian suffering; such suffering Christians are of course to avoid (4:15). Rather, they are to conduct themselves in such a way that the God they worship is praised for it (2:12; on good conduct, see also 1:15; 2:20b; 2:12; 3:2; 16).

What is interesting here for our purposes is the fact that where the vocation of Christians to suffer, following the example of Christ, is most clearly stated is in relation to the advice to household slaves (*oiketai*, 2:18–25). Not only are vocation and example explicitly stated (2:21), but the nature of Christ's suffering is given its most extended exposition (2:22–25). It is further interesting that that exposition is cast in language drawn from Isaiah 53, where the suffering servant, either Israel or its representative, is described (cf. 1 Pet 2:22 with LXX Isa 53:9; 2:24a with 54:4; 2:24c–25a with 53:9). It would appear once more that the controlling metaphor "people of God" has prompted the author to understand Christ as the model for Christian suffering, again in terms of that original chosen people.

What is even more instructive is that the description of exemplary Christian suffering, while here given as part of advice to household slaves, is not limited to them, as we saw above; such suffering is normative for Christian existence. Rather clearly, the slave has been chosen as an example of the kind of suffering that Christians, as members of that new people of God constituted by the suffering (and risen) Christ, are to expect as part of their Christian calling. In short, the slave is here a social metaphor for Christian suffering, but described in terms of the suffering Christ who constituted the new people of God, who is himself then described in terms of the larger metaphor of the people of God. The point is that just as a slave in that society could hardly avoid suffering, even unjust suffering, so the Christian in that society could expect a similar fate.[88]

The author deals in the same way with wives. While the ideal of modesty in apparel and decorum among women was widespread in the Greco-Roman world within which 1 Peter was written, as its absence was equally widely lamented,[89] the closest parallel to the language used in 1 Pet 3:3 is found not in such sources but rather in LXX Isa 3:18, 23.[90] Again, the example given for proper conduct comes from the OT, in this case Sarah (Gen 18:12). Even the forced nature of the citation points to the author's desire to find an example in the OT. It would appear therefore that our author is motivated here more by his controlling metaphor of the people of God, which led him to quote from the Scriptures of that people, than by any desire to find links with Hellenistic culture or urge Christians to accommodate their activity to its ideals.

Finally, the fact that this household code begins with comments on the behavior of all who live within the Hellenistic world (2:13–17), coupled with the choice of slaves (2:18–25) and wives (3:1–6), appears to be intended to serve as examples for those Christians who, like the three classes described, had no recourse but to suffer if they were abused. That is of course not to say there were no common people, slaves, or wives in the Christian communities being addressed, but the choice of classes and the language employed lead one to see them in terms other than their expected roles in Greco-Roman culture. Even the inclusion of husbands, and particularly the advice given them, is significant: the advice is not to maintain order,[91] but

---

[88] People of God as controlling metaphor thus makes Balch's thesis of the author's desire for Christians to seek accommodation with the Hellenistic world questionable at best.

[89] For the praise of women in this regard, see as examples Pliny *Letters* 4.19; Seneca "To Marcia on Consolation" 6.1; for the condemnation of those who showed no such characteristics, see as examples Tacitus *Annales* 3.34.54; 4.20; Juvenal *Satires* 6.362–65; 457–60, 501–11.

[90] In the NT, 1 Tim 2:9 is comparable in intent but not so much in vocabulary. The common notion that the differentiation between outer and inner beauty found in this passage was common parlance among 1 Peter's contemporaries is repeated by N. Brox (*Der erste Petrusbrief*, 145), who supports it with a citation of E. G. Selwyn (*The First Epistle*, 451 nn. 2, 3; Brox, n. 461). Selwyn cites only one reference to Jewish literature, Philo (*De migr. Abr.* 97), a fleeting reference at best, and two from Hellenistic literature, Plautus ("Mostellaria" 1.3.101–21) and Euripides ("Heraclidae" 476–77): the former speaks of the contrast in temporal sequence; the latter says silence befits a woman. More evidence than this will be necessary to demonstrate it a "common notion." On the other hand there are comments on excessive ornamentation in women in Greco-Roman sources, e.g., Seneca "To Helvetia on Consolation" 16.4; "On Benefits" 1.10.2; 7.9.4–5; Dio Chrysostom 7th (Euboean) Discourse 117, and on the abuses to which it led in the family, e.g., Juvenal *Satires* 6.501–11, but the vocabulary of 1 Pet 3:3 describing ornamentation is in fact closer to that of Isaiah than to that of such Hellenistic sources.

[91] That governing the wife was the husband's moral duty is implied by the natural order (e.g., Dio Chrysostom *Third Discourse on Kingship* 50, 62) and by the evil consequences that follow a wife's getting out of hand (e.g., Tacitus *Annales* 3.34; 4.20; Juvenal *Satires* 6.242–43, 475–80),

to regard their wives, though they are members of the "weaker sex,"[92] nevertheless as equal recipients of grace. Neglect of that conduct will lead to the husbands' forfeiture of communication with God (3:7c)! The only advice to a class in the position of ruling rather than being ruled is therefore not to use the power to dominate but rather to give it up in favor of equality.[93]

We here conclude our examination of the controlling metaphor of 1 Peter. That examination had consistently pointed is to the author's use of material from the OT, not surprising in light of the fact that the controlling metaphor itself is drawn from its contents. We have a final problem to consider, and that is the theme of the letter, which has led the author to frame his prose as he has and to make the points he does in terms of his controlling metaphor. It is to a consideration of that theme we must now turn.

The Theme of 1 Peter

While there have been discussions of the overarching theme or unifying concept(s) of 1 Peter, there has been no consensus established. Some scholars, principally those who regard the letter as a composite adapted from a baptismal homily or liturgy, have, not surprisingly, affirmed that 1 Peter has no unifying theme.[94] Others have spoken in terms of frequently occurring types of words or concepts, without seeking to determine the one word or concept that functioned as overall theme.[95]

There have been scholars, however, who have found unifying themes for 1 Peter. Some, for example, have argued for "hope" as the theme;[96] others

---

and is made explicit by direct command (e.g., Seneca [Moral Essays] "On Firmness" 1.1; Martial *Epigrammata* 8.12) as well as by the disdain shown for those peoples who allow women to rule (e.g., Tacitus *Annales* 14.11; *Agricola* 16; *Germania* 45).

[92] That women were by nature the weaker sex is virtually everywhere presumed in the Greco-Roman world; e.g., Tacitus *Annales* 3.34; Petronius *Satyricon* 110; Juvenal *Satires* 6.475–80; Seneca [Tragedies] *Hippolytus* 559, 563–64; *Octavia* 868–69; [Moral Essays] "On Anger" 3.24.3; Dio Chrysostom "74th Discourse: On Distrust" 9.

[93] This is further evidence against Balch's argument that the author of 1 Peter desires Christians to accommodate themselves to Hellenistic culture. It would be difficult to imagine any advice to husbands less in accord with the general tenor of Greco-Roman society, and hence less likely to foster accommodation to that culture than that given in 3:7.

[94] For example, F. W. Beare, *The First Epistle*, 8; a convenient summary of those holding this view is found in L. Goppelt, *Der erste Petrusbrief*, 37–40.

[95] R. W. Thurston ("Interpreting First Peter," 172) points out that words for suffering, hope, and obedience "occur very frequently"; M.-A. Chevallier ("Condition et Vocation," 390) finds as organizing concepts people of God, diaspora and election; cf. V. P. Furnish ("Elect Sojourners in Christ," 3–4) and E. G. Selwyn (*The First Epistle*, 64–115), who have discussions of leading concepts, which apparently serve in lieu of identifying a theme.

[96] E.g., N. Brox, *Der erste Petrusbrief*, 17; J. W. Thompson, " 'Be Submissive,' " 68; cf. John

have defined the theme in relation to suffering, namely as "comfort" for the persecuted[97] or as "advice" on how to act in such adversity.[98] The maintenance of social cohesion has also been proposed as the theme for the letter.[99] The problem is that each of these proposals can be defended with equal conviction on the basis of roughly the same evidence. In addition, each tends to overemphasize present (suffering, advice, cohesion) or future (hope)[100] in a letter that abounds with references to the past.

There are of course scholars who have noted the contrast between past and present and have emphasized its importance for the letter.[101] Indeed, the letter does abound with references to that contrast, to the extent that one may argue that in it we are to find the structuring theme of the letter. There are some nineteen passages in which this contrast is present. We may catalog them in the following way:

	Then	Now
Concerning Christ:		
1:20	destined	manifest
2:4	rejected by men	chosen, precious to God
3:22	went into heaven	powers subjected to him
Concerning Christ and readers:		
2:21	Christ suffered	readers suffer
2:24	Christ wounded	readers being healed
3:18	Christ dies	readers being brought to God
4:1–2	Christ suffered	readers live by God's will

Piper, "Hope as the Motivation of Love: I Peter 3:9–12," *NTS* 26 (1980) 212–31, esp. 213, 216–17.

[97] E.g., E. Lohse, "Parenesis and Kerygma," 50.

[98] D. Hill, "On Suffering," 189; cf. L. Goppelt, *Der erste Petrusbrief,* 41.

[99] This is the particular emphasis of Elliott; cf. "1 Peter," esp. 66–68; he also speaks (67) of conversion as a goal of such cohesion. He has been criticized by Balch ("Hellenization/Acculturation," 84) on this latter point.

[100] Hope is of course also a present reality, but its significance is dependent wholly on future events which will change the present hopeless conditions.

[101] W. C. van Unnik ("The Critique of Paganism in I Peter 1:28," *Neotestamentica et Semitica* [Fest. Matthew Black; ed. E. E. Ellis, M. Wilcox; Edinburgh: T. & T. Clark, 1969] 129–42, esp. 129) notes that this thematic contrast underlay the attempt to find in baptism and its results the key category for the letter; he also notes that contrast in "The Redemption," 64, 77. For further discussion of this contrast see also G. Delling, "Der Bezug der christlichen Existenz," 100, 109, 110; C. Wolff, "Christ und Welt," 335.

Concerning other biblical persons and readers:

1:10–12	Prophets spoke	events fulfilled
3:6	Sarah did right	readers to do right
3:20–21	Noah saved by ark	readers are saved by baptism

Concerning readers:

1:3	born (implied)	born anew
1:14	in ignorance	to be holy
1:18	futile ways	ransomed by Christ
1:23	born of perishable seed	born of imperishable seed
2:9	in darkness	in light
2:10	no people, no mercy	God's people, God's mercy
2:25	straying sheep	returned to shepherd
4:3	acted as Gentiles	no longer so act
4:4	joined Gentiles in profligacy	no longer join in
4:10	received gift	employ gift

It is apparent from such a table that the contrast of past and present runs throughout the entire letter, informing every aspect of it, kerygmatic as well as hortatory. Not only is the readers' own past brought into play, but the past of Christ and of other biblical characters as well. Yet major emphasis is on the readers' past, and it is given a negative evaluation. Such a stance was not one that would find favor in the eyes of non–Christians of that time, since value was to be found not in things that were new, but in things that were old. Such a stance would thus go completely counter to any kind of accommodation to Greco–Roman sensitivities. To be sure, the appeal to prophecy (1:10–12), to figures from the OT (Sarah, 3:6; Noah, 3:20), and to the antiquity of God's plan for Christ ("before the foundation of the world"; 1:20) would be appropriate for that ethos, but the negative description of past practices (e.g., *patroparadotos*, 1:18; cultural practices, 4:3–4) would cast suspicion on the faith that embodied such value judgments[102] and would go a long way to explaining the kind of negative social pressure reflected in 1 Peter.

Yet the contrast between past and present, important though it is, is not the only contrast. Equally important and equally widespread in this letter is the contrast between present and future.[103] There are some twenty references

---

[102] For a good discussion of *patroparadotos* in this context, see van Unnik, "The Critique of Paganism"; that old was preferred to recent, see Abraham J. Malherbe, *Moral Exhortation, A Greco-Roman Sourcebook* (Philadelphia: Westminster, 1986) 90; for a list of Hellenistic sources decrying a break with ancestral religion, see C. H. Talbert, "The Plan," 145.

[103] Despite occasional references to this as a key contrast (van Unnik, "Christianity according to I Peter," 83; D. W. Kendall, "The Literary and Theological Function," 113, 116), scholars for the most part simply acknowledge a future orientation for the letter: it has an eschatological

to such a contrast. They may be catalogued in the following way:

	Now	Then
Concerning Christ and readers:		
1:7	tested faith	praise, glory, honor at Christ's return
1:13	hope	revelation of Christ
Concerning God and readers:		
2:12	good conduct in the face of false accusations	glorify God on the day of visitation
4:11–12	employ gift	God glorified
5:6	be humble under God's mighty hand	God exalts you
Concerning readers:		
1:3–4	born anew	receive imperishable inheritance
1:5–6	trials	salvation
1:9	faith	salvation
2:2	long for milk	grow up to salvation
2:15	do right	put ignorance to silence
3:1	have disobedient husbands	with husbands
3:9	suffer wrong, not respond in kind	obtain blessing
3:10–11	do right	see good days
3:14	suffer for righteousness' sake	be blessed
4:12–13	suffer	rejoice as glory is revealed
4:17	judgment on house of God	judgment on those disobedient to gospel
5:2–4	tend flock well	obtain unfading crown of glory
Concerning others:		
4:4–5	gentiles live profligate lives	give account to judge
5:1	author a witness of suffering	partaker in glory revealed

(e.g., G. Delling, "Christliche Existenz," *passim*; M.-A. Chevallier, "Condition et Vocation," 396; J. W. Thompson, " 'Be Submissive,' " 73) or an apocalyptic dimension (e.g., E. Richard, "The Functional Christology," 130); the mention of hope (J. Piper, "Hope as the Motivation," 215) or of Christ's resurrection (E. Richard, "The Functional Christology," 132, 133; G. Delling, "Christliche Existenz," 112) or of glory (R. W. Thurston, "Interpreting First Peter," 181) also implies the future.

Again, it is apparent from this table that the theme of present/future also runs through the entire letter. The two are of course not unrelated. The formal parallelism between the past/present contrast and the present/future contrast informs the argument of the entire letter. The past/present contrast provides the reader with assurance that the present/future contrast will be as sure and as complete as the former has shown itself to be. Hence the great emphasis on that contrast between once and now, which serves to buttress the main intention of the letter, which is to strengthen the readers in the "now" of their suffering and persecution by assuring them that the future of glory will transform their present condition as surely as their present situation transformed them from their past. That is the burden of the exposition, the "kerygma." Closely allied to that is the exhortation not to revert to that past, lest in doing so they lose their future as well as their present. The corollary to that is the need to hold to the unpleasant present as the only path to the better future. That is the burden of the exhortation, the "parenesis." Both contrasts therefore inform and structure the kerygma and the parenesis of the letter and give it both its unity and its theological impact.

Some Conclusions

1 Peter, as we have seen, is to be read as a unity, written against the background of a hostile society for whom Christian values and behavior were interpreted as threats to the stability and religious welfare of Greco-Roman society. In this context, the author of this epistle took as metaphor for the struggling Christian communities to which he was writing the chosen people of the OT, the people of Israel.[104] Using that people and its history as controlling metaphor, the author both announced and encouraged behavior appropriate to the readers' situation. In each instance, the structure which he pursued is the comparison between past and present, with strong emphasis on the danger of reverting to past behavior, i.e., behavior in conformity with Greco-Roman norms of social and religious life. In that case, all that they had gained through their relation to Christ would be lost.[105]

---

[104] While this metaphor has on occasion been noted (e.g., M.-A. Chevallier, "Condition et Vocation," 391, 395; G. Delling, "Christliche Existenz," 97; K. R. Snodgrass, "I Peter II, 1–10," 106), it has not been understood as controlling metaphor, nor has it been combined with the dual contrasts between past and present, and between present and future. The understanding of the metaphors used in 1 Peter as we have developed them is in many ways an extension of the insights of J. H. Elliott, with the changes made necessary by our emphasis on "people of God" as the ruling metaphor.

[105] Once again, it would be hard to imagine (*pace* Balch) a structure less likely to be amenable to the notion that Christians must learn to accommodate themselves to the Greco-Roman culture within which they live.

Combined with that is the equally emphatic contrast between present and future, with strong emphasis on the need to maintain behavior appropriate to their Christian calling lest they lose the glory promised them as followers of Christ, a glory to be revealed when he returns.

The controlling metaphor and the structuring contrasts are of course not unrelated. Israel itself was constantly reminded of the significance of its present both in terms of its past and even more especially of its future. Israel itself faced the danger of reverting to practices unacceptable to the God who had called them. It too faced the danger of losing its promised future through activity in the present unacceptable to the God who had given them that promise. Again and again, from its conduct in the wilderness to its policies as a nation, Israel by its actions endangered its promised future. Therefore to be the chosen people in the OT meant always to be reminded of the danger of reverting to unacceptable behavior, which jeopardized the future God had promised them. It was therefore quite natural that when the author of 1 Peter took as his controlling metaphor the people of God, he should also take as the structure of his kerygma as well as his parenesis the contrasts of past/present and present/future and employ them as they had been employed in relation to that first chosen people, Israel. In that way, our author found the means to encourage and bear witness to his readers "of the true grace of God in which (they) stand" (5:12).

Chapter
16

The Structure and Composition
of the Matthean Beatitudes

Alexander A. Di Lella, O.F.M.
The Catholic University of America

Blessed are the peacemakers,
for they shall be called
children of God.
Matthew 5:9

THE AMOUNT OF MATERIAL that has been published on the Beatitudes in Matthew's Gospel is vast.[1] As one would expect, there has been considerable dispute about the origin, composition, form, function, and redaction of the Beatitudes. Even the extent of the Beatitudes has been the subject of debate: originally were there three, four, eight, or nine Beatitudes?[2] Most scholars today, however, view the eight Beatitudes in Matt 5:3–10 as a discrete unit; the ninth Beatitude (5:11–12), which is a shorter form (thirty-five words) of Luke's fourth Beatitude (6:22–23, fifty-one words), was not part of the original group.[3]

---

[1] Cf., e.g., the magisterial (and massive) study of J. Dupont, *Les Béatitudes: Tome I, Le problème littéraire: Les deux versions du Sermon sur la montagne et des Béatitudes* (2d ed., 1958); *Tome II, La Bonne Nouvelle* (2d ed., 1969); *Tome III, Les Évangélistes* (1973) (EBib; Paris: Gabalda, 1958–73); H. Frankemölle, "Die Makarismen (Mt 5,1–12; Lk 6,20–23): Motive und Umfang der redaktionellen Komposition," *BZ* 15 (1971) 52–75; R. A. Guelich, "The Matthean Beatitudes: 'Entrance-Requirements' or Eschatological Blessings," *JBL* 95 (1976) 415–34; and N. J. McEleney, "The Beatitudes of the Sermon on the Mount/Plain," *CBQ* 43 (1981) 1–13.

[2] Cf. R. A. Guelich ("The Matthean Beatitudes," 432) for a summary of his reconstruction of the redaction history of the present eight Beatitudes. For a different accounting of the redaction, cf. N. J. McEleney, "The Beatitudes," 10–13.

[3] Cf. J. Dupont (*Les Béatitudes*, 3. 312–16) for a discussion of those scholars who attempt to defend the theory that Matt 5:11–12 should be taken together with the eight Beatitudes. Dupont points out, correctly, that Matt 5:11–12 serves as a literary transition, which has as its purpose an appeal to the Christian community; hence the switch from the 3rd person (vv. 1–10) to the 2nd person (vv. 11–12). He writes: "Béatitude surnuméraire [vv. 11–12], elle forme ainsi le premier membre de la seconde partie de l'exorde du Sermon sur la montagne: après avoir été prévenus des persécutions dont ils auront à souffrir de la part des hommes, les disciples sont avertis qu'ils ont à remplir à leur égard un rôle comparable à celui du sel (v. 13) et à celui de la lumière (vv. 14–16)" (p. 315).

The Structure of the Beatitudes

The purpose of the present study is not to resolve disputed issues that have exercised scholars for years. The lack of consensus regarding the oral and literary prehistory of the Beatitudes, the history of their redaction, their order and arrangement in the Gospels of Matthew and Luke, etc., is itself a good indication that convincing and generally accepted solutions to these problems are not likely or possible with the currently available evidence. What I propose to do is quite modest. I shall point out several features about the structure and composition of Matt 5:3-10 that seem to have escaped the critical notice of exegetes. These features, I believe, may provide some empirical data on which hypotheses may be refined, modified, revised, or discarded.

Many authors have observed that the Matthean Beatitudes fall naturally into two sections or strophes: vv. 3-6 and vv. 7-10.[4] Each strophe has exactly thirty-six words.[5] Thus the eight Beatitudes have a total of seventy-two words.[6] But nobody seems to have noticed: (1) that each strophe has one Beatitude with six words, one with eight words, one with ten words, and one with twelve words (all even numbers); (2) that the makarioi-clause of each Beatitude in both strophes has three, five, or seven words (all odd numbers); and (3) that each hoti- clause also has three, five, or seven words. See the chart on the next page:

[4] Cf. ibid., 309-12.

[5] After I had discovered this count myself, I learned from J. Dupont (Les Béatitudes, 3. 309, n. 4) that a certain Wilhelm Weber had also made this observation.

[6] The number twelve is, of course, a significant (and often sacred) number in the NT: twelve patriarchs (Acts 7:8); twelve tribes of Israel (Matt 19:28; Luke 22:30; Acts 26:7; Jas 1:1; Rev 21:12); twelve apostles (Matt 10:1, 2, 5; 11:1, etc.); twelve stars on the head of the woman clothed with the sun (Rev 12:1); twelve years the woman suffered with a hemorrhage (Matt 9:20; Mark 5:25; Luke 8:43); twelve years, the age of Jesus in the Temple (Luke 2:42); twelve years, the age of Jairus's daughter (Mark 5:42; Luke 8:42); twelve hours in the day (John 11:9); twelve basketfuls of fragments (Matt 14:20; Mark 6:43; 8:19; Luke 9:17; John 6:13); twelve legions of angels (Matt 26:53); twelve gates in the wall of the new Jerusalem with twelve angels (Rev 21:12); twelve foundation stones (Rev 21:14); twelve crops a year from the trees of life (Rev 22:2); about twelve in the group of John's disciples at Ephesus (Acts 19:7). Apparently seventy-two (6 x 12) and thirty-six (3 x 12) were also meaningful symbolic numbers in the early Christian community. "The Lord appointed a further seventy-two and sent them in pairs [= thirty-six pairs] before him to every town and place he intended to visit" (Luke 10:1; cf. v. 17). Though the external evidence is evenly divided between "seventy-two" and "seventy" (cf. K. Aland et al. [eds.], The New Testament in Greek [3d ed.; New York: American Bible Society, 1975] 250, 252), I agree with K. Aland's argument (in B. M. Metzger, A Textual Commentary on the Greek New Testament [London: United Bible Societies, 1971] 151) that "seventy-two" is the better reading.

TOTALS

makarioi-clause			hoti-clause	

Strophe I

v. 3a	5 words	(12)	7 words	v. 3b
v. 4a	3 words	(6)	3 words	v. 4b
v. 5a	3 words	(8)	5 words	v. 5b
v. 6a	7 words	(10)	3 words	v. 6b

Strophe II

v. 7a	3 words	(6)	3 words	v. 7b
v. 8a	5 words	(10)	5 words	v. 8b
v. 9a	3 words	(8)	5 words	v. 9b
v. 10a	5 words	(12)	7 words	v. 10b

Thus there are three clauses with seven words, six clauses with five words, and seven clauses with three words. The symmetry and regularity of the word counts in this structure can hardly be accidental. This structure with its word counts provides *prima facie* evidence that the person responsible for the Matthean Beatitudes had in mind a clear and well-defined plan for formulating and arranging the present text of 5:3–10.

Support for this conclusion can be seen in vv. 3, 5, 6, and 10. In Luke (6:20) the first clause of the first Beatitude reads simply *makarioi hoi ptōchoi*, whereas in Matthew (5:3) the first clause has the additional words *tō pneumati* after *hoi ptōchoi*. This apparently peculiar feature has received a wide variety of explanations. Some scholars maintain that the phrase *tō pneumati* was appended in order to align the first Beatitude with "the poor," *ʿānāwîm*, of Isa 61:1.[7] Others hold that, on the basis of the analogous phrase *ʿanwê rûaḥ* in 1QM 14:7, *hoi ptōchoi tō pneumati* refers to an internal religious poverty that depends on God alone.[8] If, however, the structure (with its word counts) that I have observed was deliberately intended by the author of the Matthean Beatitudes, as I am convinced it was, then one of the reasons for the addition of the phrase *tō pneumati* was to give v. 3 the twelve words it would need in order to correspond to the twelve words in v. 10, with which it forms an

---

[7] Cf., e.g., E. Bammel, *"ptōchos, ptōcheia, ptōcheuō,"* TDNT 6 (1968) 888–89, 904; and R. A. Guelich, "The Matthean Beatitudes," 427. J. A. Fitzmyer (*The Gospel According to Luke [I-IX]* [AB 28; Garden City, NY: Doubleday, 1981] 632) writes: "By adding 'in spirit,' Matthew has adapted the original beatitude to the *ʿānāwîm* among the early Jewish Christians. . . ."

[8] Cf., e.g., S. Légasse, "Les pauvres en esprit et les 'volontaires' de Qumran," NTS 8 (1961–62) 336–45; E. Schweizer, *"pneuma . . . ,"* TDNT 6 (1968) 401; N. J. McEleney, "The Beatitudes," 5–6.

inclusio (see below). Moreover, it could be argued that *tǭ pneumati* was appended to suggest a connection as well as a contrast with *pneuma Theou*, "the breath [or wind] of God" that hovered over the waters of chaos (Gen 1:2) "before" creation (see below for other connections between the Matthean Beatitudes and Genesis 1). God's breath was all powerful, for it propelled the divine word to call into being and presence everything in the universe (Gen 1:3–31).[9] In contrast, *hoi ptōchoi tǭ pneumati*, "the poor in breath [or wind]," are those who have little power of their own and consequently must depend completely on God (cf. Matt 18:1–5; Mark 9:33–37; Luke 9:46–48).

The Beatitude in v. 5, *makarioi hoi praeis, hoti autoi klēronomēsousin tēn gēn*, is commonly admitted by scholars to derive from Ps 37:11; in the LXX (36:11) the text reads as follows: *hoi de praeis klēronomēsousin gēn* (cf. also vv. 9, 22, 29, 34). Note that *gēn* in Ps 36:11 is anarthrous, but in the Beatitude we find the expression with the article, *tēn gēn*. I submit the following reason for this: the author of the Beatitudes wanted to keep an odd number of words (five) in that clause as in every other clause of his composition. But there is a difficulty with v. 5 that must be addressed. Some scholars are of the opinion that the *praeis*-Beatitude may be a doublet of the first Beatitude (v. 3).[10] The reason, they argue, is that both *ptōchoi* and *praeis* seem to be translations of the same Hebrew word *'ănāwîm* in Isa 61:1; hence both Greek terms convey the same thought. In addition, Luke makes no mention of *hoi praeis* in his Beatitudes. However, though there is a problem regarding the relative position of the *praeis*-Beatitude (see below), there is no evidence at all that any of the textual witnesses omitted it. Consequently, there can be no reasonable doubt that v. 5 was an integral part of the Beatitudes. A further reason can be supplied for the inclusion of the *praeis*-Beatitude: its eight words were required for the sum of thirty-six words that comprise the first strophe. As I have indicated above, this structure of two strophes, each with thirty-six words, was intentionally conceived by the author.

In the fourth Beatitude, Matthew (v. 6) has *makarioi hoi peinōntes kai dipsōntes tēn dikaiosynēn*, whereas the parallel in Luke (6:21) has only *makarioi hoi peinōntes nyn*. Scholars have wondered why Matthew has the four extra words,[11] particularly since *dipsōntes* disrupts the *p*-alliteration found in the first clauses of the first four Beatitudes: *ptōchoi, pneumati, penthountes, praeis, peinōntes*.[12] I

---

[9] For arguments in defense of this interpretation of Gen 1:1–3, cf. A. A. Di Lella, "Genesis 1:1–10: A Formal Introduction to P's Creation Account," in *Festschrift M. Delcor*, AOAT 215 (1985) 129–32.

[10] Cf. J. Dupont (*Les Béatitudes*, 1. 251–55) for a thorough discussion, with bibliography, of this issue.

[11] Cf. N. J. McEleney, "The Beatitudes," 7–8.

[12] Cf. F. Michaelis, "Die *p*-Alliteration der Subjektsworte der ersten 4 Seligpreisungen in Mt V 3–6 und ihre Bedeutung für den Aufbau der Seligpreisungen bei Mt., Lk., und in Q," *NovT* 10 (1968) 148–61.

would say that one of the reasons, among many, that these four words were inserted is that they were necessary for the literary structure which the author had planned: seven words are required to give the first strophe thirty-six words to match the thirty-six words in the second strophe. Moreover, *dikaiosynēn* in the last Beatitude of the first strophe provides the *inclusio* with *dikaiosynēs* (v. 10a) in the last Beatitude of the second strophe. Note also that there is a double *inclusio* between the first Beatitude (v. 3) and the eighth Beatitude (v. 10): each Beatitude has twelve words, and the *hoti*-clause in each is exactly the same (*hoti autōn estin hē basileia tōn ouranōn*).

In the eighth Beatitude *dikaiosynēs* (v. 10a) is anarthrous whereas in the fourth Beatitude we find *tēn dikaiosynēn* (v. 6a). The reason for this, I submit, is that in v. 6a the article was necessary to get seven words, but in v. 10a the article before *dikaiosynēs* would have given us six words instead of the five the author needed in order to preserve the odd number of words in the clause and the total of thirty-six words in the strophe.

The Textual Problem

A closer look at the above structure may provide some evidence even for the textual problem regarding the relative position of the Beatitudes in vv. 4 and 5. The majority of the textual witnesses have the present order of the verses, i.e., *hoi penthountes* before *hoi praeis*. But an impressive number of important and early witnesses (the Alexandrian MS 33, Clement, Origen, Eusebius, Hilary, Basil, Gregory of Nyssa, Jerome, and Ammonius; the Western group: MS D, most MSS of the Old Latin, the Vulgate, Curetonian Syriac, and several witnesses of the Diatessaron, Aphraat, and Ephrem; and many MSS of the Caesarean group: 700 565 28 544 543) place the *praeis*-Beatitude (v. 5) before v. 4. Many of these witnesses go back to the second century.[13] Thus, the external textual evidence for preferring one arrangement over the other is not conclusive. The majority of scholars seem to favor the present arrangement of these two Beatitudes. But some scholars (e.g., Tischendorf, Lagrange, and Benoit in *La Bible de Jérusalem*[14] and also in its English counterpart *NJB* [1985] have concluded that v. 5 should precede v. 4. An argument for this arrangement can be seen in the following table that shows the chiastic patterning of the number of words in the Beatitudes when arranged with v. 5 before v. 4:

v. 3	12 words		6 words	v. 7
v. 5	8 words		10 words	v. 8
v. 4	6 words		8 words	v. 9
v. 6	10 words		12 words	v. 10

---

[13] Cf. J. Dupont, *Les Béatitudes*, 1. 252; and K. Aland et al. (eds.), *The Greek New Testament*, 11–12.

[14] Cf. J. Dupont, *Les Béatitudes*, 1. 252.

Another argument is that v. 3 with *tōn ouranōn* would then be followed by *tēn gēn* in v. 5, exactly the order of these nouns in the phrase *ton ouranon kai tēn gēn* found at the beginning and again at the end of the first creation account (Gen 1:1 and 2:4a). I might add that the reason why the author has given us eight Beatitudes instead of seven (one of the most sacred and cherished numbers of the Bible) may be that he took the number from the eight works of creation in Genesis 1. What he suggests in the Beatitudes, therefore, is that there are eight conditions that are met by members of the new order of creation, the kingdom of heaven inaugurated by Jesus.

A further point of contact between the Beatitudes and Genesis 1 can be seen in the choice of the verb *chortasthēsontai* in the fourth Beatitude (v. 6) at the end of the first strophe. The verb *chortazein* occurs only fourteen times in the entire LXX. Hence one could rightly wonder why this relatively rare verb was employed instead of the frequently occurring verb *(em)plēsthēsontai* (cf. Luke 6:25; John 6:12), especially since *empimplanai* and *pimplanai* are the most commonly used verbs in the LXX to render Hebrew *sb'*, "to be filled, satisfied" (cf., e.g., Exod 16:12; Lev 26:26; Deut 6:11; 8:10, 12; 14:29; 26:12; 31:20; Ruth 2:14, 18; Neh 9:25; Pss 21(22):26; 62(63):5; 77(78):29; 89(90):14; 104(105):40; Prov 12:11, 14; 18:20; 28:19). The reason why the author selected the verb *chortasthēsontai* may be that it is cognate with the noun *chortou*, "green crops," in LXX Gen 1:11–12. It is noteworthy that the phrase *botanēn chortou* occurs precisely in the account of the fourth work of creation, a work that concludes the first panel of the literary diptych comprising the eight works of creation in Genesis 1, just as *chortasthēsontai* occurs in the fourth Beatitude, which concludes the first strophe.

A final argument for making v. 5 the second Beatitude and v. 4 the third is that the verb *paraklēthēsontai* (v. 4b) would then be in the penultimate Beatitude of the first strophe to match the cognate verb *klēthēsontai* (v. 9b) in the penultimate Beatitude of the second strophe.

Conclusion

Though there is nothing earthshaking in what I have proposed here, the empirical facts I have observed and the interpretations I have offered may help scholars avoid the subjectivity and circular arguments one occasionally finds in discussions of the Beatitudes in Matthew and Luke. If there is any merit in the word counts, structures, and other points I have noted, then these should be taken seriously in the study of the literary history and redaction of the Beatitudes.

Chapter
17

The Theology of 1 Thessalonians as a Reflection of Its Purpose

Karl Paul Donfried
Smith College

1 Thessalonians is a λόγος
παραμυθητικός to a Christian
congregation suffering the
effects of persecution.

I. Introduction

DURING PAUL'S BRIEF ORIGINAL VISIT to Thessalonica, which following the chronology of John Knox[1] we would place in the early forties of the first century A.D., he aroused such hostility (Acts 17:1–9; 1 Thess 2:13–16) that he was forced to leave hurriedly. During both Paul's presence and his absence it was argued that he and his message were dangerous and fraudulent; such a critique would be equally valid from either a Jewish or a Roman perspective.[2] Following his hurried departure the persecution of his followers intensified.[3]

Paul writes this letter to the Thessalonian Christians in order to (1) console them and to encourage them to stand firm during continued persecution. Thus, we understand 1 Thessalonians not primarily as a "paraenetic" letter[4] but as a "paracletic" letter,[5] as a

---

[1] *Chapters in a Life of Paul* (New York and Nashville: Abingdon-Cokesbury, 1950) 86; see also Gerd Lüdemann, *Paulus, der Heidenapostel* I (FRLANT 123; Göttingen: Vandenhoeck & Ruprecht, 1980) 272.

[2] We understand συμφυλέτης in a local rather than in a racial sense. Thus, this reference by no means excludes those Jews who instigated the persecutions in Thessalonica. See further Karl P. Donfried, "The Cults of Thessalonica and the Thessalonian Correspondence," *NTS* 31 (1985) 336–56, especially on this point, 348.

[3] For the further details of this argument see Donfried, "Cults."

[4] Paul never uses the verb παραινέω, it is found only in Acts 27:9 and 22. For the position that 1 Thessalonians is a paraenetic letter see Abraham J. Malherbe, "1 Thessalonians as a Paraenetic Letter" (an unpublished seminar paper given at the 1972 meeting of the Society of Biblical Literature) and also his "Exhortation in First Thessalonians," *NovT* 25 (1983) 238–56.

[5] Note the frequent occurrence of this word group: 1 Thess 2:12, 13; 3:2; 4:1, 10; 5:11, 14. Interestingly enough there are only two occurrences in 2 Thess (2:16 and 3:12).

243

consolatio.[6] But in order to carry out effectively this purpose he must also (2) defend the message he proclaimed while present as originating from God and, therefore, as valid, and (3) defend himself against charges made concerning his motivation and behavior.

II. Persecution

A. External Witnesses

The theology of 1 Thessalonians is about a God who is present among his elect and suffering people and about a God who is leading them to their promised salvation. The theological themes found in the letter are a response to situations created by persecution and martyrdom as well as to the problem of living the Christian life in the midst of a pagan culture. Although the recent monograph by John S. Pobee[7] supports a position similar to the one we outlined in our 1984 SNTS lecture,[8] viz., that 1 Thessalonians is a church under attack, this has not been the usual interpretation of 1 Thessalonians to date.[9] Therefore it will be useful to review certain external data, that is, data other than 1 Thessalonians: (1) the evidence found in 2 Cor 8:1–2; (2) the witness of Acts 17:1–9; and (3) the relationship of Jewish theologies of martyrdom to the theology of 1 Thessalonians.

1. *2 Cor 8:1–2*

In these verses Paul commends the generosity of the churches in Macedonia despite their present condition: ἐν πολλῇ θλίψει. This reference is significant because it supports unequivocally the fact that there was a severe external threat present to the churches in Macedonia and that θλίψις is not simply a term indicating general eschatological woes as some would argue for 1 Thessalonians. Further, it seems improbable that Paul would be referring to the Macedonian churches and not have very clearly in mind the Thessalonian

---

[6] A further discussion of this genre will follow later in this essay.

[7] *Persecution and Martyrdom in the Theology of Paul* (JSNT 6; Sheffield: JSOT Press, 1985) esp. 13.

[8] Donfried, "Cults," esp. 347–52.

[9] There are notable exceptions, of course. Willi Marxsen writes: "Ich lasse es hier offen, wodurch es zur Verfolgung gekommen ist. Sicher aber ist, dass es eine Verfolgung gegeben hat. Die Frage, vor der nun die junge Gemeinde steht, lautet: Lohnt es sich denn überhaupt, Christ zu sein, wenn das in solche Bedrängnis führen kann? Wenn mann als Christ in der Gefahr steht, die bürgerliche Existenz—und mehr—zu verlieren, dann hört mann doch besser (wieder) auf die Goëten. Ich glaube . . . das wir es hier mit der Zentralfrage des ganzen Briefes zu tun haben" ("Auslegung von 1 Thess 4,13–18," *ZTK* 66 [1969] 24).

church,[10] which was a congregation located in the capital of the Roman province and which according to 1 Thessalonians itself (1:7) became an example to all the believers in Macedonia and beyond.

2. *Acts 17:1–9*

The account in Acts 17 of Paul's activities in Thessalonica informs us that the Jews together with some persons from the *agora* attacked the home of Paul's sponsor, Jason, with the hope of accusing Paul and his associates before the politarchs. Verses 6 and 7 continue that "when they could not find them, they dragged Jason and some of the brethren before the city authorities, crying, 'These men who have turned the world upside down have come here also, and Jason has received them; and they are all acting against the decrees of Caesar (τῶν δογμάτων Καίσαρος), saying that there is another king, Jesus.' " Elsewhere we have suggested that Luke is, in general, faithfully describing the reality of the Thessalonian situation.[11] We have also attempted to explain what might be meant by the term δογμάτα Καίσαρος.[12] In all likelihood the politarchs in Thessalonica were responsible for administering an oath of loyalty and for dealing with violations of this oath. Given the hostility of the Jews toward Paul and the unusually strong civic cult active in the city, there would have been present in Thessalonica an environment particularly hostile to Paul's proclamation of the Christian gospel. Finally, the reference to the politarchs λαβόντες τὸ ἱκανόν may well refer to some decision whereby it was agreed that Paul must leave the city immediately and not return.

3. *The Relationship between the Theology of Martyrdom in Judaism and 1 Thessalonians*

Paul's theology is apocalyptic theology modified by the Christ event.[13] Or to use the words of Beker, the coherent center of the gospel is located in the "apocalyptic interpretation of the Christ event." And thus "the *character* of Paul's contingent hermeneutic is shaped by his apocalyptic core in that in nearly all cases the contingent interpretation of the gospel points—whether implicitly or explicitly—to the imminent cosmic triumph of God."[14] It is precisely this perspective which dominates Paul's *consolatio* to the persecuted Thessalonian Christians.

---

[10] So also Victor Furnish, *II Corinthians* (AB 32A; Garden City: Doubleday, 1984) 400.

[11] Karl P. Donfried, "Paul and Judaism: 1 Thessalonians 2:13–16 as a Test Case," *Int* 38 (1984) 247; "Cults," 342ff.

[12] Donfried, "Cults," 342ff.

[13] Donfried, "Paul," 242–53.

[14] J. Christian Beker, *Paul the Apostle* (Philadelphia: Fortress Press, 1980) 18–19.

If there is to be an imminent cosmic triumph of God, there must be a battle raging at present. In much apocalyptic literature the forces of Satan are at war against the forces of God as, for example, in Dan 10:13ff. In fact, the presence of Satan is felt to be so real that it is often argued that Satan inhabits the persecutors.[15] This idea of a cosmic battle presently in progress appears to be reflected in 2:18 and 3:5. This latter verse indicates that the present is not only a time of persecution but may also be a time of apostasy, a feature which commonly occurs in the Jewish literature of persecution.

There are other related aspects of the Jewish theology of martyrdom found both in apocalyptic literature and beyond which have the possibility of illuminating a variety of themes found in 1 Thessalonians. Pobee has demonstrated that the martyr in biblical literature is characterized by three elements: (1) suffering which might or might not include death; (2) suffering as a witness to the martyr's zeal and devotion to God; and (3) a conviction about the omnipotence and transcendence of God.[16] These factors are summarized by the term *hallul hashem*, "sanctification of the Holy Name." Such was the obligation of every Jew who lived among the Gentiles. *Midrash Ps* 68.13, for example, compares Israel to a dove because she does not struggle when "they are slaughtered for the sanctification of the Name."

It is noteworthy that ἁγιασμός appears three times in 1 Thessalonians (4:3, 4, 7) and only three other times in the remainder of the Pauline corpus (Rom 6:19, 22; 1 Cor 1:30) and that ἁγιάζειν, used in 1 Thess 5:23 is found only in four other places in Paul (Rom 15:16; 1 Cor 1:2; 6:11; 7:14). It is possible that the use of this idea in discussions about Jewish persecution provided one of the reasons why it was useful for Paul to stress the theme of "sanctification" in 1 Thessalonians. Further, when Pobee observes that the "martyr was the zealot, who by his suffering advertised his God,"[17] one immediately recognizes remarkable resemblances to the thought world of 1 Thessalonians, especially to 1:7–8 and in a more limited sense to 4:10. If for Paul suffering was an advertisement for God then it followed especially that the situation of persecution was no excuse for moral laxity[18] or any behavior which would allow the non-Christian world to ridicule the work of God in Thessalonica.[19] Linked with this theme is the entire concept of reward and punishment found in both the Jewish martyriological literature and in 1 Thessalonians (5:9, ὅτι οὐκ ἔθετο ἡμᾶς ὁ θεὸς εἰς ὀργὴν ἀλλὰ εἰς περιποίησιν

[15] See, for example, 1 Kgs 22:26; *Ass. Mos.* 10:1; *Mart. Isa.* 1:8–9; 2:4–5, 8; 3:11; 4:2–3; 5:1; 7:9–10; 1QS 1:17–18; 3:23; Dan 7:2ff.; *1 Enoch* 89f.

[16] Pobee, *Persecution*, 30.

[17] Ibid.

[18] This situation provides another reason why Paul uses the term ἁγιασμός.

[19] It is for this reason that Paul includes in this *consolatio* the exhortations found in 1 Thess 4:1–12.

σωτηρίας διὰ τοῦ κυρίου ἡμῶν 'Ιησοῦ Χριστοῦ). From these selected examples it should be apparent that Paul is addressing a context quite similar to that addressed by this type of Jewish literature.[20]

B. Paul's Understanding of and Involvement with Persecution

The fact that Paul suffered and was persecuted for his apostolic work is beyond question. In addition to the important texts in 1 Thess 2:1–4, 13–16, and 3:7, there is the evidence of 2 Cor 4:7–12,[21] 2 Cor 11:23–33, Gal 6:17, and Phil 1:20.[22] Pobee's conclusion is one to which most Pauline scholars would assent, viz., that Paul's "persecution and sufferings were a *sine qua non* of Paul's apostolic ministry."[23]

The issue for us is not, then, whether Paul was persecuted; the issue rather is how Paul understood those sufferings. Was his attitude that of the Stoics, who taught that one should accept afflictions cheerfully, with fortitude and with thanks?[24] Seneca, for example, writes: *nihil aeque magnam apud nos admirationem occupet quam homo fortiter miser.*[25] He even argues that to suffer affliction can serve as an example to others.[26]

We would suggest that the apparent similarities between Paul and the Stoics at this point are at best superficial. The Stoics understand affliction as part of accepting fate;[27] for Paul, suffering is part of the cosmic struggle which is leading to God's triumphant victory. Whereas for the Stoics divinity is understood in terms of reason as the world principle,[28] for Paul God is the one who through Christ has inaugurated the imminent redemption of the created order. Thus, on the one hand, accepting persecution is a sign of

---

[20] A similar point is made in the first three chapters of Revelation: God will redeem those disciples and martyrs who do his will even though the entire world is disintegrating. Only after such obedience has been stressed in the Christian congregations of Asia Minor does the author proceed with his message of comfort and hope to those who are persecuted because of their discipleship. See further on this theme, K. P. Donfried, *The Dynamic Word* (San Francisco: Harper & Row, 1981) 187–96.

[21] On this text as well as the overall theme of suffering in Paul, see the new work by Scott J. Hafemann, *Suffering and the Spirit* (Tübingen: Mohr, 1986).

[22] A further discussion of these and related texts (such as Rom 8:17ff. and its use of πάσχειν) may be found in Pobee, *Persecution*, 93–98.

[23] Pobee, *Persecution*, 106.

[24] Seneca, *Ad Marciam* 24; *Ad Polybium* 2.1.5; *Epist.* 96.6; Cicero, *Disp. Tusc.* 3.32.77. See also the essay by R. Liechtenhan, "Die Ueberwindung des Leides bei Paulus und in der zeitgenössischen Stoa," *ZTK* 3 (1922) 368–99, esp. 377ff.

[25] Seneca, *De Consolatione* 13.6. See also his *Ad Polybium* 16.2; 1.4; and *Epist.* 21.33.

[26] *Ad Polybium* 5.4.

[27] Seneca, *Ad Marciam* 21.4.

[28] Cicero, *Tusc.* 2.21.47.

obedience to the gospel; on the other hand, accepting it with joy is a gift of God given through the Holy Spirit.

Although Paul's attitude of accepting persecution with joy (1 Thess 1:6) might be more appropriately compared with the Jewish martyrological literature where accepting sufferings with joy is an established motif,[29] there is a distinctive difference. For Paul, joy in any situation, especially in one involving persecution, is always an eschatological gift of the Spirit. It is rooted in faith and nurtured by the hope of God's imminent triumph. It is the result of a conscious relationship between the believer and Christ. No matter how difficult the immediate moment, the believer is always enabled to transcend this situation through prayer which allows the disciple to be strengthened through the eschatological gifts of the Spirit. Since these theological motifs permeate all of 1 Thessalonians, it is quite natural for Paul to write these words toward the end of his letter (5:16–19): Πάντοτε χαίρετε, ἀδιαλείπτως προσεύχεσθε, ἐν παντὶ εὐχαριστεῖτε, τοῦτο γὰρ θέλημα θεοῦ ἐν Χριστῷ Ἰησοῦ εἰς ὑμᾶς. τὸ πνεῦμα μὴ σβέννυτε. . . . For Paul, then, suffering and affliction only make sense in the context of God's eschatological revelation in Jesus Christ.

C. Persecution and the Thessalonian Church

In addition to the similar context between 1 Thessalonians and that of the Jewish persecution literature, as well as the clear indications of persecution found in 2 Cor 8:1–2 and Acts 17:1–9, we must now examine both the explicit and the implicit terminology in 1 Thessalonians which point to a situation which affected the Christian church in that city.

1. Explicit Terminology

a. 1:6: Καὶ ὑμεῖς μιμηταὶ ἡμῶν ἐγενήθητε καὶ τοῦ κυρίου, δεξάμενοι τὸν λόγον ἐν θλίψει πολλῇ μετὰ χαρᾶς πνεύματος ἁγίου.

If the Acts account of Paul's initial visit to Thessalonica is correct, as 1 Thess 2:13–16 would indicate, then it is clear that Paul's message had as its consequence immediate hostility from the Jews. This was brought to the attention of the politarchs who at the outset already took limited action against the followers of Paul. Thus Paul reminds the Thessalonian Christians about two things: when they first became Christians they did so under the most adverse conditions and that in doing so they already experienced the eschatological joy given by the Spirit. Their present situation of persecution

---

[29] 4 Macc. 10:20–21; 1:18–23; 3 Macc 4.1; Josephus, Ant. 2.299.

should not surprise them since it is in direct continuity with the original context out of which their faith arose. In addition, Paul reminds them in 3:4 that he had forewarned them of precisely this type of future.

1:6 also reminds the hearers that as they suffer for the faith, they are not only imitators of Paul, Silvanus, and Timothy, but also of the Lord. Here Jesus serves as the prototype of the martyr, a theme that is then further developed in 2:13–16.[30] Yet we must ask even more precisely in what way the Thessalonian Christians were imitators of Paul and Jesus. The δεξάμενοι clause serves as an explanation of the imitation and Pobee is to be followed when he concludes that "the content of the imitation is the fact of accepting affliction and persecution along with receiving the word of God. The point is the martyr spirit in which they accepted affliction with patience for the sake of God. Their endurance of affliction has proven them to be zealous of the Lord."[31] Contrary to other usage of the imitation motif in Greek or Jewish literature, imitatio Christi for Paul is not primarily a paraenetic emphasis but a literal one.[32]

b. 2:13–16: Ὑμεῖς γὰρ μιμηταὶ ἐγενήθητε, ἀδελφοί, τῶν ἐκκλησιῶν τοῦ θεοῦ τῶν οὐσῶν ἐν τῇ Ἰουδαίᾳ ἐν Χριστῷ Ἰησοῦ, ὅτι τὰ αὐτὰ ἐπάθετε καὶ ὑμεῖς ὑπὸ τῶν ἰδίων συμφυλετῶν καθὼς καὶ αὐτοὶ ὑπὸ τῶν Ἰουδαίων, τῶν καὶ τὸν κύριον ἀποκτεινάντων Ἰησοῦν καὶ τοὺς προφήτας καὶ θεῷ μὴ ἀρεσκόντων καὶ πᾶσιν ἀνθρώποις ἐναντίων, κωλυόντων ἡμᾶς τοῖς ἔθνεσιν λαλῆσαι ἵνα σωθῶσιν, εἰς τὸ ἀναπληρῶσαι αὐτῶν τὰς ἁμαρτίας πάντοτε. ἔφθασεν δὲ ἐπ' αὐτοὺς ἡ ὀργὴ εἰς τέλος.

---

[30] Note Cerfaux's observation on this theme in 1:6: "Can this be understood without reference to the human, or rather superhuman courage of Jesus in his passion? Have we not here the first model which is set up for our imitation—a model which is really human? . . . By accepting death Christ has set us an example (see Rom. 15.3)" (L. Cerfaux, Christ in the Theology of St. Paul [London, 1959] 182–83).

[31] Pobee's analysis of this verse in general is helpful. "The internal construction of the sentence permits two interpretations of the δεξάμενοι clause: (a) it explains μιμηταί, i.e. 'in that you received the word with much affliction, with joy inspired by the Holy Spirit'; or (b) it supplies the antecedent fact and ground of the imitation, i.e. 'after that or inasmuch as you had received. . . .' The obvious parallelism between the two parts of the verse will be destroyed unless the δεξάμενοι clause is taken as a participle of identical action. Also, the use of the two aorists, ἐγενήθητε and δεξάμενοι, in the two parts of the sentence suggests that the two are co-extensive action and the latter explicative of the former" (Persecution, 69–70).

[32] Against Malherbe, "Exhortation," 246ff.; see also Hans-Heinrich Schade, Apokalyptische Christologie bei Paulus (GTA 18; Göttingen: Vandenhoeck & Ruprecht, 1981) 118–26; see further Martin Buber, "Imitatio Dei" in Israel and the World (New York, 1963) 66ff.; J. Schoeps, Aus frühchristlicher Zeit: Religionsgeschichtliche Untersuchungen (Tübingen, 1950) esp. chap. 13; Xenophon, Mem. 1.63: οἱ διδάσκαλοι τοὺς μαθητὰς μιμητὰς ἑαυτῶν ἀποδεικνύουσιν; Letter of Aristeas, 188, 210, 281; 4 Macc 9:23.

As we have shown in detail elsewhere,[33] these verses are not a later gloss but were included by Paul intentionally. That he is dependent on tradition and formulaic material is without question, but that alone cannot be used as an argument for a later addition to the original Pauline text. Thus we understand these verses as an important and integral part of this earliest extant Christian document.

To understand 2:13–16 we need to pay careful attention to 1:6–9a. "The themes of 'imitation' and 'affliction' from those earlier verses are taken up and expanded in 2:13ff., where the behavior of the Thessalonian converts is contrasted to that of the Jews. The Thessalonians accepted the word of the apostles as the Word of God and it is therefore at work (ἐνεργεῖται) in them; the Jews in Judea (and the unbelieving Jews in Thessalonica) did not receive the apostolic proclamation as the Word of God but as the word of men. Thus, it is not at work in them, and as a result a negative description of these unbelievers is made in 2:15–16. As the Thessalonian Christians had welcomed Paul, so the Jews hindered Paul and his associates from speaking to the Gentiles. The Thessalonian church became a model for the churches not only in becoming imitators of Paul, Silvanus, and Timothy, but also in imitating the faithful endurance of the churches in Judea that were persecuted by the Jews. As the Thessalonians became an example for all the believers in Macedonia and in Achaia, so had the churches in Judea become a model for the Thessalonians. The believers in Judea and in Thessalonica had become examples of God's salvation which rescues "from the wrath to come" (1:10) whereas the unbelieving Jews had become objects of God's wrath (2:16). This is summarized at the end of the letter: "For God has not destined us for wrath, but to obtain salvation through our Lord Jesus Christ . . ." (5:9). To summarize: by following the use of the thanksgiving theme in this letter, we note how the general thanksgiving of chapter 1 is further specified in chapter 2 with regard to suffering/affliction (cf. 3:4) and in chapters 3 and 4 with regard to the problem of hope (ἐλπίς); suffering and hope are two of Paul's main concerns in this letter to the Thessalonian congregation."[34]

If we understand τῶν ἰδίων συμφυλετῶν in a local rather than racial sense, viz., as not excluding the Jews who instigated the persecution,[35] then "it makes perfectly good sense for Paul to draw a parallel between the situation of the Thessalonian church with that of the churches in Judea and to show that in both situations the Jews hindered the process of speaking to the Gentiles. Paul, having just recently experienced this rebuke at the hands of the

[33] Donfried, "Paul."
[34] Ibid., 246–47.
[35] Ibid., 248.

Thessalonian Jews, and being aware of the ongoing afflictions of the Thessalonian church (3:3–4), turns to a preexisting tradition in his denunciation of the Jews in Judea and Thessalonica."[36]

c. 3:3: τὸ μηδένα σαίνεσθαι ἐν ταῖς θλίψεσιν ταύταις. αὐτὸ γὰρ οἴδατε ὅτι εἰς τοῦτο κείμεθα.

Here we find another clear reference to the existential situation of the Thessalonians: continuing persecutions. Paul, most anxious to know how they are coping under these circumstances, sent Timothy (3:1–2) εἰς τὸ στηρίξαι ὑμᾶς καὶ παρακαλέσαι ὑπὲρ τῆς πίστεως ὑμῶν so that no one would be "beguiled away" from the faith. Chadwick [37] points to the original meaning of the hapax legomenon σαίνεσθαι as "to wag the tail," "fawn," or "flatter." Pobee suggests that its later metaphorical use as "to deceive" or "beguile" may be another of the several martyrological motifs found in 1 Thessalonians. Since beguiling is the work of Satan the use of this verb may be pointing directly to the present persecution as the work of Satan (2:18; 3:5).[38]

d. 3:4: καὶ γὰρ ὅτε πρὸς ὑμᾶς ἦμεν, προελέγομεν ὑμῖν ὅτι μέλλομεν θλίβεσθαι, καθὼς καὶ ἐγένετο καὶ οἴδατε.

Paul reminds the Thessalonian Christians that, in addition to the persecution they experienced upon accepting the gospel, he and his coworkers warned them that suffering at the hands of their fellow citizens would continue. Therefore what they are now experiencing should not be unnecessarily unsettling since it does not come as an unannounced surprise.

2. Implicit Terminology

Now that it has been established that Paul is in fact writing to a church which had and continues to be confronted by persecution, we can examine certain texts in 1 Thessalonians which confirm the same state of events, although more implicitly than the texts just reviewed.

a. 1:4: εἰδότες, ἀδελφοὶ ἠγαπημένοι ὑπὸ θεοῦ, τὴν ἐκλογὴν ὑμῶν.

The phrase τὴν ἐκλογὴν ὑμῶν is of particular interest. Ἐκλεκτός/ἐκλογή/

---

[36] Ibid., 248. For a further discussion of these conclusions see now the further elaboration in Pobee, Persecution, 35, 39ff., 70–71, 88–89.

[37] Henry Chadwick, "1 Thess. 3.3, σαίνεσθαι," JTS 1 (1950) 156–58.

[38] Pobee, Persecution, 136, n. 1.

ἐκλέγεσθαι language is not frequent in Paul[39] and always emphasizes God's initiative in choosing. The point in 1 Thess 1:4 is again to mitigate any surprise in the continued persecution of the Christians. Surely God who has chosen them is aware of their present and future suffering; this is part of the cosmic battle which leads to the ultimate triumph of God. Paul's emphasis here is quite parallel to that in Rom 8:33, τίς ἐγκαλέσει κατὰ ἐκλεκτῶν θεοῦ; θεὸς ὁ δικαιῶν, as well as to the verses that follow.[40] Thus, this widespread apocalyptic theme is used by Paul to assure the Thessalonians that the God who has selected them is the God who is the Lord of all history and who is in process of bringing it to conclusion. Persecution, then, is no cause to lose hope in God's forthcoming victory. The Holy Spirit is already present in their midst in the form of the eschatological gift of joy (1:6) and is at work in them through the gospel (2:13, ἐνεργεῖται ἐν ὑμῖν τοῖς πιστεύουσιν). We would thus agree with von Dobschütz's analysis: "Die Erwählung . . . ist für P. immer ein übergeschichtlicher, vorzeitiger Akt, der mit der πρόθεσις dem göttlichen Vorsatz Röm 9.11, 8.28, dem προορίζειν der göttlichen Vorbestimmung Röm 8.29f. zusammengehört als die Garantie der Heilsgewissheit; die Berufung κλῆσις ist davon zu unterscheiden als der geschichtliche Akt, durch den Gott seinen Heilsratschluss verwirklicht, indem er die Gnadenbotschaft wirksam an die Erwählten herantreten und das Evangelium bei ihnen Glauben wecken lässt—diese beiden Momente bringen v. 5 und v. 6 zum Ausdruck."[41]

b. 1:7: ὥστε γενέσθαι ὑμᾶς τύπον πᾶσιν τοῖς πιστεύουσιν ἐν τῇ Μακεδονίᾳ καὶ ἐν τῇ 'Αχαΐᾳ.

The Thessalonians have become an example (τύπος) precisely in having received the word in much affliction and presumably for having remained steadfast in the faith despite much suffering. Thus, they are *now* a model or pattern for the other congregations in Macedonia and Achaia to follow. This stands quite in contrast to the used of the words μιμητής and τύπος in 1 Cor

---

[39] ἐκλεκτός: Rom 8:33; 16:13; ἐκλογή: Rom 9:11; 11:5, 7; ἐκλέγεσθαι: 1 Cor 1:27–28.

[40] E.g., v 35: "Then what can separate us from the love of Christ? Can affliction (θλῖψις) or hardship . . . ?"; v. 39b: "nothing in all creation . . . can separate us from the love of God in Christ Jesus our Lord."

[41] Ernst von Dobschütz, *Die Thessalonicher Briefe* (MeyerK; Göttingen: Vandenhoeck & Ruprecht, 1974) 69–70. Similarly Holtz, "Denn wie das Folgende zeigt, blickt ἐκλογή auf das Geschehen, durch das die Erwählung sich ereignete, Gestalt gewann, wirklich wurde" (Traugott Holtz, *Der Erste Briefe an die Thessalonicher* [EKK 13; Neukirchen-Vluyn: Neukirchener, 1986] 45), and Rigaux, "L'élection et la vocation nous semblent deux facettes d'une même réalité: l'entrée concrète dans la réalisation du plan divin" (B. Rigaux, *Saint Paul: Les Épîtres aux Thessaloniciens* [EBib; Paris: Gabalda, 1956] 372).

4:16; 11:1; and Phil 3:17 where those congregations *are being urged* to become imitators; in 1 Thess 1:6–7 the Thessalonians *have already become* imitators of Jesus and Paul, not only by believing but by believing despite persecution, and thus they can serve as a model for other congregations. Once again it is apparent how persecution is a key factor in understanding the Thessalonian church and why Paul can hold them up as an example to be followed.[42]

c. 2:18: διότι ἠθελήσαμεν ἐλθεῖν πρὸς ὑμᾶς, ἐγὼ μὲν Παῦλος καὶ ἅπαξ καὶ δίς, καὶ ἐνέκοψεν ἡμᾶς ὁ σατανᾶς.

In our discussion of σαίνεσθαι above we stated that since "beguiling" is the work of Satan, the use of this verb in 3:3 may be pointing directly to the present persecution in Thessalonica as the work of Satan. If that is indeed the case then the term ὁ σατανᾶς in 2:18 may well refer to an agent of Satan, presumably an official of the Roman government, who is responsible for the persecution in Thessalonica, the expulsion of Paul and the prohibition of his further reentry into the city.[43]

d. 3:5: διὰ τοῦτο κἀγὼ μηκέτι στέγων ἔπεμψα εἰς τὸ γνῶναι τὴν πίστιν ὑμῶν, μή πως ἐπείρασεν ὑμᾶς ὁ πειράζων καὶ εἰς κενὸν γένηται ὁ κόπος ἡμῶν.

1 Thess 3:5, as we noted above, indicates that the present is not only a time of persecution but may also be a time of apostasy and, further, that this theme of apostasy is common in the Jewish literature of persecution. We have also pointed out that in this literature the presence of Satan is experienced with such reality that often it is argued that Satan inhabits the persecutors themselves. Thus whether ὁ πειράζων refers to the local source of persecution or to Satan himself is not a critical question since in this literature a sharp

---

[42] This interpretation would thus disagree with Holtz when he states: "Man wird aus einem solchen Satz keine Rückschlüsse nach beiden Richtungen ziehen dürfen, also auch auf die Situation der Glaubenden, denen die Thessalonicher zum 'Vorbild' geworden sind" (*Thessalonicher,* 50). For an exegesis parallel to ours see Willi Marxsen, *Der erste Brief an die Thessalonicher* (Zürcher Bibelkommentare; Zurich: Theologischer Verlag, 1979) 38–39.

[43] A similar understanding of this verse is articulated by Pobee, who states: "That temporary ban on his missionary activities in Thessalonica Paul considered the work of Satan. Second, since the Jews had had a hand in the situation, fomenting the trouble which cut Paul's ministry short, their action was the work of Satan, on which God's wrath is later pronounced. Whatever the historical detail, the opposition to Paul's active ministry at Thessalonica that led to his enforced departure and continued absence from Thessalonica was interpreted as the work of Satan. This is the martyrological motif which interprets persecution and martyrdom as part of the cosmic battle between the forces of God and the forces of evil" (Pobee, *Persecution,* 99). Some of the other options in understanding this phrase are given by Rigaux, *Thessaloniciens* 462. Holtz argues a position which is extreme: "Da Paulus nicht sagt oder auch nur andeutet, welcher Mittel Satan sich für sein Werk bedient hat, ist jeder Versuch, sie zu bestimmen, hoffnungslose Raterei."

distinction between Satan and his specific manifestations is often not made. That even for Paul Satan can be the specific source of temptation is evident from 1 Cor 7:5 (ἵνα μὴ πειράζη ὑμᾶς ὁ σατανᾶς), although there the context is sexual and not one of apostasy. That "the tempter" in 1 Thess 3:5 is clearly related to their afflictions is apparent from the wider context, especially verses 3 and 4.[44]

e. 4:13: περὶ τῶν κοιμωμένων . . .

Elsewhere we have suggested that the dead who are referred to in 1 Thess 4:13-18 are those who may have died in some mob-action type of persecution in Thessalonica. There we said:

It is important to ask why this issue concerning the "dead in Christ" (οἱ νεκροὶ ἐν Χριστῷ, 4:16) is so central to the letter, and, further, we must ask whether it is possible to identify those who have fallen asleep (τοὺς κοιμηθέντας, 4:14). F. F. Bruce makes a bold suggestion: ". . . perhaps those who 'fell asleep' so soon (I Th. iv. 13) were victims of this persecution [the ones referred to in Acts 17]."[45] Bruce's suggestion is an unorthodox one in view of the fact that few scholars[46] discuss the matter of death by persecution this early in Christian history. Yet there are a number of items which could give positive support to Bruce's suggestion: 1. The use of κοιμόω in Acts 7.60 is remarkable: "And as they were stoning Stephen, he prayed, 'Lord Jesus, receive my spirit.' And he knelt down and cried with a loud voice, 'Lord do not hold this sin against them.' And when he had said this, he fell asleep (ἐκοιμήθη)." In this text the verb κοιμόω refers explicitly to one who has suffered death through persecution. 2. In 1 Thess 2.14- 16 . . . Paul makes a very clear parallel between the situation of the Thessalonian church and that of the churches in Judea; they "became imitators of the churches of God in Christ Jesus which are in Judea" and they "suffered the *same things*" (τὰ αὐτὰ ἐπάθετε) from their countrymen and that clearly involves the dimension of death (2.14-15). 3. The Thessalonian congregation became an example to all the believers in Macedonia and in Achaia precisely because they "received the word in much affliction . . ." (1 Thess 1.6-8). Further they became "imitators"

---

[44] Marxsen (*Thessalonicher,* 55) is correct: "Wären die Thessalonicher, um den Bedrängnissen zu entgehen, zu einem nicht von Christus geprägten Wandel ausgewichen, hätte sich darin gezeigt, dass sie dem Versucher erlegen sind. Dann wäre die Arbeit des Paulus in nichts zerfallen."

[45] F. F. Bruce, *The Acts of the Apostles* (Grand Rapids: Eerdmanns, 1951) 327-28. Unfortunately, Bruce does not mention this suggestion in his new commentary, *1 & 2 Thessalonians* (Word Biblical Commentary 45; Waco, TX: Word, 1982). This interpretation is found at least as early as 1911 in Kirsopp Lake, *The Earlier Epistles of St. Paul* (London, 1911) 88, where in referring to 4:14 he thinks it probable "that it means martyrdom rather than a natural death. . . ."

[46] Perhaps W. H. C. Frend, *Martyrdom and Persecution in the Early Church* (Oxford: Blackwell, 1965) 83.

of Paul, Silvanus and Timothy (1 Thess 1.6) in suffering, a theme which Paul articulates in 2.2: "but though we had courage in our God to declare to you the gospel of God in the face of great opposition (ἐν πολλῷ ἀγῶνι)." Paul uses this same term, ἀγών, only once again, in a very similar context, in Phil 1.30. It is precisely in this first chapter of Philippians that the apostle expresses "full courage" so that "Christ will be honored in my body, whether by life or by death" (Phil 1.20) and it is in this same letter that Paul once again expresses the possible nearness of death: "Even if I am poured as a libation upon the sacrificial offering of your faith, I am glad and rejoice with you all" (Phil 2.17). Most commentators are agreed that Paul is alluding to the possibility of his own death as a martyr;[47] Lohmeyer goes even further than this when he suggests that Paul and the congregation are bound together in this threat of martyrdom. Referring to Paul's anticipated trip to Philippi he remarks: "Es ist eine Reise zum Martyrium, genauer zu der dauernden persönlichen Vereinigung von Apostel und Gemeinde im Martyrium."[48]

The question which, of course, arises in light of these suggestions is their persuasiveness: is it probable that the afflictions and persecutions[49] in Thessalonica could lead to occasional deaths?[50] When Paul in Romans 8:35–36 speaks of tribulation, distress, persecution, famine, nakedness, peril, and sword and then cites Ps 44:23, "For thy sake we are being killed all the day long; we are regarded as sheep to be slaughtered," is he merely speaking rhetorically? Otto Michel reminds us of an important point: "Die Aufzählung der Bedrängnisse wird bekräftigt durch das Schriftwort Ps 44.23. Das Rabbinat hat Ps 44.213 gern auf den Zeugentod (II Makk 7) gedeutet, und dies Getötetwerden galt im Judentum als Erweis echter Gottesliebe."[51] We are hard pressed to see that Paul had any other intention in mind.[52]

This suggestion concerning the identity of the dead in 1 Thess 4:13–18 is, in our judgment, a reasonable hypothesis. Given our inclination to take seriously the possibility of persecution(s)[53] in Thessalonica and elsewhere as leading to occasional death, do we have any extrabiblical evidence which

[47] Joachim Gnilka, Der Philipperbrief (HTKNT 10/3; Freiburg: Herder, 1968) 154–55; J. B. Lightfoot, Saint Paul's Epistle to the Philippians (London: Macmillan, 1891) 118–19; Ernst Lohmeyer, Der Brief an die Philipper, an die Kolosser und an Philemon (MeyerK; Göttingen: Vandenhoeck & Ruprecht, 1963) 217.

[48] Lohmeyer, Philipper, 111.

[49] See also 2 Thess 1:4.

[50] We certainly do not wish to imply any systematic persecutions.

[51] Otto Michel, Der Brief an die Römer (MeyerK; Göttingen: Vandenhoeck & Ruprecht, 1963) 217.

[52] Donfried, "Cults," 349–50.

[53] "Persecution" may be a somewhat misleading term and we should be pleased to find a more precise alternative. We have in mind neither systematic nor necessarily official persecution, but rather isolated and sporadic "mob actions."

would lend further credibility to this suggestion? The Paphlogonian oath of loyalty to the Caesarian house in 3 B.C.[54] compels Romans and non-Romans alike to report cases of disloyalty and to physically hunt down the offenders. The seriousness by which this oath is meant to be taken—even to the point of death for those who are disloyal—is clear. If this possible parallel has any relevance for the political situation in Thessalonica at the time of Paul, then certainly the Apostle's "political preaching" and his direct attack on the *pax et securitas* emphasis of the early principate was likely to place him in precarious situation.

In his publication subsequent to our 1984 SNTS lecture, John Pobee has independently reached the identical conclusion concerning the identity of οἱ κοιμώμενοι. Stressing with Nestle-Aland[26] the correctness of reading here the present rather than the perfect participle, Pobee concludes that the meaning of this present participle is that "there is a reference to the continued and protracted persecution of Christians at Thessalonica which was taking the lives of some Christians."[55]

Pobee also raises an important question concerning the interpretation of the following phrase in 4:14: καὶ ὁ θεὸς τοὺς κοιμηθέντας διὰ τοῦ 'Ιησοῦ ἄξει σὺν αὐτῷ. The issue is whether διὰ τοῦ 'Ιησοῦ goes with κοιμηθέντες which precedes or with ἄξει which follows. If the διὰ τοῦ 'Ιησοῦ is to be taken with the second half then there is an element of redundancy in the σὺν αὐτῷ phrase. Pobee is to be followed in reading οἱ κοιμηθέντες διὰ τοῦ Χριστοῦ[56] and in understanding the διὰ as expressing attendant circumstance.[57] We fully follow Pobee's conclusion with regard to this phrase when he states that it "refers to the Christians who died in their zeal for Jesus as was demonstrated by their patient endurance of persecution, before the parousia of Christ. The attendant circumstances of the death were the persecutions raging in the church of Thessalonica."[58]

III. Paul's Defense of the Gospel

It is truly remarkable to note the significant emphasis Paul places on the theme of "the word" and "the gospel" in this brief letter, the combination of

---

[54] Donfried, "Cults," 342–44.

[55] Pobee, *Persecution*, 113.

[56] Other scholars joining διὰ τοῦ 'Ιησοῦ to τοὺς κοιμηθέντας include Ephraim, Chrysostom, Calvin, Lightfoot, von Dobschütz, Dibelius, and Frame; although their understanding of διὰ τοῦ 'Ιησοῦ is certainly not identical.

[57] Pobee, *Persecution*, 113–14. See also the detailed discussion of this issue in James E. Frame, *Epistles of St. Paul to the Thessalonians* (ICC; Edinburgh: T. & T. Clark, 1912) 169–70, and especially his citation of Musculus: "The faithful die through Christ, when on his account they are slain by the impious tyrants of the world."

[58] Pobee, *Persecution*, 114.

which is probably unparalleled in his other letters when calculated proportionate to their length. Λόγος, when referring specifically to the Word of God, appears in 1:5, 6, 8; 2:13; and 4:15, 18. Εὐαγγέλιον appears in 1:5; 2:2, 4, 8, 9; and 3:2. When one observes the heavy concentration of occurrences in 1 Thess 2:1–9 it may not be amiss to conclude that Paul's apology is essentially an apology for the gospel.[59]

Nils Dahl has drawn attention to a phenomenon in 1 Thessalonians which he has referred to as "superfluous rehearsals." What he has in mind here are the repetition of the οἴδατε (and related) phrases throughout the letter, examples of which can be found, for example, in 1:5; 2:1, 2, 5, 9, 10, 11; 3:3b–4; 4:1, 2, 6, 10, 11; and 5:1.[60] Why does Paul make such frequent reference to this phrase? At issue in Thessalonica is the validity of the gospel he preached. From our previous discussion we know that a frontal assault has been launched against its veracity. As a result Paul must defend this gospel in two ways. First, he must defend it as a message originating from God. Second, and more particularly, he must bring to recollection the specific elements of his preaching and reemphasize their validity lest they be regarded as irrelevant for the situation in Thessalonica. Thus, all the οἴδατε phrases in the letter are not simply to be regarded as "superfluous rehearsals" but as key elements in Paul's defense of the gospel he preached and presented to the Thessalonians during his initial visit. We would thus suggest that the overall defense of the gospel is intimately linked with the steady rehearsal of his gospel as valid.

There is another factor which needs to be considered in this context. It appears as if Paul's defense of his message as truly a word of God and the repetition and new application of his previous proclamation and teaching, pave the way for the new and decisive information and consolation which he is about to give in 4:13–18. What is presented here is ἐν λόγῳ κυρίου. This new information attempts to console the Thessalonian Christians at a most neuralgic point: some of them have died for the faith and now some are about to jettison a critical dimension of their faith, viz., hope. Paul's word of consolation would be worthless if he had not first attempted to demonstrate the validity of his prior preaching. Only then can the word of the Lord here presented as new information be considered as an effective response to the problem of death caused by persecution.

---

[59] See Willi Marxsen, "Auslegung von 1 Thess," 22–37, who quite rightly argues that these verses are an apology for the *gospel*. A similar point is made by A. Suhl, *Paulus und seine Briefe: Ein Beitrag zum paulinischen Chronologie* (Gütersloh: Mohn, 1975) 99.

[60] For a more complete analysis of this phenomenon see Donfried, "Cults," 347–49.

IV. Paul's Defense of His Behavior

1 Thess 2:1–12 has been interpreted in the most varied ways.[61] Given our understanding of 1 Thessalonians, we would argue that it is impossible for Paul to defend his message as a word of God unless he also defends the integrity of the messenger himself. Since not only Paul's gospel but also his person is under attack in Thessalonica, both must be defended.[62]

Critical is this question: out of what context does Paul make his defense of gospel and messenger? Although Dio Chrysostom, for example, shares certain common phrases and language with Paul in distancing himself from the less than honorable popular wandering philosophers, that should not lead to the conclusion that the context of both is the same or that Paul is not involved in a real "Auseinandersetzung" with those who have falsely challenged his veracity and integrity.[63] One should not overlook the fact that the self-understanding of Paul and Dio are radically different. Paul is influenced by the conceptual world of Old Testament prophecy and the normative criteria of the true prophet which involves not only the content of teaching as deriving from God but also involves the moral behavior of the prophet as one accountable and acceptable to Yahweh.[64] The fact that in 2:6 Paul refers to himself and his two coworkers as "apostles" does not nullify this point. We would argue that it is Paul's understanding of his prophetic role which informs his developing understanding of apostolate, an understanding which is still in its infancy in 1 Thessalonians.[65] Paul, operating out

[61] See the literature cited by Collins, *Thessalonians*, 183–91.

[62] Quite correctly Holtz (*Thessalonicher*, 94): "Denn mit dem Boten steht und fällt die Botschaft."

[63] See here Abraham J. Malherbe, "Gentle as a Nurse: The Stoic Background of 1 Thess ii," *NovT* 12 (1970) 203–17. As illuminating as Malherbe's work is, the following comments by Holtz are relevant: "Indessen ist die Analogie deshalb nicht überzeugend, weil Dio tatsächlich popularphilosophischer Wanderprediger war ... und das natürlich auch wusste, während Paulus das nicht war und das ebenfalls wusste. Dio redet letzlich in eigener Autorität und musste sich daher zunächst aufbauen. Aufgrund genereller Erfahrung (die natürlich Malherbe anerkennt, 215f) konnte er das aktuell nur in Abgrenzung gegen andere Leute seiner Art tun. Paulus aber brauchte von der Sache und von der Autorität her, auf die er sich berief, eine generelle Verwechselung nicht zu fürchten. So muss eine Abgrenzung einen aktuallen Anlass haben" (Traugott Holtz, *Thessalonicher*, 93, n. 422).

[64] Literature on this theme includes: J. Murphy-O'Connor, *Paul on Preaching* (London & New York: Sheed & Ward, 1964) 104ff.; J. M. Meyers and J. D. Freed, "Is Paul Among the Prophets," *Int* 20 (1966) 40–53; David Hill, *New Testament Prophecy* (London, 1975) 111f.; James Dunn, "Prophetic 'I' Sayings and the Jesus Tradition: the Importance of Testing Prophetic Utterances within Early Christianity," *NTS* 24 (1977–78) 175–98; Collins, *Studies*, 183–85.

[65] One needs to be careful not to read Paul's later understanding of his apostolate in this early period. Although in our judgment Ernest Best ("Paul's Apostolic Authority," *JSNT* 27 [1986] 3–25) understates the importance of Paul's apostolic self-understanding in general, his criticism of the other extreme is urgently needed.

of a *prophetic context*, uses certain language also present in the popular rhetoric of the day to clarify to the Thessalonians the radical difference between himself and certain of the charletan-type popular philosophers.[66]

A. M. Denis and Traugott Holtz[67] have attempted to show the influence of Deutero-Isaiah on Paul's thought. Holtz is more interested in the influence on Paul's theology as a whole. Thus, for Holtz, the background of Gal 1:15, Paul's call to be an apostle to the Gentiles is to be found in Isa 49:1 and the interpretative background for Paul's understanding of suffering, as for example in 2 Cor 4:8ff., is to be found in Isa 50:5–7 as well as in Isa 49:4 and 7.[68] Denis is more concerned with the influence of Deutero-Isaiah on 1 Thess 2:1–6 and suggests that terms and phrases such as παράκλησις (e.g., 57:18; 66:11), ἀκαθαρσία (Isa 52:1, 11), δόλος (Isa 53:9), and ὅτι οὐ κενὴ γέγονεν (Isa 59:4) are rooted in this prophetic book. In general these observations move in a right direction, especially the observations about the use and function of παράκλησις in Second Isaiah.[69]

Earlier we suggested that 1 Thessalonians has some elements in common with the genre *consolatio* (λόγος παραμυθητικός) in classical literature. Since Isaiah 40ff. is such a book of consolation,[70] it is little wonder that we would find striking similarities between it and 1 Thessalonians. Paul's intention in writing 1 Thessalonians is not much different from Second Isaiah's announced intention in 40:1: Παρακαλεῖτε παρακαλεῖτε τὸν λαόν μου, λέγει ὁ θεός.

Where we would differ from Malherbe[71] is not by denying that there are paraenetic elements in 1 Thessalonians but in denying that this is the overriding genre. Much closer to Paul's intention is the genre *consolatio*,[72] a genre

[66] At this point one should be somewhat more cautious than Collins when he states that Paul's "language and his self-image . . . are a product of his double roots" (Collins, *Thessalonians*, 191). Are both equally important?

[67] A. M. Denis, "L'Apôtre Paul, prophète 'messianique' des Gentils. Etude thématique de 1 Thes., II,1–6," *ETL* 33 (1957) 245–318; Traugott Holtz, "Zum Selbstverständnis des Apostels Paulus," *TLZ* 91 (1966) 322–30.

[68] "So wird bei Deuterojesaja das Vorbild für das paulinische Leidensverständnis zu suchen sein." Holtz, "Selbstverständnis," 325 and 330.

[69] Earle Ellis suggests that παράκλησις has a particular connection with Christian prophecy even when that relationship is not explicitly indicated. See E. Earle Ellis, "The Role of the Christian Prophet in Acts," in *Apostolic History and the Gospel* (ed. W. W. Gasque and R. P. Martin; Exeter: Paternoster Press, 1970) 55–67.

[70] For example, John L. McKenzie, *Second Isaiah* (AB 20; Garden City: Doubleday, 1973) 16–17: "The opening words have given the Book of Second Isaiah the title of 'Book of Consolation.' Second Isaiah is much more than a book of consolation, but this is certainly a dominant theme."

[71] Malherbe, "Exhortation."

[72] For a brief discussion of the genre and further literature, see the article "Consolatio" in *The Oxford Classical Dictionary* (Oxford: Clarendon, 1970) 279. Also, Leichtenhan, "Ueberwindung des Leides bei Paulus" 368–99, esp. 371ff. and now the discussion in the new publication by Stanley Stowers, *Letter Writing in Greco-Roman Antiquity* (Philadelphia: Westminster, 1986).

which, along with many other subcategories, includes paraenesis. 1 Thessalonians is a λόγος παραμυθητικός to a Christian church suffering the effects of persecution. Παραμυθεῖσθαι is used only in 1 Thess 2:12 and 5:14 within the Pauline corpus. In fact the advice given in 5:14, παραμυθεῖσθε τοὺς ὀλιγοψύχους, is not far from the mark in describing the intention of the letter as an encouragement to the discouraged. They are discouraged precisely because "hope" has become disengaged from their faith.[73] The preservation of Thessalonians in the canon is a testimony to its effectiveness in correcting by encouragement this situation of hopelessness among some in the church of Thessalonica.

[73] See further Donfried, "Cults," 347–48. Also related to these remarks are the following comments made by W. Marxsen in connection with 1 Thess 4:13–18, "Auslegung," 32: "Aber es geht hier nicht darum, ob die Heiden Vorstellungen von der Zukunft haben, sondern darum, ob ihre ἐλπίς in der πίστις begründet ist. Die λοιποί haben deswegen keine Hoffnung, weil ihnen die πίστις und damit der Grund für die ἐλπίς fehlt. So kann die λύπη angesichts von Todesfällen in der Tat charakterisiert werden als ein ὑστέρημα τῆς πίστεως."

The New Testament Papyrus
Manuscripts in Historical Perspective

Eldon Jay Epp
Case Western Reserve University

The nineteenth Century is
the age of inscriptions;
the twentieth will be
the age of papyri.

Theodor Mommsen

I HAVE TWO MAJOR INTERESTS in NT textual criticism: history and method. These may appear to be two separate interests, but I have never been able to keep them apart. Methodology in NT textual criticism is informed by its history, and its history, in turn, is informed by the study of method. This interaction of history and method is integral to this brief and somewhat simple paper, for the question that intrigues me is this: If the NT papyri are considered to be so extraordinarily important by virtually all textual critics, then why was their importance really not recognized—or at least not widely recognized—for something like 50 or 60 years after the first discoveries? In exploring this issue, the intertwining of history and method will be both obvious and extensive.

This paper, then, has a simple thesis and a limited purpose. The thesis is that the NT papyri were surprisingly underappreciated until about 20 years ago, and the purpose is to attempt an explanation for this claim, as well as to shed some light both on the history of NT textual criticism and on text-critical theory. In the process, it will be of interest to ask, for example, what papyri were known at various critical points in NT text-critical work, to what extent they were utilized by researchers and editors, and how important they were at various historical junctures.

Theodor Mommsen (1817–1903), the great nineteenth-century classical scholar and winner of the Nobel Prize for literature in 1902—the year before his death—referred to the nineteenth century as "the age of inscriptions"; "the twentieth," he said, "will be the age of papyri."[1] Certainly this prediction was "on target" for the ancient world generally, but no less so for the NT text— particularly from our present perspective near the end of that twentieth century. Yet, our understanding of the significance of the papyri for NT textual criticism cannot be complete unless we have walked, step by step and year by year, through the period of their discovery, use, and eventual triumph. This journey begins with a general account of the use of papyrus in antiquity, which will provide background and perspective for our subject.

The Ancient Use of Papyrus and Its Modern Rediscovery

Anyone vaguely familiar with antiquity knows how the freshly cut lower stem of the papyrus plant can be peeled off in long strips, which are placed side by side—slightly overlapping—and are then covered by another set of strips laid crosswise, and how several blows from a broad mallet or a flat stone fuse the two layers together into a sheet, which, when dried and polished with pumice, produces a writing material that is light-colored, strong, flexible, and durable.[2]

Durability, of course, is a relative term. Yet, those who doubt the strength and flexibility of the papyrus stems need only be reminded of the papyrus sailing ships built and used by Thor Heyerdahl in his attempt to replicate those of antiquity. Heyerdahl's second ship, the *Ra II*, was constructed of eight tons of papyrus, held together only by rope. As many will recall, in 1970 it completed the 3,270-mile trip from Morocco to Barbados in 57 days. A year earlier the first ship, the *Ra I*, broke apart 600 miles short of its goal, but the failure was due not to the papyrus itself but to an inferior, segmented method of construction.[3] We know that light skiffs were made of papyrus in Egypt already in the 4th dynasty (around 2600 B.C.), as, for example, were sails

---

[1] E. G. Turner, *Greek Papyri: An Introduction* (Oxford: Clarendon Press, 1968) 23.

[2] Ibid., 3; H. Idris Bell, *Egypt from Alexander the Great to the Arab Conquest: A Study in the Diffusion and Decay of Hellenism* (Oxford: Clarendon Press, 1948) 6–7. For the *locus classicus* on the making of papyrus in antiquity (Pliny, *Natural History* xiii.74–82), see the text, commentary, and discussion in Naphtali Lewis, *Papyrus in Classical Antiquity* (Oxford: Clarendon Press, 1974) 34–69.

[3] Thor Heyerdahl, "The Voyage of *Ra II*," *National Geographic Magazine* 139 (January, 1971) 44–71, esp. 46–47.

and, in 480 B.C., the cables for a bridge of boats across the Hellespont.[4] The Egyptian tombs also yield examples of papyrus rope.[5]

When prepared as a writing material, papyrus retained these same characteristics of strength and flexibility, contrary to the long-standing and popular misconception that it was an especially fragile substance, which certainly — it is said — was inferior in durability to parchment. One striking confirmation that this is a misconception was the discovery that the Qumran leather scroll of Samuel (4QSam^a) had been strengthened on the back with a strip of papyrus, thereby significantly aiding the scroll's preservation. We know also that papyrus manuscripts already 250 years old were used again for new documents in the first century B.C.[6]

Papyrus does, however, become fragile when it has been alternately wet and dry. If this occurs repeatedly, papyrus disintegrates at the slightest touch.[7] Actually, papyrus manuscripts survive only when protected from moisture, either by placement in protective caves, buildings, or jars, or when buried in ordinary ground in the virtually rain-free areas of Egypt, Palestine, and Mesopotamia — provided, however, that they are neither too close to the surface, nor too deeply buried so as to be affected by water rising from below.[8] Incidentally, the new high dam at Assuan and increased irrigation will result in the gradual raising of the water-table, not merely in the immediate area, but throughout Egypt, and — most regrettably — the continued survival of any buried papyrus is thereby forever threatened.[9]

Unfortunately, too, the conditions necessary for the survival of papyrus did not prevail in the vast Delta area of Egypt, including Alexandria, which contained the greatest library of the ancient world and was a city with extensive literary activity. Ancient Alexandria, in fact, is now below sea level.[10] Moreover, blowing sand often defaces papyrus text, and white ants may devour papyrus manuscripts.[11] With all of these natural hazards — ancient and modern — it is remarkable that any considerable quantity of papyrus has survived.

---

[4] *Encyclopaedia Britannica* (1972) 19.614a; 17.296c.

[5] Ibid., 19.614a. A full account of uses of papyrus in antiquity can be found in Lewis, *Papyrus in Classical Antiquity*, 21–32; 95–97.

[6] T. C. Skeat, "Early Christian Book-Production: Papyri and Manuscripts," *Cambridge History of the Bible, Volume 2: The West from the Fathers to the Reformation* (ed. G. W. H. Lampe; Cambridge: University Press, 1969) 59–60.

[7] Turner, *Greek Papyri*, 3.

[8] Ibid., 18.

[9] Ibid , 40.

[10] Bell, *Egypt*, 10.

[11] Ibid., 61.

When human hazards are added to the natural ones, it is an even greater wonder that we have much remaining papyrus at all. One of the earliest stories of Westerners securing papyrus manuscripts comes from the late 18th century (1778) and reports that a traveler was offered at a low price some 40 or 50 papyrus rolls, but that he bought only one and that the others—so the story goes—were torn up and burned for their pleasant odor.[12] A century later, when scholars began to search systematically for papyri, masses of discarded documents were discovered in the rubbish heaps of Egypt. These were documents that had been discarded already in antiquity. Researchers, however, often discarded anew the top layers of Arabic, Coptic, and Byzantine papyri that they uncovered, and kept only the more interesting ones from earlier periods, or they discarded papyri in general in favor of ancient artifacts that might have more artistic or intrinsic worth. E. G. Turner, currently the leading expert on papyri, estimates that "many thousands, perhaps millions of texts must have been destroyed" in this process.[13] He estimates, moreover, that "in the hit-or-miss ransacking of ancient sites for [artifacts] of intrinsic value, perhaps half the papyri they contained were ruined by the coarse methods employed."[14] But even when papyri were specifically sought and valued, disaster might strike: the ship containing the entire results of an 1898 German expedition caught fire in the harbor at Hamburg, and all the papyri were destroyed.[15] Who knows what may have been lost in that unforeseen destruction!

When one recognizes the historical value that we now attach, for example, to a credit-card-sized papyrus of the Fourth Gospel, one shudders to think of what might—indeed, must—have been lost through natural causes or human negligence. I refer in this example, of course, to P52, a tiny fragment of John that can be dated to between A.D. 100 and 125 and which shows that John's Gospel was written recently enough to have been transferred to Egypt and to have been copied and circulated there at that early period.

If so much militated against the survival of papyrus manuscripts, what aided their preservation? There were, after all, tens of thousands of papyri recovered (if one counts fragments) and many thousands published.[16] It is difficult, by the way, to find statistics, but already by 1920 perhaps 20,000 papyri had been discovered, and about half of those had been published.[17] A recent estimate is that "somewhere between 15,000 and 20,000" Greek and

[12] Turner, *Greek Papyri*, 18–19.
[13] Ibid., 21.
[14] Ibid., 26.
[15] Ibid., 13; Bell, *Egypt*, 18.
[16] Bell, *Egypt*, 19.
[17] B. P. Grenfell, "The Present Position of Papyrology," *BJRL* 6 (1921–22) 155–56.

Latin papyrus documents had been published by 1968, and that this represented perhaps only half of those discovered.[18] Literary texts, of course, are far less numerous, and William H. Willis suggested as long ago as 1968 that "the number of literary papyri already published must now have exceeded 3,000."[19] Not only has much survived the hazards, but some discoveries will continue—though only tombs, or hiding places in the desert on the fringes of the Nile valley are likely to be safe preserves in the days ahead.[20]

In addition to the dry, natural conditions specified earlier, where would papyri best survive? Placing them in the semi-loose soil of a rubbish mound, or in a building partly filled with and buried in rubbish, or in a collapsed building filled with wind-blown sand, would significantly aid their survival. In 1896/97, B. P. Grenfell and A. S. Hunt, who developed a calculated method for searching these kinds of sites for papyri, excavated the ancient town of Oxyrhynchus, which is on the edge of the desert 120 miles south of Cairo, where they recovered a huge quantity of papyrus from the rubbish heaps. During two of the best days, for example, thirty-six large baskets of papyri were recovered the first day, and twenty-five more the second.[21]

A cemetery unaffected by moisture—as already intimated—was another favorable location, and some papyri were buried with the dead. Papyrus was also one of the materials used for constructing mummy cases in certain periods and in certain parts of Egypt. Layers of used papyrus were glued together to form a kind of paper maché, which was molded into shape, plastered, and painted.[22] In 1900, Grenfell and Hunt, again, were searching a cemetery for mummy cases, hoping to find such papyrus with writing on it, when one of their workmen—disgusted at finding only mummified crocodiles—struck and broke one of the crocodile cases. It was wrapped in sheets of papyrus. Within a few weeks "several thousand" crocodiles were excavated, of which about 2% contained papyrus.[23]

Of particular interest, however, are the Jewish customs of preserving manuscripts by placing them in jars and of disposing of defective or worn-out manuscripts by burying them near a cemetery. The Dead Sea Scrolls represent the best-known example of this practice. It has been suggested recently that these habits were taken over from Judaism by early Christians and that the preservation of some Christian documents must be attributed to this procedure. These views were developed by C. H. Roberts, who for a generation has been the premier palaeographer of the English-speaking

---

18 Turner, *Greek Papyri*, 128.
19 William H. Willis, "A Census of the Literary Papyri from Egypt," *GRBS* 9 (1968) 205.
20 Turner, *Greek Papyri*, 40.
21 Ibid., 27–30.
22 Bell, *Egypt*, 13–14.
23 Turner, *Greek Papyri*, 31–32; Bell, *Egypt*, 13–14.

world, though T. C. Skeat, also distinguished in the field, is skeptical of the theory.[24] It is significant, however, that only one classical manuscript has been discovered in a jar—in an archive of family papers from the sixth century A.D.,[25] while some Christian papyri were discovered in jars or other hiding places in houses, presumably to preserve them during times of persecution.[26] If this is how some NT papyri were preserved, then—at the risk of an unworthy pun and to paraphrase St. Paul in 2 Cor 4:7—"we have these treasures in earthen vessels."

The majority of papyri, however, were recovered from rubbish heaps or ruined buildings, and the vast majority, of course, are not literary texts—much less biblical texts—but rather official documents, correspondence, and records; or land surveys, census lists, and legal documents and contracts of all kinds; or even schoolboys' exercises in penmanship.[27]

This profusion of material attests to the fact that at times papyrus as a writing material was quite inexpensive. For example, an account from Ptolemaic Egypt in 257 B.C. indicates that certain offices of the prime minister used 434 rolls in just thirty-three days.[28] Lest this evidence be discounted on the ground that government officials—then or now—can hardly be expected to set standards for the economical use of supplies, consider that papyrus was often used with wide margins and large unwritten spaces, or that papyrus could be easily reused in either or both of two ways: by washing off the original writing (thus producing a *palimpsest*) or by writing on the reverse side—and yet such reuse was infrequent. Rather, vast quantities of documents that might have been used again were thrown on the rubbish heaps of Oxyrhynchus and other sites. As T. C. Skeat says, "the consumption of papyrus in the ancient world was on a scale which almost passes belief" and it is a "major misconception" that papyrus was an expensive commodity.[29]

When did papyrus become a vehicle for writing, and how long was it in use? A papyrus roll for writing has been found from 3000 B.C.,[30] and papyrus

---

[24] T. C. Skeat [review of C. H. Roberts, *Manuscript, Society and Belief in Early Christian Egypt*, 1979], *JTS* 31 (1980) 186.

[25] Colin H. Roberts, *Manuscript, Society and Belief in Early Christian Egypt* (Schweich Lectures, 1977; Oxford: University Press for the British Academy, 1979) 6–7.

[26] Ibid., 8.

[27] Bell, *Egypt*, 20–21.

[28] Turner, *Greek Papyri*, 6. For more detail on this heavy use of papyrus in finance offices in Oxyrhynchus, see Naphtali Lewis, *Greeks in Ptolemaic Egypt: Case Studies in the Social History of the Hellenistic World* (Oxford: Clarendon Press, 1986) 51–55.

[29] Skeat, "Early Christian Book-Production," 59. See also the careful assessment by Lewis, *Papyrus in Classical Antiquity*, 129–34.

[30] Turner, *Greek Papyri*, 1.

was still being manufactured in Egypt in the eleventh century A.D.[31]—a period of more than 4000 years. The earliest extant papyri with Greek writing on them go back to the fourth century B.C.,[32] and Greek papyrus manuscripts were used for literary works as late as the sixth century A.D. and for documents and letters into the early eighth century A.D.—some 1100 years overall.[33]

Greek literary works during this period were more commonly written on parchment or vellum manuscripts—carefully prepared from the skins of animals—which was probably a more expensive material and certainly a more elegant one.[34] In the pre-Christian era these Greek literary works were written on rolls. From the first century A.D. there are extant 253 such rolls, and only one writing in codex form—that is, in our form of the book as we know it, constructed of folded sheets bound at one edge. In fact, until A.D. 300, Greek literature is found on 1697 rolls and in only thirty-six codices.[35] A theory advanced thirty years ago and held with increasing certainty is that the Christians invented the codex form of the book and that the earliest codices were made of papyrus, or—if Christians did not invent the codex— they immediately adopted it as the only acceptable form for their writings. As we just observed, it is striking that Greek literary work is found on only one codex in the first century and on only four more before A.D. 200, and that the earliest Latin codex is dated about 100, with no others dating prior to about 300.[36] There are, however, eleven biblical manuscripts that Roberts and Skeat would date in the second century: six are OT texts made and used by Christians, and five are NT texts. These are "the earliest Christian manuscripts in existence. All are on papyrus and in codex form."[37] The natural conclusion that they draw is "that when the Christian Bible first emerges into history the books of which it was composed are always written on papyrus and are always in codex form."[38] This "instant and universal" adoption of the codex by the earliest Christians is all the more striking because, whether Jewish or Gentile, these early Christians would "be strongly prejudiced in favour of the roll by upbringing, education and environment."[39] Clear reasons for this Christian propensity for the codex are still

---

[31] Ibid., 16.

[32] Ibid., 1.

[33] Ibid., 16.

[34] On the "profitless debate" about which was more expensive, see Colin H. Roberts and T. C. Skeat, *The Birth of the Codex* (Oxford: University Press for the British Academy, 1983) 7.

[35] Ibid., 37.

[36] Ibid., 28.

[37] Ibid., 40–41.

[38] Ibid., 42.

[39] Ibid., 53.

matters of speculation, but if their preference achieved nothing else, it clearly differentiated Christian writings from both Jewish and secular writings, where the roll-form of the book persisted and was dominant for a considerable period.[40]

In this connection, it is interesting that Christians at about the same time invented Greek abbreviations, or—better—contractions for the so-called *nomina sacra*, or certain divine names or terms used in the NT. The contractions were marked with a superscript line, and the words so treated were GOD, LORD, JESUS, and CHRIST, but also SPIRIT, ANTHROPOS or MAN, CROSS, FATHER, SON, SAVIOR, MOTHER, HEAVEN, ISRAEL, DAVID, and JERUSALEM. This was "strictly a Christian usage unknown to Jewish or pagan manuscripts,"[41] and was carried through the Christian biblical manuscripts with rigorous uniformity. It has recently been suggested that these *nomina sacra* were theologically motivated—that the most prominent terms represented the common beliefs of all Christians: GOD, FATHER; LORD, JESUS, CHRIST, SON, SAVIOR, CROSS; and SPIRIT.[42] In any case, like the exclusive use of the papyrus codex form in the earliest period, the *nomina sacra* also set apart the Christian writings from those that were Jewish or secular. It might be said also that their development of the codex form of the book shows that the early Christians were pragmatic —looking for practical ways to place more of their writings (including the bulky Septuagint) in less space than would have been required in the scroll form of the book.

But this is to push ahead of our story. Though used over these long periods, papyrus was little known or thought about from the late Middle Ages (1100 on) through the Renaissance. Papyrus was rediscovered by the scholarly world, however, when 800 rolls turned up at Herculaneum in 1752. They had been buried in the volcanic ash from Mt. Vesuvius in A.D. 79. The elements, though, had turned them into hardened masses, and they could not immediately be unrolled in any fruitful manner.[43] In spite of this new interest, the first papyrus manuscript was edited and published only in 1787; though this publication did not meet the expectations that the discovery had generated, numerous Europeans searched for and collected papyrus manuscripts during the following century.[44] Yet, Greek (and Latin) papyri were not common: In 1891 only 200 had been published, with very

---

[40] See ibid., 60.

[41] Ibid., 57.

[42] Modified from Roberts, *Manuscript, Society and Belief*, 46–47.

[43] Turner, *Greek Papyri*, 17–18. For an extensive, popularized account of the discoveries at Herculaneum, see Leo Deuel, *Testaments of Time: The Search for Lost Manuscripts and Records* (Baltimore, MD: Penguin Books, 1970 [original, New York: Knopf, 1965]) 55–77.

[44] Turner, *Greek Papyri*, 18–20. See also Deuel, 90–93.

few literary texts among them,[45] and not even a half-dozen fragments of the NT were included. The fact remains, however, that papyri had been redis-covered in the late eighteenth century and that a hundred years of moderate interest in them then prepared the way for the great discoveries that were to burst upon us during the last few years of the nineteenth century and the first half of the twentieth century.

The Discovery and Publication of the New Testament Papyri

The discovery of NT papyri and their publication had an inauspicious and bizarre beginning, for the first claim to have found NT papyri and the first publication of these papyri took place in 1861, when a volume in large format was issued in London entitled *Fac-Similes of Certain Portions of The Gospel of St. Matthew and of the Epistles of Ss. James & Jude Written on Papyrus in the First Century*. Its editor was Constantine Simonides, and the papyri were quickly exposed by recognized experts as forgeries—this was a genuine "pious fraud." Simonides had, in fact, perpetrated other manuscript forgeries several years earlier in Germany. The most curious aspect of this unusual story, however, developed in the following year, 1862, when Simonides claimed, in a letter to *The Guardian,* that he himself had written the famous parchment Codex Sinaiticus, which Constantin Tischendorf had recently found in St. Catherine's Monastery on Mount Sinai. Though Simonides vigorously denied forging the papyrus manuscripts of Matthew, James, and Jude, he just as vigorously claimed to have forged Codex Sinaiticus— obviously in an attempt to discredit Tischendorf, whose discovery of this mid-fourth century parchment manucript was not only attracting attention in the world press but was promising to revolutionize biblical textual criticism.[46]

Several years later, in 1868, the first genuine NT papyrus text, now designated P11, was published by Tischendorf, about twenty years after he had discovered Codex Sinaiticus. Tischendorf and C. R. Gregory, who wrote the voluminous *Prolegomena* to Tischendorf's 8th critical edition (1864–72; *Prolegomena,* 1884–94), published a total of three NT papyri [P7, P8, P11], and two others [P3, P14] had been published by Carl Wessely and J. Rendel Harris prior to 1898. Of these five papyri, however, two date in the seventh century, two in the fifth, and one in the fourth century—and none is older than the great uncial manuscripts Sinaiticus and Vaticanus,

---

[45] Turner, *Greek Papyri,* 21.

[46] See J. K. Elliott, *Codex Sinaiticus and the Simonides Affair: An Examination of the Nineteenth Century Claim that Codex Sinaiticus Was Not an Ancient Manuscript* (Analecta Vlatadon, 33; Thessa-loniki: Patriarchal Institute for Patristic Studies, 1982) 26–70; 131–70.

which had dominated the construction of the critical NT texts of Tischendorf in 1869 and Westcott-Hort in 1881. Moreover, these five papyri contain a combined total of only 120 verses of the NT. It is not surprising, therefore, that they did not create great excitement in NT scholarship.

A sense of excitement was almost immediate, however, when Grenfell and Hunt, during their systematic searches for manuscripts, began to dig a low mound at Oxyrhynchus on January 11, 1897. They had purposely selected Oxyrhynchus as:

> a site where fragments of Christian literature might be expected of an earlier date than the fourth century, to which our oldest manuscripts of the New Testament belong; for the place was renowned in the fourth and fifth centuries on account of the number of its churches and monasteries.[47]

As Grenfell and Hunt began to dig, almost immediately two sheets of great significance appeared: first a leaf of "Sayings of Jesus" from an apocryphal gospel and then, nearby but "a day or two afterwards,"[48] a leaf containing parts of Matthew chapter 1, now designated P1 in the official list of NT papyri. It dates, as they had properly surmised, to the third century. When the first volume of *The Oxyrhynchus Papyri* appeared in 1898, the place of honor as their first published papyrus was given to the "Sayings of Jesus," but the papyrus of Matthew appears second, and at the time, as Grenfell and Hunt affirmed, "it may thus claim to be a fragment of the oldest known manuscript of any part of the New Testament."[49] Furthermore, it is clearly from a codex, that is, in our form of the book.

Papyrus manuscripts flowed from the Oxyrhynchus sites until they became a "torrent," and twenty-seven of our present eighty-six different NT papyrus manuscripts were found there. These Oxyrhynchus papyri contain portions of fifteen of our twenty-seven NT books; six contain portions of Matthew, four have portions of John's Gospel, three have Romans, two contain Hebrews, two have James, two have the Apocalypse, and one each has Luke, Acts, 1 Corinthians, Galatians, Philippians, 1 Thessalonians, 2 Thessalonians, 1 John, and Jude. The only major NT books not represented are Mark, 2 Corinthians, Ephesians, Colossians, and the Pastoral Epistles, though certainly that is of no significance in the kind of random situation that excavations in rubbish heaps provide. What is remarkable, however, is that

---

[47] Turner, *Greek Papyri,* 28, quoting the excavation report. See also the extended, but popular account of Grenfell and Hunt's excavations by Leo Deuel, *Testaments of Time,* 132–64.

[48] Bernard P. Grenfell and Arthur S. Hunt (eds.), *The Oxyrhynchus Papyri, Part I* (London: Egypt Exploration Fund, 1898) 4.

[49] Ibid.

nineteen of the Oxyrhynchus papyri [plus one uncial manuscript (0162) found there] were written in the second, third, or early fourth centuries, that is, prior to the great uncial manuscripts that have loomed so large for so long, such as Codices Sinaiticus, Vaticanus, Alexandrinus, and Bezae. Today there are forty-one such early papyri — and Oxyrhynchus provided almost half. These early papyri, of course, are all highly fragmentary.

But greater discoveries were yet to come, though not so much by systematic excavation and calculated searches. Such excavations are expensive, and already by 1920 Grenfell reached the conclusion "that the present time is more propitious for buying papyri found by native diggers [who are looking for] nitrous earth [to be used for fertilizer] than for digging at one's own expense."[50] He added that "America, owing to the favorable [currency] exchange, seems to be the only country which is just now in a position to face the heavy outlay for excavations in search of papyri in town sites."[51] Alas, America's "Great Depression" was only several years away.

It will be instructive to stop short of the next important discoveries in the early 1930s and to ask what papyri were available to the scholarly world in 1930. We mentioned earlier that only 200 papyri had been published by 1891, but by 1920, according to a survey of the entire scene of papyrology made by Grenfell, some sixty volumes containing nearly 10,000 texts had been published, though he estimated that this represented "probably less than half of the whole material which has been recovered."[52]

What interests us, of course, is the quantity of known *New Testament* papyri. By 1922, twenty-one of the twenty-seven Oxyrhynchus papyri of the NT had already been published, but then no more were edited until 1941, and the last two, P77 and P78, were not published until 1968. Of other NT papyri, twenty-one were edited and published by 1930 in addition to the Oxyrhynchus, for a total of forty-two (P1 through P44, minus P25 [1938] and P42 [1939]), or just under half the present number of known NT papyri. It must be emphasized again, however, that these forty-two papyri are highly fragmentary in nature. For example, many contain bits and pieces of a few or several verses; the only ones with extensive text — say, of more than two dozen verses — are P4, with about ninety-six verses of Luke (3d century); P5, with about thirty-seven verses of John (3d century); P8, with about twenty-nine verses of Acts (4th century); P11, with about sixty-four verses of 1 Corinthians, though it dates in the 7th century; P13, with about seventy-nine verses of Hebrews (3d/4th century); P15, with about twenty-seven verses of 1 Corinthians (3d century); P27, with about thirty verses of Romans (3d

---

[50] Grenfell, "Present Position," *BJRL* 6 (1921-22) 161.
[51] Ibid.
[52] Ibid., 155-56.

century); P37, with about thirty-four verses of Matthew (3d/4th century); P40, with about thirty-four verses of Romans (3d century); and P41, with about fifty-two verses of Acts, but dated in the 8th century. Yet even sections thirty, sixty, or ninety verses in length are still mere fragments. This is clear when we are reminded that the entire Gospel of Matthew has about 1070 [1068] verses, Luke has about 1150 [1149] verses, and even our shortest Gospel, Mark, has about 660 [661] verses.

Nevertheless, these ten longer papyrus texts, as well as the thirty-two that are still more fragmentary in nature, are of great significance, especially since twenty-three of them—more than half—are prior to the third/fourth century, that is, prior to the great parchment uncials upon which the NT text, by 1930, had been based already for several decades.

Now, it is this largely fragmentary character of the papyri known prior to 1930 that makes the discovery of the Chester Beatty papyri in 1930–31 and the Bodmer papyri about 1955–56 so extremely important. We know virtually nothing, however, about the origin of these and some similar collections of papyri, for they were purchased or obtained in some fashion other than excavation and other than discovery *in situ*. Sir Frederic Kenyon, who published the bulk of the Chester Beatty papyri in 1933–37, gives the following brief and often-repeated assessment of their likely place of origin:

> From their character, however, it is plain that they must have been discovered among the ruins of some early Christian church or monastery; and there is reason to believe that they come from the neighbourhood of the Fayum.[53]

Carl Schmidt, in reviewing Kenyon's work, reports that a Fayumic dealer told him in early 1933 that the manuscripts were found in a pot at Atfih, that is, ancient Aphroditopolis in the Fayum, about two-thirds of the way up the Nile from Alexandria to Oxyrhynchus.[54] Regardless of their places of origin, here for the first time were extensive portions of extraordinarily ancient NT codices. First to come to light were the three most famous Chester Beatty papyri:

P45 From the first half of the third century, P45 contains thirty leaves of an original codex of perhaps 220 leaves, which originally held all of the four Gospels and Acts. What has been preserved are sixty-one verses of Matthew; about six chapters of Mark; more than five chapters of Luke; most of John 10 and 11; and thirteen chapters of Acts.

[53] Frederic G. Kenyon, *The Chester Beatty Biblical Papyri: Descriptions and Texts of Twelve Manuscripts on Papyrus of the Greek Bible: Fasciculus I, General Introduction* (London: Emery Walker, 1933) 5.

[54] Carl Schmidt, "Die Evangelienhandschrift der Chester Beatty-Sammlung," *ZNW* 32 (1933) 225–26; I was alerted to this by Roberts, *Manuscript, Society and Belief*, 7.

P46 From about the year 200, P46 contains eighty-six leaves of an original 102. Ten epistles of Paul (but not the Pastorals) were originally included, and, though none of 2 Thessalonians has been preserved, the codex does have about eight chapters of Romans; virtually all of 1 and 2 Corinthians; all of Galatians; all of Ephesians; all of Philippians; all of Colossians; two of the five chapters of 1 Thessalonians; and all of Hebrews. The epistles, however, are not in the usual canonical order.

P47 Dating to the mid or latter third century, P47 contains ten leaves of an estimated thirty-two originally. It held the book of Revelation, of which eight chapters from the middle survive.

Then, twenty-five years later, M. Martin Bodmer, founder of the Bodmer Library near Geneva, came into possession of four codices, of which three are in some respects even more extraordinary than the Chester Beatty:

P66 Like P46, P66 dates from around 200. It contains 104 pages of the text of the Gospel of John, to which fragments of forty-six other pages were later added. All but about twenty-five verses of the first fourteen and a half chapters of the Fourth Gospel are well preserved, as well as fragments of the remaining portions.

P72 This is a small third-century codex which is the earliest known copy of 1 and 2 Peter and Jude. It contains the entire text of these three epistles, as well as a half dozen other Christian writings.

P75 From the early third century—possibly earlier—P75 contains 102 pages of its original 144, and it preserves portions of Luke 3, 4, and 5, all of chapters 6 through 17, half of chapter 18, and virtually all of chapters 22, 23, and 24. It also contains virtually all of John chapters 1 through 12, and portions of chapters 13, 14, and 15. This is the earliest known copy of Luke. As is now well known, the text of P75 is extraordinary in its identity with that of Codex Vaticanus.

P74 The fourth Bodmer papyrus is P74 (7th century), with portions of Acts, James, 1-2 Peter, 1-3 John, and Jude. A fifth Bodmer papyrus, P73, is still unedited, but contains only 3 verses of Matthew.

Given the unlikelihood of survival, the NT papyri are all genuine treasures, but they are far more than ancient artifacts that have survived the hazards and ravages of time, for they furnish us with texts that may help us unlock the secrets of the very earliest stages of our NT textual transmission. But what, more precisely, has been their reception and their influence?

The General Effect of the Papyrus Discoveries
on New Testament Textual Criticism

As is well known, from the early eighteenth century on, NT textual criticism attempted to overcome its long-standing reliance on the *textus receptus* — the text found in the mass of eighth century and later manuscripts. Slowly but surely textual critics shifted their allegiance, rather, to earlier manuscripts, and particularly to the great uncial manuscripts of the fourth and fifth centuries. From our present standpoint, therefore, we would naturally assume that when all the major NT papyri had been published, the scholarly world would revel in the extensive documentation that they provide for the early history of the NT text. After all, they fill in — from actual, datable texts — the critical period that reaches 150 to 200 years behind the great uncial manuscripts that had been the mainstay of the discipline at least since the grand days of Tischendorf and Westcott-Hort.

Moreover, these papyri seem to provide precisely what the landmark figures in textual criticism had been looking for ever since 1730, when *Bentley* and *Wettstein* enunciated the basic text-critical principle that the more ancient reading is preferable, and when *Bengel* insisted that textual witnesses must be weighed and not merely counted. This, moreover, is precisely the direction that *Lachmann* took in 1831 when he made the decisive break with the *textus receptus* — that is, when he broke the reliance on the mass of late manuscripts — and took as his aim the establishment of the NT text as it existed around A.D. 400 and, accordingly, devised his text entirely from the most ancient witnesses known to him. And it goes without saying that this is precisely the principle operative in the work of the greatest figures among textual critics, *Tischendorf* and *Tregelles* around 1850 and *Westcott-Hort* in 1881, for all of them based their work on the hard-won criterion that, as Tischendorf put it, "the text should be sought solely from ancient witnesses" and that "among disagreeing witnesses" "the oldest Greek codices" are to be placed first, for "those that excel in antiquity prevail in authority," or, as Hort put it, "older readings, manuscripts, or groups are to be preferred." These firmly held principles suggest that any newly found documents of early date would play a highly important role as NT textual criticism continued to unfold.

Yet, when numerous fragmentary papyri from the third/fourth century appeared, and even when papyri containing extensive portions of text and dating from around the year 200 came to light in the 1930s and mid-1950s, much less changed than this history of textual criticism would lead one to expect. Obviously, the papyri, by any measure, are great treasures from the past, but — as we shall see momentarily — the papyri, including the Chester Beatty, were often treated not so much as welcome illuminators of textual history, but more as intruders and as irritants to an already firmly established understanding of the history of the text. After all, textual critics in the first half of the twentieth century had carefully and confidently reconstructed the early textual history of the NT in accordance with the elegant parchment codices of the fourth and fifth centuries, and many critics simply did not wish that structure to be jeopardized by these young papyrus interlopers—these ragged-edged documents written on what seemed to some of them to be an almost unworthy vehicle for the Scripture. Yet the papyri would not and could not be ignored, and they were gradually worked into the critical editions of the numerous Greek New Testaments that were produced in the twentieth century. When the dust had settled, what was the result? I think that most will agree that the result was something unexpected rather than expected.

As noted earlier, the extraordinarily old but highly fragmentary papyri that came to light prior to about 1930 had relatively little impact on NT textual criticism. The great critical edition of Tischendorf in 1869, and the influential edition of Westcott-Hort in 1881, by the very fact of timing, could not have been much affected by papyri. Though Tischendorf published P11 (containing sixty-four verses of 1 Corinthians) a year before his 8th edition, he cites it in his apparatus (using the symbol "Q") only about six times (1 Cor 6:13, 14; 7:3, 13 bis, 14). As for Westcott-Hort, they do not refer to the six papyri known before the second edition of their *Introduction* was issued in 1896, even though they do take special note of an Old Syriac manuscript discovered in 1892, and its readings were incorporated into their notes; also, they mention three uncial manuscripts reported by Gregory in his *Prolegomena* to Tischendorf's edition, but they do not mention the two papyri Gregory published for the first time in that very same work.[55]

The logical conclusion to be drawn from these sparse data is that in this early period the papyri did not make an impact as a new and important category of NT manuscripts. The reasons were obvious enough: these first six papyri to become available (P3 [6th/7th century]; P4 [3d century, but considered 6th century when published; revised to 4th century in Gregory, 1909]; P7 [4th/6th centuries?]; P8 [4th century]; P11 [7th century]; and P14 [5th century]) were all dated at that time from the 4th to the 7th century (though one [as noted] was later revised to the 3d century), with the result that they were viewed as being no older—and in most cases much later—than the great uncials upon which Tischendorf and Westcott-Hort relied. Along with this perception were three others: first, the highly fragmentary nature of the papyri; second, the fact that they provided texts from only Luke, Acts,

[55] B. F. Westcott and F. J. A. Hort, *The New Testament in the Original Greek* (Cambridge/London: Macmillan, 1881–82) 2.325–30.

and 1 Corinthians; and, third, the difficulty of readily identifying them with the major text-types recognized by the textual scholars of that period. All of this, then, combined to make these scraps of papyrus appear less than startling, and at the time they did not appear to be revolutionary discoveries. If one adds to this the extraordinary confidence possessed by the textual critics of that day—such as the almost total confidence that Westcott-Hort placed in the mid-fourth-century Codices Vaticanus and Sinaiticus—then it is understandable that the papyri caused little excitement, either then or during the following years when that same confidence was the hallmark of the discipline.

Indeed, thirty years after Westcott-Hort, Sir Frederic Kenyon, who was later to edit the Chester Beatty papyri, spoke of the nineteen papyri known to him in 1912 as follows: "Valuable as such copies may be, chiefly on account of their age, we cannot look to them with any confidence for purity of text."[56] Why? Because, he went on to say, "The papyrus period . . . may be summarily characterized as the period when the textual problems came into being, which we have to try to solve with the help of the evidence afforded by the later periods." Then, just two paragraphs before Kenyon listed the nineteen known papyri, of which at least nine dated in the third/ fourth century, he dared to say that "up to the present time, no evidence worth mentioning is extant which comes from within this [papyrus] period itself." Next, in a prophetic passage, Kenyon says that it is possible, even probable, "that Egypt . . . may yet bring to light a Gospel or an Epistle written in the second or third century"—which indeed happened only twenty years later. Kenyon goes on to remark, however, that "such a discovery would be full of interest . . . ; but it would have to be received with caution . . . [for] it might contain a text inferior in quality to that of some existing manuscripts." Therefore, he concludes, "the best preparation for dealing judiciously with such new testimony is a sound knowledge of the evidence already in existence."[57] And what does he mean? He immediately begins to describe in glowing terms the great uncial manuscripts of the fourth century. That is what the papyri were up against: the overwhelming dominance of the uncials and of their preeminent place in NT textual theory as it was then understood.

How were the papyri treated in the following years? When the next full critical edition appeared, that of von Soden in 1913, only twelve papyri were in his apparatus,[58] though twenty had been published. George Milligan, the

---

[56] Frederic G. Kenyon, *Handbook to the Textual Criticism of the New Testament* (2d ed.; London: Macmillan, 1912) 40.

[57] Ibid., 40–41.

[58] *Apud* Benedikt Kraft, *Die Zeichen für die wichtigeren Handschriften des griechischen Neuen Testaments* (3d ed.; Freiburg im Br.: Herder, 1955) 11–30. According to J. K. Elliott, *A Survey*

Scottish papyrologist, could list twenty-three NT papyri in 1913, but he is quite clear in stating that their real significance comes with the light they cast on the nature of the *koine* Greek language,[59] and even ten years later he states that the papyri "present us with no new readings of special interest."[60] The text-critical handbooks of Eberhard Nestle—the standard manuals of their time—follow the lead of Gregory and list the NT papyri at the end of the list of uncials. The second edition, which was translated into English in 1901, includes six papyri;[61] the third edition of 1909 lists fourteen papyri and calls attention to the fact that the author has added "an entirely new section, the papyri," to Gregory's conventional way of listing the NT manuscripts, and for the first time includes two plates of NT papyrus manuscripts (P1 and P10).[62] Yet, in these editions the papyri are still listed at the end of the uncial list. After Nestle's death in 1913, the authorship of the Nestle handbook eventually fell to Ernst von Dobschütz, and the fourth edition appeared in 1923. It reveals a significant change: von Dobschütz places the papyri at the head of the list of manuscripts, "in distinction," as he says, "from Gregory and Nestle" (and the two plates reproducing P1 and P10 also are dutifully moved to the beginning of that section at the end of the volume!). Then follow entries for 32 papyri.[63] Interestingly, Nestle is quick to point out—as was true at the time—that "our very oldest manuscripts" are the deluxe [parchment] codices of the fourth century.[64] Beyond this, very little attention is paid to the papyri by these handbooks of Nestle and von Dobschütz.

Goodspeed, in 1937, after the publication of the Chester Beatty papyri, does refer to these and other papyrus discoveries as "remarkable" and "sensational," but concludes that "it is not these discoveries of Biblical papyri, however dazzling," that most affect the biblical text; rather—again—it is the discovery of the thousands of everyday papyrus documents that illuminate

---

of Manuscripts Used in Editions of the Greek New Testament (NovTSup 57; Leiden: Brill, 1987) 3–4, cf. xiii–xiv, twenty-one papyri were *theoretically* available to von Soden. Why P3 is included in neither list is unclear, for it was published by Wessely in 1882.

[59] George Milligan, *The New Testament Documents: Their Origin and Early History* (London: Macmillan, 1913) 60–62; 248–54.

[60] George Milligan, *Here and There among the Papyri* (London: Hodder & Stoughton, 1923) 121.

[61] Eberhard Nestle, *Introduction to the Textual Criticism of the Greek New Testament* (tr. from the 2d German ed. by W. Edie; ed. A. Menzies; Theological Translation Library, 13; London: Williams and Norgate; New York: Putnam, 1901) xv, 74, 80; cf. 81–82.

[62] Eberhard Nestle, *Einführung in das Griechische Neue Testament* (3d ed.; Göttingen: Vandenhoeck & Ruprecht, 1909) 61, 88–89, plates 11–12.

[63] Ernst von Dobschütz, *Eberhard Nestle's Einführung in das Griechische Neue Testament* (4th ed.; Göttingen: Vandenhoeck & Ruprecht, 1923) 85–86, plates 1–2.

[64] Same in both of Nestle's editions referred to in nn. 61 and 62, above: English, p. 82; German, p. 90.

the NT language.[65] Kenyon, also writing in 1937, after he had himself published the Chester Beatty papyri, still spoke of the previously discovered NT papyri as follows: ". . . Small fragments, individually of slight importance, but collectively of some value," and "Though their evidence with regard to particular readings does not amount to much, they are of value as throwing a little light on the general character of the . . . types of text current in Egypt during this period." Naturally, he speaks more glowingly of the Chester Beatty, a discovery, as he puts it, "which threw all the others in the shade and which is indeed only to be rivalled by that of the Codex Sinaiticus."[66] Yet the *independent* significance of these papyri—as we shall observe in a moment—was not championed even by Kenyon.

Continuing our asssessment of critical editions of the Greek NT, it is understandable that the large critical apparatus of Mark by Legg in 1935 cited only one papyrus, the Chester Beatty P45, for Mark is poorly represented among the papyri. It is found in only three: P45, which had been published only two years prior to Legg's edition; in another fragment published in 1972; and in one still unedited. However, the succeeding volume by Legg on Matthew in 1940 cites only six papyri when nine of Matthew were known. In the popular Nestle Greek New Testament (*Novum Testamentum Graece*), the 1936 edition [16th] cited only fifteen papyri, including the recently discovered Chester Beatty, though altogether nearly fifty were known at the time. The number of papyri cited increased rapidly, however, with each succeeding Nestle edition, so that twenty-eight appeared in the 1952 edition [21st]; thirty-seven in that of 1963 [25th], which was after the Bodmer papyri were published; and finally all eighty-six were cited in the current 26th edition of 1979, when completeness was finally considered a virtue and the papyri had come fully into their own.

But—perhaps to our considerable surprise—this "coming into their own" did not occur even with the finding of the extensive texts of the Chester Beatty papyri, for the nature of the text found in the early third century P45 did not conform to the type of text in either of the two text-types identified by Westcott-Hort as very early (i.e., the so-called "Neutral" and the so-called "Western"), nor—of course—to their later Syrian (or Byzantine) text-type. Rather, P45 seemed to fall midway between these two texts, and seemed at the time (that is, in the mid-1930s when it was found) to confirm the Caesarean text-type, which recently had been identified by textual critics as a text-type additional to those marked out by Westcott-Hort in their

[65] Edgar J. Goodspeed, *New Chapters in New Testament Study* (New York: Macmillan, 1937) 92–101.

[66] Frederic Kenyon, *The Story of the Bible: A Popular Account of How It Came to Us* (New York: Dutton, 1937) 110–13.

depiction of NT textual history. The Caesarean text, though considered at the time to be an early, local text, was not thought to be as early as either the "Neutral" or the "Western" text-types; hence identifying P45 with the Caesarean text did not thereby confer on P45 any preponderant authority. There was no general agreement, however, as to the exact nature of the text of P45 *vis à vis* the established text-types—the subject of a complicated and extended discussion in the mid-1930s by F. G. Kenyon, R. V. G. Tasker, M.-J. Lagrange, P. L. Hedley, C. C. Tarelli, H. Lietzmann, and others, which was summarized by A. F. J. Klijn in 1949.[67] But that is the point: mostly these discussions of P45 were *vis à vis* the established text-types, rather than in terms of the *independent* significance of the papyrus for the history and method of the NT text. Lietzmann, for instance, in two articles in 1934 (on P46) and in 1935 (on P45), says in each that these very welcome discoveries confirm both the reliability of our textual tradition and of our present knowledge, and he states quite bluntly that they teach us neither anything radically new nor anything we did not already know.[68] Lagrange, in his 1935 analysis, does at one juncture assign methodological significance to P45 when he says that "the independence of the papyrus in relation to the *D* [text-]type is of the highest importance for the history of the text."[69] Yet, this judgment, too, is in the context of fitting the newly discovered manuscript into the current textual formulation—a pattern disclosed and reinforced almost invariably as one peruses the scores of assessments of P45 in the period preceding the discovery of the Bodmer papyri. Klijn, at the conclusion of his 1949 overview, seems almost apologetic when he states that "on the surface it may seem that this rather long discussion of the inquiry into the text of P45 may have originated in an overrating of a newly discovered text," but the statement that follows is one of the few that give P45 a right to independent status; he continues, "This is seen to be false once we grasp that Egypt appears to be more and more important for the history of the text, and since P45 takes a central place in the text of Egypt, it requires thorough study."[70] Here, at last, is a clear recognition that this papyrus and, by implication, the other early papyri have independent and fundamental significance in tracing out the history of the NT text.

For the most part, the second Chester Beatty papyrus, P46 of the Pauline

---

[67] A. F. J. Klijn, *A Survey of the Researches into the Western Text of the Gospels and Acts* (Utrecht: Kemink, 1949) 132–46.

[68] Hans Lietzmann, "Zur Würdigung des Chester-Beatty-Papyrus der Paulusbriefe," SPAW, phil.-hist. Klasse, 25 (1934) 775, reprinted in his *Kleine Schriften, II: Studien zum Neuen Testament* (ed. K. Aland; TU 68; Berlin: Akademie-Verlag, 1958) 171; and "Die Chester-Beatty-Papyri des Neuen Testament," *Antike* 11 (1935) 147, reprinted in *Kleine Schriften, II,* 168.

[69] M.-J. Lagrange, *Critique textelle: II. La critique rationnelle* (EBib; Paris: Gabalda, 1935) 415.

[70] Klijn, *Survey,* 145.

epistles, received treatment similar to that accorded P45 by most scholars: its readings were assessed in comparison with the prevailing manuscripts and within the traditional framework of text-types, yielding the general conclusion that P46 sides with the "Neutral" text over against the "Western." Yet, to Kenyon, the editor of the Chester Beatty papyri, P46's major significance appeared to be in sharpening the already well-established distinction between the Neutral and Western text-types, and his overall assessment is that the papyrus "in general confirms the integrity of the text that has come down to us, and offers no sensational variants." The concluding paragraph of his edition of P46 reads:

> It therefore seems clear that, while our modern texts are an advance on those which preceded them, we have not reached finality. The papyrus affects the balance of evidence in many cases; and while it can by no means claim a predominant authority (since, so far as we know, it is only a text circulating in provincial Egypt), it shows that the margin of doubt in details is greater than was supposed, and that the exercise of critical judgement and the search for further evidence are still required.[71]

Henry A. Sanders, in his publication of the forty then-known leaves of P46 (out of the eighty-six eventually recovered), follows the usual procedure of evaluating them against all the relevant later manuscripts and text-types.[72] It is of interest, too, that a footnote in a 1953 article by Kenneth Clark affirms that "the contribution [of P46] to the textual criticism of the New Testament has not been fully exploited"—and this was already twenty years after P46 was discovered and is another evidence that the significance of these extensive papyri had not been appreciated even by the mid-1950s.[73]

There was, however, a notable—and perhaps singular—exception to all of this, a substantial work published in the same year as Kenneth Clark's comment: G. Zuntz's *The Text of the Epistles*.[74] Zuntz turned then-current procedures upside down: he began his study with "the oldest manuscript" of the Pauline corpus, P46, which he calls "the decisive material accession" to our resources,[75] and proposes to employ it "as a foil in assessing the value of,

[71] Frederic G. Kenyon, *The Chester Beatty Biblical Papyri: Descriptions and Texts of Twelve Manuscripts on Papyrus of the Greek Bible: Fasciculus III Supplement; Pauline Epistles, Text* (London: Emery Walker, 1936) xxii.

[72] Henry A. Sanders (ed.), *A Third-Century Papyrus Codex of the Epistles of Paul* (University of Michigan Studies, Humanistic Series, 38; Ann Arbor: University of Michigan Press, 1935) 23–32.

[73] Kenneth W. Clark, "Textual Criticism and Doctrine," *Studia Paulina in honorem Johannis de Zwaan septuagenarii* (Haarlem: Bohn, 1953) 56, reprinted in K. W. Clark, *The Gentile Bias and Other Essays* (ed. John L. Sharpe, III; NovTSup 54; Leiden: Brill, 1980) 94.

[74] G. Zuntz, *The Text of the Epistles: A Disquisition upon the* Corpus Paulinum (Schweich Lectures, 1946; London: Oxford University Press for the British Academy, 1953).

[75] Ibid., 11.

and the interrelation between, the other witnesses."[76] Then, for more than half of his large volume, he uses that papyrus as the standard against which all other manuscripts are measured. This is the "exception [as we say— though with questionable logic] that proves the rule." Still, it was 1953 before this quite reasonable approach appeared in print (even though Zuntz's Schweich Lectures were delivered originally in 1946), and it represents a direction and an emphasis taken by very few others in this period.

As to the third Chester Beatty codex, P47, containing the text of Revelation, Kenyon—as late as 1948—says merely that "the textual variants in Revelation are not of great importance, but the papyrus [P47] must take its place as one of the principal . . . authorit[ies] for the book," since it is the oldest.[77] Josef Schmid in 1955, in the leading work on the Greek text of the Apocalypse, did find that this most ancient, extensive manuscript permitted the older text of Revelation to be divided into two distinct text-groups, that it helped to confirm the mixed character of Codex Sinaiticus, and that it established more precisely the superior value of the Codices A and C group over the Sinaiticus–P47 group.[78] Yet, in his extensive investigations, the readings of P47 are largely fed into the existing textual classifications and utilized as would those of any other newly found witness.

Such assessments of these three extensive papyri (with the notable exception of Zuntz's procedure) hardly suggest that they were considered revolutionary discoveries destined to change the world of textual criticism. And this lack of enthusiasm strikes us as rather surprising when the quantity of known NT text on papyrus had suddenly been multiplied many times over by the appearance of the Chester Beatty papyri and when the date of extensive documentary evidence had been pushed back 100 to 150 years behind the great uncials. We can understand, of course, why the other papyri then known attracted relatively little attention, for they were extremely fragmentary, and—due primarily to their fragmented state—did not solidify the currently identified textual configurations; they seemed, therefore, to be factors of confusion in the textual theory of the time, rather than vehicles for clarification. Yet, this would appear also to be the main reason why the Chester Beatty papyri did not generate as much excitement as we would have expected: in the Gospels, Acts, and Epistles, these papyri introduced

---

[76] Ibid., 17.

[77] Frederic G. Kenyon, *The Text of the Greek Bible: A Student's Handbook* (Studies in Theology; 2d ed.; London: Duckworth, 1949) 191; cf. 188–91.

[78] Josef Schmid, *Studien zur Geschichte des griechischen Apokalypse-Textes. 2. Teil: Die alten Stämme* (Münchener theologische Studien, 1. Ergänzungsband; Munich: Karl Zink, 1955) 12, 251. See now Kurt Aland and Barbara Aland, *The Text of the New Testament: An Introdction to the Critical Editions and to the Theory and Practice of Modern Textual Criticism* (tr. E. F. Rhodes; Grand Rapids: Eerdmans; Leiden: Brill, 1987) 59: P47 is related to Codex Sinaiticus, not to codices A or C.

complicating factors rather than greater clarity in textual history and theory as they were then understood.

Hindsight might suggest, nevertheless, that these papyri all should have been viewed as more important than they were in the 1930s and 1940s — and even in the early 1950s — but the necessary catalyst for recognizing their critical importance came only with the discovery of the Bodmer papyri in the mid-1950s. P66, but especially P75, raised them all to a new level of visibility and significance. Why? Primarily because P75, a codex of John and Luke from the year 200 or earlier, contains a text extraordinarily similar to Codex Vaticanus and yet dates at least a 150 years earlier. That made textual critics sit up and take notice, for the common view after Westcott and Hort had been that the text represented in Codex Vaticanus was the result of revision over time and thus presented a refined, smoothened version of an older, rougher text. Rather than confirming that hypothesis, P75 demonstrated — in an actual, datable document — that already at or before 200 this very text existed in Egypt.

But P66 also attracted attention, though in a different way. This codex of John, also from about the year 200, was viewed as a mixed text "with elements which are typically Alexandrian and Western,"[79] that is, with textual characteristics that are typical of the two early but sharply distinguishable text-types that Westcott-Hort had identified. (This assessment was later modified and P66 is now usually linked with the P75-B kind of text, though recognizing that it is a rather "wild" member of that group.[80]) Here again, however — with respect to both P75 and P66 — we encounter that almost universal shortcoming among textual critics who approach new papyri discoveries, which J. N. Birdsall so forcefully pointed out in 1958, when he spoke of the fault "common to many contemporary scholars who attempt to discuss and define such early evidence as this by standards of later witnesses." He continues:

> Beyond the fourth century the divisions of "Neutral," "Western," "Caesarean," "Byzantine" (or corresponding terms) are apposite: but in the early period, which such a papyrus as p66 reveals to us, these concepts are out of place. The task of present-day criticism is to inaugurate an era in which we begin from the earliest evidence and on the basis of its interpretation discuss the later.[81]

[79] As reflected, e.g., in the description of P66 offered by Bruce M. Metzger, *The Text of the New Testament: Its Transmission, Corruption, and Restoration* (2d ed.; New York/Oxford: Oxford University Press, 1968) 40.

[80] See Gordon D. Fee, "P76, P66, and Origen: The Myth of Early Textual Recension in Alexandria," *New Dimensions in New Testament Study* (ed. R. N. Longenecker and M. C. Tenney; Grand Rapids: Zondervan, 1974) 30–31; idem, *Papyrus Bodmer II (P66): Its Textual Relationships and Scribal Characteristics* (SD 34; Salt Lake City: University of Utah Press, 1968) 35.

[81] J. Neville Birdsall, *The Bodmer Papyrus of the Gospel of John* (Tyndale New Testament Lecture, 1958; London: Tyndale Press, 1960) 7.

This statement has been widely quoted—and rightly so—but has not yet been widely heeded. Less well known are similar sentiments expressed a decade earlier—before the Bodmer papyri had been discovered—by Kenneth Clark at a Chicago conference to honor Edgar J. Goodspeed. Referring to the Chester Beatty papyri, he reported that "the only studies made thus far seem to approach these texts by reversing the centuries. We require a new mental attitude, wherein we . . . approach these earliest materials *de novo*," and Clark offered the further admonition that "we should study the third-century witnesses in their own right."[82]

As was the case with the Chester Beatty papyri, this faulty and illogical procedure of judging the earlier by the later was the one normally applied also to P66 and P75. Yet there was a difference here, as will be noted presently.

More significant than its textual character, however, was the observation that P66 contains four to five hundred scribal corrections, most of which are the scribe's own corrections of his errors, though others appear to be corrections made by comparison with another exemplar, that is, comparison of the finished product with another manuscript. Thus, P66 presents a kind of early textual history of its own, showing how scribes worked, how they made corrections, and how different textual complexions can be found in the same manuscript.[83]

These findings gave the Bodmer and all early papyri a new status: P75 connected Codex Vaticanus (B)—generally considered the preeminent NT manuscript—directly to the earliest level of textual history, thereby bestowing new significance on both manuscripts, but new significance not only as witnesses but also in terms of text-critical methodology. The same was true of P66: it acquired a fresh, independent importance for its disclosure of the character of the early transmission process. New Testament papyri, therefore, had finally come into their own with the analysis of the Bodmer discoveries. At last they could stand on their own merit and be judged on their own terms. It is no coincidence that the first entirely new critical edition to be produced after their appearance, the *United Bible Societies Greek New Testament* (*UBSGNT*), first issued in 1966, contained a list of all the known papyri—the first Greek NT to do so. Moreover, all the papyri were newly collated for this edition and cited in every case where they offer data for variant readings. This full citation of the textual evidence in the papyri is now standard procedure.

[82] Kenneth W. Clark, "The Manuscripts of the Greek New Testament," *New Testament Manuscript Studies: The Materials and the Making of a Critical Apparatus* (ed. M. M. Parvis and A. P. Wikgren; Chicago: University of Chicago Press, 1950) 20–21.

[83] See Fee, *Papyrus Bodmer II*, 35, 56, 76–83.

This is where this paper should end, for its purpose—as indicated in the title—was to provide historical perspective on the NT papyri. That included an assessment of papyrus as a writing material for manuscripts, a review of their discovery, but particularly a scrutiny of their reception and use by NT textual critics from their first appearance down to the present time. Those tasks have been performed, though with what success is for the reader to judge.

At the very time, however, when the NT papyri seemed finally to have achieved independent status and to have been fully utilized in NT textual criticism, a quite unexpected and disquieting discovery made its appearance, raising serious questions about the actual, practical impact of the papyri upon NT text-critical method and upon the critical editions of our own time that have been the beneficiaries of these precious documents from the distant past. Were it not for this turn of events, the succeeding section might not be necessary.

The Proper Place of the Papyri in New Testament Textual Criticism

The unexpected and disquieting development to which I refer can be quickly described. When these half dozen early and extensive NT papyrus manuscripts had finally been analyzed, utilized, and incorporated into the texts and into the textual apparatuses of our latest critical editions, what was the result? As demonstrated by several assessments of the post-Bodmer editions of the Nestle-Aland text and of the United Bible Societies text, as well as others, it was discovered that these NT texts in general usage actually differed only moderately from the Greek text of Westcott-Hort in 1881. Kenneth Clark demonstrated this already in a 1956 publication—before the Bodmer papyri had been worked into our critical texts—and again in 1968 —after all the major papyri had been fully utilized.[84] The analysis done at Duke University led to the following forthright conclusion:

> Since 1881 [that is, since Westcott-Hort's text] twenty-five editors have issued about seventy-five editions of the Greek New Testament. The collation of these many "critical" texts consistently exposes the fact that each of them is basically a repetition of the Westcott-Hort text.... Indeed, we have continued for eighty-five years to live in the era of Westcott-Hort, our *textus receptus* ["the text received by all"].[85]

[84] Kenneth W. Clark, "The Effect of Recent Textual Criticism upon New Testament Studies," *The Background of the New Testament and Its Eschatology* (ed. W. D. Davies and D. Daube; Cambridge: University Press, 1956) 33–36, reprinted in K. W. Clark, *The Gentile Bias,* 71–74; and K. W. Clark, "Today's Problem with the Critical Text of the New Testament," *Transitions in Biblical Scholarship* (Essays in Divinity, 6; ed. J. C. Rylaarsdam; Chicago: University of Chicago, 1968) 158–60, reprinted in K. W. Clark, *The Gentile Bias,* 121–23.

[85] K. W. Clark, "Today's Problem with the Critical Text," 160 = Clark, *The Gentile Bias,* 123.

Now it is 107 years later than Westcott-Hort, and yet essentially the same statement must be made today. That is a striking conclusion to be drawn after a hundred years of vigorous text-critical work and after a hundred years of extraordinary papyrus discoveries, to say nothing of the discovery of numerous other influential manuscripts and versions. Indeed, it is a shocking and therefore sobering conclusion, and one not lost on a number of us who work in the field. *If Westcott-Hort did not utilize papyri in constructing their NT text, and if our own modern critical texts, in fact, are not significantly different from that of Westcott-Hort, then why are the papyri important after all?* And have they really "come into their own" and been fully and *appropriately* utilized in the text-critical discipline? While there is one sense, then, in which the NT papyri have come into their own—they have been fully incorporated into our critical editions—there is another real sense in which their expected impact has not yet been fully felt.

To raise this question in a different way, the great achievement of NT textual criticism over the past 250 years—since 1730—was the departure from and triumph over the *textus receptus,* that is, the long struggle to accredit the few older manuscripts as superior witnesses to the original text over against the mass of later manuscripts. That was achieved by the rudimentary and preparatory—and yet monumental—work of those mentioned earlier (Bentley, Wettstein, Bengel, and Griesbach), whose labors were characterized, for example, by the insistence that textual witnesses must be weighed and not merely counted (Bengel), followed by the decisive break with the *textus receptus* in Lachmann's Greek NT of 1831. During the succeeding fifty years—until the 1881 appearance of Westcott-Hort's *New Testament in the Original Greek* (as they called it)—giants like Tischendorf and Tregelles pressed home the principles that "the text should be sought solely from ancient witnesses" (Tischendorf), that textual witnesses "that excel in antiquity prevail in authority" (Tischendorf) and that the NT text should be formed "on the authority of ancient copies without allowing the 'received text' any prescriptive rights" (Tregelles). Hort then produced the *tour de force* in his *Introduction* to the Greek NT, in which he effectively argued that the "original" text is to be found in the "best" manuscripts, and that the "best" manuscripts are, first, Codex Vaticanus (B) and, second, Codex Sinaiticus (ℵ), the two great parchment codices that originated in the mid-fourth century. All of this was achieved without the assistance of the early papyri.

Textual criticism did not, of course, stand still during the intervening fifty years until the Chester Beatty papyri were discovered, yet little had occurred to alter the basic understanding of the development of the text as Hort had outlined it, except that a Caesarean text had been proposed as a type of text midway between Hort's two early text-types, the "Neutral" and the "Western." Moreover, really nothing had occurred to dislodge Codices Vaticanus and Sinaiticus from their preeminent place in the whole structure. The Chester Beatty papyri, as we have seen, provided readings that supported the general theory of these three earliest text-types, and then later the Bodmer papyri attested an earlier stage of the Vaticanus text in P75, as well as another example, in P66, of a text basically supportive of the P75-B type of text, but also showing elements of other identifiable texts as they are found in the Westcott-Hort framework. It is only natural, then, to expect the critical texts of the NT to resemble Westcott-Hort's 1881 text, and that, essentially, is what they did, despite numerous claims that great advances had been made since the papyri had made their appearance.

I repeat, therefore, the question: *If Westcott-Hort did not utilize papyri in constructing their NT text, and if our own modern critical texts, in fact, are not significantly different from that of Westcott-Hort, then why are the papyri important after all?*

This point might have been made in another way. In the process of describing and extolling the work of Eberhard Nestle in producing his long series of hand-editions of the Greek NT, Kurt and Barbara Aland compare Nestle's early editions (that of 1898—the first—and those that quickly followed) with the so-called "Standard Text" in their own Nestle-Aland twenty-sixth edition of 1979. They say—somewhat surprisingly—that Nestle "produced a text that not only lasted seventy years, but on the whole truly represents the modern state of knowledge. It is significant that in its 657 printed pages the early Nestle text differs from the modern 'Standard text' in merely seven hundred passages."[86] By the nature of the circumstances, the papyri could play only the smallest role in these early Nestle editions, so the small difference between their text and that of the latest Nestle-Aland raises the same question: why should the papyri be credited with great importance?

So we are left with the somewhat disappointing conclusion that the significance of the strikingly early and even the strikingly extensive NT papyri has not yet been clarified by NT textual critics — contrary to the expectations so reasonably elicited as each new papyrus came to light. If this is the case, where do we go from here?

In contemporary NT textual criticism, nearly everyone talks about the "monumental" importance of the NT papyri, and Kurt Aland has claimed repeatedly in recent years that in the forty papyri prior to about A.D. 300 the history of the NT text "can be studied in the original."[87] More recently he has claimed that in the Nestle-Aland 26th edition "the goal of an edition . . . 'in the original Greek' seems to have been reached."[88] Yet, this critical text

---

[86] Aland and Aland, *The Text of the New Testament*, 20.

[87] Kurt Aland, "The Twentieth-Century Interlude in New Testament Textual Criticism," *Text and Interpretation: Studies in the New Testament Presented to Matthew Black* (ed. E. Best and R. McL. Wilson; Cambridge/New York: Cambridge University Press, 1979) 11 [A reply, in German, to the author's Hatch Memorial Lecture of the same title, *JBL* 93 (1974) 386–414].

[88] Kurt Aland, "Der neue 'Standard Text' in seinem Verhältnis zu den frühen Papyri und

which he has edited (most recently with Barbara Aland) also falls under the same judgment rendered a few moments ago: it is among those that differ little from the Westcott-Hort text of 1881,[89] which was constructed without benefit of the papyri. At the same time, the Nestle-Aland text (which is identical to that of the *UBSGNT*) is widely accepted and, by some, is even acclaimed as the new "standard text"[90] of the NT.

So our discipline faces an interesting situation: on the one hand, we have a widely used and generally accepted NT text of good quality — no one denies that — but a text that would not be much different if the NT papyri had not been dicovered; on the other hand, we have new manuscript treasures of great antiquity with extensive coverage of the NT text that — contrary to their intrinsic and expected worth — appear to be underutilized and even undervalued when one looks at their actual influence on text-critical history and method. So a pointed question arises: Should there not be a more *dynamic* relationship between the two — between the early papyri and the critical text? That is, should not current methodology be more *actively* and more *radically* affected by these startling new discoveries? And should not the current critical text be more *directly* based on principles and theories that issue more *immediately* from an assessment of the textual character of the earliest papyri? The challenge that results is this: Can we find a way, methodologically, to use these papyri to break through in a new fashion to an earlier state of the NT text? Some think that this has already happened — as noted above — but it would appear that the papyri have been fed into the critical editions almost in a passive manner and in accordance with theories of the NT text formulated before the early, extensive papyri were ever discovered. A more logical approach — as intimated above — would be to establish a history and theory

---

Majuskeln," *New Testament Textual Criticism: Its Significance for Exegesis: Essays in Honor of Bruce M. Metzger* (ed. E. J. Epp and G. D. Fee; Oxford: Clarendon Press, 1981) 274–75.

[89] The close relationship between the texts of Nestle-Aland[25] (1963) and of Westcott-Hort (1881) is demonstrated vividly in a chart in Aland and Aland, *The Text of the New Testament*, 26–27. In a comparison of Nestle-Aland with the editions of Westcott-Hort, Vogels, Merk, and Bover (as well as Tischendorf), Nestle-Aland[25] shows strikingly fewer variants from Westcott-Hort than from any of the others. The numbers of variants from Nestle-Aland[25] are as follows: Westcott-Hort (1881) = 558 variants; Merk[9] (1965) = 770 variants; Bover[5] (1968) = 1161 variants; and Vogels[4] (1950) = 1996 variants [as a matter of interest, Tischendorf[8] (1869) differs by 1262 variants].

[90] Notice the pervasive use of the term "Standard Text" in Aland and Aland, *The Text of the New Testament*, especially pp. 20–36. They hasten to point out that "this name did not come from the editors but from reviews of the new Nestle-Aland[26] in the popular press and in scholarly journals" (p. 30). The matter is by no means undisputed, however, as evidenced, e.g., by Ian A. Moir, "Can We Risk another 'Textus Receptus'?" *JBL* 100 (1981) 614–18; or H.-W. Bartsch, "Ein neuer Textus Receptus für das griechische Neue Testament?" *NTS* 27 (1980–81) 585–92, to which Kurt Aland replied, under the same title, in *NTS* 28 (1982) 145–53.

of the NT text, or reconfirm an existing one, by beginning with the early papyri and then basing the critical text on the resultant theory. That, of course, is a highly complex subject, which I have treated, though only in a preliminary fashion, in more than one publication.[91] Space does not permit repetition of those proposals here, but suffice it to say that the papyri can and should play a fundamental role in at least three areas:

(1) The papyri can be employed to isolate the earliest discernible text-types, which is feasible because the papyri vary in their textual complexions and can be placed into groups.

(2) By using the resulting text-types, the papyri can help us to trace out the very early history of the NT text, thereby opening the way for more objective methods of judging the quality of witnesses than are presently available.

(3) Finally, the papyri can aid in refining the canons of criticism—the principles by which we judge variant readings—for they open to us a window for viewing the earliest stages of textual transmission, providing instances of how scribes worked in their copying of manuscripts.

All of this confirms our sense that the papyri are of extraordinary importance for writing the history of the NT text and for guiding the development of its proper methodology.[92]

---

[91] See E. J. Epp, "Textual Criticism," *The New Testament and Its Modern Interpreters* (ed. E. J. Epp and †G. W. MacRae; The Bible and Its Modern Interpreters, 3; Atlanta: Scholars Press; Philadelphia: Fortress, 1988) 97–106; "The Twentieth Century Interlude in New Testament Textual Criticism," *JBL* 93 (1974) 397–99.

[92] The issues raised here have been explored by the present writer in a paper presented at the international conference on "Gospel Traditions in the Second Century" at the University of Notre Dame, 15–17 April 1988, entitled, "The Significance of the Papyri for Determining the Nature of the New Testament Text in the Second Century: A Dynamic View of Textual Transmission," scheduled for publication in 1989 in a volume of the Notre Dame series, Studies in Christianity and Judaism in Antiquity, ed. by William L. Petersen.

This paper draws a fair measure of material from the author's Kenneth W. Clark Lectures at Duke University in April, 1986, but its particular thrust was developed for presentation at the Annual Meeting of the Society of Biblical Literature in November of that year. Following that reading, Gordon D. Fee graciously alerted me to a serious deficiency, which I have corrected for this version, and I am grateful to him.

Professor Fitzmyer presided at the session in which I read my very first paper at a learned society—at the Society of Biblical Literature in December of 1960—and that paper became my first publication (*HTR* 55 [1962] 51–62). In the same year Professor Fitzmyer published an article on P75 (*CBQ* 24 [1962] 170–79)—noting some of the methodological points emphasized now in this paper—and his magisterial commentary on *The Gospel according to Luke* (2 vols.; AB 28; Garden City, NY: Doubleday, 1981–85)—unlike many—is fully informed by text-critical discussion. During Professor Fitzmyer's six-year term (1971–76) as Editor of the *Journal of Biblical Literature,* I was privileged to serve as Associate Editor for NT book reviews, and my already high admiration for him as a scholar was enlarged to include admiration also as a fair-minded and meticulous editor and as a good friend and colleague.

The Narrative Meshalim in the Old Testament Books and in the Synoptic Gospels

Birger Gerhardsson
Lunds Universitet

And God gave Solomon depth of wisdom and insight, and understanding as wide as the sand on the sea-shore, so that Solomon's wisdom surpassed that of all the men of the east and of all Egypt. For he was wiser than any man. . . . He uttered three thousand meshalim and his songs numbered a thousand and five.

1 Kings 5:9–12 (4:29–31)

What is here is greater than Solomon.

Matt 12:42 par.

IT IS WELL KNOWN that the synoptic Gospels have a common, general designation (*parabolē*, *parabolai*) for the independent units of the proper sayings-tradition ("parables" as well as "logia"). Such an application indicates that they are uninfluenced by the classical rhetoricians' definitions of a παραβολή but have in mind the Hebrew *māshāl* (*měshālîm* in the plural).[1] This is a very broad designation, covering oral and written "words" and texts of many different kinds: aphorisms, proverbs, similitudes, parables, allegories, fables, riddles, folk songs, prophetical sayings, etc.[2] It is admittedly difficult to characterize a genre which includes such a variety of texts, but

[1] The Aramaic equivalent *mathlā'* is not very interesting. Of course, Jewish teachers formulated meshalim even in Aramaic, but it is rather striking that the extant rabbinic "parables" are almost exclusively in Hebrew (and stemming from Palestine); cf. D. Flusser, *Die rabbinischen Gleichnisse und der Gleichniserzähler Jesus* (Judaica et Christiana 4, Part 1; Bern, Frankfurt am Main, Las Vegas: P. Lang, 1981) 18.

[2] Cf. J. Jeremias, *Die Gleichnisse Jesu* (9th ed., Göttingen: Vandenhoeck & Ruprecht, 1977) 16–17. On the OT meshalim, cf. O. Eissfeldt, *Der Maschal im Alten Testament* (BZAW; Giessen: Töpelmann, 1913); J. Pirot, "Le '*māšāl*' dans l'Ancien Testament," *RSR* 37 (1950) 565–80; A. S. Herbert, "The 'Parable' (*Māšāl*) in the Old Testament," *SJT* 7 (1954) 180–96; and J. Hempel, *Jahwegleichnisse der israelitischen Propheten* (Apoxysmata; Berlin: Töpelmann, 1961) 1–29. On the meshalim in the so-called intertestamental literature, see E. Hammershaimb, "Om lignelser og billedtaler i de gammeltestamentlige Pseudepigrafer," *SEA* 40 (1975) 36–65. On the rabbinic meshalim, see now, in addition to A. Feldman, *The Parables and Similes of the Rabbis* (2d ed.; Cambridge: University Press, 1927) and the well-known works by P. Fiebig, Flusser, *Die rabbinischen Gleichnisse*.

but I believe one can say that all verbal meshalim have three characteristics in common: they are texts (oral texts primarily, but also written ones)—not free streams of words; they are brief—not entire books; and they have an artistic design—differing from careless colloquial speech.

I feel that usage of the term "mashal" in the exegetical work as an overall designation of the independent units within the synoptic sayings-tradition is recommended. This would help us to do justice to the fact that "logia" and "parables" have important characteristics in common.

On the other hand, the variations are great. We must, of course, for our analytical aims categorize the synoptic meshalim more closely and divide them into convenient subgroups. I am not going to suggest a detailed division at this time, but just a simple separation of that which we conventionally call "logia" and "parables." I would suggest the designations *aphoristic*[3] *meshalim* and *narrative meshalim*, respectively.[4] In both cases the appellation is simplified. Aphoristic does not always strike the character of a "logion" quite well, and some "parables" paint a picture rather than narrating a story. Nevertheless, I think the two designations are reasonable; allowing for a more accurate, yet simple nomenclature.

This article's purpose is twofold. First, presentation and characterization of the narrative meshalim found in the OT books, followed by an elucidation of the narrative meshalim in the synoptic Gospels by way of comparison. Especially the contrasts are revealing. I will also address the subject of aphoristic meshalim now and then, but only incidentally.

This article is dedicated—in appreciation and admiration—to my old friend Joe Fitzmyer, who has given us so many important works concerning the NT and the world around it, and even shed light on many parables.[5]

The Narrative Meshalim
in the Old Testament Books

The OT books contain an enormous number of texts, which are either called meshalim or might rightly be called so. The majority are aphoristic, e.g., those which are gathered in the book of Proverbs, where older collections have been brought together.[6] Only very few texts qualify for the

---

[3] For the term, cf. J. D. Crossan, *In Fragments: The Aphorisms of Jesus* (San Francisco: Harper & Row, 1983); see also V. K. Robbins, "Picking up the Fragments," *Forum* 1, 2 (1985) 32–36.

[4] In the second edition of his book *Jesus als Lehrer* (WUNT 2 R. 7; Tübingen: Mohr, 1984), R. Riesner uses the designations "Lehrsummarien" and "Besinnungstexte" respectively (392–93).

[5] Fitzmyer's interpretations of all the Lucan "parables" are now readily available in his great commentary, *The Gospel According to Luke* (AB 28–28A, 2 vols; Garden City, NY: Doubleday, 1981, 1985).

[6] See Prov 1:1; 10:1; (22:17); 24:23; 25:1; 30:1; 31:1.

designation "narrative meshalim." There are a number of borderline cases,[7] but it seems reasonable to accept but five texts as belonging to the category of "narrative meshalim":[8]

(1) Jotham's mashal of the Trees in Judg 9:7–15 (7–21),
(2) Nathan's mashal of the Poor Man's only Lamb in 2 Sam 12:1–4 (1–15),
(3) Jehoash's mashal of the Thistle in 2 Kgs 14:9 (8–14),
(4) Isaiah's mashal of the Vineyard in Isa 5:1–6 (1–15), and
(5) Ezekiel's mashal of the Vine and the Eagles in Ezek 17:3–10 (1–24).

Numbers 1, 3, and 5 are fables; #4 is an allegorizing parable, while #2 is a narrative parable of a sort we find often in the synoptic Gospels.

The majority of the five texts are strikingly artificial. They are not unforced analogies, taken from the general course of nature or human life. The three fables are remarkably strained works of art: the trees anoint a king over them, the thistle seeks a son-in-law, the eagle plants a vine. Animals and plants speak a human language and are occupied with human concerns. The mashal of the Vineyard (#4) is less artificial, and the mashal of the Poor Man's Lamb (#2) is almost unforced; but, to the extent they are formulated in that way, they are atypical. Thus the narrative meshalim in the OT must be regarded as deliberately devised products of art, not as spontaneous analogies.[9]

They are texts but rather artless texts: they start directly and end directly, without a special introduction or ending and lacking a strict structure. In one case (#5) the narrative theme is taken up in the continuation of the speech and brought a step further, but this does not change the character of the mashal.

The mashal illuminates the topic of a speech with a narrative picture and thus implies a comparison, but none of the five examples is introduced by any formula which indicates the comparison (". . . is like . . ." or something similar). The narration starts nakedly, directly. In the following, discursive part of the speech, the comparison is easy to see, however, especially in the two cases when the speaker explicitly states whom he is aiming at: "You are the man" (#2), "The vineyard of the Lord of hosts is Israel" (#4). But we miss altogether interpretative and applicative elements of the type, "So you also. . . ."

Each of the five meshalim is especially constructed for the speech to which it belongs. This notwithstanding, the mashal is an independent part of the

---

[7] E.g., 2 Sam 14:5–7; Prov 9:1–6, 13–18; Isa 28:23–29; Ezek 15:1–18; 16:1–54; 19:2–9, 10–14; 23:1–19; 24:3–14.

[8] Thus also M. D. Goulder, *Midrash and Lection in Matthew* (London: SPCK, 1974) 47.

[9] It is misleading when Goulder writes, "The OT parables are essentially comparisons between the human-divine situation and an analogy in nature" (*Midrash*, 51). Flusser, on the other hand, emphasizes rightly the "pseudo-realistic" character of the "parables" (*Gleichnisse*) (*Die rabbinischen Gleichnisse*, 31–49).

speech. There is no transitional formula which links the mashal to the following portions, except in one case (#5).

In all five cases the mashal appears first, as a kind of proem, if we disregard the fact that the first of them is prefaced by a call to attention.

The message of the speech is then immediately presented in plain language. We do not get the impression that the mashal is put forward separately as an enigmatic story, which the listeners get time to ponder. Instead, the message follows directly after the mashal and without much regard to it. Thus the mashal is not made the object of exegesis or explicit textual commentary. It might be said that, when the proper message is presented, the mashal is superfluous. In two cases (##1 and 5) it is seen that some metaphor or phrase from the mashal comes up in the discursive portion of the speech, but even then we search in vain for a proper exposition of the mashal itself.

It is herein apparent that the mashal form has least of all been chosen because the content of the message could not be articulated in plain language. For the task of conveying the factual content of the message the introductory mashal lacks substantial importance; it is dispensable. In two cases one might believe that the mashal is, in fact, the central message. Isaiah begins his mashal (#4) with the declaration that he will now sing a love song concerning his friend's vineyard. In the continuation, however, the song (mashal) is not treated as a basic text, to be interpreted and applied. Ezekiel's mashal (#5) is preceded by a notice to the effect that the prophet gets God's command to speak a mashal to the house of Israel, but this mashal is not treated as the focal point of the speech. Even here the mashal is nothing more than a didactic means and one that in itself could be dispensed with.

What role precisely do the five narrative meshalim play within their respective speeches? Concrete and visual as they are, they catch the interest and engagement of the listeners and provoke them to react as the speaker wishes. This is especially easy to see when the listeners are exhorted to "judge" the message of the mashal (#4), or when David's anger is kindled and he condemns the man of the mashal (#2). The narrative mashal can play this role because it drapes the truth in a metaphoric, epic presentation so that the listener does not notice that he is judge in his own case.[10] Perhaps we might say that the mashal is a means to convince the listeners, a kind of argumentation, a metaphoric and epic *argumentum ad hominem*.

The speech to which the narrative mashal belongs is in all five cases a speech which partly censures the listener for something that has been done,

---

[10] The narrative meshalim in the OT are heterogeneous; the genre has many roots. One is obviously the presentation of a legal case before a tribunal. For interesting intermediate forms, see 2 Sam 14:5–7; 1 Kgs 20:39–40. Note also 2 Sam 12:1–4!

and partly predicts the punishments and evils which soon will come, the later element having a certain ring of prophecy. That the way of repentance is open nevertheless belongs to the religious axioms. The condemnation and the warnings are presented in plain language, but the soil has been prepared psychologically—or shall we say emotionally—with the introductory mashal. This awakens the listeners to attention, commitment, and decision.

It is very important to note that the narrative meshalim in the OT—not to mention the aphoristic meshalim—are not at all bound to be used only for religious aims or for teaching about celestial things. The aphoristic meshalim deal extremely often with highly mundane matters. And if we look at the narrative meshalim we see that Jotham's mashal censures the political ungratefulness of the citizens of Shechem against Jerubbaal, while Nathan's mashal rebukes David for his personal cruelty against Uriah. Jehoash's mashal depicts Amaziah's political presumption and warns him for going too far, and Ezekiel's mashal condemns Zedekiah's political unfaithfulness toward the Babylonian king. Only Isaiah's mashal has a directly religious theme: Israel's disobedience in the covenant with God. Of course the teaching is in all five cases presented within the limits of a world view in which God is the most important factor, but the mashal is not per se specifically tied to the religious sphere or to religious themes. Thus the narrative meshalim—as well as the aphoristic ones—are didactic means for proclaiming or teaching, irrespective of the content of the message to be presented.[11]

In the OT there are collections of aphoristic meshalim, brought together in the book of Proverbs. On the other hand there is no collection of narrative meshalim. This is hardly a mere coincidence. The type of narrative meshalim we have considered here—it is easy to imagine other types—is specially made for serving its purpose within a specific speech. Therefore they cannot be lifted out from this particular context without more ado and used for other aims. They are not totally independent units, not so generally applicable and "timeless" as the aphoristic meshalim usually are.

I said, "not without more ado." It is obvious that some of them can be reformulated and so made apt for a more general use. Isaiah's mashal about the Vineyard can be shortened and made useful for more general teaching; in fact the synoptic meshalim about the Vineyard[12] seem to have initially gained their figurative material from this text. And Nathan's little story about the Poor Man's Lamb could be used as an ethically summoning mashal

---

[11] In the rabbinic literature the narrative mashal is mostly used in a rather dry, technical way. There are, however, also examples of an older, more existential type of narrative mashal. Thus correctly Flusser, who thinks that the fundamental divide can be set to about 120 A.D., with exceptions naturally, *Die rabbinischen Gleichnisse*, 17–29.

[12] Mark 12:1–12 parr.; Matt 20:1–16; 21:28–32; cf. Luke 13:6–9.

without much alteration. This mashal is the one of the five which comes closest to the narrative meshalim of the synoptic tradition. The three fables cannot, however, be used for general aims without extremely deep reworking. Generally we know that the more strained a text has been made for serving a specific purpose, the harder it is to use it for something else.

The Narrative Meshalim
in the Synoptic Gospels

Mark, Matthew, and Luke are in good consonance with ancient Jewish tradition when they judge aphoristic and narrative meshalim as all being alike. They call all the independent units of the proper sayings-tradition *parabolai* in the sense *meshalim*. They put aphoristic and narrative meshalim together, side by side, in their sayings-dominated sections. And their information that Jesus used to teach ἐν παραβολαῖς[13] does not mean "in parables" but "in meshalim," including not only narrative but also aphoristic texts, not only long but also brief, not only elaborated but also dense sayings.[14] Mark 4 is the best example of this.

In the OT books the narrative meshalim are very few, while in the synoptic Gospels they are numerous, with the entire account of Jesus' specified teaching consisting of meshalim—aphoristic and narrative ones—with clarifying accessories. They are of many different types, though none of them are fables.[15]

As I pointed out above, most of the narrative meshalim in the OT are not only very artificial but also very artless, being rather unsophisticated in composition, structure, and wording. The same can certainly be said about some of the narrative meshalim in the synoptic Gospels as well, but these are exceptions. The bulk of the narrative meshalim in the Gospels are designed with quite another artistic skill than the OT examples. It is true that the narrative body of the synoptic mashal often *ends* nakedly, directly, but there usually follows a rounding off with an interpretive or applicative element. Some of the narrative meshalim in the Gospels also *start* directly—in Luke nearly half of them—without an introductory formula, but this is done in such cases with finesse. And in Mark and Matthew a formula normally stands

---

[13] Cf. Mark 3:23; 4:2, 10, 13, 33–34; 7:17; Matt 13:3, 10, 13, 34–35, 53. Luke uses the word παραβολή only once in the plural (8:10) against 17 times in the singular.

[14] In addition to "the parable chapter" (Mark 4:1–34; Matt 13:1–52; Luke 8:4–18), see especially Mark 12:1; Matt 21:45; 22:11. Clear examples of the use of *parabolē* in the meaning "aphoristic mashal" (maxim, aphorism, proverb, etc.) are Mark 7:17; Matt 15:15; Luke 4:23; 6:39. Mark 13:28 parr. may be meant otherwise.

[15] Inversely, note, e.g., that there is not a single king-mashal in the OT (Hempel, *Die Jahwegleichnisse*, 7).

introduction to the narrative. Moreover, the very narration is in most cases characterized by rhythm and poignancy; many of the narrative meshalim in the Gospels are little gems.[16]

In Mark and Matthew very often it is also said in the introduction to a narrative mashal that a comparison of some kind is intended. This element can be redundant ("With what can we compare the kingdom of God, or what parable shall we use for it? It is like . . .," e.g., Mark 4:30 parr., RSV) or a simple particle[17] or something between these extremes. The interpretive or applicative elements after the narrative body indicate the comparison more specifically: "So it will be . . ." or something similar.[18] As we have seen, comparative elements of the former kind are totally lacking in the OT texts under review, an intended comparison notwithstanding. The latter kind has, on the other hand, a certain counterpart in two cases ("You are the man," "The vineyard of the Lord of hosts is Israel").

In contrast to all the OT examples not one of the narrative meshalim in the synoptic Gospels is an organic part of a particular speech. Together with some fittings all of them are independent texts, which may be used each by itself in different connections and even put together in chain-like collections or composed into secondary, fictive "speeches."

The speeches are, however, but fictive. Strictly speaking, there is not one proper speech held by Jesus in the synoptic Gospels. Even the Sermon on the Mount (Matthew 5–7) is something other than a proper, explicated speech; despite being presented as a speech with an editorial formula before (5:1–2) and one after (7:28–29), without anything of the kind in between. It is a mosaic of ready-made pieces from the Jesus tradition. The pieces have been reworked—we disagree about to what extent—but they have nevertheless retained their character of finished meshalim, briefer or longer, simple or compound, dense or elaborate, propositional or metaphoric, aphoristic or narrative. The same can even more correctly be said about the other sayings-dominated sections of the synoptic Gospels, where small redactional elements often reveal that the presentation is a secondary composition, not a proper speech. The so-called eschatological speech (Mark 13:1–37; Matt 24:1–25:46; Luke 21:1–36) has in one way a coherent main theme, but not even this meets the criteria for classification as a uniform, explicated speech.

---

[16] Flusser finds a certain loquacity (*Plauderhaftigkeit*) in the "parable" genre, even in the "parables" of Jesus (*Die rabbinischen Gleichnisse*, 299; cf. 290–91 and 306). It is difficult to agree. Unnecessary words appear very rarely in the narrative meshalim of the Gospels. I can hardly give more examples than Matt 25:22–23, 37–39, 44, and Luke 15:21, where, possibly, repetitions could have been replaced by summarizing words.

[17] ὡς, Mark 13:34; ὥσπερ, Matt 25:14.

[18] Matt 13:49; cf., e.g., 18:14 par., 35, 20:16; Luke 15:10; 17:10. Note also Luke 11:8; 16:8; 18:6–8. Very often this element lacks a formula, e.g., Matt 11:18–19 par., 21:31–32.

Yet Matthew has often followed the principle of grouping together elements of tradition which are akin as to form or content. It is typical for him that he presents not fewer than 16 of his 21 narrative meshalim in three blocks (13:1–52; 21:23–22:14; 24:42–25:46), while—faithful to his specific redactional program (1:1–4)—Luke almost always presents his narrative meshalim one by one. Only four of his 29 narrative meshalim stand successively (15:1–16:14), and he has also refrained from divorcing two couples (13:18–21; 14:28–33). The remaining 21 narrative meshalim are put forward individually, in certain cases even prefaced by a brief indication of situation, cause, or aim.[19] It should perhaps be mentioned that Matthew and Luke have not themselves invented their way of presenting the narrative meshalim. In the older collections the narrative meshalim were on occasion presented in groups, while at other times one by one. The two evangelists have each fortified one tendency in the collections they have used.

One might get the idea that the placing together of meshalim in the synoptic Gospels—or in the older collections we glimpse behind them—is analogous to the OT collections of *aphoristic* meshalim, e.g., the book of Proverbs. This is not the case. Collections of that type contain meshalim of somewhat variegating form, but are on the whole rather homogeneous. In the synoptic tradition, on the other hand, the transmitted sayings-material has many different forms—as does the so-called Q-material—and has also been included together with narratives about Jesus. The evangelists have been forced into a much more complicated editorial endeavor than the men who made assembled collections such as the book of Proverbs. (For analogies we might instead look at some sections of the prophetic books.)

I have shown that the narrative mashal in the OT books is used as a kind of proem to a speech which is then explicated in plain language. I also mentioned the purpose it serves in this connection and the limited importance that it has within the speech. In conveying the factual content of the message it is, strictly speaking, superfluous. In the synoptic Gospels, on the contrary, we find not a single example of a section in which a narrative mashal stands as a proem to a properly explicated speech. In the two cases where a narrative mashal begins a fictive speech or sayings-dominated section (Mark 4:1–9 parrs., Luke 15:3–7), it is only the first important element of this, not a proem. And the narrative meshalim may appear anywhere in the body of the "speech." Very often a text of this kind comes as a forceful final element in a "speech" or section of sayings,[20] but the placement may vary quite freely.

This also means that the narrative meshalim in the synoptic Gospels play

---

[19] Luke 14:7; 15:1–3; 18:1, 9; 19:11. I think 8:4 too should be seen in this light.

[20] Mark 4:30–32; 13:33–37; Matt 7:24–27 par.; 11:16–19 par.; 13:47–50; 18:23–35; 20:1–16; 21:33–44; 22:11–14; 25:31–46; Luke 6:46–49; 7:31–35; Luke 12:58–59; 13:20–21; 14:16–24; 16:19–31; 17:7–10; 19:11–27.

a much more substantial role in conveying the factual content of the message than do the OT examples. In the account of Jesus' specified teaching, the majority is given in mashal form, in aphoristic or narrative meshalim furnished with due fittings, calculated to facilitate understanding. Thus the narrative meshalim of the Gospels are didactic means with a very substantial function; they are vital carriers of the material content of the teaching.

One cannot exclude the possibility that Jesus on occasion held proper speeches, in which he explicated at length a coherent theme. John may have—beneath his characteristic distinctiveness—preserved a reminiscence of that. But in that case recollection has disappeared completely from within the synoptic tradition. All the way through we are presented the image of Jesus conveying his proper teachings in short texts—aphoristic and narrative meshalim—the meaning of which he clarifies with the aid of different interpretive and applicative fittings, when necessary. And one thing is especially plain: that the teaching of Jesus has been *transmitted within Early Christianity* in the form of meshalim with accessories, which facilitate understanding and oral exposition.

There follows a listing of what I term the fittings or accessories of the narrative meshalim. The evangelist can indicate the theme of a mashal by its place in the Gospel as a totality and in a certain local context. In addition he can help the readers understand the sense of the mashal with one or more of the following accessories:

(1) a directly preparing editorial notice (e.g., Luke's preparative sentences, in which he indicates the birth situation of the mashal or its cause or aim[21]),

(2) some didactic phrase in the mouth of Jesus before the very narrative (e.g. the set formula: "With what can we compare . . . ?"),

(3) an introductory formula to the narrative body of the mashal (e.g. "The kingdom of God is like the case of . . ."),

(4) a concluding question, proper or rhetorical (point 2 above can also have question form),

(5) a generalizing conclusion,

(6) a proper interpretation or application (sometimes even introduced by a set formula: "So it will be . . ." etc.),[22]

(7) a conclusion (e.g., "Watch therefore . . ."),

(8) one or more complementary, kindred statements, which may not be intended as a proper interpretation of the main point of the mashal,[23]

(9) a subsequent frame notice.[24]

---

[21] See above, n. 19.

[22] See above, n. 18.

[23] E.g., Luke 16:9–13. These statements are hardly given as proper interpretations of the mashal itself.

[24] E.g., Mark 12:12 parr.

(10) "The factual half" can penetrate "the figurative half" at certain places so that some elements — terms, expressions, sentences, motifs — at one and the same time express both "the figurative half" and "the factual half" (e.g., "Cast the worthless servant into the outer darkness . . ."[25]).

(11) Sometimes didactic elements (questions, answers, admonitions) are integrated into the narrative text of the mashal. Luke does so several times, Mark only once, and Matthew twice[26] These interferences occasion more than the others that the inherited wording of the narrative text is changed. (Sometimes, however, this element may be original.)

Only one of the narrative meshalim in the synoptic Gospels stands nakedly, without at least one of these interpretative accessories (Luke 16:19–31). Most of them have several.

These fittings have as a rule been more variable than the narrative text of the mashal. It is easy to see in the preserved texts that many of them have been reworked during the process of transmission, use, and redaction. Yet I think it is a great mistake to believe that Jesus himself generally put forward his narrative meshalim without such accessories — of course he may have done that in exceptional situations[27] — and that his narrative meshalim have been transmitted without them at any stage of tradition before the evangelists. Without them the narrative text is a riddle, and nothing indicates that Jesus' attitude to his people was such that he visited a place, conveyed a number of riddles, and then went away. Consequently, it is one thing to recognize that these fittings have been variable and in fact reworked during the course of tradition and exposition in Early Christianity and at the final editing of the Gospels, and quite another thing to maintain that Jesus himself put forward his narrative meshalim without such clarifying fittings.

Michael Goulder has drawn our attention to the fact that some "parables" in the Gospels are indicative and some imperative[28] This is a fruitful observation, but I do not think that we have to do here with alternatives. The narrative body of a mashal has almost without exception an elucidative function, with the aspect here being indicative. When a narrative mashal has an imperative character, it has that in addition, and it is mostly due to the fact that the accessories have been formulated to that effect. Only in a minority of cases, most of them in Luke, has the imperative aspect also been included in the narrative body itself of the mashal, but even then this aspect has only been added to the indicative one.

---

[25] Matt 25:30; further, e.g., 24:46, 48, 51; 25:5–6, 19, 21, 23.
[26] Mark 13:33–37; Matt 24:43–44, 45–51; cf. Luke, e.g., 12:35–38, 41–46, 58–59; 13:24–30; 14:7–11; 18:9–14; 20:9–19.
[27] Cf., e.g., Mark 12:12 parr.
[28] Goulder, *Midrash*, 48–50.

The narrative meshalim of the synoptic Gospels have a strikingly homogeneous *theme*. The key term is βασιλεία τοῦ θεοῦ, "the kingdom/rule of God," which is not to be taken in the narrow meaning of "the coming kingdom/rule." Rather as a broad designation of God's ruling the world, his people, and the individual human being, as well as the obedience or disobedience he gets from "the children of the kingdom." Sometimes the focus is on how God acts, either himself or through some representative, other times it is on the human part of the relation, and on some occasions both are referred to. Solely human or interhuman problems are not at stake; when human issues are brought up, the will of God is the first concern of the mashal.[29] There is one possible exception in the synoptic Gospels—the mashal of the Good Samaritan—but this is debatable.[30]

The theme "the kingdom/rule of God" is not secondarily pressed upon the meshalim with the aid of new, foreign fittings. Even the narrative body of the mashal is always formed in order to elucidate the relationship of God and men. It seems to me beyond discussion that the narrative meshalim in the synoptic Gospels, without exception, have been created to elucidate different aspects of the teaching about the rule of God. They are all "parables of the Kingdom."

This is not at all a trivial fact, something self-evident with regard to the original milieu of the material. The theme has been chosen deliberately; it mirrors a conscious concentration upon "the one necessary thing." As we have seen, it did not at all belong to the nature of the mashal that it should elucidate religious or heavenly matters. It could serve whatever message one wished to present. When, in spite of their familiarity with the broad Jewish mashal tradition, Jesus and early Christianity concentrated upon "the kingdom/rule of God" they must have made their choice of theme quite intentionally. It cannot be said that other problems—personal, social, political, and other secular questions—were outside their horizon. The fact to be considered is that they did in reality not bring up such subjects.[31]

I have emphasized the great importance of the narrative meshalim within the synoptic tradition, stating that they were essential elements in the

---

[29] The mashal of the Unmerciful Servant (Matt 18:23–35) elucidates the necessity of forgiving our debtors, but the central point is that God retracts his great forgiveness, if we do not forgive others. This is typical.

[30] Cf. my old study *The Good Samaritan—the Good Shepherd?* (CN 16; Lund: Gleerup; Copenhagen: Munksgaard, 1958). I have more sense now of the complications of the transmission and editing process behind Luke 10:25–37, but I still find it difficult to interpret this mashal as a *Beispielerzählung*, which just presents a model for right behavior.

[31] In itself it is, of course, possible that Jesus said more about mundane matters than the early church has preserved, but a thesis to that effect is not very probable and can hardly be substantiated.

teaching of Jesus according to the synoptists. This evaluation must now be qualified. In one respect the narrative meshalim are only secondary elements in Jesus' activity in Israel. These sayings are not elementary nor proclamative. Neither do they belong to that which Jesus preaches initially. They do not belong to his *kerygma* and are not present until Jesus explains himself more closely. They are important texts, but only in the more specific teaching—the *didache*—of Jesus.[32]

This is true to form in one sense. The narrative meshalim are by nature elucidative, illuminative. For direct, elementary proclamation one needs first of all plain language. There are also certain types of aphoristic meshalim which are fit for use: dense sayings of the kind close to religious plain language. When the synoptic evangelists account for Jesus' elementary proclamation to his people they use rather straightforward statements: "The time is fulfilled, and the kingdom of God is at hand; repent, and believe the gospel" (Mark 1:15, RSV), or "Repent, for the kingdom of heaven is present" (Matt 4:17, RSV). And when they present that which Jesus does and says in front of the individual human being, they depict a man who speaks in plain language: "I will; be clean," "My son, your sins are forgiven," "Come out of the man, you unclean spirit," "Talitha cumi" (Mark 1:41; 2:5; 5:8, 41; RSV; cf. parr.). This is plain language. In the basic proclamation and actions of Jesus, narrative meshalim were not in place. According to the synoptic Gospels, neither has Jesus followed the traditional pattern, familiar from the OT, of using narrative meshalim as fanfares, provoking attention and interest before a proclamatory speech.

Some Hermeneutical Reflections

In conclusion I would like to note some simple hermeneutical reflections based upon my historical observations.

Among the interesting things going on in theology today are the attempts some scholars make to penetrate behind the Gospels to the historical Jesus himself, scrutinizing his genuine utterances with the aid of modern literary and linguistic analysis.[33] One course of action they take is to isolate and analyze the narrative body and the aphoristic core of those "parables" and

---

[32] I do not believe that it is only due to the subsequent development within the early church that the Gospels present narrative meshalim solely within the more specific teaching of Jesus. Nor do I think that Jesus himself primarily used his "parables" as weapons for attack and defense; contra Jeremias, *Die Gleichnisse*, 17–18 and 29–39, who keeps the multitudes together with the Pharisees and the scribes.

[33] I am especially thinking of those American scholars whom we associate with the journals *Semeia* and *Forum*, but similar approaches are common even in many other countries, as is well known.

"logia" which can be derived from Jesus himself with a high degree of probability. By way of this concentration one wishes to get hold of Jesus' intentions on safe basic points; at the same time one hopes to release new possibilities of interpretation in the sayings of Jesus.

I can very well understand both the historical and the practical motives for this program. Yet I think this course of reasoning is extraordinarily hazardous and might lead to self-deception, if Jesus is interpreted along these lines. The impending risk is that such interpretations are only superficially and apparently connected with Jesus, and are in fact only products of the general mentality of our time.[34]

For my part I do not think it is possible to get hold of the message of Jesus with any reasonable degree of certainty if the early Christian tradition has departed significantly from it. Our only alternative in this case would be speculation. I feel that we have, properly speaking, only two options: either to trust that the early Christian tradition has understood the intentions of Jesus within acceptable limits and has preserved his proclamations and teaching fairly well, or to admit that our historical reconstructions are hardly more than guesses.[35] As for myself, I think that there is satisfactory evidence for the first alternative.

I do not feel that it is proper to proceed directly from general theories about the metaphor or the narrative, taken as linguistic and aesthetic objects, to the "logia" and "parables" in the Gospels. In my opinion a historical restriction is necessary already at the beginning of our work with the texts, 2000 years old. Thus I think we must respect the fact that the evangelists call the independent units of the synoptic sayings-tradition *parabolai* in the meaning *meshalim,* and that they do so with historical right. The first classification has therefore been made already. I also believe it is fruitful for our exegetical work that we call these texts meshalim ourselves. When we do so, we state their literary identity correctly and also express something substantial about their character. Furthermore, I think it is important that we keep the "logia" and the "parables" of Jesus together by way of dividing them solely with a qualifying attribute, such as "aphoristic meshalim" and "narrative meshalim." In this way it becomes natural to consider their kinship and similarities and to interpret them in the light of each other.

The genre which is covered by the designation mashal is wide and variegated. It is therefore not easy to say that a text must be interpreted in a certain

---

[34] I am not polemicizing against any particular scholar now, just discussing tendencies which I find hazardous.

[35] It is difficult to share the expectation that "the Gnostic library" or other recent text discoveries will give us much help in the questions of the historical Jesus or the earliest phases of the Gospel tradition.

way because it is a mashal. A number of characteristics are, however, so general that we can say about *some* interpretations at least that they seem to be reasonable, and about *some* others that they appear to be rather strange as renderings of a mashal.

Many theorists maintain today that the metaphor or the narrative is intended to say something that the speaker cannot express in a more theoretical, discursive way.[36] This cannot be said about the narrative mashal. It is quite clear that the mashal is frequently created as a means for a message, which in itself could just as well be conveyed in plain language. In the Jewish and early Christian documents from antiquity it consistently occurs that a narrative mashal is formed to elucidate a special point and that a comparison of some kind is intended. This means that the speaker knows what he wants to say and often also states it in plain language. The mashal is taken into use as a didactic means. That which comes first is accordingly not a fascinating text to be interpreted. That which comes first is the "message" the speaker wants to convey. In relation to this "message" the mashal is logically secondary.

Of course there are cases where the narrative text comes first: e.g., when it is received as a pure riddle or an account of a dream—or as an unprefaced, totally foreign text, which one meets for the first time.[37] But these are special cases.

Of course it is also true that nobody can say in plain language *all* that might be conveyed in a well-designed mashal. A certain loss of both meaning and effect occurs when we change linguistic means of expression. But to make this insight absolute and maintain that we cannot express *at all* in plain language what we say in a mashal seems to me to be an untenable and very misleading exaggeration, however fascinating the idea may be in itself.

Turning to the narrative meshalim in the synoptic Gospels we can get some insights into their meaning solely by analyzing their narrative body—structure, usage, etc. But a fairly safe grasp of their meaning may only be gained from the elements I have herein called accessories or fittings. With these we can see, at least roughly, what the narrative body elucidates. We may find, sometimes, that these accessories, or at any rate some of them, pass by the point the narrative body seems to have in itself when analyzed in isolation. We do not find, however, that the point has been moved outside the theme with which all the synoptic meshalim deal, "the kingdom/rule of

[36] For an acute analysis of current theories about the metaphor and the parable, see M. Stiller Bjärgaard, *Metaphor and Parable: A Systematic Analysis of the Specific Structure and Cognitive Function of the Synoptic Similes and Parables qua Metaphors* (Acta Theologica Danica 19; Leiden: Brill, 1986).

[37] C. S. Lewis's distinction between "the Master's metaphor" and "the Pupil's metaphor" is also of great interest in this connection, but I cannot discuss it now, "Bluspels and Flalansferes" (*The Importance of Language,* ed. M. Black; Englewood Cliffs: Prentice Hall, 1962) 36–50.

God." In the main, the indications of the accessories accord rather well with the structure and expressions of the narrative body itself, if we read it without pettiness.

It is easy to see, when analyzing narrative meshalim of the independent type we find in the synoptic Gospels, that very foreign interpretations are possible, if one removes these fittings. In that case one holds a naked narrative, which can be supplied with new accessories, placed in quite another context, and so put into the service of some totally different message. One quotes a text, but its message may now have very little to do with the intentions of the text's originator. Responsible interpreters have discussed for centuries the question of when a fresh interpretation is in fact not an interpretation at all, but a new message. In this case the risk of unintentional unfaithfulness is impending.

The fact that the narrative meshalim of the Gospels have one homogeneous, concentrated *theme* is worthy of more attention than it usually receives. It has been pointed out above that it does not at all belong to the nature of the ancient Jewish meshalim that they deal with God or some other religious theme. They treat all kinds of subjects, widely different themes. Nor is it true that nonreligious questions lacked importance and interest in the milieus where Jesus and the early Christianity were active. This means that their choice of theme is deliberately made. They concentrated themselves consciously upon a subject, which was to them "the one necessary thing." This must mean that we leave our historical base if we interpret these texts today as if they treated other themes. A secularized use of Jesus' meshalim today may have its value, but it must be made quite clear that in that case the interpreter has left the original "message" of the ancient texts and has performed a μετάβασις εἰς ἄλλον τόπον.

One additional observation. We have seen in the Gospels, and found it quite probable, when viewed in its historical context, that the narrative meshalim of the Gospels do not give us the *elementary* message of Jesus, his initial, basic proclamation. They play a subsidiary role and do not come until Jesus acts in his "secondary" activity and explains himself more closely. Even this is a memento for our interpretation today. It is—if my point is allowed—possible to overestimate the narrative meshalim as representatives of the message of Jesus. They must be seen as subordinated to that which Jesus says in plain language and in aphoristic meshalim of the most direct and propositional type. Moreover, even the information which the evangelists mediate to us with their total presentation of Jesus' mission and message, with their episodal narratives, their passion and resurrection narratives, and their editorial statements as well, must be taken into consideration, if we want to see and preserve that which was basic and decisive for Jesus. Even these insights forbid us to build freely on the bodies of Jesus' narrative meshalim.

Thus I do not believe that we can reach the message and teaching that the historical Jesus presented during his short activity on earth in any other way than by utilizing the positive tradition his closest adherents have transmitted to us. If their documents are based on unreliable information and serious misunderstandings, then the historical truth about Jesus of Nazareth is lost to us without hope of recovery.

A Qualifying Parenthesis
(Rom 5:13-14) and Its Context

Charles Homer Giblin, S.J.
Fordham University

No man is an Iland, intire
of it selfe . . . any mans
death diminishes me, because
I am involved in Mankinde;
And therefore never send to
know for whom the bell tolls;
It tolls for thee . . . but
this bell, that tells me of
[another's] affliction . . .
applies . . . to mee: if by
this contemplation of anothers
danger, I take mine owne into
contemplation and so secure
my selfe, by making recourse
to my God, who is our onely
securitie.

John Donne (1624)

AMONG THE MANY COMMENTARIES dealing with the second half of Romans 5, Joseph A. Fitzmyer's in the *JBC*[1] stands out for its lucidity and theological perspicacity. In this essay honoring my colleague and friend, I shall discuss a few points regarding Paul's argumentation in Rom 5:11–21 which may in large measure support Fitzmyer's interpretation. In particular, I offer some observations regarding his view of the purpose of what he calls "the digression" in 5:12c–14: "The point . . . seems to be precisely to define Adam's relation to all men."[2] I find that relationship defined functionally, and in a way which can be interpreted as a universal, "corporate" sinfulness which followed automatically for all mankind. It was not "personal" sinfulness, as Adam's indeed was. In short, Paul is denying that, on the score of sinfulness, every man becomes Adam for himself. Paul makes a parenthetical qualification (5:13–14) prompted by the need to dissociate himself from a Pharisaic tradition which would compromise his own view of a corporate solidarity in sinfulness that automatically followed upon Adam's sinful act, a solidarity which could be remedied only by a free acceptance of God's gracious life-giving act in

---

[1] J. A. Fitzmyer, "The Letter to the Romans," *Jerome Biblical Commentary* (ed. R. E. Brown, J. A. Fitzmyer, R. E. Murphy; Englewood Cliffs, NJ: Prentice Hall, 1968) 53:52–60.

[2] Ibid., 53:56.

one man, Jesus Christ. In a more general context, I shall also proceed to submit a view of the way Rom 5:12–21 makes better sense not as a passage taken by itself, but as integrated into the context of 5:1–11.

In attempting to situate and thus clarify Paul's argumentation, A. J. M. Wedderburn[3] discussed the background of Paul's views in Rom 5:12. He rightly ruled out gnosticism, but then opted for Judaism. He assumed that Paul endorsed the Pharisaic position concerning Adam and accordingly concluded that Paul meant by ἐφ' ᾧ πάντες ἥμαρτον the responsible, active sinning of all men.[4] Recently, however, Hans Weder[5] has made use of passages from 4 Ezra to illustrate in Romans 5 a "qualitative leap" in Paul's notion of universal sinfulness following from Adam. Since Paul sees justice as coming solely through Christ, sin is not defined simply in terms of what is opposed to law but as what is contrasted with grace.[6] In particular, where 4 Ezra admits that the law does not prevent sins, Paul holds what 4 Ezra cannot allow, that the law *multiplied* the fall.[7] Weder also argues that Rom 5:13–14 confirms his view that law no longer *defines* sin, and that there is a sinfulness which cannot be defined on the model of Adam's sin, which consisted in the transgression of [a] law.[8]

Weder's theological exegesis is solid. In the same vein, however, one should also bring to bear on Rom 5:13–14, as Weder unfortunately fails to do, the position adopted by the Jewish *2 Baruch* 54:15, 19. A. F. J. Klijn places the work about the first decade of the second century, but admits that it draws on earlier Jewish traditions, even those before A.D. 70.[9] According to *2 Baruch* 54:15, 19, each one, as far as sinfulness goes, has become his own Adam; Adam is not the cause of universal judgment, but only of judgment for himself. Such a view, if espoused by Paul, would demolish the Apostle's

---

[3] A. J. M. Wedderburn, "The Theological Structure of Romans V. 12," *NTS* 19 (1973) 339–54.

[4] Ibid., 340, 351.

[5] Hans Weder, "Gesetz und Sünde: Gedanken zu einem qualitativen Sprung im Denken des Paulus," *NTS* 31 (1985) 357–76.

[6] Ibid., 362–63.

[7] Ibid., 369.

[8] Ibid., 362.

[9] A. F. J. Klijn, "2 (Syriac Apocalypse of) Baruch: A New Translation and Introduction," *The Old Testament Pseudepigrapha*. Vol. I, *Apocalyptic Literature and Testaments* (ed. J. H. Charlesworth; Garden City, NY: Doubleday, 1983) 615–52, 616–17.

As R. H. Charles points out (*Apocrypha and Pseudepigrapha of the Old Testament*, Vol II, *Pseudepirapha* [Oxford: Clarendon, 1913] 511), vv. 16 and 18 break the context in *2 Baruch* 54. The passages on Adam in vv. 15 and 19, however, fit well into the more "original" document, the "Prayer of Baruch" in the context of the apocalypse of the clouds (*2 Baruch* 53–74[76]). Charles dates *2 Baruch* 53–74 between A.D. 50 and 70; ibid., 510.

The difference between Paul's viewpoint and that of *2 Baruch* 54:15, 19 has briefly been noted by H. Schlier, *Der Römerbrief* (HTKNT 6; Freiburg: Herder, 1977) 163.

argument, which entails an Adam–Christ antithesis rooted elsewhere and earlier in his writings.[10]

The distinction which Paul works out to dissociate himself from this Pharisaic view may be termed "functional." That is, Paul clarifies by contrasted instances called for by an ambiguous term or phrase in something he has just said how he himself understands the matter he has referred to, so that further issues may be placed in proper perspective. To illustrate: Rom 4:3 contains a scriptural reference (a quotation from Gen 15:6) which speaks of a reckoning for justice in the case of Abraham. In v. 4, Paul begins to clarify his understanding of the matter. He admits a kind of reckoning according to what is owed in a case where one performs a work. By the antithetical v. 5, however, he specifies the kind of reckoning which he sees operative in Gen 15:6, namely, the setting-right of a sinner who, by believing (trusting), actually throws himself on the mercy of the judge. Paul's further argumentation (vv. 6–8) develops the latter portion of his "casuistic" distinction. In a casuistic or "case-based" way (vv. 4–5), Paul has distinguished "commutative justice" (as in a wage-contract) from a new, paradoxical, "divinely creative" justice (for "to justify the impious" is a crime if done by a human person) that mercifully sets right for a new life the unjust, godless man.

Before turning to another casuistic distinction (that in Rom 5:13–14), one should address a number of debated points in Rom 5:12. Rather than encumber this essay with detailed arguments for and against the options chosen, I shall select the interpretations which I judge to be most plausible in the context of the whole line of Paul's argument. For the greater intelligibility of the whole literary unit provides the ultimate justification for these particular exegetical choices.

---

[10] Cf. 1 Cor 15:22, 45; cf. also Rom 7:4–7a, and Rom 7:7b–25 as answered by Rom 8:1–2.

Rom 3:23–24 speaks of men's need for the glory of God even as they are being justified (pres. ptc.) by grace through redemption in Christ. Paul does not refer to the supposed glory of (the first) Adam, but to the glory of *God,* which he later clarifies (5:2, 7–10) as deliverance from final wrath and as a share in the resurrection of God's Son. *Contra* U. Wilckens (*Der Brief an die Römer* [EKK 6/1; Neukirchen: Benziger, 1978] I, 188), Paul implicitly dissociates himself from the Jewish views of Adam's being created in glory. Adam was sinless "*once upon a time*" (Rom 7:9–11a); for Paul, "glory" is imperishable as God's abiding justice (2 Cor 3:7–4:6).

Paul, of course, supposed that Adam was an individual human being. The Apostle's position, however, does not require that supposition. As elsewhere, especially in apocalyptically-cast scenarios, the negative "foil" for rhetorical presentation of God's positive, redemptive act in a historical situation (e.g., the death and resurrection of Jesus Christ) must be portrayed so as to set in relief the positive, doctrinal affirmation. That there has occurred a final and definitive recreation of humanity through Jesus Christ which is intended for all requires vivid representation of the situation truly remedied, reversed, overcome, etc. The kind of representation employed is inevitably conditioned by the resources of the theologian in question and by his immediate audience's powers of comprehension. Cf. C. H. Giblin, "Revelation 11:1–13, Its Form, Function, and Contextual Integration," *NTS* 30 (1984) 433–59, 452.

First, διὰ τοῦτο ("therefore") should in context be taken as introducing the explanation for something which Paul has just said.[11] An understanding of this connection will be offered more fully below. Suffice it here to note that the summary (5:18–21) which begins with ἄρα οὖν (v. 18) should help the reader perceive aright the line of argumentation begun with v. 12. That line of thought explains a *felix culpa*: sin of one and sins of many triumphantly countered (in a dynamic imbalance attesting the overwhelming, "superabundant" power of God's grace) by justification of many through life-giving justice imparted through one. "Therefore" introduces the grounds for the boast in v. 11.

Second, sin, death, law, and grace are presented largely as apocalyptic, personified "power figures." Sin "enters" (εἰσελθεῖν, v. 12a) and through it (enters) death; death "spreads/'moves throughout' " (διελθεῖν, v. 12b); law (first mentioned in v. 13 and implied by mention of Moses in v. 14) "enters later" (παρεισελθεῖν, v. 20) to multiply the personal fall (which was that of one with the consequence of death for many, cf. v. 20). Death "reigns" (βασιλεῦσαι, v. 14a); sin "reigns (βασιλεῦσαι) in death" once sin has multiplied thanks to law (v. 20). The "reign (βασιλεῦσαι) of grace (v. 21)" is one through justice for eternal life, effectively overcoming the compounded reign of sin in death. That Paul depicts sin, death, law, and grace as personified powers does not mean that he considers them to be ungrounded in actual deeds or states of being. Rather, by these concrete, apocalyptic symbols he transcends a merely particularistic viewpoint according to which, (a) sin amounts only to a personally committed transgression, defined by law; (b) death supposes merely physical death, not also a state of alienation from the living, life-giving God; and (c) gracious justification constitutes only an individual blessing, and has, essentially, no communitarian aspects. For Paul, the reign of grace requires our becoming a new, integrated collectivity under "our Lord," for it derives through that *one* alone. The justice transmitted amounts to a new kind of life, which is meant to last forever. The staging of this drama begins in vv. 12–14, but the drama itself appears in full perspective only with the introduction of the eschatological antitype (Jesus Christ) in v. 14c.

Third, v 12 begins to establish the connection between "one" and "all/the

---

[11] C. E. B. Cranfield (*The Epistle to the Romans* [ICC; Edinburgh: T. & T. Clark, 1980] I, 271) holds that διὰ τοῦτο introduces the conclusion to be drawn from vv. 1–11, because Paul's vision now includes not just believers but the whole of humanity. Nevertheless, the recapitulation of the themes of justification (v. 1; later specified in vv. 10 and 11 as reconciliation) and of boasting (vv. 2, 3, 11 suggests that the explanation begun with v. 12 refers more specifically to v. 11. Besides, the mention of "him who was to come" (v. 14) bears out the eschatological perspective announced by the emphatically-placed "now/at this present time" of v. 11. Cf. also Egon Brandenburger, *Adam und Christus: Exegetisch-religionsgeschichtliche Untersuchung zu Röm 5:12–21 (1 Kor 15)* (Neukirchen: Moers, 1962) 263.

many" which becomes essential to the honed comparisons and contrasts in vv. 13–21: "As through one man sin entered the world and through sin death, even so (or 'even thus') (καὶ οὕτως) did death spread to all because all sinned." Καὶ οὕτως introduces not a mere comparison (as though it were "so, too," οὕτως καί) but a demonstrative clause of result, "even thus," namely, through one man.[12] It implies (by being correlated with the opening phrase ὡς δι' . . .) that the spread of death to all is somehow the result of one man's sin, whereby death entered in the first place. "Somehow," but precisely how? Perplexingly, a further aspect of the spread of death includes also as its reason or causal circumstances universal sinfulness. At this point, one should exercise caution, since Paul may not as yet have said precisely what he means by universal sinfulness. Moreover, one should not prejudge Paul's argumentation as inconsistent, confused, or even loose. To do so would preclude understanding a man who regularly writes concisely and tightly, albeit in a highly condensed way. If one were to understand universal sinfulness as Paul states it in v. 12c as individual sinful acts, one would seem to reverse or seriously to compromise what Paul affirms in v. 12 as a whole, for the actions of "one" and of "all" would loosely be *paralleled,* not causally related from one to all. On the other hand, taking v. 12c as "because all became sinners" suggests a coherent, consistent line of argumentation: a universal solidarity in sinfulness which a new solidarity in grace through justification for life can overcome.

Perhaps exegetes have been over-eager to determine the exact sense of ἐφ' ᾧ when Paul himself may have recognized its ambiguity, especially as introducing πάντες ἥμαρτον. He had dissociated himself from Jewish theology regarding Abraham's justice,[13] and he shows us elsewhere that he dissociated himself from Jewish views concerning the "glory of Adam." Apropos of Rom 5:12, especially its concluding phrase, he seems disputatiously to articulate his own position regarding universal sinfulness consequent upon Adam's sin and the spread of death to all men. 'Εφ' ᾧ functions as a causal connective, though a relatively flexible one in that it can refer to circumstances rather than deliberate, personal agency.[14]

Granting that ἐφ' ᾧ πάντες ἥμαρτον has a general causal sense (and excluding

---

[12] Cf. Gal 6:2; Rom 11:26; 1 Thess 4:17; 1 Cor 7:17, 36b. Translating καὶ οὕτως in 5:12b as "and so" needlessly obscures its consecutive sense and suggests that v. 12 is an anacoluthon. The translation "even thus" or "and thus" brings out the balance and coherence of the sentence and obviates any need to construe it as an anacoluthon; schematically:

| as through one | sin | | causing death, |
| even thus (sc., through one) | death | to all | because of sinfulness of all. |

[13] Paul regularly appeals to Gen 15:6 instead of Genesis 17 in order to dissociate Abraham's being justified from his being circumcised. Cf. U. Wilckens, *Der Brief an die Römer,* I, 259–60.

[14] Cranfield, *Romans,* I, 274–79, provides a convenient survey of the various senses discerned in ἐφ' ᾧ. Elsewhere in Paul, the connective seems to refer to "objective circumstances" (2 Cor 5:4; Phil 3:12; 4:14).

mainly the grammatically unwarranted equation of ἐφ' ᾧ with ἐν ᾧ[15]), vv. 13–14 may be taken as a parenthesis casuistically clarifying that phrase. Verse 13a affirms that sin was (present) in the world up to the time of law. This "power figure," sin, was operative on a cosmic scale. By implication, it dominated all men. Verse 13b, whether δέ be construed as concessive or as explicative, then insists that sin is not "chalked up" as a personal account[16] when there is no law. In effect, the universal sinfulness that was indeed present in the world was not, in Paul's view, what we would call "personal" sin, namely, one deliberately committed in violation of law or of its instance, a precept. How, then, can Paul affirm the existence of universal sinfulness prior to the law? What evidence proves its presence? Verse 14 provides the answer by introducing the attendant power-figure, death. Death, which concretely manifests sinfulness, notably as the result of sin (6:23), held sway from Adam up to Moses even over those who had not sinned precisely as Adam did, namely, by transgressing a precept.[17]

Paul is not saying that there were no "personal sins" committed between the time of Adam and that of Moses. In his generalizing (and apocalyptic) perspective he must be content to prescind from detailed questions (e.g., the brutality of Cain and Lamech or the exceptional lot of a righteous figure like Enoch). He remains concerned with a large canvas for his argument: the

---

[15] To rule out this ungrammatical equation in Greek (and its Latin equivalent, equating *quia* with *in quo*) does not mean ruling out the notion of a kind of corporate identity or solidarity of "all" with "one." How that solidarity is to be explained remains a question to preoccupy the attention especially of speculative theologians. Paul seems content to state the fact, to explain the sin of all as real sinfulness, attested by death, and to insist that it was not specifically personal sinfulness on the part of Adam's descendants. Perhaps, for Paul, it may be regarded as a "legacy" lost, a legacy of the life which Adam could have had and could have passed on to his progeny had he not sinned and brought about an intrinsically hopeless, "dead-end" situation for all his people. The biblical-theological exposition of solidarity in Adam, notably as the counterpart of the dominant pole of the contrast, solidarity in Christ, may well have to be worked out in terms of ψυχή, σάρξ, σῶμα, πνεῦμα, and the like.

[16] Phlm 18. In Rom 5:13b there may well be an apocalyptic allusion to the heavenly books; cf. E. Käsemann, *An die Römer* (HNT 8a; Tübingen: Mohr, 1973) 140.

[17] Käsemann, *An die Römer*, 141. The cycle in Rom 5:12 is consistently enunciated: sin, therefore death; death, because of sin. But the *kind* of sin in each case should not be assumed to have a univocal sense. Other Pauline texts (viz., attesting the use of first or second aorists) do not determine the sense of 5:12b. Paul himself determines the sense in this unique context by introducing a somewhat obtrusive parenthesis (vv 13–14).

Again (cf. n. 15), how this *peccatum originale originatum* should be construed cannot be treated at length here. It may suffice to consider it an automatic "legacy" of injustice and a situation of "death" (lack of genuine life, with a consequent hopelessness for human survival—a state which is true even of one who is physically "still living" as a person; cf. Rom 4:19; 7:10a, 24).

C. Clifton Black II helpfully points out various shades of meaning for death in Romans 5:12–21 ("Pauline Perspectives on Death in Romans 5–8," *JBL* 103 [1984] 413–33, 420–21, 429–31). Nevertheless, he confusingly construes 5:12c ("all sinned") univocally as "individual responsibility and guilt" (ibid., 420–21).

universal need for justification through Jesus Christ alone as the new, different, eschatological Adam, the sole channel for a new humankind. Paul endeavors to clarify his understanding of "because all sinned" as a universal sinfulness independently of personal actions by Adam's descendants. His parenthesis functions as a casuistic distinction which he needs to make in order to set up the following contrast: Adam and all of an "automatically established/constituted" collectivity, namely, he and his descendants, *versus* the antitype, "the one who was to come," Jesus Christ, and the collectivity of those who "freely accept God's freely-given justice" in him. The "Adamite collectivity" may continue and may temporally coexist with the "Christological collectivity." Nevertheless, a new human interrelationship has been effected eschatologically (cp. νῦν, v. 11; and τοῦ μέλλοντος, v. 14) on a radically different basis, that of grace, namely, an undeserved, unexpected gift which must be accepted freely and appreciatively.

Much more could and perhaps should be said, even in an article of limited compass, about exegetical refinements in Rom 5:12–21. My own penchant, however, is to try to capture the larger perspective of a passage rather than to risk "painting myself into a corner" by needlessly specifying and insisting upon one of various viable options concerning given words or phrases. The admittedly awkward διὰ τοῦτο which introduces Rom 5:12 and, indeed, the line of thought subsequently developed through the concluding remarks in vv. 18–21, may suggest that 5:12–21 has been brought in by Paul from another context in his missionary repertoire.[18] Be that as it may, in the context of Rom 1:16–8:39 it surely introduces neither a kind of excursus nor a "self-standing" literary portion of Paul's exposition of his gospel. Elsewhere, I have indicated my own position concerning Rom 1:16–8:39 and, admitting the need for certain, minor modifications, reaffirm it here.[19] The whole of Romans 5 marks a pivotal point in 1:16– 8:39. For the first time, Paul introduces the element of exhortation to compound the alternating pattern of exposition, then controversy.[20] In Rom 5:1–2 the element of

---

[18] Fitzmyer, "Letter to the Romans," *JBC* 53:54.

[19] C. H. Giblin, *In Hope of God's Glory: Pauline Theological Perspectives* (New York: Herder and Herder, 1970) 318–98, esp. 318–21. Up until Rom 3:27, Paul is addressing an *unconverted* audience (which is not necessarily hostile — and probably more dumbstruck than indignant — if the exegete may be allowed to imagine the situation). From that point onwards, and certainly from 5:1 onwards, he supposes that his hearers have been converted. The change of audience makes sense by reasonably supposing that Paul is offering in Rom 1:16–8:39 a concentrated example of his gospel (a kind of "crash course") to the Romans, not directed against the Romans, but staged for their benefit, before he arrives in Rome.

[20] The sections I labeled "controversy," *In Hope of God's Glory*, 320–21 (Rom 2:1–3:20; 3:27–4:25; 6:1–7:25) even that which is addressed to an "unconverted" audience (2:1–3:20), should not be construed as addressed to "opponents." As S. K. Stowers has shown (*The Diatribe and Paul's Letter to the Romans* [SBLDS 57; Chico, CA: Scholars Press, 1981] 175–84), Paul employs the diatribe as a protreptic process, supposing a teacher–student relationship rather than the

exhortation is introduced for the first time, and here colors the whole exposition of the consequences of a state of grace based on justification by faith. In Romans 5, as apparently in Rom 3:27–4:25, Paul now addresses a *converted* audience in offering the Romans a sample of his evangelical preaching.

What establishes the relationship between 3:27–4:25 and Rom 5:1–21 is formulated as a characteristically Pauline paradox regarding boasting (καυχᾶσθαι), not in men, but in God (cf. 1 Cor 1:29–31; 3:21; 2 Cor 10:12–18). Also, Paul moves from controversy to exposition (with the additional element of exhortation in the latter passage, thanks to the theological basis for "boasting"). Self-assertive boasting has been excluded both on principle (3:27–31) and on historical precedent (4:1–25). In Rom 5:1–2, recapitulating his gospel as stated in 3:21–26 (an exposition) and confirmed in 3:27–4:25 (a conciliatory controversy with those who might demur), Paul encourages boasting in the hope of God's glory, namely, the resurrection still to be realized in us (Rom 5:10; 8) and already realized in Christ (Rom 6:4). This boast, based on faith, not surprisingly works out through human weaknesses energized by hope and, basically, by the love granted us in the Holy Spirit (5:3–5). It is achieved, in spite of prior sinfulness and enmity toward God (5:6–10) through the unique (5:7–8) proof of divine love, Christ's death for us sinners (5:8), God's Son's reconciliation of God's enemies (5:10).

Now, the boast enunciated in 5:2 contains two developments, as the use of the verb καυχᾶσθαι (vv. 3 and 11 consequent upon v. 2) attests. The first stage of the boast runs from v. 3 through v. 10. The second stage of the boast begins with v. 11. Again, it takes account of human sinfulness and its remedy, but it enlarges the perspective to take stock of the fate of all humankind, beginning with its foregoing servitude to cosmic powers. Once more, the proof of God's sovereign, salvific power will center on his action in and through Jesus Christ for us. This time, however, Paul employs a kind of "epic"—more exactly "apocalyptic"—framework which encompasses the prospects for the whole of humanity, not just the experience of the Christian community. Sin, death, and law (*de facto,* another oppressive force, since it articulates human moral impotence, 3:9–20; 7:21) have been overcome in Christ, who defines in his being human the free gift of grace (5:15b: ἡ δωρεὰ ἐν χάριτι τῇ τοῦ ἑνὸς ἀνθρώπου Ἰησοῦ Χριστοῦ). Admittedly, these adversaries have not as yet been overcome fully (as a subsequent exposition, Romans 8, will explain), but the victory of grace is both present and ongoing, "for life

---

the mass propaganda of the wandering Cynic street-preacher. Nevertheless, Stowers's approach slights the kerygmatic preaching of the gospel by a Christian missionary like Paul, especially as attested by the Apostle's opening gambit: "I am not ashamed of the gospel" (1:16a). Paul adapts learned discourse to his own purposes, not *vice versa,* and does so in a creative way which defies pat classification according to any ancient form of oratory or philosophical discourse.

everlasting" (5:21), thanks to the one through whom it has come. Romans 6–7 will pick up (through controversy combined with exhortation) the implications for Paul's converted audience of what was said in Rom 5:11–21. Romans 8 will continue to develop the implications of Rom 5:1–21 (by exposition coupled with exhortation), but mainly by emphasizing the dynamic activity of the Spirit, both now and in the apocalyptically-conceived future.

After surveying this larger perspective, one may return with the hope of keener insight to the connection between 5:12–21, especially as introduced by διὰ τοῦτο, and 5:11, the opening of the second portion of Paul's boast as governed by 5:1–2 (the first portion being 5:3–10). The second portion of the boast, which must certainly include v. 11, begins not indirectly, with a boast in our weakness (v. 3), but quite forthrightly with a boast in God himself. The participle introducing v. 11 is not an *Anhang*. True, it must thematically be correlated with the terms preceding it (vv. 2 and 3: καυχώμεθα [v. 2] and καυχώμεθα or καυχώμενοι [v. 3]); at the same time, it equivalently begins a new sentence.[21] Paul encourages us to boast in God through our Lord Jesus Christ, through whom we have obtained reconciliation *at this present time*. He is introducing a new dimension of the counseled "boast." Paul hardly intends to let this thought remain undeveloped, especially since its theocentric orientation *vis-à-vis* the programmatic vv. 1–2 is more pronounced than is the indirect approach used at the beginning of the first portion (v. 3ff.) of the development. The Christological focus of God's love in 5:3–10 and of God's grace in 5:12–31 requires no further discussion here other than to observe that there occurs a "personal" note in both passages although differentiated according to context. In 5:6–10, the emphasis falls not just on justification of sinners through Christ and deliverance from the (final) wrath (judgment), but on reconciliation of enemies through the death of God's Son, with consequent confidence for a share in his Son's risen life. Paul moves in v. 10 *vis-à-vis* vv. 8–9 to a more intensely personal and positive statement of justification as personal reconciliation, and does so on several counts.[22] Later, in 5:15–17, in the context of a new order in creation, he

---

[21] Rom 5:2, 3, 11. The ptc. in v. 11 may be construed as equivalently a finite verb, Zerwick-Smith, *Biblical Greek* (Rome: Pontifical Biblical Institute, 1963) § 374; Blass-Debrunner-Funk, *Greek Grammar of the New Testament* (Chicago: University of Chicago, 1961) § 468. Ultimate dependence on the well-attested subject of v. 2 and occurrence in an *a fortiori* construction paralleling v. 3 (where the more probable reading is a subject), suggest that the ptc. in v. 11 be construed as a hortatory subject. Granted the initial, well-attested subject of v. 2, however, a different modal construction of the other two forms of the same verb (again, acknowledging the aspects of parallelism in the whole passage) would not invalidate the exposition offered in this paper.

[22] Giblin, *In Hope of God's Glory*, 367.

emphasizes the role of "the one (man) Jesus Christ" and on free reception of abundant grace and unmerited justification. A new, personal point which he introduces just before his "*in somma*," amplified conclusion (vv. 18–21) is that of ongoing *acceptance* (pres. ptc.) of the abundance of grace (v. 17).

"Boasting in God," however, merits more attention. It suggests a clearer, theocentric focus in line both with what Paul announced in 5:1–2 and with the way he argues elsewhere, as Thüsing has shown.[23] This central concern entails the picture of a cosmic reversal thanks to God's grace (5:15), specified as that in the incarnate Jesus Christ. That ὁ θεός is not mentioned elsewhere in 5:12–21 does not in the least diminish the importance of the theocentric aspect of Paul's discourse. From the boast centered on God in v. 11 through the scenario of world domination through reversing the catastrophic effects of Adam's sin so that everlasting life would reign supreme, and by insistent use of terms for grace (χάρις, χάρισμα), which originates from God the Father, Paul's theocentric view coherently governs his whole exposition from v. 11 through v. 21.

Furthermore, Paul insists on boasting in God through our Lord Jesus Christ, through whom we have received reconciliation *now*. Why at this present time? Proof for his statement requires further exposition on his part. Given the fact that his boast centers on God, he starts *ab ovo*, from the beginning of human existence. He shows how, starting with Adam, sin leads to death, to widening death in a state of sinfulness even independently of personally committed sins (transgressions of law/precept) (vv. 12–14)[24] and to more, personal sins in addition to all that (v. 16), so that the triumph of God's grace in Christ for the constitution of a new humanity may shine forth for what it really is, a *current, eschatological triumph* over a catastrophic human situation dominated by sin and death. At the same time, he explains the eschatological polarity: what is now available in Christ through free acceptance of God's grace is intended to remain a lasting share in a kingdom for life eternal (cp. vv. 17b, 21). The future (as Romans 8 will set forth) emerges as the eschatological realization of the eschatological (final and definitive) present reality of life by God's grace through Jesus Christ. Although further

---

[23] W. Thüsing, *Per Christum in Deum: Studien zum Verhältnis von Christozentrik und Theozentrik in den Paulinischen Hauptbriefen* (Münster: Aschendorff, 1965) 183–84, 187, 256–70.

[24] The "state" of sinfulness enunciated in vv. 13–14 is borne out as follows: In the first set of contrasts (v. 15), Paul uses an image of "collective death" (οἱ πολλοὶ ἀπέθανον). Although οἱ πολλοί need not exclude the sense "all" (πάντες), it more appropriately refers to a collectivity, *in casu*, a *society* (not a "sandpile" of individuals) under the "reign of death." In the second set of contrasts (vv. 16–17), general condemnation is explained (v. 17) as expressly including a reign of death, and the summary clarifies that condemnation as the collectivity's being "constituted sinners." It is when law enters the picture that sin as a personal transgression (παράπτωμα) is multiplied (v. 20, retrospectively clarifying ἐκ πολλῶν παραπτωμάτων of v. 16b).

developments (Romans 6–7 and especially Romans 8) call for qualifications and expansions of this perspective, Paul's argument even within Romans 5, notably 5:11–21, stands as unified, coherent, and well-focused.

By way of conclusion, Rom 5:13–14 functions as a polemic clarification of universal sinfulness consequent upon Adam's personal transgression of a precept. Employing a casuistic, "case-based" distinction, Paul dissociates himself from Pharisaic views of the consequences of Adam's sin (somewhat as he casuistically dissociated himself from Pharisaic views concerning the nature and consequences of Abraham's first encounter with God). The Apostle affirms a corporate solidarity in sinfulness even apart from personal acts (transgressions of law/precept). Perhaps, as Albert Schweitzer is reported to have said, Paul is never more difficult to understand than when he tries to explain what he means. Nonetheless, his explanation makes good sense, especially in the wider context of his argument: the contrast between two "human collectivities, unified under one man" which he goes on to develop from the concluding, relative clause of 5:14 through v. 21, and the relation of his reasoning in 5:12–21 to 5:11, to the rest of Romans 5, and, as far as could be pursued here, to the rest of Rom 1:16–8:39, especially the argument following Romans 5.

Birth Narratives in Pseudo-Philo's Biblical Antiquities and the Gospels

Daniel J. Harrington, S.J.
Weston School of Theology

Behold, an angel of
the Lord appeared to him
in a dream.

Matt 1:20

THE BIRTH OF HEROES has long been a topic of great fascination in world literature, especially in religious writings. The biblical stories of the births of the patriarchs in Genesis, Moses, Samson, Samuel, John the Baptist, and Jesus provide important examples of this motif. There is abundant evidence that in intertestamental Judaism the Old Testament birth narratives were particularly attractive and were retold by way of addition and mutual influence.[1]

Ps.-Philo's *Biblical Antiquities* contains examples of developments of biblical birth narratives. Starting from the biblical text, ps.-Philo "improved" the biblical narratives by adding new motifs and explaining mysterious elements. Since some of his procedures offer good parallels to Matthew 1–2 and Luke 1–2, it may be useful to see what light *Biblical Antiquities* can shed on the Gospel texts.

After introductory remarks about ps.-Philo's *Biblical Antiquities,* I will present English translations of its versions of the birth of Moses (9:9–16) and the announcement of Samson's birth (42:1–7). The discussions accompanying the English versions will focus on points at which ps.-Philo departed from the biblical text. The second part of the article will examine parallels between the texts in

[1] C. Perrot, "Les récits d'enfance dans la haggada antérieure au IIe siècle de notre ère," *RSR* 55 (1967) 481–518.

Biblical Antiquities and the infancy Gospels, with particular attention to those departures and their New Testament correspondences. It will also reflect on the significance of these parallels.

I do not envision a relationship of direct dependence between these texts, nor do I believe that one writer knew the other's work. Rather, the importance of ps.-Philo's birth narratives is that they reveal the devices that one Jewish writer in first-century Palestine used in telling how biblical heroes were born and thus illustrate some patterns that the Evangelists used in writing about the birth of Jesus.

Ps.-Philo's Birth Narratives

Biblical Antiquities[2] tells the story of Israel from Adam to David. It uses the framework of biblical books from Genesis to 2 Samuel and selectively expands and contracts certain episodes. Although the primary language in which it now exists is Latin (the Hebrew fragments in *Chronicles of Jerahmeel* seem to be medieval retroversions), it was composed in Hebrew and translated into Greek before the Latin version was made. The ascription to Philo is purely accidental, as several factors indicate: the composition in Hebrew, the different methods of treating the biblical text, and the contradictions to Philo's genuine works. A Palestinian origin is suggested by its composition in Hebrew, use of a Palestinian biblical text, knowledge of Palestinian geography, literary parallels to *4 Ezra* and *2 Baruch,* and theological interests.

The original date of composition is controverted. A date around the turn of the era is likely for the following reasons: the silence about the destruction of the Second Temple, the assumption that the Temple cult was still going on, and the use of an Old Testament text that seems to have been suppressed after A.D. 100. Those who argue for a late-first or early-second-century A.D. origin point to the parallels with *4 Ezra* and *2 Baruch* (both post-A.D. 70 works), and find in the reference to the destruction of "the place where the people will serve me" for 740 years on the seventeenth day of the fourth month (see *Bib. Ant.* 19:7) an allusion to the fall of the Second Temple. Whichever dating is accepted, it is clear that ps.-Philo's *Biblical Antiquities* was composed at roughly the same period when the Gospels of Matthew and Luke were written.

Efforts at connecting ps.-Philo's *Biblical Antiquities* with a specific Jewish group (e.g., Essenes, Pharisees, Samaritans, anti-Samaritans) have not been successful. Rather, the work seems to reflect the ethos of the Palestinian synagogues at the turn of the era. It shows us how Jews were reading the

[2] The next three paragraphs summarize introductory information set forth in D. J. Harrington, J. Cazeaux, C. Perrot, and P.-M. Bogaert, *Pseudo-Philon: Les Antiquités Bibliques* (SC 229–230; Paris: Cerf, 1976).

Bible, tells us something about the popular theology of the day, and transmits motifs and legends not found elsewhere in ancient Jewish literature.

Ps.-Philo's method of dealing with the biblical text can be seen easily from his account of Moses' birth in *Bib. Ant.* 9:9–16. The story, of course, takes its narrative framework from Exod 2:1–10. In retelling the biblical narrative, ps.-Philo retained some phrases from the text as a framework for telling a longer and (presumably in his mind) more interesting tale. The italicized words in the following translation indicate expressions taken over directly from Exod 2:1–10; the rest represents ps.-Philo's own contribution.[3]

9. *And* Amram *of the tribe of Levi went out and took a wife* from his own tribe. When he had taken her, others followed him and took their own wives. And this man had one son and one daughter; their names were Aaron and Miriam. 10. And the spirit of God came upon Miriam one night, and she saw a dream and told it to her parents in the morning saying: "I have seen this night, and behold a man in a linen garment stood and said to me: 'Go and say to your parents: "Behold he who will be born from you will be cast forth into the water; likewise through him the water will be dried up. And I will work signs through him and save my people, and he will exercise leadership always." ' " And when Miriam told of her dream, her parents did not believe her.

11. The strategy of the king of Egypt, however, prevailed against the sons of Israel, and they were humiliated and worn down in making bricks. 12. *Now* Jochebed *conceived* from Amram *and hid him* in her womb *for three months. For she could not conceal him any longer,* because the king of Egypt appointed local chiefs who, when the Hebrew women gave birth, would immediately throw their male children into the river. *And she took* her child and *made for him an ark* from the bark of a pine tree *and placed the ark at the bank of the river.*

13. Now that child was born in the covenant of God and the covenant of the flesh. 14. And when they had cast him forth, all the elders gathered and quarreled with Amram saying: "Are not these our words that we spoke: 'It is better for us to die without having sons than that the fruit of our womb be cast into the waters?' " And Amram did not listen to those who were saying these words.

15. *Now Pharaoh's daughter came down to bathe in the river,* as she had seen in dreams, *and* her maids *saw the ark. And she sent* one, *and she fetched and opened it. And when she saw the boy* and while she was looking upon the covenant (that is, the covenant of the flesh), *she said: "It is one of the Hebrew children."* 16. And she took him and nursed him. And he became her son, and she called him by the name Moses. But his mother called him Melchiel. And the chid was nursed and became glorious above all other men, and through him God freed the sons of Israel as he said.

[3] My translations of this and the following text appeared in J. H. Charlesworth (ed.), *The Old Testament Pseudepigrapha* (vol. 2; Garden City, NY: Doubleday, 1985). They are based on my critical edition of the Latin text in *Pseudo-Philon: Les Antiquités Bibliques.*

One of ps.-Philo's concerns was to clear up problems in the biblical text. Thus he supplied the names of Moses' parents — Amram and Jochebed — from Exod 6:20 (see *Bib. Ant.* 9:9, 12). He also explained why Pharaoh's daughter according to Exod 2:6 could have recognized Moses as "one of the Hebrews' children": Moses was born circumcised, i.e., "in the covenant of the flesh" (see *Bib. Ant.* 9:13, 15). Finally, he solved the problem posed by the Egyptian background of Moses' name (see Exod 2:10) and the feeble attempt at etymology in the biblical text. He attributed the Egyptian name Moses to Pharaoh's daughter and the Hebrew name Melchiel ("God is my king" or perhaps "God is my counsel") to Moses' mother (see *Bib. Ant.* 9:16). Moses had both an Egyptian and a Jewish name.

There are, however, elements in ps.-Philo's version of Moses' birth that are neither derived from the biblical text nor attempts at solving an exegetical problem. Several motifs without foundation in Exod 2:1–10 also occur in the New Testament infancy narratives: The spirit of God initiates the sequence of events that result in Moses' birth (see *Bib. Ant.* 9:10). Both Miriam (see 9:10) and Pharaoh's daughter (see 9:15) know what to do because God's will has been communicated to them in dreams. In Miriam's dream, a "man in a linen garment" (presumably an angel) appears and tells her what to say to her parents about the child to be born to them (9:10).

Two other features have some basis in the biblical text but are more fully developed by ps.-Philo. The mission of Moses as an adult takes its starting point from the fanciful etymology based on the Hebrew root *mšh* ("I drew him out of the water") in Exod 2:10 and is stated in great detail: ". . . through him the water will be dried up. And I will work signs through him and save my people" (9:10). Also, the slaughter of the Hebrew children, which was threatened in Exod 1:16–22, is described as a reality in *Bib. Ant.* 9:12: ". . . the king of Egypt appointed local chiefs who, when the Hebrew women gave birth, would immediately throw their male children into the river."

This look at ps.-Philo's story of the birth of Moses gives a good introduction to the author's methods of composition. He interweaves biblical phrases, exegetical traditions, motifs foreign to the biblical narrative, and expansions of the biblical text into a new literary creation. His attitude toward the biblical text is free and flexible. His aims appear to have been entertainment and edification.

Bib. Ant. 42:1–7 retells the story of the birth of Samson found in Judg 13:2–14. Again the words and phrases of the biblical text serve as the framework for an expanded version. The italicized material in the following translation again represents expressions clearly taken from Judg 13:2–14. The remainder comes from ps.-Philo. Many of the same procedures are followed as in the Moses' story, though it is harder to find cases of exegetical problem-solving here.

1. *Now there was a man from the tribe of Dan, whose name was Manoah,* son of Edoc, son of Odon, son of Eriden, son of Fadesur, son of Dema, son of Susi, son of Dan. And he had a wife whose name was Eluma the daughter of Remac, and she *was sterile and did not bear children* to him. And every day Manoah her husband was saying to her: "Behold the Lord has shut up your womb so that you may not bear children, and now let me go that I may take another wife lest I die without fruit." And she said: "Not me has the Lord shut up that I may not bear children, but you that I may not bear fruit." And he said to her: "Would that this could be tested and proved!" 2. And they were quarreling daily, and both were very sad because they were without fruit. One night the wife went up to the upper chamber and prayed saying: "Behold you, Lord God of all flesh, reveal to me whether it has not been granted to my husband or to me to produce children, or to whom it may be forbidden or to whom it may be allowed to bear fruit in order that whoever is forbidden may weep over his sins because he remains without fruit. Or if both of us have been deprived, then reveal to us also so that we might bear our sins and be silent before you."

3. And the Lord heard her voice and sent his angel to her in the morning, *and he said to her: "You are the sterile one* who *does not bring forth,* and you are the womb that is forbidden so as not to bear fruit. But now the Lord has heard your voice and paid attention to your tears and opened your womb. *And behold you will conceive and bear a son, and* you will *call his name Samson. For* this one *will be dedicated* to your Lord. *But see* that he *does not taste from any fruit of the vine and eat any unclean thing because* (as he himself has said) *he will free Israel from the hand of the Philistines."* And when the angel of the Lord had spoken these words, he departed from her.

4. *And she came* into the house *to her husband and said* to him: "I am placing my hand upon my mouth, and I will be silent before you all the days because I have boasted in vain and have not believed your words. For the angel of the Lord *came to me* today and *revealed* to me, saying: 'Eluma, *you are sterile, but you will conceive and bear a son.'* " 5. And Manoah did not believe his wife, and being perplexed and sad he himself also went to the upper chamber and *prayed and said:* "Behold I am not worthy to hear the signs and wonders that God has done among us or to see the face of his messenger." 6. And while he was speaking these words, *the angel of the Lord came again to* his *wife. But she was in the field, and Manoah* was in his house. And the angel said to her: "Run and announce to your husband that God has accounted him worthy to hear my voice." 7. *And the wife ran and called to her husband, and* he hurried to *come* to the angel in the field. The angel said to him: "Go into your wife and do all these things." And he said: "I am going, but see to it, sir, that *your word be accomplished* regarding your servant." And he said: "It will be accomplished."

The first and most obvious contribution made by ps.-Philo is the construction of a genealogy for Samson. Whereas Judg 13:2 simply describes Manoah as a Danite from Zorah, *Bib. Ant.* 42:1 supplies the generations between Manoah and Dan (Edoc, Odon, Eriden, Fadesur, Dema, Susi). None of the names has any biblical or even extrabiblical foundation. It also supplies

Samson's mother with a name — Eluma, which also has no parallel in Jewish literature.

The angel's appearance to Eluma and his declaration of her sterility is prefaced in *Bib. Ant.* 42:2 by the report of daily quarrels between Manoah and Eluma and by Eluma's prayer. These insertions have the literary effect of heightening suspense and giving more background for the angelic announcement. That Manoah should request a divorce from his wife ("now let me go that I may take another wife") is unusual in a Jewish context (see Deut 24:1–4). Eluma's prayer for enlightenment regarding the couple's lack of children is an example of ps.-Philo's fondness for constructing prayers and placing them on the lips of biblical figures.

Most of the material in *Bib. Ant.* 42:3 repeats biblical expressions but there are a few interesting developments: Samson's birth is the answer to Eluma's prayer ("the Lord has heard your voice . . . and opened your womb"). As in the biblical story, the child's name and mission are given even before his birth. Samson is the one who must abstain from drinking wine and eating unclean things, not his mother as in Judg 13:4–5, 13.

While *Bib. Ant.* 42:4–7 follows the basic outline of Judg 13:6–14 (the wife's report to her husband, Manoah's prayer, the angel's second appearance to the woman, the angel's confirmation to Manoah), ps.-Philo makes several changes along the way. Eluma vows perpetual silence with regard to her husband ("I will be silent before you all the days") because she failed to believe him (42:4). The angel's appearance to Manoah (42:7) serves to resolve his doubt about his wife and his confusion (42:5), though his statement "See to it, sir, that your word be accomplished" suggests less than complete acceptance of the angel's statement.

Again we see an example of ps.-Philo's free and flexible attitude toward the biblical text, as well as his concern to entertain and edify. Using the framework supplied by Judg 13:2–14, ps.-Philo has created a new and (to his mind) more interesting story concerning the birth of Samson.

New Testament Parallels and Their Significance

Even a superficial reading of ps.-Philo's accounts of the births of Moses and Samson is sufficient to make one aware of the similarities to the New Testament infancy narratives. Some similarities are due simply to the use of the same biblical models. It has long been acknowledged that there is a Moses-Jesus typology in Matthew 1–2 and that the announcement of Samson's birth in Judges 13 has influenced the announcements of the births of John the Baptist and Jesus in Luke 1.[4] The more intriguing similarities stem

---

[4] For a comprehensive treatment of the New Testament infancy stories, see R. E. Brown, *The*

from the appearance of the same kinds of literary forms (e.g., genealogies, prayers) and motifs (e.g., communication by dreams, silence, doubt). In making an inventory of the parallels between ps.-Philo's birth narratives and the Gospel infancy stories, I will focus first on Matthew 1–2 and then on Luke 1:5–38.

The genealogy in Matt 1:1–17 situates Jesus in Israel's history with special reference to Abraham, David, and the Babylonian Exile. The names up to Abiud (1:13) are found in the Old Testament, but those from Eliakim (1:13) to Jacob (1:16) have no biblical basis and cannot be reconciled with Luke 3:23–27. We have no way of knowing what genealogical resources were at the disposal of the evangelists. But we do know that a contemporary Jewish writer like ps.-Philo had no hesitation about filling in genealogical gaps for Samson (see *Bib. Ant.* 42:1) and other biblical characters. In fact, the early chapters of *Biblical Antiquities* are full of such genealogies.

The Matthean story of the announcement of Jesus' birth (Matt 1:18–25) contains several parallels to ps.-Philo's birth stories. Just as the spirit of God set in motion the events leading up to Moses' birth (see *Bib. Ant.* 9:10), so Mary was found pregnant "from the Holy Spirit" (Matt 1:18). Joseph's bewilderment (Matt 1:19) is paralleled by Manoah's doubt and confusion about his wife (*Bib. Ant.* 42:5, 7). In both cases the resolution of doubt comes about through the appearance of an angel (Matt 1:20; *Bib. Ant.* 42:7).

The idea of divine communication by dreams (see Matt 1:20–23; 2:12, 13–14, 19–20) finds a resonance in the dream visions granted to Miriam and Pharaoh's daughter (*Bib. Ant.* 9:10, 15). In both instances, angels deliver God's message: "an angel of the Lord" according to Matt 1:20, and "a man in a linen garment" according to *Bib. Ant.* 9:10. The divine message concerns the child's name and mission: Jesus will save his people from their sins (Matt 1:21); Moses/Melchiel will dry up the waters (*Bib. Ant.* 9:10); and Samson will free Israel from the hand of the Philistines (*Bib. Ant.* 42:3).

Apart from the dream instructions in Matt 2:12, 13–14, 19–20, the one remaining parallel of substance involves the slaughter of the innocent children. Whereas Exod 1:16–22 implies that the massacre was going to happen, *Bib. Ant.* 9:12 and Matt 2:16–18 describe it as an actual event connected with the birth of Moses and Jesus, respectively.

The Lucan parallels with the birth stories in ps.-Philo's *Biblical Antiquities* occur chiefly in the announcements of the births of John the Baptist and Jesus. Elizabeth's sterilty (Luke 1:7) parallels Eluma's sterility (*Bib. Ant.* 42:1), though this is a common biblical motif (e.g., Sarah, Rebecca, Rachel, Hannah). Just as Samson's birth was announced as an answer to his parents'

Birth of the Messiah (Garden City, NY: Doubleday, 1977). See also J. A. Fitzmyer, *The Gospel According to Luke* (AB 28A; Garden City, NY: Doubleday, 1981).

prayers (*Bib. Ant.* 42:2, 5), so John's birth was announced when all the people were praying (Luke 1:10). An angel makes the birth announcement (*Bib. Ant.* 9:10; 42:3; Luke 1:13) and describes the child's future mission (*Bib. Ant.* 9:10; 42:3; Luke 1:15–18). Contrary to the Hebrew text of Judg 13:4–5, 13, Samson according to *Bib. Ant.* 42:3 will abstain from wine and strong drink. Likewise, John the Baptist "shall drink no wine or strong drink" (Luke 1:15). Whereas Zechariah was struck silent as a sign because he did not believe the angel's words (Luke 1:20, 22), Eluma vows to be silent before her husband because she failed to believe him (*Bib. Ant.* 42:4).

The announcement of Jesus' birth (Luke 1:26–38) contains some motifs found in the announcement of John's birth (Luke 1:5–25), and so displays parallels with ps.-Philo's *Biblical Antiquities*. The angel Gabriel conveys the announcement to Mary (see *Bib. Ant.* 9:10; 42:3; Luke 1:11). The angel announces the child's name and his future mission (see *Bib. Ant.* 9:10, 16; 42:3; Luke 1:13–17). In Jesus' birth the Holy Spirit is the agent: "The Holy Spirit will come upon you" (Luke 1:35). The references to the Holy Spirit in Moses' birth (see *Bib. Ant.* 9:10) and John's birth ("he will be filled with the Holy Spirit," Luke 1:15) are considerably weaker.

This inventory of parallels between the birth narratives in ps.-Philo's *Biblical Antiquities* 9:9–16 and 42:1–7 and the New Testament infancy narratives (Matt 1:1–2:23; Luke 1:5–38) calls for interpretation. What is the significance of the parallels? What do they tell us about the New Testament infancy stories?

Paul Winter[5] was so impressed by the parallels between *Bib. Ant.* 42:1–7 and Luke 1:5–38 that he concluded to Luke's literary dependence on ps.-Philo's work. Nevertheless, the impressive array of intertestamental Jewish birth narratives assembled by Charles Perrot[6] reveals a more complicated situation, making claims of direct dependence very unlikely. That ps.-Philo depended on Luke is even less likely, for the Latin version of *Biblical Antiquities* (which was probably made by Christians and certainly circulated among Christians) contains no evidence of Christian elements or allusions to Christianity. Therefore a relationship of direct dependence does not appear to be an adequate explanation of the parallels.

The best approach to these parallels is to view them as independent developments.[7] At this point, it may be useful to recall the definition of parallel lines or planes in Euclidean geometry: "lying evenly everywhere in

---

[5] P. Winter, "The Proto-Source of Luke I," *NovT* 1 (1956) 184–99.

[6] Perrot, "Les récits."

[7] As Perrot suggested. See also S. Muñoz Iglesias, "El procediemento literario del anuncio previo en la Biblia," *EstBíb* 42 (1984) 21–70, esp. 34–53.

the same direction, but never meeting, however far extended."[8] Parallels by definition never meet. In a literary study such as this one, parallels tell us what was "in the air," i.e., literary forms, expressions, motifs, devices, etc. available to writers of the time.

The Gospel infancy narratives present a difficult hermeneutical problem. They are clearly blends of historical, theological, and "midrashic" or "haggadic" elements. They recount events that happened to real people (Jesus, Joseph, Mary, John the Baptist, Elizabeth, Zechariah) at the time of Herod the Great (before 4 B.C.) in Palestine. They were written, however, from this side of Easter and in the light of Christian confessions about Jesus' person and ministry. They used Old Testament models to portray the births of John the Baptist and Jesus as being in line with those of Moses and Samson. The hermeneutical problem comes in trying to determine in what category (historical, theological, midrashic-haggadic) this or that element belongs.

I have introduced the terms "midrashic" and "haggadic" with much hesitation. These terms are often used carelessly with reference to the New Testament infancy accounts, as if the words themselves explained what was going on in the text. I prefer the narrow, classical understanding of midrash as a systematic explication of a biblical text (somewhat like a modern biblical commentary).[9] But the Gospel infancy narratives are stories about Jesus, not explications of biblical texts. The biblical texts quoted in them are devices to highlight the significance of Jesus. The term "haggadic" labors under the same difficulties. Understood widely, "haggada" refers to rabbinic anecdotes, legends, and expanatory narratives. Taken narrowly (as I prefer), it refers to imaginative expositions of biblical texts not related to the Torah ("halakha").

When the words "midrashic" and "haggadic" are used with reference to the New Testament infancy narratives, they are employed loosely to describe their basis in the Old Testament, their concern with explaining exegetical problems, and their aim at suiting the bibical message to contemporary needs. The parallels assembled in this article are sometimes proposed as proofs that the Gospels' infancy accounts are midrashic or haggadic.

I take a more cautious attitude. I imagine that ps.-Philo had before him the Hebrew texts of Exod 2:1–10 and Judg 13:2–14 when he composed the texts studied in this paper, whereas the authors of the Gospels relied on biblical memories or at best collections of biblical testimonia. Ps.-Philo was concerned primarily with illuminating and enlivening the biblical texts, whereas the evangelists sought mainly to identify the person of Jesus. The parallels show that roughly contemporary writers with differing methods and concerns used some of the same literary devices and motifs in telling the stories about the births of their heroes. This modest conclusion is enough for me.

---

[8] *Webster's New International Dictionary of the English Language. Second Edition. Unabridged* (ed. W. A. Neilson; Springfield, MA: G. & C. Merriam, 1942) 1772.

[9] A. G. Wright, *The Literary Genre Midrash* (Staten Island, NY: Alba House, 1967).

1 Thessalonians and
Hellenistic Religious Practices

Pheme Perkins
Boston College

Jewish Missionary among the Greeks

I have become all things to
all persons so that I might at any
rate save some.

1 Corinthians 9:22

ATTEMPTS TO FERRET OUT the conceptual structures of Pauline thought continue to leave us
with a dichotomy. On the one hand, there is
the apostle who employs conceptual and
rhetorical patterns of popular Hellenistic
philosophy.[1] On the other, there is the Paul
who recasts Jewish exegetical traditions and
conceives the salvation from the Lord in
apocalyptic categories of salvation history
and judgment.[2] Professor Fitzmyer's knowledge of first-century Palestinian Judaism has
done much to illuminate the apostle's Jewish
context. He has argued that the Greco-Roman
language of metamorphosis has been explicated by Paul using the "rhetoric" of Jewish
midrash and conceptual categories exemplified in the Qumran material in which God
illumines the teachers of the sect.[3] He has
insisted that the categories in which Paul
wrestles with the role of the law are shaped by
Paul's polemical situation and his exegetical
methods. They do not represent the intrusion

[1] As in A. J. Malherbe, "Exhortation in First Thessalonians," *NovT* 25 (1983) 238–56; idem,
" 'Gentle as a Nurse': The Cynic Background to I Thess ii," *NovT* 12 (1970) 203–17; and H. D.
Betz, *Der Apostel Paulus und die sokratische Tradition* (BHT 45; Tübingen: Mohr-Siebeck, 1972).

[2] See J. Baumgarten, *Paulus und die Apokalyptik: Die Auslegung apokalyptischer Überlieferung in den
echten Paulusbriefen* (WMANT 44; Neukirchen: Erziehungsverein, 1975); and the apocalyptic
reconstruction of Pauline theology in J. C. Becker, *Paul, the Apostle: The Triumph of God in Life
and Thought* (Philadelphia: Fortress, 1980).

[3] J. A. Fitzmyer, "Glory Reflected on the Face of Christ (2 Cor 3:7–4:6) and a Palestinian
Jewish Motif," *TS* 42 (1981) 630–44.

the intrusion of a Hellenistic understanding of "law of nature" or a gnosticizing anthropology.[4] On the other hand, Paul does not share the fascination with purity and sectarian isolation evident in the interpolated passage in 2 Cor 6:14–7:1.[5]

How then is the interplay between the two ways of portraying Paul and his teaching to be understood? Father Fitzmyer's work suggests one approach. Conceptual categories and rhetorical techniques that have their origins in the Greco-Roman world are subordinated to and sometimes reshaped by Paul in a distinctively Jewish vein. In this regard, Paul is much closer to traditions of Palestinian Judaism than to the assimilation of Hellenistic speculation in someone like Philo.[6] Following this lead, we propose to examine the interplay between the pluralism of Greco-Roman philosophic and religious thought and a decidedly Jewish understanding of apocalyptic holiness in 1 Thessalonians.

1 Thessalonians clearly presents Christianity as a Jewish movement, centered on expectations of salvation at the parousia, which Paul and others had been spreading to Gentiles. Scholars have recognized in 1 Thess 1:9b–10 a creedal summary of the basic message of this mission.[7] Alan Segal has proposed that Christianity's success among the Gentiles lay in its ability to transform the sentiments and practices of apocalyptic sectarianism into a religion of personal piety. Apocalyptic fervor was not abandoned but channeled into the formation of cohesive, stable communities among persons of very diverse backgrounds. Rather than serve as the focus of intensified apocalyptic speculation and antinomianism, Paul is able to present the resurrection of Christ as the foundation of this new view of community.[8]

Conversion and community focus our attention on the two aspects of the early Christian experience which most clearly separated it from the moral exhortation of pagan philosophy and the cultic associations of the Hellenistic cities. Conversion implied a break, a separation from one's past and social environment, which frequently led to hostility. Persecution reinforced the solidarity of the group as is evident in 1 Thessalonians (e.g., 1:6–8; 2:14–16).[9]

---

[4] J. A. Fitzmyer, "Paul and the Law," *To Advance the Gospel* (New York: Crossroad, 1981) 186–201.

[5] See J. A. Fitzmyer, "Qumran and the Interpolated Paragraph in 2 Cor 6:14–7:1," *Essays on the Semitic Background of the New Testament* (SBLSBS 5; Missoula: Scholars, 1974) 205–17.

[6] Fitzmyer, "Glory on the Face of Christ," 643–44.

[7] See, for example, E. Best, *The First and Second Epistles to the Thessalonians* (London: Black, 1972) 82–86.

[8] See A. Segal, *Rebecca's Children: Judaism and Christianity in the Roman World* (Cambridge: Harvard University Press, 1986) 94–115.

[9] See W. A. Meeks, *The Moral World of the First Christians* (Philadelphia: Westminster, 1986) 125–26.

Apocalyptic imagery reinforces the sense of an absolute obligation to the ethos of the new community. The distinctiveness of members of that community is made evident in eschatological images (e.g., 5:5–8).[10] Even though the ethical expectations of Pauline paraenesis are often not different from an "enlightened paganism," the imagery of apocalyptic holiness makes the Christian community the only sphere in which such goals may be obtained.

Christianity among the Cults

1 Thess 1:9a presents conversion as primarily a cultic issue, not a turn toward philosophic enlightenment. Baptism and other ritual forms of practice and speech, about which we know much less than we would like, served to define the community as much as teaching did.[11] Opposition to idols was an established theme within Judaism and could even serve to define the sectarian purity of the Qumran sect over against the larger Jewish community (e.g., 1QS 2:16–17).[12] When Paul employs this theme again in Gal 4:8–9, he depends on a Hellenistic Jewish formulation of the argument against the idols that had taken over euhemeristic explanations for the existence of "gods." Paul may even have known a form of that tradition which linked the "gods" with demonic powers.[13] However, the focus on "purity" in the paraenetic section of 1 Thessalonians suggests that here the associations are drawn in a way that is closer to the Qumran tradition in which idolatry and impurity are equated.[14]

Conversion does not appear to involve intellectual enlightenment as much as a decisive shift in cultic practice. Inscriptional evidence attests that in the first half of the second century A.D. the public cult of the Egyptian god Anubis can count high-ranking Roman citizens among the majority of functionaries listed.[15] Karl Donfried has argued that both religious and civic cults enjoyed a high degree of visibility in Thessalonica. He suggests that the accusations of "impurity" associated with cultic practice could be supported by the use of phallic symbols and sexual symbols in a number of the cults.[16] Were

---

[10] See Meeks, *Moral World*, 128.

[11] See the description of the ritual elements in the self-identity of Pauline churches in W. A. Meeks, *The First Urban Christians* (New Haven: Yale, 1983) 140–63.

[12] See Fitzmyer, "Qumran and the Interpolated Paragraph," 213–15.

[13] See the discussion in H. D. Betz, *Galatians* (Philadelphia: Fortress, 1979) 213–15.

[14] See M. Newton, *The Concept of Purity at Qumran and in the Letters of Paul* (SNTSMS 53; Cambridge: University Press, 1985) 102–4.

[15] See J. E. Stambaugh and D. L. Balch, *The New Testament in Its Social Environment* (Philadelphia: Westminster, 1986) 136.

[16] K. Donfried, "The Cults of Thessalonica and the Thessalonian Correspondence," *NTS* 31 (1985) 336–41.

Christianity merely another imported cult, it would presumably have attracted no more attention than Judaism or the Samaritan community in Thessalonica.[17]

However, it is evident that conversion to Christianity was not perceived as association with yet another foreign cult. Donfried proposes that the hostility Christianity evoked must be linked to the civic cults. The close ties between Thessalonica and Rome led to cultic practices honoring the city's Roman benefactors as early as the first century B.C. Coins from 27 B.C. show the head of the divinized Julius and his son Augustus. During Augustus's reign a temple to the divinized Caesar was built, which had its own staff of priests and functionaries.[18] Since Christianity required withdrawal from all forms of cultic association, its new adherents could not but offend the civic sentiments of their fellows. Donfried speculates that the politarchs mentioned in Acts 17:7–8 might also have been responsible for administering oaths of loyalty (reverence and obedience) such as those attested for the Cypriots and the inhabitants of Paphlagonia. The latter swore to spare nothing of themselves in imperial service and to report anyone whose activities might represent rebellion against the emperor.[19]

The very language of Christian preaching has overtones which are politically suspicious in such an environment.[20] Christian cult centers on Jesus Christ, the kyrios (1:1, 3, 6; 2:15, 19; 3:11–13; 4:1, 2, 6, 15, 17; 5:2, 9, 12, 23, 27, 28). Not only have his followers received instructions from the kyrios (1:6; 4:2, 15; 5:27) and spread "the word" to others (1:8), they are bound by affirmations of loyalty (3:8); have persons "over you in the Lord" (4:12) and await the parousia (arrival of a visiting dignitary) of the Lord whom they will gather to meet (2:14; 3:13; 5:23). For an outsider, who was not aware that the "Lord" had died, the apocalyptic overtones of the parousia language would raise even more suspicions. Certain persons are "crowned" at his coming (2:19) while he acts with vengeance against outsiders and disloyal members of the sect (4:6). Even worse, the parousia will not be a public approach to the city, but the stealthy act of a thief coming in the night (5:2). Taken out of context in this way, there is quite enough in the language of Christian belief to arouse suspicion and even hostility without presuming that Christians engaged in any direct polemic against the civic cult.

Suffering and the Apostolic Example

The theme of "imitation" runs throughout the epistle. Its recipients are praised for having become "imitators" of the apostle and of the Lord by

[17] On the existence of Jews and Samaritans in this region, see Meeks, *Urban Christians,* 46.
[18] Donfried, "Cults of Thessalonica," 344–46.
[19] Ibid., 342–44.
[20] Ibid., 343.

suffering for the word (1:6–8; 2:13–14)[21] and this imitation is to carry through into the ethical obedience with which they await the coming of the Lord (4:1). Imitation of noble examples, sometimes of a father or ancestor; sometimes of the philosopher whose life embodies his preaching, was an established element in Greco-Roman ethical preaching.[22]

Malherbe notes that while Paul confidently speaks of his addressees as imitators of himself, Stoic philosophers were reticent to make claims for themselves as examples. The Cynics, by contrast, did speak of their own example of endurance and their Herculean labors as support for the "rough speech" they used in preaching to others. Paul draws a link between "speech" and imitation in 1 Thess 1:5–6. However, the "deeds" by which Paul's preaching is vindicated are not his own apostolic labors but the way in which the gospel message came to his converts.[23] The description of his own ministry in 1 Thess 2:1–13 continues in this vein. Like the true philosopher, Paul speaks frankly, without flattering his audience or distorting the truth for material gain. Like them, he can also insist that he has a divine mission in speaking. However, Paul differentiates himself from the majority of Cynic preachers by playing down the "boldness" or "harshness" of his speech. Apostolic boldness is evident not in speech but in perseverance in preaching despite affliction. Instead, Paul uses the figure of a "nurse" caring for children and of a "father" encouraging and exhorting them to describe his own position. Malherbe notes that the image of the philosopher-nurse carries ambiguous overtones in the philosophic tradition. While it may reflect a healing concern for one's audience, it may also represent the "soft speech" of the flatterer.[24]

Donfried rejects the philosophic background of this image in favor of one from the cult. The myth of Dionysus included the story of how the infant was nursed by nymphs, while in the version of the Cabrius cult known from Samothrace, Tethys, the spouse of Okeanos, is described as "nurse and provider of all things." Both cults are attested for Thessalonica. If the contrast between Christianity and its pagan environment is primarily cultic, then the apostle's self-presentation as nurse expresses a "divine protectiveness," which his converts might otherwise have found in their devotion to particular deities.[25]

---

[21] This is the only case in which Paul speaks of his addressees as "having become" imitators already (see G. Lyons, *Pauline Autobiography: Toward a New Understanding* [SBLDS 73; Atlanta: Scholars, 1985] 190).

[22] See A. Malherbe, *Moral Exhortation: A Greco-Roman Sourcebook* (Philadelphia: Westminster, 1986) 38, 135–36; idem, "Exhortation in First Thessalonians," 246–49; Meeks, *Moral World*, 127.

[23] Malherbe, "Exhortation in First Thessalonians," 246–47.

[24] Malherbe, "Gentle as a Nurse," 205–13.

[25] Donfried, "Cults of Thessalonica," 337–41.

There is a more characteristically Jewish side to Paul's presentation of suffering as well. Paul claims to have already told the Thessalonians to expect sufferings (3:2–4). The basis for such a confident prediction is not a theoretical principle about the "content" of his preaching and the ignorant vanity of humanity such as one finds in the Hellenistic moralists. Rather Paul's assertion is based on a broad pattern of "sufferings" that connect the Thessalonians' experience with that of the apostle, whose treatment at Philippi they may have heard about when he preached among them (2:2), that of Christians elsewhere and of Christ himself (2:14).[26] In the Pauline context, suffering retains a decidedly apocalyptic rendering.

Lyons's study of Paul's use of autobiography has also called attention to the cultic and communal implications of Paul's presentation of his mission. He suggests that the contrast between the "boldness" of Paul's founding mission and "weakness" was directed against idolatry. Anti-idol polemic in Jewish circles described them as "empty, false, without spirit and strength" (e.g., Jer 10:14–15; 18:15; Wis 11:15; 12:24; 14:22–26). Idol cults are a source of uncleanness and immorality (Wis 14:12–26). Vice lists in the Pauline tradition regularly associate uncleanness, idolatry, and sexual immorality (Gal 5:19–21; Col 3:5; Eph 5:3–6). Ability to surmount affliction is evidence for the "power" which the apostle and his converts have received from the true God (1:5–9). This power could never come from the error, uncleanness, and deceit of a pagan cult (2:3).[27]

Using parallels from the Qumran material, M. Barré has argued that "weakness" in Paul always refers to specific events of hostility from outsiders, never to the physical health of the apostle. The *Hodayot* present the Teacher of Righteousness as one whose weaknesses and stumbling are caused by his enemies, through whom Satan is attempting to destroy the elect (e.g., 1QH 9:25–27). God is the one who steps in to heal the wounds of the afflicted teacher and to make the teacher a sign of divine power. The apocalyptic reading of such persecution is evident in 1QH 2:23–25:

> You allowed them [= the congregation of Belial] to assemble against me. So that you might be glorified in the judgment of the wicked. And you might manifest your power through me in the presence of the children of men, for by your grace I stand firm.

Both the suffering and "standing firm" are ultimately signs of God's eschatological power acting through the Teacher of Righteousness. A similar pattern is evident in the way in which Paul presents his own ministry.[28]

---

[26] See Meeks, *Urban Christians*, 174.
[27] Lyons, *Pauline Autobiography*, 191–96.
[28] M. L. Barré, "Qumran and the Weakness of Paul," *CBQ* 42 (1980) 216–27.

Paul's reference to opposition at Philippi (2:2; see also Phil 1:27–30) indicates that the afflictions about which he is speaking result from the actions of human opponents. Acts 17:1–9 presumes that hostility from members of the Jewish community led to Paul's departure from Thessalonica. Certainly his assertion that "Satan" prevents his returning to visit the church there (1 Thess 2:18–19) not only suggests human opposition but casts that opposition in apocalyptic categories. Satan is attempting to destroy Paul's work (also see 3:5), the "crown" in which he can boast at the judgment. Within this context, Timothy's positive report that the community is "standing firm" and Paul's own prayer to visit there soon (3:6–10) imply an impending victory of divine power.[29]

Donfried suggests that the specific forces of opposition in Thessalonica were linked to the civic cult. Paul's departure from the city may have resulted in some criticism. Dio Chrysostom (*Or.* 32,11) contrasts true "boldness" with those philosophers who behave in a timid way lest they be sent packing. It might also have been suggested that Paul had not adequately warned the community about the persecutions to come.[30] Paul both denies the charges that he seeks to avoid "affliction himself" and claims to have spoken a "prophetic word" about the future afflictions (3:4).[31] Only the appropriation of an eschatological understanding of his mission, revelation, suffering, and divine power enables Paul to turn the potentially devastating effects of external hostility and persecution into effective support for the faithfulness and love shown in the Thessalonian community.[32]

Exhortation in 1 Thessalonians

Both the rejection of idolatrous cult and impurity and the imitation of apostolic example point toward the paraenetic section of the letter. The Spirit active in Paul's preaching and the Thessalonians' reception of the gospel has been given them so that they will lead lives of holiness, not uncleanness (1:5–6; 4:7–8). Such a life is also evidence of heeding God, not humans (2:1–4, 13; 4:8; 5:19). Paul himself has set an example for avoiding *akatharsia* (2:3; 4:1, 7).[33] He has also set them an example for specific elements of the

---

[29] Lyons, *Pauline Autobiography*, 210–15.

[30] Donfried, "Cults of Thessalonica," 347–51.

[31] Paul's treatment of the afflictions in 1:5–2:11 uses the pattern "word from the apostle—divine wording—imitation" twice (see Lyons, *Pauline Autobiography*, 191). The apostle claims to transmit a divine word explicitly in 1 Thess 4:13–18 (see J. Gillman, "Signals of Transformation in 1 Thessalonians 4:13–18," *CBQ* 47 [1985] 271). Though 1 Thess 3:4 does not use the technical vocabulary of prophecy, the community's experience is invoked to attest to the truth of what Paul had previously told them.

[32] See Meeks, *Urban Christians*, 174–75.

[33] Lyons, *Pauline Autobiography*, 195.

paraenesis in working as an expression of love for his converts and so as not to burden others (2:8–12; 4:9–12).[34]

As Malherbe has observed, the exhortation in 4:3–8 has been shaped by the "motivation" given for Christian behavior, "holiness" (vv. 3, 7 and "holy spirit" in v. 8).[35] Noting parallels between this section and 1 Pet 1:1–2:3, 11–12, Hodgson has suggested that Paul has redacted a form of the "holiness code" with the ethos of "philosophic retirement" from the Hellenistic moralists in 4:10b–11.[36] The theme of holiness returns as the conclusion to the paraenetic section (5:23–24). There, it is clearly the condition in which the Christian participates in the coming of the Lord,[37] and further evidence of the power of God which has been operative since the Thessalonians were "called."

Participation in the "Lord's coming" is the primary issue behind the pericope on fate of those who have died (4:13–18).[38] This section begins a compilation of elements of early Christian apocalyptic tradition, which speak to the situation of those living as the community which is to participate in the Lord's coming (4:13–5:11).[39] Paul may be presuming the pessimistic language of tombstone inscriptions and the "consolations" of Hellenistic moralists in drawing the contrast between Christians and "those who have no hope."[40] He has a "better hope" to offer. Instead of permanent "separation" of the living and dead, the community is to be brought together with the Lord.[41] At the same time, Paul is able to use the images of apocalyptic separation to sharpen the distinction between the Christian community and outsiders that is already presupposed in the "holiness tradition" with which the paraenetic section begins.[42]

---

[34] Ibid., 199–201.

[35] Malherbe, "Exhortation in First Thessalonians," 250–51.

[36] R. Hodgson, "1 Thessalonians 4:1–12 and the Holiness Tradition," SBL Seminar Papers (ed. K. Richards; Chico, CA: Scholars, 1982) 199–214. R. F. Collins ("The Unity of Paul's Paraenesis in 1 Thess 4.3–8, 1 Cor 7,1–7, A Significant Parallel," NTS 29 [1983] 420–25) argues that this section reflects a fixed pattern in Pauline ethical teaching.

[37] U. Schnelle, "Der erste Thessalonicherbrief und die Entstehung der paulinischen Anthropologie," NTS 32 (1986) 209.

[38] See Gillman, "Signals of Transformation," 268–74; P. Perkins, Resurrection (Garden City, NY: Doubleday, 1984) 296–98; A. F. J. Klijn, "I Thessalonians 4.13–18 and its Background in Apocalyptic Literature," Paul and Paulinism: Essays in honour of C. K. Barrett (ed. M. D. Hooker and S. G. Wilson; London: SPCK, 1982) 67–69.

[39] See Meeks, Urban Christians, 175; Klijn, "1 Thessalonians 4.13–18," 72.

[40] So Malherbe, "Exhortation in First Thessalonians," 254–56.

[41] Ibid., 256 n. 84; Meeks, Urban Christians, 175.

[42] For an attempt to reconstruct the pre-Pauline traditions behind this section, see W. Harnisch, Eschatologische Existenz: Ein exegetischer Beitrag zum Sachanliegen von 1 Thessalonicher 4,13–5,11 (FRLANT 110; Göttingen: Vandenhoeck & Ruprecht, 1973) 39–124.

The distinction between the community destined for salvation "with the Lord" and not for "wrath" in 5:9–10 recalls the formula of 1 Thess 1:9–10. Throughout 1 Thessalonians, Paul has insisted on the obligation of Christians to separate themselves from their idolatrous past and to exemplify that separation in the solidarity of their new community. The apocalyptic imagery at the conclusion of the letter intensifies the boundaries which have already been drawn in the earlier references to suffering and to holiness.[43] 1 Thess 5:10 picks up the conclusion of the section on those who have died (4:17). The Christian hope of "being with the Lord" already relativizes the distinction between the living and dead for the community.[44] The "separation" entailed by "holiness" in the Christian community of common love and exhortation is presented as overcoming a more radical separation in human experience.

The gospel called upon people to turn away from the pagan cults to the true God. We have seen that this call had sufficient impact to arouse hostility against both its messengers and those who followed their summons. Understood as evidence of the eschatological power of God, such affliction did not weaken the new Christian community but strengthened its perception of a divine calling to holiness and salvation. Some scholars have even speculated that those Christians whose death is referred to in 1 Thess 4:13–18 had in some way died because of the hostility.[45] Whether or not that is the case, Paul will later confront the possibility of such death in his own case, where he again uses the same relativizing of the categories life and death (Phil 1:20–26) and in the "generalized case" where he insists that nothing separates the Christian from the "love of God/Christ" (Rom 8:31–39).

Paul's solution to the practical problems of the community living in the presence of persecution is a quietist withdrawal reminiscent of Epicurean preaching (4:11–12), though Paul does not invoke other Epicurean topoi on friendship, on the pleasant life or freedom from fear of death or the gods.[46] Repetition and reapplication of the paraenesis on "quietness and work" by the Paulinist author of 2 Thessalonians (2 Thess 3:12) show that this advice played an ongoing role in shaping the understanding of an appropriate way of life for Thessalonian Christians. There it appears to be invoked against possibility of a "quiet idleness" as an appropriate response to the impending parousia. In 1 Thessalonians, on the other hand, Paul seems to be primarily

---

[43] See Meeks, *Urban Christians,* 128–29.

[44] Donfried, "Cults of Thessalonica," 352.

[45] J. A. Fitzmyer, "Paul and the Law," *To Advance the Gospel* (New York: Crossroad, 1981) 186–201.

[46] Malherbe (*Social Aspects of Early Christianity* [Baton Rouge: Louisiana State University Press, 1977] 25–27) even suggests that Paul wanted to prevent the Thessalonians from turning in that direction; also see Meeks, *Moral World,* 129.

concerned with alleviating suspicions and the tension the community experiences from outsiders.

Quite unlike his moralist counterparts, Paul does not recommend "living quietly" on the grounds that it frees the individual from the ambitions, cares, and dangers of public life. He does not have the "moral education" of individuals in view.[47] Paul does presume that the larger community can recognize in Christian behavior that which the larger society considered "decent" and may be influenced in how it reacts to Christians accordingly.[48] But from beginning to end, 1 Thessalonians shows us the precarious process by which a new Christian community carves out its place among the cults and associations of the Greco-Roman city. The most basic categories and images which Paul gives his readers to understand their common experience stem from his Jewish heritage.

[47] See also Meeks, *Moral World*, 130. Meeks notes that the communal dimension looms much larger in Paul than it does in civic-minded Greek ethics. One finds a similar concern with community only among Pythagoreans and Epicureans.

[48] Meeks, *Moral World*, 129.

The "Itinerary" as a Form in Classical
Literature and the Acts of the Apostles

John Reumann
Lutheran Theological Seminary

In our voyage along the shore (*paraplous*) we passed many other countries but put in at the Morning Star, then being colonized. And landing there, we procured water. Embarking for the Zodiac, we passed the Sun on the port side, sailing close by the shore. . . . Sailing the next day and night, toward evening we reached Lychnopolis (Lamptown). . . . This city lies between the Pleiades and the Hyades in the air.

Lucian, *Alēthōn diēgmatōn* (*Verae Historiae*) 1.28,29

LUCAN STUDIES HAVE LONG OCCUPIED the scholar honored in these pages.[1] Father Joseph A. Fitzmyer, S.J., has always been meticulous in his caution about use of evidence from antiquity, whether Semitic or Greek. The purpose of these pages is to further the reexamination of the often-proposed "itineraria" as a form and source in the book of Acts by looking into what evidence exists for such a literary phenomenon. Accuracy in what we say about the world in which the Bible spoke its original witness is a heritage from this friend and colleague in NT studies and ecumenical dialogue, and it behooves us to test constantly what modern interpreters say to see if these things are really so (cf. Luke 1:4).

The notion of the "itinerary" often intertwines with a device noted in Acts at least since Irenaeus (*Adv. Haer.* 3.1, 1; 3.10, 1; and 3.14, 1–14),[2] the use of the first person plural pronoun "we" in certain passages concerning travel, often by sea (16:10–17; 20:5–15; 21:1–18; 27:1–28:16; plus 11:28 in the Western text). Space does not permit here a detailed report on the history of research on the use of

---

[1] Besides AB 28 and 28A, *Luke*, one recalls "Acts of the Apostles," *JBC* 45:1–8, 35–119, especially, in connection with the topic below, 6 and 81 on a "diary" or "notes from the journey" as a source in Acts.

[2] Cf. AB 28:37–38, in connection with discussion of the "we"-sections.

"we,"[3] but as modern criticism developed, especially in the nineteenth century, appeal was widely made to a "we"-source, travel diaries, or an itinerary, often to defend Luke's authorship and the accuracy of the Acts accounts. For the author of this "we"-material was often taken to be also the author of the book of Acts.

A Review of Research on the Itinerary

It was Martin Dibelius who popularized the view that the travel diary or "itinerary" was the appropriate form from Luke's day to explain a great deal in those passages. In a 1923 Festschrift article Dibelius defined the form as

> an itinerary of stations where Paul stopped, an itinerary which we may suppose to have been provided with notes of his journeys, of the founding of communities and of the result of evangelising.[4]

The form did not depend, he said, on the presence of "we," so that 16:6–9 could also have belonged to an itinerary, for example. Some sixteen years later Dibelius expanded his view to include the underlying document behind Acts 13:1–14:28; 15:35–21:16, containing

> information about the stations on the journey, the hosts, the preaching and the results of preaching, the founding of communities, disputes and either voluntary or forced departures—all these constantly recur . . . as the constituent parts of this itinerary. We cannot imagine that these records, with their concise and impartial style, were written down for the purpose of edifying or of entertaining. Nor are they colorful enough to be regarded as the local traditions of individual communities.[5]

---

[3] Cf. Jacques Dupont, *Les Sources du Livre des Actes* (Bruges: Desclée de Brouwer, 1960), cited from the Eng. trans. by Kathleen Pont, *The Sources of Acts: The Present Position* (London: Darton, Longman & Todd, 1964); Ward Gasque, *A History of the Criticism of the Acts of the Apostles* (BGBE 17; Tübingen: Mohr-Siebeck, 1975); rev. ed., *A History of the Interpretation of the Acts of the Apostles* (Peabody, MA: Hendrickson, 1989)..

[4] "Stilkritisches zur Apostelgeschichte," *Eucharisterion. Studien zur Religion und Literatur des Alten und Neuen Testaments Hermann Gunkel . . . dargebracht,* ed. H. Schmidt (FRLANT 36, N.F. 19; Göttingen: Vandenhoeck & Ruprecht, 1923) 2. 27–49, repr. in Dibelius's *Aufsätze zur Apostelgeschichte,* ed. H. Greeven (FRLANT N.F. 42; Göttingen: Vandenhoeck & Ruprecht, 1951) 9–28; cited from trans. by Mary Ling, "Style Criticism of the Book of Acts," in Dibelius's *Studies in the Acts of the Apostles* (London: SCM, New York: Scribner, 1956) 1–25, quotation from p. 5.

[5] "Paulus auf dem Areopag," Sitzungsberichte der Heidelberger Akademie der Wissenschaft; Philosophisch-historische Klasse, 1938–39, fasc. 2 (Heidelberg: C. Winter, 1939), repr. in Dibelius's *Aufsätze,* 29–70; cited from "Paul on the Areopagus," in *Studies* (1956) 26–77, quotation from p. 69.

Then in 1947 Dibelius proposed a reason why such an "account of the stations" was treasured: so that, if "the journey were to be repeated, the way and former hosts could be found once more."[6]

Ever since Dibelius's pioneer work on some of the "we"-passages as form-critically "itineraries," opinions have varied and debates often waxed vigorous on this putative form. One of the anomalies to be noted is that we are not likely dealing with an oral form but a *written* one, yet "Form-geschichte in Acts" was the designation used. Independently of Dibelius, Henry Cadbury, too, spoke of an "itinerary" source.[7] Alfred Wikenhauser, among Catholic scholars, came also to allow for such a diary source.[8] Bauernfeind's commentary spoke of "the so-called Itinerary, the travel report" as the source behind Acts 16–28.[9] Kümmel's influential *Introduction* took over the hypothesis but also noted opposition to it.[10] Arthur Darby Nock's review of Dibelius's *Aufsätze* preferred not "*the* Itinerar" but "several distinct travel-diaries."[11]

Haenchen at first followed the itinerary theory[12] but later moved away from it, rejecting any single long itinerary source and expressing doubt again and again—this section (e.g., 15:36–18:22) was no itinerary or that (e.g., 18:23–21:17; 27–28) was by no means a diary verbatim.[13] E. Trocmé avoided

[6] "Der erste christliche Historiker," *Schriften der Universität Heidelberg*, 3: *Aus der Arbeit der Universität, 1946–1947* (Heidelberg: Springer, 1948) 112–25, repr. in Dibelius's *Aufsätze*, 108–19; cited from "The First Christian Historian," in *Studies* (1956) 123–37, quotation from p. 126.

[7] *The Making of Luke-Acts* (New York: Macmillan, 1927, repr. London: SPCK, 1958); "Acts of the Apostles," *IDB* 1:35.

[8] Compare Wikenhauser's *New Testament Introduction*, trans. of 2d German ed. of 1956 by J. Cunningham (New York: Herder and Herder, 1960) 327–28, with his earlier *Die Apostel-geschichte und ihr Geschichtswert* (NTAbh 8/3–5; Münster: Aschendorff, 1921) and his commentary, *Die Apostelgeschichte* (RNT 5; Regensburg: Pustet, 1938, 2d. ed. 1951) 12.

[9] *Die Apostelgeschichte* (THKNT 5; Leipzig) 7, a view not changed in the revision on which he was working at his death, published in his *Kommentar und Studien zur Apostelgeschichte* (WUNT 22; Tübingen: Mohr-Siebeck, 1980) 300–301.

[10] *Introduction to the New Testament*, trans. A. J. Matill, Jr., from the 14th German ed. 1965 (New York & Nashville: Abingdon, 1966) 131, cf. p. 126, in contrast to the 9th ed. by Feine and Behm of this *Einleitung* (1950) 87. Kümmel's view remains the same in the German 17th ed., trans. H. Kee (1975) 177–78 and 184.

[11] *Gnomon* 25 (1953) 497–506, repr. in Nock's *Essays on Religion and the Ancient World*, ed. Zeph Stewart (Cambridge: Harvard University Press, 1972) 2. 821–32. The reference is to pp. 499–501 in the *Gnomon* pagination (retained in the reprint).

[12] "Tradition und Komposition in der Apostelgeschichte," *ZTK* 52 (1955) 205–25, especially 220–22; repr. in Haenchen's *Gott und Mensch: Gesammelte Aufsätze* (Tübingen: Mohr-Siebeck, 1965) 206–26, especially 221–23.

[13] The changes in his views can be traced out in Haenchen's *Apostelgeschichte* (MeyerKEK; Göttingen: Vandenhoeck & Ruprecht, 10th ed. 1956) through the 14th ed. (1965) that was translated into English as *The Acts of the Apostles* (Philadelphia: Westminster, 1971), above all in

the term "itinerary," preferring instead the notion of a travel diary kept by various persons.[14] But Gottfried Schille attacked head-on the pillars upon which the itinerary-theory rested, calling it "nothing other than a final vestige of those source theories that M. Dibelius has so sharply denounced."[15]

Yet Dupont inclined nonetheless to the theory,[16] Erich Grässer has stood by it,[17] and so did Vielhauer.[18] Conzelmann spoke of it in a nuanced way,[19] but Stählin[20] and Weiser[21] in their commentaries more positively. Similarly Gerhard Schneider,[22] so that to say, as one survey has concluded, "nowadays, the hypothesis has been generally abandoned"[23] is untrue.

More recently Eckhard Plümacher explained the "we"-passages as basically a literary device by Luke, imitating classical practice, especially in sea voyage accounts to show firsthand acquaintanceship with the subject matter.[24] Vernon K. Robbins has carried further the view that in antiquity sea voyages were often couched in first person narration.[25] He cites sailing manuals in particular, the *periplus* form, and rests on four examples where there is a shift from third person to first plural and "the narrator is not the

---

his "Das 'Wir' in der Apostelgeschichte und das Itinerar," *ZTK* 58 (1961) 329–66, repr. in Haenchen's *Gott und Mensch*, 227–64, trans. J. Wilson, " 'We' in Acts and the Itinerary," in *JTC* 1, *The Bultmann School of Biblical Interpretation: New Directions?* ed. R. Funk (Tübingen: Mohr-Siebeck, New York: Harper & Row, 1965) 64–99.

[14] *Le "Livre des Actes" et l'Histoire* (Études d'Histoire et Philosophie Religieuses 45; Paris: Presses Universitaires de France, 1957).

[15] "Die Fragwürdigkeit eines Itinerars der Paulusreisen," *TLZ* 84 (1959) 165–74; *Die Apostelgeschichte des Lukas* (THKNT 5; Berlin: Evangelische Verlagsanstalt, 1983) 352–53, 366–67.

[16] *Sources*, 157–67, though he speaks of the "fragmentation" of the itinerary theory.

[17] *TRu* 26 (1960) 124–27 and 41 (1976) 188–90.

[18] *GGA* 221 (1969) 4–7; *Geschichte der urchristlichen Literatur* (Berlin & New York: de Gruyter, 1975) 389–90, 392, cf. 71 and 76.

[19] *Die Apostelgeschichte* (HNT 7; Tübingen: Mohr-Siebeck, 1963) 5–6; trans. James Limburg, A. Thomas Kraabel, and Donald H. Juel, ed. Eldon Jay Epp with Christopher R. Matthews, from 2d German ed. of 1972, *Acts of the Apostles* (Hermeneia; Philadelphia: Fortress, 1987) xxxviii–xl. Note among other classical passages Lucian *Verae Historiae* 1.28, where an itinerary is satirized as a "space journey." See below, n. 51.

[20] *Die Apostelgeschichte* (NTD 5; Göttingen: Vandenhoeck & Ruprecht, 10th ed. 1962) 215; similarly J. Roloff, 17th ed. (1981) 10, 238–39.

[21] Alfons Weiser, *Die Apostelgeschichte* (ÖTKNT 5/1; Gütersloh: Mohn, Würzburg: Echter, 1981) 36–38 and Exkurs 7.4; 5/2 (1985) 405–6.

[22] *Die Apostelgeschichte* (HTKNT 5/1–2; Freiburg: Herder, 1980, 1982) 1:89–95, 2:204.

[23] Gasque, *History*, 240 n. 112.

[24] "Wirklichkeitserfahrung und Geschichtsschreibung bei Lukas: Erwägungen zu den Wir-Stücken der Apostelgeschichte," *ZNW* 68 (1977) 1–22. See further Plümacher's "Acta Forschung 1974–1982 (Fortsetzung und Schluss)," *TRu* 49 (1984) 125–28.

[25] "The We-Passages in Acts and Ancient Sea Voyages," *BR* 20 (1975) 5–18; "By Land and Sea: The We-Passages and Ancient Sea Voyages," in *Perspectives on Luke-Acts*, ed. Charles H. Talbert (Perspectives in Religious Studies, Special Studies Series 5; Danville, VA: Association of Baptist Professors of Religion; Edinburgh: T. & T. Clark, 1978; repr. Macon, GA: Mercer University Press, 1981) 215–42.

main actor." But on this reading the "we" turns out to be redactoral, not from a source. Susan Marie Praeder has rebutted this position,[26] rather effectively in my view, observing that two of Robbins's four examples are later than Acts (the *Antiochene Acts of the Martyrdom of Ignatius* and the Nag Hammadi *Acts of Peter and the Twelve Apostles*) and the "parallels" in the *Periplous of Hanno* and a papyrus text about episodes from the Third Syrian War become less impressive upon examination.[27] Most impressive, while Robbins presented some examples of texts about sea voyages, Praeder lists some forty-five authors providing accounts of trips by sea from the fifth century B.C. until the fourth A.D. Her own "narrative theology" approach to Acts 27–28 leaves open who the "I" behind the "we"-passages is beyond "a Christian of the first century." It is not possible to examine here the implications for all these views from the survey which follows.[28]

Classical References to "Itineraries"

It is surprising that relatively few of those who have debated whether an itinerary form or source or something of the sort stood behind the second half of Acts and was intertwined with the "we"-passages took pains to document such a form in Greco-Roman literature of the period. (Robbins and Praeder are happy exceptions.) It is therefore understandable that Schille in 1959 went so far as to ask whether such a Gattung existed in Paul's day.

In terms of modern scholarship Julius Wellhausen had used the term "itinerary" as early as 1907 in an essay.[29] Eduard Norden, though he did not employ the term "itinerary," cited a great many classical parallels for the "we"-sections in his discussion of the composition of Acts. In *Agnostos Theos*

[26] "The Narrative Voyage: An Analysis and Interpretation of Acts 27–28" (diss., Graduate Theological Union, Berkeley, CA: 1980); "Acts 27:1–28:16: Sea Voyages in Ancient Literature and the Theology of Luke-Acts," *CBQ* 46 (1984) 683–706, especially 683–84 n. 3; 686–89; 693–95, on Robbins, itineraries, and ancient novels. Richard I. Pervo (*Profit with Delight: The Literary Genre of the Acts of the Apostles* [Philadelphia: Fortress, 1987] 57) sides with Robbins against Praeder on Luke's "Itinerary style." Gerd Lüdemann (*Das frühe Christentum nach den Traditionen der Apostelgeschichte: Ein Kommentar* [Göttingen: Vandenhoeck & Ruprecht, 1987] 20–22, 28, 170–71, 184, 190, 192, 269, and *passim*) reckons with "Itinerar" and "Reisestationen"; trans., *Early Christianity According to the Traditions in Acts* (Philadelphia: Fortress, 1988).

[27] The Ignatian text is in J. B. Lightfoot, *The Apostolic Fathers, Part II, S. Ignatius, S. Polycarp*, Vol. 2, Sect. 1 (London: Macmillan, 1885) 573, Greek on pp. 483–85. The Acts of Peter, in *The Nag Hammadi Library in English*, ed. James M. Robinson (New York: Harper & Row, 1977) 265–70. For the *Voyage of Hanno*, see below, under C. 3. The papyrus text is Flinders Petri Papyri II, III: XLV and CXLIV (246 B.C.).

[28] I hope to do so in the Anchor Bible *Philippians*, which will also deal with the founding mission in Acts 16.

[29] "Noten zur Apostelgeschichte," Nachrichten von der königlichen Gesellschaft der Wissenschaften zu Göttingen, Philologisch-historische Klasse, 1907 (Berlin, 1907) 21, and then in his "Kritische Analyse der Apostelgeschichte," Abhandlungen der königlichen Gesellschaft der Wissenschaften zu Göttingen, Philologisch-historische Klasse, NF 15/2 (Berlin: Weidmannische Buchhandlung, 1914) 39.

he listed the following examples of the two possible types of "memoirs" (*hypomnēma*) which he thought might lie behind Acts[30]:

hypomnēma

I.	II.
Pure "We" or "I" Style	"We" or "I" Style combined with a report
Travel reports:	Reports on expeditions:
e.g., Odysseus in the	e.g., Ptolemy I Soter,
realms of Alcinous	Ptolemy III Exergetes, Nearchus
periploi (see below),	Caesar and Cicero, letters
apodēmiai ("trips abroad")	to the Senate
novels (Lucan, Dio	Trajan's *Dacian Wars*
[Chrysostom] of Prusa	
gnostic Acts of the Apostles	Arrian's *Periplus* [*of the Euxine Sea*]
	for Hadrian
	Historical works and similar
	works:
	e.g., Velleius Paterculus
	Dio Cassius
	Ammianus Marcellinus
	novels on Alexander the Great
	NT writings
	the underlying source
	(*Grundschrift*) of the canonical
	Acts; apocryphal Gospels.

Norden put all future investigators in his debt by detailing so many places in classical literature where first person forms existed, especially for sea voyages like the *periploi*. Sometimes these first singulars or plurals in narratives were interspersed with third person reports, the model (II above) that Acts obviously follows in its present form. An example occurs, e.g., at Philippi, 16:6ff., where the "we" of the eyewitness and the third plural both occur. By analogy with what happened to the memoirs of Ezra and Nehemiah in the OT, Norden concluded the redactor of Acts had reworked a first-person source.[31]

---

[30] Eduard Norden, *Agnostos Theos. Untersuchungen zur Formgeschichte religioser Rede* (Leipzig & Berlin: Teubner, 1913, repr. 1923) 311–32, chart on p. 326.

[31] Ezra begins in the third person but from 7:29 through 9:15 employs the pronoun "I" for Ezra. Nehemiah 1:1–7:5; 12:31, and 13:4–31 is first person singular, but the rest is told in the third person. The relation of first-person singular memoirs and the third person "he source" continues to be debated in Ezra-Nehemiah studies; cf. *JBC* 24:83 and Jacob M. Myers, *Ezra, Nehemiah* (AB 14; Garden City, NY: Doubleday, 1965) xxxviii–xli, xlix.

Dibelius, in proposing the "itinerary" form, referred to Norden but offered no ancient itineraries as evidence.[32] Haenchen did no differently in his several treatments.[33] The most impressive additional primary evidence probably comes in A. D. Nock's review of Dibelius's *Aufsätze* on Acts, but his documentation in *Gnomon* 25 (1953) 499 dealt with diaries, not "itineraries."[34] Yet that *Gnomon* reference is what Vielhaur cites to refute Schille's question about whether there was such a Gattung in antiquity.[35]

In defense of many of the scholars involved, NT professors always used to be trained classicists and would from school days have known Xenophon's constant refrain, "Then Cyrus marched so and so many stages, so many parasangs and came to a city named . . ." (*Anabasis* 1.2.5, 6, 7, 10, 13, etc., usually *enteuthen exelaunei stathmous . . . parasangas . . .*), or were familiar with the first-person accounts in Homer's *Odyssey*, such as, "I am Odysseus. . . . My home is under the clear skies of Ithaca. Our landmark is the wooded peak of windswept Neriton. For neighbors we have many peopled isles" (9.19–23)[36] or the first-person account of a storm at sea (9.67ff.).

Such knowledge can no longer be taken for granted, however, and given the dearth of references in the NT literature for proving or disproving an itinerary form in antiquity, the following observations and assessments of the evidence are in order.

A. *Encyclopedia articles.* By the time Dibelius wrote, major articles, based on considerable research by classicists, had appeared in such reference works as the *Encyclopaedia Britannica* (in the famous 11th edition, of 1910–11) and the Pauly-Wissowa *Real-Enzyklopädia der classischen Altertumswissenschaft* (hereafter, "PW"), specifically an article by W. Kubitschek, 1916.[37] Subsequently, smaller works like *The Oxford Classical Dictionary* (G. H. Stevenson in the 1949 edition; E. Badian in the 2d ed.), *Der Kleine Pauly* (G. Radke and F. Lasserre), and even *The Oxford Companion to Classical Literature*, contain references.[38] We are dealing with terms, then, that are well-known in some quarters but that are not treated in much depth in NT discussions.

B. The term in Latin, *itineraria*, which is derived from the noun *iter, itineris,*

---

[32] See above, nn. 4, 5, and 6.

[33] See above, nn. 12 and 13.

[34] See above, n. 11.

[35] See above, n. 18; *Geschichte*, p. 389.

[36] Trans. by E. V. Rieu, *The Odyssey* (Baltimore: Penguin, 1946) 139.

[37] "Itinerarien," PW 9, 2 (1916) 2308–63. Also, "Itinerarium Alexandri," 9,2:2363–66, and the section on "Itinerarkarten" (## 68–72) in his article on "Karten," PW 10, 2 (1919) 2113–21.

[38] G. H. Stevenson, "Itineraries," *OCD* (1949) 463; E. Bedian, "Itineraries," *OCD* 2d ed. (1970) 558. G. Radke, "Itineraria," *Der Kleine Pauly*, ed. K. Ziegler and W. Sontheimer (Stuttgart: Alfred Druckenmuller) 2 (1967) cols. 1488–90, and F. Lasserre, "Periplus," 4 (1972) cols. 640–41. In the *Oxford Companion to Classical Literature*, ed. Paul Harvey (Oxford: Clarendon Press, 1937), see "Itineraria," p. 226, and "Periplous," p. 314.

"road," occurs specifically in the military writer Vegetius in the late fourth century A.D. with the sense that a good general ought to have *itineraria,* i.e., maps showing routes, etc., for all regions in which war is to be waged.[39] In Vegetius one is also informed that there existed both *itineraria adnotata,* i.e., in book form, annotated as to roads, stations, cities, etc., and *itineraria picta,* ornamental maps with symbols for such features, perhaps in color, and similar devices. Earlier in the century, about A.D. 325, Aelius Lampridius, one of the authors of the *Historia Augusta,* in his Life of Alexander Severus, emperor A.D. 222–35, praised the ruler because of his careful planning for a campaign: Severus kept the plan for a campaign secret but publicly announced the length of march (*itinerum*) each day; "he would even issue a proclamation two months beforehand, in which was written 'On such and such a day, and at such and such an hour, I shall depart from the city, and, if the gods so will, I shall tarry at the first halting-place.' Then were listed all the halting-places [*mansiones*], next the camping-stations [*stativae*], and next the places where provisions were to be found. . . ."[40]

The nub of the problem is precisely how much earlier "itineraries" existed and exactly what their contents included. A significant piece of evidence involves four silver cups found at Vicarello, Italy, long in the Museo Kircheriano, in Rome. They were dedicated by travellers from Spain upon completing their journey to Rome. Three of the cups (*CIL* 11.3281, 3282, 3283) have inscriptions about the *itinerarium* (3281) or *itinerare* (3282 and 3283) from Gades (modern Cadiz, Spain) to Rome and the number of miles, *sum(ma) m(ilia) p(assuum)* [or *passus*] *1841* or *1842.* The fourth, smaller vase (11.3284) traces a similar route from Spain via Corduba to Tarraco to Narbo (in southern France) and then Tourinos, but there the inscription breaks off; the total is given, for the miles, as *summa 1835.* These texts have been compared with stations and distances in the *Itinerarium Antoninianum* (see D, below). The vases date certainly to the fourth century A.D., though attempts have been made to place them in the third century, thus making them the oldest written testimonies to itineraries.[41]

The question is, on what did such itinerary references to routes, cities, and distances rest? We may pass over here such bits and driblets of evidence as the inscription on a dish found in Wiltshire, England, giving several place names in northwest Britain (also found in reverse order in the Ravenna *Cosmographia ca.* AD 700); and inscriptional evidence from columns,

[39] 3.6; so G. Radke, in *Der Kleine Pauly,* 2:1488.

[40] *Scriptores Historiae Augustae,* trans. David Magie, LCL (New York: G. P. Putnam's Sons), Vol. 2 (1924) 269.

[41] See G. Radke, *Der Kleine Pauly,* 2:1488–89, who regards the earlier date as questionable; fuller discussion and older literature in W. Kubitschek, PW 9,2 (1916) 2318–19.

milestones, and the like. Perhaps the most significant is that found at Autun, France, in 1706, a fragmentary list of route place names (not earlier than the 3d cent. A.D.).[42] What, from ancient sources, can serve as data will be discussed below (point D).

For the Latin term *itinerarium,* evidently post-NT in origin, there seems no Greek equivalent. At least the standard reference articles cite none. Perhaps the closest one can point to are *apodēmiai* ("trips abroad," as in Norden's list above); *periēgēsis,* literally, "leading around," as by guides with explanation; therefore, a geographical description; the *Persistasen*-catalogues (a list of crises or sufferings, as at 2 Cor 6:4–5, 8–10; 11:2–33; 12:10[43]); or *periodoi* ("travels," accounts of a land journey).[44] But none of these are precise parallels to what are labeled *itineraria* in Roman sources.

If one asks why no Greek equivalent term existed, the answer probably is that the *itinerarium* arose out of data from Roman roadbuilding, milestones, and mapping activities such as was possible only in the Roman times, and indeed from the first or second century A.D. on, at that.

Hellenistic origins in the east are, however, suggested in remarks made by M. Rostovtzeff.[45] He speaks of "military and administrative itineraries" in the Hellenistic monarchies in the east after Alexander, "which were based . . . on similar Persian itineraries." Termed *stathmoi* or "stations," they may have been accompanied by maps. One is extant, the *Stathmoi Parthikoi,* by Isidore of Charax, written in Greek probably about two decades before the birth of Jesus.[46] The author, probably from a port city near the mouth of the Tigris, wrote on geography (Pliny *Natural History* 2.112, passim) and according to Athenaeus (3.46) also produced a *Periēgēsis Parthias* or "Journey around Parthia," from which the list of stations is derived. They trace a route from Zeugma and Apamia on the Euphrates (east of Antioch in Syria) through Parthia to "White India" far to the east, with typical entries like "From that place, Chalonitis, 21 schoeni [i.e., parasangs, a unit of 3 to 3 and ½ miles]."

---

[42] *CIL* 13.2681 = H. Dessau, *Inscriptiones Latinae selectae* [1892–1916] 5838. See PW 9,2:2314–18, and *Der Kleine Pauly* 2:1489 for a later judgment rejecting some of the inscriptions as evidence for itineraries.

[43] Cf. A. Fridrichsen, as summarized in H. Lietzmann, W. G. Kümmel, *An die Korinther I–II,* HNT 9 (Tübingen: Mohr-Siebeck, 4th ed. 1949) 211, and Robert Hodgson, "Paul the Apostle and First Century Tribulation Lists," *ZNW* 74 (1983) 59–80.

[44] Cf. Vielhauer, *Geschichte der urchristichen Literatur,* 699 and 716, relevant to the apocryphal acts.

[45] *The Social and Economic History of the Hellenistic World* (Oxford: Clarendon Press, 1941) 2:1032–45, with notes in 3:1582–85.

[46] Text in *Geographi Graeci Minores,* ed. C. Müller (Paris: Didot, 1855–61) Vol. 1, pp. 244–56 (hereafter GGM); trans., Wilfred H. Schoff, *Parthian Stations by Isidore of Charax* (Philadelphia: The Commercial Museum, 1914) 2–9. Cf. M. Cary and E. Warmington, *The Ancient Explorers* (London: Methuen, 1929; rev. ed., Baltimore: Penguin, 1963) rev. ed. 95, 194–95, 224.

It is possible that Isidore gathered his data for the Roman Emperor Augustus in connection with a projected military campaign against Parthia.[47]

While Persian and other Near Eastern roads and mapping practices might be considered as background—in part on the grounds that Norden found the Ezra-Nehemiah parallel helpful on diagnosing the "we"-sections—we are dubious about any direct influence from there, since Paul and Luke are to be seen in the setting of the *Roman* empire, and *itinerarium*, the "form" we are investigating, is a Latin term and a demonstrable phenomemon later only in the empire (certainly fourth and third centuries A.D.).

C. The starting point in the Greek world for seeking any "form" behind the Acts material must be with the *periplus*, a category already mentioned above and documentable in sources from Homer on, described in numerous encyclopedia articles.[48] The category was the one with which Norden began in his treatment of Acts 27.[49]

From the verb "to sail" (*pleō*, as at Acts 21:3) comes the compound form "to sail around, circumnavigate" (*peripleō*, not found in the NT) and hence the masculine noun *ho periploos*, contracted form *periplous*; pl., *hoi periploi*, as in *The Oxford Classical Dictionary* entry. While the term may mean (1) "circumnavigation" and was applied to a certain type of maneuver in ancient naval battles,[50] it more commonly referred to (2) an account of a sea voyage along the coast, often of an unexplored region. Lucian, in "How to Write History" (*Quomodo Historia Conscribenda sit*) 31, refers to one historian who promised "to write of the circumnavigation [*periplus*] of the outer sea."[51]

Such accounts might more accurately have been called *paraploi*, "voyages *along* the shore," or *anaploi*, "trips *up* the coast," in many cases, but *periploi* is the term that became the technical designation, even used in book titles. In some cases there is an extended use—2b, alongside (a) "reports of pioneers along unexplored coasts"—namely "(b) manuals for the use of navigators, which collected and systematized the information of previous travellers."[52]

---

[47] Schoff, p. 17. Cf., further, Weissbach, PW 9:2064-68; W. Spoerri, "Isidoros 5," *Der Kleine Pauly* 2:1461.

[48] PW 19, 1 (1937) 842-50 (F. Gisinger) and *The Oxford Classical Dictionary* (E. H. Warmington, 1949 ed., p. 665, and 2d ed., p. 802); more recently, F. Lasserre, "Periplus," in *Der Kleine Pauly*, 4 (1972) 640-41.

[49] *Agnostos Theos*, 313, 323-24.

[50] F. Miltner, PW 19, 1:839-41.

[51] Trans. K. Kilburn, LCL *Lucian*, 6, p. 47; cf. Cary and Warmington, *Ancient Explorers*, rev. ed. p. 245, under "Humorous Reaction" in antiquity to travel accounts, including this one and *Verae Historiae* 1.28 (LCL *Lucian*, 1, pp. 280-83) about space voyages to the moon!

[52] E. H. Warmington, *OCD* articles; for the term and the examples that follow, see Cary and Warmington, *Ancient Explorers*, rev. ed. pp. 44, 91, 224-26; 29-30 (Odyssey); 224 and 248 n. 24 (*Stadiasmus Maris Magni*, there dated to the early 3d cent. A.D.); and other pages cited below.

This second sense comes closest to what we have in passages like Acts 16:11 or 21:1–3.

The following examples, extant at least in fragmentary state, may be listed as illustrative of the *periploi* as a genre or gattung.

(1) *Odyssey* 9.105–92, about the land of the Cyclopes, seen from a ship, and the epic of the Argonauts, often retold, as by Apollonius Rhodius (3d cent. B.C.) and Valerius Flaccus (*ca.* A.D. 90), are prototypes.

(2) Description of the Mediterranean coast from Tartessus in Spain to Massalia (modern Marseilles), by a Massalian sea captain, on flora and fauna, 6th cent. B.C., preserved in the iambic verses of Festus Ruf(i)us Avienus's *Ora Maritima* (4th cent. A.D.); there are also references from voyages in the Atlantic, to Britain and Ireland, by Greek and Carthaginian sailors.

(3) A voyage by the Carthaginian, Hanno, along the west coast of Africa, as far as Sierra Leone, before 480 B.C., is preserved in a Greek translation of the Punic account.[53]

(4) Scylax of Caryanda was said (a) by Herodotus 4.44 to have commanded ships sent by Darius I to explore eastwards to India, and he is quoted as an "ancient writer" on India by Aristotle (*Politics* 1332b 23) and on Troad geography by Strabo. There is (b) a *Periplous* extant in his name[54] that is a fourth-century B.C. compilation dealing with the Mediterranean and Black Seas. It mentions the Neapolis of Acts 16:11, among other places, and is said to cite the name "Rome," in its rather complete section on the Italian peninsula, for the first time in any extant author. It is possible the work was epitomized in the third century or later.[55]

(5) Nearchus of Crete, a friend of Alexander the Great, wrote an account about his ships cruising the coast from the Indus River to the Tigris River in 325–324 B.C. It was used in the *Anabasis Alexandri* and is preserved in the *Indica* (21–42) by Flavius Arrianus in the second century A.D.[56]

(6) There are references in Strabo (*Geography* 1.4.2–5; 2.1.12, 18; 2.3.5;

---

[53] Trans. by Wilfred H. Schoff, *The Periplus of Hanno: A Voyage of Discovery Down the West African Coast by a Carthaginian Admiral of the Fifth Century* BC (Philadelphia: Commercial Museum, 2d ed., 1912) and in Cary and Warmington, *The Ancient Explorers*, 47ff., rev. ed. 63–68.

[54] *GGM* 1, 15–96. L. Casson (*Ships and Seamanship in the Ancient World* [Princeton: Princeton University Press, 1971] 245 n. 83) describes it and the *Stadiasmus Maris Magni*, mentioned below, as "true coast pilots" for merchant skippers.

[55] Cf. H. F. Tozer, *A History of Ancient Geography*, 2d ed., ed. M. Cary (Cambridge: University Press, 1935) 118–21; Cary and Warmington, *Ancient Explorers*, rev. ed. 39, 78–79, 122, 227–28; Kurt von Fritz, *Die griechische Geschichtsschreibung* (Berlin: de Gruyter, Vol. 1, 1967) 33, 52–53.

[56] Text and trans. by E. Iliff Robson, LCL, *Arrian*, 2 vols. (New York: Putnam, 1929 and 1933), especially Books 4 and 6, and 7 of the *Anabasis Alexandri*. Cf. also *The Life of Alexander the Great by Arrian*, trans. Aubrey de Sélincourt (Baltimore: Penguin, 1958), especially pp. 161, 194–95, 205–13, 221, 227, 229, 245, and 247. Cf. Cary and Warmington, *Ancient Explorers*, rev. ed. 80–86, bibliography in n. 21.

2.4.1, 2; 2.5.8, 43; 3.2.11; 4.5.5, and *passim*), as well as in Diodorus and Pliny, *Natural History* 2.187, 217; 4.95, about Pytheas, a Greek navigator from Massalia who described a voyage about 310–306 B.C. through the Pillars of Hercules and along the Atlantic shore to Britain, which he circumnavigated, and to islands beyond ("Thule," i.e., Norway or Iceland). His *Periplus ōkeanou* was doubted by some but could reflect actual accomplishments.[57]

(7) Another Greek, Patrocles, explored the Caspian Sea for the Selucid kings in the early third century B.C.[58]

(8) The previously mentioned Flavius Arrianus (see (5) above), a Greek who was a Roman army officer and legate in Cappadocia, also himself wrote a *Periplus of the Euxine* [Black] *Sea* in A.D. 132.[59]

(9) There is extant a *Periplus Maris Erythraei,* about the Arabian Sea, stemming from the first century A.D. and describing coastal routes from Egypt to India and along the East African shore, perhaps to Zanzibar. The text provides "a firstclass document for the orient and its economic connections with the Roman empire."[60]

(10) There was a likely earlier description of the coasts of the Red Sea by Agatharchides of Cnidus, about 110 B.C., referred to in Diodorus Siculus 3.11.2; 3.18.4–5; and 3.48.4; and by Photius in the 9th century.[61] Among later texts we may mention:

(11) the *Stadiasmus Maris Magni* (4th century A.D.?), with details on harbors, places to take on water, and distances from one place to another; and

(12) Marcianus, on the "Outer Sea" (Atlantic and Indian Oceans, in contrast to the Mediterranean or *Mare Internum*), about A.D. 400, compiled from Ptolemy's *Geography* (first half of the second century A.D.).

A few other anonymous examples occur in *GGM,* and there are some "*periplus*-like descriptions of the world such as Varro's *Ora maritima* which are no more *periploi.*"[62] Warmington claims as "manuals for navigators" numbers (4b), (9), (10), and (11) and (12) above.

Literary characteristics of the *periploi* have been summarized by Gisinger.[63] At their simplest, they were pilots' handbooks, describing the coastal waters

---

[57] Cf. Cary and Warmington, *Ancient Explorers,* 33ff., rev. ed. 47–56.

[58] Cf. Strabo 2.68–70, 74; 11.508–9; 15.689; Cary and Warmington, *Ancient Explorers,* 51–52, rev. ed. 185–86.

[59] Cf. E. Iliff Robson, LCL *Arrian.* Cf. Cary and Warmington, *Ancient Explorers,* rev. ed. 224.

[60] F. Lasserre, *Der Kleine Pauly* 4:641–42. Text *GGM* 1, 257–305. Trans. by Wilfred H. Schoff, *The Periplus of the Erythraean Sea: Travel and Trade in the Indian Ocean by a Merchant of the First Century* (New York: Longmans, Green & Co., 1912). Cf. Cary and Warmington, *Ancient Explorers,* rev. ed. 224. Casson (*Ships,* 245 n. 83) terms it "a trader's handbook."

[61] Text in *GGM* 1, 111–95. Cf. Cary and Warmington, *Ancient Explorers,* rev. ed. 90, 225.

[62] F. Lasserre, *Der Kleine Pauly* 4:641.

[63] PW 19, 1:843–44.

for safe navigation, with attention to dangers to the ship, details about harbors, and so forth. They can be akin in Gattung to related writings called *Peri limenōn,* "Concerning Harbors." Stylistically they could be similar also to the guidebook-style or geographical descriptions of the *periēgēsis*-technique. There are typical connectives like "after," "(in)to," "from," "as far as," "then," "next," and "thence" (*enthen;* in *Odyssey* 9.62–105, all three sections each start with it). Verbs occur such as "comes next," "stretches along," "we have neared," and the like. First-person forms sometimes occur. The Gattung, finally, often shows a mercantile purpose, for merchant seafarers: to get safely and as swiftly and smoothly as possible to a goal. *Periploi* material of course benefitted also the map-maker and geographer.

Given the demonstrated existence of this form, the "(circum)navigation account" or manual, in the first century A.D., it is entirely possible that the author of Acts and/or an earlier companion of Paul knew of it and used it. Some of what we call "itinerary-material" could have arisen from its influence, as Norden sensed. Certain verses in Acts, like 16:11–12; 18:18, 22; 20:3–6, 13–15; 21:1–3, 7; and 27:2–3a, 4 8, 13–20, 27–32, 39–44; 28:11–13, or portions thereof, could reflect a source or composition by the final author of the book, modeled on this Gattung.

Gisinger suggests[64] that the Greek *periploi* lived on in the Latin *itineraria,* though he is also aware of Kubitschek's insistence that a treatment of sea-voyages will have a different character from that of land travel (PW 9, 2:2350), besides whether distance is reckoned in time (so many days, as in early texts, like *Odyssey* 9.82–83), or, as later, in Greek stades (each over 600 feet or 200 meters), or in Roman miles (7–1/2 stades = 1 mile, 11/12 of an English mile).

D. *Roman "Itineraries."* We noted above, in section B, the statement from the fourth century A.D. that there existed *itineraria adnotata* (or *scripta*) and *itineraria picta,* respectively something like modern guides for auto travelers or cyclists and like maps. A few examples of such itineraries survive, all of them unfortunately later in date than the time of Paul and Luke. We shall note this significant evidence, however, before asking what the likelihood is that the form existed in the first century A.D.

(1) Pride of place goes to a document called "the Antonine Itinerary" (*Antonini Itinerarium;* its full title is *Itinerarium Provinciarum Antonini Augusti*). It consists of a list of seventeen routes throughout provinces of the Roman Empire, including North Africa, Sardinia, Corsica, Sicily, Italy, and stretching as far as England; section XI, e.g., Milan to Boulogne (862 miles), and XII Milan to northwest Spain (1257 miles). Route X from which we shall

---

[64] PW 19, 1:850.

make citations below, traces the Via Egnatia from Dyrrhachium on the Adriatic Sea to Byzantium. Attached to these "Itineraries of the Provinces" is a shorter *itinerarium maritimum,* giving a few sea routes. The text was published as early as 1735 (by Petrus Wesseling, 1692–1764, who edited texts of Herodotus and Diodorus Siculus), then in 1848 by G. F. C. Parthey and M. E. Pindar. We quote below from the edition of Otto Cuntz.[65]

Arranged in columns, the itinerary takes the form of a listing of place-names of cities or halting places, with a reference to the distance between them, usually in terms of Roman miles. Over 53,000 miles are said to be included in the survey. Usually the abbreviation "m.p." (for *milia passuum,* "a thousand paces" = one Roman mile or 1620 yards) is used, with the figure in Roman numerals. We translate some sample listings:

> The route (*iter*) which leads from Dyrrachium [the northern of the two terminus cities of the Via Egnatia on the Adriatic] through Macedonia and Thrace as far as Byzantium [on the European side of the Bosphorus]: from Brindisium [in Italy], the passage as far as Dyrrachium   number of stades, 1400

from Dyrrachium to Byzantium	754 miles, thus:
Clodiana	33 miles
Scampis	20 miles
Tres Tabernas [cf. the "Three Taverns" of Acts 28:15]	28 miles
Licnido	27 miles
Nicia	34 miles
Heraclea	11 miles
Cellis	34 miles
Edessa	28 miles
Pella	28 miles
Thessalonica	27 miles
Mellissurgin	20 miles
Apollonia	17 miles
Amphipoli	30 miles
Philippis	33 miles
Neopoli	12 miles
Acontisma	9 miles
[19 more names to follow, via Hadrianopolis, with a total of	344 miles
before the final entry, from Melantrada to] Byzantium	19 miles.[66]

Another segment traces the route from the Apollonia on the Adriatic, which is the southern terminus for the Via Egnatia, to Byzantium through Philippi, Acontisma, and thence to the east. The pertinent lines read thus:

[65] *Itineraria Romana.* Vol. 1. *Itineraria Antonini Augusti et Burdigalense* (Leipzig: Teubner, 1929).
[66] Wesseling, 317–23; Cuntz, 48–49.

from Dioclitianopolis,

Thessalonica	29 miles
Apollonia	36 miles
Amphipoli	32 miles
Philippis	32 miles
Acontisma	21 miles.[67]

The date of this *Antonini Itinerarium* is debated. The Antoninus in the title could be any of several of the Antonines who ruled the empire, Antoninus Pius (A.D. 138–61), Marcus Aurelius Antoninus (161–80), or Marcus Aurelius Antoninus called Caracalla (ruled 211–17, succeeding Septimus Severus, first of the Severi emperors). However, reference to Diocletianopolis, mentioned above, means the present form of the text cannot be earlier than the time of that emperor, for whom the city was named, and Diocletian ruled 284–305. Tozer cites details in the text that may reflect the period of Constantine, around 325.[68] All in all, we seem to have a document perhaps from Caracalla's time and later interpolated with other additions. The question remains, what is the origin of such an itinerary?

As we shall see (below, E), this itinerary may rest upon official documents from a survey ordered by Julius Caesar and carried out under Augustus. The *Antonini Itinerarium,* however, likely is not an official compilation. It seems rather a badly done version from the third century at the earliest. Perhaps Caracalla promoted the undertaking, but later hands have certainly been at work, obviously in the time of Diocletian.[69] Kubitschek rejects the notion it was intended for Christian pilgrims[70] but allows a connection of the text as transmitted to us with the later efforts of Cassiodorus in the sixth century to preserve classical learning and indeed develop a cosmography, among other parts of an encyclopedia of knowledge, in his monastic community at Virarium in southern Italy.[71] The author, he argues, was "no scholar, no geographer, no military or public official," but it is an excerpt, perhaps from a map, by an amateur or student.[72] But there may well have been many works of this type, all others having subsequently perished.

The *itinerarium maritimum* attached to it is much briefer.[73] It haphazardly gives routes—for example, from Achaia to Africa via Sicily—and lists islands

---

67 Wesseling, 330–31; Cuntz, 50.
68 Tozer, *A History of Ancient Geography,* 307.
69 *Encyclopaedia Britannica,* 11th ed., 2:148.
70 PW 9, 2:2331–32.
71 PW 9, 2:2321–22.
72 PW 9, 2:2329–30; cf. 10,2:2113.
73 In Cuntz's edition, 1, pp. 76–85.

like Samothrace (Acts 16:11). But it errs in making Mt. Parnassus an island too. Descended from the *periploi,* it differs from the land itineraries in its freedom and variety in routes and therefore times and distances.[74]

(2) A more widely known text from the fourth century is the *Itinerarium Burdigalense* or *Hierosolymitanum.*[75] It describes the route of an unnamed Christian pilgrim from Bordeaux in France to Jerusalem, with a homeward journey via Rome. It can be dated to A.D. 333.

The Bordeaux Pilgrim traces a route via Milan, Italy, and Sirmium in Pannonia (modern Yugoslavia) to Constantinople. Thus the journey eastwards goes north of the Via Egnatia and Philippi. The trip across Asia Minor goes through Tarsus, Paul's home city (Acts 22:3), a fact which the itinerary notes. The most detailed section deals with Palestine, where sites for OT and NT events are identified. There are "tourists' notes" on such things as the fact that no fish live in the Dead Sea.[76] The return journey goes through Caesarea on the coast of Palestine and then picks up an alternate route through Macedonia. There are references to places familiar from Acts 16 and 17. Each is designed as a city (*civitas*), a station or halting-place with night quarters (*mansio*), or a point where one changed horses, etc. (*mutatio*), and to this extent it is more detailed than the Antonine Itinerary. We cite a sample section:

mutatio Neapolim [Neapolis, Acts 16:11]	mil. VIII	
[8 miles from Hercontroma to the east]		
civitas Philippi [Philippi],	mil. X	[10 miles]
where Paul and Silas were in prison,		
mutatio Ad Duodecimum	mil. XII	[12 miles]
mutatio Domeros [cf. perhaps	mil. VII	[7 miles]
Acts 20:4, Gaius, *a Derbean*]		
civitas Amphipholim [Acts 17:1]	mil. XIII	[13 miles]
mutatio Pennana	mil. X	[10 miles]
mutatio Peripidis, where Euripides		
the poet is honored	mil. X	[10 miles]
mansio Appollonia [Acts 17:1]	mil. XI	[11 miles]
mutatio Heracleustibus	mil. XI	[11 miles]
mutation Duodea	mil. XIIII	[14 miles]
civitas Thessalonica [Acts 17:1]	mil. XIII	[13 miles].[77]

[74] PW 9, 2:2350.
[75] Published in the same editions as the *Antonini Itinerarium,* i.e., those of Wesseling; Parthey and Pindar; cited here from Cuntz, 1, pp. 86–102.
[76] Wesseling, 597, 9.
[77] Wesseling 603, 9–605, 4; Cuntz, 99.

The crossing of the Adriatic Sea was made from Apollonia, the southern terminus of the Via Egnatia, to Brindisi, and thence to Rome. Kubitschek (PW 9, 2:2352–63) compares this itinerary with the Antonine Itinerary. At points their routes are very similar, leading to Wesseling's conjecture that it was a later edition of the *Antonini Itinerarium* itself. The details in it are such that one should not suppose it, however, to be simply a book of remembrances (Erinnerungs-Itinerar), for the author assumes practical use of it by the reader (col. 2354).[78]

(3) The *Itinerarium Alexandri* stems from the period A.D. 340–345 and was part of the preparations of the Emperor Constantius for an invasion of Persia. The document draws on the writings of Arrianus (see above, C, items (5) and (8) in the list of *periploi*) and other writers in describing the earlier expeditions of Alexander the Great and Trajan against the same enemy. The first half or so of the document that is preserved makes clear that it is as much a depiction of the life and character of Alexander as a presentation of his military campaigns.[79]

(4) Among examples of such "road-books" some would also list later Christian pilgrim texts.[80] The best known example is "Pilgrimage of Etheria" (or Egeria) by a Spanish nun or abbess to Egypt, the Holy Land, Edessa, Asia Minor, and Constantinople (but not Greece). The Latin text stems from the late fourth century.[81] For further examples of such literature, see John Wilkinson, *Jerusalem Pilgrims Before the Crusades;*[82] e.g., "The Piacenza Pilgrim," *ca.* A.D. 570: "At Ptolemais we left the coast and travelled into the Galilee region to a city called Diocaesarea. . . . We travelled on to the city of Nazareth, where many miracles take place. In the synagogue there is kept the book in which the Lord wrote his ABC . . ." (p. 79). However, texts of this sort are, in our judgment, too late to be of any help in discerning an itinerary form that Paul or Luke might have known, and the pilgrim literature with its air of later piety is influenced by the NT and patristic Christianity, rather than providing a genre for the Acts itinerary.

---

[78] For the text of the *Itinerarium Burdigalense,* see also the critical edition of P. Geyer in CSEL 39 (1889) 1–33, and by P. Geyer and O. Cuntz in CSL 175 (1965) 1–26. Trans. by A. Stewart, with notes by C. W. Wilson in the *Library of the Palestine Pilgrim's Text Society* (1877); partial trans. by John Wilkinson in *Egeria's Travels* (London) 153–61.

[79] Cf. W. Kubitschek, PW 9, 2:2363–66; G. Radtke, *Der Kleine Pauly* 2:1490; text, Dietrich Volkmann, Program Schulpforta 1871.

[80] Cf., e.g., G. Schille, TLZ 84 (1959) 174, or J. O. Thompson, *History of Ancient Geography* (Cambridge: University Press, 1948) 377.

[81] Ed. A. Franceschini and R. Weber, CSL 175 (1965) 37–90. Trans. by George E. Gingras, *Egeria: Diary of a Pilgrimage* (Ancient Christian Writers, 38; New York: Newman Press, 1970); J. Wilkinson (cited above) 91–147, 180–210.

[82] Westminster, England: Aris & Phillips, 1977.

(5) Besides these possible examples of *itineraria adnotata* or written route-books, there existed *itineraria picta* or maps, according to ancient testimony cited above. One example is preserved, the "Peutinger Table," named for Konrad Peutinger (1465–1547), humanist, scholar, and city councillor of Augsburg. He received it from a friend, Conrad Celtes. It was copied by a monk in Colmar (Alsace) in 1265. This medieval replica of a Roman map represents the world from Spain to the Ganges in India on twelve pieces of parchment, 13–1/3 inches (0.34 meters) in breadth, 22 feet (268 inches, 6.82 meters) in length. The southeast corner of Britain shows. The Mediterranean is like an elongated canal.

The chief purpose of the Peutinger Table was to exhibit the roads of the Roman Empire. Cities, stations, and distances are marked, using such symbols as a few houses for a town, walls and towers for a city like Thessalonica, a bath-house and tank for watering-places, and a figure on a throne for Rome, Constantinople, and Antioch (probably the three successors of Constantine the Great, his sons Constantine II, Constantius II, and Constans), about A.D. 338. While east-west distances are exaggerated and north-south ones compressed, the map employs color (red, rose, green, yellow, blue and black) and makes some effort to represent rivers and mountains. The two forests that the monk has included are the ones he could see from Colmar, the Vosages and the Black Forest.

How far back one can trace the examplar that this monk was copying is uncertain. Obviously it comes from at least late Roman times. One theory is that it stems from a map from Castorius about A.D. 366, based on the prominence of Rome, Constantinople, and Antioch.[83] A second theory is it goes back to an earlier map about the year A.D. 170; so Kubitschek and Cuntz. Indeed, Kubitschek reconstructed a genealogy for three extant and three putative documents[84]:

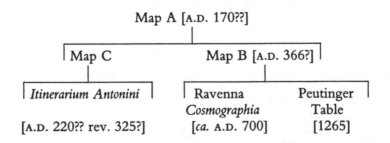

Map A [A.D. 170??]

Map C   Map B [A.D. 366?]

Itinerarium Antonini   Ravenna   Peutinger
     Cosmographia   Table
[A.D. 220?? rev. 325?]   [*ca.* A.D. 700]   [1265]

---

[83] Cf. K. Miller, *Die Peutingerische Tafeln* (1916) and *Itineraria Romana* (1916).
[84] PW 9, 2:2336; 10, 2:2118.

Radke[85] thinks the fourth-century date preferable. The Peutinger Table is now in the Imperial Library, Vienna. One of its sections is reproduced in the *Encyclopaedia Britannica*, 11th ed., 17 (1911) 637. It adds a bit more knowledge about the form Roman itineraries could have taken.

E. *The Rise of the itinerary Form*. Without conjecturing what road maps or route descriptions may have existed in the east, in Persia or Parthia (see above, in the discussion of Isidore's *Parthian Stations*), the form which writers of the Roman Empire refer to as *itinerarium* arose out of military needs and commercial concerns for travel over the Roman road system and the Mediterranean and other seas. Radtke suggests that as early as 52 B.C. Julius Caesar consulted such an itinerary to determine how he might most quickly get to his legions.[86] This same Caesar is said to have commanded a map of the Roman Empire to be made, a project which was completed in the time of Augustus. It was placed, we know, engraved in marble, in the Porticus of Octavia, the sister of Augustus, in Rome (Pliny *Natural History* 3.2.17: "a plan of the world, . . . from the design and commentaries of Marcus Agrippa," probably about 7 B.C.). E. G. Ravenstein took this and other ancient references to mean that Marcus Vipsanius Agrippa, the son-in-law of Augustus, superintended the work until his death in 12 B.C. and wrote a commentary on the map.[87] The map would have been based on the work of army surveyors, road-building records, and expeditions sent out by government officials such as were noted above. This "official" map in Rome could then have been produced, in whole or in part, throughout the empire, in *itineraria picta* and *itineraria adnotata*.

There are occasional, tantalizing references to such possible itineraria between the time of Augustus and the later evidence cited above (D) from the third century A.D. and later, where clear and extant texts exist. Propertius (4.21.29) in the late first century B.C. might refer to such maps, and Vitruvius (8.2.6), the military engineer and architect under Julius and Augustus Caesar, seemingly speaks of a world map in picture and writing.[88] Suetonius (early second century A.D.) says in his *Life of Domitian* 10.3, "It was commonly reported that [Mettius Pompusianus] carried about a map of the world on parchment"; unfortunately this senator was put to death because the emperor suspected the map meant the senator hoped to rule the world in his place. Strabo possibly and Pliny (already cited) repeatedly refer to the map and its data.[89]

---

[85] *Der Kleine Pauly* 2:1489–90.
[86] *Der Kleine Pauly* 2:1489, with reference to *Gallic Wars* 5.11.
[87] *Encyclopaedia Britannica*, 11th ed., Vol. 17 (1911) 637, in his article on "Map."
[88] Cf. Kubitschek, PW 10, 2:2121–22.
[89] Thompson, *History of Ancient Geography*, 332–33.

The Vicarello cups, described above (see section B), reflect the sort of information travelers could have obtained from itineraries based on the map and commentary of Agrippa. In the outpost of Dura-Europus, on the eastern frontier of the Roman Empire, the shield has been found of a Palmyrene archer, stationed there (before A.D. 235); painted on the shield is a list of stations and distances (in miles) of his marches north and east of Byzantium, and his journey by ship on the Black Sea, together with a simple sketch map with blue for sea and rivers.[90] Does this mean other travelers might have kept similar records, drawing on *itineraria* and *periploi* for information? J. Oliver Thomson speaks of road-books or *itineraria* as providing "a lowly kind of geography,"[91] but for the traveler their information would have been a boon.

We may conclude our survey of evidence that enhances the likelihood of the existence of *itineraria* between the time of Augustus's map and the Antonine Itinerary by looking at two references, both of which refer to the area traversed by Paul in going to Philippi.

The text of (pseudo-)Scylax discussed above (C, 4[b], under *Periploi*) provides a running account of places on the coast, including rivers, promontories, and cities. The sequence moves from Thessalia and Magnetes, on the Aegean Sea, going north from Athens and then east along the coasts of Macedonia and Thrace.[92] (This would roughly parallel the route of the Pauline party in Acts 20:3-6.) Beginning with a reference to the city mentioned at Acts 17:1, the passage goes thus:

> [66] . . . Apollonia, a Greek city. There are also other cities of Macedonia inland. It [the coastline] is full of bays [*kolpōdēs*, "winding"]. To sail by, around the bays, takes two days. After Macedonia, the Strymon River; this divides Macedonia and Thrace.
> [67] Thrace. Thrace extends from the Strymon River as far as the Istros River which [empties] in the Black Sea. There are in Thrace the following Greek cities: Amphipolis [Acts 17:1], Phargēs, Galēpsos, Oisymē, and other trade centers of the Thracians. Opposite these is Thasos, an island with a city and two harbors, one of which is excellent. But I return to the point at which I turned aside. Neapolis [Acts 16:11]; opposite this, Datos, a Greek city, which Kallistratos Athēnaios colonized; and the Nestos River, Abdēra, the Koudētos River, and the cities of Dikaia and Marōneia. Opposite these, Samothrace, an island with a harbor [Acts 16:11]. . . .

The traveler (or writer) could thus glean information from such texts about routes and the landscape. Philippi would not be mentioned in such a text

---

[90] Cf. F. Cumont, *Fouilles de Doura-Europos 1922-1923* (Paris, 1926) 335, and *Syria* 6 (1925) 1-15; Rostovtzeff, *Hellenistic World*, 2:1038 and 3:1583 n. 3.

[91] *History of Ancient Geography*, 376.

[92] *GGM* 1:15-96, sections 64-67.

because it is (a) inland and (b), if this *periplous* is fourth-century B.C., Philippi was only beginning to become a Greek city after Philip II of Macedon took it from the Thracians.

While itineraries and *periploi* would tell a traveler some things, they would not always provide the information needed to insure a successful trip. An interesting insight is provided for the late second century in a reference by the physician Galen of Pergamum (*ca.* A.D. 129–199) to his trip from Asia Minor to Rome and return. Galen, who spent part of his career as court physician to the Emperor Marcus Aurelius, wished, while en route to Rome, to stop at the island of Lemnos, in the Aegean Sea, in order to see the Temple of Hephaestus. He describes his efforts in the first person singular.

> Going by foot through Thrace and Macedonia to arrive at Rome the second time, I sailed first from Alexandrian Troas [Acts 16:11] to Lemnos, having met with a ship sailing to Thessalonica, the captain agreeing to land first at Lemnos. But he landed not at the city which was required. For at first I did not understand that there are two cities on the island but supposed, as with Samos, Chios, Cos, Andros, and Tenos and all the other islands in the Aegean, that Lemnos too would have one city of the same name for the whole island. When we disembarked from the boat, I learned that the city was called Myrina but that there was no hill connected with Philocletes or Temple of Hephaestus in the region of that city, but in another city called Hephaistias, and this was not near that city of Myrina. Further, the ship captain could not wait for me. I put off seeing Hephaistias till afterwards, when I returned from Rome.
>
> This was done for me just as I hoped and planned. For after I had crossed over from Italy into Macedonia and had journeyed through almost all of it, I was in Philippi, which is a neighboring city to Thrace. From there, having gone down to the sea nearby 120 stades, I sailed first to Thasos nearby, about 200 stades, and from there to Lemnos 700 stades and then from Lemnos to Alexandrian Troas the same distance of 700 stades. Accordingly I am writing carefully about the voyage and the stades, in order that if anyone wishes to see Hephaistias, as I myself similarly did, learning carefully its location, that person should thus prepare for the voyage.[93]

Perhaps Galen had nothing more to rely on originally than the sort of information in the *Periplus* attributed to Scylax. In any case, in applying it he was at the mercy of chance as to what ship he could find going where he wanted and the arrangements that could be worked out with the captain. Perhaps in Rome he was able to plan his journey more carefully after consulting the "official" map and commentary. Just possibly in Philippi he might

---

[93] Galen, *Peri tēs tōn haplōn pharmakōn kraseōs kai dynameōs*, Book 1; in *Medicorum Graecorum Opera Quae Exstant*, ed. C. G. Kühn (Leipzig: C. Cnobloch) Vol. 12, *Claudii Galeni* (1826) 171–73.

have had access to an *itinerarium maritimum* or at Neapolis to pilots who used such guides and knew the mileage accurately. Galen's is vivid testimony both to the vicissitudes of travel and to what literary materials we regard as likely to have existed in the first century A.D., namely *periploi* and *itineraria,* in accord with the evidence presented above.

F. *The itinerary form in Acts.* Based on the facts and possibilities just sketched, we believe it entirely possible that the author of material in the latter half of Acts—certainly chapters 16-21, very likely 27-28, possibly 13-14—knew of the *periploi* and *itineraria* of the ancient world.

The *periploi* was a recognized form in Greek antiquity and has been noted by several scholars in connection with Acts; cf. references above, in section C, to Norden's original proposal; as well as Cadbury's mention in 1927 of the sea journey style of the *periplous;* and E. Trocmé, who noted that the first-person plural sections in Acts are almost entirely maritime journeys and that this form, as in Arrian, is more literary than that of Norden's *hypomnēmata.*[94]

Unless one invokes possible lists of Parthian stations along a road or Hellenistic origins in the east for such lists of places as appear in an itinerary (see above, D, in the discussion of Isidore of Charax and the views of Rostovtzeff), the background for *itineraria* lies in the mapping of the Roman Empire under Augustus and the written lists or map-like charts that are clearly attested from the third century A.D. (like the *Antonini Itinerarium*) but that likely also existed in the first century A.D.

The *periploi* listed and sometimes described coastlines, islands, rivers, promontories, and cities. The *itineraria* gave cities, overnight stopping places, and stations where horses might be changed, and so forth. For sea captains and travelers (or authors) there were thus handbooks, though evidence for charts is conjectural.

In our opinion, verses like Acts 16:11 and 20:6, 13–15a, but especially 21:1–3, 7 and 27:2–8, 12, and 28:11–13 could derive both information and their vocabulary and style from the *periploi.* Acts 16:7–8, 12; 17:1; and 28:15, among others, might reflect data and the style of an itinerary. It has probably been a disservice to scholarship to lump all possible material together under the heading of "(the) itinerary."

In allowing for such forms behind the Acts material, we must add two important qualifications on this finding.

(1) Identification of such forms tells us nothing definite in answer to the question, At which stage in the tradition were the *periploi-itineraria* forms employed?

It is possible, on the one hand, that the final author-editor of Acts (Luke the Hellenist, even if a non-Jewish Semite?), knowing of such classical

---

[94] See above, nn. 30 and 14 (Trocmé, 125) respectively.

models, opted to reflect them as part of his polished Hellenistic historian's style. He could not merely have made use of the literary style to good advantage, but might also have consulted such material to ascertain the most likely route, so as to link more convincingly the source materials he had about Paul in Asia Minor, Paul in Philippi, in Thessalonica, and elsewhere. Thus use of the *itineraria* and related forms could be entirely redactoral. On the other hand, it is possible that the author of the "we"-sections or the diarist who accompanied Paul on some of his missionary travels (Luke or someone else) inevitably fell into the style of *periplous* and of the *itinerarium*, either as a natural device imitating a format the traveler knew from the world of the day or as a reflection of the route-maps which the party consulted or the charts they saw the ship captain use or phrases they heard him employ ("We're making a straight run toward Samothrace").

To sum up, the influence of these forms could have come at the source or redactoral levels in the composition of Acts. The influence could be through an eyewitness or from a later hand who was far removed from the happenings themselves.

(2) Neither the *periplous* nor the itinerary as a form demands or explains the use of the first person plural, such as we find in Acts.

The *itineraria*, certainly in the map form (*picta*) and likely also in the route format (*adnotata* or *scripta*), used no verbs in most instances known to us. The Antonine Itinerary is a dry-as-dust list of cities and towns, with rarely even a phrase such as "the road which leads to. . . ." The Bordeaux Pilgrim's *itinerarium* lists cities, overnight stopping-places, and stations to change horses; when comments appear, they are in the third-person vein ("where Paul and Silas were in prison" or "where the Lord was baptized by John"). True, Galen can tell in the first person singular about his experiences in getting to the Temple of Hephaestus, but then any other narrative about himself is also thus presented. (Pseudo-)Scylax may make an aside in his *Periplous,* about returning to the point where he began his digression, but that is very different from the "we" in Acts.

The most that can be said is that sometimes the *periploi* make use of a first person plural in narrating a sea voyage. But the forms themselves do not carry with them any requirement of a plural first person verb. If "we" occurred in some examples above (cf. *Odyssey* 9.67ff., of a storm at sea, or certain of the documents listed in C), it was at a point natural to the flow of the narrative and not because of any requirement of the form per se. To this extent we must decline the notion that "we" for a sea voyage was a "classical convention" in antiquity, let alone a necessary feature of style.

Chapter 24

Assessing Omissions as Redaction: Luke's Handling of the Charge against Jesus as Detractor of the Temple

Frank Connolly-Weinert
St. John's University

καὶ ἔσται ὁ οἶκός μου
οἶκος προσευχῆς.
Luke 19:46 (cf. Isa 56:7)

OVER THE PAST 30 YEARS, as redaction criticism has come into widespread use for analyzing biblical texts, the results for the study of the Gospels have been rich and manifold. Above all, this discipline, which focuses on the Gospel writers' mentality and motives in presenting their material, has established these authors in their own right as significant contributors to the Christian theological tradition.[1]

Not surprisingly, refinement of the method has been marked by growing complexity. But an overview of redaction-critical study shows that there are still only four basic ways in which a redactor can handle material received from a tradition. The redactor may: (1) preserve the material as it is; (2) preserve the

---

[1] The methodology and importance of redaction criticism is treated in detail in N. Perrin, *What Is Redaction Criticism?* (Philadelphia: Fortress, 1969); on this topic also see R. Stein, "What Is Redaktionsgeschichte?" *JBL* 88 (1969) 45–56, or, more recently, D. Carson, H. Hoehner, V. Poythress, D. Scholer, "Redaction Criticism: Is It Worth the Risk?" *Christianity Today* 29 (1985) 55–66; C. Bussmann, D. van der Sluis, *Die Bibel studieren. Einführung in die Methoden der Exegese* (Munich: Kösel Verlag, 1982); R. Soulen, *Handbook of Biblical Criticism* (2d ed.; Atlanta: John Knox, 1981) 165–66; D. Harrington, *Interpreting the New Testament* (Wilmington, DE: Glazier, 1979) 96–107.

On the role of redaction criticism in Lucan studies, see E. Richard, "Luke—Writer, Theologian, Historian: Research and Orientation of the 1970s," *BTB* 13 (1983) 3–15; C. H. Talbert, "Shifting Sands: The Recent Study of the Gospel of Luke," *Int* 30 (1976) 381–95; P.-G. Muller, "Conzelmann und des Folgen. Zwanzig Jahre redaktionsgeschichtliche Forschung am Lukas-Evangelium," *BK* 28 (1973) 138–42; C. H. Talbert, "The Redactional Critical Quest for Luke the Theologian," *Perspective* 11 (1970) 171–222; R. Edwards, "The Redaction of Luke," *JR* 49 (1969) 392–495.

content, but rearrange its elements; (3) add to the received material; or (4) omit the material altogether. Among these options (or their various mixes) omission remains the most difficult to explain. The reason is that omission usually forces interpreters to argue from silence.

From a redaction-critical standpoint, then, evaluating omissions demands special care. The larger the omission, the more numerous and potentially complex become the author's possible reasons, and the less positive evidence is available for determining them. The result is interpretation that becomes increasingly vague, spotty, and diffuse.

Nevertheless, there is a systematic, fourfold procedure which can help to reveal, by inference, the purpose behind even large omissions. First, the omission must be shown to be the redactor's own doing; otherwise, any discussion of deliberate editorial intent is moot. Second, one must then search the immediate narrative context of the episode containing the omission, looking for those editorial themes that show up most clearly in close proximity to the episode. Third, one must identify the dominant editorial themes within the episode itself. Finally, one must look for positive traces of redactional activity in the material immediately before and after the omission itself, that is, in the bridge the editor uses to close the gap created by the omission. Redactional evidence from the bridge, the episode, and its narrative context may thus be compared to determine by successive approximation those editorial motives that are most probably responsible for the omission. Once these steps are complete, other data may be weighed for added verification.

Luke's handling of the charge against Jesus as detractor of the Temple (cf. Mark 14:57–58; 15:29–30; Acts 6:13–14) provides a useful test case for this procedure. Here Luke departs from his tradition by failing to offer a significant charge leveled against Jesus in the course of his trial and death. On the other hand, Luke does preserve the episodes in which these charges otherwise appear in the Synoptic tradition. One is naturally led to ask why. But Lucan commentators show no real consensus on this point, and the complexity of the issue has led many to dispatch the question rather summarily.[2]

---

[2] Most scholars simply note these omissions with only the briefest explanations. For example, in Jesus' arraignment J. Blinzler sees Luke's editing as part of his omission of witnesses at large, probably because such allegations "did not influence the outcome of the trial decisively" (*The Trial of Jesus* [2d ed.; Westminster, MD: Newman, 1959] 101 n. 27). P. Walasky says Luke omitted such charges in order to show the illegitimacy of the hearing ["The Trial and Death of Jesus in the Gospel of Luke," *JBL* 94 (1975) 81–93, esp. 82–83]. H. Conzelmann (*Die Mitte der Zeit: Studien zur Theologie des Lukas* [BZHT 17; 5th ed,; Tübingen: Mohr-Siebeck, 1964] 76–77), sees any false testimony as superfluous for Luke since: (a) Jesus' messianic claim already was public knowledge, (b) in Luke Jesus is tried on the basis of truth, i.e., his own testimony, and (c) Luke's main interest in presenting Jesus' hearing is christological, not juridical. For V. Taylor, *The Passion Narrative of St. Luke* (SNTSMS 19; London: Cambridge University, 1972) these omissions simply reflect

From the outset there are four solid reasons for regarding the absence of such charges in Luke as deliberate. First, the Lucan narrative lacks the same material twice, in two separate contexts: once in Jesus' arraignment before the Sanhedrin (22:66–71), and again in Jesus' crucifixion (23:33–43). This greatly reduces the chance that such a feature is accidental or is due to the peculiarities of special Lucan source material.[3] Second, in Acts 6:13–14 Luke's wording of the accusation against Stephen is remarkably similar to Mark 14:57–58a; this strongly suggests that Luke knew about such Jewish charges concerning Jesus and the Temple, and knew them in a form much like that offered by Mark. Third, in both cases Luke lacks only a well-defined portion of an episode that he otherwise preserves from Mark.[4] Finally, the larger narrative context of both episodes shows other clear signs of special Lucan redactional work.[5]

A more difficult issue is the task of determining *why* Luke deleted this material. Luke's elaborate editing of both Marcan episodes containing charges about Jesus and the Temple suggests complex motivation, complicating the search for Luke's reasoning still more.[6] In each case, however, systematic study of the main redactional concerns in the broader narrative context, the immediate episode itself, and in the bridge Luke constructs to repair each omission helps greatly to answer this question.

Luke's use of non-Marcan sources (pp. 82, 92). E. E. Ellis, *The Gospel of Luke* (rev. ed.; London: Oliphants, 1974) says that Luke drops such charges because he prefers to affirm the Christian's corporate exaltation with Christ by means other than such a Temple saying (p. 269). Somewhat more positively, A. Vanhoye, *Structure and Theology of the Accounts of the Passion in the Synoptic Gospels* (Collegeville, MN: Liturgical Press, 1967) sees the omission at Jesus' trial as resulting from Luke's stress on the revelation of Jesus' person (p. 17) and, at his death, to Luke's interest in the immediate interior effects that derive from personal relations with Christ (p. 35).

[3] V. Taylor (*Passion Narrative*) speculates on Luke's use of a connected non-Marcan source throughout this portion of his Gospel. For substantial arguments against Taylor's hypothesis see W. G. Kümmel, *Introduction to the New Testament* (rev. Eng. ed.; Nashville: Abingdon, 1975) 130–35 or, more recently, F. J. Matera, "The Death of Jesus According to Luke: A Question of Sources," *CBQ* 47 (1985) 469–85.

[4] From Mark 14:55–64, Luke drops vv. 55b–61a, 62b–63a, 64b; Luke also removes vv. 24d–30 from their present place in Mark 15:22–32. Some of this material appears elsewhere in Luke (v. 26 [= Luke 23:38]; v. 27 [= Luke 23:33b]; v. 30a [= Luke 23:37b]), and Luke creates his own equivalent for 15:29a (cf. Luke 23:35ab).

[5] Luke alters Mark's passion sequence three main places: (a) the Last Supper account (22:14–38, cf. Mark 19:17–25); (b) Jesus' capture to his appearance before Pilate (22:54–23:1, cf. Mark 14:53–15:1), and (c) Jesus' crucifixion and death (23:32–49, cf. Mark 15:22–41). Luke's omission of charges about Jesus and the Temple (Mark 14:57–58; 15:29–30) occur in (b) and (c).

[6] At Jesus' hearing Luke omits both Mark 14:57–58 and 14:55b–56, 59–61a; he also transposes 15:1a to replace 14:55a. At Jesus' crucifixion, Luke not only disposes of Mark 15:29–30, but also omits 15:24d–25a, transposes 15:26, 27, 30a, and replaces 15:29a with Luke 23:35ab.

1. The Lucan Omission of Mark 14:57–58

In his general narrative of Jesus' capture, detention, arraignment before the Sanhedrin, and its outcome (22:54–23:1; cf. Mark 14:53–15:1), Luke reworks Mark's unified, chiastic structure[7] into a series of three, smaller, more personal vignettes which juxtapose first Jesus and Peter (22:54–62), then Jesus and the guard (22:63–65), and finally Jesus with the entire Sanhedrin (22:66–23:1).[8] In each episode, Jesus' personal stature and the force of his prophetic word move to the center of Luke's presentation. Along the way, the charge that Jesus opposed the Temple disappears from Luke 22:67–71. At this level of analysis, Luke's omission agrees with his wish to focus on Jesus' own words rather than on patent distortions by false witnesses. The omission also corresponds to Luke's portrayal of the events underway in terms of personal opposition; elsewhere in his Gospel Luke clearly is reluctant to personify the Temple, especially as the embodiment of opposition to Jesus in Israel (cf. 21:5–7 // Mark 13:1–4).

In 22:66–71 proper, Luke's account of Jesus' appearance before the Sanhedrin exhibits five main redactional concerns, any one of which might explain his dropping the charge from Mark 14:57–58 that Jesus threatened the Temple. First, Luke presents this hearing as an affair conducted in closed court by the same Jewish leaders who (in contrast to the people at large) opposed Jesus from the very start of his otherwise popular, unhindered, and successful ministry in the Temple (22:66–67a; cf. 19:47). A charge that Jesus promised to destroy the site that served him so well simply clashes too sharply with Luke's effort elsewhere to dissociate the Temple itself from the true source of opposition to Jesus (19:47–48; 20:1, 19; 21:5–7; 22:53).

Second, Luke's emphasis on Jesus' personal, prophetic testimony about his true christological stature[9] would discourage inclusion of distracting (and possibly misleading) evidence from false witnesses. Instead, Luke prefers to stress Jesus' own words on this important issue. In the process, Luke also plays down the potential christological symbolism of the Temple, just as he does in his handling of Mark's text concerning the "desolating abomination" (Mark 13:14; cf. Luke 21:20).

Third, in order to portray Jesus' eschatological authority as a present and

---

[7] The chiasmus in Mark 14:53–15:1 as a whole, i.e.: (A–A′) = 14:53a, 15:1c; (B–B′) = 14:53b, 15:1ab; (C–C′) = 14:54a, 14:66–72; (D–D′) = 14:54b, 14:65b; (E–E′) = 14:56–59, 14:63–65a, reaches its crux in (F–F′) = 14:59–61a; 14:61b–62. There the high priest's first question to Jesus draws only silence, while his second question elicits Jesus' reply.

[8] A. Vanhoye, *Structure,* 17.

[9] So Conzelmann, *Mitte,* 76–78, and others. Walasky, "Trial and Death of Jesus," 82–83, brings out the specifically religious import of Jesus' messianic claim as Luke presents it here.

enduring affair (22:69),[10] in this episode Luke otherwise tempers Mark's suggestion that this authority remains to be demonstrated by imminent future events (cf. Mark 14:58, 62c). For Luke, Jesus' authority as Son of Man is already effective. As such it looks neither to the destruction nor to the replacement of the Temple, nor even to the parousia, for its inauguration.

Fourth, Luke reduces the apocalyptic import of the proceedings against Jesus by dropping Mark's reference in 14:62c to the Son of Man's "coming with the clouds of heaven." Elsewhere Luke already has avoided Mark's reference to the desecration of the Temple as an apocalyptic symbol for the arrival of the End (Mark 13:14; cf. Luke 21:20). In the same vein Luke now drops a potentially similar apocalyptic allusion from Mark 14:58.

Finally, in this episode Luke wishes to affirm Jesus' innocence of any valid charges before this court and to portray him as the victim of a legal sham.[11] To this end he leaves out any testimony against Jesus, including that concerning the Temple. In the same vein, Luke also omits any charge of blasphemy or formal verdict in Jesus' case.[12]

But which of these concerns represents Luke's main reason for dropping Mark 14:57–58? The most positive clue lies in Luke 22:66–67, in the way Luke bridges the gap resulting from his omission of the charges concerning Jesus and the Temple. In these verses Luke reshapes his Marcan source to produce a single, daytime interrogation of Jesus by the whole Sanhedrin as a group. The resulting account strikingly resembles an earlier confrontation between Jesus and this same group of officials over the very issue of his activity in the Temple (20:1–8).[13]

In that episode Jesus effectively asserts his prophetic authority for using the Temple to successfully complete his teaching ministry to Israel. When these Jewish officials collectively challenge Jesus to show his credentials for teaching Israel this way (20:1–2), Jesus thwarts their challenge with a riposte (20:3–4) that exposes their self-interest (20:5–6) and lack of discernment (20:7). Luke thereby shows that Jesus' opposition in Israel comes not from the people, or from the nature of the Temple, but from those Jewish leaders who already intend to destroy him (20:1, cf. 19:47). Luke also suggests that

---

[10] The Lucan addition *apo tou nyn de estai* (22:69) not only points to the present state of affairs, but also combines with the present participle (*kathēmenos*) in the citation from Dan 7:13, creating a periphrasis for the future which emphasizes the duration of the action in view. For this sense of the construction *einai* (future) + pres. ptc., see BDF p. 180, #353(7).

[11] Walasky, "Trial and Death of Jesus," 83. Luke 22:69 also implies that this court is exceeding its competence by trying to judge, in God's name, the very one to whom such authority already has been given.

[12] Walasky, "Trial and Death of Jesus," 83.

[13] The parallels between these passages may be outlined as follows: 22:66 (cf. 20:1); 22:76a (cf. 20:2); 22:67b–68a (cf. 20:3a, 5b, 3b); 22:68b (cf. 20:7).

although they are using their official authority for immediate personal and political ends (20:6), the larger question is prophetic and religious. The real issue here is the power to judge whose action truly comes from God (20:4). And for Luke, in this area Jesus' opponents are impotent (20:7).

Similarly, as the official proceedings against Jesus begin in 22:66, Luke has Jesus, freshly abused by the guard as a would-be prophet (22:63–65), stand before the Sanhedrin.[14] Once again, these officials stand apart in Israel as the group that embodies Jesus' primary opposition. Again they collectively demand a personal accounting from him (22:67–67a).[15] And once again Jesus exposes their incompetence to judge him in God's name, not only because they have abdicated such responsibility for the sake of self-interest (22:67b–68; cf. 20:5–7), but also because Jesus' present prophetic and eschatological authority supersedes theirs (22:69; cf. 20:8).

In this light, Luke's main reason for omitting the charges from Mark 14:57–58 emerges as his wish to focus sharply on the conflict between those authorities who represent the opposition to Jesus in Israel, and Jesus in his present authority as Son of Man. A close corollary is Luke's desire to affirm Jesus' honor and blamelessness before this court, which shortly will be bringing him up on charges before Pilate (23:1–2, 5). Accordingly Luke omits all third parties from Jesus' trial before the Sanhedrin (which transpires in closed session) and any suggestions of antagonism between Jesus and the Temple.[16]

2. The Lucan Omission of Mark 15:29-30

Concerning Jesus' crucifixion and death, the Marcan and Lucan accounts (Mark 15:20b–41; Luke 23:26–49) both offer the same broad scenario. But the timing and arrangement of the action in each Gospel shows how differently each evangelist views these events. Mark, for example, begins Jesus' passion with his crucifixion at the third hour (15:25). Unrelieved abuse of

---

[14] Luke's transposition of this abuse (which uses irony to stress Jesus' prophetic identity) to the beginning from the end of the hearing (23:63–65, cf. Mark 14:65) further highlights the prophetic dimension of Jesus' stature and words in the material that follows.

[15] The expression *to presbyterion tou laou* denotes the combined leadership of Israel; together with Luke's specific reference to the chief priests and scribes, it focuses on the religious nature of the hearing; it also recalls Luke's earlier contrast between the authorities' attitude and that of the people toward Jesus (19:47–48; 20:1, 6, 19; 21:38 and 22:2). Only Luke portrays their interrogation of Jesus in strictly collective terms (Vanhoye, *Structure,* 17) and in the form of a command (*legontes eipon hēmin*).

[16] The apocalyptic reason for dropping this reference to the Temple, though valid, is less important for Luke here than the personal honor-shame confrontation between Jesus and his foes. For the importance of honor-shame encounters in Mediterranean cultures as a way of expressing one's view of someone's character, see B. Malina, *The New Testament World: Insights from Cultural Anthropology* (Atlanta: John Knox, 1981) 25–50, esp. 39.

Jesus follows until the sixth hour (15:29-33, esp. 15:33), and even throughout the apocalyptic approach of Jesus' death throes at the ninth hour (15:34) his tormentors still are active (15:35-37).

Luke, however, edits his version to center around the sixth and the ninth hours (23:32-43, 46-49),[17] punctuating his account with Jesus' prophetic and prayerful words (23:28-31, 34,[18] 43, 46), and separating both phases with a brief narrative interlude (23:44-45). The resulting Lucan narrative of Jesus' execution, though longer than Mark's, is more dramatically compact, and spans a period of three rather than six hours.

On the whole, Luke's thematic development of this material is manifold and complex. In addition to at least seven scriptural references (all but one from the Psalms), Luke emphasizes seven other themes through repeated reference.[19] Despite their apparent complexity, however, many of these themes actually coalesce to underscore three main Lucan interests. First, the frequent allusions to Scripture (especially the Psalms) correspond to Luke's wider redactional stress on *prayer* throughout his Gospel. Yet they also join with other themes (such as repeated mention of the co-crucified wrongdoers, taunts that Jesus save himself, acknowledgment of Jesus' blamelessness, and references to the witnesses) to affirm *Jesus' innocence,* and his death as the inevitable fulfillment of Scripture (cf. 22:37; Isa 53:12). Finally, the scriptural references also combine with sayings of Jesus and questions raised about his identity as Messiah and king, to dramatize Luke's thinking about the true nature of *Jesus' messiahship.*

Along these lines, the themes of prayer, of Jesus' innocence, and his messianic identity help to explain Luke's omission of the taunt in Mark 15:29 against Jesus as opponent of the Temple. Because Luke places special stress on the Temple as a true house of prayer (cf. 19:45), at this critical moment he can well avoid any suggestion of antipathy between Jesus and such a place.

---

[17] Luke tends to subsume even his burial narrative temporally to the events immediately surrounding Jesus' death by eliminating Mark's note of delay between Jesus' death at midafternoon (Mark 15:34) and the initiative of Joseph of Arimathea on his behalf at dusk (Mark 15:42).

[18] Several good manuscript witnesses omit 23:34a (p75, ℵa, B, D*, W, Θ, 0124, ita,d syrs, sa, bo, Cyril). But the early as well as widespread evidence for this text (ℵ*,c A, C, Db, K, L, Γ, Δ, Λ, Φ, itb,c,ff2, syrc,p, bo, Heg, Marcion, Iren, Clem, Or, Eus, Jer, Aug) tends to weigh in favor of its authenticity.

[19] Namely: (1) 23:30-31 (cf. Hos 10:8; Ezek 21:3); (2) 23:34 (cf. Ps 21:19 [LXX]); (3) 23:35 (cf. Ps 21:8 [LXX]); (4) 23:35 (cf. Ps 21:9b [LXX]); (5) 23:36 (cf. Ps 68:22 [LXX]); (6) 23:46 (cf. Ps 30:6 [LXX]); (7) 23:49 (cf. Ps 37:12; 87:1 [LXX]). Luke sounds seven other themes at least three times. These include: (1) reference to the co-crucified wrongdoers (*kakourgoi*, 23:32, 33, 39); (2) sayings of Jesus (23:34, 43, 46); (3) taunts that Jesus save himself (23:35, 37, 39); (4) the question of Jesus' identity (23:35, 37, 39); (5) references to Jesus' kingship (23:37, 38, 42); (6) acknowledgment of Jesus' innocence (23:41, 47, 48); and (7) the witnesses to these public events (23:26, 35, 47, 48, 49).

And considering Luke's other efforts in this context to affirm Jesus' innocence and messianic stature as benign, prophetic king, any charges of impiety toward the national religious shrine now would thwart Luke's main concerns here.

The account of events surrounding Jesus' crucifixion proper (23:32–44a) provides the immediate setting for Luke's second omission of the charge concerning Jesus and the Temple. Here again many of the themes expressed in the broader Lucan context reappear. And once again, the pattern of major Lucan emphases, as reflected in themes sounded more than once, is quite complex. For example, in this section alone Luke alludes three separate times to Scripture (23:34, 35, 36), to the co-crucified evildoers (kakourgoi, 23:32, 33, 39), to Jesus' kingship (23:37, 38, 42),[20] questions about his messianic identity (23:35, 37, 39), and taunts from antagonists concerning his saving power (23:35, 37, 39). Lucan touches that appear twice include reference to Jesus' word (23:34, 43) and omission of the taunt that Jesus descend from the cross (23:35, cf. Mark 15:30b, 32b).

Again, Luke's actual presentation of these themes simplifies the search for his main emphases. The references to Scripture and to the co-crucified evildoers actually combine in Luke to affirm Jesus' innocence. This coincides with Luke's earlier interpretation of Jesus' fate (Luke 23:37) as the blameless servant from Second Isaiah, who nevertheless is to be reckoned with lawless men (cf. Isa 53:12). And the call by opponents for Jesus to prove concretely his messianic identity by saving himself joins all the other themes, with particular focus on the true nature of Jesus' saving power.[21]

Either of these thematic clusters might well explain Luke's omission of the charge about Jesus and the Temple. For example, in his wish to stress Jesus' innocence, Luke can well avoid suggesting that Jesus provoked his own fate by opposing the Temple. But Luke might just as well have dropped the allusion to Jesus as potential destroyer of the Temple (along with the challenge that Jesus descend from the cross) as too materialistic, impersonal, and grossly self-serving to reflect Jesus' true power to save.[22]

The most probable and immediate Lucan motive for deleting Mark 15:29, however, emerges from the way in which Luke bridges the gap that this

[20] For the identification of the title "Christ" with that of King (of the Jews), see Luke 23:2–3.

[21] Luke hardly agrees with Jesus' foes in Mark 15:31, who see Jesus as bereft of any saving power. In fact Luke changes this taunt from an outright denial (heauton ou dynatai sōsai) to a more open-ended expression of skeptical mockery (sōsatō heauton ei houtos estin ho christos, 23:35). Luke 23:43 then settles the question of Jesus' stature and fate by asserting his present and continuing power to save, ironically turning the taunts of his enemies into affirmations of his true identity.

[22] By separating the downfall of the Temple from validation of Jesus' salvific claim Luke avoids the destructive and vindictive note suggested by Mark in favor of stress on Jesus' forgiveness.

omission creates in his Marcan source. In a variety of ways (mainly by omission and transposition) Luke eliminates six verses of Marcan material between the dividing of Jesus' garments (Mark 15:24b) and the scoffing by religious leaders (Mark 15:31).[23] Luke then closes the gap with 23:35.

In the process Luke follows Mark 15:29a, using Ps 21:8 (LXX) to identify Jesus' tormentors; but Luke goes on to distinguish the people (who watch) from the rulers (who mock), thus altering both Mark and the OT to suit his own editorial concerns. Luke also changes the ruler's taunt, in line with Ps 21:9, from the indicative in Mark (*ou dynatai sōsai*) to the imperative (*sōsatō*); along with his substitution of *tou theou ho eklektos* for *ho basileus Israel* (Mark 15:32), this shows that Luke sees the issue of Jesus' messianic claim primarily as a challenge to their religious authority.[24]

Luke's editing condenses and personalizes Mark's account by identifying the rulers (*hoi archontes*) as Jesus' primary tormentors, simultaneously separating the people's action from that of their leaders. By using Psalm 21 (LXX) for this purpose Luke allows himself, like Mark, to present the abuse of Jesus at his death as the fulfillment of Scripture. Along the way Luke also brings forward the issue of Jesus' messianic standing and especially his saving power.

The same spirit which leads him elsewhere to distinguish the leaders' approach to Jesus from that of their people (19:47–48) and from the interests of the Temple (22:52–53) also brings Luke to drop the charge about Jesus and the Temple (cf. Mark 15:29). For Luke, Jesus' attitude toward the Temple is not the true cause of the abuse he suffers nor of his death, for he is innocent of any wrongdoing in this respect, whether real or imagined. The events surrounding Jesus' death instead represent the inevitable fulfillment of Scripture. But they also remain the responsibility of those Jewish leaders who act out of personal opposition to the challenge of Jesus' messianic claim. As such they actually have gone beyond the support of the people and have abused their authority with respect to the Temple.

3. Comparison of Results
Regarding Both Lucan Omissions

Luke's double omission of the charge about Jesus and the Temple actually

---

[23] Luke omits Mark 15:24d–25, 29b, 30b, and transposes 15:26 (cf. Luke 23:38), 15:27 (cf. Luke 23:33b), and 15:30a (cf. Luke 23:37b); he also replaces 15:29b with an equivalent text of his own (Luke 23:35ab). The manuscript tradition shows that 15:28 was not in Luke's Marcan source but was borrowed later from Luke 23:37 (cf. Isa 53:12).

[24] The expression *ho christos tou theou ho ekletos* (23:35) recalls Luke's distinctive rendering of Peter's messianic testimony to Jesus earlier in the Gospel (9:20, cf. Mark 8:29) and also corresponds to Luke's version of Jesus' transfiguration (9:35, cf. Mark 9:7). Along these lines also see Luke 18:7, where the issue is God's speedy vindication of those elect who cry out to him (in prayer) constantly.

derives from a constellation of possible motives. This should not be surprising; Luke's manifest concern about careful transmission of his tradition (1:1–4) surely would incline him to use omission as a last resort and only for suitably serious reasons. Such complex motivation also helps to explain the varied opinions offered by Lucan interpreters on this point.

Within this Lucan complex of motives, however, three dominant threads recur that tend to absorb the other possibilities. First, Luke's presentation of Jesus as the object of limited, mainly official, opposition, combined with Jesus' acceptance by the people at large, helps to establish his reputation and authority as a matter of widespread public recognition. Second, Luke clearly wants to show that Jesus' behavior is upright, blameless, and innocent of any impiety or wrongdoing. Third, there is Luke's characterization of Jesus' messiahship as a form of royalty that is basically religious and prophetic (i.e., divinely authorized), already effective, and demanding of personal discernment. Such kingship is essentially benign in that it looks to salvation rather than destruction and is founded on service rather than self-interest.[25]

Correspondingly Luke separates the Temple's violent fate from the issue of Jesus' messianic authority and its confirmation. Having dissociated Jesus' trial and death from the support of the people of Israel and from the destruction of the Temple, Luke frees himself to use both of these themes in a constructive rather than polemical way. This enables him in turn to build a more positive sense of religious origins for his contemporary audience.

One curious result of our analysis is to show the important role that Jesus' *innocence* plays in Luke's Christology.[26] Another is that the three themes just

---

[25] For Luke, Jesus' messianic status is a present and irreversible reality; it is also personal in that it is uniquely his, exercised directly by him, and represents an authority over human affairs, especially human fate (22:69–70; 23:43).

Luke tends to distinguish the political from the religious aspect of Jesus' messianic office and to stress the latter (Luke 22:67a, 69–70 [cf. Mark 14:61b]; Luke 23:35, 37 [cf. Mark 15:32]). But perception of this authority requires discernment that hinges on belief rather than incontestable signs (22:67b–68, cf. 20:2, 5–7, and the omission of *kai opsesthe* in 22:69 [cf. Mark 14:61a] and of *katabato . . . pisteusomen* in 22:35 [cf. Mark 15:32]). For Jesus' messianic judgment, see the omission of *kai erchomenon . . . ouranou* in 22:69 (cf. Mark 14:64), and also 23:34a, 43. Finally, Jesus' messianic power is characterized by service to others rather than self-interest. This is only implicit in 22:68 (cf. 20:5–7) but comes through more clearly in 23:34a, 43, as well as in Luke's omission of Mark 15:30b, 32b (*katabas/katabatō apo tou staurou*).

[26] R. Karris, "Luke 23:47 and the Lucan View of Jesus' Death," *JBL* 105 (1986) 65–74 rightly recognized that Jesus' innocence has religious as well as legal import. On the dynamic understanding of Jesus' innocence in Luke as a function of martyrdom, see R. Michiels, "Het passieverhaal volgens Lucas," *Collationes* 30 (1984) 191–210. J. B. Tyson, *The Death of Jesus in Luke-Acts* (Columbia, SC: University of South Carolina, 1986) offers a carefully nuanced treatment of the Lucan passion account which brings out the importance of Jesus' innocence in Luke's scheme.

mentioned (official opposition, innocence, and Jesus' messianic stature) all coalesce in a complementary way if we see Luke as trying to portray Jesus as a truly extraordinary man of honor. By our standards this may seem rather tame — how much more politically dramatic it is to picture Jesus as the victim of a miscarriage of justice forced on a Roman official by unruly provincials; how much more theologically sophisticated it seems to be able to view Jesus as the Servant of Second Isaiah, reckoned with transgressors as he goes to his death! And these points are valid, as far as they go. In the last analysis, however, it is not by our standards or even our needs that we must begin to judge Luke's work, but rather those of *his* world. And in that light this study seeks to provide an added tool for advancing such understanding.

Chapter 25   The Son of Man Sayings in the Sayings Source

Adela Yarbro Collins
University of Notre Dame

In him dwells the spirit of wisdom, and the spirit which gives understanding, and the spirit of knowledge and of strength.

1 Enoch 49:3

RECENT WORK ON THE SAYINGS SOURCE[1] and the Sermon on the Mount has tended to deemphasize their eschatological and apocalyptic aspects.[2] Among the many factors which may account for this state of affairs, three may be mentioned that relate to the history of scholarship.[3]

---

[1] For the purposes of this study, the solution of the Synoptic problem usually referred to as the Two Source Theory is presupposed, namely, that the authors of Matthew and Luke (hereafter, for convenience often referred to as simply Matthew and Luke) used, in addition to a gospel very close to what has been preserved as the Gospel of Mark, another written document. The latter document may be reconstructed from material common to Matthew and Luke which was not derived from Mark. This document will be referred to in this study as the Sayings Source or Q. The occasionally considerable variations in wording between Matthew and Luke in Q material can be explained (1) by the probability that, after Q was received by the communities in which Matthew and Luke were written, it underwent further editorial modification; (2) by the likelihood that the authors of Matthew and Luke made editorial changes as they incorporated Q into their works. In order to avoid undue speculation, only material found in both Matthew and Luke will be attributed to Q. On the adaptation of Q by the communities of Matthew and Luke, see Dieter Lührmann, *Die Redaktion der Logienquelle* (WMANT 33; Neukirchen-Vluyn: Neukirchener Verlag, 1969) Appendix.

[2] James M. Robinson, "LOGOI SOPHON: On the Gattung of Q," in *Trajectories through Early Christianity* (Philadelphia: Fortress, 1971) 71–113; Hans Dieter Betz, "Eschatology in the Sermon on the Mount and the Sermon on the Plain," *Society of Biblical Literature 1985 Seminar Papers* (ed. Kent H. Richards; Atlanta: Scholars Press, 1985) 343–50, John S. Kloppenborg, "The Function of Apocalyptic Language in Q," *Society of Biblical Literature 1986 Seminar Papers* (ed. Kent H. Richards; Atlanta: Scholars Press, 1986).

[3] Joseph A. Fitzmyer has contributed greatly to the study of the Son of Man sayings by his philological research and observations. See his "The New Testament Title 'Son of Man' Philologically Considered," *A Wandering Aramean: Collected Aramaic Essays* (SBLMS; Missoula, MT: Scholars Press, 1979) 143–60; and "Another View of the 'Son of Man' Debate," *JSNT* 4 (1979) 58–68. These contributions were duly noted in an essay in an earlier volume dedicated to Professor Fitzmyer: John R. Donahue, S.J.; "Recent Studies on the Origin of 'Son of Man' in the Gospels," in *A Wise and Discerning Heart: Studies Presented to Joseph A. Fitzmyer, S.J. In Celebration of His Sixty-Fifth Birthday, CBQ* 48/3 (July 1986) 484–98.

The Sayings Source and Wisdom

One factor is that James M. Robinson, in his influential article "LOGOI SOPHON: On the Gattung of Q," defined the genre of the Sayings Source on the basis of only one of the four types of sayings material which make up its content, namely, wisdom sayings in the narrower sense.[4] Bultmann, whose form-critical work provided Robinson's point of departure, classified the tradition of the sayings of Jesus into two major types, apophthegms and dominical sayings (sayings of the Lord). He then divided the dominical sayings into three groups, primarily on the basis of content, but also to some degree of form: (1) sayings or *logia* in the narrower sense, that is, wisdom sayings; (2) prophetic and apocalyptic sayings; and (3) laws and community regulations.[5] The Sayings Source apparently contained five apophthegms: the question of John the Baptist (Matt 11:2–19/Luke 7:18–35),[6] two brief dialogues on discipleship (Matt 8:19–22/Luke 9:57–60), and two miracle stories transformed into dialogues, the centurion from Capernaum and the dispute about exorcism (Matt 8:5–13/Luke 7:1–10 and Matt 12:22–30/Luke 11:14–23).[7] Among the sayings discussed by Bultmann under the rubric of "prophetic and apocalyptic sayings" are twenty which may confidently be attributed to the Sayings Source.[8] Six of the sayings designated "legal sayings and church rules" belonged to Q.[9] The material in the Sayings Source that fits

---

[4] Robinson, "LOGOI SOPHON," 71–74.

[5] Rudolf Bultmann, *The History of the Synoptic Tradition* (rev. ed.; New York: Harper & Row, 1968) 11, 69.

[6] The actual apophthegm is only Matt 11:2–6/Luke 7:18–23 (see Bultmann, *History,* 23); as often, the apophthegm has been expanded with additional related sayings. In this study, reference is made to the full versions of both Matthew and Luke as an indication that they both give evidence for the form of the passage in Q; such references do not imply a particular, precise reconstruction of the wording of Q.

[7] See Bultmann, *History,* 28–29, 56–57, 61, 38, 13.

[8] The relevant sayings are listed here, organized by means of Bultmann's categories; "Preaching of Salvation": Luke 10:23–24/Matt 13:16–17; Luke 6:20–23/Matt 5:3–12; Matt 11:5–6/Luke 7:22–23; Matt 3:11–12/Luke 3:16–17; "Minatory Sayings": Matt 10:32–33/Luke 12:8–9; Matt 11:21–24/Luke 10:13–15; Luke 11:31–32/Matt 12:41–42; Luke 11:43, 46, 52, 42, (39), 44, 47/Matt 23:(4, 6), 13, 23, 25, 27, 29; Luke 11:49–51/Matt 23:34–36; Matt 23:37–39/Luke 13:34–35; Luke 12:54–56 (Matt 16:2–3); Matt 8:11–12/Luke 13:28–29; Luke 6:46/Matt 7:21; Matt 7:22–23/Luke 13:26–27; Matt 24:37–41/Luke 17:26–27, (28–30), 34–35; Matt 3:7–10/Luke 3:7–9; Matt 12:39–40/Luke 11:29–30; "Admonitions": Matt 24:43–44/Luke 12:39–40, Matt 24:45–51/Luke 12:42–46; "Apocalyptic Predictions": Luke 17:23–24/Matt 24:26–27; see Bultmann, *History,* 109–22.

[9] Sayings which may fit the categories of wisdom sayings or prophetic and apocalyptic sayings, but which also express a position in regard to the law on Jewish piety: Matt 12:31–32/Luke 12:10; Matt 23:23–24/Luke 11:42; Matt 23:25–26/Luke 11:39–41; sayings formulated in legal style: Matt 5:17–19/Luke 16:17; prescriptions for the Christian community: Matt 18:15–17, 21–22/Luke 17:3–4; Matt 10:40/Luke 10:16; Matt 10:5–16/Luke 10:2–12; see Bultmann, *History,* 130–45.

under the rubric of wisdom sayings in the narrower sense consists of about thirty-six sayings.[10] Thus, almost half of the material in Q that is presented as teaching of Jesus does not fit in the category of wisdom sayings in the narrower sense (about thirty-one sayings).[11] The largest portion of this material may be described as prophetic and apocalyptic sayings.

Although Robinson defined the genre of Q in terms of the *logia* as a form of wisdom literature, his major examples of the genre from Jewish literature roughly contemporary with Q do not support a narrow definition of "sayings of the wise" as a genre of proverbial or didactic wisdom. The work that fits such a narrow definition best is *'Aboth*, the *Sayings of the Fathers*, a tractate of the Mishna. Robinson suggested that there was an overlap of the genre "testament" and the genre "sayings of the wise," which is evident in the opening lines of the individual testaments in the *Testaments of the Twelve Patriarchs.*[12] In five cases the individual unit is referred to as a *diathēkē*. In seven cases, the work is introduced as the patriarch's *logoi*. Then the patriarch's experiential wisdom is given "in analogy to wisdom literature."[13] It should be pointed out, however, that there is also an overlap of wisdom and apocalyptic material within the framework of the testament in this work. The *logoi*

---

[10] (1) "Principles": (a) Material Formulations: Matt 12:34b/Luke 6:45b; Matt 24:28/Luke 17:37; Matt 10:26/Luke 12:2; Luke 12:3/Matt 10:26; Matt 12:25–26/Luke 11:17–18; Matt 6:22–23/Luke 11:34–36; Luke 6:43–44/Matt 7:16–20, 12:33; (b) "Personal Formulations": Luke 10:7b/Matt 10:10b; Matt 17:20/Luke 17:6; Luke 11:23/Matt 12:30; Matt 12:35/Luke 6:45a; Matt 10:39/Luke 17:33; Matt 6:24/Luke 16:13; Matt 10:24–25/Luke 6:40; Matt 8:20/Luke 9:58; (d) "Arguments *a maiore ad minus*": Matt 6:26, 30/Luke 12:24, 28; Matt 7:11/Luke 11:13; Matt 10:29–30/Luke 12:6–7a; (2) "Exhortations": Matt 8:22b/Luke 9:60; Luke 6:31/Matt 7:12a; Matt 10:28/Luke 12:4–5; Matt 6:19–21/Luke 12:33–34; Matt 7:13–14/Luke 13:24; Luke 17:3–4/Matt 18:15, 22; (3) "Questions": Matt 6:27/Luke 12:25; Luke 6:39/Matt 15:14; Matt 5:15/Luke 11:33; (4) "Longer Passages": Matt 5:39b–42/Luke 6:29–30; Matt 5:44–48/Luke 6:27–28, 32–36; Matt 7:1–5/Luke 6:37–38, 41–42; Matt 7:7–11/Luke 11:9–13; Matt 6:25–26, 28b–33/Luke 12:22–24, 27–31; see Bultmann, *History*, 73–81.

[11] Another category of sayings material represented in Q is rabbinic haggada; such seems to be the form of the Temptation Story (Matt 4:1–11/Luke 4:1–13); see Bultmann, *History*, 254–57.

[12] This study assumes that the *Testaments of the Twelve Patriarchs*, a work preserved in Greek, was originally a Jewish work, which has been edited and expanded by one or more Christians. Fragments of a related work(s) in Aramaic have been found. See J. Becker, *Untersuchungen zur Entstehungsgeschichte der Testamente der zwölf Patriarchen* (Leiden: Brill, 1970); idem, *Die Testamente der zwölf Patriarchen* (JSHRZ 3/1; Gütersloh: Mohn, 1974); for the view that the work is essentially Christian, see M. de Jonge, *The Testaments of the Twelve Patriarchs* (Assen: van Gorcum, 1953); idem, *Studies in the Testaments of the Twelve Patriarchs* (Leiden: Brill, 1975). See now also H. W. Hollander and M. de Jonge, *The Testaments of the Twelve Patriarchs: A Commentary* (Leiden: Brill, 1985). On testaments in general, see E. von Nordheim, *Die Lehre der Alten: I, Das Testament als Literaturgattung im Judentum der Hellenistisch-Römischen Zeit* (ALGHJ 13; Leiden: Brill, 1980) and *II, Das Testament als Literaturgattung im Alten Testament und im Alten Vorderen Orient* (ALGHJ 18; Leiden: Brill, 1985).

[13] Robinson, "LOGOI SOPHON," 106.

of the patriarchs include both. The *Testament of Levi,* for example, is introduced as the *logoi* of Levi (1:1). The account of Levi's experience that follows, however, includes a heavenly journey (chaps. 2–5), which contains an eschatological prophecy of judgment and salvation (chap. 4) and a vision of the heavenly temple and the Most High on a throne of glory (chap. 5). The *Testament of Judah,* introduced as the *logoi* of Judah, contains both moral exhortation of a proverbial wisdom type (chaps. 13–19) and apocalyptic eschatology (chaps. 24–25).

The Coptic Gnostic *Apocalypse of Adam* (CG V, 5) is also cited as evidence for the overlap of the genres testament and sayings of the wise. The overall genre of this work is indeed the testament, because its framework describes the handing on of (esoteric in this case) wisdom from father (Adam) to son (Seth; see 64:1–7; 85:20–32). But this framework affects the body of the work only slightly. The work as a whole is very similar in form and content to other works recognized as apocalypses.[14] The mixing of genres here is analogous to the presentation of the New Testament apocalypse as a letter. In any case, the proverbial element in *Apoc. Adam* is virtually nonexistent.

Ethiopic Enoch (1 Enoch) is also presented by Robinson as analogous to the *T. 12 Patr.* As is well known, *1 Enoch* is a composite of at least six originally independent works. All but one of these (the Epistle of Enoch or the Book of Exhortation; *1 Enoch* 91–104 or 105, excluding the Apocalypse of Weeks, i.e., 93:3–10; 91:12–17) are apocalypses.[15] At various points in the work in its present form, as Robinson points out, the term "words" is associated with the notion of "wisdom." It should be kept in mind, however, that the type of wisdom contained in *1 Enoch* is not the proverbial type which dominates Proverbs, Ecclesiastes, Aḥiqar, and Sirach. The wisdom of *1 Enoch* is closer to the wisdom of Joseph (Genesis 37, 40–41) and Daniel (Daniel 2, 4 and 5), which has aptly been called "mantic wisdom."[16] The words of wisdom in the Book of the Watchers (*1 Enoch* 1–36) and in the Similitudes (chaps. 37–71) concern visions, heavenly journeys, angels, and eschatological judgment and salvation. The Epistle of Enoch (chaps. 91–104) is the closest to the Synoptic Sayings Source in form and content. Its original form may have been a testament (91:1) or a letter (93:1).[17] Its content in part may be characterized as parenesis.[18] It is important to keep in mind that exhortation or parenesis may

---

[14] Francis T. Fallon, "The Gnostic Apocalypses," *Semeia* 14 (1979) 124–27.

[15] John J. Collins, "The Jewish Apocalypses," *Semeia* 14 (1979) 31–32, 37–40, 45.

[16] See H.-P. Müller, "Mantische Weisheit und Apokalyptik," in *Congress Volume: Uppsala, 1971* (VTSup 22; Leiden: Brill, 1972) 268–93. See also John J. Collins, *The Apocalyptic Imagination* (New York: Crossroad, 1984) 17, 21–22, 73, 121.

[17] Matthew Black, *The Book of Enoch or 1 Enoch* (SVTP 7; Leiden: Brill, 1985) 11–12.

[18] Ibid., 21–22.

be proverbial (Luke 6:31/Matt 7:21a),[19] prophetic (Matt 8:22/Luke 9:60),[20] or apocalyptic (Matt 3:8–9a/Luke 3:8a).[21] The exhortation of the Epistle of Enoch may be characterized as apocalyptic in its present form, because it is placed in the context of the expectation of eschatological woes, universal judgment, and eternal rewards and punishments (100:1–6; 102:2–3; 103:4).

Because of the presence of "the Sophia myth" in *1 Enoch* (chap. 42), Robinson concludes that "we are directed a step further back, into the wisdom literature in the narrower sense."[22] This step certainly makes sense for a diachronic study of the genre *logoi sophōn,* which is Robinson's main concern. But it should not preclude synchronic studies which, along with recognition of the variety in Q's content, could bring out the affinities of the genre with prophetic and apocalyptic tradition. The notion of personified or hypostatized wisdom is certainly part of the heritage of Gnosticism. But this notion could also be combined with philosophical mysticism (Philo) and apocalypticism (Similitudes of Enoch). The presence of this motif in Q (Luke 11:49), therefore, does not necessarily mean that the genre *logoi sophōn* or the Sayings Source itself is proto-Gnostic or gnosticizing. Robinson points out the close association of wisdom and apocalypticism in early Judaism to explain the shift from an apocalyptic Jesus to a wisdom-oriented sayings collection. His article is very helpful in its illumination of the affinities of Q with wisdom traditions, including esoteric wisdom. But the affinities of Q with apocalyptic tradition should not be overlooked. One should probably reckon with subtypes of the genre *logoi sophōn,* which can be distinguished on the basis of what constitutes *sophia* in each case. From this point of view, it is interesting to note that Polycarp placed the small collection of Jesus' sayings which he quotes in an apocalyptic context (Pol. *Phil.* 2.3; cf. 7.1–2) and that Justin Martyr associates Jesus' *logia* with the *logia* of the prophets (*1 Apol.* 63.14; *Dial.* 139.5; 18.1).[23]

The Son of Man Sayings in the History of the Tradition of Q

The second reason for the recent deemphasis on the eschatological and

[19] Bultmann classified this parenetic saying among the *logia,* wisdom sayings in the narrow sense (*History,* 77).

[20] Bultmann characterized this saying along with Matt 10:28/Luke 12:4; Matt 5:39–40/Luke 6:29; Matt 17:13–14/Luke 13:23–24 as warnings among the *logia* which are characteristically prophetic (*History,* 119). David Aune questions the transmission of these sayings by early Christian prophets, not the prophetic character of the sayings themselves (*Prophecy in Early Christianity and the Ancient Mediterranean World* [Grand Rapids: Eerdmans, 1983] 242–45).

[21] See also Matt 24:43–44/Luke 12:39–40 and Matt 24:45–51/Luke 12:42–46; see Bultmann, *History,* 119.

[22] Robinson, "LOGOI SOPHON," 108–9.

[23] Cited by Robinson, ibid., 99.

apocalyptic characteristics of the Sayings Source is that the constitutive and central role of the eschatological sayings in that document has been challenged. Heinz Eduard Tödt, following Bultmann, understood Q to be thoroughly eschatological in orientation.[24] Further, he argued that the Son of Man sayings were constitutive for the Christology of Q, which he described as a Son of Man Christology.[25] Tödt also argued that the sayings about the coming Son of Man had an important place in the structure of Q as a whole. They were not simply placed together because of a similarity in content; rather, their placement reflects an editorial plan and attention to nuances of meaning.[26] Although Tödt accepted the form-critical conclusion that Q had a long history of development, he did not consider the possibility that the placement of the Son of Man sayings was not the work of the editor who gave Q the form presupposed by Matthew and Luke, but of an earlier editor whose perspective may have been different. The reason why Tödt did not consider this possibility is that he apparently assumed that behind the whole process of the development of the Sayings Source was a single community with a unified perspective. Insofar as he recognizes change in perspective in the history of the tradition of Q, he emphasizes continuity rather than discontinuity.

Rather than emphasize the process of the formation of the tradition related to the Sayings Source, Dieter Lührmann focused on fixed points, such as the composition of Q at a specific point in time. He also proposed that behind Q one particular community be imagined, which possessed Q and few other traditions. Unlike Tödt, Lührmann does not assume that the interests of the redactional stage of Q were the same as those of earlier stages.[27] Nevertheless, he confirms the interpretation of Q as thoroughly eschatological; in fact, he uses the term "apocalyptic." Lührmann concludes that the beatitudes had a prominent place in the structure of the Sayings Source; they constituted the beginning at least of a large complex of Q-material and possibly of the document as a whole. He attributed the last, longest beatitude (Matt 5:11–12/ Luke 6:22) to the redaction of Q. The significance of this conclusion is that the theme of opposition between Jesus along with his followers and outsiders comes early in the document and is prominent. It also means that the rest of

---

[24] For Bultmann's judgment, see, e.g., *Theology of the New Testament* (New York: Scribner, 1951) 1. 42. Heinz Eduard Tödt, *Der Menschensohn in der synoptischen Überlieferung* (Gütersloh: Mohn, 1959) 217, 245–46. Siegfried Schulz also emphasized the apocalyptic character of Q in its earliest form. See his *Q: Die Spruchquelle der Evangelisten* (Zurich: Theologischer Verlag, 1972) 168, 487.

[25] Tödt, *Der Menschensohn*, 207–15, 228–32, 239–42, 265–67.

[26] Ibid., 246–47.

[27] Lührmann, *Redaktion*, 14–22.

the programmatic speech of Jesus, which is largely parenesis, is placed in an eschatological framework.[28] Like Bultmann and others, Lührmann concluded that Q ended with an eschatological section (Matt 24:23, 26–28, 37–41/Luke 17:23–37).[29] Unlike Tödt, Lührmann did not argue that the Son of Man sayings were constitutive for the theology of Q. He agreed with Tödt that the major christological motif in Q is its perceived mandate to continue the preaching of Jesus. But the message of Jesus, according to Lührmann, was interpreted in such a way that the announcement of judgment became central. Although the Son of Man is not one of the primary motifs of the Q-redaction in Lührmann's interpretation, it plays a key role in the theological schema which he infers from the text: the content of the proclamation in Q is the coming judgment in which Jesus as Son of Man will rescue his community.[30] Unlike Tödt and Robinson, Lührmann attempted to show how the wisdom elements in Q are related to the apocalyptic elements. He made a case for the use of the Old Testament in Q being a wisdom-type interpretation of historical material in Scripture with a parenetic aim. He also showed that the wisdom motifs in Q serve to substantiate the apocalyptic announcement of judgment; for example, personified wisdom in Luke 11:49–51 is the speaker of a prophetic threat.[31]

This perspective on Q as an eschatological or apocalyptic document has been challenged by Heinz Schürmann.[32] His basic thesis was that the Son of Man title appears only in introductory and concluding sayings in the traditions of Q. He related this hypothesis to his view of the stages of growth of the Sayings Source. First, individual sayings of Jesus circulated independently. Then certain sayings were interpreted by appending a second saying attributed to Jesus which functioned as a "Kommentarwort" upon the first.[33] Then groups of sayings were gathered because of similarity of content or in accordance with catchwords. Next, speeches were composed in relation to the needs of particular Christian communities. Finally, Q was composed, which is a collection of such speeches.

The question Schürmann posed is whether the Son of Man sayings function primarily to comment on the individual saying which they precede or

---

[28] Ibid., 55–56.
[29] Ibid., 89.
[30] Ibid., 93–96.
[31] Ibid., 98, 100.
[32] Heinz Schürmann, "Beobachtungen zum Menschensohn-Titel in der Redequelle: Sein Vorkommen in Abschluss- und Einleitungswendungen," in *Jesus und der Menschensohn: Für Anton Vögtle* (ed. R. Pesch and R. Schnackenburg with O. Kaiser; Freiburg: Herder, 1975) 124–47.
[33] Schürmann first worked out this idea in *Das Lukasevangelium,* Part One (HTKNT 3/1; Freiburg: Herder, 1969). Joachim Wanke develops the notion in " 'Kommentarworte': Älteste Kommentierungen von Herrenworten," *BZ* n.s. 24 (1980) 208–33.

follow and interpret or whether their main function is to interpret larger
units in the final redaction of Q.[34] He examined ten Son of Man sayings
which he attributed to Q[35] and concluded that it is difficult to recover the
use of these sayings in the formation of small groups of sayings and in the
composition of speeches which predate Q. But he believed that he had shown
conclusively that the Son of Man sayings in every case were attached to other
individual sayings and that in no case can they be attributed with any certainty to the final redaction of Q. He argued that, in most cases, the link was
made before the pair of sayings was incorporated into a larger unit.[36]

In only one case does Schürmann's thesis hold without modification: the
saying about the Son of Man eating and drinking was added as an interpretation to the similitude about children playing in the marketplace (Matt
11:16–19a/Luke 7:31–34). The link was probably made before this unit was
joined with the other sayings about John the Baptist, since the similitude
would not have been included otherwise. The Son of Man saying itself is not
the climax of the larger unit on John the Baptist; rather, the wisdom saying
(Matt 11:19b/Luke 7:35) plays this role. There is then, nothing to suggest
that the Son of Man saying should be linked in a special way to the composition of Q.

In the other cases, some reservations or corrections must be expressed in
relation to Schürmann's conclusions, at times serious ones. The last beatitude
is a Son of Man saying in its Lucan form, which probably represents Q (Matt
5:11–12/Luke 6:22–23).[37] This saying is not associated simply with another
individual saying which requires interpretation. Rather it is joined to a small
collection of three sayings, all of which have the same form. The addition of
the last beatitude does indeed suggest a particular meaning for the first three,
but this result is less obvious than in the case discussed above and may not
have been intentional. Further, the absence of the phrase Son of Man in the
rest of the unit (Luke 6:20b–23, 27–49) does not prove that the Son of Man
saying cannot be attributed to the redaction of Q or that the last beatitude
circulated with the other three at one time as an independent unit. Its
difference in form from the other three, as well as its length and complexity,
suggests that it belongs to a written, rather than oral, stage of tradition.
Although it may not be possible to demonstrate that this Son of Man saying
was composed in the course of the redaction of Q, one can at least point out

---

[34] Schürmann, "Beobachtungen," 124, 128–29.

[35] One of the ten should probably be attributed to special Matthean material rather than to
Q (Matt 10:23), since it has no parallel in Luke.

[36] Schürmann, "Beobachtungen," 140–41.

[37] The assumption is made here that Q contained the phrase *tou huiou tou anthrōpou* and that
Matthew changed it to *emou*, as elsewhere.

that the theme of the mistreatment of the prophets is not confined to this saying; indeed, it was rather prominent in Q (see Matt 23:29/Luke 11:47; Matt 23:34/Luke 11:49; Matt 23:37/Luke 13:34).

Contrary to Schürmann's conclusion, it seems prudent to infer that the short dialogue about putting one's hand to the plow was not part of Q at the point at which it was received independently by the congregations in which Matthew and Luke were written, since it does not appear in Matthew. Therefore, rather than supposing that the saying about the Son of Man having nowhere to lay his head was prefixed as an introduction to a double anecdote about discipleship, it could more appropriately be viewed as a "Kommentarwort" on the saying about leaving the dead to bury the dead. If it was originally attached to a single saying, it may well have followed it as "Kommentarworte" usually do. If it did, then the order may have been reversed when the two sayings as a unit were prefixed to introduce the missionary speech (Luke 10:2–12 par.).[38] The inverting of the order would signify that, at some redactional stage, possibly a late one, the Son of Man saying was significant in interpreting the whole unit. Lack of a home in the Son of Man saying is indeed analogous to various elements of the missionary speech: carrying no purse, bag, or sandals (Luke 10:4 par.), traveling from town to town, being dependent on hospitality and vulnerable to rejection and thus to lack of shelter (Luke 10:5–8, 10 par.). Schürmann is correct that the link between the Son of Man saying (Matt 8:19–20/Luke 9:57–58) and the missionary speech is secondary in relation to the link between that saying and the one about the dead burying the dead. But the observations above suggest, contrary to Schürmann, that the secondary link was intentional and significant.

Lührmann had argued that the saying comparing Jonah and the Son of Man (Luke 11:30)[39] was composed by the editor of Q as a bridge between the apophthegm about the request for a sign (Matt 12:38–39/Luke 11:29)[40] and the warnings about the role that the queen of the South and the Ninevites would have at the judgment (Matt 12:41–42/Luke 11:31–32). Schürmann disagreed, because in Luke 11:32 par. Jesus, like Jonah, is only a preacher of judgment and not the Judge as he is in v. 30. If v. 30 were added after v. 29 was joined to vv. 31–32, it would have referred more clearly to the earthly Jesus as the "more than Jonah."[41] Schürmann, however, did not pay sufficient

---

[38] See Wanke, " 'Kommentarworte,' " 216–17.

[39] The assumption is made here that something close to Luke 11:30 appeared in Q; the parallel in Matt 12:40 is secondary relative to the Lucan (Q) formulation.

[40] Lührmann, *Redaktion*, 41–42; but note that the saying is an apophthegm only in Matthew; see Bultmann, *History*, 117, 335.

[41] Schürmann, "Beobachtungen," 133. Schürmann, Lührmann, and Tödt are correct in viewing Luke 11:30 as a reference to the future, apocalyptic Son of Man and not to the present,

attention to the fact that vv. 31–32 claim that some*thing* greater (*pleion*) than Jonah is here, not some*one* (*pleiōn*). Even though vv. 31–32 are placed in the mouth of Jesus, the use of the neuter allows a broader reference than one to the person of the earthly Jesus alone. When the sayings circulated independently, the referent of the *pleion* was most likely the Holy Spirit (*to pneuma to hagion*). Another possible referent is the proclamation of the early church (*to kerygma;* this term is used in v. 32). Since vv. 31–32 need not refer narrowly to the earthly Jesus in a minimally or pre-Christological sense, the possibility that v. 30 was added by the editor of Q cannot be excluded.[42]

According to Schürmann, the saying about the Son of Man acknowledging and denying human beings before the angels of God (Luke 12:8–9)[43] was added as a "Kommentarwort" to the sayings on whom to fear (Luke 12:4–5) and on anxiety (vv 6–7). It "concluded" the theme of lack of fear and anxiety with a promise of reward. Later, vv. 8–9 became the conclusion to the larger unit Luke 12:2–3, 4–7 par., but the saying about the Son of Man was not added because of vv. 2–3; rather vv. 8–9 became the ending of the larger composition by chance. Later v. 10 was added to correct vv. 8–9 in the light of a new situation, the preaching of the early church. Thus, a Son of Man saying once again was made a conclusion. Finally, he argued, it is not possible to demonstrate that there was a redactional intention at work in adding v. 10, that is, that it was supposed to serve as a conclusion to the whole unit (Luke 12:2–9).[44] Schürmann is probably correct in seeing Luke 12:4–9 par. as an early unit later incorporated into a somewhat larger composition. Although vv. 4–7 constitute a double rather than an individual saying and even though the two sayings do not call for an interpretation as obviously as the similitude about the children in the marketplace, it is plausible that vv. 8–9 were attached in order to conclude the exhortation with a promise of reward (and

---

earthly Son of Man, as P. Vielhauer argued. Since the original meaning of v. 29, when it was an independent saying, is obscure, one cannot assert, as Vielhauer did, that the *dothēsetai* does not refer to the eschatological future. In any case, when v. 30 was added, it served to (re)interpret v. 29, not vice versa. There is no reason to conclude that the *estai* of v. 30 is something other than a real future. A reference to the eschatological future is the most natural reading. See Philipp Vielhauer, "Jesus und der Menschensohn," *ZTK* 60 (1963) 133–77; reprinted in idem, *Aufsätze zum Neuen Testament* (Munich: Kaiser, 1965) 92–140, the relevant discussion of Luke 11:30 is on p. 112. Contrast Lührmann, *Redaktion,* 40; and Tödt, *Der Menschensohn,* 49.

[42] Lührmann's conclusion, however, that the reference to Jonah in Luke 11:29 is secondary, is dubious. This conclusion is based on the judgment that the Marcan form of the saying is more original (Mark 8:12). On the contrary, Mark's omission of the reference to Jonah can be explained either (1) because the allusion to Jonah was no longer understood or (2) as a means of heightening the theme in Mark of the "messianic secret." See Lührmann, *Redaktion,* 41–42.

[43] The assumption is made here that the phrase *ho huios tou anthrōpou* appeared in the Q-formulation of this saying and that Matthew changed it to *kagō* (see above, n. 37).

[44] Schürmann, "Beobachtungen," 135–36.

a threat of punishment in v. 9, which ties in with v. 5). Beyond this point, however, Schürmann's reconstruction of the formation of the larger composition (Luke 12:2–10) is not necessarily the most probable one. It is at least equally probable that vv. 2–3 and v. 10 were added at the same time, as an introductory and concluding framework, in order to place the earlier unit (vv. 4–9) more clearly in the situation of early Christian preaching (vv. 2–3). The contrasts of hidden and revealed (v. 2), darkness and light, whispering and proclamation (v. 3), Son of Man (earthly Jesus) and Holy Spirit (Spirit-led mission of the early church) (v. 10) serve to highlight the present time of the Christian proclamation as humanity's last and best chance to repent, which builds on and completes the proclamation of Jesus, God's penultimate word. Verses 11–12 either stood in Q and were added at the same time as vv. 2–3 and 10 or were placed here by Luke. If this reconstruction is plausible, as it seems to be, the possibility that vv. 2–3 and 10 (11–12) were added by the editor of Q cannot be ruled out.

Schürmann's treatment of Luke 17:23–30 is very problematic.[45] He assumed that the saying in v. 23 ("And they will say to you, 'Lo there!'. . .") was originally an independent saying, because of the parallel in Mark 13:21. But it is highly unlikely that Mark 13:21 or Luke 17:23 ever circulated independently. Rather, Mark 13:21–22 and Luke 17:23–24 are more likely variants of a unified, individual saying.[46] Thus, Luke 17:24 is not a "Kommentarwort" at all. In this case a Son of Man saying (Luke 17:23–24 par.) is the "Bezugwort," the logically prior saying in need of interpretation.[47] It is likely that in Q this saying was followed by the one about the corpse and vultures (Matt 24:28/Luke 17:37). The author of Luke probably moved the latter saying, in order to break the potentially offensive link between the Son of Man and the corpse (Luke has *to sōma* rather than *to ptōma* as Matthew does) and to create a literary *inclusio* by returning at the end of the eschatological discourse to the theme expressed at the beginning, the question regarding location (cf. Luke 17:37 with vv. 21 and 23).[48] Thus, if there was a "Kommentarwort" in this unit as it appeared in Q, it was the saying about the vultures, not the saying about the Son of Man.

As Wanke points out in his essay building on Schürmann's work, "Kommentarworte" must be distinguished from secondary expansions (composed

---

[45] Ibid., 139–40.
[46] See Bultmann, *History*, 122, 125, 152; it is difficult to imagine that the saying-fragment preserved in Mark 13:21; Matt 24:23; Matt 24:26; and Luke 17:23 ever circulated independently.
[47] Wanke, " 'Kommentarworte,' " 211.
[48] Tödt, *Der Menschensohn*, 44; Lührmann, *Redaktion*, 72.

for the context) and analogous formations.[49] Schürmann implied that the sayings comparing the days of Noah and Lot to the days of the Son of Man (Luke 17:26–27 par. and 17:28–30) were "Kommentarworte" on the previous Son of Man saying (Luke 17:23–24 par.).[50] It is questionable whether these exegetical, quasi-scribal sayings (vv. 26–27 par., 28–30) ever circulated independently. It seems more prudent, therefore, to conclude that they are sayings formed by analogy with 17:23–24 par. for this particular context, that is, secondary expansions. This conclusion is supported by the likelihood that only the saying about Noah was in Q at the point at which that document was received by Matthew's community (Matthew does not have the saying about Lot). This probable fact suggests that 17:23–24 par. was expanded first with the saying about Noah, and then later, in the continuing editorial modification of Q in Luke's community, with the saying about Lot. The addition of the Noah saying would have taken place at a relatively late redactional stage (after the saying about the corpse had been linked to the Son of Man saying). Therefore, one cannot exclude the possibility that the saying about Noah was added by the editor of Q. If such was the case, the title Son of Man would indeed have been used emphatically by that editor, contrary to Schürmann's claim.[51]

One more Son of Man saying comes into question here, the one about his coming at an unexpected hour (Matt 24:44/Luke 12:40). It is likely, as Schürmann concludes, that this saying was appended as an allegorizing interpretation to the aphorism about the thief (Matt 24:43/Luke 12:39) at a stage in the formation of the tradition prior to the editing of Q.[52] It is doubtful, however, that the Son of Man saying circulated independently prior to its appearance in this context.[53] It was probably composed as an interpretation of the aphorism.[54] It is unlikely, however, contrary to Schürmann's view, that v. 40 par. was added at the same time as a conclusion to the whole unit of Luke 12:35–39, which he claims Matthew must have read in some form. Since Matthew has no reasonably close parallel to Luke 12:35–38, it is prudent to conclude that those verses did not appear in Q when it was received by Matthew's community. Schürmann's claim that the unit containing the Son

---

[49] Wanke, " 'Kommentarworte,' " 211. See now also his book *Bezugs-und Kommentarworte in den synoptischen Evangelien* (Erfurter Theologische Studien 44; Erfurt: St. Benno, 1981).

[50] Schürmann, "Beobachtungen," 139–40.

[51] Ibid., 140.

[52] Ibid., 138.

[53] Compare the variant of the saying about the thief in *Gos. Thom.* 21:3, which has a different interpretation attached (probably a secondary expansion) and the similar saying with no interpretation in *Gos. Thom.* 103.

[54] See Bultmann, *History,* 119, 171.

of Man saying was originally a conclusion to the series Luke 12:35-39, which then gradually "grew," is thus unwarranted. The unit about the thief (Luke 12:39-40 par.) may be in its present position because of a catchword association with the preceding saying about treasure (Matt 6:19-21/Luke 12:33-34) which mentions a thief (thieves in Matthew). Alternatively, it may have been placed before the admonition about the faithful and wise slave/ steward (Matt 24:45-51/Luke 12:42-46) as its introduction. In that case, the Son of Man saying would serve as an allegorizing interpretation of the master (*kyrios*) in the admonition and would be constitutive of its meaning at a relatively late stage of the process of transmission.

In conclusion, one may note that, of the ten Son of Man sayings in the Saying Source discussed by Schürmann, one should be eliminated because of a reasonable doubt that it appeared in Q (Matt 10:23). Of the remaining nine, two are "Kommentarworte," that is, originally independent sayings attached to another individual saying in order to interpret or reinterpret it (Matt 11:18-19a/Luke 7:33-34 and Matt 8:20/Luke 9:58). A third functions in a way similar to the "Kommentarworte"; it is an originally independent saying that was added as a conclusion to a small collection of previously independent sayings (Luke 12:8-9; cf. Matt 10:32-33).

Six of the Son of Man sayings in Q do not fit under the rubric "Kommentarwort." In one case, the Son of Man saying does not seem to have been attached to another previously independent individual saying; rather, it is probably the second part of an originally unitary two-part saying (Matt 24:27/Luke 17:24). In three cases the Son of Man sayings seem to be secondary expansions, either composed to interpret an earlier saying in an allegorical and admonitory manner (Matt 24:44/Luke 12:40) or composed by analogy to (an) older saying(s) in an elaborative style (Luke 6:22-23; cf. Matt 5:11-12 and Matt 24:37-39/Luke 17: 26-27). In two cases there is evidence for the use of Son of Man sayings in redactional activity. In one case a saying that was probably independent originally (Matt 12:32/Luke 12:10; cf. Mark 3:28-29) was used by an editor along with other sayings in the construction of an introductory and concluding framework for an older small collection of sayings. In the other case, the Son of Man saying may be a redactional composition (Luke 11:30).

This study based on a critical assessment of Schürmann's theses suggests that the Son of Man sayings are found at virtually every stage of the formation of the tradition included in the Sayings Source. One saying represents the oldest stage, that is, an independent saying which is the starting point for an eschatological discourse (Matt 24:26-27/Luke 17:23-24). Three sayings represent the next stage, the attachment of sayings to other individual sayings. The attached sayings may be originally independent sayings (Matt 8:20/Luke 9:58) or secondary expansions (Matt 24:44/Luke 12:40 and probably Matt 11:18–19a/Luke 7:33–34). The next stage would seem to be the formation of small collections. As we have seen, one Son of Man saying in Q appears to have been the conclusion of such a collection (Luke 12:8–9; cf. Matt 10:32–33). The last two stages, the composition of individual speeches and the composition of Q, are difficult to distinguish. Four Son of Man sayings appear to have been involved in editorial activity and so belong to one or the other of these two late stages: Luke 6:22–23; cf. Matt 5:11–12; Matt 12:32/Luke 12:10; Matt 24:37–39/Luke 17:26–27; Luke 11:30; cf. Matt 12:40. Apocalyptic Son of Man sayings are found at the earliest (Matt 24:26–27/Luke 17:23–24) and at the latest stages (Matt 24:37–39/Luke 17:26–27 and Luke 11:30; cf. Matt 12:40). These observations render unlikely the hypothesis that the apocalyptic Son of Man sayings represent an early stage of tradition that was no longer of interest to the editor of Q.[55]

Q and the Gospel of Thomas

The observations made above about the place of the Son of Man sayings in the history of the tradition of Q also call into question the hypothesis that an early form of the Sayings Source was nonapocalyptic. This hypothesis, presented by Helmut Koester, is another reason for the recent shift of scholarly interest from the apocalyptic to the wisdom elements of Q.[56] Against those who argued that the *Gospel of Thomas* was a late work, dependent on the canonical Gospels and representative of a new Gnostic genre, created by selecting congenial material and omitting uncongenial material from the narrative Gospels, Koester argued, like Robinson, that the *Gospel of Thomas* is an early work similar in literary form to the Sayings Source. He suggested that both Q and the *Gospel of Thomas* were dependent on an older "sayings gospel," which lacked not only the passion narrative but also the expectation of the apocalyptic Son of Man. Koester argued that this early version of Q was close to proverbial wisdom and proto-Gnostic. It was subsequently revised in an apocalyptic direction in order to combat the tendency toward a Gnostic use of the document.

In support of this hypothesis, Koester pointed out that Q and the *Gospel of Thomas* share some eschatological sayings,[57] but notably not the future Son of Man sayings.[58] These observations do not support the conclusion that the

---

[55] Implied by Schürmann, "Beobachtungen," 142–47.

[56] Helmut Koester, "GNOMAI DIAPHOROI: The Origin and Nature of Diversification in the History of Early Christianity," in *Trajectories through Early Christianity*, 138; "One Jesus and Four Primitive Gospels," in *Trajectories*, 169–72, 186–87; and "Apocryphal and Canonical Gospels," *HTR* 73 (1980) 112–19.

[57] Koester, "One Jesus," 169–70.

[58] Ibid., 170–71.

editor of *Thomas,* or compilers of its traditions at earlier stages, knew some form of Q, the Synoptic Sayings Source. The evidence cited supports at most the hypothesis that these compilers and editor(s) knew a pre-Q collection of eschatological sayings presented in Luke 12:35–56, as well as individual sayings preserved in Q.[59]

If the compilers or editor(s) of the *Gospel of Thomas* knew a pre-Q eschatological speech preserved in Luke 12:35–56,[60] it is odd that none of the corresponding sayings in the *Gospel of Thomas* have the same order as those in Q, whose order is probably represented by Luke.[61] It is also noteworthy that two Q-sayings from this context have no parallel in the *Gospel of Thomas.*[62] On the question of order, it is noteworthy that, of all the parallels between Q and the Gospel of Thomas, the same two sayings are linked in both documents in only two cases. The saying about carrying one's cross follows the saying about hating relatives in both works (Luke 14:26–27; cf. Matt 10:37–38/*Gos. Thom.* 55:1–2). The beatitude about the hungry and the one about the persecuted are in sequence, although the order in the *Gospel of Thomas* is the reverse of Q (Luke 6:21a, 22–23/Matt 5:6, (10)11–12/*Gos. Thom.* 69:2; 68, 69:1). The data concerning order suggest that the primary stage at which Q and the *Gospel of Thomas* share tradition is the stage of free-floating individual sayings in the oral tradition. Beyond that, they seem to share only two very small units of two sayings each.

In his more recent work, Koester has discussed the relation between Q and the *Gospel of Thomas* in more nuanced ways. In an essay prepared for an international conference on Gnosticism at Yale in 1978, he examined sayings about "seeking and finding" in canonical and extracanonical gospels.[63] He concluded that "it is extremely difficult to establish any relationships among [all the variants of the sayings] in terms of dependence and development. The most plausible explanation would assume that there were several different sayings about "seeking" circulating as part of the tradition of sayings of Jesus.[64] Since the sayings in Q interpreted the "seeking and finding" as prayer,

---

[59] Ibid., 169–70.

[60] It is doubtful that Luke 12:35–38, 41, 47–48, 49 and 50 belonged to Q, since they have no parallels in Matthew. On the other hand, Luke 12:58–59/Matt 5:25–26 probably did belong to Q. If it followed Luke 12:54–56 in Q, as seems likely, it would have had an eschatological significance in that context.

[61] Luke 12:39–40/*Gos. Thom.* 21:3; cf. *Gos. Thom.* 103; Luke 12:51–53/*Gos. Thom.* 16; Luke 12:54–56/*Gos. Thom.* 91:2.

[62] Luke 12:42–46/Matt 24:45–51 and Luke 12:58–59/Matt 5:25–26.

[63] The essay has been published as "Gnostic Writings as Witnesses for the Development of the Sayings Tradition," in *The Rediscovery of Gnosticism:* Vol. 1, *The School of Valentinus* (ed. Bentley Layton; Studies in the History of Religions 41.1; Leiden: Brill, 1980) 238–56.

[64] Ibid., 243.

it cannot be the source of the other sayings which allude to the religious quest.[65] After discussing unsatisfactory explanations, Koester concludes, "Therefore, if one must explain the occurrence of these sayings in several writings as due to a common source, it is best to posit a written (and/or oral?) tradition of sayings which was not unrelated to, but still different from Q and the *Gospel of Thomas*."[66]

There seem to be no positive reasons for positing such a source. The attractiveness of such a hypothesis might be greater if the variants in John were consistently similar to those in *Thomas*. One (John 7:33–34) does seem related to the notion of the religious quest. The other (16:24), however, is best understood in the context of prayer, as in Q. The preceding verse (23), which is closely linked to v 24, makes this context clear.[67] Therefore, Koester's original suggestion is preferable, that there were several different sayings about "seeking" in circulation.

In the same essay, Koester discussed a number of revelation sayings which appear in the canonical Gospels, the *Dialogue of the Savior,* the *Gospel of Thomas,* and 1 Corinthians 1–4.[68] On the basis of the interconnections among these sayings, he concluded that their ultimate source was a sapiential writing or wisdom book attributed to an authoritative figure of the Old Testament (this attribution would explain why the document was cited as scripture in 1 Cor 2:9 and Matt 13:35).[69]

In emphasizing these interconnections, Koester has made a significant contribution by building on the work of previous scholars in exploring some links between the gospel tradition and the situation in Corinth.[70] The suggestion of the existence of such a wisdom book is intriguing in the light of Matt 13:35 and 1 Cor 2:9. But it is doubtful that Q was dependent on such a

[65] Ibid., 238–39, 243.

[66] Ibid., 244.

[67] So also Ernst Haenchen, *A Commentary on the Gospel of John* (Hermeneia; Philadelphia: Fortress, 1984) 2. 145. One may infer from Raymond E. Brown's interpretation that the older idea of prayer is taken in the direction of the religious quest by the author or editor of John (*The Gospel according to John XIII-XXI* [AB 29A; Garden City, NY: Doubleday, 1970] 722–23, 734).

[68] Matt 11:25–26 = Luke 10:21; Matt 11:27 = Luke 10:22; Matt 13:16–17 = Luke 10:23–24; Matt 11:18–30; John 3:35; 14:7–10; *Dial. Sav.* 134:14–15; *Gos. Thom.* 90; *Dial. Sav.* 141:3–6; Mark 4:22 pars.; *Gos. Thom.* 5; 6; Matt 13:35; 1 Corinthians 1–4; especially 1:19; 2:7, 9, 10; 3:1, 13; 4:5; *Gos. Thom.* 17; *Dial. Sav.* 140:2–4.

[69] Koester, "Gnostic Writings," 249–50. For assessments of Koester's hypothesis concerning a wisdom book, see M. Eugene Boring, *Sayings of the Risen Jesus: Christian Prophecy in the Synoptic Tradition* (Cambridge: University Press, 1982) 157–58; James M. Robinson, "On Bridging the Gulf from Q to the Gospel of Thomas (or Vice Versa)," in *Nag Hammadi, Gnosticism and Early Christianity* (ed. Charles W. Hedrick and Robert Hodgson; Peabody, MA: Hendrickson, 1986) 149–57.

[70] See the literature cited, ibid., p. 244, nn. 18 and 19.

source. A case for such dependence could be made only by demonstrating that Matt 11:28–30 and 13:35 were included in Q. It is hard to see how any such demonstration could achieve a high degree of probability. The *Gospel of Thomas* has no close parallel to the material that can be attributed to Q with confidence (Matt 11:25–27 = Luke 10:21–24).[71]

In the light of the literary relations (and the equally important lacks thereof) between Q and the *Gospel of Thomas,* Koester's description of their relationship in his *Introduction to the New Testament* is more satisfactory than that in the essays in *Trajectories through Early Christianity*. In the *Introduction* he referred to some overlap between them, but presented them as two separate traditions of the interpretation of the sayings of Jesus.[72] But he continued to suggest that the Son of Man sayings were characteristic only of the stage of the final composition and redaction of Q, a theory that is improbable in the light of the history of the tradition of Q, as it can be inferred from an analysis of Matthew and Luke.[73]

Koester turned once again to the question of the relationship between the *Gospel of Thomas* and Q in an article entitled "Überlieferung und Geschichte der frühchristlichen Evangelienliteratur."[74] This long article is closely related to the Shaffer Lectures which he presented at Yale in 1980.[75] In these lectures, Koester characterized the *Gospel of Thomas* as "an old Christian sayings collection, or else based upon an older collection, which is more closely related to the genre of the wisdom book than the second common source of Matthew and Luke."[76] Questions arise in connection with this statement similar to those discussed in relation to Robinson's work (see the first section of this essay). What is a "wisdom book"? Does Koester have in mind an example of the genre "sayings of the wise"? Does a wisdom book contain primarily proverbial sayings, aphorisms, and the like? The issue once again is what kind of wisdom is referred to and how content (type of wisdom) relates to form (the designation of the genre). A book that emphasizes

---

[71] The fourth part of *Gos. Thom.* 61 is a distant parallel.

[72] Helmut Koester, *Introduction to the New Testament:* Vol. 2, *History and Literature of Early Christianity* (Philadelphia: Fortress, 1982) 147–48, 150.

[73] Ibid., 147–48. See the section on "The Son of Man Sayings in the History of the Tradition of Q" above.

[74] Published in *Aufstieg und Niedergang der römischen Welt* (ed. Wolfgang Haase; New York: de Gruyter, 1984) 2. 25.2, pp. 1463–1542.

[75] Koester's Shaffer Lectures are not yet published. He allowed James M. Robinson to quote excerpts in his article "On Bridging the Gulf from Q to the Gospel of Thomas (or Vice Versa)." In it he cites the typescript of Koester's lectures under the title "Tradition and History." I am grateful to Professor Robinson for sharing the page proofs of the article with me prior to its publication.

[76] Cited by Robinson, "On Bridging the Gulf," 127.

revealed heavenly wisdom should probably not receive the identical generic label as a book that emphasizes proverbial or aphoristic wisdom.

In connection with 1 Corinthians 1–4, Koester suggests that "the wisdom teaching of Jesus was understood as a secret teaching for the perfect. . . ."[77] Similarly, the parables of Jesus came to be understood "as special revelation to the elect which had been hidden until now and remains hidden for those outside."[78] This understanding represents, according to Koester, a shift from the earlier understanding of the parables as prophetic proclamation of a new age to a kind of wisdom theology.

The term "wisdom theology" is misleading, because it can be read as referring primarily to proverbial wisdom. The pattern of ideas in which Koester is primarily interested, however, the notion of previously hidden wisdom which is now revealed to a chosen few, is a typically apocalyptic motif. It has roots in didactic wisdom (Wis 7:21; Sir 1:30; 4:18), but the pattern described by Koester is clearest and most common in apocalyptic writings. In the book of Daniel, for instance, various types of wisdom traditions are placed in an apocalyptic framework. The courtly tales of Daniel 1–6, with their emphasis on mantic wisdom (wisdom revealed through dreams and visions and the gift of their interpretation), serve as an introduction to the apocalyptic visions of Daniel 7–12. As in Mark 4:11 and 1 Cor 2:7, the term "secret" or "mystery" is used in Dan 2:19, 27–30, 47 to describe heavenly knowledge, previously hidden, but now revealed to Daniel as a wise man of God.[79]

In one of the oldest apocalypses, the Book of the Heavenly Luminaries (1 Enoch 72–82), things normally hidden are revealed to Enoch by the angel Uriel (80:1). Enoch in turn revealed these heavenly secrets to his son Methuselah and his children (82:1–2). These secrets are called wisdom (82:2–3).

In another very old apocalypse, the Book of the Watchers (1 Enoch 1–36), wisdom is the eschatological gift to the elect (5.8–9). Like Paul in 1 Corinthians, this work distinguishes types of wisdom and sets them in opposition. The wisdom revealed by the fallen angels is useless (9:5–6; 16:3), whereas Enoch received the true wisdom (implied, e.g., by 14:1–3; 15:1; 36:4). The saying quoted by Paul in 1 Cor 2:9 claims that no one has seen or heard what God has prepared for the righteous. Enoch claims to have seen the end of

---

[77] Cited by Robinson, ibid., 128.

[78] Ibid. Reference is made to Mark 4:10–12, 33–34 and to Gos. Thom. 62–65.

[79] On the term "mystery" see Raymond E. Brown, The Semitic Background of the Term "Mystery" in the New Testament (Philadelphia: Fortress, 1968). See also Helmut Koester, "History and Development of Mark's Gospel (From Mark to Secret Mark and 'Canonical' Mark)," in Colloquy on New Testament Studies: A Time for Reappraisal and Fresh Approaches (ed. Bruce Corley; Macon, GA: Mercer University Press, 1983) 47–49.

everything (punishments of the wicked) and that no one has seen what he has seen (19:3).[80] He has also seen what God has prepared for the righteous (25:7).

In the Similitudes of Enoch (*1 Enoch* 37–71), an apocalypse to be dated to the late first century B.C.E. or early first century C.E.,[81] wisdom is said to dwell in heaven because she could find nowhere among humanity to dwell (42:1–3). Also in heaven is "that Son of Man" who will be revealed in the last days (51:1–5). In the meantime the wisdom of the Lord of Spirits has revealed that Son of Man to the righteous (the elect), although he remains hidden for everyone else (48:6–10). The revelation of heavenly secrets (hidden things) is a major theme (52:5; 59:1–3; 60:10–11; 61:5; 62:7; 69:26). Like the Book of the Watchers, this work also speaks of an unauthorized revelation of secrets by the evil angels which led humans astray (64:1–2; 65:6, 11; 69:8).

The Epistle of Enoch (*1 Enoch* 91–104), which dates to the first century B.C.E., is an exhortation by Enoch to his son which is permeated by apocalyptic eschatology. Like the Book of the Watchers, it speaks of wisdom as an eschatological gift to the righteous (91:10). It refers to itself as "this complete wisdom teaching" (92:1). The reward of the righteous and the punishment of the wicked beyond the grave are mysteries revealed to Enoch through reading the heavenly tablets (103:2). Enoch reveals two further mysteries: that the impious will write false books and that the righteous will derive wisdom from Enoch's writings (104:10–13).

According to 4 Ezra, God revealed to Abraham the end of the times, secretly by night (3:14). Like the Similitudes of Enoch, 4 Ezra speaks of wisdom withdrawing from the earth in the last days (5:9–10). Like the Book of the Watchers, 4 Ezra describes what God has prepared for the righteous (8:51–54; 9:13). Many secrets are revealed to Ezra, including the heavenly Jerusalem, which he sees "as far as it is possible for your eyes to see it, and afterward you will hear as much as your ears can hear. For you are more blessed than many, and you have been called before the Most High as but few have been" (10:55–57; cf. 1 Cor 2:9). Ezra is judged worthy to be shown the end of the times (the eagle vision) and to learn the secret of the Most High (the interpretation of the vision, including the revelation of the hidden Messiah; 12:9, 32, 36; cf. 13:26). Ezra is instructed to write down these secrets for the instruction of the wise (12:37–38). Finally, just as Moses made some divine revelations public and kept some secret (14:3–5), so is Ezra to do (14:26, 45–46). The seventy secret books written by Ezra contain "the fountain of wisdom" and are to be revealed only to the wise (14:47).

The conversation between Paul and his addressees in Corinth fits nicely

---

[80] Some manuscripts read "will see" for "has seen."
[81] See the discussion and literature cited by John J. Collins, "The Jewish Apocalypses," 39.

into the thought-world of the apocalypses just discussed. Instead of positing a "wisdom book" as the source of the revelation sayings reflected in the canonical gospels, the *Dialogue of the Savior*, the *Gospel of Thomas*, and 1 Corinthians 1–4, Koester could more plausibly speak of an apocalypse attributed to an authoritative figure of the Old Testament (see the discussion above related to nn. 68 and 69). If the interpretation of the parables in Mark and *Thomas* is more apocalyptic-oriented than wisdom-oriented (or if the orientation is to apocalyptic wisdom), the "shift" from the presentation of the parables as prophetic proclamation seems to be a smaller step and a natural one.

If the *Testaments of the Twelve Patriarchs* and the Epistle of Enoch could combine proverbial wisdom, revealed wisdom, apocalyptic revelation, and apocalyptic eschatology (see the first section of this essay), the "dual character" of the Synoptic Sayings Source (wisdom material and apocalyptic Son of Man sayings) appears in a different light.[82] This dual character need not be seen as the result of editing, but may be seen as a typical characteristic of sapiential apocalypses, apocalyptic sayings collections, testaments, and other genres of the period.

The hypothesis that the Son of Man sayings belong to a late stage in the formation of Q seems to be reinforced by the assumption that the expectation of the Son of Man is quite different from and more recent than the expectation of the coming of the kingdom of God.[83] This sharp distinction was argued by Philipp Vielhauer.[84] In the introduction to his forthcoming edition of the *Gospel of Thomas*, Koester concludes: "If the sayings of Jesus about the kingdom indeed belong to an older stage of the sayings tradition than the Son of Man sayings, the sayings of the *Gospel of Thomas* derive from a stage of the developing sayings tradition which is more original than Q."[85]

Those who deny that the expectation of the Son of Man goes back to Jesus usually conclude that this expectation arose in one of the very earliest forms of Christian faith.[86] This position leaves open the possibility that some Son

---

[82] Koester, "Tradition and History," cited by Robinson, "On Bridging the Gulf," 128. The question of the relation of wisdom and apocalyptic elements in Q is discussed by John S. Kloppenborg, *The Formation of Q: Trajectories in Ancient Wisdom Collections* (Studies in Antiquity and Christianity; Claremont, 1987). See the review by A. Y. Collins in *CBQ* 50 (1988) 720–22. See also his "Tradition and Redaction in the Synoptic Sayings Source," *CBQ* 46 (1984) 34–62.

[83] Ibid.

[84] Philipp Vielhauer, "Gottesreich und Menschensohn in der Verkündigung Jesu," in *Festschrift für Günther Dehn* (Neukirchen Krs. Moers: Verlag der Buchhandlung des Erziehungsvereins, 1957) 51–79; reprinted in idem, *Aufsätze zum Neuen Testaments*, 55–91; reference herein is to the latter. See also "Jesus und der Menschensohn," in *Aufsätze*, 92–140.

[85] Cited by Robinson, "On Bridging the Gulf," 126.

[86] Vielhauer, "Gottesreich und Menschensohn," 90–91; Norman Perrin, *Rediscovering the Teaching of Jesus* (New York: Harper and Row, 1967) 175–76.

of Man sayings may have been formulated by followers of Jesus as a response to his death and in the conviction of his vindication and ongoing significance. If one assumes that no collections of Jesus' sayings were made during his lifetime, these early Son of Man sayings could well have been incorporated into some of the earliest collections.

When Koester speaks of "an older stage of the sayings tradition," however, he apparently means sayings that go back to the historical Jesus. Thus, the discussion of the relationship between the *Gospel of Thomas* and Q leads to the question of the relation of the Son of Man sayings to the historical Jesus.[87]

Conclusions

The major conclusions of the part of this study on "The Sayings Source and Wisdom" are the following: (1) The genre *logoi sophōn* should not be viewed as a genre of proverbial or didactic wisdom alone. Its affinities with prophetic and apocalyptic tradition should be taken into account, so that "the wise" include not only teachers but also prophets and visionaries. (2) Material that can be attributed with confidence to the Sayings Source contains about twenty prophetic and apocalyptic sayings presented as spoken by Jesus. Almost half of the sayings attributed to Jesus in Q do not fit under the rubric of wisdom sayings in the narrow sense.

The main conclusion of the section on "The Son of Man Sayings in the History of the Tradition of Q" is: The sayings about the coming Son of Man in the Sayings Source are neither a relic from the past, handed on with little relevance for the later stages of Q, nor a new arrival at a relatively late stage. Coming Son of Man sayings play an important role at virtually every stage: (a) the oldest layer of individual sayings (Matt 24:26–27/Luke 17:23–24); (b) the stage at which individual sayings are linked to other independent sayings or expanded by sayings composed for the context (Matt 24:44/Luke 12:40); (c) the stage at which sayings are added as introductions or conclusions to small collections of sayings (Luke 12:8–9); and (d) editorial activity in the composition of larger speeches, including the editing of Q as a whole (Matt 24:37–39/Luke 17:26–27; Luke 11:30).

The section on "Q and the *Gospel of Thomas*" concludes: (1) The primary stage at which there was contact between the tradition that found its way into the Sayings Source and the tradition that ultimately was included in the *Gospel of Thomas* was the stage of free-floating individual sayings in the oral tradition. (2) Nothing in the relationship between Q and the *Gospel of Thomas* precludes the possibility that the coming Son of Man sayings are among the most primitive of the post-Easter formulations.

[87] See Adela Yarbro Collins, "The Origin of the Designation of Jesus as 'Son of Man,'" *HTR* 80 (1987) 391–407 and idem, "Daniel 7 and Jesus," forthcoming in the *Journal of Theology* 93 (1989).

Bibliography of Joseph A. Fitzmyer, S.J.

1943

1. "Nicholas Copernicus: 1543–1943," *America* 69 (15 May 1943) 148–50.

1949

2. "The Function of the Papacy," *AER* 121 (1949) 34–44.
3. "Recent Controversy on Genesis 3,15 and the Immaculate Conception," *Theologian* 5 (1949) 1–14.

1952

4. "Introduction à l'étude du grec par Homère: Un nouveau système américain," *Etudes classiques* 20 (1952) 378–91.

1955

5. "The Qumrân Scrolls, the Ebionites and Their Literature," *TS* 16 (1955) 335–72 [see #12].
6. "Battle of the Scrolls," *Commonweal* 63 (9 December 1955) 260–61 [review of E. Wilson, *The Scrolls from the Dead Sea* (New York: Oxford University, 1955); M. Burrows, *The Dead Sea Scrolls* (New York: Viking, 1955)].

1956

7. "L^e as a Preposition and a Particle in Micah 5,1 (5,2)," *CBQ* 18 (1956) 10–13.
8. "The New Testament and the Dead Sea Scrolls," *Commonweal* 64 (29 June 1956) 327–28 [review of G. Graystone, *The Dead Sea Scrolls and the Originality of Christ* (New York: Sheed and Ward, 1956)].

1957

9. "The Syntax of *kl, kl'* in the Aramaic Texts from Egypt and in Biblical Aramaic," *Bib* 38 (1957) 170–84.
10. "The Dead Sea Scrolls," *Catholic Encyclopaedia Supplement* II, section 9 (1957) 16½ columns (9 pages, unpaginated).
11. "Excellent Survey," *Commonweal* 66 (31 May 1957) 238–39 [review of G. Vermès, *Discovery in the Judean Desert* (New York: Desclée, 1957)].
12. "The Qumran Scrolls, the Ebionites and Their Literature," in K. Stendahl, *The Scrolls and the New Testament* (New York: Harper, 1957) 208–31, 291–98 [reprint, in slightly abridged form, of #5].
13. "A Feature of Qumrân Angelology and the Angels of I Cor. xi. 10," *NTS* 4 (1957–58) 48–58.
14. "'4Q Testimonia' and the New Testament," *TS* 18 (1957) 513–37.

1958

15. "Maryland Province Jesuit Works on the Dead Sea Scrolls," *Jesuit* (1958) 6–7.
16. "Ébionites," *Dictionnaire de spiritualité* 4/25 (1958) 32–40.
17. "'Peace upon Earth among Men of His Good Will' (Lk 2:14)," *TS* 19 (1958) 225–27.
18. "The Second Phase," *Commonweal* 68 (1 August 1958) 454–55 [review of F. M. Cross, Jr., *The Ancient Library of Qumran and Modern Biblical Studies* (Garden City, NY: Doubleday, 1958)].
19. "The Aramaic Suzerainty Treaty from Sefîre in the Museum of Beirut," *CBQ* 20 (1958) 444–76.
20. "The Book of Books," *Commonweal* 69 (5 December 1958) 253–55 [review of H. Daniel-Rops, *What Is the Bible?* (New York: Hawthorn Books, 1958)].
21. "The Second Edition of the *Lexikon für Theologie und Kirche*," *TS* 19 (1958) 572–85 [under the signature of W. J. Burghardt; mine is the partial review of NT articles," appearing on 574 ("Among the longer . . .")–576 (". . . fortunate.")].
22. Review of J. Carmignac, *La règle de la guerre des fils de lumière contre les fils de ténèbres*, vol. 1 (Paris: Letouzey et Ané, 1958), *TS* 19 (1958) 606–8.
23. Review of A. Wikenhauser, *New Testament Introduction* (New York: Herder & Herder, 1958), *TS* 20 (1959) 114–16.

1959

24. "Scholars on Scrolls," *Commonweal* 70 (3 April 1959) 30–32 [review of J. van der Ploeg, *The Excavations at Qumran* (London: Longmans, Green, 1958); J. Daniélou, *The Dead Sea Scrolls and Primitive Christianity* (Baltimore: Helicon, 1959)].
25. "The Aramaic Qorbān Inscription from Jebel Ḥallet eṭ-Ṭûri and Mark 7.11/Matt 15.5," *JBL* 78 (1959) 60–65.
26. Review of J. T. Milik, *Ten Years of Discovery in the Wilderness of Judaea* (SBT 26; Naperville: Allenson, 1959), *TS* 20 (1959) 448–51.
27. Review of M.-A. Chevallier, *L'Esprit et le Messie dans le Bas-Judaïsme et le Nouveau Testament* (Paris: Presses universitaires, 1958), *TS* 20 (1959) 451–55.
28. Review of F.-W. Eltester, *Eikon im Neuen Testament* (BZNW 23; Berlin: Töpelmann, 1958), *TS* 20 (1959) 459–62.
29. Review of *Bibliographie biblique* (Montreal: Facultés de Théologie et de Philosophie S.J., 1958), *TS* 20 (1959) 480–81.
30. Review of O. Karrer, *Neues Testament, übersetzt und erklärt* (Munich: Ars Sacra, 1959), *Woodstock Letters* 88 (1959) 433.
31. "The Oxyrhynchus *Logoi* of Jesus and the Coptic Gospel according to Thomas," *TS* 20 (1959) 505–60.

1960

32. Review of L. Cerfaux, *Christ in the Theology of St. Paul* (New York: Herder and Herder, 1959), *TS* 21 (1960) 164–65.
33. Review of A. Adam, *Die Psalmen des Thomas und das Perlenlied als Zeugnisse vorchristlicher Gnosis* (BZNW 24; Berlin: Töpelmann, 1959), *TS* 21 (1960) 165.
34. Review of F. F. Bruce, *Biblical Exegesis in the Qumran Texts* (Grand Rapids: Eerdmans, 1959), *CBQ* 22 (1960) 234–36.
35. Review of C. E. B. Cranfield, *The Gospel according to Saint Mark* (Cambridge: University Press, 1959), *TS* 21 (1960) 285–88.

36. Review of E. Hennecke-W. Schneemelcher, *Neutestamentliche Apokryphen in deutscher Übersetzung,* vol. 1 (Tübingen: Mohr, 1959), *TS* 21 (1960) 292–94 [see #121].
37. Review of R. M. Grant, *Gnosticism and Early Christianity* (New York: Columbia University, 1959), *TS* 21 (1960) 294–97.
38. Review of A. Guillaumont, H.-Ch. Puech, G. Quispel, W. Till and Y. 'Abd-al-Masîh, *The Gospel according to Thomas* (Leiden: Brill; New York: Harper, 1959), *TS* 21 (1960) 297–99.
39. "Some Observations on the Genesis Apocryphon," *CBQ* 22 (1960) 277–91.
40. Review of K. Grobel, *The Gospel of Truth: A Valentinian Meditation on the Gospel* (Nashville: Abingdon, 1960), *CBQ* 22 (1960) 358–59.
41. Review of U. Wilckens, *Weisheit und Torheit* (BHT 26; Tübingen: Mohr, 1959), *TS* 21 (1960) 468–70.
42. Review of B. M. Metzger, *Index to Periodical Literature on the Apostle Paul* (NTTS 1; Leiden: Brill, 1960), *TS* 21 (1960) 643–44.

1961

43. "Simon, Saint," *Encyclopaedia Britannica* 20 (1961) 695.
44. Review of E. P. Arbez and M. R. P. Maguire, *Guide to the Bible* (2d ed.; New York: Desclée, 1960), *TS* 22 (1961) 151.
45. "The Date of the Qumran Scrolls," *America* 104 (18 March 1961) 780–81.
46. (Co-authored with G. S. Glanzman) *An Introductory Bibliography for the Study of Scripture* (Woodstock Papers 5; Westminster, MD: Newman, 1961).
47. Review of J. M. Allegro, *The Treasure of the Copper Scroll* (Garden City, NY: Doubleday, 1960), *TS* 22 (1961) 292–96.
48. Review of B. M. Metzger et al., *A Bibliography of Bible Study for Theological Students* (Princeton Seminary Pamphlets 1; 2d rev. ed.; Princeton: Princeton Theological Seminary, 1960), *TS* 22 (1961) 329–30.
49. Review of S. Wagner, *Die Essener in der wissenschaftlichen Diskussion* (BZAW 79; Berlin: Töpelmann, 1960), *TS* 22 (1961) 333–34.
50. Review of L. Morris, *The First and Second Epistles to the Thessalonians* (NICNT; Grand Rapids: Eerdmans, 1959), *Bibbia e Oriente* 3 (1961) 118.
51. "Qumrân and the Interpolated Paragraph in 2 Cor 6,14–7,1," *CBQ* 23 (1961) 271–80 [see #383].
52. Review of O. Betz, *Offenbarung und Schriftforschung in der Qumransekte* (WUNT 6; Tübingen: Mohr, 1960), *CBQ* 23 (1961) 373–74.
53. "The Use of Explicit Old Testament Quotations in Qumran Literature and in the New Testament," *NTS* 7 (1960–61) 297–333.
54. "A Recent Roman Scriptural Controversy," *TS* 22 (1961) 426–44 [reprinted by offset at P.I.B. in Rome at time of Vatican Council II for distribution to English-speaking bishops].
55. Review of J. Dupont, *Les sources du livre des Actes* (Bruges: Desclée de Brouwer, 1960), *TS* 22 (1961) 468–70.
56. "A Note on Ez 16,30," *CBQ* 23 (1961) 460–62.
57. Review of G. Eichholz, *Glaube und Werk bei Paulus und Jakobus* (Theologische Existenz heute 88; Munich: Kaiser, 1961) *CBQ* 23 (1961) 524–25.
58. Review of A. Adam, *Antike Berichte über die Essener* (KlT 182; Berlin: de Gruyter, 1961), *CBQ* 23 (1961) 528 [see #243].
59. Review of H. Conzelmann, *The Theology of St. Luke* (New York: Harper, 1961), *TS* 22 (1961) 663–65.

60. Review of E. de Strycker, *La forme la plus ancienne du Protévangile de Jacques* (Brussels: Société des Bollandistes, 1961), *TS* 22 (1961) 707-8.

1962

61. Review of G. E. Wright and D. N. Freedman, *The Biblical Archaeologist Reader* (Chicago: Quadrangle Books, 1961), *CBQ* 24 (1962) 98-99.
62. "The Padua Aramaic Papyrus Letters," *JNES* 21 (1962) 15-24.
63. (Co-authored with G. S. Glanzman) *An Introductory Bibliography for the Study of Scripture* (Woodstock Paper 5; Westminster: Newman, 1962) [2d printing, slightly corrected].
64. Review of J. Carmignac and P. Guilbert, *Les textes de Qumran traduits et annotés I* (Paris: Letouzey et Ané, 1961), *TS* 23 (1962) 109-11 [see ##105, 118].
65. Review of S. E. Johnson, *A Commentary on the Gospel According to St. Mark* (HNTC; New York: Harper, 1961), *TS* 23 (1962) 113-15.
66. "The Aramaic Inscriptions of Sefîre I and II," *JAOS* 81 (1961, appeared in March 1962) 178-222.
67. "Papyrus Bodmer XIV: Some Features of Our Oldest Text of Luke," *CBQ* 24 (1962) 170-79.
68. Abstract of "A Recent Roman Scriptural Controversy," *NTA* 6 (1961-62) 161-62 (#378).
69. Review of *Quaestiones disputatae 1,2,3* (New York: Herder and Herder, 1961), *Perspectives* 7 (1962) 51-52.
70. Review of J. Pfammatter, *Die Kirche als Bau: Eine exegetisch-theologische Studie zur Ekklesiologie der Paulusbriefe* (AnGreg 110; Rome: Gregorian University, 1960), *TS* 23 (1962) 288-90.
71. Review of J. D. Yoder, *Concordance to the Distinctive Greek Text of Codex Bezae* (NTTS 2; Leiden: Brill, 1961), *TS* 23 (1962) 341-42.
72. Review of *La sainte Bible . . .* (Jean, Epîtres catholiques, Apocalypse, Epîtres de la captivité, Luc) (Paris: Cerf, 1959-61), *TS* 23 (1962) 343-44.
73. "The Spiritual Exercises of St. Ignatius and Recent Gospel Study," *Woodstock Letters* 91 (1962) 246-74 [reprinted separately by "Program to Promote the Spiritual Exercises," Jersey City, NJ].
74. Review of P. Benoit, *Exégèse et Théologie I-II* (Paris: Cerf, 1961), *JAOS* 82 (1962) 80-81.
75. "Memory and Manuscript: The Origins and Transmission of the Gospel Tradition," *TS* 23 (1962) 442-57 [reprinted separately by the Theology Department of John Carroll University, Cleveland, Ohio].
76. Review of R. Schnackenburg, *La théologie du Nouveau Testament: Etat de la question* (Bruges: Desclée de Brouwer, 1961), *TS* 23 (1962) 461-63.
77. Review of E. Lövestam, *Son and Saviour* (ConNT 18; Lund: Gleerup, 1961), *TS* 23 (1962) 467-69.
78. Review of *"Mélanges offerts au Père René Mouterde pour son 80e anniversaire I* (= *MUSJ* 37 [1960-61]), *TS* 23 (1962) 502-3 [see #97].
79. Review of *La sainte Bible . . .* (Matthieu, Marc) (Paris: Cerf, 1961), *TS* 23 (1962) 506-7.
80. Review of J. Levie, *The Bible, Word of God in Words of Men* (New York: Kenedy, 1962), *Woodstock Letters* 91 (1962) 403-4.

1963

81. Review of J. Carmignac, *Christ and the Teacher of Righteousness* (Baltimore: Helicon, 1962), *America* 108 (5 January 1963) 26.

82. "The Bar Cochba Period," *The Bible in Current Catholic Thought: Gruenthaner Memorial Volume* (ed. J. L. McKenzie; New York: Herder and Herder, 1962) 133–68.
83. "Foreword" to L. Alonso Schökel, *Understanding Biblical Research* (tr. by P. J. McCord; New York: Herder and Herder, 1963) v–ix.
84. "The Name Simon," *HTR* 56 (1963) 1–5.
85. Review of J. E. Ménard, *L'évangile de vérité* (Paris: Letouzey et Ané, 1962), *CBQ* 25 (1963) 195–96.
86. Review of M. Bouttier, *En Christ: Etude d'exégèse et de théologie pauliniennes* (Paris: Presses universitaires de France, 1962), *TS* 24 (1963) 296–99.
87. Review of C. F. Pfeiffer and E. F. Harrison (eds.), *The Wycliffe Bible Commentary* (Chicago: Moody, 1962), *TS* 24 (1963) 328–29.
88. Review of J. A. T. Robinson, *Twelve New Testament Studies* (SBT 34; Naperville: Allenson, 1962), *TS* 24 (1963) 331.
89. Review of F. W. Maier, *Paulus als Kirchengründer und kirchlicher Organisator* (Würzburg: Echter-Verlag, 1961), *TS* 24 (1963) 332.
90. Review of H. E. W. Turner and H. Montefiore, *Thomas and the Evangelists* (SBT 35; Naperville: Allenson, 1962), *TS* 24 (1963) 335.
91. "'Now This Melchizedek . . .' (Heb 7, 1)," *CBQ* 25 (1963) 305–21.
92. Review of B. Rigaux, *Saint Paul et ses lettres* (Bruges: Desclée de Brouwer, 1962), *TS* 24 (1963) 473–76.
93. Review of J. Barr, *Biblical Words for Time* (SBT 33; Naperville: Allenson, 1962), *TS* 24 (1963) 524–25.
94. Review of M. E. Dahl, *The Resurrection of the Body: A Study of I Corinthians 15* (SBT 36; Naperville: Allenson, 1962), *TS* 24 (1963) 528–29.
95. Review of J. Steinmann, *The Life of Jesus* (New York: Little, 1963), *America* 109 (9 November 1963) 597–98.
96. Review of R. M. Grant, *A Historical Introduction to the New Testament* (New York: Harper & Row, 1963), *TS* 24 (1963) 671–73.
97. Review of *Mélanges offerts au Père René Mouterde . . . II* (= *MUSJ* 38), *TS* 24 (1963) 714 [see #78].

1964

98. "The Name Simon—A Further Discussion," *HTR* 57 (1964) 60–61.
99. "The Story of the Dishonest Manager (Lk 16:1-13)," *TS* 25 (1964) 23–42.
100. Review of L. F. Hartman (ed.), *Encyclopedic Dictionary of the Bible* (New York: McGraw-Hill, 1963), *TS* 25 (1964) 75–77.
101. Review of A. Feuillet, *L'Apocalypse: Etat de la question* (Bruges: Desclée de Brouwer, 1963), *TS* 25 (1964) 82–85.
102. Review of R. Bultmann, *The History of the Synoptic Tradition* (New York: Harper & Row, 1963), *TS* 25 (1964) 133–34.
103. "The Gospel Truth," *America* 110 (20 June 1964) 844–46 [translated into Polish: "Nowa instrukcja Papieskiej Komisji Biblijnej," *Znak* 16 (1964) 1399–1404].
104. Review of R. Schnackenburg, *Neutestamentliche Theologie* (Munich: Kösel, 1963), *TS* 25 (1964) 309–10.
105. Review of J. Carmignac, H. Cothenet and H. Lignée, *Les textes de Qumran traduits et annotés II* (Paris: Letouzey et Ané, 1963), *CBQ* 26 (1964) 362–63 [see ##64, 118].
106. "Letter to Editor," *America* 111 (8 August 1964) 119.

107. "The Biblical Commission's Instruction on the Historical Truth of the Gospels," *TS* 25 (1964) 386–408 [see ##119, 120, 133]. My translation reprinted: *Bible Interpretation* (Official Catholic Teachings; ed. J. J. Megivern; Wilmington, NC: McGrath Publ. Co., 1978) 391–98. Chinese translation: "Tsungtsuo Shenshing Weiyüanhuei tuei Fuyin lishihtsing te shyüin shih," *Collectanea theologica universitatis Fujen* (Taiwan) 4 (1970) 171–84.

108. Review of G. Kittel (ed.), *Theological Dictionary of the New Testament,* vol. 1 (tr. G. W. Bromiley; Grand Rapids: Eerdmans, 1964), *TS* 25 (1964) 424–27.

109. Review of T. de Kruijf, *Der Sohn des lebendigen Gottes* (AnBib 16; Rome: Biblical Institute, 1962), *TS* 25 (1964) 427–30.

110. "Andrew, Saint," *Encyclopaedia Britannica* (1964 printing), 1. 908 [revised form: 1966 printing, 1. 908].

111. "Bartholomew, Saint," *Encyclopaedia Britannica* (1964 printing), 3. 206.

112. "Luke, Saint," *Encyclopaedia Britannica* (1964 printing), 14. 475–76; (1967 printing) 14. 409–10.

113. "Nathanael," *Encyclopaedia Britannica* (1964 printing), 16. 134; (1967 printing) 16. 50.

114. "Simon, Saint," *Encyclopaedia Britannica* (1964 printing), 20. 695; (1967 printing) 20. 552.

115. Review of B. Gerhardsson, *Tradition and Transmission in Early Christianity* (ConNT 20; Lund: Gleerup, 1964), *CBQ* 26 (1964) 407 [cf. also *TS* 26 (1964) 685].

116. Review of B. M. Metzger, *The Text of the New Testament* (New York: Oxford, 1964), *TToday* 21 (1964) 386–88.

117. Review of L. Deiss, *Synopse de Matthieu, Marc et Luc avec les parallèles de Jean* (2 vols.; Bruges: Desclée de Brouwer, 1963–64), *TS* 25 (1964) 683–84.

118. Review of J. Carmignac, E. Cothenet, and H. Lignée, *Les textes de Qumran traduits et annotés II* (Paris: Letouzey et Ané, 1963), *TS* 25 (1964) 684–85 [see #105].

119. "The 1964 Biblical Commission Instruction on the Historical Truth of the Gospels," *Pathways Through Scripture* (tapes), ser. 2, #5–6 (in two parts) (Purchase, NY: CBA Audio-Visual Aids, 1964) [see #107].

1965

120. *The Historical Truth of the Gospels: The 1964 Instruction of the Biblical Commission* (Paulist Pamphlet; Glen Rock, NJ: Paulist Press, 1965). Pp. 32 [reprint, with slight corrections, of #107].

121. Review of E. Hennecke-W. Schneemelcher, *Neutestamentliche Apokryphen,* vol. 2 (3d ed.; Tübingen: Mohr, 1964), *TS* 26 (1965) 116–18 [see #36].

122. "Letter to the Editor," *The Catholic Standard and Times* (Philadelphia, 12 March 1965) 4.

123. "The Aramaic Letter of King Adon to the Egyptian Pharaoh," *Bib* 46 (1965) 41–55.

124. Review of P. Gaechter, *Das Matthäus-Evangelium: Ein Kommentar* (Innsbruck: Tyrolia, 1964), *TS* 26 (1965) 300–303.

125. Review of *Ecole des langues orientales de l'Institut Catholique de Paris: Mémorial du cinquantenaire 1914–1964* (Paris: Bloud et Gay, 1964), *TS* 26 (1965) 338–39.

126. Review of *Apophoreta: Festschrift für Ernst Haenchen* (BZNW 30; Berlin: Töpelmann, 1964), *TS* 26 (1965) 508–9.

127. Review of G. Kittel (ed.), *Theological Dictionary of the New Testament,* vol. 2 (1965), *TS* 26 (1965) 509–10 [see #108].

128. *The Study of the Synoptic Gospels: New Approaches and Outlooks* by Augustin Card. Bea, S.J. (London/Dublin: Geoffrey Chapman; New York: Harper and Row, 1965). Pp. 95 [my revised English translation of *The Historicity of the Gospels* (mimeographed; Rome, 1962), following *La storicità dei Vangeli* (Brescia: Morcelliana, 1964)].

129. "The Aramaic 'Elect of God' Text from Qumran Cave IV," *CBQ* 27 (1965) 348–72.

130. "Anti-Semitism and the Cry of 'All the People' (Mt 27:25)," *TS* 26 (1965) 667–71.

131. Review of *The New Testament of Our Lord and Savior Jesus Christ: Revised Standard Version—Catholic Edition* (Collegeville: St. John's Abbey, 1965), *TS* 26 (1965) 672–75.

132. Review of C. Burchard, *Bibliographie zu den Handschriften vom Toten Meer II* (BZAW 89; Berlin: Töpelmann, 1965), *TS* 26 (1965) 718–19.

133. *Die Wahrheit der Evangelien* (SBS 1; Stuttgart: Katholisches Bibelwerk, 1965). Pp. 56 [German translation and adaptation of #107 and part of #103; 2d slightly corrected German edition, 1966] [see #191].

1966

134. Review of P. Benoit and M.-E. Boismard, *Synopse des quatre évangiles en français avec parallèles des apocryphes et des pères* (Paris: Cerf, 1965), *TS* 27 (1966) 152–53.

135. "Jewish Christianity in Acts in Light of the Qumran Scrolls," *Studies in Luke-Acts: Essays Presented in Honor of Paul Schubert* (ed. L. E. Keck and J. L. Martyn; Nashville: Abingdon, 1966) 233–57.

136. Review of L. H. Feldman, *Josephus, Jewish Antiquities, Books XVIII-XX* (LCL; Cambridge, MA: Harvard University, 1965), *TS* 27 (1966) 311.

137. *The Genesis Apocryphon of Qumran Cave I: A Commentary* (BibOr 18; Rome: Biblical Institute, 1966). Pp. xvi + 232 [see #218].

138. "A Sample of Scrollduggery," *America* 115 (3 September 1966) 227–29 [see #254].

139. Review of B. Gärtner, *The Temple and the Community in Qumran and the New Testament* (SNTSMS 1; Cambridge: University Press, 1965), *TS* 27 (1966) 448–51.

140. Review of A. Isaksson, *Marriage and Ministry in the New Temple* (ASNU 24; Lund: Gleerup, 1965), *TS* 27 (1966) 451–54.

141. "Philip, Saint," *Encyclopaedia Britannica* (1966 printing), 17. 832.

142. "Letter to the Editor," *Harper's Magazine* 233 (October 1966) 6 [mutilated!].

143. "The Son of David Tradition and Matthew 22, 41–46 and Parallels," *Concilium 20: The Dynamism of Biblical Tradition* (Glen Rock, NJ: Paulist Press, 1967) 75–87 [British version: "The Son of David Tradition and Matt. 22. 41–46 and Parallels," *Concilium* 10/2 (December 1966) 40–46; French translation: "La tradition du Fils de David en regard de Mt 22, 41–46 et des écrits parallèles," 67–78; German translation: "Die Davidssohn-Überlieferung und Mt 22,41–46 (und die Parallelstellen)," 780–86; Portuguese translation: "A tradição do filho de David e *Mateus* 22: 41–46 e lugares paralelos," 68–80; Spanish translation: "La tradicion sobre el hijo de David en Mt 22, 41–46 y paralelos," 434–48; Dutch translation: "De Zoon van David-traditie en Mt. 22,41–46 en parallelplaatsen," 74–87].

144. "The Phoenician Inscription from Pyrgi," *JAOS* 86 (1966) 285–97.

1967

145. "Further Light on Melchizedek from Qumran Cave 11," *JBL* 86 (1967) 25–41.

146. Review of the *Jerusalem Bible* (ed. A. Jones; Garden City, NY: Doubleday, 1966), *TS* 28 (1967) 129–31.

147. Review of B. M. Metzger, *Index to Periodical Literature on Christ and the Gospels* (NTTS 6; Leiden: Brill, 1966), and of A. J. Mattill, Jr., and M. B. Mattill, *A Classified Bibliography of Literature on the Acts of the Apostles* (NTTS 7; Leiden: Brill, 1966), *TS* 28 (1967) 140–41.

148. Review of *The Oxford Annotated Bible with the Apocrypha: Revised Standard Version* (ed. H. G. May and B. M. Metzger; New York: Oxford University, 1965), *TS* 28 (1967) 173.

149. Review of *The Greek New Testament* (ed. K. Aland et al.; New York: American Bible Society, 1966), *TS* 28 (1967) 178–79.

150. Review of G. Kittel (ed.), *Theological Dictionary of the New Testament*, vol. 3 (1965), *TS* 28 (1967) 179–80 [see ##108, 127].

151. "Aramaeans," *New Catholic Encyclopedia* (New York: McGraw-Hill, 1967), 1. 735–36.

152. "Aramaic Language, Ancient," *NCE*, 1. 736–37.

153. "Bar Kokhba, Simon (Bar Cocheba)," *NCE*, 2. 82–83.

154. "Dead Sea Scrolls," *NCE*, 4. 676–81.

155. "Qumran Community," *NCE*, 12. 33–35.

156. "Romans, Epistle to the," *NCE*, 12. 635–39.

157. "St. Paul and the Law," *The Jurist* 27 (1967) 18–36.

158. *Pauline Theology: A Brief Sketch* (Englewood Cliffs, NJ: Prentice-Hall, 1967). Pp. viii + 88 [see ##182, 256; Portuguese translation: *Linhas fundamentais da teologia paulina* (Coleção bíblica; São Paulo: Edições Paulinas, 1970)].

159. Review of A. R. C. Leaney, *The Rule of Qumran and Its Meaning: Introduction, Translation and Commentary* (Philadelphia: Westminster, 1966), *TS* 28 (1967) 363–65.

160. *The Aramaic Inscriptions of Sefire* (BibOr 19; Rome: Biblical Institute, 1967). Pp. xiv + 208 + pls.

161. Review of P. Benoit, *Passion et résurrection du Seigneur* (Lire la Bible, 6; Paris: Cerf, 1966), *CBQ* 29 (1967) 597–99.

162. Review of G. Kittel (ed.), *Theological Dictionary of the New Testament*, vol. 4 (1967), *TS* 28 (1967) 873–74 [see ##108, 127, 150].

163. Review of F. Rosenthal (ed.), *An Aramaic Handbook* (Porta linguarum orientalium, 10; Wiesbaden: Harrassowitz, 1967), *JBL* 86 (1967) 478–79.

1968

164. "The Spiritual Exercises of St. Ignatius and Recent Gospel Study," *Jesuit Spirit in a Time of Change* (ed. R. A. Schroth et al.; Westminster, MD: Newman, 1968) 153–81 [reprint of #73].

165. Review of K. Rahner, *Belief Today* (Theological Meditations 3), *Religious Education* 63 (1968) 149–50.

166. Review of M. Yizhar, *Bibliography of Hebrew Publications on the Dead Sea Scrolls 1948–1964* (HTS 23; Cambridge: Harvard University, 1967), *JBL* 87 (1968) 116.

167. Review of B. Vawter, *The Four Gospels: An Introduction* (Garden City, NY: Doubleday, 1967), *TS* 29 (1968) 318–20.

168. Review of M. McNamara, *The New Testament and the Palestinian Targum to the Pentateuch* (AnBib 27; Rome: Biblical Institute, 1966), *TS* 29 (1968) 322–26.

169. Review of M. Black, *An Aramaic Approach to the Gospels and Acts* (3d ed.; Oxford: Clarendon, 1967), *CBQ* 30 (1968) 417–28.

170. Review of A.-M. Denis, *Les thèmes de connaissance dans le Document de Damas* (Studia hellenistica, 15; Louvain: Publications universitaires, 1967), *JBL* 87 (1968) 341–43.

171. Review of F. V. Filson, *'Yesterday': A Study of Hebrews in the Light of Chapter 13* (SBT 2/4; Naperville: Allenson, 1967), *TS* 29 (1968) 565–67.

172. (Co-edited with R. E. Brown, S.S., and R. E. Murphy, O.Carm.), *The Jerome Biblical Commentary* (2 vols. in one; Englewood Cliffs, NJ: Prentice-Hall, 1968). Pp. xxxviii + 638 + 889 [the following ten articles in the *JBC* were authored (in whole or in part) by Joseph A. Fitzmyer, S.J.].

173. "Acts of the Apostles," *JBC*, art. 45; 2. 165–214 [co-author: R. J. Dillon].

174. "A Life of Paul," *JBC*, art. 46; 2. 215–22.

175. "New Testament Epistles," *JBC*, art. 47; 2. 223–26.

176. "The Letter to the Galatians," *JBC*, art. 49; 2. 236–46.

177. "The Letter to the Philippians," *JBC*, art. 50; 2. 247–53.
178. "The Letter to the Romans," *JBC*, art. 53; 2. 291–331.
179. "The Letter to Philemon," *JBC*, art. 54; 2. 332–33.
180. "The First Epistle of Peter," *JBC*, art. 58; 2. 362–68.
181. "A History of Israel," *JBC*, art. 75; 2. 692–702 [co-authors: A. G. Wright, S.S., and R. E. Murphy, O.Carm.].
182. "Pauline Theology," *JBC*, art. 79; 2. 800–827 [a slightly revised form of #158].
183. "A Feature of Qumran Angelology and the Angels of 1 Cor 11:10," *Paul and Qumran: Studies in New Testament Exegesis* (ed. J. Murphy-O'Connor; London: Chapman; Chicago: Priory, 1968) 31–47 [with a postscript of 1966 (pp. 45–47); otherwise a reprint of #13].
184. "Thoughts About Preaching on the Gospels," *Insta* 28 (1968) 45–47. [*Insta:* San Jose Seminary, Quezon City, P.I.]

1969

185. "A Bibliographical Aid to the Study of the Qumran Cave IV Texts 158–186," *CBQ* 31 (1969) 59–71.
186. Review of I. de la Potterie, *De Jésus aux Evangiles: Tradition et rédaction dans les évangiles synoptiques* (BETL 25; Gembloux: Duculot, 1967), *TS* 30 (1969) 117–20.
187. Review of A. Sand, *Der Begriff "Fleisch" in den paulinischen Hauptbriefen* (Biblische Untersuchungen, 3; Regensburg: Pustet, 1967), *TS* 30 (1969) 122–23.
188. Review of G. Friedrich (ed.), *Theological Dictionary of the New Testament,* vol. 5 (1967), *TS* 30 (1969) 158–59 [see ##108, 127, 150, 162].
189. Review of L. Hartman, *Prophecy Interpreted* (Coniectanea biblica, NT ser. 1; Lund: Gleerup, 1966), *Interpretation* 23 (1969) 249–51.
190. Review of J. M. Allegro, *Qumran Cave 4: I (4Q158-4Q186)* (DJD 5; Oxford: Clarendon, 1968), *CBQ* 31 (1969) 235–38.
191. "Die Wahrheit der Evangelien," *Theologisches Jahrbuch* (ed. A. Dänhardt; Leipzig: St. Benno-Verlag) 12 (1969) 121–38 [reprint of #133].
192. Review of V. P. Furnish, *Theology and Ethics in Paul* (Nashville: Abingdon, 1968), *Perkins School of Theology Journal* 22 (1969) 113–15.
193. Review of J. W. Etheridge, *The Targums of Onkelos and Jonathan ben Uzziel on the Pentateuch with the Fragments of the Jerusalem Targum* (New York: Ktav, 1968), *TS* 30 (1969) 370.
194. Review of H. Haag, *Is Original Sin in Scripture?* (New York: Sheed and Ward, 1969), *CBQ* 31 (1969) 430–31.
195. Review of B. Rigaux, *The Letters of St. Paul: Modern Studies* (tr. S. Yonick; Chicago: Franciscan Herald, 1968), *TS* 30 (1969) 546–47.
196. Review of R. Bultmann, *Faith and Understanding I* (New York: Harper & Row, 1969), *TS* 30 (1969) 547–48.
197. Review of *In Memoriam Paul Kahle* (ed. M. Black and G. Fohrer; BZAW 103; Berlin: Töpelmann, 1968), *JBL* 88 (1969) 346–48.
198. "The Catholic Biblical Quarterly Monograph Series: An Experimental Policy," *CBQ* 31 (1969) 533–35.
199. Review of M. D. Johnson, *The Purpose of the Biblical Genealogies with Special Reference to the Setting of the Genealogies of Jesus* (SNTSMS 8; Cambridge: University Press, 1969), *TS* 30 (1969) 700–704.
200. Review of W. R. Farmer, *Synopticon: The Verbal Agreement between the Greek Texts of Matthew, Mark and Luke Contextually Exhibited* (Cambridge: University Press, 1969), *TS* 30 (1969) 742–43.

201. Review of G. Friedrich (ed.), *Theological Dictionary of the New Testament*, vol. 6 (1968), *TS* 30 (1969) 743–44 [see ##108, 127, 150, 162, 188].

202. "A Further Note on the Aramaic Inscription Sefîre III.22," *JSS* 14 (1969) 197–200.

1970

203. Review of A. Díez Macho, *Neophyti 1: Targum palestinense. Ms de la Biblioteca Vaticana. Tomo I: Génesis* (Textos y estudios, 7; Madrid: Consejo superior de investigaciones científicas, 1968), *CBQ* 32 (1970) 107–12 [see ##241, 305, 378].

204. "'To Know Him and the Power of His Resurrection' (Phil 3.10)," *Mélanges bibliques en hommage au R. P. Béda Rigaux* (ed. A. Descamps and A. de Halleux; Gembloux: Duculot, 1970) 411–25.

205. Review of K. Stendahl, *The School of St. Matthew and Its Use of the Old Testament with a New Introduction by the Author* (Philadelphia: Fortress, 1968), *JBL* 89 (1970) 250.

206. "The Priority of Mark and the 'Q' Source in Luke," *Jesus and Man's Hope* (Pittsburgh: Pittsburgh Theological Seminary, 1970), 1. 131–70 [never given opportunity to proofread!].

207. Review of P. van der Osten-Sacken, *Gott und Belial* (SUNT 6; Göttingen: Vandenhoeck & Ruprecht, 1969), *CBQ* 32 (1970) 468–69.

208. "Marinating the Mushroom," *America* 123 (26 September 1970) 206–7.

209. Review of J. Finegan, *The Archeology of the New Testament* (Princeton: Princeton University, 1969), *Journal of Church History* 39 (1970) 391–92.

210. "Prolegomenon," Reprint of S. Schechter, *Documents of Jewish Sectaries* (The Library of Biblical Studies; 2 vols. in one; New York: Ktav, 1970) 9–37.

211. Review of R. J. Austgen, *Natural Motivation in the Pauline Epistles* (Notre Dame: University of Notre Dame, 1969), *TS* 31 (1970) 584–85.

212. "The Languages of Palestine in the First Century A.D.," *CBQ* 32 (1970) 501–31.

213. Review of B. Peckham, S.J., *The Development of Late Phoenician Scripts* (HSS 20; Cambridge, MA: Harvard University, 1968), *JSS* 15 (1970) 267–68.

214. Review of R. Degen, *Altaramäische Grammatik der Inschriften des 10.-8. Jh. v. Chr.* (Abh. f. d. Kunde des Morgenlandes im Auftrage d. deut. morgenl. Gesellschaft, 38/3; Wiesbaden: DMG, 1969), *Orientalia* 39 (1970) 580–84.

215. "New Testament Biblical Preaching for the 70's," *Preaching* 5/5 (1970) 1–18 [beware of howlers!].

216. *Essays on the Semitic Background of the New Testament* (London: Chapman, 1971). Pp. xx + 524 [see #271].

217. "A Re-Study of an Elephantine Aramaic Marriage Contract (*AP* 15)," *Near Eastern Studies in Honor of William Foxwell Albright* (ed. H. Goedicke; Baltimore/London: Johns Hopkins, 1971) 137–68.

218. *The Genesis Apocryphon of Qumran Cave I: A Commentary* (BibOr 18A; 2d rev. ed.; Rome: Biblical Institute, 1971). Pp. xvi + 260 [see #137].

219. Review of E. C. Colwell, *Studies in Methodology in Textual Criticism of the New Testament* (NTTS 9; Grand Rapids: Eerdmans, 1969), *TS* 32 (1971) 346.

220. Review of L. Rost, *Einleitung in die alttestamentlichen Apokryphen und Pseudepigraphen, einschliesslich der grossen Qumran-Handschriften* (Heidelberg: Quelle und Meyer, 1971), *JBL* 90 (1971) 346–47.

221. Review of B. Mazar et al., *Encyclopaedia of Archaeological Excavations in the Holy Land* (2 vols.; Jerusalem: Israel Exploration Society, 1970), *JBL* 90 (1971) 349–50.

222. Review of M. Barth et al., *Foi et salut selon S. Paul (Épître aux Romains 1, 16)* (AnBib 42; Rome: Biblical Institute, 1970), *JBL* 90 (1971) 375.

223. Review of *Der Ruf Jesu und die Antwort der Gemeinde: Festschrift für Joachim Jeremias* (ed. E. Lohse et al.; Göttingen: Vandenhoeck & Ruprecht, 1970), *JBL* 90 (1971) 376.
224. Review of *Mélanges offerts à M. Maurice Dunand I* (= *MUSJ* 45 [1969, appeared 1970]), *JBL* 90 (1971) 376–77 [see #250].

1972

225. Review of L. Moraldi, *I manoscritti di Qumrān* (Turin: Unione Tipografico, 1971), *CBQ* 34 (1972) 95–97.
226. *Commentario biblico 'San Jeronimo'* (5 vols.; Madrid: Ediciones Cristiandad, 1972) [Spanish version of #172].
227. Review of John C. L. Gibson, *Textbook of Syrian Semitic Inscriptions: Volume 1, Hebrew and Moabite Inscriptions* (Oxford: Clarendon, 1971), *JBL* 91 (1972) 109–12 [see #327].
228. Review of G. Friedrich (ed.), *Theological Dictionary of the New Testament*, vol. 7 (1971), *TS* 33 (1972) 172–73 [see ##108, 127, 150, 162, 188, 201].
229. Review of J. Bowker, *The Targums and Rabbinic Literature: An Introduction to Jewish Interpretations of Scripture* (Cambridge: University Press, 1969), *JNES* 31 (1972) 54–56.
230. Review of A. G. Lamadrid, *Los descubrimientos del Mar Muerto* (BAC 317; Madrid: La editorial católica, 1971), *JBL* 91 (1972) 277.
231. Review of *Index to Festschriften in Jewish Studies* (ed. C. Berlin; New York: Ktav, 1971), and of *Index of Articles Relative to Jewish History and Literature Published in Periodicals, from 1665 to 1900* (ed. M. Schwab; New York: Ktav, 1971), *JBL* 91 (1972) 277–78.
232. Review of E. Käsemann, *Perspectives on Paul* (Philadelphia: Fortress, 1971), *TS* 33 (1972) 325–28.
233. "A Qumran Fragment of Mark?" *America* 126 (24 June 1972) 647–50.
234. "David, 'Being Therefore a Prophet' (Acts 2:30)," *CBQ* 34 (1972) 332–39.
235. "The Use of *Agein* and *Pherein* in the Synoptic Gospels," *Festschrift to Honor F. Wilbur Gingrich: Lexicographer, Scholar, Teacher and Committed Christian Layman* (ed. E. H. Barth and R. E. Cocroft; Leiden: Brill, 1972) 147–60.
236. Review of R. Brownrigg, *Who's Who in the New Testament* (New York: Holt, Rinehart, and Winston, 1971), *JBL* 91 (1972) 438–39.
237. Review of E. Haenchen, *The Acts of the Apostles: A Commentary* (Philadelphia: Westminster, 1971), *TS* 33 (1972) 582–85.
238. Review of E. Lohse, *Colossians and Philemon* (Hermeneia; Philadelphia: Fortress, 1971), *Review of Books and Religion* 2 (October 1972) 10.
239. Review of M. Martin, *Three Popes and the Cardinal* (New York: Farrar, Straus and Giroux, 1972), *CBQ* 34 (1972) 515–16.
240. "1972 Report of the Editor of the Journal of Biblical Literature," *CSR Bulletin* 3/5 (1972) 21–26.
241. Review of A. Díez Macho, *Neophyti 1: Targum palestinense, Ms. de la Biblioteca Vaticana. Tomo II: Exodo, JBL* 91 (1972) 575–78 [see ##203, 305, 378].
242. Review of B. Mazar et al., *Encyclopaedia of Archaeological Discoveries in the Holy Land* (Jerusalem: Israel Exploration Society, 1970), *Ariel* 31 (1972) 119–20 [reprint of #221; also in the Spanish edition of *Ariel* 25 (1972) 119–20; French, *Ariel* 27 (1972) 117–18 (slightly abridged)].
243. Review of A. Adam, *Antike Berichte über die Essener* (2d ed. rev. by C. Burchard; KIT 182; Berlin: de Gruyter, 1972), *JBL* 92 (1973) 155 [see #58].
244. Review of G. Friedrich (ed.), *Theological Dictionary of the New Testament*, vol. 8 (1972), *TS* 34 (1973) 147–48 [see ##108, 127, 150, 162, 188, 201, 228].

1973

245. Review of J. C. O'Neill, *The Recovery of Paul's Letter to the Galatians* (London: SPCK, 1972), *TS* 34 (1973) 150–52.
246. Review of J. A. Ziesler, *The Meaning of Righteousness in Paul: A Linguistic and Theological Enquiry* (SNTSMS 20; Cambridge: University Press, 1972), *TS* 34 (1973) 154–57.
247. Review of A. Díez Macho, *El Targum: Introducción a las traducciones aramaicas de la Biblia* (Barcelona: Consejo Superior de Investigaciones científicas, 1972), *CBQ* 35 (1973) 233–35.
248. Review of F. Montagnini, *Rom. 5,12-14 alla luce del dialogo rabbinico* (Supplementi alla Rivista biblica 4; Brescia: Paideia, 1971), *CBQ* 35 (1973) 255–56.
249. Review of E. Osty, *La Bible* (Lausanne: Ed. Rencontre, 1970–72), *JBL* 92 (1973) 279–80.
250. Review of *Mélanges offerts à M. Maurice Dunand II* (= *MUSJ* 46 [1970–71]), *JBL* 92 (1973) 321–22 [see #224].
251. Review of M. Didier (ed.), *L'évangile selon Matthieu* (BETL 29; Gembloux: Duculot, 1972), *JBL* 92 (1973) 322.
252. "How to Exploit a Secret Gospel," *America* 128 (23 June 1973) 570–72.
253. Review of E. Vogt, *Lexicon linguae aramaicae Veteris Testamenti* (Rome: Biblical Institute, 1971), *Bib* 54 (1973) 131–35.
254. "A Sample of Scrollduggery," *Christianity for the Tough-Minded: Essays in Support of an Intellectually Defensible Religious Commitment* (ed. J. W. Montgomery; Minneapolis: Bethany Fellowship, 1973), Appendix B, pp. 272–79 [revised form of #138].
255. "Letter to the Editor: Reply to Morton Smith," *America* 129 (4 August 1973) 64–65 [apropos of #252].
256. *Paulinsk teologi: En introduktion* (Stockholm: Almqvist & Wiksell, 1973). Pp. 104 (tr. H. Backman; Swedish translation of #158].
257. Review of B. M. Metzger, *A Textual Commentary on the Greek New Testament* (New York: United Bible Societies, 1971), *TS* 34 (1973) 522–23.
258. Review of B. Jongeling, *A Classified Bibliography of the Finds in the Desert of Judah 1958–1969* (Leiden: Brill, 1971), *JBL* 92 (1973) 624–26.
259. Review of *Scrolls from Qumran Cave I: The Great Isaiah Scroll, the Order of the Community, the Pesher to Habakkuk* (Jerusalem: Albright Institute of Archaeological Research and the Shrine of the Book, 1972), *JBL* 92 (1973) 628–30.
260. "The Virginal Conception of Jesus in the New Testament," *TS* 34 (1973) 541–75.
261. Review of K. Aland (ed.), *Synopsis of the Four Gospels: Greek-English Edition of the Synopsis Quattuor Evangeliorum* (Stuttgart: UBS, 1972), *TS* 34 (1973) 756–57.

1974

262. Review of B. Grossfeld, *A Bibliography of Targum Literature* (Bibliographica judaica, 2; Cincinnati: HUC, 1972), *JBL* 93 (1974) 135–36.
263. Review of J. M. Robinson (ed.), *The Future of Our Religious Past: Essays in Honor of Rudolf Bultmann* (New York: Harper & Row, 1971), *JBL* 93 (1974) 152–53.
264. Review of *Solomon Zeitlin's Studies in the Early History of Judaism* (New York: Ktav, 1973), *JBL* 93 (1974) 153–54 [see ##284, 306].
265. Review of F. Neirynck (ed.), *L'Evangile de Luc: Problèmes littéraires et théologiques: Mémorial Lucien Cerfaux* (Gembloux: Duculot, 1973) *JBL* 93 (1974) 154.
266. (Co-edited with R. E. Brown and R. E. Murphy) *Grande commentario biblico* (Brescia: Queriniana, 1973). Pp. 1974 [Italian translation of #172].
267. "Some Notes on Aramaic Epistolography," *JBL* 93 (1974) 201–25 [see #399].

268. Review of the *Annual of the Swedish Theological Institute 9 (1973): Festschrift Hans Kosmala* (Leiden: Brill, 1974), *JBL* 93 (1974) 487.

269. Review of J.-E. Ménard (ed.), *Exégèse biblique et judaïsme* (Strasbourg: Faculté de théologie catholique, 1973), *JBL* 93 (1974) 487.

270. "The Contribution of Qumran Aramaic to the Study of the New Testament," *NTS* 20 (1973-74) 382-407.

271. *Essays on the Semitic Background of the New Testament* (SBLSBS 5; Missoula, MT: Scholars Press, 1974). Pp. xix + 524 [paperback reprint of #216].

272. Review of *The Oxford Dictionary of the Christian Church* (ed. F. L. Cross and E. A. Livingstone; Oxford: Clarendon, 1974), *JBL* 93 (1974) 481-82.

273. Review of G. Friedrich (ed.), *Theological Dictionary of the New Testament,* vol. 9 (1973), *TS* 35 (1974) 550-52 [see ##108, 127, 150, 162, 188, 201, 228, 244].

274. "Belief in Jesus Today," *Commonweal* 101 (15 November 1974) 137-42.

275. Review of S. G. Wilson, *The Gentiles and the Gentile Mission in Luke-Acts* (SNTSMS 23; Cambridge: University Press, 1973), *TS* 35 (1974) 741-44.

276. Review of E. Käsemann, *An die Römer* (HNT 8a; Tübingen: Mohr, 1973), *TS* 35 (1974) 744-47.

277. Review of B. Porten, *Archives from Elephantine* (Berkeley, CA: University of California, 1968), *JARCE* 10 (1973 [appeared January 1975]) 123-25.

278. "Some Observations on the Targum of Job from Qumran Cave 11," *Patrick W. Skehan Festschrift* (= *CBQ* 36/4 [1974] 503-24).

279. Review of D. M. Hay, *Glory at the Right Hand: Psalm 110 in Early Christianity* (SBLMS 18; Nashville: Abingdon, 1973), *CBQ* 36 (1974) 594-95.

1975

280. "Methodology in the Study of the Aramaic Substratum of Jesus' Sayings in the New Testament," *Jésus aux origines de la Christologie* (ed. J. Dupont; BETL 40; Gembloux: Duculot; Louvain: Leuven University, 1975) 73-102.

281. Review of *Studies in Jewish Legal History in Honour of David Daube* (= *JJS* 25/1, Special Issue, February 1974), *JBL* 94 (1975) 161.

282. Review of *Opuscula exegetica aboensia in honorem Rafael Gyllenberg octogenarii* (Åbo: Åbo Akademi, 1973), *JBL* 94 (1975) 161.

283. "Correction," *CBQ* 37 (1975) 238.

284. Review of *Solomon Zeitlin's Studies in the Early History of Judaism,* vol. 2 (New York: Ktav, 1974), *JBL* 94 (1975) 322-23 [see ##264, 306].

285. Review of *Harper's Bible Dictionary* (ed. M. S. Miller and J. L. Miller; 8th ed.; New York: Harper & Row, 1973), *JBL* 94 (1975) 323.

286. Review of *The Jewish People in the First Century: Historical Geography, Political History, Social, Cultural and Religious Life and Institutions* (Philadelphia: Fortress, 1974), *TS* 36 (1975) 335-38.

287. *The Dead Sea Scrolls: Major Publications and Tools for Study* (SBLSBS 8; Missoula: Scholars Press, 1975). Pp. xiv + 171.

288. *Teología de san Pablo: Síntesis y perspectivas* (Epifanía, 19; Madrid: Ediciones cristiandad, 1975). Pp. 202 [Spanish translation of #158, revised and expanded to include "A Life of Paul" (*JBC* #46)].

289. Review of S. H. Levey, *The Messiah: An Aramaic Interpretation: The Messianic Exegesis of the Targum* (Monographs of Hebrew Union College, 2; Cincinnati: Hebrew Union College, 1974), *JBL* 94 (1975) 473-77.

290. Review of N. A. Dahl, *The Crucified Messiah and Other Essays* (Minneapolis: Augsburg, 1974), *JBL* 94 (1975) 483.
291. Review of *Sparsa Collecta: The Collected Essays of W. C. van Unnik: Part One: Evangelia— Paulina—Acta* (NovTSup 29; Leiden: Brill, 1973), *JBL* 94 (1975) 483–84.
292. Review of G. J. Botterweck and H. Ringgren, *Theological Dictionary of the Old Testament 1: 'ābh—bādhādh* (Grand Rapids: Eerdmans, 1975), *TS* 36 (1975) 510–13 [see #331].
293. "Paul and the Law," *A Companion to Paul: Readings in Pauline Theology* (ed. M. J. Taylor; Staten Island, NY: Alba House, 1975) 73–87 [an abridgement of #157].
294. Review of P. Grelot, *Documents araméens d'Egypte* (Paris: Cerf, 1972), *Bib* 56 (1975) 254–56.
295. "Reconciliation in Pauline Theology," *No Famine in the Land: Studies in Honor of John L. McKenzie* (ed. J. W. Flanagan and A. W. Robinson; Missoula, MT: Scholars Press, 1975) 155–77.
296. "Der semitische Hintergrund des neutestamentlichen Kyriostitels," *Jesus Christus in Historie und Theologie: Neutestamentliche Festschrift für Hans Conzelmann* (ed. G. Strecker; Tübingen: Mohr, 1975) 267–98.
297. Review of R. de Vaux, *Archaeology and the Dead Sea Scrolls* (New York: Oxford University, 1973), *JBL* 94 (1975) 628.
298. Review of *Josephus-Studien: Untersuchungen zu Josephus, dem antiken Judentum und dem Neuen Testament: Otto Michel zum 70. Geburtstag gewidmet* (ed. O. Betz et al.; Göttingen: Vandenhoeck & Ruprecht, 1974), *JBL* 94 (1975) 641.
299. Review of *IATG: Internationales Abkürzungsverzeichnis für Theologie und Grenzgebiete* (Berlin: de Gruyter, 1974), *JBL* 94 (1975) 641–42.
300. "The Kerygmatic and Normative Character of the Gospel," *Evangelium—Welt—Kirche: Schlussbericht und Referate der römisch-katholisch/evangelisch-lutherischen Studienkommission "Das Evangelium und die Kirche", 1967–1971 auf Veranlassung des Lutherischen Weltbundes und des Sekretariats für die Einheit der Christen* (ed. H. Meyer; Frankfurt am M.: O. Lembeck und J. Knecht, 1975) 111–28.

1976

301. Review of P.-E. Dion, *La langue de Ya'di* (Editions SR; Waterloo, Ont.: Corporation pour la publication des études académiques en religion au Canada, 1974), *CBQ* 38 (1976) 98–100.
302. Review of *The Published Works of William Foxwell Albright: A Comprehensive Bibliography*, prepared by David Noel Freedman et al. (Cambridge: ASOR, 1975), *JBL* 95 (1976) 168–69.
303. Review of G. Vermes, *Post-Biblical Jewish Studies* (SJLA 8; Leiden: Brill, 1975), *JBL* 95 (1976) 169.
304. "The Matthean Divorce Texts and Some New Palestinian Evidence," *TS* 37 (1976) 197–226.
305. Review of A. Díez Macho, *Neophyti 1: Targum palestinense. Ms de la Biblioteca Vaticana. Tomo III: Lévitico. Edición principe, introducción general y versión castellana* (Textos y estudios, 9; Madrid/Barcelona: Consejo superior de investigaciones científicas, 1971); *Tomo IV: Números* (Textos y estudios, 10; 1974), *JBL* 95 (1976) 315–17 [see ##203, 241, 378].
306. Review of S. Zeitlin's *Studies in the Early History of Judaism*, vol. 3: *Judaism and Christianity* (New York: Ktav, 1975), *JBL* 95 (1976) 328 [see ##264, 284].
307. Review of J. Ernst, *Die Briefe an die Philipper, an Philemon, an die Kolosser, an die Epheser* (Regensburg: Pustet, 1974), *TS* 37 (1976) 485–87.
308. Review of J. O'Callaghan, *Los papiros griegos de la cueva 7 de Qumrân* (BAC 353; Madrid: Editorial católica, 1974), *JBL* 95 (1976) 459.

309. Review of B. Mazar (ed.), *Spr Nlswn Glyq: Nelson Glueck Memorial Volume* (Eretz-Israel, 12; Jerusalem: Israel Exploration Society, 1975), *JBL* 95 (1976) 521–22.

310. Review of J.-E. Ménard, *L'Evangile selon Thomas* (Nag Hammadi Studies, 5; Leiden: Brill, 1975), *CBQ* 38 (1976) 574–76.

311. Review of *La Bible de Jérusalem: La Sainte Bible traduite en français sous la direction de l'Ecole biblique de Jérusalem* (rev. ed.; Paris: Cerf, 1973), *JBL* 95 (1976) 640–41.

312. Review of K. Aland et al., *Vollständige Konkordanz zum griechischen Neuen Testament*, Bd. I, Lief. 1: *A—astheneō* (Berlin: de Gruyter, 1975), *JBL* 95 (1976) 679–81 [see #348].

313. Review of M. de Jonge (ed.), *Studies on the Testaments of the Twelve Patriarchs: Text and Interpretation* (SVTP 3; Leiden: Brill, 1975), *JBL* 95 (1976) 691–92.

314. Review of F. M. Cross and S. Talmon (eds.), *Qumran and the History of the Biblical Text* (Cambridge/London: Harvard University, 1975), *JBL* 95 (1976) 692–93.

315. Review of *Disputation and Dialogue: Readings in the Jewish-Christian Encounter* (ed. F. E. Talmage; New York: Ktav, 1975), *JBL* 95 (1976) 693–94.

1977

316. Review of H. N. Ridderbos, *Paul: An Outline of His Theology* (Grand Rapids: Eerdmans, 1975), *Interpretation* 31 (1977) 75–80.

317. Review of L. H. Schiffman, *The Halakhah at Qumran* (SJLA 16; Leiden: Brill, 1975), *CBQ* 39 (1977) 133–35.

318. Review of N. A. Dahl, *Jesus in the Memory of the Early Church* (Minneapolis: Augsburg, 1976), *JBL* 96 (1977) 155.

319. Review of E. Lipiński, *Studies in Aramaic Inscriptions and Onomastics I* (Louvain: Leuven University, 1975), *CBQ* 39 (1977) 262–63.

320. "Implications of the New Enoch Literature from Qumran," *TS* 38 (1977) 332–45.

321. *The Dead Sea Scrolls: Major Publications and Tools for Study. With an Addendum (January 1977)* (SBLSBS 8; Missoula: Scholars Press, 1977) [Addendum to #287].

322. Review of *Theological Dictionary of the New Testament, 10: Index Volume* (compiled by R. E. Pitkin; Grand Rapids: Eerdmans, 1976), *TS* 38 (1977) 402–3 [see ##108, 127, 150, 162, 188, 201, 228, 244, 273].

323. Review of Michael Grant, *Saint Paul* (New York: Scribner, 1976), *Commonweal* 104/14 (1977) 442–44 [see #325].

324. Review of F. L. Horton, Jr., *The Melchizedek Tradition: A Critical Examination of the Sources to the Fifth Century A.D. and in the Epistle to the Hebrews* (SNTSMS 30; Cambridge: University Press, 1976), *CBQ* 39 (1977) 436–38.

325. "Letter to the Editors," *Commonweal* 104/17 (19 August 1977) 543 [see #323].

326. Review of *The New International Dictionary of New Testament Theology*, Vols. 1–2 (ed. C. Brown; Grand Rapids: Zondervan, 1975–76), *TS* 38 (1977) 560–63.

327. Review of J. C. L. Gibson, *Textbook of Syrian Semitic Inscriptions: Volume II, Aramaic Inscriptions, Including Inscriptions in the Dialect of Zenjirli* (Oxford: Clarendon, 1975), *JBL* 96 (1977) 425–27 [see #227].

328. "Biblical Commission," *Oxford Dictionary of the Christian Church* (2d ed., reprinted; Oxford: Clarendon, 1977) 173.

1978

329. Review of J. Hoftijzer and G. van der Kooij, *Aramaic Texts from Deir 'Alla* (Documenta et monumenta orientis antiqui, 19; Leiden: Brill, 1976), *CBQ* 40 (1978) 93–95.

330. Review of J. K. Elliott (ed.), *Studies in New Testament Language and Text: Essays in Honour of George D. Kilpatrick* (NovTSup 44; Leiden: Brill, 1976), *JAAR* 46 (1978) 370–71.

331. Review of *Theological Dictionary of the Old Testament 1: 'abh—bādhādh; 2: bdl—gālāh* (rev. ed.; Grand Rapids: Eerdmans, 1977), *TS* 39 (1978) 154–56 [see #292].

332. Review of R. de Vaux and J. T. Milik, *Qumrân grotte 4, II: I. Archéologie; II. Tefillin, mezuzot et targums (4Q128—4Q157)* (DJD 6; Oxford: Clarendon, 1977), *TS* 39 (1978) 158–60.

333. Review of W. C. van Unnik (ed.), *La littérature juive entre Tenach et Mischna: Quelques problèmes* (Recherches bibliques, 9; Leiden: Brill, 1974), *JBL* 96 (1977) 625.

334. Review of *The Nag Hammadi Library in English* (ed. J. M. Robinson; New York: Harper & Row, 1978), *America* 138/15 (22 April 1978) 330–31.

335. "Jesus the Lord," *Chicago Studies* 17 (1978) 75–104.

336. Review of *The Interpreter's Dictionary of the Bible: Supplementary Volume* (ed. K. Crim; Nashville: Abingdon, 1976), *JBL* 97 (1978) 105–6.

337. Review of L. Ginzberg, *An Unknown Jewish Sect* (New York: JTSA, 1976), *JBL* 97 (1978) 154–55.

338. Review of J. A. T. Robinson, *Redating the New Testament* (Philadelphia: Westminster, 1976) and *Can We Trust the New Testament?* (Grand Rapids: Eerdmans, 1977), *Interpretation* 32 (1978) 309–13.

339. "Judaic Studies and the Gospels: The Seminar," *The Relationship among the Gospels: An Interdisciplinary Dialogue* (Trinity University Monograph Series in Religion, 5; ed. W. O. Walker, Jr.; San Antonio: Trinity University, 1978) 237–58.

340. (Co-edited with R. E. Brown, K. P. Donfried, and J. Reumann) *Mary in the New Testament* (Philadelphia: Fortress; New York: Paulist, 1978). Pp. xii + 323.

341. (Co-authored with D. J. Harrington, S.J.) *A Manual of Palestinian Aramaic Texts (Second Century B.C.—Second Century A.D.)* (BibOr 34; Rome: Biblical Institute, 1978). Pp. xix + 373.

342. "The Composition of Luke, Chapter 9," *Perspectives on Luke-Acts* (ed. C. H. Talbert; Special Studies Series, 5; Danville, VA: Association of Baptist Professors of Religion; Edinburgh: Clark, 1978) 139–52.

343. "Divorce among First-Century Palestinian Jews," *H. L. Ginsberg Volume* (Eretz-Israel 14; Jerusalem: Israel Exploration Society, 1978) 103*–110* (with an abstract in modern Hebrew, p. 193).

344. "Crucifixion in Ancient Palestine, Qumran Literature, and the New Testament," *CBQ* 40 (1978) 493–513.

345. "The Targum of Leviticus from Qumran Cave 4," *Maarav* 1 (1978) 5–23.

346. Review of B. Jongeling, C. J. Labuschagne, and A. S. van der Woude (eds.), *Aramaic Texts from Qumran with Translations and Annotations* (Semitic Study Series 4; Leiden: Brill, 1976), *JBL* 97 (1978) 464.

347. Review of S. Safrai and M. Stern (eds.), *The Jewish People in the First Century*, vol. 2 (Compendia rerum iudaicarum ad Novum Testamentum, 1/2; Philadelphia: Fortress, 1976), *TS* 39 (1978) 769–71.

348. Review of K. Aland et al., *Vollständige Konkordanz zum griechischen Neuen Testament, Bd. I, Lief. 2, 3–4, 5; Bd. II, Spezialübersichten* (Berlin/New York: de Gruyter, 1976–77, 1978), *JBL* 97 (1978) 604–6 [see #312].

1979

349. "Aramaic Kepha' and Peter's Name in the New Testament," *Text and Interpretation: Studies in the New Testament Presented to Matthew Black* (ed. E. Best and R. McL. Wilson; Cambridge: University Press, 1979) 121–32.

350. "Neudatierung der neutestamentlichen Schriften?" *Theologie der Gegenwart* 22 (1979) 39-42 [abridged translation of #338].
351. Review of P.-E. Langevin, *Bibliographie biblique . . .* (Quebec: Université Laval, 1978), *TS* 40 (1979) 345-47.
352. Review of C. Brown (ed.), *The New International Dictionary of New Testament Theology 3: Pri-Z* (Grand Rapids: Zondervan, 1978), *TS* 40 (1979) 347-49 [see #326].
353. Review of J. Ernst, *Das Evangelium nach Lukas* (RNT; Regensburg: Pustet, 1977), *TS* 40 (1979) 349-51.
354. Review of H. Schlier, *Der Römerbrief* (HTKNT 6; Freiburg im Br.: Herder, 1977), *TS* 40 (1979) 354-56.
355. Review of F. W. Dillistone, *C. H. Dodd: Interpreter of the New Testament* (Grand Rapids: Eerdmans, 1977), *Catholic Historical Review* 65 (1979) 331-32.
356. *A Wandering Aramean: Collected Aramaic Essays* (SBLMS 25; Missoula, MT: Scholars Press, 1979). Pp. xvii + 290.
357. Review of *A Greek-English Lexicon of the New Testament and Other Early Christian Literature: Second Edition Revised and Augmented*, by F. W. Gingrich and F. W. Danker (Chicago: University of Chicago, 1979), *TS* 40 (1979) 533-35.
358. Review of C. Morrison, *An Analytical Concordance to the Revised Standard Version of the New Testament* (Philadelphia: Westminster, 1979), *TS* 40 (1979) 572.
359. "Another View of the 'Son of Man' Debate," *Journal for the Study of the New Testament* 4 (1979) 58-68.
360. "The Gospel in the Theology of Paul," *Interpretation* 33 (1979) 339-50.
361. "John Paul II, Academic Freedom and the Magisterium," *America* 141/13 (3 November 1979) 247-49.
362. "Letter to the Editor (Father Fitzmyer responds)," *America* 141/19 (15 December 1979) 377.

1980

363. "The Gnostic Gospels according to Pagels," *America* 142/6 (16 February 1980) 122-24.
364. "The Office of Teaching in the Christian Church according to the New Testament," *Teaching Authority & Infallibility in the Church* (Lutherans and Catholics in Dialogue, 6; ed. P. C. Empie, T. A. Murphy, and J. A. Burgess; Minneapolis: Augsburg, 1980) 186-212, 328-35.
365. "Letter to the Editor," *America* 142/10 (15 March 1980) 198.
366. Review of F. Zimmerman, *The Aramaic Origin of the Four Gospels* (New York: Ktav, 1979), *TS* 41 (1980) 193-95.
367. Review of G. J. Botterweck and H. Ringgren (eds.), *Theological Dictionary of the Old Testament 3: gillûlîm—hāras* (Grand Rapids: Eerdmans, 1978), *TS* 41 (1980) 229-30 [see #292].
368. "The Aramaic Language and the Study of the New Testament," *JBL* 99 (1980) 5-21.
369. Review of S. Lund and J. R. Foster, *Variant Versions of Targumic Traditions within Codex Neofiti 1* (SBL Aramaic Studies 2; Missoula: Scholars Press, 1977), *JAAR* 48 (1980) 279.
370. "Az újszövetségi iratok új datálása?" *Mérleg* 80/3 (1980) 266-74. ["New Dating of New Testament Documents?" Full Hungarian translation of #338].
371. Review of Moulton-Geden-Moulton, *A Concordance to the Greek Testament* (Edinburgh: Clark, 1978), *TS* 41 (1980) 767-69.
372. Review of J. B. van Zijl, *A Concordance to the Targum of Isaiah* (SBL Aramaic Studies 3; Missoula, MT: Scholars Press, 1979), *CBQ* 42 (1980) 554-55.

1981

373. "Nouveau Testament et christologie—Questions actuelles," *Nouvelle revue théologique* 103 (1981) 18–47, 187–208 [revised and expanded form of #335].

374. "The Gospel in the Theology of Paul," *Interpreting the Gospels* (ed. J. L. Mays; Philadelphia: Fortress, 1981) 1–13 (reprint of #360).

375. Review of *The International Standard Bible Encyclopedia, Volume 1: A—D* (ed. G. W. Bromiley; Grand Rapids, MI: Eerdmans, 1979), *TS* 42 (1981) 135–36.

376. *An Introductory Bibliography for the Study of Scripture: Revised Edition* (Subsidia biblica 3; Rome: Biblical Institute, 1981). Pp. xi + 154.

377. Review of M. A. Knibb, *The Ethiopic Book of Enoch* (2 vols.; Oxford: Clarendon, 1978), *JBL* 99 (1980) 631–36.

378. Review of A. Díez Macho, *Neophyti 1: Targum palestinense, Ms. de la Biblioteca Vaticana. Tomo V: Deuteronomio. Edición príncipe, introducción y versión castellana* (Madrid: C.S.I.C., 1978), *JBL* 99 (1980) 640–41 [see ##203, 241, 305].

379. *To Advance the Gospel: New Testament Studies* (New York: Crossroad, 1981). Pp. xiii + 265.

380. Review of A. George, *Etudes sur l'oeuvre de Luc* (Sources bibliques; Paris: Gabalda, 1978), *TS* 42 (1981) 292–93.

381. Review of B. M. Metzger, *New Testament Studies: Philological, Versional, and Patristic* (NTTS 10; Leiden: Brill, 1980), *TS* 42 (1981) 295–98.

382. Review of E. Käsemann, *Commentary on Romans* (Grand Rapids, MI: Eerdmans, 1980), *TS* 42 (1981) 331–32.

383. "Qumran und der eingefügte Abschnitt 2 Kor 6,14—7,1," *Qumran* (Wege der Forschung 410; ed. K. E. Grözinger et al.; Darmstadt: Wissenschaftliche Buchgesellschaft, 1981) 385–98 [German translation of #51 above].

384. Review of C. F. D. Moule, *The Origin of Christology* (Cambridge: University Press, 1977), *CBQ* 43 (1981) 475–77.

385. Review of K. Aland et al. (eds.), *Vollständige Konkordanz zum griechischen Neuen Testament*, Bd. I, Lief. 6–10, *JBL* 100 (1981) 147–49 [see ##312, 348].

386. *The Gospel according to Luke (I–IX)* (Anchor Bible 28; Garden City, NY: Doubleday, 1981). Pp. xxvi + 837.

387. Review of G. B. Caird, *The Language and Imagery of the Bible* (Philadelphia: Westminster, 1980), *New Catholic World* 224 (1981) 239.

388. *Maria im Neuen Testament: Eine Gemeinschaftsstudie von protestantischen und römisch-katholischen Gelehrten* (Stuttgart: Katholisches Bibelwerk, 1981). Pp. 304 [tr. U. Schierse; German version of #340].

389. "Kyrios, kyriakos," *Exegetisches Wörterbuch zum Neuen Testament* (3 vols.; ed. H. Balz and G. Schneider; Stuttgart: Kohlhammer, 1980–83), 2. 811–20.

390. Review of M. F. Unger and W. White, Jr. (eds.), *Nelson's Expository Dictionary of the Old Testament* (Nashville: Nelson, 1980) and W. E. Vine, *An Expository Dictionary of New Testament Words, With Their Precise Meanings for English Readers* (Nashville: Nelson, n.d.), *Verbatim* 8 (1981) 23–24.

391. "Hvad ved vi om Kristus? 16 aktuelle spørgsmål om Nytestamentlig kristologi," *Magasin* 4–5 (1981) 1–67 [Danish version of #373, which was itself a revised form of #335].

392. "Glory Reflected on the Face of Christ (2 Cor 3:7—4:6) and a Palestinian Jewish Motif," *TS* 42 (1981) 630–44.

393. Review of F. Bovon, *Luc le théologien: Vingt-cinq ans de recherches (1950–1975)* (Neuchâtel: Delachaux et Niestlé, 1978), *TS* 42 (1981) 670–71.

394. Review of *Theological Dictionary of the Old Testament 4: z^e 'ēbh — ḥms* (tr. D. E. Green; Grand Rapids: Eerdmans, 1980), *TS* 42 (1981) 707 [see ##292, 331, 367].

395. "Monogenēs," *Exegetisches Wörterbuch zum Neuen Testament*, 2. 1081–83 [see #389].

396. "Monos," ibid., 2. 1083–88 [see ##389, 395].

397. "Habakkuk 2:3-4 and the New Testament," *De la Tôrah au Messie: Etudes d'exégèse et d'herméneutique offertes à Henri Cazelles pour ses 25 années d'enseignement à l'Institut Catholique de Paris (Octobre 1979)* (ed. J. Doré et al.; Paris/Tournai: Desclée, 1981) 447–55 [see #379, pp. 236–46].

398. "The Dead Sea Scrolls and the New Testament after Thirty Years," *Theology Digest* 29/4 (Winter 1981) 351–67. [see ##403, 405].

399. "Aramaic Epistolography," in *Studies in Ancient Letter Writing* (ed. J. L. White; Semeia 22; Chico, CA: Scholars, 1982) 25–57 [revised form of #267 and of chap. 8 of #356, pp. 183–204].

400. "Parthenos, ou, hē und ho," *Exegetisches Wörterbuch zum Neuen Testament* (ed. H. R. Balz und G. Schneider), 3. 93–95 [see ##389, 395-96].

401. *A Christological Catechism: New Testament Answers* (Ramsey, NJ/New York: Paulist, 1982). Pp. viii + 160 [expanded form of #335; see ##373, 391].

402. "Nuevo Testamento y cristología," *Selecciones de teología* 21 (1982) 163–85 [Spanish abstract of #373; cf. #391].

403. "New Testament Illustrated by Dead Sea Scrolls," *Biblical Archaeology Review* 8 (1982) 6–8 [unauthorized abstract of *TD* 29/4 (1981) 351–67 (#398)].

404. Review of F. W. Beare, *The Gospel according to Matthew* (New York: Harper & Row, 1981), *New Catholic World* 226 (1982) 242–43.

405. "Dödahavsrullarna och Nya testamentet efter trettio år," *Svensk Teologisk Kvartalskrift* 58 (1982) 117–30 [Swedish version of #398; talk given on day before honorary degree at the University of Lund].

406. Review of B. M. Metzger, *Manuscripts of the Greek Bible: An Introduction to Greek Palaeography* (Oxford: Oxford University, 1981), *TS* 43 (1982) 706–7.

407. Review of G. Schneider, *Die Apostelgeschichte, I. Teil* (HTKNT 5/1; Freiburg im B.: Herder, 1980), *TS* 43 (1982) 709–12.

408. Review of J. Finegan, *The Archeology of the New Testament* (Boulder, CO: Westview, 1981), *TS* 43 (1982) 745.

409. Review of Lee I. Levine (ed.), *Ancient Synagogues Revealed* (Jerusalem: Israel Exploration Society, 1981), *TS* 43 (1982) 745–46.

410. "The Biblical Basis of Justification by Faith: Comments on the Essay of Professor Reumann," in J. Reumann, *"Righteousness" in the New Testament: "Justification" in the United States Lutheran—Roman Catholic Dialogue (with Responses by Joseph A. Fitzmyer, Jerome D. Quinn)* (Philadelphia: Fortress; Ramsey, NJ/New York: Paulist, 1982) 193–227.

1983

411. *Vingt questions sur Jésus-Christ* (Dossiers libres; Paris: Cerf, 1983). Pp. 129 [French version of #401, using that of #373 and building on it, but omitting its appendix].

412. Review of M. Aberbach and B. Grossfeld, *Targum Onkelos to Genesis* (New York: Ktav, 1982), *TS* 44 (1983) 132–34.

413. Review of G. W. Bromiley (ed.), *The International Standard Bible Encyclopedia, Volume Two: E—J* (Grand Rapids: Eerdmans, 1982), *TS* 44 (1983) 168–69 [see #375].

414. Review of J. R. Kohlenberger III, *The NIV Triglot Old Testament* (Grand Rapids: Zondervan, 1981), *TS* 44 (1983) 169.

415. Review of J. M. Robinson, *The Problem of History in Mark and Other Marcan Studies* (Philadelphia: Fortress, 1982), *New Catholic World* 226 (1983) 140–41.
416. *Maria en el Nuevo Testamento* (Salamanca: Sigueme, 1982) [Spanish version of #340].
417. Review of I. Drazin, *Targum Onkelos to Deuteronomy: An English Translation . . .* (New York: Ktav, 1982), *TS* 44 (1983) 497–98.
418. Review of G. Schneider, *Die Apostelgeschichte 2: Kommentar zu Kap. 9, 1 – 28,31* (HTKNT 5/2; Freiburg im B.: Herder, 1982), *TS* 44 (1983) 695–97 [see #407].
419. Review of J. Carmignac (ed.), *The Four Gospels Translated into Hebrew by William Greenfield in 1831* (Traductions hébraïques . . . 1; Turnhout: Brépols, 1982); *Evangiles de Matthieu et de Marc traduits en Hébreu en 1668 par Giovanni Battista Iona, retouchés en 1805 par Thomas Yeates* (Traductions hébraïques . . . 2); *Evangiles de Luc et de Jean traduits en hébreu en 1668 par Giovanni Battista Iona, retouchés en 1805 par Thomas Yeates* (Traductions hébraïques . . . 3), *TS* 44 (1983) 700–703.
420. Review of K. Aland, *Vollständige Konkordanz zum griechischen Neuen Testament . . . , Bd. I, Lief. 11-12: ho - polys* (Berlin/New York: de Gruyter, 1981), *JBL* 102 (1983) 639–40 [see ##312, 318, 385].

1984

421. Review of J. M. Lindenberger, *The Aramaic Proverbs of Ahiqar* (Baltimore/London: The Johns Hopkins University Press, 1983), *CBQ* 46 (1984) 315–17.
422. "Nieuw Testament en Christologie: Actuele vragen," *Collationes* 14 (1984) 6–30, 131–60; 15 (1985) 5–32 (Flemish translation of #373).

1984

423. Review of J. D. Crossan, *In Fragments: The Aphorisms of Jesus* (New York: Harper & Row, 1983), *New Catholic World* 227 (1984) 140–41.
424. Review of J. Murphy-O'Connor, *St. Paul's Corinth: Texts and Archaeology* (Wilmington, DE: Glazier, 1983), *TS* 45 (1984) 388–89.
425. Review of A. Abou-Assaf et al. (eds.), *La statue de Tell Fekherye et son inscription bilingue assyro-araméenne* (Paris: Editions Recherche sur les Civilisations, A.D.P.F., 1982), *JBL* 103 (1984) 265–67.
426. Review of B. Z. Wacholder, *The Dawn of Qumran: The Sectarian Torah and the Teacher of Righteousness* (Cincinnati: Hebrew Union College, 1983), *TS* 45 (1984) 556–58.
427. Review of G. L. Archer and G. Chirichigno, *Old Testament Quotations in the New Testament* (Chicago: Moody, 1983), *TS* 45 (1984) 591–92.
428. "The Ascension of Christ and Pentecost," *TS* 45 (1984) 409–40.
429. *Catecismo cristológico: Respuestas del nuevo testamento* (Biblia y catequesis 4; Salamanca: Ediciones Sígueme, 1984). Pp. 159 (Spanish translation of #401).
430. "Christology and the Biblical Commission," *America* 151/20 (22 December 1984) 417–20.
431. Review of *Commentary on the Gospel of Saint Luke* by Cyril of Alexandria (tr. R. Payne Smith; Astoria, LIC, NY: Stoudion, 1983), *TS* 45 (1984) 768.
432. Review of M. Sokoloff (ed.), *Arameans, Aramaic and the Aramaic Literary Tradition* (Ramat-Gan: Bar-Ilan University, 1983), *Religious Studies Review* 10 (1984) 386–88.

1985

433. "Reply to Letter," *Biblical Archaeology Review* 11 (1985) 10–12 (written at request of the editor).

434. (With R. E. Brown), "Danger Also from the Left," *The Bible Today* 23 (1985) 105-10.

435. Review of J. M. Allegro, *The Dead Sea Scrolls and the Christian Myth* (Buffalo: Prometheus Books, 1984), *TS* 46 (1985) 130-32.

436. Review of L. Smolar et al., *Studies in Targum Jonathan to the Prophets* (New York: Ktav, 1983), *TS* 46 (1985) 170.

437. *The Gospel According to Luke (X-XXIV): Introduction, Translation, and Notes* (AB 28A; Garden City, NY: Doubleday, 1985).

438. "Justification by Faith and 'Righteousness' in the New Testament," *Justification by Faith* (Lutherans and Catholics in Dialogue 7; ed. H. G. Anderson et al.; Minneapolis: Augsburg, 1985) 77-81, 338-39.

439. "More about Elijah Coming First," *JBL* 104 (1985) 295-96.

440. Review of K. Aland et al. (eds.), *Vollständige Konkordanz zum griechischen Neuen Testament, Bd. I, Lief. 13/14: polys - ōphelimos* (Berlin/New York: de Gruyter, 1983) *JBL* 104 (1985) 360-62 [see ##312, 348, 385, 420].

441. "The Biblical Commission and Christology," *TS* 46 (1985) 407-79 [see #450].

442. "Scrolls, The Dead Sea," *Harper's Bible Dictionary* (ed. P. J. Achtemeier; San Francisco: Harper & Row, 1985) 915-17.

443. Review of E. G. Clarke, *Targum Pseudo-Jonathan of the Pentateuch: Text and Concordance* (Hoboken, NJ: Ktav, 1984), *TS* 46 (1985) 712-14.

444. Review of *Traductions hébraïques des évangiles rassemblées par Jean Carmignac 4: Die vier Evangelien ins Hebräische übersetzt von Franz Delitzsch* (Turnhout: Brépols, 1984), *TS* 46 (1985) 746 [see #419].

445. "*Abba* and Jesus' Relation to God," *A cause de l'évangile: Etudes sur les Synoptiques et les Actes offertes au P. Jacques Dupont, O.S.B. à l'occasion de son 70ᵉ anniversaire* (LD 123; Paris: Cerf, 1985) 15-38.

446. (With coeditors, R. E. Brown, K. P. Donfried, and J. Reumann), *Maria nel Nuovo Testamento: Una valutazione congiunta di studiosi protestanti e cattolici* (Assisi: Cittadella, 1985), Pp. 341. (Italian translation of #340).

447. "The Priority of Mark" and "Luke's Use of Q," *The Two-Source Hypothesis: A Critical Appraisal* (ed. A. J. Bellinzoni, Jr.; Macon, GA: Mercer University Press, 1985) 37-52 and 245-57 (reprint in two parts of #206)

1986

448. "Prepare the Way of the Lord," *CUA Communiqué* 2/1 (Winter 1986) 3-4 (homily preached in the Shrine of the Immaculate Conception on 8 December 1985, at Mass at which the Patronal Medal was conferred).

449. "La Comisión Bíblica y la Cristología," *Estudios eclesiásticos* 61 (1986) 71-77 (Spanish translation of #430).

450. *Scripture and Christology: A Statement of the Biblical Commission with a Commentary* (New York/Mahwah, NJ: Paulist, 1986). (see #441)

451. Review of P.-E. Langevin, *Bibliographie biblique . . . III: 1930-1983* (Quebec: Université Laval, 1985), *TS* 47 (1986) 301-3 [see #351].

452. Review of D. Townsley and R. Bjork, *Scripture Index to the New International Dictionary of New Testament Theology* (Grand Rapids: Zondervan, 1985), *TS* 47 (1986) 341-42.

453. Review of J. B. Segal, *Aramaic Texts from North Saqqâra: With Some Fragments in Phoenician* (London: Egypt Exploration Society,1983), *CBQ* 48 (1986) 541-44.

454. Review of Y. Yadin, *The Temple Scroll: Vol. I, Introduction; Vol. II, Text and Commentary; Vol. III, Plates and Text* (Jerusalem: Israel Exploration Society, 1983 [vols. I, II], 1977 [vol. III]), *CBQ* 48 (1986) 547-49.

455. *Raktiniai Klausimai apie Kristu: Naujojo Testamento Atsakymai* (tr. Jurgis Strazdas; Putnam, CT: Krikščionis Gyvenime, 1986). Pp. 198. (Lithuanian translation of #401)
456. Review of W. R. Garr, *Dialect Geography of Syria-Palestine, 1000–586 B.C.E.* (Philadelphia: University of Pennsylvania, 1985), *TS* 47 (1986) 510–12.
457. Review of M. E. Stone (ed.), *Jewish Writings of the Second Temple Period* (Compendia rerum iudaicarum ad Novum Testamentum II/2; Assen: Van Gorcum; Philadelphia: Fortress, 1984), *TS* 47 (1986) 512–15.
458. Review of Y. Yadin, *The Temple Scroll: The Hidden Law of the Dead Sea Sect* (New York: Random House, 1985), *TS* 47 (1986) 515–18.
459. Review of G. J. Botterweck and H. Ringgren (eds.), *Theological Dictionary of the Old Testament 5: ḥmr – YHWH* (Grand Rapids: Eerdmans, 1986), *TS* 47 (1986) 740.
460. *El evangelio según Lucas: I. Introducción general* (Madrid: Ediciones Cristiandad, 1986). Pp. 1–475 (tr. Dionisio Mínguez).

1987

461. Review of G. Luedemann, *Paul, Apostle to the Gentiles: Studies in Chronology* (Philadelphia: Fortress, 1984, *TS* 48 (1987) 160–64.
462. "Kommentar," in P. G. Müller, *Bibel und Christologie: Ein Dokument der Päpstlichen Bibelkommission in Französisch und Latein: Mit deutscher Übersetzung und Hinführung von Paul-Gerhard Müller, einem Kommentar von Joseph A. Fitzmyer und einem Geleitwort von Kardinal Joseph Ratzinger* (Stuttgart: Katholisches Bibelwerk, 1987) 199–258 (German translation of the commentary in ##441, 450)
463. *Geloven in vraag en antwoord: De historische Jezus en de Christus van het geloof volgens het Nieuwe Testament* (tr. A. Vansteeland, A. Denaux, and F. Lefevre; Antwerp/Amsterdam: Patmos. 1987). Pp. 171 (Flemish translation of #401)
464. *El evangelio según Lucas II: Traducción y commentarios, Capitulos 1–8,21* (Madrid: Ediciones Cristiandad, 1987) Pp. 1–766 [see #460].
465. "Jesus in the Early Church through the Eyes of Luke-Acts," *Scripture Bulletin* 17 (1987) 26–35.
466. "The Dead Sea Scrolls and the Bible: After Forty Years," *America* 157/12 (31 October 1987) 300–303.
467. "The Resurrection of Jesus Christ according to the New Testament," *The Month* 258 (1987) 402–10.
468. Review of *The International Standard Bible Dictionary 3: K–P* (ed. G. W. Bromiley; Grand Rapids: Eerdmans, 1986), *TS* 48 (1987) 784 [see ##375, 413].
469. *Domande su Gesù: Le riposte del Nuovo Testamento* (Universale teologica 20; Brescia: Queriniana, 1987). Pp. 115. [Italian translation of #401, without the appendix].
470. "Aramaic Evidence Affecting the Interpretation of *Hosanna* in the New Testament," *Tradition and Interpretation in the New Testament: Essays in Honor of E. Earle Ellis for His 60th Birthday* (ed. G. F. Hawthorne with O. Betz; Grand Rapids, MI: Eerdmans; Tübingen: Mohr [Siebeck], 1987) 110–18.
471. Review of D. M. Golomb, *A Grammar of Targum Neofiti* (HMS 34; Chico, CA: Scholars, 1985), *JBL* 106 (1987) 748–49.

1988

472. Review of G. J. Brooke, *Exegesis at Qumran: 4QFlorilegium in Its Jewish Context* (JSOTSup 29; Sheffield: University of Sheffield, 1985), *JBL* 107 (1988) 130–31.

473. Review of C. Newsom, *Songs of the Sabbath Sacrifice: A Critical Edition* (HSS 27; Atlanta, GA: Scholars Press, 1985), *JBL* 107 (1988) 315–16.

474. "The Aramaic Background of Philippians 2:6-11," *CBQ* 50 (1988) 470–83.

475. *Paul and His Theology: A Brief Sketch* (2d ed.; Englewood Cliffs, NJ: Prentice-Hall, 1989) [appeared August 1988].

476. "The Pauline Letters and the Lucan Account of Paul's Missionary Journeys," *SBL Seminar Papers 1988* (ed. D. J. Lull; Atlanta, GA: Scholars Press, 1988) 82–89.

477. Review of D. J. Harrington and A. J. Saldarini, *Targum Jonathan of the Former Prophets;* B. D. Chilton, *The Isaiah Targum;* R. Hayward, *The Targum of Jeremiah;* S. H. Levey, *The Targum of Ezekiel* (The Aramaic Bible 10-13; Wilmington, DE: Glazier, 1987), *TS* 49 (1988) 735–39.

478. Review of J. T. Sanders, *The Jews in Luke-Acts* (London: SCM, 1987), *New Blackfriars* 69 (1988) 461–62.

479. "The Qumran Scrolls and the New Testament after Forty Years," *Mémorial Jean Carmignac: Etudes Qumrâniennes* (= *RevQ* 13; Paris: Gabalda, 1988) 609–20.

1989

480. "Historical Criticism: Its Role in Biblical Interpretation and in Church Life," *TS* 50 (1989) 244–59.

481. *Luke the Theologian: Aspects of His Teaching* (New York/Mahwah, NJ: Paulist, 1989). Pp. xiii + 250 (The Martin D'Arcy Lectures, Campion Hall, Oxford University, Hilary Term 1987).

482. "Preaching in the Apostolic and Subapostolic Age," *Preaching in the Patristic Age: Studies in Honor of Walter J. Burghardt, S.J.* (ed. D. G. Hunter; New York/Mahwah, NJ: Paulist, 1989) 19–35.

483. (Co-edited with R. E. Brown, S.S., and R. E. Murphy, O.Carm.), *The New Jerome Biblical Commentary* (Englewood Cliffs, NJ: Prentice-Hall, 1990 [off the press in August 1989]). Pp. xlix + 1484. [The following articles in the *NJBC* were authored (in whole or in part) by J. A. Fitzmyer, S.J.]

484. "Introduction to the New Testament Epistles," *NJBC*, art. 45, 768–71.

485. "The Letter to the Galatians," *NJBC*, art. 47, 780–90.

486. "The Letter to the Romans," *NJBC*, art. 51, 830–68.

487. "The Letter to Philemon," *NJBC*, art. 52, 869–70.

488. (Co-authored with A. G. Wright, S.S., and R. E. Murphy, O.Carm.), "A History of Israel," *NJBC*, art. 75, 1219–52, esp. 1243–52.

489. "Paul," *NJBC*, art. 79, 1329–37.

490. "Pauline Theology," *NJBC*, art. 82, 1382–1416.

Index of Names

Colophon

*To Touch the Text: Biblical and Related Studies
in Honor of Joseph A. Fitzmyer, S.J.*
was designed by Maurya P. Horgan and Paul J. Kobelski.
The type for the text is 10-point Bembo and
the display type is Goudy Old Style, condensed.
The type was set by The Scriptorium, Denver, Colorado.